PLANTAGENET ANCESTRY OF
SEVENTEENTH-CENTURY COLONISTS

*P*LANTAGENET *A*NCESTRY OF SEVENTEENTH-CENTURY COLONISTS

The Descent from the Later Plantagenet Kings of England,
Henry III, Edward I, Edward II, and Edward III,
of Emigrants from England and Wales
to the North American Colonies
before 1701

DAVID FARIS

Copyright © 1996
David Faris
213 East Gowen Avenue
Philadelphia, PA 19119
All Rights Reserved
Published by Genealogical Publishing Co., Inc.
1001 N. Calvert St., Baltimore, MD 21202
Library of Congress Catalogue Card Number 96-76348
International Standard Book Number 0-8063-1518-0
Made in the United States of America

TABLE OF CONTENTS

Introduction vii

Acknowledgments xi

Colonists xii

Text .... 1 – 294

Bibliography .... 295 – 301

English Abbreviations 301

Latin Abbreviations and Phrases 301

Index .... 302 – 324

INTRODUCTION

PURPOSE: This book is intended to provide summary information about the legitimate descent from an Angevin (i.e., Plantagenet) King of England of about one hundred individuals who emigrated from England and Wales to the North American colonies by the end of the seventeenth century and who are believed to have many descendants living in this country today. Wherever possible, all descents from the Plantagenet kings have been included. This information has been gathered principally for the interest of those who do not have ready access to information that has been published about their English ancestry.

BACKGROUND: This book is a successor in part to *Ancestral Roots of Certain American Colonists Who Came to America before 1700* (7th edition, 1992). The content of that book had evolved through the previous six editions from 1950 to 1988 through the dedicated genealogical work of Frederick Lewis Weis and his successor Walter Lee Sheppard, Jr. The available pertinent information on the ancestry of American colonists in New England, together with the interest in extending coverage to other colonies, has outgrown the size of a single volume.

PUBLICATION PLAN: With the retirement of Mr. Sheppard, it has been decided to replace *Ancestral Roots*, and its companion volume *The Magna Charta Sureties, 1215*, with a series of books providing information about the descent of 17th-century colonists from the Plantagenet kings of England, from the Magna Charta Sureties of 1215, from the earlier feudal English barons, and from the Emperor Charlemagne. The succeeding volumes will include many 17th-century colonists without Plantagenet ancestry. Bold face cross-references in this book show many of the ancestral connections to the companion volumes now in preparation. *Ancestral Roots* will remain in print until this process is completed.

ORGANIZATION: The 137 ancestral lines in this book include the consecutive generations of married couples with the spouse of Plantagenet descent on the left margin, each such individual being the child of the previous generation. Generation 1 names the parents of an emigrant, and the preceding generations are numbered back in time to the Plantagenet kings. Of these lines, 72 end with an emigrant or with a related group of emigrants. The remaining lines provide the ancestry linking the emigrant lines with the basic PLANTAGENET line. Each line is preceded by a summary of previous generations found in full in the indicated line. When both spouses are of Plantagenet descent their lines are cross-referenced.

CONSTRUCTION OF LINES: The lines have been constructed according to three principles: (1) maximizing the length of patrilineal generations (except when it would obscure a descent from King Edward III), (2) maintaining lines of at least two generations in length, and (3) restricting as much as practical the inclusion of grandchildren, and even great-grandchildren, within a line.

LINE NAMES: Lines ending with the emigrant receive that emigrant's surname (with the one exception of STAPLETON for Thomas and Phillip Nelson, as NELSON is used for the emigrant John Nelson). Lines not ending with an emigrant receive a surname, usually that of the first male in the line. With the duplication of some surnames, the place of residence or title has occasionally been used, as with Elsing, Ightfield, Lancaster, Letheringham, Norfolk, Over Peover, Wilton and York. Variation in spelling has allowed the distinction between Mainwaring and Manwaring lines.

INTRODUCTION

COMPLETENESS: This book, as with others of its nature, depends almost entirely on the finding and copying of information developed and published by researchers, with the compilation of this information generously supported by friends and colleagues. Nevertheless, much information readily available has not been consulted in time for the present publication. The author welcomes the contribution of additions, corrections, and citations to sources for future editions.

DOCUMENTATION: The cited sources are mostly confined to published secondary sources which may be consulted for their underlying primary sources. The quality and specificity of the documentation in the cited secondary sources varies widely. The documentation is provided for each generation in the descent, a practice that occasionally betrays the thinness of the documentation. The reference sections include some indication of editorial position by the inclusion of contradictory or alternate statements, and by the use of the word "state" to indicate warning, and the word "assert" to indicate disagreement. The abbreviations of sources examined appear in italics. The sources carried over from *Ancestral Roots* but not as yet examined are distinguished by the lack of italics.

NAMES AND SPELLING: Proper names in their first appearance and in the index are spelled in accordance with editorial conventions. In a few cases names have been spelled according to their evolution over time (as from Éléonore and Alianore to Eleanor). Some Latin sources, such as visitations and writs, are quoted to indicate the spelling and style of the name used. The contemporary English spelling of the names of many individuals and their places of residence is quoted where possible from a printed will written in English, from the listed entry in a will index, or from the pardon rolls in the published Letters and Papers of King Henry VIII. No attempt has been made to include all possible variations in spelling of surnames and place names. British spelling (as, "baptised") and punctuation have generally (but not always consistently) been used, particularly in passages taken almost verbatim from a printed source, with American spelling (as "baptized") and punctuation used for colonists once in the New World.

SELECTION OF EMIGRANTS: Emigrants have been included on the basis of published material that is believed to support the described relationship. The quality of documentation depends on the skill of the researcher (often a present-day descendant), and does not always rise to the level of the completely persuasive. Some of the American colonists included in the text, such as Essex Beville, have not been documented as being the individual with the same name in England of an undoubted Plantagenet descent. Some emigrants adequately documented in England before emigration do not have unquestioned Plantagenet ancestry. The process of providing a secure basis for all the links in these descents continues, and particular acknowledgment should be made to individuals, such as Charles M. Hansen, who are engaged in the methodical review of previously published material.

USE OF UNPUBLISHED SOURCES: There are three exceptions to the decision to include only emigrants documented in published sources. The most problematical is that of Governor Thomas Dudley (see DUDLEY for rationale for inclusion in this work). The publication of the immediate ancestry of Maria Johanna Somerset has been supplemented by excerpts from manuscript material in the Maryland Historical Society (the inclusion of Maria permits the presentation of the later generations of the Plantagenets). The immediate ancestry of Thomas Gerard has been provided by Claude W. Faulkner supplementing material contributed to *Ancestral Roots* (1992).

INTRODUCTION

CHILDREN: The listing of all the children in a family, including those who have no American descendants, is limited to the families of the male-line descendants of the Kings of England (including the Beauforts), and to the children of the emigrants (sometimes to the siblings of the emigrant). A few others, principally the wives of King Henry VIII, have also been included. The text usually states the total number of children for each couple. Those other children are named, often with their spouses, and sometimes with some or many of their descendants, in one or more of the sources cited.

ILLEGITIMATE DESCENTS: The legitimate descents included in this work are indicated by the bold face used for the names of Plantagenet descendants and spouses at first appearance in the text. Legitimacy is defined as birth to a married couple, the children of marriages later annulled being regarded as legitimate for purposes of descent. The children of post-birth marriages or of no marriage are regarded as illegitimate without regard to any later legitimization. Nevertheless, some descents from illegitimate children have been included, notably the Beauforts, with the names lacking bold face until there is a marriage to a legitimate descendant. The only emigrant included without a legitimate descent is Thomas Gerard.

COMPLEXITY: The attempt to present all descents from the Plantagenet kings creates unavoidable complexity. Most of this complexity is caused by two factors: (1) cousin marriages (indicated by cross-references to the ancestry of the spouse), and (2) multiple marriages of individuals, with or without Plantagenet ancestry, with spouses of Plantagenet ancestry, with children by more than one marriage.

CONSISTENCY: An attempt has been made to treat the material drawn from many sources in a consistent fashion (in such areas as spelling of name, place of residence, possession of manors, honorific titles, religious houses and the like), but many inconsistencies undoubtedly remain. Many dates found ambiguously in a source have been transferred to the text as found in the source.

ABBREVIATIONS: Abbreviations have been limited principally to months in dates including the day of the month, "co." in places of residence, and certain abbreviations of Latin words or phrases (see page 301).

COUNTY NAMES: The names of the English counties (or shires) are presented according to three systems: (1) formal: as, Hampshire or Staffordshire, (2) conventional abbreviation in places of residence: as, co. Hants, or co. Stafford, and (3) informal abbreviations, as in references to visitations: as, Hants or Staffs. Shires not named for a borough are named without "co.": Cornwall, Cumberland, Dorset, Durham, Essex, Kent, Middlesex, Norfolk, Northumberland, Rutland, Somerset, Suffolk, Surrey, Sussex, and Westmorland.

SPECIAL COLLATERAL RELATIONSHIPS: Two undocumented sources have been included as a means to determine a non-Plantagenet relationship:

The Lineage and Ancestry of H.R.H. Prince Charles, Prince of Wales, by Gerald Paget (1977), provides information for eighteen generations of the ancestry of the Prince of Wales, including that of his mother, Queen Elizabeth II, and his maternal grandmother, the Queen Mother. The latter shares many ancestors in Tudor times with the emigrants to the American colonies. The most recent generation including a page reference to that work indicates that another but unnamed child in the family was an ancestor of the Queen Mother, and that the Paget work provides that descent.

INTRODUCTION

Stemmata Chicheleana, or A Genealogical Account of Some of the Families Derived from Thomas Chichele of Higham-Ferrers in the County of Northampton; All Whose Descendants are Held to be Entitled to Fellowship in All Souls College, Oxford; by Virtue of their Consanguinity to Arch-bishop Chichele, the Founder (1765), shows the consanguinity to several emigrants, although Charles Scott (grandfather of Henry Fleete) is the only ancestor listed in this work who was admitted to fellowship in All Souls College.

IMPLIED WORDS: There are many implied words, including principally "his wife" in the naming of parents-in-law, "parish" in many places of residence, "Church" in places of baptism, marriage and burial (unless otherwise specified), and "lord of the manor" frequently in the naming of the seat of residence.

WORDS WITH LIMITED MEANING: "Baron" is used in the limited sense of an individual who was a tenant-in-chief to the King. "Lord" is used (often in brackets as found in the *New Complete Peerage*) in the limited sense of an individual summoned to Parliament by writ, but who in earlier times was not so addressed, but is presently and conventionally so called. Both such lords and those possessed of manors are generally but indiscriminately called lord in many sources.

PARISH NAMES: The spelling of parish names has been taken from *The Phillimore Atlas and Index of Parish Registers* (1984), based on James Bell's *A New and Comprehensive Gazetteer of England and Wales* (1834). Many places of residence have not been located by parish. In some cases, this spelling differs from that of a family resident there or from that usually included in printed sources.

BIOGRAPHICAL INFORMATION: Keeping this book to practical size precludes the inclusion of anything more than minimal biographical information. Much additional biographical information is found in the historical and genealogical literature cited in this work. For this essentially genealogical work, customary information is included, with biographical information favoring personal and domestic life if available. Many individuals were leading participants in the complex political and military activities of the times (in particular the War of the Roses), but that often can be barely discerned in the text. The lives of the higher ranking individuals included here reveal the astonishing number of deaths in battle or by execution (with and without trial), and the machinations of land owners. The course of domestic life is not frequently available, but the author prefers to believe that many lives were not directed primarily to property acquisition, litigation, and self-aggrandizement. To illustrate, the following is the filial tribute of Sir Edward Rodney writing in the seventeenth century of his father (see RODNEY 3, p. 240):

> Hee had borne all the Country Offices, which were proper to the best sort of Gentlemen, and at last being highe Shiriffe at the Assizes at Charde, dyed on the sixth day of August 1612 ... He was very temperate in his diet, just in all his dealings, chaste in Wedlocke, a good Maister to his Servants, very Hospitable in his port & manner of living, and generally an honest man and a good Christian, Whose soule by Gods mercy enjoys the beatificall vision.

MEDIEVAL AND GENEALOGICAL TERMS: No glossary has been provided for the many specialized or obsolete words and phrases, some in Latin, that appear in the text. General comprehensive dictionaries and encyclopedias contain many of them, and genealogical sections of libraries often have specialized dictionaries and other aids. Knowing the meaning of all of them, however, is not essential to understand the genealogical relationships included in this work.

ACKNOWLEDGMENTS

PRIORITY OF PUBLICATION: A complete analysis of the development of evidence for Plantagenet descents has not been possible for this edition, but the following individuals (of the present and of earlier generations) have been important, either substantively or incrementally, in the collection of evidence: Arthur Adams, Sarah Cantey Whitaker Allen, Robert Behra, Ross Boothe, Jr., Howard M. Buck, Henry DeSaussure Bull, Meredith Bright Colket, Jr., Leander Howard Crall, Walter Goodwin Davis, Katharine Dickson, Winifred Lovering Holman Dodge, John Frederick Dorman, Lucy L. Erwin, Claude W. Faulkner, Thomas Allen Glenn, Rebecca Irwin Graff, Charles M. Hansen, James L. Hansen, Mrs. Napier Higgins, Henry Bainbridge Hoff, Alvahn Holmes, Rodney T. Hood, John G. Hunt, Donald Lines Jacobus, Alfred Rudulph Justice, David Humiston Kelley, Asselia Strobhar Lichliter, William Daniel Ligon, E.L. Lomax, George Englert McCracken, Robert H. Montgomery, Patrick W. Montague-Smith, George Andrews Moriarty, Jr., Paul C. Reed, Douglas Richardson, Gary Boyd Roberts, Milton Rubincam, Herbert Furman Seversmith, Walter Lee Sheppard, Jr., Neil D. Thompson, Anthony R. Wagner, and Frederick Lewis Weis. There are doubtless others, and acknowledgment of the contributions of all must be postponed to future publication. Correspondence is welcome on this subject.

ACKNOWLEDGMENTS: Thanks are due to all the aforementioned individuals (and others not named) for the contribution of their published work in the preparation of this book, but particular immediate thanks are due to five individuals, Gary Boyd Roberts, Henry B. Hoff, Marshall Kirk, Claude W. Faulkner, and Douglas Richardson, who have reviewed this work in draft with valuable additions, corrections, questions, and warnings (not all of them sufficiently heeded). Much help has been derived from the differing approach each takes to the critique of work in progress. In addition, specific thanks are due for these individual contributions: Henry B. Hoff for relaying information from Anthony Hoskins about Maria Johanna Somerset, Marshall Kirk for a summary of his analysis of the ancestry of Thomas Dudley, Douglas Richardson for reference to the Percy ancestry of Arthur Harris and assistance in conventional names and places, Claude W. Faulkner for unpublished information about Thomas Gerard, and for proof-reading, and Robert Barnes for examination of manuscript material concerning Maria Johanna Somerset. Thanks and acknowledgment of a different order are due Gary Boyd Roberts for his publication of *The Royal Descents of 500 Immigrants* ... (1993) which reaches beyond the scope of this work in nearly all dimensions and provides an extraordinary number of welcome references to available sources in the printed literature in the identification of royal descents.

The immediate credit for the present approach to the preparation of these ancestral lines lies with those scholars who developed *Ancestral Roots* during the years 1950 through 1992, Frederick Lewis Weis and Walter Lee Sheppard, Jr. As Mr. Sheppard noted in his introductions to the sixth and seventh editions, the reputation of Dr. Weis lay elsewhere than in the incidental documentation of royal descents. The reputation of Mr. Sheppard also rests on his extensive genealogical publication (the bibliography notes his large-scale work on the ancestry of Edward Carleton and Ellen Newton). The meticulous attention to documentation underlying the larger genealogical work of these men was brought, with appropriately skeptical consideration of previous publications in the field, to the review of royal and Magna Charta Surety ancestry, and provides a basis for continued evolution of this aid to the summary presentation of the work of many genealogists in the field.

COLONISTS

The following alphabetized list includes the names of the seventeenth-century emigrants whose Plantagenet ancestry is the subject of this book, together with several emigrants after 1701 who have been incidentally noted in the text or a footnote. The names of women have been provided with a cross-reference to the surname of the husband.

Abbott, Anne (Mauleverer) 191	Deighton, Katherine (see Hackburne,
Abell, Robert 2	Dudley, Allin) 86
Abney, Dannett 3	Digges, Edward 87
Allin, Katherine (Deighton) 86	Dudley, Katherine (Deighton) . . . 86
Alston, John 202	Dudley, Thomas 93
Asfordby, William 4	Eddowes, Ralph 101
Ball, Elizabeth (Harleston) 132	Eddowes, Sarah (Kenrick) 74,75
Barham, Charles 112	Ellis, Rowland 97
Batt, Anne (Baynton) 12	Farrar, William 100
Baynton, Anne (see Batt) 12	Farwell, Olive (Welby) 276
Beckwith, Marmaduke 148	Fenwick, John 101
Bernard, Richard 21	Fisher, John 104
Bernard, William 21	Fleete, Henry 112
Beville, Essex 22	Foliot, Edward 165
Bolles, Joseph 27	Gerard, Thomas 114
Bosvile, Elizabeth (see Pelham) . . 31	Gill, Mary (Mainwaring) 183
Bourchier, Mary (see Whitaker) . . 34	Gorsuch, Anne (Lovelace) 172
Brent, George 35	Gurdon, Muriel (see Saltonstall) . 123
Brent, Giles 35	Gye, Mary (see Maverick) 124
Brent, Robert 36	Hackburne, Katherine (Deighton) 86
Brewster, Thomas (or Sackford) . . 130	Harleston, Elizabeth (see Ball) . . . 132
Brooke, Mary (Wolseley) 285	Harleston, John 131
Bulkeley, Grace (Chetwode) 60	Haviland, Jane (see Torrey) 137
Bull, Stephen 41	Haynes, Elizabeth (Cooke) 139
Burrough, Nathaniel 44	Horsmanden, Warham 245
Calvert, Charles 49	Humphrey, Anne (see Palmes) . . . 145
Carleton, Edward 53	Hutchinson, Anne (Marbury) 186
Carter, Sarah (Ludlow) 175	Jennings, Edmund 147
Chetwode, Grace (see Bulkeley) . 60	Kemp, Edmund 152
Clarke, Jeremy 65	Kemp, Matthew 151
Claypoole, James 67	Kemp, Richard 152
Clopton, William 69	Kenrick, Sarah (see Eddowes) . 74,75
Codd, St.Leger 246	Launce, Mary (see Sherman) 161
Cooke, Elizabeth (Haynes) 139	Lewis, Elizabeth (Marshall) 189
Coytemore, Elizabeth (see Tyng) . 75	Ligon, Thomas 166
Crowne, Agnes (Mackworth) 180	Littleton, Nathaniel 168
Culpeper, Katherine (Saint Leger) 245	Lloyd, Thomas 170
Dade, Francis 78	Lovelace, Anne (see Gorsuch) . . 172
Dale, Diana (Skipwith) 254	Ludlow, Gabriel 176
Davie, Humphrey 82	Ludlow, Roger 175
Deighton, Frances (see Williams) . 85	Ludlow, Sarah (see Carter) 175
Deighton, Jane (see Lugg) 85	Lugg, Jane (Deighton) 85
Deighton, Jane (see Negus) 85	Lunsford, Thomas 178

COLONISTS

Mackworth, Agnes (see Crowne) . 180
Mainwaring, Mary (see Gill) 183
Manwaring, Oliver 183
Marbury, Anne (see Hutchinson) . 186
Marbury, Catherine (see Scott) . . 186
Marshall, Elizabeth (see Lewis) . . 189
Mauleverer, Anne (see Abbott) . . 191
Maverick, Mary (Gye) 124
Negus, Jane (Deighton) 85
Nelson, John 202
Nelson, Margaret (see Teackle) . . 202
Nelson, Philip 258
Nelson, Thomas 258
Owen, Joshua 210
Oxenbridge, John 213
Palgrave, Richard 215
Palmes, Anne (Humphrey) 145
Pelham, Elizabeth (Bosvile) 31
Pelham, Herbert 217
Peyton, Robert 221
Pynchon, Amy (Wyllys) 291
Randolph, Henry 236
Randolph, William 237
Reade, George 239
Rodney, William 241
Saint Leger, Katherine 245
Saltonstall, Muriel (Gurdon) 123
Saltonstall, Richard 248
Savage, Anthony 290
Scott, Catherine (Marbury) 186
Sherman, Mary (Launce) 161
Skipper, William 252
Skipwith, Diana (see Dale) 254
Skipwith, Grey 254
Smith, Maria Johanna (Somerset) 256
Somerset, Maria Johanna 256
Spencer, Nicholas 89
Stockman, John 260
Teackle, Margaret (Nelson) 202
Throckmorton, John 267
Torrey, Jane (Haviland) 137
Tyng, Elizabeth (Coytemore) 75
Washington, John 275
Washington, Lawrence 275
Washington, Richard 274
Welby, Olive (see Farwell) 276
West, John 144
Whitaker, Mary (Bourchier) 34
Williams, Frances (see Deighton) . 85
Wingfield, Thomas 283

Wolseley, Mary (see Brooke) 285
Wyatt, Hawte 289
Wyllys, Amy (see Pynchon) 291

xiii

ABELL

EDWARD I OF ENGLAND, King of England, married **ALIANORE DE CASTILLE**.
JOAN OF ENGLAND [*of Acre*], married **GILBERT DE CLARE**, Earl of Gloucester.
MARGARET DE CLARE, married **HUGH DE AUDLEY**, Earl of Gloucester.
MARGARET DE AUDLEY, married **RALPH DE STAFFORD**, Earl of Stafford.
KATHERINE DE STAFFORD, married **JOHN DE SUTTON**, Baron of Dudley.
JOHN DE SUTTON, Baron of Dudley, married **JOAN** _____.
JOHN SUTTON, Baron of Dudley, married **CONSTANCE BLOUNT**.
JOHN SUTTON, Knt., Lord Dudley, married **ELIZABETH BERKELEY**.
JANE SUTTON, married **THOMAS MAINWARING** of Ightfield [see MAINWARING 6].

4. CECILY MAINWARING, was married to **JOHN COTTON**, Esq., of Cotton in Wem, co. Salop, son of William Cotton, of Cotton, co. Salop, by Agnes, daughter of Philip Yonge, of Cainton, co. Salop. He was born about 1465.

Wotton (1741) 3:611 (Cotton arms: *Azure*, a chevron between three cotton-hanks, *argent*). *H.S.P.* 29:348 (1889) (1623 Vis. Salop) (names two sons but no daughters of Thomas Mainwaring). *TG* 5:163-165 (1984).

3. GEORGE COTTON, Knt., of Combermere, co. Chester, Sheriff of Denbighshire, Esquire of the Body to King Henry VIII, second son, was born at Cotton, co. Salop, about 1505. He was married before 11 Nov. 1537 to **MARY ONLEY**, daughter of John Onley, Esq., of Catesby, co. Northampton, by Jane Pontesbury, daughter of Thomas Pontesbury, of Albrighton, co. Salop. They had one son and four daughters. He and his wife were granted the abbey of Combermere by the King, and the manors of Wilkesley and Pulton, co. Chester. SIR GEORGE COTTON died at Combermere on 25 Mar. 1545. His widow died at Combermere on 14 Mar. 1559/60.

Wotton (1741) 3:611-612. *C.P.* 4:210 (1916). *TG* 5:151, 163 (1984).

2. RICHARD COTTON, Esq., of Combermere, son and heir, was born about 1540 (aged twenty-one and more at mother's death). He built the Combermere manor house in 1563, incorporating the remains of the Abbey. He was married for the first time at Combermere on 6 Jan. 1559/60 to **MARY MAINWARING**, daughter of Arthur Mainwaring, Knt. (**descendant of King Edward I**), by Margaret, daughter of Randall Mainwaring, Knt., of Over Peover [see MAINWARING 3]. She was born at Ightfield, co. Salop, about 1541. They had three sons and four daughters. She died before 14 June 1578. He was married for the second time at St. Olave's, Old Jewry, London, on 14 June 1578 to **JANE SULLIARD**, daughter of William Sulliard, by his wife Joan Todd. She died before 20 Feb. 1603/4 leaving one daughter Jane. He was married for the third time to **PHILIPPA** _____, widow (with issue John and Elizabeth Dormer) of John Dormer, and a "poor, yet very near kinswoman" to Sir Robert Cecil, later the Earl of Salisbury. RICHARD COTTON, ESQ., died intestate at Stoke, co. Warwick, on 14 June 1602. The will of his widow was dated 30 May 1625 and proved 18 Aug. 1631.

Wotton (1741) 3:612. *H.S.P.* 29:349 (1889) (*Maria uxor Georgii Cotton de Combermere*). *TG* 5:158-160 (1984) (information on his wives and children, supplementing past varied and confusing accounts, principally from the 1613 Visitation of Cheshire, and Ormerod).

1. FRANCES COTTON, daughter, evidently, by the first marriage, was born about 1573. She was married about 1598 to **GEORGE ABELL**, Gent., of Hemington in Lockington, co. Leicester, son of Robert Abell, of Stapenhill, co. Derby. He was born at Stapenhill about 1561. He matriculated 8 Dec. 1578 at Brasenose College, Oxford, and was admitted to the Middle Temple in 1581. GEORGE ABELL, GENT., was buried at Hemington on 13 Sep. 1630. His will, dated 8 Sep. 1630 and proved 7 Feb. 1630/1 (P.C.C., 10 St. John), made this bequest: "I bequeath unto my second sonne Robert Abell onelie a Twentie shillings peece for his childs parte in regard of ye charges I have beene at in placeing him in a good trade in London wch

ABELL (cont.)

hee hath made noe use of and since in furnishing him for newe England where I hope he now is". The will also names his brothers, Andrew Cotton, Gent., of Combermere, and George Cotton, Esq., of Combermere. She was probably dead by 16 Apr. 1646, when Dorothy, "sister of George Cotton of Combermere", made a bequest to her "cousin Mary Abell".

NEHGR 106:165 (July 1952) (Abell arms: Silver on a saltire engrailed azure nine fleurs-de-lis gold.
TG 5:158-171 (1984) (additions to ancestry of Frances Cotton) (evidence that Frances was daughter of first marriage).

Children of George Abell, by Frances Cotton:
  i. MARY ABELL, born about 1600, living 16 Apr. 1646, probably died unmarried.
  ii. GEORGE ABELL, eldest son, born about 1602; married MARY STANFORD. Issue.
  iii. ROBERT ABELL, second son, born about 1605, early settler of Weymouth and Rehoboth, Massachusetts, died Rehoboth, 20 June 1663; married JOANNA _____.
  iv. RICHARD ABELL, born about 1610, third son, an apprentice in 1631.

* * *

ABNEY

EDWARD I OF ENGLAND, King of England, married ALIANORE DE CASTILLE.
JOAN OF ENGLAND [*of Acre*], married GILBERT DE CLARE, Earl of Gloucester.
MARGARET DE CLARE, married, second, HUGH DE AUDLEY, 8th Earl of Stafford.
MARGARET DE AUDLEY, married RALPH DE STAFFORD, 2nd Lord Stafford.
KATHARINE DE STAFFORD, married JOHN DE SUTTON, Baron of Dudley.
JOHN DE SUTTON, Baron of Dudley, married JOAN DE _____.
JOHN SUTTON, Baron of Dudley, married CONSTANCE BLOUNT.
JOHN SUTTON, Knt., Lord Dudley, married ELIZABETH BERKELEY.
ELEANOR SUTTON, married, GEORGE STANLEY.
ANNE STANLEY, married JOHN WOLSELEY [see WOLSELEY 5].

4. ELLEN WOLSELEY, sixth daughter, was married to **GEORGE ABNEY**, Esq., of Willesley, co. Derby. They had eleven sons and ten daughters. She died on 3 Dec. 1571. GEORGE ABNEY, ESQ., died testate on 1 Mar. 1577/78. They were buried in the chancel of Willesley Chapel, with monumental inscriptions.

H.S.P. 2:154 (1870) (1619 Vis. Leic.) (Abney arms: *Or*, on a chief *gules* a lion passant *argent*).
Yeatman (1907), p. 56. *TG* 5:145 (1984).

3. EDMUND ABNEY, Gent., fourth son, was Freeman of Leicester in 1594, member of Council in 1599. He was married in 1587 to **KATHERINE LUDLAM**, daughter of William Ludlam, Alderman & Mayor of Leicester. They had two sons and two daughters. "Edmond Abnye, gent., of borow of Leicester" was buried testate (P.C.C., 65 Harte) at St. Mary's, Leicester, on 1 Apr. 1604.

H.S.P. 2:154 (1870). Yeatman (1907), pp. 53,94-95. *TG* 5:145 (1984).

2. PAUL ABNEY, eldest son, apprenticeship expiring at the Feast of the Purification of our Lady in 1607, was married in 1611 to **MARY BROKESBY**, daughter of George Brokesby, of Stapleford, co. Leicester. They had six sons and seven daughters. He entered pedigree in Visitation of Leicester 1634. PAUL ABNEY was buried at Leicester on 10 June 1635 (will proved 18 June 1635).

H.S.P. 2:154 (1870). Yeatman (1907), p. 94-95. *TG* 5:145 (1984).

1. GEORGE ABNEY, eldest son, was baptised at St. Mary's, Leicester, on 11 July

ABNEY (cont.)

1613. He was married to **BATHUSA** _____. They had five sons. **GEORGE ABNEY** was buried at St. Mary's, on 3 May 1661. His widow was married for the second time to REV. JOSEPH LEE, rector of Cotesbach near Lutterworth, co. Leicester, who had a daughter Mary Lee by a previous marriage. Her will was dated 2 Jan. 1706, and proved at Leicester on 22 Sep. 1712.
H.S.P. 2:154 (1870). *Yeatman* (1907), p. 94. *TG* 5:145-146 (1984).

Children and grandchildren of George Abney, by Bathusa _____:

i. **PAUL ABNEY**, baptised St. Mary's, 14 Jan. 1652/3, benefitted by the influence of his kinsman Sir Thomas Abney to become a merchant in the Virginia trade, Lieutenant of Frigate *Josiah* under Captain Sharpe in 1679; engaged before sailing for Virginia to his mother's stepdaughter, who joined him later in Virginia, she sailing in the company of his younger brother Dannett; married **MARY LEE**. Perhaps parents of George Abney, of Henrico County, Virginia.

ii. **DANNETT ABNEY**, died in infancy.

iii. **GEORGE ABNEY**, citizen of London, living 1689.

iv. **ABRAHAM ABNEY**, baptised 12 Apr. 1658, citizen of London, will dated 28 June 1689.

v. **DANNETT ABNEY**, baptised St. Mary's, 26 Feb. 1659/60, legatee of brother Abraham 1689 and mother 1716; patented land in Spotsylvania, Virginia, 28 Sep. 1728, will proved 5 Mar. 1733; married, second, about 1702, **MARY LEE**, widow of his brother Paul, and daughter of Rev. Joseph Lee (husband's stepfather) by his first wife. Issue.

   a. **DANNETT ABNEY**, of Hanover County, Virginia, married **MARY** _____. Issue.

   b. **ABRAHAM ABNEY**, resided South Carolina; married. Issue.

   c. **PAUL ABNEY**, of Goochland County, Virginia.

   d. **ABNER ABNEY**, of Albemarle County, Virginia, married **ANN** _____. Three children.

* * *

AGARD see BULL

ANDREWS see LUDLOW

APPLETON see TYRRELL

ARUNDEL see BROWNE

ARUNDELL see CALVERT

* * *

ASFORDBY

EDWARD I OF ENGLAND, King of England, married, second, **MARGUERITE DE FRANCE**.
THOMAS OF NORFOLK [of *Brotherton*], married **ALICE DE HALES**.
MARGARET OF NORFOLK, married **JOHN DE SEGRAVE**, 4th Lord Segrave.
ELIZABETH DE SEGRAVE, married **JOHN DE MOWBRAY**, 4th Lord Mowbray.
ALIANOR DE MOWBRAY, married **JOHN DE WELLES**, Knt., 5th Lord Welles.
EUDO DE WELLES, married **MAUD DE GREYSTOKE**.

ASFORDBY (cont.)

LIONEL DE WELLES, Knt., 6th Lord Welles, married, first, JOAN DE WATERTON.
MARGARET DE WELLES, married THOMAS DYMOKE, Knt.
LIONEL DYMOKE, Knt., married JOAN GRIFFITH.
ALICE DYMOKE, married WILLIAM SKIPWITH, Knt. [see SKIPWITH 4].

4. JOHN SKIPWITH, Esq., of Walmsgate, second son, was married to **ELEANOR KINGSTON**, daughter and heiress of John Kingston, of Great Grimsby, co. Lincoln. The administration of the estate of JOHN SKIPWITH, ESQ., was granted to his widow on 5 Nov. 1585. The will of "Elinearne Skipwith" of Walmsgate, "late wyfe of John Skipwith", dated 4 June 1599 and proved 31 Dec. 1599, named "my Doughter Newcomen" "John Newcomen my sonn in lawe" and her Newcomen grandchildren.
> H.S.P. 51:716 (1903) (Maddison Linc. Ped.). *Allaben* (1908), pp. 191-198.

3. MARY SKIPWITH, was married to **JOHN NEWCOMEN**, of Saltfleetby, co. Lincoln, son of John Newcomen, of Saltfleetby, by Alice, daughter of John Gascoigne, of Lasingcroft, co. York. They had four sons and five daughters. JOHN NEWCOMEN died testate and was buried at Saltfleetby on 1 May 1621. The will of his widow was dated 12 Mar. 1626/7 and proved 2 Oct. 1627.
> *Gen.* 4:260 (1880). H.S.P. 50:46 (1902), 51:716 (1903). *Allaben* (1908), pp. 151-152 (Newcomen arms: *Argent*, a lion's head erased *sable* between three crescents *gules*).

2. ELEANOR NEWCOMEN, was baptised at Saltfleetby on 10 Nov. 1576. She was married at Saltfleetby on 20 Apr. 1597 to **WILLIAM ASFORDBY**, of Saltfleetby, and of Newark-on-Trent, co. Nottingham, son of Edward Asfordby, Gent., of Asfordby in Bilsby, co. Lincoln, by Katherine, daughter of William Sandon, of Ashby-by-Partney, co. Lincoln. They had one son and seven daughters. WILLIAM ASFORDBY was buried at Saltfleetby in May 1623. His widow was buried at Saltfleetby on 19 Nov. 1634.
> H.S.P. 50:45-46 (1902) (Asfordby arms: *Or*, a saltire engrailed *sable*). H.S.P. 51:716 (1903).

1. JOHN ASFORDBY, of Saltfleetby, son and heir, was married at Cumberworth, co. Lincoln, on 14 Oct. 1634 to **ALICE WOLLEY**, daughter of William Wolley, of Cumberworth, by Anne (**descendant of King Edward I**), daughter of Roger Leming, of Barnetby le Wold, co. Lincoln. She was baptised at Cumberworth on 14 Dec. 1610 [see GIRLINGTON 1 for her ancestry]. They had eight sons and four daughters. She was buried on 16 June 1638. JOHN ASFORDBY was living on 11 Nov. 1657.
> H.S.P. 50:46 (1902) (John Asfordby signed the 1634 Lincolnshire pedigree). *Allaben* (1908), p. 95-100, 358. NEHGR 107:267 (Oct. 1953) (Asfordby arms).

Children & grandchildren of John Asfordby, by Alice Wolley:

i. ELIZABETH ASFORDBY, baptised 21 Jan. 1635/6, buried 28 Mar. 1646.

ii. WILLIAM ASFORDBY, baptised Saltfleetby, 29 Mar. 1638, of Stayne-in-the-Marsh, co. Lincoln, emigrated before 1674, bringing a parchment pedigree of twelve generations of ancestors, dated 1562; resided Kingston and Marbletown, Ulster County, New York, member of the first New York Assembly and sheriff of Ulster County, will proved 1698; married MARTHA BURTON, daughter of William Burton, of Burgh-in-the-Marsh, co. Lincoln.

    a. MARTHA ASFORDBY, legatee of her grandmother, 18 Mar. 1667/8.

    b. CHARLES ASFORDBY, baptised Mablethorpe 29 Oct. 1668, died in infancy.

    c. SUSANNA ASFORDBY, baptised Mablethorpe 3 Nov. 1669, buried 4 Nov. 1669.

    d. SUSANNA ASFORDBY, died Frederick County, Maryland, married JOHN BEATTY. Ten children.

    e. ELEANOR ASFORDBY, baptized Ulster County, New York, 26 Feb. 1682, married THOMAS COOK.

    f. ANNE ASFORDBY, baptised Ulster County, New York, 2 Mar. 1684, died before 1711, unmarried.

ASFORDBY (cont.)

    g. **PROVIDENCE ASFORDBY** [twin to Anne], baptized 2 Mar. 1684, died before 1711, unmarried.

    h. **CATHERINE ASFORDBY**, baptized Ulster County, 9 Nov. 1685, living New York City 1711, unmarried.

  iii. CHARLES ASFORDBY, baptised 14 Jan. 1640/1, buried 28 June 1649.

  iv. THOMAS ASFORDBY, baptised 28 June 1642, married MILDRED EMERSON. Issue in England.

   v. EDWARD ASFORDBY, baptised 4 Apr. 1644, buried 2 Dec. 1675.

  vi. MARY ASFORDBY, baptised 20 Apr. 1646, married THOMAS COOPER.

 vii. ANNE ASFORDBY, baptised 12 Dec. 1647, buried 4 Aug. 1649.

viii. SIMEON ASFORDBY, baptised 10 July 1649.

  ix. BENJAMIN ASFORDBY [twin], baptised 10 July 1649, buried 8 Aug. 1649.

   x. ELEANOR ASFORDBY, baptised 8 Feb. 1651/2.

* * *

AUCHER see LOVELACE

* * *

AUDLEY

EDWARD I OF ENGLAND, King of England, married **ALIANORE DE CASTILLE**.
JOAN OF ENGLAND [*of Acre*], married **GILBERT DE CLARE** [see CLARE 12].

13. MARGARET DE CLARE, was born, probably, at Caerphilly Castle in October 1292 (aged twenty-two at her brother's death), and was second sister and co-heiress of Gilbert de Clare, last Earl of Gloucester of that family. She was married on 1 Nov. 1307 to **PETER DE GAVESTON**, son, probably, of Sir Ernaud de Gaveston, by Clarmunda de Marsau et de Louvigny. He was born at Béarn, Gascony, about 1284. They had two daughters. He became a favourite of King Edward II and was created **Earl of Cornwall**. He was beheaded without trial on 19 June 1312. She was married for the second time at Windsor on 28 Apr. 1317 to **HUGH DE AUDLEY**, second son of Hugh Audley, of Stratton Audley, co. Oxford (**descendant of Charlemagne**), by Isolt, daughter of Edmund de Mortimer, Knt., **Baron** of Wigmore, co. Hereford (**descendant of Charlemagne**). He was born about 1289. He was summoned to Parliament *v.p.*, on 30 Nov. 1317 by writ directed *Hugoni Daudele juniori* whereby he may be held to have become **Lord Audley**. In right of his wife, he was created **Earl of Gloucester** on 16 Mar. 1336/7. MARGARET DE CLARE died on 9 Apr. 1342. HUGH DE AUDLEY, Earl of Gloucester, died on 10 Nov. 1347 *s.p.m.*, and was buried at Tonbridge Priory.

    C.P. 1:346-7 (1910). *C.P.* 3:434 (1913). *C.P.* 5:715-719 (1926). *C.P.* 12(1):177 (1953). *TAG* 35:100-102 (Apr. 1959). *TAG* 40:95-99 (Apr. 1964). *TAG* 69:138. *Paget* (1957) 17:2-3.

12. MARGARET DE AUDLEY, Baroness Audley, daughter and heiress, was born about or before 1325 (aged eighteen before 1343). She was married before 6 July

AUDLEY (cont.)

1336 to **RALPH DE STAFFORD, Baron** of Stafford, co. Stafford, 2nd Lord Stafford, son and heir of Edmund Stafford, **Baron** of Stafford, co. Stafford, by Margaret, daughter of Ralph Basset, Lord Basset of Drayton, co. Stafford (**descendant of Charlemagne**). He was born on 24 Sep 1301. He had been married previously about 1326/7 to Katherine de Hastang, daughter of John de Hastang, Knt., of Chebsey, co. Stafford, by his wife Eve. They had one daughter. Ralph's first wife, Katherine, died well before 6 July 1336 on which date a commission was appointed to enquire into a complaint by Hugh de Audley, Lord Audley, soon to be created Earl of Gloucester, that Ralph de Stafford and others (mostly relatives) broke his close at Thaxted, Essex, carried away his goods, abducted Margaret his daughter and heiress, and married her against her will. Margaret was then aged about twelve. King Edward III intervened to protect Ralph, and, after making his peace, Ralph and Margaret were given the reversion to a large part of the Gloucester inheritance. They had two sons and five daughters. MARGARET DE AUDLEY died on 16 Sep. 1348 (perhaps following the birth of her youngest child Katherine), and was buried at Tonbridge, Kent. Ralph was summoned to Parliament from 29 Nov. 1336 as *Radulpho Baroni de Stafford*, and was a Founder Knight of the Order of the Garter on 23 Apr. 1349. He was created **Earl of Stafford** on 5 Mar. 1350/1. RALPH DE STAFFORD, Earl of Stafford, died testate on 31 Aug. 1372, and was buried at Tonbridge, with his second wife, at the feet of Margaret's parents.

Banks (1844), p. 408. C.P. 3:161 (1913). C.P. 5:313, 710 (1926). C.P. 11:101 (1949). C.P. 12(1):174-177 (1953). TG 5:131-133 (1984).

Children of Ralph de Stafford, by Margaret de Audley:
   i. **ELIZABETH DE STAFFORD**, married **JOHN DE FERRERS** [see FERRERS 11].[1]
   ii. **BEATRICE DE STAFFORD**, married, second, **THOMAS DE ROS** [see ROS 11].[2]
   iii. **JOAN DE STAFFORD**, married **JOHN DE CHERLETON** [see CHERLETON 12].[3]
   iv. **HUGH DE STAFFORD**, Knt., born about 1342 [see next].
   v. **KATHERINE DE STAFFORD**, born 1347/8, married **JOHN DE SUTTON** [see DUDLEY 9].[4]

11. HUGH DE STAFFORD, K.G., 2nd Earl of Stafford, 3rd Lord Stafford, Lord Audley, second but first surviving son and heir, was born in or before 1342. He was married before 1 Mar. 1350/1 to **PHILIPPE DE BEAUCHAMP**, daughter of Thomas de Beauchamp, of Elmley, co. Worcester, 11th Earl of Warwick (of **Magna Charta Surety descent** and **descendant of Charlemagne**) by Katherine (of **Magna Charta Surety descent**), daughter of Roger de Mortimer, 1st Earl of March, **Baron** of Wigmore, co. Hereford (**descendant of Charlemagne**). He was summoned to Parliament on 8 Jan. 1370/1 *v.p.* His wife died before 6 Apr. 1386. On 27 Mar. 1386 he was licenced to voyage overseas to Jerusalem. HUGH STAFFORD, Earl of Stafford, died testate on the Isle of Rhodes on 16 Oct. 1386. They were buried at Stone.

---

[1] Ancestors of **Robert Abell, Grace Chetwode, Anne & Catherine Marbury**.

[2] Ancestors of **Elizabeth Bosvile, Charles Calvert, Francis Dade, Humphrey Davie, Henry Fleete, Muriel Gurdon, John Harleston, Agnes Mackworth, Philip & Thomas Nelson, William Randolph, George Reade, William Rodney, Richard Saltonstall, William Skepper, Olive Welby, Thomas Wingfield, Hawte Wyatt**, and, probably, **Thomas Dudley, Jane Haviland**.

[3] Ancestors of **Nathaniel Littleton, Thomas Lloyd, Agnes Mackworth, John Nelson, Philip & Thomas Nelson, John Washington**, and, probably, **Thomas Dudley**.

[4] Ancestors of **Robert Abell, Dannett Abney, Elizabeth Marshall, Agnes Mackworth, John Washington, Mary Wolsesley**, and probably **Thomas Dudley**.

AUDLEY (cont.)

C.P. 12(1):177-179 (1953).

Children of Hugh de Stafford, by Philippe de Beauchamp:
  i. **EDMUND DE STAFFORD**, fourth son, born 2 Mar. 1377/8 [see next].
  ii. **MARGARET DE STAFFORD**, married, **RALPH NEVILLE** [see NEVILLE 10].[1]
  iii. **KATHERINE DE STAFFORD**, married **MICHAEL DE LA POLE** [see POLE 12].[2]

10. EDMUND DE STAFFORD, K.B., K.G., 5th Earl of Stafford, 6th Lord Stafford, fourth son, was born on 2 Mar. 1377/8. He was married to **ANNE OF GLOUCESTER**, the childless widow of his brother Thomas, 3rd Earl of Stafford (died 4 July 1392 *s.p.*), and daughter and eventual sole heiress of Thomas of Gloucester [*of Woodstock*], Duke of Gloucester (**son of King Edward III**), by Alianor, elder daughter and co-heiress of Humphrey de Bohun, 7th Earl of Hereford, 6th Earl of Essex and 2nd Earl of Northampton. She was born in April 1383. EDMUND DE STAFFORD, Earl of Stafford, was slain at the Battle of Shrewsbury on 21 July 1403, and was buried at Austin Friars', Stafford. His widow was married for the third time to **WILLIAM BOURGCHIER**, Comte d'Eu in Normandy [see LAUNCE 8 for her ancestry, and for descendants of this marriage]. She died testate between 16 and 24 Oct 1438.

C.P. 5:208 (1926). *C.P.* 6:475-477 (1926). *C.P.* 12(1):180-181 (1953).

9. HUMPHREY STAFFORD, Knt., K.G., 6th Earl of Stafford, 7th Lord Stafford, was born on 15 Aug. 1402. He was created **Duke of Buckingham** on 14 Sep. 1444. He was married, before 18 Oct. 1424 to **ANNE NEVILLE**, daughter of Ralph Neville, of Raby, Durham, 1st Earl of Westmorland, by Joan Beaufort, the legitimized daughter of John of Lancaster [*of Gaunt*], Duke of Lancaster [see BEAUFORT 11.iv.g for her ancestry]. HUMPHREY STAFFORD, Duke of Buckingham, a zealous Lancastrian, was slain at the battle of Northampton on 10 July 1460, and was buried in the Grey Friars' at Northampton (P.C.C., 21 Stokton). His widow was married for the second time in 1467 to Walter Blount, 1st Baron Mountjoy (died 1 Aug. 1474). She died testate (P.C.C., 2 Logge) 20 Sep. 1480, and was buried at Pleshey, Essex.

C.P. 2:388-389 (1912). *C.P.* 11:706 (1949). *C.P.* 12(1):48 footnote *a*, 181 (1953). *Paget* (1977), p. 424.

8. HUMPHREY STAFFORD, styled Earl of Stafford, first son and heir apparent, was married to **MARGARET BEAUFORT**, daughter, and in her issue heiress, of Edmund Beaufort, Duke of Somerset (**descendant of King Edward I**), by Alianor, second daughter of Richard Beauchamp, Earl of Warwick (**descendant of King Edward I**) [see BEAUFORT 9.v for her ancestry]. HUMPHREY STAFFORD died *v.p.*, said to have been slain on the Lancastrian side on 22 May 1455 at the first Battle of St. Albans. His widow was married for the second time to RICHARD DARELL, Knt., of Lillingstone Dayrell, co. Buckingham, and had issue. She died in 1474.

C.P. 1:342 (1910). *C.P.* 2:389 (1912). *C.P.* 12(1):182 (1953). *Paget* (1957) 500:3. *Paget* (1977), p. 257.

7. HENRY STAFFORD, K.B., K.G., 2nd Duke of Buckingham, Earl of Stafford, only son and heir, was born posthumously on 4 Sep. 1455. He was married to **KATHERINE WYDEVILLE**, daughter of Richard Wydevile, Earl Rivers, by Jacquette, daughter of Pierre de Luxembourg, Comte de Saint-Pol et de Brienne

---

[1]Ancestors of **Richard & William Bernard, Edward Carleton, John Fenwick, Thomas Lunsford, Agnes Mackworth, Anne Mauleverer, George Reade, Richard Saltonstall**.

[2]Ancestors of **William Asfordby, William Farrar, John Nelson, William Skepper**.

AUDLEY (cont.)

(**descendant of Charlemagne**). She was sister of Elizabeth, Queen Consort of King Edward IV. Having joined in the plot to place the Earl of Richmond on the throne, **HENRY STAFFORD**, Duke of Buckingham, was beheaded aged twenty-eight (without legal trial) at Salisbury on 2 Nov. 1483, and was buried at the Grey Friars'. His widow was married before Nov 1485 to JASPER TUDOR, Duke of Bedford, who died on 21 Dec. 1495 *s.p. legit.* She was married for the third time, as his first wife, to RICHARD WINGFIELD, K.G. (died 22 July 1525).

Banks (1844), p. 409 ("He was Shakespear's Buckingham, in his celebrated tragedy of king Richard III."). *C.P.* 2:389-390 (1912). *C.P.* 12(1):182 (1953). *Paget* (1957) 500:3. *Paget* (1977), p. 176.

Children of Henry Stafford, by Katherine Wydeville:
  i. **EDWARD STAFFORD**, married **ALIANOR PERCY** [see SAINT-LEGER 5].[1]
  ii. **ANNE STAFFORD**, married **GEORGE HASTINGS** [see HASTINGS 6].[2]

* * *

BARDOLF

EDWARD I OF ENGLAND, King of England, married **ALIANORE DE CASTILLE**.
JOAN OF ENGLAND [*of Acre*], married **GILBERT DE CLARE**, Earl of Gloucester.
ELIZABETH DE CLARE, married **ROGER DAMORY**, Lord Damory [see BURGH 13].

11. ELIZABETH DAMORY, Lady Damory, daughter and heiress, was born shortly before 23 May 1318. She was married before 25 Dec. 1327 to **JOHN BARDOLF**, Knt., of Wormegay, Norfolk, 3rd Lord Bardolf, son of Thomas Bardolf, Knt., 2nd Lord Bardolf, **Baron** of Wormegay, Norfolk (**descendant of Charlemagne**), by Agnes, daughter, probably, of William de Grandison, Seigneur de Grandison on Lake Neufchâtel, Switzerland, 1st Lord Grandison (**descendant of Charlemagne**). He was born on 13 Jan. 1313/14. She was living in 1360 and died before 1363. He was summoned to Parliament 1336-1363 with writs directed *Johanni Bardolf de Wirmegey*. JOHN BARDOLF, Lord Bardolf, died aged fifty-one at Assisi in Italy on 29 July 1363.

C.P. 1:418-419 (1910). *C.P.* 4:45-46 (1916).

10. WILLIAM BARDOLF, 4th Lord Bardolf, of Wormgay, son and heir, was born on 21 Oct. 1349. He was summoned to Parliament from 1375 by writs directed *Willelmo Bardolf de Wirmegeye*. He was married to **AGNES DE POYNINGS**, daughter of Michael de Poynings, Lord Poynings, by Joan (of **baronial** descent), daughter of Richard Rokesley, Knt. Their daughters were born at Tattershall Castle, co. Lincoln. WILLIAM BARDOLF, Lord Bardolf, died testate aged thirty-six on 29 Jan. 1385/6 (will requesting burial at the Friar Carmelites at Lynn, Norfolk). His widow was married for the second time shortly after 10 Apr. 1386 to Thomas Mortimer, Knt., who was dead 9 Jan. 1402/3. She died testate on 12 June 1403 (will dated 9 Jan. 1402/3, requesting burial at Trinity Priory, Aldgate, London).

C.P. 1:419-420 (1910). *C.P.* 5:397 (1926).

---

[1]Ancestors of **St.Leger Codd, Edward Digges, Warham Horsmanden, Katherine Saint Leger**.
[2]Ancestors of **Maria Johanna Somerset**.

BARDOLF (cont.)

9. CECILY BARDOLF, was married to **BRIAN STAPLETON**, Knt., of Ingham, Norfolk, and Bedale, co. York, son of Miles Stapleton, Knt., of Ingham and Bedale (**descendant of Charlemagne**), by Ela, daughter of Edmund Ufford, Knt. (of **Magna Charta Surety descent** and **descendant of Charlemagne**). He was born in 1379 (aged forty and more in 1419). He fought in the French Wars, and was at Agincourt in 1415. He was a prisoner for five years until ransomed. He was M.P., and Sheriff of Norfolk and Suffolk, 1424. She died on 29 Sep. 1432. SIR BRIAN STAPLETON died testate on 7 Aug. 1438. They were buried in Ingham Priory (with monumental brass, now lost).
    C.P. 5:397 (1926). *NEHGR* 148:255-256 (July 1994) (arms: *Argent*, a lion rampant *sable*).

Children of Brian Stapleton, by Cecily Bardolf:
    i. **MILES STAPLETON**, Knt., born about 1408 [see next].
    ii. **BRIAN STAPLETON**, Esq., born about 1410, married **ISABEL** _____ [see HAYNES 8].[1]

8. MILES STAPLETON, Knt., of Ingham and Bedale, was born about 1408 (aged thirty and more in 1438). He was married for the first time to an unidentified wife. He was married for the second time to **KATHERINE DE LA POLE**, daughter (and in 1430 heiress) of Thomas de la Pole, Knt., of Grafton Regis, co. Northampton, by Anne, daughter of Nicholas Cheney. She was born about 1416 (aged fourteen and more in 1430). SIR MILES STAPLETON died testate on 30 Sep. or 1 Oct. 1466, and was buried in Ingham Priory (will dated 4 Aug. 1442, proved on 17 Nov 1466). His widow was married for the second time to Richard Harcourt, Knt., of Wytham, co. Berks (died 1 Oct. 1486). She died on 13 or 14 Oct. 1488, and was buried in Rowley Abbey (will dated 7 July, 5 Sep. 1488, proved 23 Jan. 1488/9).
    Swyncombe and Ewelme (1858), pp. 310-311 (first wife identified as Elizabeth, daughter of Sir Simon Felbrigg). *C.P.* 5:397 (1926).

Children of Miles Stapleton, by Katherine de la Pole:
    i. **ELIZABETH STAPLETON**, born about 1441 [see next].
    ii. **JANE STAPLETON**, married **CHRISTOPHER HARCOURT** [see HARCOURT 7].[2]

7. ELIZABETH STAPLETON, elder daughter and co-heiress, was born about 1441 (aged twenty-five in 1466). She was married before 7 Mar. 1463/4 to **WILLIAM CALTHORPE**, Knt., of Burnham Thorpe, Sheriff of Norfolk, son of John Calthorpe, Knt., by Anna, daughter of John Withe, Knt. He was born at Burnham on 30 Jan. 1409/10. He had been married previously to Elizabeth Grey (died 1437), daughter of Reynold, Lord Grey of Ruthin. SIR WILLIAM CALTHORPE died testate aged eighty-five on 15 Nov. 1494 to be buried at White Friars', Norwich. His widow was married for the second time to JOHN FORTESCUE, Knt., of North Mimms, co. Hertford (died 28 July 1500). She was married for the third time to EDWARD HOWARD, Knt., K.G., Lord High Admiral (slain off Brest 25 Apr. 1513). She died on 18 Feb. 1504/5.
    H.S.P. 16:295 (1881) (1563 Vis. Yorks). *Chester of Chicheley* (1878), p. 140. *C.P.* 6:397 (1926).

Children of William Calthorpe, by Elizabeth Stapleton:
    i. **ANNE CALTHORPE** [see next].
    ii. **ELIZABETH CALTHORPE**, married **FRANCIS HASILDEN**, Esq. [see HASILDEN 6].[3]

---

[1] Ancestors of **Elizabeth Haynes**.
[2] Ancestors of **Muriel Gurdon**.
[3] Ancestors of **George & Robert Brent, Robert Peyton**.

BARDOLF (cont.)

6. ANNE CALTHORPE was married to **ROBERT DRURY**, Knt., of Hawstead, Suffolk, M.P. for Suffolk, Speaker of the House of Commons, son and heir of Roger Drury, Knt., of Hawstead, by Felice, daughter of Walter Denston, of Besthorpe, Norfolk. They had two sons and three daughters. He was legatee of the "Ellesmere Chaucer" (which bears the signature of Robert Drury on the fly-leaf) from John de Vere, Earl of Oxford. She was living on 31 May 1494 when mentioned in the will of her father. He was married for the second time to Anne Jerningham, widow of Edward, Lord Gray, and _____ Berkeley, and daughter of Edward Jerningham of Somerleyton, Suffolk, by whom he had no issue. SIR ROBERT DRURY died testate (P.C.C., 32 Hogen) on 2 Mar. 1535/6, and was buried with his first wife at St. Mary's, Bury St. Edmunds, Suffolk. His widow was married for the fourth time to Edmund Walsingham, Knt., of Scadbury and died before 1 Mar. 1558.

H.S.P. 16:295 (1881). *Chester of Chicheley* (1878), p. 140. *Muskett* (1900), p. 354. *Campling* (1937), pp. 43-47. *Clopton* (1939), pp. 57-58. *TG* 9:192 (1988).

Children of Robert Drury, by Anne Calthorpe:

  i. **WILLIAM DRURY**, Knt., born 1500, married **ELIZABETH SOTHILL** [see DRURY 5].[1]
  ii. **ANNE DRURY**, married, first, **GEORGE WALDEGRAVE**, Knt. [see KEMPE 4].[2]

* * *

BARENTYN see TUCHET

BARKHAM see JENNINGS

BASSET see DEIGHTON

* * *

BAYNTON

HENRY III OF ENGLAND, King of England, married **ÉLÉNORE DE PROVENCE**.
EDMUND OF LANCASTER *Crouchback*, Earl of Lancaster, married, **BLANCHE D'ARTOIS**.
HENRY OF LANCASTER, Duke of Lancaster, married **MAUD DE CHAWORTH**.
ALIANOR OF LANCASTER, married **RICHARD FITZ ALAN**, Earl of Arundel.
JOHN DE ARUNDEL, Lord Arundel, married **ALIANOR MALTRAVERS**.
JOAN DE ARUNDEL, married **WILLIAM DE ECHINGHAM**, Knt. [see ECHINGHAM 9].

6. JOAN DE ECHINGHAM, daughter, it is said, was married to **JOHN BAYNTON**, Knt., of Falstone, co. Wilts, Sheriff of Wiltshire, M.P. for Wiltshire, son of Nicholas de Baynton, Esq., of Falstone (of **baronial** descent), by Joan (**descendant of Charlemagne**), daughter of John de la Roche, Knt., of Roche in Bromham, co. Wilts. He was born about 1407 (aged four at the time of the death of his maternal

---

[1] Ancestors of **John Harleston, Robert Peyton**.
[2] Ancestors of **Nathaniel Burrough, William Clopton, Edmund Kempe**.

BAYNTON (cont.)

grandmother, and of age in 1428). They had five sons. He was married for the second time to Katherine Payne, widow of John Stourton, M.P., of Preston Plucknet, Somerset, and daughter of Thomas Payne, of Payneshay, co. Devon. SIR JOHN BAYNTON died on 20 June 1465. His widow was married for the third time to William Carent, Esq., of Toomer in Henstridge, Somerset (died 8 Apr. 1476). She died in 1473.

H.S.P. 105:6 (1954) (1623 Vis. Wilts) *(Johes Bainton miles fil: et haer temp: E. 4 = Jana filia Willi Ichingham mil:). Abel Lunt* (1963), pp. 209-223 (Bayton arms: *Sable*, a bend fusilly *argent*).

Children of John Baynton, by Joan de Echingham:

  i. ROBERT BAYNTON, Knt., born about 1439 [see next].

  ii. HENRY BAYNTON, married [see GYE 4].[1]

5. ROBERT BAYNTON, Knt., of Falstone, co. Wilts, said to be son of Joan de Echingham, was born about 1439 (aged over twenty-six on his father's death). He was married, evidently, to **ELIZABETH HAUTE**, daughter of William Haute, of Waddenhall in Waltham, Kent, by Joan, daughter of Richard Wydeville, of Grafton, co. Northampton. She was a cousin of Elizabeth Wydeville, Queen of King Edward IV. As a Lancastrian he fought for King Henry VI at Tewkesbury. He was taken prisoner by the forces of King Edward IV, declared a traitor and attainted 1471-2. SIR ROBERT BAYNTON died before 6 Oct. 1472.

H.S.P. 105:6 (1954). *Abel Lunt* (1963), pp. 222-226. *Paget* (1977), p. 436.

4. JOHN BAYNTON, Knt., of Falstone, co. Wilts, was born about 1460. He was married to **JOAN DIGGES**, daughter of Thomas Digges, of Chilham, Kent. They had four sons and three daughters. On 1 July 1504 he obtained a reversal of the attainder of his father for high treason committed at Tewkesbury, with a restoration in blood and inheritance and thus recovered the many family manors. He succeeded to the estate of Bromham, co. Wilts, as heir to his second cousin once removed, Richard Beauchamp, Lord St. Amand, in 1508, and he appears to have resided thereafter at Bromham. SIR JOHN BAYNTON died testate (P.C.C., 17 Porch) on 31 Oct. 1516, to be buried at St. Nicholas', Bromham, co. Wilts.

H.S.P. 105:6-7 (1954). *Abel Lunt* (1963), pp. 226-229 (his brass shows his arms as Baynton, de la Mere, Roche, and evidently those of his wife: *Gules*, on a cross *argent* five eagles displayed *sable*). *Paget* (1977), p. 263.

3. EDWARD BAYNTON, Knt., of Bromham, co. Wilts, Sheriff of Wiltshire, M.P., son and heir, was born about 1480. He was married for the first time about 1505 to **ELIZABETH SULLIARD**, daughter of John Sulliard, Knt., of Weston, Norfolk, Lord Chief Justice of the Common Pleas, by his second wife Anne (descendant of King Edward I), daughter of John Andrews, Esq., of Baylham, Suffolk. They had three sons and four daughters. He was married for the second time about 18 Jan. 1531/2 to **ISABEL LEIGH**, daughter of Ralph Leigh, of Stockwell in Lambeth, Surrey, by Joyce Culpeper **(descendant of King Edward I)** [see STOCKMAN 6]. They had two sons. Sir Edward Baynton was Vice Chamberlain to three of the wives of King Henry VIII (Anne Boleyn, Jane Seymour and Anne of Cleves). He built a new manor house at Bromham and twice entertained there King Henry VIII and his court, once in 1535 when Henry was courting Jane Seymour. When, in the summer of 1540, King Henry was married to her half sister Katherine Howard, Isabel Baynton became a Lady of the Privy Chamber. He (and presumably Isabel as well) was present at the marriage of King Henry and Katherine Parr. SIR EDWARD

---

[1]Ancestors of **Mary Gye**.

BAYNTON (cont.)

BAYNTON died testate (P.C.C., 28 Pynnyng) on 27 Nov. 1544, probably in France on the ill-considered invasion of France. His widow was married for the second time to JAMES STUMPE, Knt., of Malmesbury, co. Wilts (died testate 1563), and for the third time to THOMAS STAFFORD, Esq. She died on 16 Feb. 1572/3.

H.S.P. 105:7 (1954). *Abel Lunt* (1963), pp. 229-244. *Mary Isaac* (1955), pp. 352-353. *Paget* (1977), p. 178.

2. **HENRY BAYNTON**, of Chelsea, Middlesex, elder son by second marriage, was born about 1536 (aged nine and more in 1545). Most, if not all, of the manors and lands by which his father had attempted to provide for Henry were sold by his mother and her second and third husbands, with Henry's consent. He was married to **ANNE CAVENDISH**, daughter of William Cavendish, Knt., by Margaret, daughter of Edmund Bostock, of Whatcroft, co. Chester. They had three sons.

H.S.P. 105:8 (1954). *Abel Lunt* (1963), pp. 244-246.

1. **FERDINANDO BAYNTON**, Gent., third son, was baptised at Bromham on 28 May 1566. He was married, possibly at Calne, co. Wilts, about 1598, as her second husband, to **JOAN WEARE** (or **BROWNE**), widow (with eight children) of John Hinckley, of Salisbury, and daughter of John Weare *alias* Browne, of Calne. Ferdinando and Joan had eight children. He became an innholder through the inheritance of his wife from her grandfather, William Weare *alias* Browne, innholder of Salisbury. Ferdinando Baynton was living on 4 Nov. 1616.

H.S.P. 105:8 (1954). *NEHGR* 112:248 (Oct. 1958) ("Bainton" arms). *Abel Lunt* (1963), pp. 169-171, 180-188, 246-247 (comment by Mr. Davis on page 247: Because in all probability no other seventeenth-century English emigrant to America had so many close kinsmen of high rank as Anne possessed, they are partially listed here. Through her great-aunt Bridget Baynton, Anne was the second cousin of the Countess of Suffolk, the Countess of Lincoln and the Countess of Rutland, and the second cousin, once removed, of the Duchess of Buckingham. Through her great-grandfather Sir William Cavendish, she was a great-niece of the Earl of Devonshire, the Countess of Shrewsbury and the Countess of Lennox, and the first cousin, once removed, of Lady Arabella Stuart, the Duke of Newcastle and the Earl of Kingston-upon-Hull. This constitutes an outstanding example of the fluidity of English society.).

Children & grandchildren of Ferdinando Baynton, by Joan Weare:

    i. ELIZABETH BAYNTON, died young.

    ii. KATHERINE BAYNTON, born 21 July 1602, living 1623.

    iii. ANNE BAYNTON, born 23 Sep. 1602, died testate 1679; married St. Edmund's, Salisbury, 12 Oct.1629 **CHRISTOPHER BATT**, of Boston, Massachusetts, baptised St. Edmund's, Salisbury, 6 July 1601, emigrated with family on the *Bevis* of Southampton in May 1638, merchant in Boston, died testate Boston, Massachusetts, 10 Aug. 1661, son of Thomas Batt, of Salisbury, co. Wilts, by Joan, daughter of Henry Byley, tanner, of St. Edmund's, Salisbury.

        a. **ANNE BATT**, baptised St. Edmund's 1 Aug. 1630, married 12 June 1657 **EDMUND ANGIER**, merchant of Cambridge, Massachusetts. Eight children.

        b. **JANE BATT**, baptised St. Edmund's December 1631, married **DR. PETER TOPPAN**, of Newbury.

        c. **CHRISTOPHER BATT**, baptised St. Martin's 22 Sep. 1633, of Dover, New Hampshire, died 1712 *s.p.*

        d. **THOMAS BATT**, baptised St. Martin's 23 July 1635, tanner, of Boston, Massachusetts, died 1678-79; married **LYDIA BENJAMIN**. Three children.

        e. **ELIZABETH BATT**, baptised St. Martin's 1 Nov. 1636, died Newbury 6 July 1652.

        f. **SAMUEL BATT**, born in New England probably about 1639, B.A., Queen's College, Oxford, rector of Coulston, co. Wilts, vicar of Steeple Aston, co. Wilts, died England 1684-1690; married in England MARY _____. Four children.

        g. **JOHN BATT**, born Salisbury, Massachusetts, 4 Mar. 1641, died young.

        h. **PAUL BATT** [twin], born Salisbury 18 Feb. 1643, glazier of Boston, Massachusetts, died July

BAYNTON (cont.)

1678; married SARAH _____. Three children.
- i. **BARNABAS BATT** [twin], born 18 Feb. 1643, died London, England, 1671.
- j. **TIMOTHY BATT**, born about 1645, tailor of Boston, Massachusetts, died January 1678/9; married before 1671 **ABIGAIL BAYES**. Three children.
- iv. HENRY BAYNTON, buried 23 May 1607.
- v. BAMFIELD BAYNTON, baptised 8 Sep, buried 9 Sep. 1606.
- vi. FERDINANDO BAYNTON, baptised 16 Aug, buried 31 Dec. 1608.
- vii. ELIZABETH BAYNTON, born 10 Nov. 1609, living 1623.
- viii. HENRY BAYNTON, baptised 31 Mar. 1611, buried 9 Apr. 1612.

* * *

BEAUCHAMP

EDWARD I OF ENGLAND, King of England, married **ALIANORE DE CASTILLE**.
JOAN OF ENGLAND [*of Acre*], married **GILBERT DE CLARE**, Earl of Gloucester.
ELIZABETH DE CLARE, married **THEOBALD DE VERDUN**, Lord Verdun.
ISABEL DE VERDUN, married **HENRY DE FERRERS**, 2nd Lord Ferrers of Groby.
WILLIAM DE FERRERS, Lord Ferrers, married **MARGARET DE UFFORD** [see CLARKE9].

10. MARGARET DE FERRERS, was married before April 1381 to **THOMAS DE BEAUCHAMP**, K.G., Earl of Warwick *de facto*, Hereditary Sheriff of Worcestershire, and Chamberlain of the Exchequer, younger son of Thomas de Beauchamp, of Elmley, co. Worcester, 11th Earl of Warwick, **Baron** of Salwarpe, co. Worcester, of Hanslope, co. Buckingham, of Flamstead, co. Hertford, and of Warwick, co. Warwick (of **Magna Charta Surety descent** and **descendant of Charlemagne**), by Katherine, daughter of Roger de Mortimer, 1st Earl of March, **Baron** of Wigmore, co. Hereford (**descendant of Charlemagne**). He was born before 16 Mar. 1338/9. He may have joined in the alleged plot of the Earls Gloucester and Arundel for which he was arrested on a charge of high treason, being banished to the Isle of Man for life until liberation on the accession of King Henry IV. THOMAS BEAUCHAMP, Earl of Warwick, died testate aged over sixty-two on 8 Apr. 1401. His widow died on 22 Jan. 1406/7. They were buried at St. Mary's, Warwick (M.I.).
D.N.B. (1908) 2:32. *C.P.* 12(2):375-378 (1959).

9. RICHARD DE BEAUCHAMP, Knt., K.B., K.G., 13th Earl of Warwick, Hereditary Sheriff of Worcestershire and Chamberlain of the Exchequer, son and heir, was born at Salwarpe, co. Worcester on 25 or 28 Jan. 1381/2. He served in Wales against Owen Glendower, defeating him near Machynlleth, co. Montgomery, and capturing his banner, in 1402 (dated by the appearance of Halley's comet at the time). He was married for the first time, with covenant dated September 1392 but before 5 Oct. 1397, to **ELIZABETH DE BERKELEY**, daughter and heiress of Thomas de Berkeley, 5th Lord Berkeley (**descendant of King Edward I**), by Margaret, daughter and heiress of Warin de Lisle, 2nd Lord Lisle (of Kingston Lisle) and Lord Teyes [see DEIGHTON 9.i for her ancestry]. She was born about 1386 (aged under seven in 1392). He was present at the death-bed of King Henry V, 30-31 Aug. 1422, who made him an executor, and bequeathed to his care the education of his infant son, Henry VI. His wife Elizabeth died *s.p.m.* on 28 Dec. 1422, and was buried in Kingswood Abbey, co. Gloucester (or Wilts). He was married for the second time

13

BEAUCHAMP (cont.)

at Hanley Castle, co. Worcester on 26 Nov. 1423 to **ISABEL LE DESPENSER**, widow of his cousin Richard de Beauchamp, Earl of Worcester (died *s.p.m.* March 1421/2) [see OXENBRIDGE 6 for descendants of this marriage], only surviving sister and heiress of Richard le Despenser, *de jure* Lord Burghersh (who died 7 Oct. 1414 *s.p.*), posthumous daughter and eventually sole heiress of Thomas le Despenser, Earl of Gloucester and Lord le Despenser, by Constance, daughter of Edmund of York [*of Langley*, Duke of York, **fifth son of King Edward III**). She was born at Cardiff on 26 July 1400 [see CLARE 8 for her ancestry]. From 1 June 1428 till 19 May 1436 Richard de Beauchamp was Tutor and Governor to the young King, whom he bore to Westminster Abbey for his Coronation on 6 Nov. 1429. On 16 July 1437 he was appointed lieutenant of France and Normandy, the most serious responsibility of his life, remaining in France thereafter. "Richard Beauchamp therl of Warwyk" died testate (P.C.C., 19 Rous) aged fifty-seven at Rouen on 30 Apr. 1439, and was buried in St. Mary's, Warwick, being afterwards removed to the Lady Chapel, where is a superb monument to him. His widow died testate aged thirty-nine at Friars Minoresses, London, on 27 Dec. 1439, buried in Tewkesbury Abbey.

D.N.B. (1908) 2:29-31 ("a brave and chivalrous warrior in an age of chivalry"). *C.P.* 2:131 footnote *c* (1912). *C.P.* 4:282 (1916). *C.P.* 8:54-55 (1932). *C.P.* 12(2):378-382 (1959).

Children of Richard de Beauchamp, by Elizabeth de Berkeley:
  i. **ALIANOR DE BEAUCHAMP** [see ROS 9],[1] & [see BEAUFORT 9].[2]
  ii. **ELIZABETH DE BEAUCHAMP**, born about 1418 [see next].

Child of Richard de Beauchamp, by Isabel le Despenser:
  iii. **ANNE DE BEAUCHAMP**, married **RICHARD NEVILLE** [see MONTHERMER 8.i].[3]

8. **ELIZABETH DE BEAUCHAMP**, daughter and co-heiress, was born about 1418 (aged twenty-two in 1439), and inherited Stowe and other lands in Northamptonshire. She married for the first time before Id. Feb. 1436/7 to **GEORGE NEVILLE**, Knt., younger son of Ralph Neville, 1st Earl of Westmorland, by Joan Beaufort, legitimised daughter of John of Lancaster [*of Gaunt*], Duke of Lancaster [see BEAUFORT 11.iv.d for his ancestry]. He was summoned to Parliament from 25 Feb. 1431/2 by writs directed *Georgio Latymer chivaler*, whereby he is held to have become **Lord Latimer**. He became a lunatic before 11 June 1451, when custody of his lands was given to his brother, Richard Neville, Earl of Salisbury, but apparently had lucid intervals. GEORGE NEVILLE, Lord Latimer, died on 30 or 31 Dec. 1469, and was buried at Well, co. York. She was married for the second time to THOMAS WAKE, Esq., of Blisworth, who died on 20 May 1476. She made her will on 20 Sep. 1480, desiring to be buried in the Beauchamp Chapel (St. Mary's), Warwick, beside her son. She died before 2 Oct. 1480.

C.P. 7:479-480, 480 footnote *k* (1929).

Child of George Neville, by Elizabeth de Beauchamp:
  i. **HENRY NEVILLE**, Knt., married **JOAN BOURCHIER** [see BOSVILE 6].[4]

---

[1] Ancestor, by first husband Thomas de Ros, of **Philip & Thomas Nelson**.

[2] Ancestor, by second husband Edmund Beaufort, of **St. Leger Codd, Edward Digges, Warham Horsmanden, Anne Humphrey, Herbert Pelham, Katherine Saint Leger, John West**.

[3] Ancestors of **Maria Johanna Somerset**.

[4] Ancestors of **Elizabeth Bosvile, George, Giles & Robert Brent, Anne Mauleverer**.

BEAUCHAMP OF BERGAVENNY see OXENBRIDGE

BEAUMONT see MARSHALL

* * *

BEAUFORT

EDWARD III OF ENGLAND, married PHILIPPE DE HAINAUT [see PLANTAGENET 12].

11. JOHN OF LANCASTER [*of Gaunt*], Duke of Lancaster, fourth son, was married for the third time [see LANCASTER 10 for earlier marriages and descendants by those marriages] at Lincoln Cathedral on 13 Jan. 1395/6 to KATHERINE DE ROËT, widow of Hugh Swynford, Knt., of Coleby and Ketelthorpe, co. Lincoln (died 1372), and younger daughter and co-heiress of Pain de Roët, Knt., Guienne King of Arms, a Hainaulter, and one of the knights of Queen Philippe's household. She was born, probably in Hainault, about 1350 and had formerly been the governess to his daughters, and then his mistress, and by her he had children, born before marriage. The marriage was ratified and confirmed during the Great Schism by the Roman pope, Boniface IX. Their three sons were legitimised, with the assent of Parliament, on 9 Feb. 1396/7, the patent confirmed by King Henry IV on 10 Feb. 1406/7, but with a saving clause barring them from succession to the throne. Their children were given the name Beaufort from their father's (lost) castle in Champagne which had devolved on him through his first wife, Blanche of Lancaster, a descendant of Blanche d'Artois who had purchased the lordship of Beaufort in 1270. His widow died on 10 May 1403, and was buried at Lincoln Cathedral.

C.P. 7:415 footnote *i* (1929). *C.P.* 12(1):39-45 (1953). *TAG* 32:9-10 (Jan. 1956) (Philippe de Roët, sister of Katherine, was wife of the poet Geoffrey Chaucer).

Children & grandchildren of John of Lancaster [*of Gaunt*], by Katherine Roët:

i. JOHN BEAUFORT, eldest son, born about 1371 [see next].

ii. HENRY BEAUFORT, born about 1375, ordained priest, Bishop of Lincoln, 19 July 1398, Lord Chancellor of England, Cardinal Bishop of Winchester 14 Mar. 1405, Cardinal-Priest of the titular church of San Eusebio, 24 May 1426, Papal legate in England, died testate at Winchester 11 Apr. 1447, buried at Winchester Cathedral (will dated 20 Jan. 1446/7). His will names his daughter and her husband. The mother of his daughter was said to have been Alice fitz Alan, wife of John Cherleton, 4th Lord Cherleton of Powis (died 19 Oct. 1401 *s.p.*). *D.N.B.* 2:41-48 ("Beaufort was ambitious, haughty, and impetuous ... seems to have clung unduly to his office as trustee of the family estates of the House of Lancaster, which must have given him command of a considerable sum of money ... His speeches in parliament are marked by a constitutional desire to uphold the crown by the advice and support of the estates of the realm. ... Family relationships gave him a place in Europe such as was held by no other statesman, and made him the fittest representative of his country abroad"). *TAG* 32:10-11 (Jan. 1956) ("participated (shamefully) in the trial of St. Jeanne d'Arc at Rouen, 24 May 1431").

   a. JOAN BEAUFORT, base-born, married EDWARD STRADLING.[1]

iii. THOMAS BEAUFORT, born about January 1377, K.G. about 1400, Chancellor of England, Admiral of England, Ireland and Aquitaine, created *Earl of Dorset*, at siege of Harfleur, created *Duke of Exeter*, at siege of Rouen, and of Melun, died testate at his manor of Greenwich 31 Dec. 1426 *s.p.s.*, buried Bury St. Edmunds; married before 15 Feb. 1404 MARGARET

---

[1] Ancestors of Elizabeth Coytmore (see *TAG* 32:9-17 (Jan. 1956)).

BEAUFORT (cont.)

NEVILLE, born about 1385, daughter and heiress of Thomas Neville, Knt., of Hornby, having issue a son Henry, died young. *D.N.B.* 3:49-50 (1908). *C.P.* 4:417 (1916). *C.P.* 5:200-204 (1926).

iv. JOAN BEAUFORT, born about 1379, died testate Howden 13 Nov. 1440, buried (with her mother) at Lincoln Cathedral; married, first, before 30 Sep. 1390 ROBERT DE FERRERS, Knt., of Willisham and Wem, 2nd Lord Ferrers, born about 1373 (aged eight in December 1380), died before 29 Nov. 1396 *v.m.*; married, second, RALPH NEVILLE, Earl of Westmorland [see NEVILLE 10 for descendants of his first marriage]. *Arch.Cant.* 11:105 (1870) ("Ralph ... first differenced the arms of Nevill, a white cross of St. Andrew on a red field, by the Lancastrian device of the red rose, which was said to be an allusion to his mother, Joan Beaufort"). *C.P.* 2:233 (1912). *C.P.* 6:196 (1926).

    a. MARY DE FERRERS, born about 1394, married **RALPH NEVILLE** [see NEVILLE 9].[1]
    b. RICHARD NEVILLE, born 1400, married **ALICE MONTAGU** [see MONTHERMER 8].[2]
    c. WILLIAM NEVILLE, Knt., K.G., of Alnwick, Northumberland, sixth son, summoned to Parliament from 3 Aug. 1429 by writs directed *Willelmo de Nevill' chivaler*, later directed *Willelmo de Nevill' de Faucomberge militi*, commanded the vanguard of the Yorkist army at the battles of Northampton and Towton, created **Earl of Kent** 1 Nov. 1461, died, most probably at Alnwick, 9 Jan. 1462/3 *s.p.m.l.*, buried Guisborough Priory; married before 28 Apr. 1422 JOAN FAUCONBERG, born at Skelton, co. York, 18 Oct. 1406, "a fool and idiot from birth", died aged eighty-four on 11 Dec. 1490, daughter and heiress of Thomas Fauconberg, of Skelton, co. York (of Magna Charta Surety descent and descendant of Charlemagne), by his second wife, Joan, daughter of Thomas Brounflete, Knt., of Londesborough and Weighton, co. York (she married, second, with pardon for marrying without royal licence dated 14 Mar. 1462/3, two months after the death of her first husband, JOHN BERWYKE, and survived all her children). *C.P.* 5:281-287.

        ELIZABETH NEVILLE [see STRANGEWAYS 7].[3]
        ALICE NEVILLE, born about 1437, married **JOHN CONYERS** [see CONYERS 7].[4]
    d. GEORGE NEVILLE, married **ELIZABETH DE BEAUCHAMP** [see BEAUCHAMP 8].[5]
    e. EDWARD NEVILLE [see OXENBRIDGE 6][6] [& see MOWBRAY 8.ii].[7]
    f. ALIANOR NEVILLE, married **HENRY PERCY** [see KEMPE 9].[8]
    g. ANNE NEVILLE, married, **HUMPHREY STAFFORD** [see AUDLEY 9].[9]
    h. CECILY NEVILLE, married **RICHARD PLANTAGENET** [see YORK 7].[10]

10. JOHN BEAUFORT, Knt., K.G., eldest base-born son, was born about 1370/1. He was created **Earl of Somerset** on 10 Feb. 1396/7, and **Marquess of Dorset** on 29

---

[1] Ancestors of **Edward Carleton, Anne Mauleverer, George Reade, Richard Saltonstall**.

[2] Ancestors of **Elizabeth Bosvile, Stephen Bull, Charles Calvert, Grace Chetwode, John Nelson, John Oxenbridge, Maria Johanna Somerset, Thomas Wingfield**, and, probably, **Thomas Dudley**.

[3] Ancestor, by husband Richard Strangeways, of **Edward Carleton**.

[4] Ancestors of **Philip & Thomas Nelson**.

[5] Ancestors of **Elizabeth Bosvile, George, Giles & Robert Brent, Anne Mauleverer**.

[6] Ancestor, by first wife Elizabeth Beauchamp, of **St. Leger Codd, Edward Digges, John Fisher, Warham Horsmanden, John Oxenbridge, Katherine Saint Leger, Maria Johanna Somerset**.

[7] Ancestor, by second wife Katherine Howard, of **Henry Fleete, Muriel Gurdon, William Randolph, Hawte Wyatt**.

[8] Ancestors of **St. Leger Codd, Edward Digges, Warham Horsmanden, Anne Mauleverer, John Nelson, Katherine Saint Leger, George Reade, Richard Saltonstall, Maria Johanna Somerset**, and, probably, **Jane Haviland**.

[9] Ancestors of **St. Leger Codd, Warham Horsmanden, Philip & Thomas Nelson, Maria Johanna Somerset, Katherine Saint Leger**.

[10] Ancestors of **Philip & Thomas Nelson**.

BEAUFORT (cont.)

Sep. 1397. He was summoned to Parliament on 17 Sep. 1397. He was married before 28 Sep. 1397 to **MARGARET DE HOLAND**, daughter of Thomas de Holand [*of Woodstock*], 2nd Earl of Kent (**descendant of King Edward I**), by Alice (**descendant of King Henry III**), daughter of Richard fitz Alan, 5th Earl of Arundel. She was sister and co-heiress of Edmund de Holand, Earl of Kent [see HOLAND 8 for her ancestry]. JOHN BEAUFORT, Earl of Somerset, died testate in the hospital of St. Catherine-by-the-Tower on 16 Mar. 1409/10, and was buried in St. Michael's chapel in Canterbury Cathedral. His widow was married for the second time (with Papal mandate dated 16 Aug. 1410) to THOMAS, Duke of Clarence, second son of King Henry IV (died 22 Mar. 1420/1 *s.p.legit.*, being slain at the Battle of Baugé in Anjou). She died in the Monastery of St. Saviour's, Bermondsey, Surrey, on 30 Dec. 1429, and was buried with her two husbands in Canterbury Cathedral. *C.P.* 4:416 (1916). *TAG* 19:198 (Apr. 1943). *C.P.* 12(1):39-45 (1953).

Children & grandchildren of John Beaufort, by Margaret de Holand:

    i. HENRY BEAUFORT, son and heir, born Oct. 1401, 2nd Earl of Somerset, died 25 Nov. 1418, unmarried, *s.p.*

    ii. JOHN BEAUFORT, K.G., second son, born before 25 Mar. 1404, created **Duke of Somerset**, 28 Aug. 1443, Captain-General in Aquitaine and Normandy, returned to England disgraced after failure of French campaign, and died soon after testate on 27 May 1444 *s.p.m.*, buried Wimborne Minster; married in or about 1442 MARGARET BEAUCHAMP, died at a great age shortly before 3 June 1482, widow of Oliver St. John, Knt., and daughter and heiress of John Beauchamp, Knt., of Bletsoe, co. Bedford, by Edith, daughter of John Stourton, Knt. She married, second, about April 1447, as second wife, Lionel Welles, 6th Lord Welles (a Lancastrian, slain at Towton 29 Mar. 1461). *D.N.B.* 3:48 (1908) ("died by his own hand it is said being unable to brook the disgrace of banishment from court"). *C.P.* 4:207 (1916). *C.P.* 6:180 (1926). *C.P.* 12(1):46-28 (1953).

        a. MARGARET BEAUFORT, born at Bletsoe 31 May 1443, founder of Christ's and St. John's Colleges, Cambridge University, died at Westminster 29 June 1509 (three months after the death of her son King Henry VII), buried Westminster Abbey; married, first, as a child, before 18 Aug. 1450 JOHN DE LA POLE, 2nd Duke of Suffolk (born 27 Sep. 1442, died 1491-2), marriage dissolved; married, second, EDMUND TUDOR, Earl of Richmond (born at Hadham about 1430, died at Carmarthen 3 Nov. 1456), son of Owen Tudor, by Katherine, daughter of Charles VI, Roi de France; married, third, before 1464 HENRY STAFFORD, Knt. (died 4 Oct. 1471), younger son of Humphrey, 1st Duke of Buckingham; married, fourth, before October 1473 THOMAS STANLEY, 1st Earl of Derby (died at Lathom 29 July 1504). *D.N.B.* 3:48-49 (1908) ("she was a valuable and early patron to Caxton ... She was one of the few worthy and high-minded members of the aristocracy, in an essentially selfish and cruel age"). Son and heir by second marriage:

            HENRY TUDOR, Earl of Richmond, born posthumously 28 Jan. 1456/7, defeated King Richard III at Bosworth on 22 Aug. 1485, ascended the throne as **King Henry VII**. Ancestor of Tudor and later Kings and Queens of England.

        b. THOMASINE, base-born daughter, married REYNOLD GREY [see WILTON 7].[1]

    iii. THOMAS BEAUFORT, born 1405, styled Earl of Perche, died unmarried 1432.

    iv. EDMUND BEAUFORT, born about 1405-6 [see next].

    v. JOAN BEAUFORT, died at Dunbar 15 July 1445, married, first, at St. Mary Overy's, Southwark 2 or 13 Feb. 1423/4 JAMES I OF SCOTLAND, King of Scotland, born Dumferline December 1394, crowned 21 May 1424 at Scone, murdered 21 Feb. 1436/7 at Perth, buried there in the Carthusian Church; second, 1439 JAMES STEWART, Knt. [*the Black Knight of Lorne*].

    vi. MARGARET BEAUFORT, married THOMAS COURTENAY, 5th Earl of Devon.

9. EDMUND BEAUFORT, K.G., younger son, was born about 1405-6, and held

---

[1]Ancestors, probably, of **Jane Haviland**.

BEAUFORT (cont.)

military command in the French wars from 1431 to 1453. He was married, without license, about 1435 (pardon dated 7 Mar. 1438) to **ALIANOR DE BEAUCHAMP**, widow of THOMAS ROS, 8th Lord Ros (died 18 Aug. 1430) [see ROS 9 for descendants of this marriage], and daughter of Richard de Beauchamp, 5th Earl of Warwick (**descendant of King Edward I**), by his first wife Elizabeth, only daughter and heiress of Thomas Berkeley, 10th Lord Berkeley (**descendant of King Edward I**). She was born at Edgenoch, co. Warwick, in 1407 [see BEAUCHAMP 9 for her ancestry]. He was created **Earl of Dorset** on 28 Aug. 1441, and was summoned to Parliament from 13 Jan. 1444/5. He was created **Duke of Somerset** on 31 Mar. 1448. EDMUND BEAUFORT, Duke of Somerset, was slain on the Lancastrian side at the first Battle of St. Albans on 22 May 1455, and was buried in the Abbey Church. His widow was married for the second time to WALTER ROKESLEY, Esq., and died at Baynard's Castle, London, on 6 Mar. 1466/7.

> *D.N.B.* 2:38-39 (1908) ("His blood was the first shed in the war of the Roses, which proved fatal to his sons, and ended the male line of the Beauforts"). *C.P.* 2:131 footnote *c* (1912). *C.P.* 4:417 (1916). *TAG* 19:199 (Apr. 1943). *C.P.* 12(1):49-58 (1953) (said to have been slain by Warwick; he was accused by the Duke of York of having been the sole cause of the civil war; he was marked by extreme avarice, although a very rich man, being the heir of his uncle Henry).

Children of Edmund Beaufort, by Alianor Beauchamp:

i. HENRY BEAUFORT, 2nd Duke of Somerset, son and heir, born 26 Jan. 1436 [see next].

ii. EDMUND BEAUFORT, 3rd Duke of Somerset, born about 1439, fled after the Battle of Tewkesbury on 4 May 1471 to take refuge in Tewkesbury Abbey, beheaded by the Yorkists in the town of Tewkesbury on 6 May 1471, buried in the Abbey Church. With him the house of Beaufort became extinct.

iii. JOHN BEAUFORT, styled Earl of Dorset, slain at Tewkesbury 4 May 1471.

iv. THOMAS BEAUFORT, died young before 1463.

v. **MARGARET BEAUFORT**, married **HUMPHREY DE STAFFORD** [see AUDLEY 8].[1]

vi. **ALIANOR BEAUFORT**, married **ROBERT SPENCER** [see CARY 5].[2]

vii. ANNE BEAUFORT, married WILLIAM PASTON, Knt.

viii. JOAN BEAUFORT, married, ROBERT ST. LAWRENCE, Lord Howth, RICHARD FRY, Knt.

ix. ELIZABETH BEAUFORT, died before 1492; married HENRY LEWES, Knt.

x. MARY BEAUFORT, married _____ BURGH.

8. HENRY BEAUFORT, 2nd Duke of Somerset, son and heir, was born on 26 Jan. 1436. He was with his father at the 1st Battle of St. Albans, at which he was severely wounded, on 22 May 1455. He commanded the victorious Lancastrian army at the Battle of Wakefield on 30 Dec. 1469, and defeated the Yorkists at the 2nd Battle of St. Albans 17 Feb. 1460/1. After defeat at the Battle of Towton on 29 Mar. 1461, he fled to Scotland; attainted, 1461, and all honours forfeited; pardoned 10 Mar. 1462/3; but at end of 1463 deserted King Edward IV, and fled to Alnwick; defeated and captured at the Battle of Hexham. HENRY BEAUFORT was beheaded by the Yorkists at Hexham on the same day 15 May 1464, unmarried, and was buried Hexham Abbey.

> *C.P.* 4:417 (1916). *C.P.* 12(1):54-57 (1953).

7. CHARLES SOMERSET, Knt., K.G., Lord Chamberlain of the Household of King Henry VII, base-son by Jane Hill, was born about 1460. He was married for the first

---

[1] Ancestors of **St. Leger Codd, Edward Digges, Warham Horsmanden, Maria Johanna Somerset, Katherine St. Leger.**

[2] Ancestors of **Anne Humphrey, Herbert Pelham, John West.**

BEAUFORT (cont.)

time on 2 June 1492 to ELIZABETH HERBERT, daughter and heiress of William Herbert, Earl of Huntingdon, by Mary, daughter of Richard Wydeville, Earl Rivers. She was born about 1476 (said to be aged sixteen in 1491, and thirty and more in 1507). He was summoned to Parliament from 17 Oct. 1509 by writ directed *Carolo Somerset de Herbert Chivaler*. She died between 29 Jan. 1508/9 and 21 Mar. 1512/3, and was buried at St. George's Chapel, Windsor. He was married for the second time to ELIZABETH WEST, daughter of Thomas West, 8th Lord la Warre, by Elizabeth, daughter of Hugh Mortimer, of Mortimer's Hall, co. Hants. They had three children. He was married for the third time to ELEANOR SUTTON, daughter of Edward Sutton, 2nd Lord Dudley, by Cecily, daughter of William Willoughby, Knt. They had no children. He distinguished himself at the sieges of Thérouanne and Tournai in France in 1513, and for his services was created Earl of Worcester on 1 Feb. 1513/4. As Lord Chamberlain he was largely responsible for the arrangements at the Field of Cloth of Gold in 1520. "Charles Somerset, erle of Worcestour, lord Herbert of Gower and of Chepstoe, K.G." died testate (P.C.C., 13 Porch) aged about sixty-six on 15 Apr. 1526, and was buried at St. George's Chapel (M.I.). His widow was married for the second time to Leonard Gray, Viscount Grane.

C.P. 12(1):846-850 (1953).

6. HENRY SOMERSET, Knt., Earl of Worcester, son and heir by first marriage, was married for the first time, with Papal dispensation dated 15 June 1514, to MARGARET COURTENAY, daughter of William Courtenay, Earl of Devon, by Katherine, daughter of King Edward IV. She died before 15 Apr. 1526 *s.p.* He was married for the second time before 1527 to **ELIZABETH BROWNE**, daughter of Anthony Browne, Knt., by Lucy, daughter of John Neville, Marquess of Montagu (**descendant of King Edward I**) [see BROWNE 7 for her ancestry]. HENRY SOMERSET, Earl of Worcester, died aged about fifty-three on 26 Nov. 1549. The will of his widow was dated 20 Apr. and proved 23 Oct. 1565 (P.C.C., 28 Morrison). They were buried at Chepstow (M.I.s).

C.P. 12(1):851-852 (1953).

5. **WILLIAM SOMERSET**, K.B., K.G., Earl of Worcester, son and heir by second marriage, was born about 1527. He was married before 29 Jan. 1549/50 to **CHRISTIAN NORTH**, first daughter of Edward North, 1st Lord North, of Kirtling, co. Cambridge, by Alice, daughter of Oliver Squire, of Southby, near Portsmouth. She was living on 20 Mar. 1563/4. He was married for the second time to THEOPHILA NEWTON, daughter of John Newton, Knt., of East Harptree, Somerset, by Margaret, daughter of Anthony Poyntz, Knt., of Iron Acton, co. Gloucester. WILLIAM SOMERSET, Earl of Worcester, died testate (P.C.C., 89 Leicester) aged about sixty-two at his house "by St. John's, near London" on 21 Feb. 1588/9, and was buried at Raglan (M.I.). His widow is said to have been married for the second time to William Paratt, of Pantglas.

C.P. 12(1):852-854 (1953).

Child of William Somerset, by Christian North:
  i. **EDWARD SOMERSET**, married **ELIZABETH HASTINGS** [see SOMERSET 4].[1]

---

[1]Ancestors of **Maria Johanna Somerset**.

BEAUMONT see MARSHALL

BERKELEY see DEIGHTON

* * *

BERNARD

EDWARD I OF ENGLAND, King of England, married ALIANORE DE CASTILLE.
JOAN OF ENGLAND [of Acre], married GILBERT DE CLARE, Earl of Gloucester.
MARGARET DE CLARE, married HUGH DE AUDLEY, Earl of Gloucester.
MARGARET DE AUDLEY, married RALPH DE STAFFORD, 1st Earl of Stafford.
HUGH DE STAFFORD, 2nd Earl of Stafford, married PHILIPPE DE BEAUCHAMP.
MARGARET DE STAFFORD, married RALPH NEVILLE, Earl of Westmorland.
MARGARET NEVILLE, married RICHARD LE SCOPE, 3rd Lord Scope.
HENRY LE SCROPE, 4th Lord Scrope, married ELIZABETH LE SCROPE [see SCROPE 6].

5. **MARGARET LE SCROPE**, was married for the first time to WILLIAM PENNYTON, for the second time to HUGH STAFFORD, and for the third time to JOHN BERNARD, Esq., of Abington, co. Northampton, son and heir of Thomas Bernard, Esq., of Clare, Suffolk, by his wife Margaret Mauntell. He was born about 1437 (aged twenty-eight at father's death in 1465). They had five sons. JOHN BERNARD, ESQ., died about 1485/6. The will of his widow was dated 1496.

H.S.P. 16:279 (1881) (1563 Vis. Yorks). *Metcalfe* (1887), p. 3 (1564 Vis. Northants). *Bernard* (1903), pp. 11-19 (Bernard arms: *Argent*, a bear rampant *sable*, muzzled *or*). *Clay* (1913), p. 200 (married, first, "William Plessington").

4. **JOHN BERNARD**, Esq., of Abington, son and heir, was born in 1469. He was married to **MARGARET DAUNDELYN**, daughter and heiress of William Daundelyn, of Doddington and Earl's Barton, co. Northampton. JOHN BERNARD, ESQ., died on 20 Aug. 1508.

H.S.P. 16:280 (1881). *Metcalfe* (1887), p. 3. *Bernard* (1903), pp. 20-24.

3. **JOHN BERNARD**, son and heir, was born about 1490 (aged eighteen at father's death). He was married to **CECILY MUSCOTE**, daughter of John Muscote, Gent., of Earl's Barton, by Alice, daughter and heiress of Christopher Beaufew, of Hitchin, co. Hertford. They had two sons and four daughters. JOHN BERNARD died in 1549. His widow died in 1557. They were buried at Abington.

Metcalfe (1887), p. 3. *Bernard* (1903) 24-34.

2. **FRANCIS BERNARD**, Esq., of Abington, was born in 1526. He was married to **ALICE HASLEWOOD**, daughter of John Haslewood, Esq., of Maidwell, co. Northampton, by Katherine, daughter and heiress of William Marmion, of Ringston, co. Lincoln. They had five sons and seven daughters (two daughters dying in infancy). FRANCIS BERNARD, ESQ., died on 21 Oct. 1602.

Gen. 1:48,53 (1877). *Metcalfe* (1887), p. 3 (1618-9 Vis. Northants). *Wm. & Mary Quart.* 5:62-64 (July 1896), 5:181-185 (Jan. 1897). *Bernard* (1903), pp. 34-43. *VMHB* 24:384-385 (Oct. 1916).

Children & grandchildren of Francis Bernard, by Alice Haslewood:

  i. **FRANCIS BERNARD**, Esq., of Kingsthorpe, co. Northampton, third son, born 1558 [see next].

  ii. **RICHARD BERNARD** of Great Doddington, co. Northampton, and Turvey, co. Bedford, fifth son; buried 24 Apr. 1613, will dated 20 Feb. 1612/3, proved London 16 June 1613; married, first, at Astwood, co. Buckingham, 24 Oct. 1600/1 ALICE CHIBNALL, buried Turvey 24 Apr. 1606, widow of William Adam, and daughter of John Chibnall, of Astwood, co. Buckingham; married,

BERNARD (cont.)

second, **ELIZABETH WOOLHOUSE**, daughter of Anthony Woolhouse, of Glasswell, co. Derby, haberdasher of London, by Millicent, daughter of John Strelley, of London, vintner (sister of Mary Woodhouse, wife of Francis Bernard). Two sons and one daughter.

    a. **RICHARD BERNARD**, born about 1608, admitted to Lincoln's Inn 1 Mar. 1628/9 as of Great Missenden, co. Buckingham, Gent., called to the bar 17 May 1636; in York County, Virginia, in 1647, dead by 1652; married, first, **DOROTHY ALWEY**, second, **ANNE CORDRAY** (or **COWDRAY**). Issue. *Wm. & Mary Quart.* 5:62-63 (July 1896).

1. FRANCIS BERNARD, Esq., of Kingsthorpe, co. Northampton, third son, was born in 1558. He was married to **MARY WOOLHOUSE**, daughter of Anthony Woolhouse, of Glasswell, co. Derby, haberdasher of London, by Millicent, daughter of John Strelley, of London, vintner. FRANCIS BERNARD, ESQ., died in 1630. *Metcalfe* (1887), p. 3. *VMHB* 6:407-409 (Apr. 1899). *Adventurers* (1987), pp. 117-119.

Children & grandchildren of Francis Bernard, by Mary Woolhouse:

    i. ROBERT BERNARD, Knt., Bart., of Brampton Hall, co. Huntingdon, will, dated 5 Dec. 1665, proved 15 May 1666, bequeathed "to my brother William's son, now at Brampton, £100 if he lived to be eighteen; and I leave him to my son John to bring up, and some care to be had to enquire what his father left him in Virginia".

    ii. JOHN BERNARD.

    iii. JAMES BERNARD.

    iv. **COL. WILLIAM BERNARD**, born co. Northampton, England, 1603; emigrated in the ship *Furtherance* to Virginia in 1622, commissioner of Isle of Wight County, 1646, served in the Council 1641-65, died 31 Mar. 1665; married by 1655, **LUCY (HIGGINSON) BURWELL**.

        a. GEORGE BERNARD, residing England 1665, with his uncle Sir Robert Bernard.

        b. LUCY BERNARD, married, first, DR. EDMUND GWYN, second, EDWARD CREFFIELD, JR. One daughter by first marriage.

        c. ELIZABETH BERNARD, married THOMAS TODD. Eleven children.

* * *

BERNEY see JENNINGS

* * *

BEVILLE

EDWARD III OF ENGLAND, King of England, married, second, **PHILIPPE DE HAINAUT**.
THOMAS OF GLOUCESTER [of *Woodstock*], married **ALIANOR DE BOHUN**.
ANNE OF GLOUCESTER, married **WILLIAM BOURGCHIER**, Comte d'Eu.
JOHN BOURGCHIER, Lord Berners, married **MARGERY BERNERS**.
HUMPHREY BOURGCHIER, Knt., married **ELIZABETH TILNEY**.
MARGARET BOURGCHIER, married **THOMAS BRYAN**, Knt.
ELIZABETH BRYAN, married **NICHOLAS CAREW**, Knt. [see LAUNCE 6].

3. ISABEL CAREW, fourth daughter and co-heiress, was married at St. Mary's, Beddington, Surrey, on 28 May 1560 to **NICHOLAS SAUNDERS**, Esq., of Ewell, Surrey, son and heir of William Saunders, of Ewell, by his first wife, Joan, daughter of William Merston of Horton, near Epsom, Surrey. They had two sons and three

BEVILLE (cont.)

daughters. He studied law at the Inner Temple, London. On 30 Apr. 1578 he was committed as a known recusant (being absent from his parish church services) to Fleet Prison by the Bishop of London until his release on 23 June 1578. After Isabel's death he was married for the second time to Margaret Bostock, of Newington, Surrey. NICHOLAS SAUNDERS, ESQ., died testate (P.C.C., 7 Rutland) on 17 Dec. 1587.

H.S.P. 43:17,69 (1899). *Beville* (1976), pp. 257,391,399,404,411,415-427 (Saunders arms: *Sable*, a chevron ermine between 3 bulls heads cabossed *argent*).

2. **MARY SAUNDERS**, was married to **ROBERT BEVILLE**, of Sawtry, co. Huntingdon, son of John Beville, of Sawtry, by Frances, daughter of Henry Lacy, Esq., of Stamford, co. Lincoln. They had two sons and five daughters born between May 1593 and January 1611. ROBERT BEVILLE died about 1613. His widow probably died before 1618.

Camden Soc. 43:8-9 (1849) (1613 Vis. Hunts) (signed by Robert Beville). *Beville* (1976), p. 257-262, 427.

1. **JOHN BEVILLE**, was born on 6 Jan. 1611. After the death of his parents he probably resided with his father's cousin Robert Beville, K.B., at Chesterton, co. Huntingdon. He was married, the bride's father officiating, at St. Michael's Church, Chesterton, co. Huntingdon, on 15 Apr. 1638 to **MARY CLEMENT**, daughter of Rev. John Clement, Rector of St. Michael's. They had two sons. JOHN BEVILLE was last of record in 1666 paying hearth tax at Stanground, co. Huntingdon.

Camden Soc. 43:9 (1849). *Beville* (1976), pp. 261-273,436 (John's second cousin, Robert Beville [the younger], of Chesterton, was married to Essex Cheeke. Both of the latter's children, including one named Essex, died young).

Children & grandchildren of John Beville, by Mary Clement:

i. **ESSEX BEVILLE**, baptised Chesterton 15 Mar. 1639/40, presumably the settler of that name in Henrico County, Virginia, by 1671, died testate 1682; married, probably about 1669, **AMY BUTLER**.

   a. **JOHN BEVILLE**, married **MARTHA COLSON**. Six children.
   b. **ESSEX BEVILLE**, married **ELIZABETH KENNON**. Six children.
   c. **MARY BEVILLE**.
   d. **AMY BEVILLE**.
   e. **ELIZABETH BEVILLE**.

ii. JOHN BEVILLE, baptised St. Augustine's, Woodstone, co. Huntingdon, 1 Jan. 1646/7.

* * *

BIGOD

EDWARD I OF ENGLAND, King of England, married **ALIANORE DE CASTILLE**.
JOAN OF ENGLAND [*of Acre*], married **GILBERT DE CLARE**, Earl of Gloucester.
MARGARET DE CLARE, married **HUGH DE AUDLEY**, Earl of Gloucester.
MARGARET DE AUDLEY, married **RALPH DE STAFFORD**, Earl of Stafford.
HUGH DE STAFFORD, 2nd Earl of Stafford, married **PHILIPPE DE BEAUCHAMP**.
MARGARET DE STAFFORD, married **RALPH NEVILLE**, Earl of Westmorland.
MARGARET NEVILLE, married **RICHARD LE SCROPE**, 3rd Lord Scrope of Bolton.
HENRY LE SCROPE, 4th Lord Scrope, married **ELIZABETH LE SCROPE** [see SCROPE 6].

7. **ELIZABETH LE SCROPE**, was married to **JOHN BIGOD**, Knt., of Settrington,

BIGOD (cont.)

co. York, son of Ralph Bigod, Knt., of Settrington, co. York (of **Magna Charta Surety** descent and **descendant of Charlemagne**), by Anne, daughter of John Greystoke, 4th Lord Greystoke (of **Magna Charta Surety descent** and **descendant of Charlemagne**). He was born about 1431. They had two sons. SIR JOHN BIGOD was slain, aged under thirty, with his father, at the battle of Towton, on 29 Mar. 1461. She was married for the second time to HENRY ROCHFORD, of Stoke Rochford, co. Lincoln, with issue, and for the third time to OLIVER ST. JOHN, of Lydiard Tregoz, co. Wilts, with issue. She died testate on 31 May 1503 (will dated 26 May 1503 requesting burial at Stoke with third husband).

    Clay (1913), p. 200. *Sur.Soc.* 144:139 (1930) (1480-1500 Vis. North). *York.Arch.Jour.* 32:195 (1936). *Paget* (1957) 65:2. *Carleton* (1978), chart 8.

6. RALPH BIGOD, Knt., of Settrington, co. York, Constable of Sheriff Hutton Castle, was born about 1457 (aged four at father's death, but aged twenty-one on 2 Feb. 1474). He was married for the first time before February 1482 to **MARGARET CONSTABLE**, daughter of Robert Constable, Knt., of Flamborough, East Riding, co. York, by Agnes (of **Magna Charta Surety descent** and **descendant of Charlemagne**), daughter of Roger Wentworth, Knt., of North Elmsall, co. York. They had five children. He was married for the second time to ALICE _____, and for the third time to AGNES CONSTABLE, of Dromonby. SIR RALPH BIGOD died testate on 22 Apr. 1515 (will requesting burial at Settrington).

    H.S.P. 16:24 (1881) (1563 Vis. Yorks). *Sur.Soc.* 144:159 (1930) (1480-1500 Vis. North). *York.Arch.Jour.* 32:195-198 (1936). *Carleton* (1978), chart 8.

5. JOHN BIGOD, of Settrington, co. York, was married, with licence dated 20 Jan. 1488/9, to **JOAN STRANGEWAYS**, daughter of James Strangeways, Knt., of Whorlton, North Riding, co. York (**descendant of King Edward I**), by Alice (**descendant of Charlemagne**), daughter of Thomas Le Scrope, 5th Lord Scrope of Masham [see STRANGEWAYS 6 for her ancestry]. JOHN BIGOD died *v.p.* before 22 Jan. 1514/5, probably slain at Flodden on 9 Sep. 1513. His widow was married, with licence dated 7 Nov. 1522, to WILLIAM MAULEVERER, Knt., of Wothersome (died testate on 11 Aug. 1551). She died on 15 Nov. 1546.

    H.S.P. 16:24,300 (1881). *C.P.* 4:68 (1916). *York.Arch.Jour.* 32:198 (1936). *Carleton* (1978), chart 8.

4. ELIZABETH BIGOD, was married, with marriage covenant dated 1505-06 (21 Hen. VII), to **STEPHEN HAMMERTON**, Knt., son and heir of John Hammerton, Esq., of Hellefield Peel and Wigglesworth, co. York (of **Magna Charta Surety descent** and **descendant of Charlemagne**), by Elizabeth, daughter of Thomas de Middleton, Knt., of Lonsdale. He was born about 1494 (aged twenty-one and more in 1515). SIR STEPHEN HAMMERTON, being implicated in *the Pilgrimage of Grace*, was attainted and executed by hanging on 25 May 1537. The will of his widow was dated 3 May 1538.

    Craven (1805) Hamerton chart. *Foster (1874)* (identifies son and heir Henry only). *H.S.P.* 16:153 (1881) (1563 Vis. Yorks). *Carleton* (1978), chart 7.

    Child of Stephen Hammerton, by Elizabeth Bigod:

        i. **AGNES HAMMERTON**, married, evidently, **WALTER STRICKLAND** [see CARLETON 3].[1]

---

[1] Ancestors of **Edward Carleton**.

BLENNERHASSET see THROCKMORTON

BLOUNT see ECHINGHAM

* * *

BOHUN

EDWARD I OF ENGLAND, married ALIANORE DE CASTILLE [see PLANTAGENET 14].

12. ELIZABETH OF ENGLAND was born at Rhudlan Castle, co. Caernarvon, on 7 Aug. 1282. She was married for the first time on 7 Jan. 1296/7 to Johann, Graf von Holland (died 10 Nov. 1299). She was married for the second time at Westminster on 14 Nov. 1302 to HUMPHREY DE BOHUN, Baron of Kington, co. Hereford, lord of half the barony of Trowbridge, co. Wilts, Earl of Hereford and Essex, Hereditary Constable of England, son and heir of Humphrey de Bohun, Baron of Pleshey, Essex, Baron of Kington, co. Hereford, Earl of Hereford and Essex, Hereditary Constable of England (of Magna Charta Surety descent and descendant of Charlemagne), by Maud, daughter of Enguerrand de Fiennes, Seigneur de Fienes in Guisnes (descendant of Charlemagne). He was born about 1276 (aged twenty-two at father's death). He served in Scotland and was present at the siege of Carlaverock on 1 July 1300. He fought at Bannockburn, and was taken prisoner at Bothwell. He was exchanged for Elizabeth de Burgh, wife of Robert de Bruce, King of Scotland. ELIZABETH OF ENGLAND died on 5 May 1316, and was buried at Walden Abbey, Essex. HUMPHREY DE BOHUN, Earl of Hereford and Essex, joined the rebellion against King Edward II, and was slain in battle at Boroughbridge on 16 Mar. 1321/2, and was buried in the church of the Friars Preachers at York (will dated 11 Aug. 1319 desired burial at Walden near the body of his wife).

C.P. 4:324 (1916). C.P. 5:135 (1926). C.P. 6:467-472 (1926) (his seal to the Barons' Letter to the Pope, 12 Feb. 1300/1, shows arms: "[azure] with a bend of [silver] and cotises of [gold] between six [golden] lioncels." The counterseal has "the arms of Bohun hung by a strap from the back of the Bohun swan). Paget (1957) 73:6-7.

Children of Humphrey de Bohun, by Elizabeth of England:
    i. WILLIAM DE BOHUN, Knt., born about 1312 [see next].
    ii. MARGARET DE BOHUN, married HUGH DE COURTENAY [see COURTENAY 10].[1]
    iii. ALIANOR DE BOHUN [see BUTLER 10][2] & [see BUTLER 10].[3]

11. WILLIAM DE BOHUN, Knt., K.G., fifth and youngest son, was born about 1312. He assisted King Edward III in the seizure of the Earl of March in 1330, and from that time was one of the King's most active councillors. He was created Earl of Northampton on 16 Mar. 1336/7. On 24 June 1340 he took a leading part in the King's victory at Sluys, and was with him at the siege of Tournay. He fought at

---

[1] Ancestors of Humphrey Davie, Edmund Jennings, Gabriel, Roger & Sarah Ludlow, John Oxenbridge, William Randolph, Hawte Wyatt.

[2] Ancestor, by first husband James Butler, of Robert Abell, Edward Carleton, Grace Chetwode, Anne Humphrey, Thomas Lunsford, Anne & Catherine Marbury, Philip & Thomas Nelson, Herbert Pelham, John West, and, probably, Mary Launce, and Jane Haviland.

[3] Ancestor, by second husband Thomas de Dagworth, of John Nelson.

BOHUN (cont.)

Crécy on 26 Aug. 1346, and participated in the siege of Calais. In later years he frequently had licences to export wool, both as a means of recouping his expenses and on the King's behalf. He was married 1335/1338 to **ELIZABETH DE BADLESMERE**, widow of Edmund de Mortimer, Knt., Lord Mortimer of Wigmore (died 1331), and daughter of Bartholomew de Badlesmere, by Margaret, daughter of Thomas de Clare, of Thomond in Connaught, Ireland (of **Magna Charta Surety descent** and **descendant of Charlemagne**). She was born in 1313, and was sister and co-heiress of Giles de Badlesmere. She died testate in 1356, and was buried at Black Friars', London. WILLIAM DE BOHUN, Earl of Northampton, died on 16 Sep. 1360, and was buried in Walden Abbey, Essex.

C.P. 1:244-245, 373 footnote *c* (1910). *C.P.* 6:472 (1926). *C.P.* 9:664-667, 665 footnote *a* (1936) (in the mandate (1335) for a dispensation for his marriage with Mortimer's widowed daughter-in-law, Mortimer is described as having been murdered by William and his accomplices, and the marriage said to be arranged to put an end to the enmity between the two families). *Paget* (1957) 73:8.

Children of William de Bohun, by Elizabeth de Badlesmere:
  i. **HUMPHREY DE BOHUN**, son and heir [see next].
  ii. **ELIZABETH DE BOHUN**, married **RICHARD FITZ ALAN** [see FITZ ALAN 12].[1]

10. **HUMPHREY DE BOHUN**, K.G., Earl of Northampton, Hereford and Essex, Hereditary Constable of England, was born on 25 Mar. 1341/2. He was married after 9 Sep. 1359 (Papal dispensation being related in the fourth degree) to **JOAN FITZ ALAN**, daughter of Richard Fitz Alan, 3rd Earl of Arundel (**descendant of Charlemagne**), by his second wife Alianor, daughter of Henry, Earl of Lancaster (**grandson of King Henry III**) [see FITZ ALAN 13 for her ancestry]. HUMPHREY DE BOHUN, Earl of Northampton, died testate aged thirty-two on 16 Jan. 1372/3 s.p.m. His widow died on 7 Apr. 1419. They were buried in Walden Abbey. His vast estates were divided between his two daughters: Brecknock and the Lordships in the Marches descending through the elder to the family of Stafford; and the Dukedom of Hereford becoming merged in the Crown, on the accession of Henry IV to the Throne.

C.P. 5:727 (1926). *C.P.* 6:473-474 (1926). *Paget* (1957) 73:9-10.

Children of Humphrey de Bohun, by Joan fitz Alan:
  i. **ALIANOR DE BOHUN**, married **THOMAS OF GLOUCESTER** [see LAUNCE 9].[2]
  ii. **MARY DE BOHUN**, married **HENRY IV, King of England**) [see LANCASTER 9].

* * *

BOLEYN see BUTLER

---

[1]Ancestors of **Robert Abell, Charles Calvert, Grace Chetwode, St. Leger Codd, Elizabeth Coytemore, Edward Digges, Muriel Gurdon, Warham Horsmanden, Anne Humphrey, Thomas Ligon, Thomas Lunsford, Oliver Manwaring, John Nelson, Joshua & Rebecca Owen, Richard Palgrave, Herbert Pelham, William Randolph, Katherine Saint Leger, John West, Thomas Wingfield, Hawte Wyatt, Amy Wyllys.**

[2]Ancestors of **Essex Beville, Elizabeth Bosvile, George, Giles & Robert Brent, Muriel Gurdon, Mary Launce, Anne Mauleverer.**

BOLLES

EDWARD I OF ENGLAND, King of England, married, second, **MARGUERITE DE FRANCE**.
THOMAS OF NORFOLK [of *Brotherton*], married **ALICE DE HALES**.
MARGARET OF NORFOLK, married **JOHN DE SEGRAVE**, 4th Lord Segrave.
ELIZABETH DE SEGRAVE, married **JOHN DE MOWBRAY**, 4th Lord Mowbray.
ALIANOR DE MOWBRAY, married **JOHN DE WELLES**, Knt., 5th Lord Welles.
EUDO DE WELLES, married **MAUD DE GREYSTOKE**.
LIONEL DE WELLES, Knt., 6th Lord Welles, married, first, **JOAN DE WATERTON**.
MARGARET DE WELLES, married **THOMAS DYMOKE**, Knt.
LIONEL DYMOKE, Knt., married **JOAN GRIFFITH** [see SKIPWITH 5].

4. **ANNE DYMOKE**, younger daughter and co-heiress, was married to **JOHN GOODRICK**, of East Kirkby, co. Lincoln, Sheriff of Lincolnshire, son and heir, of William Goodrick, of East Kirkby, by his wife Jane, daughter and heiress of William Williamson, Esq., of Boston, co. Lincoln. They had three sons and two daughters.
   Wotton (1741) 2:257 (1741) (Goodrick arms: *Argent*, on a fess *gules* between two lions passant guardant, *sable*, a fleur de lis, *or*, between two crescents, *argent*). *Gen.* 4:19,31 (1880) (1562 Vis. Linc.). *Goodricke* (1885), p. 4. *H.S.P.* 51:416 (1903) (Maddison Linc. Ped.). *TAG* 37:114 (Oct. 1961). *AR* (1992) 202-36 ("Early Chancery Proceedings, Bundle 444/43 which identifies her as Anne and her mother as Johanne").

3. **LIONEL GOODRICK**, Esq., of East Kirkby, co. Lincoln, was married for the first time to **BRIDGET JERMYN**, daughter of Thomas Jermyn, Knt., of Rushbrooke, Suffolk, and had no issue. He was married for the second time to **WINIFRED SAPCOTT**, widow of _____ Borton, Esq., and daughter of Henry Sapcott, Mayor of Lincoln, by Jane, daughter and heiress of Robert Smith. "Lion Gudric, esquire, Este Kirkebye, Lincoln" died testate (P.C.C., 31 Loftes) on 29 Aug. 1561. His widow was married for the second time to Humphrey Littlebury, Esq., of East Kirkby (will proved 20 Jan. 1568/9). She was living in 1568.
   Gen. 4:31 (1880). *Goodricke* (1885), pp. 4-5. *H.S.P.* 4:24-25 (1871) (1614 Vis. Notts). *H.S.P.* 51:416 (1903) (He married, third, _____ Robinson, daughter of Nicholas Robinson, of Boston.). *H.S.P.* 52:852-853 (1904). *TAG* 37:114 (Oct. 1961).

2. **ANNE GOODRICK**, daughter by second marriage, was married to **BENJAMIN BOLLES**, of Osberton, co. Nottingham, son of William Bolles, of Osberton, by Lucy, daughter and heiress of John Watts, grocer of London. They had two sons and three daughters.
   Gen. 4:31 (1880). *H.S.P.* 4:24-25 (1871) (Bolle arms: *Azure*, three boars' heads *argent* on dishes *or*, a mullet for difference *or*). *H.S.P.* 51:416 (1903). *TAG* 37:114 (Oct. 1961).

1. **THOMAS BOLLES**, of Osberton, was born at Osberton on 22 Dec. 1576. He was married for the first time to **ELIZABETH PERKINS**, daughter of Thomas Perkins, of Fishlake, co. York. Their children were baptised at Worksop, co. Nottingham. He was married for the second time to **MARY WITHAM**, of Ledston, co. York.
   Goodricke (1885), p. 5. *H.S.P.* 4:24-25 (1871). *NEHGR* 82:152 (Apr. 1928). *GDMNH* (1928-1939), p. 101. *TAG* 37:114 (Oct. 1961). *Williams* (1970), pp. 4,14-31.

Children & grandchildren of Thomas Bolles, by Elizabeth Perkins:

   i. BENJAMIN BOLLES, baptised 5 Oct. 1598.
   ii. ANNE BOLLES, baptised 20 Jan. 1599.
   iii. SAMUEL BOLLES, baptised 20 Jan. 1600, married MARTHA WOODHOUSE. Three children.
   iv. WINIFRED BOLLES, baptised 1601, died 1601.
   v. ELIZABETH BOLLES, baptised 1602, married WILLIAM REDSHAW.
   vi. JOHN BOLLES, Esq., of St. James, Clerkenwell, Middlesex, baptised 3 July 1603, will dated 1 July 1665, bequeathed £300 "unto my brother, Joseph Bolles, living in New England".
   vii. JUDITH BOLLES, baptised 28 Oct. 1605, married THOMAS SHAVER.

BOLLES (cont.)

viii. ABIGAIL BOLLES, baptised 14 Dec. 1606, married THOMAS AYSCOUGH.

ix. JOSEPH BOLLES (or BOWLES), baptised Worksop 19 Feb. 1608, settled Winter Harbor, Maine, 1640, later of Welles, Maine, died there 1678; married MARY HOWELL.

    a. MARY BOLLES, born 7 Aug. 1641, married COL. CHARLES FROST. Ten children.

    b. THOMAS BOLLES, born 1 Dec. 1644, resided New London, Connecticut, married, first, ZIPPORAH WHEELER, second, REBECCA WALLER. Three children by first marriage.

    c. SAMUEL BOLLES, born 12 Mar. 1646, resided Rochester, Massachusetts; married MARY DYER. Nine children.

    d. HANNAH BOLLES, born 25 Nov. 1649, married, first, CALEB BECKE, second, NATHANIEL WRIGHT.

    e. ELIZABETH BOLLES, born 15 Jan. 1652, married, first, JOHN LOCKE, second, WILLIAM PITNAM, of Portsmouth, New Hampshire. Four children by each marriage.

    f. JOSEPH BOLLES, born 15 Mar. 1654, resided Wells, married MARY CALL. Two children.

    g. SARAH BOLLES, born 20 Jan. 1657, married HUMPHREY CHADBOURNE. Five children.

    h. MERCY BOLLES, born 11 Aug. 1661, died unmarried.

* * *

BONNER see WYLLYS

* * *

BONVILLE

EDWARD I OF ENGLAND, King of England, married ALIANORE DE CASTILLE.
JOAN OF ENGLAND [of Acre], married GILBERT DE CLARE, Earl of Gloucester.
MARGARET DE CLARE, married HUGH DE AUDLEY, 8th Earl of Gloucester.
MARGARET DE AUDLEY, married RALPH DE STAFFORD, Earl of Stafford.
BEATRICE DE STAFFORD, married THOMAS DE ROS, 4th Lord Ros [see ROS 11].

10. MARGARET DE ROS, was married soon after 25 Nov. 1378 to REYNOLD GREY, 3rd Lord Grey of Ruthin, son and heir of Reynold de Grey, 2nd Lord Grey of Ruthin, co. Denbigh (of **Magna Charta Surety descent** and **descendant of Charlemagne**), by Alianor, daughter of Roger le Strange, Knt., of Knockin, co. Salop (**descendant of Charlemagne**). He was born about 1362 (aged twenty-six and more at his father's death in 1388). He was summoned to Parliament from 6 Dec. 1389 by writs directed *Reginaldo de Grey de Ruthyn chivaler*. He was married for the second time, before 7 Feb 1414/5, to JOAN ASTLEY, widow of Thomas Raleigh, of Farnborough, co. Warwick (died 18 Oct. 1404), and daughter and heiress of William de Astley, 4th Lord Astley, of Astley, co. Warwick (of Magna Charta Surety descent and descendant of Charlemagne), by Joan, daughter of John Willoughby [2nd Lord Willoughby of Eresby] [see GREY 7 for descendants of this marriage]. REYNOLD GREY, Lord Grey, died on 18 Oct. 1440. His widow died on 3 Sep. or 12 Nov. 1448.

    C.P. 6:155-159 (1926). C.P. 11:101 footnote *e* (1949).

    Children of Reynold Grey, by Margaret de Ros:

BONVILLE (cont.)

    i. JOHN GREY, Knt., married CONSTANCE HOLAND [see GURDON 7].[1]
    ii. MARGARET GREY [see next].

9. MARGARET GREY, was married, with marriage contract dated 12 Dec. 1414, to **WILLIAM BONVILLE**, Knt., K.G., of Chewton Mendip, Somerset, Sheriff of Devonshire, M.P. for Somerset and Devonshire, son and heir of John Bonville, Knt., of Shute, co. Devon, by Elizabeth, daughter and heiress of John fitz Roger, lord of Chewton, Somerset (of **Magna Charta Surety descent** and **descendant of Charlemagne**), by his wife Alice. He was born at Shute, near Colyton, co. Devon, on 31 Aug. 1393. They had one son and three daughters. She was living in 1426. He was married for the second time about 9 Oct. 1427 to Elizabeth Courtenay, widow of John, Lord Harington, of Aldingham in Furness and Porlock, Somerset (died 11 Feb. 1417/8), and daughter of Edward Courtenay, Earl of Devon, by Maud, daughter of Thomas Camoys, Lord Camoys. He was summoned to Parliament from 10 Mar. 1448/9 by writs directed (mostly) *Willelmo Bonville domino Bonville et de Chuton*, whereby he is held to have become **Lord Bonville of Cheston**. Despite previous appearance of loyalty to King Henry VI, he appeared on the Yorkist side at the battle of Northampton in July 1460, and witnessed the deaths of his only son William and his grandson William at the Battle of Wakefield on 30 Dec. 1460. WILLIAM BONVILLE, Lord Bonville, was, after the Lancastrian victory at St. Albans, beheaded the next day, aged sixty-seven, on 18 Feb. 1460/1. His widow died on 24 Oct. 1471 *s.p.*

    C.P. 2:218-219 (1912) (no identification of parents of first wife Margaret). Paget (1957) 273:2.
    Roskell (1992) 2:284-288 ("one of the most active of the country gentlemen of the south-west, often charged to investigate reports of lawless enterprises on land and sea").

    Children of William Bonville, by Margaret Grey:
    i. **WILLIAM BONVILLE**, son and heir apparent [see next].
    ii. **ELIZABETH BONVILLE**, married WILLIAM TAILBOYS [see TAILBOYS 6].[2]

8. WILLIAM BONVILLE, son and heir apparent, was married in or before 1442 to **ELIZABETH HARINGTON**, daughter and heiress of William Harington, 5th Lord Harington (of **Magna Charta Surety descent** and **descendant of Charlemagne**), by Margaret, daughter of John Hill, Knt., of Hill's Court, near Exeter. She died before 1458 *v.p.* WILLIAM BONVILLE died *v.p.*, being slain with his son at the battle of Wakefield on 30 Dec. 1460.

    C.P. 6:320 (1926). Paget (1957) 273:2.

7. WILLIAM BONVILLE, son and heir apparent, was born in 1442 (aged sixteen at the death of his grandfather, William, Lord Harington, in 1458). He was married in or before 1458 to **KATHERINE NEVILLE**, fifth daughter of Richard Neville, Earl of Salisbury, by Alice (**descendant of King Edward I**), daughter and heiress of Thomas Montagu, Earl of Salisbury [see MONTHERMER 8 for her ancestry]. WILLIAM BONVILLE was slain aged twenty at Wakefield with his father on 30 Dec. 1460 *s.p.m.* His widow was married for the second time to WILLIAM HASTINGS, Lord Hastings (beheaded on a charge of high treason on 13 June 1483) [see HASTINGS 8 for descendants of this marriage]. The will of "Kateryn Hastings, formerly wife of William Bonville, lord Harrington", directing burial at Ashby-de-la-Zouch, was dated 22 Nov. 1503 and proved on 25 Mar. 1504 (P.C.C., 7 Holgrave).

---

[1] Ancestors of **Muriel Gurdon**, and, probably, **Jane Haviland**.
[2] Ancestors of **George Reade**, **Richard Saltonstall**, **Olive Welby**.

BONVILLE (cont.)

C.P. 6:320 (1926). *Paget* (1957) 273:2. *Paget* (1977), p. 435.

Child of William Bonville, by Katherine Neville:
  i. **CECILY BONVILLE**, born about 1461, married **THOMAS GREY** [see GREY 5].[1]

* * *

BOSVILE

EDWARD III OF ENGLAND, King of England, married, second, **PHILIPPE DE HAINAUT**.
THOMAS OF GLOUCESTER [of *Woodstock*], married **ALIANOR DE BOHUN**.
ANNE OF GLOUCESTER, married **WILLIAM BOURGCHIER**, Comte d'Eu.
JOHN BOURGCHIER, Lord Berners, married **MARGERY BERNERS** [see LAUNCE 7].

6. **JOAN BOURGCHIER**, was married about 1467 to **HENRY NEVILLE**, Knt., son and heir apparent of George Neville, Lord Latimer, by Elizabeth, daughter of Richard de Beauchamp, 13th Earl of Warwick (**descendant of King Edward I**) [see BEAUCHAMP 8 for his ancestry]. SIR HENRY NEVILLE died on 26 July 1469 *v.p.*, being slain at the battle of Edgecote, near Banbury, and was buried in the Beauchamp Chapel, Warwick. His widow died testate on 7 Oct. 1470. Her will, as Dame Jane Nevill, dated 2 Oct., proved 16 Oct. 1470 (P.C.C., 31 Godyn) bequeathed jewels to her brothers, Sir Humphrey Bourgchier and Thomas Bourgchier, and her sister Dame Elizabeth, Lady Welles, and "to my sonne Lord Latymer, my wedding rynge".

Sur.Soc. 41:20 (1862) (1530 Vis. North) ("Syr Henry Nevill, son of George, whiche was slayne, the father lyving, maried doughter of John Lord Barnesse, called Bourser"). *H.S.P.* 16:225 (1881) (1563 Vis. Yorks). *C.P.* 7:481 (1929). *Paget* (1977), p. 440.

5. **RICHARD NEVILLE**, K.B., of Sinnington, North Riding, co. York, 2nd Lord Latimer, son and heir, was born about 1468 (aged one year at his grandfather's death). He was summoned to Parliament from 12 Aug. 1491 by writs directed *Ricardo Nevill de Latimer chivaler*. He was married for the first time about 1490 to **ANNE STAFFORD**, daughter of Humphrey Stafford, Knt., of Grafton, co. Worcester (**descendant of Charlemagne**), by Katherine, daughter of John Fray, Knt., Chief Baron of the Exchequer. They had fifteen children. He was married for the second time, with licence dated 5 July 1522, to MARGARET _____, widow of James Strangwishe, Knt., who died on 16 Dec. 1521. RICHARD NEVILLE, Lord Latimer, died between 12 and 28 Dec. 1530, at Snape Castle, co. York, and was buried with his first wife at Well.

Sur.Soc. 41:21-21 (1862) (1530 Vis. North) (Latimer arms: *Gules*, semee of hearts *argent*). *H.S.P.* 16:225 (1881). *C.P.* 7:481-482 (1929). *TAG* 69:163 (July 1994) ("a distinguished soldier and a prominent courtier under King Henry VIII").

Children & grandchild of Richard Neville, by Anne Stafford:
  i. **MARGARET NEVILLE**, born 9 Mar. 1494/5 [see next].
  ii. **ELIZABETH NEVILLE**, born 28 Apr. 1500; married **CHRISTOPHER DANBY**, Knt., of Thorpe, co. York, Sheriff of Yorkshire, born about 1505, died 14 June 1571, son of Christopher Danby,

---

[1] Ancestors of **Elizabeth Bosvile, Charles Calvert, Thomas Wingfield**, and, probably, **Thomas Dudley**.

BOSVILE (cont.)

Knt., by Margeret, daughter and co-heiress of Thomas le Scrope, 5th Lord Scrope of Masham (of **Magna Charta Surety descent** and **descendant of Charlemagne**). Six sons and eight daughters. *Sur Soc.* 41:87-88 (1862) (Danby arms: *Argent*, per chief, in chief three mullets *sable*). *H.S.P.* 16:88 (1881) (1563 Vis. Yorks). *TAG* 69:163 (July 1994).

    a. **MARY DANBY**, married EDMUND MAULEVERER [see MAULEVERER 4].[1]

4. MARGARET NEVILLE, first daughter, was born on 9 Mar. 1494/5. She was married, with dispensation dated 22 Nov. 1505, to **EDWARD WILLOUGHBY**, son and heir apparent of Robert Willoughby, Knt., 2nd Lord Willoughby de Broke in Westbury, co. Wilts (of **Magna Charta Surety descent** and **descendant of Charlemagne**), by his first wife Elizabeth, first daughter and co-heiress of Richard Beauchamp), 2nd Baron Beauchamp of Powick. EDWARD WILLOUGHBY died testate in November 1517 *v.p., s.p.m.* His daughters were co-heiresses to their grandmother's considerable pourparty of the Beauchamp inheritance, which included Alcester, but not to the Willoughby family estate.

    H.S.P. 12:29 (1877) (1619 Vis. Warwick). *C.P.* 12(2):687-688 (1959). *Paget* (1977), p. 180.

3. ELIZABETH WILLOUGHBY, Baroness Willoughby de Broke *de jure suo jure*, daughter and heiress, was eventual sole heiress of her grandfather Robert Willoughby, 2nd Lord Willoughby de Broke, receiving eventually all of her grandmother's Beauchamp inheritance. She was married shortly before 11 Apr. 1526 to **FULK GREVILLE**, Knt., of Beauchamp's Court in Alcester, co. Warwick *jure uxoris*, Sheriff of Warwickshire and Leicestershire, M.P. for Warwickshire, second son of Edward Greville, Knt., of Milcote, co. Warwick, by his wife Jane Forster. They had three sons and four daughters. SIR FULK GREVILLE died testate on 10 Nov. 1559 (P.C.C., 59 Mellershe). His widow died (apparently) on 9 Nov. 1562. They were buried at Alcester with monumental inscription.

    Collins-Brydges (1812) 4:336-343. *H.S.P.* 12:29 (1877) (identifies wife of Edward Greville as "Anne Da. of John Denton of Amersden"). *H.S.P.* 62:9 (1911) (1682 Vis. Warwick) (identifies only first two sons). *C.P.* 12(2):688-689 (1959). *Paget* (1977), p. 123.

    Children of Fulk Greville, by Elizabeth Willoughby:

    i. EDWARD GREVILLE, Knt., third son [see next].

    ii. KATHERINE GREVILLE, married GILES REED [see BRENT 3].[2]

2. EDWARD GREVILLE, Knt., of Harold Park in Waltham Holy Cross, Essex, third son, was married to **JANE GREY**, daughter of John Grey (**descendant of King Edward I**), by his wife Mary, daughter of Anthony Browne, K.G., of Battle Abbey and Cowdray, Sussex (**descendant of King Edward I**) [see GREY 3 for her ancestry]. They had three sons and eight daughters.

    Collins-Brydges (1812) 4:342 ("Edward ... married Elizabeth, daughter of Lord John Grey ... widow of Henry Denny, Esq.").

1. MARGARET GREVILLE, was married to **COL. GODFREY BOSVILE**, Esq., of Gunthwaite, co. York, and Wroxall, co. Warwick, son and heir of Captain Ralph Bosvile, of Gunthwaite (of **Magna Charta Surety descent**), by Mary, daughter of Christopher Copley, Esq., of Wadsworth. He was baptised at Sprotbrough, West Riding, co. York, on 12 Apr. 1596. He was Justice of the Peace, a member of the Long Parliament for Warwick, colonel of a regiment of foot in the Parliament Army, and treasurer for lame soldiers in the West Riding. COLONEL GODFREY

---

[1]Ancestors of **Anne Mauleverer**.

[2]Ancestors of **George, Giles & Robert Brent**.

BOSVILE (cont.)

BOSVILE died in 1658.
Collins-Brydges (1812) 4:342. *Foster* (1874), Bosvile chart. *TAG* 18:139 (Jan. 1942).

Children & children of Godfrey Bosvile, by Margaret Greville:

   i. WILLIAM BOSVILE, Esq., of Gunthwaite, born about 1620, married MARY WILKINSON. Six children.

   ii. ELIZABETH BOSVILE, born about 1617, married, first, LT.-COL. ROGER HARLAKENDEN, Esq., of Cambridge, Massachusetts, 1635, second HERBERT PELHAM, Esq.

      a. ELIZABETH HARLAKENDEN, born Cambridge, December 1636, married St. Augustine's, London, 2 Feb. 1659/60 GUTHLACH TOLLIOT.

      b. MARGARET HARLAKENDEN, born Cambridge, September 1638.

    For children by second marriage, see PELHAM 1.

   iii. MARY BOSVILE, married GEORGE JAMES SEDASCUE.

* * *

BOTREAUX

HENRY III OF ENGLAND, King of England, married ÉLÉNORE DE PROVENCE.
EDMUND OF LANCASTER, Earl of Lancaster, married BLANCHE D'ARTOIS.
HENRY OF LANCASTER, Earl of Lancaster, married MAUD DE CHAWORTH.
ALIANOR OF LANCASTER, married JOHN BEAUMONT, 2nd Lord Beaumont.
HENRY BEAUMONT, 3rd Lord Beaumont, married MARGARET DE VERE.
JOHN BEAUMONT, 4th Lord, married KATHERINE EVERINGHAM [see MARSHALL 8].

12. ELIZABETH BEAUMONT, was married before 1411 to WILLIAM DE BOTREAUX, 3rd Lord Botreaux, of Boscastle, Cornwall, son and heir of William de Botreaux, 2nd Lord Botreaux (**descendant of Charlemagne**), by Elizabeth, daughter and co-heiress of John Saint Lo, Knt., of Newton Saint Lo, co. Wilts. He was born at Walton, Kilmersdon, Somerset, on 20 Feb. 1388/9. They had three children. He was summoned to Parliament from 1 Dec. 1412. William de Botreaux was married for the second time, before 1458, to Margaret Ros, daughter of Thomas, Lord Ros, by Alianor, daughter of Richard Beauchamp, Earl of Warwick. WILLIAM DE BOTREAUX, Lord Botreaux, died on 16 May 1462 *s.p.m.s.*, and was buried at Cadbury, Somerset (M.I.). His widow was married for the second time between May 1462 and 1464 to THOMAS, Lord Burgh. She died in 1488, and was buried at Gainsborough.

   C.P. 2:242 (1912). *C.P.* 6:617 (1926).

11. MARGARET DE BOTREAUX, Baroness Botreaux *suo jure*, only daughter and heiress, was born before 1422 (aged over forty at her father's death) (but evidently before 1412). She was married at Heytesbury, co. Wilts, to ROBERT HUNGERFORD, of Heytesbury and Hamatethy, Cornwall, 2nd Lord Hungerford, son of Walter Hungerford, Knt., of Farleigh Hungerford, Somerset, and Heytesbury, 1st Lord Hungerford (**descendant of Charlemagne**), by Katherine, daughter and co-heiress of Thomas Peverell, of Parke, Hamatethy, and Penhale, Cornwall. He was born about 1409 (aged forty and more on 9 Aug. 1449) or about 1413 (aged twenty-six and more at the death of his aunt Eleanor Talbot). He was summoned to Parliament from 5 Sep. 1450 by writs directed *Roberto Hungerford seniori militi*. ROBERT HUNGERFORD, Lord Hungerford, died testate (P.C.C., 17 Stokton) on

BOTREAUX (cont.)

18 May 1459. She survived both her son and grandson and died testate on 7 Feb. 1477/8. They were buried in Salisbury Cathedral.

H.S.P. 21:89 (1885). *C.P.* 2:242-243 (1912) (she styled herself *Margareta, d'na Botreaux*). *C.P.* 6:617-618 (1926). *H.S.P.* 105:91 (1954) (1623 Vis. Glos.). *Roskell* (1992) 3:447.

Children of Robert Hungerford, by Margaret de Botreaux:
   i. **ROBERT HUNGERFORD**, son and heir, born before 1429 [see next].
   ii. **KATHERINE HUNGERFORD**, married **RICHARD WEST** [see HUMPHREY 7].[1]

10. ROBERT HUNGERFORD, 3rd Lord Hungerford, son and heir, was born before 1429 (found to be aged thirty and more in June 1459, but must have been considerably older). He was married before 5 Nov. 1440 to **ALIANOR MOLEYNS**, daughter and heiress of William Moleyns, Knt., of Stoke Poges, co. Buckingham, by Anne, daughter of John Whalesborough, of Whalesborough, Cornwall. She was born in 1425. Presumably in consequence of his marriage, he was summoned to Parliament *v.p.* from 13 Jan. 1444/5 by writs directed *Roberto Hungerford militi domino de Moleyns*, whereby he is held to have become **Lord Moleyns**. He served in France and was taken prisoner, remaining in the Duchy of Aquitaine for several years, not being released till a large ransom had been paid. After the Lancastrian defeat at Hexham on 15 May 1464, ROBERT HUNGERFORD, Lord Hungerford and Lord Moleyns, was taken prisoner and beheaded at Newcastle, Northumberland, on 18 May 1464. He was buried in Salisbury Cathedral. His widow was married for the second time, perhaps in or about 24 Mar. 1468/9, to Oliver Manyngham, Knt. (died testate 1499, P.C.C., 35 Horne), and is said to have died in 1476, and was buried at Stoke Poges (M.I. reciting her two marriages).

H.S.P. 21:89 (1885). *C.P.* 6:618-612 (1926). *H.S.P.* 105:91 (1954). *Paget* (1957) 297:2. *Paget* (1977), p. 434. *Roskell* (1992) 3:447,452,753.

9. THOMAS HUNGERFORD, Knt., of Rowden in Chippenham, son and heir, would have been, but for the forfeiture of his father's honours in 1461, 4th Lord Hungerford and 2nd Lord Moleyns. He was married before 16 Oct. 1460 to **ANNE PERCY**, daughter of Henry Percy, 3rd Earl of Northumberland (**descendant of King Edward III**), by Alianor, Baroness Poynings, daughter of Richard Poynings [see KEMPE 8 for her ancestry]. Having taken part with the Lancastrians, SIR THOMAS HUNGERFORD was attainted and put to death near Salisbury as a traitor early in 1469. His widow was married for the second time, as his second wife, to **LAURENCE RAYNSFORD**, Knt. (died testate 1490). She died on 5 July 1522.

H.S.P. 21:89 (1885). *C.P.* 2:243 (1912). *C.P.* 6:621 (1926). *H.S.P.* 105:91 (1954). *Paget* (1977), p. 440.

Child of Thomas Hungerford, by Anne Percy:
   i. **MARY HUNGERFORD**, born about 1467, married **EDWARD HASTINGS** [see HASTINGS 7].[2]

* * *

---

[1] Ancestors of **John West, Herbert Pelham, Anne Humphrey, John Stockman**.

[2] Ancestors of **John Nelson, Maria Johanna Somerset**.

BOURCHIER

EDWARD I OF ENGLAND, King of England, married ALIANORE DE CASTILLE.
JOAN OF ENGLAND [of Acre], married GILBERT DE CLARE, Earl of Gloucester.
ALIANOR DE CLARE, married HUGH LE DESPENSER, 2nd Lord Despenser.
EDWARD LE DESPENSER, Knt., married ANNE DE FERRERS.
EDWARD LE DESPENSER, 4th Lord le Despenser, married ELIZABETH DE BURGHERSH.
ANNE LE DESPENSER, married HUGH HASTINGS, Knt.
MARGARET HASTINGS, married JOHN WINGFIELD, Knt.
ROBERT WINGFIELD, Knt., married ELIZABETH RUSSELL.
ROBERT WINGFIELD, Knt., married ELIZABETH GOUSHILL.
JOHN WINGFIELD, married ELIZABETH FITZ LEWIS [see HANKFORD 6].

4. ELIZABETH WINGFIELD, the younger daughter of that name, was married to **FRANCIS HALL**, of Grantham, co. Lincoln, Comptroller of Calais, son of Thomas Hall, of Grantham, by Alice, daughter of John Bramswell. They had six sons and one daughter.

Gen. 4:23 (1880) (1562 Vis. Linc.). *H.S.P.* 51:440-441 (1903) (Hall arms: *Argent*, a chevron engrailed between three talbots' heads erased *sable*). *H.S.P. (n.s.)* 3:217-219 (1984) (1561 Vis. Suffolk) (citing East Anglian N. & Q. 4:205).

3. FRANCIS HALL, of Grantham, Surveyor of the works of Calais to King Henry VIII, was married to **URSULA SHERINGTON**, daughter of Thomas Sherington. They had three sons and three daughters. FRANCIS HALL died in July 1553. His widow was married for the second time to JOHN BANISTER, and was buried at Grantham on 5 July 1569.

Gen. 4:24 (1880). *H.S.P.* 16:30 (1881) (1563 Vis. Yorks). *H.S.P.* 51:441 (1903).

Children of Francis Hall, by Ursula Sherington:

i. ELIZABETH HALL [see next].
ii. JANE HALL, married HENRY SKIPWITH [see SKIPWITH 3].[1]

2. ELIZABETH HALL was married to **RALPH BOURCHIER**, Knt., of Benningborough, co. York, son and heir of James Bourchier, Knt., by Mary, daughter of Humphrey Banister, Knt., of Calais [see LAUNCE 6.i for his probable ancestry]. They had two sons and four daughters. He was married for the second time to CHRISTIAN SHAKERLEY, widow of John Harding, Esq., Alderman of London, and daughter of Rowland Shakerley, of London. SIR RALPH BOURCHIER was living in 1584.

Sur Soc. 36:140 (1859) (1665 Vis. Yorks). *Gen.* 4:24 (1880). *H.S.P.* 16:30 (1881) (names children William, Ursula, Bridget and Lucy, but not John). *H.S.P.* 51:441 (1903). *Allen* (1935), chart between pp. 58-59.

1. JOHN BOURCHIER, Knt., of Lambeth, Surrey, second son, was born after 1563. He was admitted to Gray's Inn on 23 Nov. 1584. He appears in 1620 in the list of adventurers for Virginia. He was knighted on 2 July 1609. He was married to **ELIZABETH** _____. The administration of SIR JOHN BOURCHIER was granted to "Mary Bouchier, alias Whitaker, wife of Jabez Whitaker, daughter of Sir John Bouchier, late of the Parish of Lambeth, County Surrey, deceased, to administer the goods of said deceased, Dame Elizabeth Bourchier, relict having renounced".

Sur Soc. 36:140 (1859) ("Sr John Bourchier of Hanging Grimston in com. Ebor. Kt") (names only four sons: Raphe, Richard, Will'm, Verney). *Allen* (1935), p. 58-65 (eight sons, James, Ralph,

---

[1] Ancestors of **William Asfordby, Diana & Grey Skipwith.**

BOURCHIER (cont.)

Richard, Robert, Verney, William, Henry and George, all knights, listed in "Register of Admissions to Gray's Inn 1521-1881"). *NEHGR* 112:169 (July 1958) (Bourchier arms: Silver a cross engrailed gules between four water-bougets sable).

Child & grandchild of John Bourchier, by Elizabeth:

i. **MARY BOURCHIER**, only daughter, born about 1598, married **JABEZ WHITAKER**, emigrated to Virginia before 1620.

   a. **WILLIAM WHITAKER**, born about 1618, died James City County, Virginia, 1662; married. Two sons.

* * *

BOURGCHIER see LAUNCE

BRANDON see PALGRAVE

BRAYBROOKE see WYATT

* * *

BRENT

EDWARD III OF ENGLAND, King of England, married **PHILIPPE DE HAINAUT**.
THOMAS OF GLOUCESTER [*of Woodstock*], married **ALIANORE DE BOHUN**.
ANNE OF GLOUCESTER, married **WILLIAM BOURGCHIER**, Comte d'Eu.
JOHN BOURGCHIER, Lord Berners, married **MARGERY BERNERS**.
JOAN BOURGCHIER, married **HENRY NEVILLE**, Knt.
RICHARD NEVILLE, 2nd Lord Latimer, married **ANNE STAFFORD**.
MARGARET NEVILLE, married **EDWARD WILLOUGHBY**.
ELIZABETH WILLOUGHBY, married **FULKE GREVILLE**, Knt. [see BOSVILE 3].

3. **KATHERINE GREVILLE**, was married to **GILES REED**, Esq., of Mitton, co. Worcester. They had thirteen children.

   Collins-Brydges (1812) 4:342-343. *Brent* (1946), pp. 36-37 (Giles Reed, Lord of Tusburie and Witten) (memorial brass at St. Mary's, Ilmington, erected after 20 June 1667 states: "Richard Brent Married Elizabeth Daughter of Giles Reed Esquier & Katherine Grevill His Wife Anno 1594 ... ").

2. **ELIZABETH REED**, was married to **RICHARD BRENT**, Esq., of Larkstoke in Ilmington, co. Warwick, son of Richard Brent, by Mary, daughter of John Huggeford, Esq. He was Sheriff of Gloucestershire in 1614, and subscribed to the building of the bridge at Stratford-upon-Avon in 1618. In 1623 he leased Larkstoke for fourteen years to Fulk Reed and others. In 1629 Richard and Elizabeth and their son Fulk conveyed by fine the manor of Admington, co. Gloucester, which he had inherited from his grandfather William, to the executors of Fulk Greville, Lord Brooke, his wife's cousin. Two thirds of his estate was sequestered in 1644 for his recusancy. His wife was buried at Bredon. **RICHARD BRENT, ESQ.**, was buried at St. Mary's, Ilmington on 1 May 1652. The administration of the estate of Richard Brent, late of Larkstoke, co. Gloucester, widower, deceased, was granted to his son George on 21 May 1652.

BRENT (cont.)

DAB 3:18-19 (1929) (Margaret Brent, "America's first feminist"). *Brent* (1946), pp. 36-37 (they also had children Foulke (died *s.p.*), Richard, son and heir, husband of Margaret Peshall, William, Edward, Catherine, Elizabeth, Eleanor, Jane and Anne), p. 42 (the will of his son Giles calls him "my Honored Father Richard Brent, Esquire, deceased antiently Lord of the Mannors of Admington and Lark Stoke in the County of Gloucestershire in England").

Children of Richard Brent, by Elizabeth Reed:

i. **COL. GILES BRENT**, third son, born 1600, Roman Catholic, at Jamestown, Virginia 23 May 1625, removed to Maryland 22 Nov. 1638 with his brother Fulk and sisters Margaret and Mary, received grant of the manor of Kent Fort on Kent Island, member of the Maryland Assembly, Deputy Governor of Maryland in 1643 when Governor Leonard Calvert returned to England; maintained allegiance to King Charles, and in 1645, as Governor Giles Brent, was seized prisoner under letters of marque from Parliament, and taken captive to London; returned to Maryland, but settled on Aquia Creek, Stafford County, Virginia, in 1646; died testate at his home *Retirement*, Stafford County, Virginia (will dated 31 Aug. 1671, proved 15 Feb. 1671/2); married, first, **KITTAMAQUUND** (baptized as **MARY**), daughter of the Tayac of the Picataway Indians; married, second, FRANCES (WHITGREAVES) HARRISON, relict of Dr. Jeremy Harrison, of St. Runwald's Parish, Colchester, England, and Westmoreland County, Virginia, and daughter of Thomas Whitgreaves, of co. Stafford, England. Issue by first marriage.

    a. RICHARD BRENT, died *v.p.*

    b. **GILES BRENT**, born 5 Apr. 1652, died Middlesex County, Virginia, 2 Sep. 1679; married, first, his cousin **MARY BRENT**, second, **FRANCES HAMMERSLEY**. Issue.

    c. MARY BRENT, died *s.p.*; married CAPT. JOHN FITZHERBERT.

ii. **GEORGE BRENT**, sixth son [see next].

vii. **MARGARET BRENT**, born about 1601, emigrated November 1638, first woman in Maryland to hold land in her own right, capable business woman, not only in the management of her own and her sister Mary's affairs, but also as executrix of the deceased governor, Leonard Calvert, as agent and representative of her brother Giles, died 1671 at her home *Peace*, Westmoreland County, Virginia, unmarried.

viii. **MARY BRENT**, emigrated to Maryland with her sister Margaret and brother Giles, died in Virginia 1658 unmarried.

1. GEORGE BRENT, of Defford, co. Worcester, sixth son, was born in 1602. He was married to **ANNE PEYTON**, daughter of John Peyton, Knt., of Doddington, co. Cambridge, by Alice, daughter of John Peyton, Knt., of Isleham, co. Cambridge **(descendant of King Edward I)** [see HASILDEN 2 for her ancestry]. She was unmarried in 1635. GEORGE BRENT died in 1671.

Chester of Chicheley (1878), p. 318. *Brent* (1946), p. 43 (1740 statement identifies wife; he married twice later, leaving several children by these last marriages, none of whom settled in Maryland or Virginia), pp. 64-82.

Children of George Brent, by Anne Peyton:

i. **GEORGE BRENT**, born about 1640, Roman Catholic, agent with William Fitzhugh for the Proprietors of the Northern Neck, died Woodstock, Stafford County, Virginia 1694-1700; married, first, about 1670 **ELIZABETH GREENE**, born 1654/5, died in childbed of a girl 26 Mar. 1686, buried Aquia cemetery, daughter of Capt. William Green, by Mary, daughter of William Layton, Knt., of Feckenham, co. Worcester, second, 27 Mar. 1687 MARY SEWALL, born 1658/9, died in childbed 12 Mar. 1693/4, relict of Col. William Chandler, of Charles County, Maryland, daughter of Henry Sewall, Secretary of Maryland, by Jane Lowe, Lady Baltimore.

    a. GEORGE BRENT, died 2 Sep. 1708 unmarried.

    b. NICHOLAS BRENT, died 18 Dec. 1711 *s.p.*; married JANE MUDD, daughter of Capt. Thomas Mudd of Charles County, Maryland.

    c. ROBERT BRENT, went to Bermuda 1701, returned to Virginia with his wife; married 8 May 1702 SUSANNAH SEYMOUR. Eight children [eldest son George prepared family statement in 1740].

    d. ANNA MARIA BRENT, born 8 May 1677, died 17 Feb. 1685.

BRENT (cont.)

    e. ELIZABETH BRENT, died November 1719; married THOMAS LANGMAN, Esq., of Bristol. Five children.
    f. HENRY BRENT, by second marriage, died 24 Dec. 1709; married JANE THOMPSON, daughter of Mr. William Thompson, of Charles County, Maryland. Issue.
    g. MARY BRENT, died December 1716, married OSWALD NEALE. Three children.
    h. MARTHA BRENT, died April-May 1715 unmarried.
  ii. JOHN BRENT, died young.
  iii. HENRY BRENT, died January 1694; married ANN (CALVERT) BROOKE, relict of Baker Brooke, and daughter of Gov. Leonard Calvert. No surviving children.
  iv. WILLIAM BRENT, died unmarried.
  v. EDWARD BRENT, died while at College of Douay in Flanders.
  vi. ROBERT BRENT, born 1660, emigrated with wife in 1686, settled in Stafford County, Virginia; attorney practising with his brother George; died Stafford County, Virginia, 19 Jan. 1695/6, buried Aquia cemetery; married ANNE BAUGH, daughter of Edmond Baugh, of Penson, co. Worcester.
    a. RICHARD BRENT, died s.p.
    b. ELIZABETH BRENT, married JESSE DOYNE, of Charles County, Maryland. Issue.
    c. ANNE BRENT, died s.p.
  vii. ANNE BRENT, married JAMES CLIFTON, Esq., of co. Lancaster.
  viii. ELIZABETH BRENT, died unmarried.
  xi. DOROTHY BRENT.
  xii. MARY BRENT, married her cousin GILES BRENT.
  xiii. MARGARET BRENT, died unmarried.
  xiii. URSULA BRENT, married CHARLES UMFRAVILLE. Issue in France.

* * *

BROOKE see WYATT

* * *

BROWNE

HENRY III OF ENGLAND, King of England, married ÉLÉONORE DE PROVENCE.
EDMUND OF LANCASTER *Crouchback*, Earl of Lancaster, married, BLANCHE D'ARTOIS.
HENRY OF LANCASTER, Duke of Lancaster, married MAUD DE CHAWORTH.
ALIANOR OF LANCASTER, married RICHARD FITZ ALAN [see FITZ ALAN 13].

11. JOHN DE ARUNDEL, of Betchworth, Surrey, younger son, was married on 17 Feb. 1358/9 to **ALIANOR MALTRAVERS**, younger daughter and co-heiress of John Maltravers, Knt. (of **Magna Charta Surety descent** and **descendant of Charlemagne**), by his wife Gwenthlian. She was born about 1345 (aged nineteen in 1364), and was granddaughter and eventual sole heiress of John Mautravers, Knt. In consequence, probably, of the marriage, he was summoned to Parliament from 4 Aug. 1377 by writs directed *Johanni de Arundell'*, whereby he may be held to have become **Lord Arundel**.

He was Marshal of England in 1377. Being in command of a naval expedition in aid to the Duke of Brittany, he defeated the French fleet off the coast of Cornwall. JOHN DE ARUNDEL died testate at sea on 15 Dec. 1379, being wrecked and drowned in the Irish Sea, and was buried in Lewes Priory. His widow was married for the second time as his second wife in 1380 to Reynold Cobham, 2nd Lord Cobham, of Sterborough in Lingfield, Surrey (died 6 July 1403), and had issue. "Alianore Arundell de Lytchett" died testate (will dated 26 Sep. 1404) on 12 Jan. 1404/5, and was buried with her first husband.

Top. & Gen. 2:317-325,336 (1853). *C.P.* 1:247, 259-260 (1910). *C.P.* 3:353-354 (1913). *C.P.* 8:585-586 (1932). *C.P.* 11:103 (1949).

Children of John de Arundel, by Alianor Maltravers:
 i. **JOHN DE ARUNDEL**, Knt., son and heir, born 30 Nov. 1364 [see next].
 ii. **RICHARD DE ARUNDEL**, Knt., married **ALICE** _____ [see WILLOUGHBY 7].[1]
 iii. **JOAN DE ARUNDEL**, married **WILLIAM DE ECHINGHAM** [see ECHINGHAM 9].[2]
 iv. **MARGARET DE ARUNDEL**, married **WILLIAM ROS**, 6th Lord Ros [see ROS 10].[3]

10. **JOHN DE ARUNDEL**, of Arundel, Knt., 2nd Lord Arundel, son and heir, was born on 30 Nov. 1364. He was with the army in Scotland in 1383 and with the English Fleet in 1388 under his uncle, Richard, Earl of Arundel, Admiral of England. He was married before 1385 to **ELIZABETH LE DESPENSER**, daughter of Edward le Despenser, Knt., Lord Despenser (**descendant of King Edward I**), by Elizabeth, daughter and heiress of Bartholomew de Burghersh, Lord Burghersh [see CLARE 9 for her ancestry]. They had three sons. JOHN DE ARUNDEL, Lord Arundel, died testate on 14 Aug. 1390, and was buried at Missenden Abbey, co. Buckingham. His widow was married for the second time to William la Zouche, Lord Zouche of Harynworth (died 13 May 1396), with no surviving issue. "Elizabeth la Zouche" died testate on 11 Apr. 1408, her will requesting burial at Tewkesbury Abbey, co. Gloucester.

Top. & Gen. 2:325-330. *C.P.* 1:247, 253, 260 (1910). *C.P.* 11:103 (1949). *TG* 5:137 (1984) (not summoned to Parliament as Baron Maltravers because his mother outlived him).

9. **THOMAS DE ARUNDEL**, Knt., third son, Steward of the Household to King Henry VI, was granted Beechworth, Surrey, by his father. He was married to **JOAN MOYNE**, daughter of Henry Moyne. They had two children, William, died "beyond sea" before 1436-7, and Alianor. SIR THOMAS DE ARUNDEL died "over sea" about 1430-1. His widow was married for the second time before 1437 to John Burdens, Esq.

Top. & Gen. 2:336 (1853), 3:253 (1858). *H.S.P.* 14:732-733 (1879) (Misc. Essex Ped.).

8. **ALIANOR DE ARUNDEL**, daughter and heiress, was married for the first time about 1431 to **THOMAS BROWNE**, Knt., of Betchworth Castle, Surrey *jure uxoris*, son of Richard Browne, Knt. He was Treasurer of the Household to King Henry VI, and Sheriff of Kent 1440 and 1460. They had seven sons and two daughters. SIR THOMAS BROWNE was convicted of high treason on 20 July 1460, and immediately beheaded. She was married for the second time in 1461 to THOMAS VAUGHAN, Esquire of the Body to King Edward IV.

---

[1]Ancestors, probably, of **Thomas Dudley**.

[2]Ancestors of **Alice Baynton, Mary Gye, Gabriel, Roger & Sarah Ludlow, John Oxenbridge**.

[3]Ancestors of **Francis Dade, Henry Fleete, Muriel Gurdon, Philip & Thomas Nelson, William Randolph, Hawte Wyatt**.

BROWNE (cont.)

Wotton (1741) 3:5. *Top. & Gen.* 2:267 (pedigree prepared in 1585 by Walter Brown, grandson of George Browne, Knt., eldest son of Thomas & Alianor), 2:336 (1853). *H.S.P.* 14:732-733 (1879). *Kemp* (1902), p. 24 (Browne arms: Sable, three lions passant in bend between two double cotises argent). *Yeatman* (1903), pp. 21-40.

Children of Thomas Browne, by Alianor de Arundel:
  i. ANTHONY BROWNE, Knt., fourth son [see next].
  ii. ROBERT BROWNE, Esq., fifth son [see OLLANTIGH 5][1].

7. ANTHONY BROWNE, Knt., of Calais, fourth son, Standard Bearer to King Henry VII, was married for the first time to ALICE ____. She died *s.p.* He was married for the second time after 1490, perhaps in 1500, to **LUCY NEVILLE**, daughter and co-heiress of John Neville, Knt., Marquess of Montagu (**descendant of King Edward I**), by Isabel (**descendant of King Edward I**), daughter of Edmund Ingoldisthorpe, Knt., of Borough Green, co. Cambridge [see MONTHERMER 7 for her ancestry]. She had previously been married, with issue, to THOMAS FITZ WILLIAM, Knt., of Aldwark, co. York. Anthony & Lucy had one son and two daughters. SIR ANTHONY BROWNE died testate with will dated 25 Sep. 1505 (P.C.C., Adeane 15), requesting burial at St. Nicolas', Calais, with his first wife. "Lady Lucye Browne, formerly Fitzwilliam" died testate (P.C.C., 15 Hogen) on 25 Mar. 1534, and was buried at Tickhill, co. York.

Wotton (1741) 3:5-6. *Top. & Gen.* 2:267 (1853). *Yeatman* (1903), pp. 55-56. *C.P.* 9:93 footnote *i* (1936). *C.P.* 12(1):118-119 footnote *g* (1953). *Paget* (1977), p. 264.

Children of Anthony Browne, by Lucy Neville:
  i. ANTHONY BROWNE, Knt. [see next].
  ii. ELIZABETH BROWNE, married HENRY SOMERSET [see BEAUFORT 6].[2]

6. ANTHONY BROWNE, Knt., K.G., of Battle Abbey and Cowdray, Sussex, Standard Bearer to King Henry VIII, Master of the Horse, was married for the first time to **ALICE GAGE**, daughter of John Gage, K.G., by Philippe, daughter of Richard Guildford, Knt. They had seven sons and three daughters. She died after July 1540. He was married for the second time to ELIZABETH FITZ GERALD, youngest daughter of Gerald Fitz Gerald, 9th Earl of Kildare, by his second wife Elizabeth, daughter of Thomas Grey, Marquess of Dorset. They had two sons who died in infancy. "Sir Anthonye Browne, K.G., of Battell, Sussex" died testate (P.C.C., 10 Coode) on 6 May 1548, and was buried at Battle. His widow was married for the second time to Edward Clinton, K.G., 9th Lord Clinton, Earl of Lincoln, Lord High Admiral of England (died 16 Jan. 1584/5). She died testate in March 1589/90.

Wotton (1741) 3:6-7. *Top. & Gen.* 2:267 (1853). *Yeatman* (1903), pp. 52-62. *C.P.* 7:692 (1929). *C.P.* 9:97 footnote *b* (1936). *C.P.* 12(1):119 footnote *g*. *Paget* (1977), p. 179.

Child of Anthony Browne, by Alice Gage:
  i. ANTHONY BROWNE, born about 1528, married JANE RADCLIFFE [see NELSON 5].[3]
  ii. MARY BROWNE, married JOHN GREY, of Pirgo, Essex [see GREY 3].[4]

---

[1] Ancesotrs of **St. Leger Codd, Edward Digges, Henry Fleete, Warham Horsmanden, Katherine Saint Leger, Diana & Grey Skipwith**.

[2] Ancestors of **Maria Johanna Somerset**.

[3] Ancestors of **John Nelson**.

[4] Ancestors of **Elizabeth Bosvile**.

BRYAN see LAUNCE

* * *

BULL

EDWARD I OF ENGLAND, King of England, married ALIANORE DE CASTILLE.
JOAN OF ENGLAND [of Acre], married RALPH DE MONTHERMER, Lord Monthermer.
THOMAS DE MONTHERMER, 2nd Lord Monthermer, married MARGARET _____.
MARGARET DE MONTHERMER, married JOHN DE MONTAGU, Lord Montagu.
JOHN DE MONTAGU, 3rd Earl of Salisbury, married MAUD FRANCIS.
THOMAS DE MONTAGU, 4th Earl of Salisbury, married ALIANOR DE HOLAND.
ALICE DE MONTAGU, married RICHARD NEVILLE, Earl [see MONTHERMER 8].

8. ALICE NEVILLE, was married to HENRY FITZ HUGH, 5th Lord Fitz Hugh, of Ravensworth, co. York, son and heir of William Fitz Hugh, 4th Lord Fitz Hugh (of **Magna Charta Surety descent** and **descendant of Charlemagne**), by Margery, daughter of William de Willoughby, 5th Lord Willoughby, of Eresby, co. Lincoln (of **Magna Charta Surety descent** and **descendant of Charlemagne**). He was born about 1429 (aged twenty-three and more at his father's death), and appears to have been but a lukewarm member of the Lancastrian party. They had five sons and five daughters. He was summoned to Parliament from 26 May 1455 by writs directed *Henrico fitz Hugh' militi*. He had licence on 18 Feb. 1467/8 for four years to go to the Holy Sepulchre at Jerusalem. HENRY FITZ HUGH, Lord Fitz Hugh, died on 8 June 1472. His widow was living on 22 Nov. 1503.

Clay (1913), p. 75. *C.P.* 5:428-432, 428 footnote *h* (1926), 432 chart. *C.P.* 11:397 footnote *l*. *Paget* (1977), p. 402.

7. ELIZABETH FITZ HUGH, second daughter, was married to WILLIAM PARR, K.G., of Kendal, Westmorland, M.P. for Westmorland, son of Thomas Parr, Knt., of Kirkby Kendall & Parr, Westmorland (of **Magna Charta Surety descent** and **descendant of Charlemagne**), by Alice, daughter of Thomas Tunstall, Knt., of Thurland Castle, co. Lancaster. He was born in 1434. He was Comptroller of the Household to King Edward IV. He had been married previously to Joan Trusbut, widow (with a son John) of Thomas Colt, of Roydon, Essex. She died in August 1473. William & Elizabeth had three sons and one daughter. SIR WILLIAM PARR died shortly before 26 Feb. 1483/4. His widow was married for the second time 1483-6 to NICHOLAS VAUX, Knt., of Harrowden, co. Northampton, Sheriff of Northamptonshire, Lieutenant of Rockingham Forest, Lieutenant of Guisnes, son of William Vaux, Esq., of Harrowden, co. Northampton, by Katherine, daughter of George Peniston, of Coverto Pramote, in the Piedmont, Italy. He was born about 1460, and grew up in poverty after the attainder of his father. The attainder was reversed on the accession of King Henry VII in 1485, and the forfeited lands restored. They had three daughters. ELIZABETH FITZ HUGH was living in 1501 and died before 29 Jan. 1507/8. Nicholas Vaux was married for the second time about 1508 to Anne Greene, daughter and co-heiress of Thomas Greene, Knt., of Boughton and Norton. She was born in 1490. They had two sons and three daughters. She predeceased her husband. He was created **Lord Vaux of Harrowden**, in 1523. "Nicholas Vaus, lord Harowdon, of Harowdon, Northants" died testate

BULL (cont.)

(P.C.C., 11 Bodfelde) on 14 May 1523.
Top. & Gen. 3:354 (1858) (Parr arms: *Argent*, two bars *azure*, a bordure engrailed *sable*). *Clay* (1913), p. 157. *C.P.* 5:432-433 (1926). *Throckmorton* (1930), pp. 114-115. *C.P.* 10:309 (1945). *Vaux* (1953), pp. 2-17 ("Gregory Penison of Courtesello, Italy") (Vaux arms: Chequy *argent* and *gules*, on a chevron *azure* three roses *or*). *TAG* 52:15-16 (Jan. 1976). *Paget* (1977), p. 247.

Child of William Parr, by Elizabeth fitz Hugh:

   i. **WILLIAM PARR**, second son [see next].

Child and grandchildren of Nicholas Vaux, by Elizabeth fitz Hugh:

   ii. **KATHERINE VAUX**, married **GEORGE THROCKMORTON**, Knt., of Coughton, co. Warwick, son and heir of Robert Throckmorton, Knt., of Coughton, by his second wife, Katherine, daughter of William Marrow, Knt., Lord Mayor of London. They had nine sons and ten daughters. He was high steward of the Abbey of Evesham, and Sheriff of Warwickshire. SIR GEORGE THROCKMORTON died testate (P.C.C., 22 Tashe) on 6 Aug. 1552. They were buried at Coughton. *H.S.P.* 12:87 (1877) (1619 Vis. Warwick). *Throckmorton* (1930), pp. 105-113. *Vaux* (1953), p. 8 ("it is said that ... there did accompany her funeral eleven score lineally descended from her"; "among her descendants were four of the Gunpowder Plot conspirators, and the wife of a fifth"). *Wotton* (1741) 2:356-358. *NEHGR* 108:178 (July 1954). *Paget* (1977), p. 167.

     a. **CLEMENT THROCKMORTON**, mar **KATHERINE NEVILLE** [see OXENBRIDGE 3].[1]

6. **WILLIAM PARR**, Knt., of Horton, co. Northampton *jure uxoris*, second son, Esquire to the Body to Kings Henry VII & VIII, and Knight of the Body to the latter, Sheriff of Northamptonshire, M.P. for Northamptonshire, was married before 1511 to **MARY SALISBURY**, daughter and co-heiress of William Salisbury, Knt., of Horton, by Elizabeth, daughter and co-heiress of Thomas Wylde, of Bromham, co. Bedford. They had four daughters. He took a prominent part in the suppression of the Lincolnshire rebellion in 1536. He was created **Lord Parr of Horton**, co. Northampton, on 23 Dec. 1543, being then Chamberlain to his niece Katharine Parr, sixth and last Queen Consort of King Henry VIII. "Sir Wylliam Parr, Knighte, lord Parr, of Horton, Northants" died testate (P.C.C., 6 Populwell) about November 1546 *s.p.m.* His widow died on 10 July 1555. They were buried at Horton.

Top. & Gen. 3:354 (1858). *Clay* (1913), p. 157. *C.P.* 10:309-310 (1945). *Paget* (1957) 429:1. *TAG* 52:15-16 (Jan. 1976).

5. **ELIZABETH PARR**, daughter and co-heiress, was married about 1523 to **NICHOLAS WODHULL**, Esq., of Warkworth, co. Northampton, son and heir of Fulk Wodhull, of Warkworth and Thenford (of **baronial** descent), by Anne, daughter of William Newenham, of Thenford, co. Northampton. He was born in 1482. He had been married previously about 1508 to **MARY RALEIGH**, daughter of Edward Raleigh, Esq. (descendant of King Edward I), of Farnborough, co. Warwick [see CHETWODE 4 for descendants of this marriage]. Nicholas Wodhull was appointed Sheriff of Northamptonshire in 1514 and 1523. She predeceased her husband. NICHOLAS WODHULL, ESQ., died testate on 6 May 1531 (will requesting burial in the chapel of Warkworth church).

Top. & Gen. 3:354 (1858). *Metcalfe* (1887), p. 56 (1564 Vis. Northants). *Bulkeley* (1933), pp. 61-62 ("Mary, m. Richard Barnaby, of Walford, co. Northampton"). *Bull* (1961), p. 93 (no mention of Plantagenet descent). *TG* 7:41-42 (1987).

4. **ANNE WODHULL**, second daughter, was married to **RICHARD BURNABY**, Esq., of Watford and Mount Sorel, co. Northampton, son of Thomas Burnaby, of Watford, by Elizabeth, daughter of _____ Taylor. They had two sons and one daughter.

---

[1] Ancestors of **John Oxenbridge**.

BULL (cont.)

She received bequests from her father and half-brother Anthony. He was married for the second time to Susanna Dixwell, daughter of William Dixwell, of Cotton, co. Warwick, and had two sons and one daughter.

H.S.P. 12:146 (1877) (1619 Vis. Warwick) (names as the first wife: *Anna filia Odall consanguinea Wm. Parr Marchionis, Northamp*"). *Metcalfe* (1887), pp. 7,8,56,172 (Susan Dixwell first wife) (Burnaby arms: *Argent*, two bars and in chief a lion passant-gardant *gules*). *Bull* (1961), p. 93. *TG* 7:42 (1987), 102 footnote 466.

3. **THOMAS BURNABY**, of Watford, co. Northampton, was married to **ELIZABETH SAPCOTT**, daughter of Edward Sapcott, of Lincoln, co. Lincoln, by Anne, daughter of Thomas Burton, of Coates near Stow. They had eight sons and four daughters. THOMAS BURNABY died 1609-10.

H.S.P. 12:146 (1877). *Metcalfe* (1887), p. 56. *H.S.P.* 52:852-853 (1904) (Maddison Linc. Ped.). *Bull* (1961), p. 93.

2. **SUSAN BURNABY**, was married to **STEPHEN AGARD**, Gent., of Broughton, co. Northampton, son of Ambrose Agard, Gent., of Broughton, co. Northampton.

Metcalfe (1887), pp. 165,172. *Bull* (1961), p. 94.

1. **KATHERINE AGARD**, was married to **JOSIAS BULL**, Gent., of Kinghurst Hall, near Coleshill, co. Warwick, Attorney, son of William Bull, of Sheldon Hall, co. Warwick, by Sarah, daughter of Lawrence Nowell, Dean of Lichfield. He was baptised on 1 Oct. 1592. JOSIAS BULL, GENT., died testate (P.C.C., 141 Hare) in his seventy-ninth year on 6 May 1671, and was buried at Coleshill. His widow died at Maxtock on 7 Dec. 1681, and was buried in the chancel at Maxtock.

H.S.P. 62:28-29 (1682 Vis. Warwick). *NEHGR* 108:33 (Jan. 1954) (Bull arms: *Gules*, a cubit arm in armor fesswise couped the hand in a gauntlet grasping a sword erect all *argent*, pomel and hilt *or*). *Bull* (1961), pp. 1-16, 75-76, 82-84, 89 (Bull arms: *Gules*, a dexter arm in armour couped in fess proper, the hand grasping a sword erect *argent*, pommelled and hilted, *or*).

Children of Josias Bull, by Katherine Agard:

 i. SUSANNA BULL, baptised 27 Nov. 1634, died *s.p.*; married NATHANIEL BRICE.

 ii. **STEPHEN BULL**, son and heir, baptised 30 Nov. 1635, attorney-at-law, emigrated in 1670 on ship *Carolina* to South Carolina, married after emigration, "now at Carolina in ye west Indies aet: 46 ann: 1681"; resided "Ashley Hall" on Ashley River, near Charlestown, died testate about 1706, will (lost) dated 24 Dec. 1701.

   a. WILLIAM BULL, eldest son, born 1683, Lieutenant Governor of South Carolina, died at Sheldon 21 Mar. 1755; married **MARY QUINTEN**. Five children.

   b. BURNABY BULL, second son, resided Prince William's Parish, buried 7 Nov. 1754; married LUCIA BELLINGER. Five children.

   c. JOHN BULL, born Ashley Hall 1693, resided Bull's Island, died 16 Aug. 1767; married MARY BRANFORD. Three children.

   d. CATHERINE BULL, born 1699, died September 1734; married _____ WILSON.

 iii. WILLIAM BULL, of Kinghurst Hall, baptised 14 May 1637, died 15 June 1723; married, first, ANNE BIRCH, second, ELIZABETH BRACEBRIDGE. Four children in England by first marriage.

 iv. JOSIAS BULL, baptised 4 Dec. 1638, ironmonger in London, died 1 Feb. 1700/1.

 v. MARY BULL, baptised 12 Apr. 1640, emigrated to Carolina after death of second husband; married, first, JEREMIAH WEBB, Gent., second, **JOHN LIMBREY**, third, in South Carolina, JOHN QUINTEN. One surviving daughter by each marriage.

   a. KATHERINE WEBB, born 1668.

   b. MARY LIMBREY, born 1673, emigrated to Carolina.

   c. _____ QUINTEN.

 vi. RICHARD BULL, baptised 9 Mar. 1642, resided Maxtock Priory, died 13 Feb. 1704/5.

 vii. LETTICE BULL, baptised 9 Mar. 1642, died 18 Mar. 1708/9; married SAMUEL DALE, broad

BULL (cont.)

silkweaver, London. Issue.

viii. JOHN BULL, baptised 24 Mar. 1643, milliner and feather dresser in London, died 9 July 1709; married, first, SARAH ALLIBOND, second, ELIZABETH BURTON. Nine children by first marriage. Four children by second marriages.

ix. AGARD BULL, baptised 28 Sep. 1644, packer in London, died 18 Dec. 1680; married MARY MANTELL. Five children.

x. KATHERINE BULL, baptised 6 Oct. 1646, died young.

xi. DIGBY BULL, baptised 10 Oct. 1648, M.A., Sidney College, Cambridge, 1676, Rector of Sheldon.

xii. BURNABY BULL, baptised 4 June 1650, "now [1681] in Carolina in the West Indies aet. 31 an.".

xiii. GODITHA BULL, baptised 30 Dec. 1652, died *s.p.*; married JOHN BAILY, of Wick, co. Wilts.

xiv. CLEMENT BULL, baptised 11 June 1656, "went master of a ship to Guinea about the year 1679 and died there about two years after".

* * *

BURGH

EDWARD I OF ENGLAND, King of England, married ALIANORE DE CASTILLE.
JOAN OF ENGLAND [*of Acre*], married GILBERT DE CLARE [see CLARE 12].

13. ELIZABETH DE CLARE, third and youngest daughter, was born at Tewkesbury on 16 Sep. 1295 and was sister and co-heiress of Gilbert de Clare, **Baron** of Clare, 7th Earl of Gloucester and Hertford (died 1314), inheriting the Lordship of Clare. She was married on 30 Sep. 1308 to **JOHN DE BURGH**, son and heir apparent of Richard de Burgh, 3rd Earl of Ulster (of **Magna Charta Surety descent** and **descendant of Charlemagne**), by Margaret, daughter, perhaps, of Arnoul III, Comte de Guines. He was born about 1290. They had one son. JOHN DE BURGH died on 18 June 1313 *v.p.* She was married for the second time near Bristol on 4 Feb. 1315/6, against the King's will and without his licence, to **THEOBALD DE VERDUN**, Knt., of Alton, co. Stafford, 2nd Lord Verdun, lord of half the barony of Weobley, co. Hereford, Justiciar of Ireland, son and heir of Theobald de Verdun (or le Botiler) (of **Magna Charta Surety descent** and **descendant of Charlemagne**), by his wife Margery. He was born on 8 Sep. 1278. They had one daughter. He was summoned to Parliament *v.p.* from 29 Dec. 1299 by writs directed (till his father's death) *Theobaldo de Verdun junior*, whereby he also is held to have become **Lord Verdun**. He had been married previously at Wigmore, co. Hereford, on 29 July 1302 to Maud de Mortimer, daughter of Edmund de Mortimer, Knt., of Wigmore, by Margaret, daughter of William de Fiennes, Knt., and had three daughters (and she died at Alton on 17 or 18 Sep. 1312 after childbirth, and was buried at Croxden Abbey). THEOBALD DE VERDUN, Lord Verdun, died aged thirty-seven at Alton on 27 July 1316, and was buried at Croxden Abbey. Their daughter Isabel was born posthumously at Amesbury, co. Wilts, in 1317. ELIZABETH DE CLARE was married for the third time about April, before 3 May 1317 to **ROGER DAMORY**, of Bletchington, co. Oxford, younger son of Robert Damory, of Bucknell, co. Oxford. They had one daughter. He was summoned to Parliament from 20 Nov. 1317 by writs directed *Rogero Damory*, whereby he is held to have become **Lord Damory**. He took an active part in "pursuing" the Despensers, for which he received a pardon on

BURGH (cont.)

20 Aug. 1321. On the retreat before the King's forces, being sick, or mortally wounded, he was left behind at Tutbury, where he was captured on 11 March, tried and condemned to death. ROGER DAMORY, Lord Damory, died at Tutbury Castle "in rebellion" on 13 or 14 Mar. 1321/2. His widow endowed University Hall, Cambridge, on 8 Apr. 1336. She died testate aged sixty-five on 4 Nov. 1360, and was buried with her third husband in the aisle of St. Mary's, Ware (M.I.).

Banks (1844), p. 445. *C.P.* 2:426 (1912). *C.P.* 4:42-46 (1916) (Damory arms: Barry undy of six, *argent* and *gules*, a bend *azure*). *C.P.* 5:346 (1926). *C.P.* 12(2):250-252 (1959).

Child of John de Burgh, by Elizabeth de Clare:

  i. **WILLIAM BURGH**, born 17 Sep. 1312 [see next].

Child of Theobald de Verdun, by Elizabeth de Clare:

  ii. **ISABEL DE VERDUN**, married **HENRY DE FERRERS** [see CLARKE 10].[1]

Child of Roger Damory, by Elizabeth de Clare:

  iii. **ELIZABETH DAMORY**, married **JOHN BARDOLF** [see BARDOLF 11].[2]

12. WILLIAM DE BURGH, Knt., 4th Earl of Ulster, lord of Connaught in Ireland and of Clare in England, was born on 17 Sep. 1312. He was married, with Papal dispensation dated 1 May 1327, to **MAUD OF LANCASTER**, daughter of Henry, Earl of Lancaster (**grandson of King Henry III**), by his first wife, Maud, daughter of Patrick de Chaworth, Knt., of Kidwelly [see LANCASTER 13 for her ancestry]. He was summoned to Parliament from 10 Dec. 1327 by writs directed *Willelmo de Burgh*, whereby he is held to have become **Lord Burgh**. WILLIAM DE BURGH, Earl of Ulster, was murdered at Le Ford (now Belfast), aged twenty, on 6 June 1333. His widow, with their daughter, fled to England, where she was married for the second time by 8 Aug. 1343 to RALPH DE UFFORD, Knt., Justiciar of Ireland. They had one daughter. He died at Kilmainham, Ireland, on 9 Apr. 1346. His widow died on 5 May 1377, and was buried with her second husband at Campsey Priory, Suffolk. *C.P.* 12(2):178-179 (1959).

Child of William de Burgh, by Maud de Lancaster:

  i. **ELIZABETH DE BURGH**, married **LIONEL OF CLARENCE** [see PLANTAGENET 11].[3]

* * *

BURNABY see BULL

BURNELL see POLE

---

[1] Ancestors of **Alice Baynton, Elizabeth Bosvile, George, Giles & Robert Brent, Charles Calvert, Edward Digges, Warham Horsmanden, Anne Humphrey, Anne Mauleverer, Philip & Thomas Nelson, Herbert Pelham, John Stockman, Katherine Saint Leger, John West, Thomas Wingfield**, and, probably, **Thomas Dudley**.

[2] Ancestors of **George & Robert Brent, Nathaniel Burrough, William Clopton, Muriel Gurdon, John Harleston, Elizabeth Haynes, Edmund Kempe, Robert Peyton**.

[3] Ancestors of **St. Leger Codd, Humphrey Davie, Edward Digges, William Farrar, John Harleston, Warham Horsmanden, Agnes Mackworth, Anne Mauleverer, John Nelson, Philip & Thomas Nelson, George Reade, William Rodney, Katherine Saint Leger, Richard Saltonstall, William Skepper, Thomas Wingfield**, and, probably, **Jane Haviland**.

BURROUGH

EDWARD I OF ENGLAND, King of England, married ALIANORE DE CASTILLE.
JOAN OF ENGLAND [*of Acre*], married GILBERT DE CLARE, Earl of Gloucester.
ELIZABETH DE CLARE, married ROGER DAMORY, Lord Damory.
ELIZABETH DAMORY, married JOHN BARDOLF, 3rd Lord Bardolf.
WILLIAM BARDOLF, 4th Lord Bardolf, married AGNES DE POYNINGS.
CECILY BARDOLF, married BRIAN STAPLETON, Knt.
MILES STAPLETON, Knt., married KATHERINE DE LA POLE.
ELIZABETH STAPLETON, married WILLIAM CALTHORPE, Knt.
ANNE CALTHORPE, married ROBERT DRURY, Knt.
ANNE DRURY, married GEORGE WALDEGRAVE, Esq. [see WALDEGRAVE 3].

3. PHYLLIS WALDEGRAVE, was married to **THOMAS HIGHAM** (or **HEIGHAM**), Esq., of Higham Green in Gazeley, Suffolk, son of John Higham, Knt., of Higham. They had five sons and two daughters. THOMAS HIGHAM, ESQ., was buried at Gazeley on 14 Dec. 1559.

   Muskett (1900), pp. 311-314, 395 (descent from King Edward I). *NEHGR* 108:174-175 (July 1954). *H.S.P.* (n.s.) 2:95 (1981) (1561 Vis. Suffolk).

2. BRIDGET HIGHAM, second daughter, was married for the first time to **THOMAS BURROUGH**, Gent., of Wickhambrook, Suffolk, son of William Burrough, Gent. He had been married previously to Elizabeth Burrell, daughter of Thomas Burrell, of Dullingham, co. Cambridge, with two children. Thomas & Bridget had three sons and one daughters. He was granted arms on 20 June 1586 (*Argent*, two chevronels *vert* between three chaplets of the second, the roses *or*). "Thos. Burro, gent., Wickhambrooke, Suff." died testate (P.C.C., 48 Cobham) on 19 June 1597. She was married for the second time at Wickhambrook on 2 Dec. 1597 to THOMAS FRENCH, of Wethersfield, Essex (will proved 1599, P.C.C., 73 Kidd).

   Muskett (1900), pp. 310-314.

1. REV. GEORGE BURROUGH, was baptised at Wickhambrook, Suffolk, on 26 Oct. 1579. He entered Corpus Christi College, Cambridge University, in 1594, LL.B., Trinity Hall, 1600; Rector of Pettaugh, 1604, and of Gosbeck, 1621. He was married to **FRANCES SPARROW**, daughter of Nicholas Sparrow, of Wickhambrook. They had four sons and one daughter. REV. GEORGE BURROUGH was buried at Pettaugh on 24 Feb. 1653.

   Waters (1885) 1:737. *Muskett* (1900), pp. 301, 311-314. *GDMNH* (1928-1939), p. 122. *NEHGR* 106:260 (Oct. 1952) (Burrough arms). *TAG* 56:43-45 (Jan. 1980). *TAG* 60:140-142 (July 1984).

   Children and grandchild of George Burrough, by Frances Sparrow:

   i. WILLIAM BURROUGH, married. Issue.

   ii. CHARLES BURROUGH, of Ipswich, born about 1612, married AMY _____. Issue.

   iii. THOMAS BURROUGH, Vicar of Newchurch, Isle of Wight.

   iv. FRANCES BURROUGH, died unmarried.

   v. NATHANIEL BURROUGH, merchant mariner, settled on the Patuxent River in Calvert County, Maryland by 1651/2, resided alternately at Roxbury, Massachusetts and in Maryland where last of record on 22 May 1676, returned to England, resided Limehouse in Stepney, Middlesex, will dated 13 Dec. 1681, proved 23 Mar. 1682 (P.C.C., 32 Drax) ("my son George Burrough of New England"); married about 1649 (?REBECCA) STYLE. Her brother John Style, Gent., of Stepney, Middlesex, in his will dated 1685 bequeathed "to my nephew Mr. George Burrough of New England, clerke, all my books".

   a. **GEORGE BURROUGHS**, born about 1650, A.B., Harvard College, 1670, tried and condemned for witchdraft, hanged at Gallows Hill, Salem, 19 Aug. 1692; married, first, **HANNAH** _____ (three daughters) died September 1681, second, **MARY (HATHORNE) RUCK** (three sons), third, **MARY** _____ (one daughter).

BUTLER

EDWARD I OF ENGLAND, King of England, married **ALIANORE DE CASTILLE**.
ELIZABETH OF ENGLAND, married **HUMPHREY DE BOHUN** [see BOHUN 12].

10. ALIANOR DE BOHUN, second daughter, was married in 1327 to **JAMES BUTLER** (or **LE BOTILLER**), K.B., Hereditary Chief Butler of Ireland, son and heir of Edmund Butler, Knt., by Joan, daughter of John Fitz Thomas Fitz Gerald, 1st Earl of Kildare. He was born about 1305 (aged under three in December 1325), and was hostage in Dublin Castle for his father in 1317. In 1326 he received a protection in England on going over to Ireland. As James le Botiller of Ireland he was created **Earl of Ormond** on 2 Nov. 1328 (Ormond was the northern part of co. Tipperary). JAMES BUTLER, Earl of Ormond, died on 6 Jan. 1337/8, and was buried at Gowran (the chief seat of the family before the purchase of Kilkenny Castle). His widow was married for the second time before 20 Apr. 1344, with licence dated 24 Jan. 1343/4 to marry in the chapel of her manor of La Vacherie, in Cranley, Surrey, to **THOMAS DE DAGWORTH**, Knt., younger son of John de Dagworth, of Dagworth, Suffolk, and Bradwell, Essex (of **Magna Charta Surety descent**), by Alice, elder daughter and co-heiress of William Fitz Warin. He was one of the most famous captains of his time, and defeated Charles de Blois at the battle of La Roche-Derien, near Tréguier, on 20 June 1347, and took him prisoner. He was summoned to Parliament from 13 Nov. 1347 by writs directed *Thome de Dagworth'*, whereby he is held to have become **Lord Dagworth**. THOMAS DE DAGWORTH, Lord Dagworth, died in July or Aug. 1350, being slain treacherously, in time of truce, in a skirmish near Aurai in Brittany. His widow died on 7 Oct. 1363.

C.P. 2:450 (1912). *C.P.* 4:27-31 (1916) (Dagworth arms: *Ermine*, on a fesse *gules* three roundlets *or*). *C.P.* 5:479, footnote *b* (1926). *C.P.* 10:116-119 (1945). *C.P.* 12(1):615 (1953).

Children of James Butler, by Alianor de Bohun:

　i. **JAMES BUTLER**, born 4 Oct 1331 [see next].

　ii. **PERNEL BUTLER**, married **GILBERT TALBOT**, Knt. [see TALBOT 9].[1]

Child of Thomas de Dagworth, by Alianor de Bohun:

　iii. **ALIANOR DE DAGWORTH**, married **WALTER FITZ WALTER** [see FITZ WALTER 11].[2]

9. JAMES BUTLER (or **LE BOTILLER**), 2nd Earl of Ormond, was born at Kilkenny on 4 Oct. 1331. He resided chiefly in Ireland, distinguishing himself in the wars there, and receiving many grants for his good services. He was several times Chief Governor of Ireland. He was married (with papal dispensation dated 15 May 1346, the parties being related in the fourth degree) to **ELIZABETH DARCY**, daughter of John Darcy, Knt., of Knaith (of **baronial** descent), probably by his second wife Joan, fourth daughter of Richard Burgh, Earl of Ulster (of **Magna Charta Surety descent** and **descendant of Charlemagne**). JAMES BUTLER, Earl of Ormond, died aged fifty-one in his castle of Knocktopher on 18 Oct. (or 6 Nov.) 1382, and was buried at Gowran. His widow was married between 28 Dec. 1383 and 30 Mar. 1384 to Robert de Hereford, Knt. She died on 24 Mar. 1389/90.

Ancient Deeds 3:456-457 (1900) (D.440: his will). *C.P.* 10:119-121 (1945) (he was called *The Noble Earl*, with reference to his royal descent, and (by the Irish) *The Chaste*).

---

[1]Ancestors of **Robert Abell, Edward Carleton, Grace Chetwode, Anne & Catherine Marbury, Philip & Thomas Nelson**, and, probably, **Mary Launce, Jane Haviland**.

[2]Ancestors of **John Nelson**.

BUTLER (cont.)

8. **JAMES BUTLER** (or **LE BOTILLER**), 3rd Earl of Ormond, son and heir, was born after 1360. He was in England to do homage on 28 Oct. 1385, and was returning in June 1386 to Ireland, where he mostly resided. Like his father, he was several times Chief Governor of Ireland. He was married before 17 June 1386 to **ANNE WELLES**, daughter of John de Welles, Knt., 3rd Lord Welles (**descendant of Charlemagne**), by Maud, daughter of William de Ros, Lord Ros of Helmsley, co. York (of **Magna Charta Surety descent** and **descendant of Charlemagne**). She was living in 1396. JAMES BUTLER, Earl of Ormond, died at Gowran on 6 or 7 Sep. 1405, and was buried there.
    C.P. 10:121-123 (1945).

7. **JAMES BUTLER** (or **LE BOTILLER**), 4th Earl of Ormond, Lieutenant of Ireland, was born probably in 1390. He was married for the first time on or before 28 Aug. 1413 to **JOAN DE BEAUCHAMP**, daughter of William de Beauchamp, Lord Bergavenny, by Joan (**descendant of King Edward I**), daughter of Richard Fitz Alan, 4th Earl of Arundel (**descendant of King Henry III**). She died on 3 or 5 Aug. 1430, and was buried in the chapel of St. Thomas Acon, London [see FITZ ALAN 12.iii for her ancestry]. He was married for the second time, with Papal dispensation dated 29 Apr. 1432, though the parties were doubly related, to **ELIZABETH FITZ GERALD**, widow of John Grey, Knt., Lord Grey of Codnor, and daughter of Gerald FitzGerald, 5th Earl of Kildare, by his second wife Agnes Darcy. She was born about 1398 and died on 6 Aug. 1452 *s.p.* JAMES BUTLER, Earl of Ormond, died at Ardee on 23 Aug. 1452, and was buried in St. Mary's Abbey, near Dublin.
    C.P. 10:123-130 (1945) (called *The White Earl*). *C.P.* 11:705 (1949).
    Children of James Butler, by Joan de Beauchamp:
      i. **THOMAS BUTLER**, Knt. [see next].
      ii. **ELIZABETH BUTLER**, born 1420, married **JOHN TALBOT** [see TALBOT 6].[1]

6. **THOMAS BUTLER (ORMOND** or **LE BOTILLER)**, K.B., 7th Earl of Ormond, was brother and heir of John Butler, 6th Earl of Ormond. He was married for the first time before 11 July 1445 to **ANNE HANKFORD**, daughter and co-heiress of Richard Hankford, Knt., of Hewish, co. Devon, etc., by his second wife Anne, eldest daughter of John de Montagu, Knt., Earl of Salisbury (**descendant of King Edward I**) [see HANKFORD 7 for her ancestry]. She was born early in 1431, and died on 13 Nov. 1485. He was married for the second time before November 1496 to **LORA BERKELEY**, widow of Thomas Montgomery, K.G. (died January 1494/5 *s.p.*), relict of John Blount, 3rd Lord Mountjoy (died 12 Oct. 1485), and daughter of Edward Berkeley, Knt., of Beverton, co. Gloucester, by Christian, daughter of Richard Holt, Esq., of Coldrey in Froyle, co. Hants. She was born about 1466 (aged thirty and more at time of marriage) and died before 30 Dec. 1501, buried with her second husband in New Abbey. "Sir Thomas Ormond, knt., erle of Ormonde" died testate (P.C.C., 8 Holden) on 3 Aug. 1515 *s.p.m.*, and was buried in the chapel of St. Thomas Acon, London.
    Banks (1844), p. 359 ("Thomas Butler, seventh earl of Ormond, in Ireland, had summons to parliament as a baron, in the peerage of England, from 11 Hen. VII. by writ addressed *Thome Ormond de Rochford Chev'* "). *C.P.* 10:131-133, 137 (1945).

5. **MARGARET BUTLER**, younger daughter and co-heiress, was born about 1465 (aged twenty in 1485). She was married in 1485 to **WILLIAM BOLEYN**, Knt., K.B.,

---

[1] Ancestors of **Robert Abell, Grace Chetwode**.

BUTLER (cont.)

of Blicking, Norfolk, son of Geoffrey Boleyn, Knt., Lord Mayor of London, by Anne, daughter and co-heiress of Thomas Hoo, Knt., Lord Hoo of Hoo, co. Bedford (**descendant of Charlemagne**). "Sir William Boleyn, knt., of Blyklying" died testate (P.C.C., 40 Holgrave) in 1505. His widow died between 30 Sep. 1539 (on which date it was found that she had for twenty years past been incapable of managing her affairs) and 20 Mar. 1539/40.

> *Banks* (1844), p. 359-360. *C.P.* 10:133 footnote *b*, 137 (1945). *C.P.* 12(2):739 (1959). *Paget* (1977), p. 456.

Children and grandchild of William Boleyn, by Margaret Butler:

  i. **THOMAS BOLEYN**, Knt., son and heir, born about 1477 [see next].
  ii. **MARGARET BOLEYN**, married **JOHN SACKVILLE**, Esq., of Withyham and Chiddingley, Sussex, son and heir, born about 1484 (aged forty and more in 1524), M.P., Sheriff of Sussex and Surrey, buried, testate, Withyham 5 Oct. 1557, son of Richard Sackville, Esq., of Withyham, by Isabel, daughter of John Digges, Esq., of Barham, Kent. *Collins-Brydges* (1812) 2:101-107 (wife "Anne" named in will). *Coll. Top. & Gen.* 4:141 (1837) (wife called "Margaret"). *Arch. Cant.* 38:6-7 (1926) (wife called "Margaret").
    a. **MARY SACKVILLE**, married **JOHN LUNSFORD** [see LUNSFORD 3].[1]

4. **THOMAS BOLEYN**, Knt., K.B., K.G., of Hever, Kent, and Blicking, Norfolk, Sheriff of Kent, son and heir, was born about 1477. With his father, he was in arms against the Cornish rebels at Blackheath in June 1497. He was married by 1506, probably about 1500, to **ELIZABETH HOWARD**, elder daughter of Thomas Howard, Knt., 2nd Duke of Norfolk (**descendant of King Edward I**), by his first wife Elizabeth, daughter and heiress of Frederick Tilney, Knt., of Ashwellthorpe, Norfolk [see MOWBRAY 6 for her ancestry]. He was Knight of the Body to King Henry VIII, and by 1512 was rapidly rising in royal favour. He was Ambassador to the Emperor Maximilian in the Low Countries, P.C. 1518, Ambassador to France January 1518/9, appointed to be present at the Field of Cloth of Gold, Comptroller of the Household 1520, and Treasurer thereof, 1522-25. His acquisition of numerous Stewardships and Keeperships and gradually of high honours marks the progress of the favour which his daughters Mary and Anne, in turn, found in the eyes of King Henry VIII. He was created **Viscount Rochford** on 18 June 1525, **Earl of Wiltshire** in England and **Earl of Ormond** in Ireland on 8 Dec. 1529. He was present at the baptism of his grand-daughter Princess Elizabeth on 10 Sep. 1533. His wife died at the Abbot of Reading's place, beside Baynard's Castle, on 3 Apr. 1538, and was buried in the Howard aisle in Lambeth Church. He was still at Court in 1538 but had lost most of his influence. THOMAS BOLEYN, Earl of Wiltshire, died aged sixty-one at Hever on 12 Mar. 1538/9 *s.p.m.s.*, and was buried there.

> *C.P.* 10:137-142 (1945) ("his besetting vice was avarice"). *C.P.* 12(2):739 (1959). *Paget* (1977), p. 273.

Children & grandchild of Thomas Boleyn, by Elizabeth Howard:

  i. **MARY BOLEYN**, married **WILLIAM CARY** [see CARY 3].[2]
  ii. **ANNE BOLEYN**, born about 1507; married 25 January 1533 **HENRY VIII OF ENGLAND**, **King of England**; she was beheaded on Tower Green on 19 May 1536, for alleged adultery.
    a. **ELIZABETH TUDOR**, born at Greenwich 7 Sep. 1533, succeeded her half-sister Mary, crowned **Queen of England** 15 Jan. 1559, died at Richmond 24 Mar. 1603, unmarried, buried at Westminster Abbey.

---

[1] Ancestors of **Thomas Lunsford**.

[2] Ancestors of **Anne Humphrey, Herbert Pelham, John West**.

BUTLER see also WASHINGTON

CALTHORPE see BARDOLF

* * *

CALVERT

EDWARD I OF ENGLAND, King of England, married ALIANORE DE CASTILLE.
JOAN OF ENGLAND [of Acre], married GILBERT DE CLARE, Earl of Gloucester.
ELIZABETH DE CLARE, married THEOBALD DE VERDUN, Lord Verdun.
ISABEL DE VERDUN, married HENRY DE FERRERS, 2nd Lord Ferrers of Groby.
WILLIAM DE FERRERS, 3rd Lord Ferrers of Groby, married MARGARET DE UFFORD.
HENRY FERRERS, 4th Lord Ferrers of Groby, married JOAN DE HOO.
WILLIAM DE FERRERS, 5th Lord Ferrers of Groby, married PHILIPPE DE CLIFFORD.
HENRY FERRERS, Knt., married ISABEL MOWBRAY.
ELIZABETH FERRERS, married EDWARD GREY, Lord Ferrers of Groby.
JOHN GREY, Knt., married ELIZABETH WYDVILLE.
THOMAS GREY, Lord Ferrers of Groby, married CECILY BONVILLE. [see GREY 5].

5. ELEANOR GREY, was married to JOHN ARUNDELL, Knt., K.B., of Lanherne, co. Cornwall, son and heir of Thomas Arundel, Knt. (of **Magna Charta Surety descent** and **descendant of Charlemagne**), by Katherine, daughter of John Dinham, Knt. They had two sons. He was made Knight Banneret in 1514 for valour at the sieges of Thérouanne and Tournai. He was married for the second time to Jane Granville, daughter of Thomas Granville, Knt., and had one daughter. SIR JOHN ARUNDELL died on 8 Feb. 1545, and was buried at St. Mary Woolnoth, London.
   Collins-Brydges (1812) 7:42-43.

4. THOMAS ARUNDELL, Knt., K.B., of Wardour Castle, co. Wilts, was married to MARGARET HOWARD, daughter and co-heiress of Edmund Howard (**descendant of King Edward I**), by Joyce, daughter of Richard Culpeper, of Oxenhoath in West Peckham, Kent (**descendant of King Edward I**) [see MOWBRAY 5 for her ancestry]. They had one son and one daughter. SIR THOMAS ARUNDELL, being charged, with Edward, Duke of Somerset, for conspiring the murder of John Dudley, Duke of Northumberland, was beheaded on 26 Feb. 1552. His widow died in 1571, and was buried, with monumental inscription, at Tisbury, co. Wilts.
   Collins-Brydges (1812) 7:43-44. *C.P.* 1:263-264 (1910).

3. MATTHEW ARUNDELL, Knt., of Wardour Castle, son and heir, was married to MARGARET WILLOUGHBY, daughter of Henry Willoughby, Knt., of Wollaton, co. Nottingham, by Anne, daughter of Thomas Grey, 2nd Marquess of Dorset (**descendant of King Edward I**) [see GREY 4.ii for her ancestry]. They had two sons. SIR MATTHEW ARUNDELL died testate (P.C.C., 12 Kidd) in December 1598, and was buried, with monumental inscription, at Tisbury.
   Collins-Brydges (1812) 7:44. *C.P.* 1:263 (1910).

2. THOMAS ARUNDELL, Knt., son and heir, was born about 1560. He was imprisoned in the summer of 1580 for his zeal in the cause of his communion. He was married for the first time, with settlement dated 19 June 1585, to MARY WRIOTHESLEY, daughter of Henry Wriothesley, 2nd Earl of Southampton, by Mary, daughter of Anthony Browne, 1st Viscount Montague. They had two sons and

CALVERT (cont.)

one daughter. He was known as *the Valiant*, and served in 1588 as a volunteer with the Imperial army in Hungary against the Turks, and, having taken a standard from the enemy at Gran, in Hungary, was created by the Emperor Rudolph II, on 14 Dec. 1595, a Count of the Holy Roman Empire. He was created **Baron Arundell of Wardour**, co. Wilts, on 4 May 1605. His first wife was buried at Tisbury, co. Wilts, on 27 June 1607. He was married for the second time at St. Andrew's, Holborn, on 1 July 1608 to **ANNE PHILIPSON**, daughter of Miles Philipson, of Crook, Westmorland, by Barbara, sister and co-heiress of Francis Sandys, of Conishead, co. Lancaster. They had three sons and six daughters. She died at Lennox House, Drury Lane, on 28 June 1637. THOMAS ARUNDELL, Lord Arundell of Wardour, died testate aged about seventy-nine at Wardour Castle on 7 Nov. 1639. They were buried, with monumental inscriptions, at Tisbury.

Collins-Brydges (1812) 7:44-48. *C.P.* 1:263-264, 393 (1910).

Children of Thomas Arundell, by Anne Philipson:
    i. **MARY ARUNDELL**, married **JOHN SOMERSET**, Knt. [see SOMERSET 2].[1]
    ii. **ANNE ARUNDELL** [see next].

1. ANNE ARUNDELL, was married, with marriage settlement dated 20 Mar. 1627/8, to **CECIL (or CECILIUS) CALVERT**, 2nd Lord Baltimore, son and heir of George Calvert, Knt., 1st Lord Baltimore, of Danby Wiske, North Riding, co. York, member of the Virginia Company, by Anne, daughter of George Mynne, of Hertingfordbury, co. Hertford. He was baptised at Boxley, Kent, on 2 Mar. 1605/6, being named after his godfather, the Earl of Salisbury. He entered Trinity College, Oxford University, in 1621, and was admitted to Gray's Inn on 8 Aug. 1633. As heir to the charter promised his father, he promoted, though in England, the settlement of Maryland. ANNE ARUNDELL died in her thirty-fourth year on 23 July 1649, and was buried, with monumental inscription, at Tisbury, co. Wilts. CECIL CALVERT, Lord Baltimore, died testate on 30 Nov. 1675, and was buried at St. Giles-in-the-Fields, Middlesex.

Collins-Brydges (1812) 7:47-48. *Glover-Foster* (1875), p. 500 (1612 Vis. Yorks) (Calvert arms: Paly of six *or* and *sable*, a bend counterchanged). *C.P.* 1:393-395 (1910). *DAB* 3:427 (1929) (Charles Calvert). *NEHGR* 86:269 (July 1932) (Calvert arms). *Adventurers* (1987), pp. 153-159.

Children & grandchildren of Cecil Calvert, by Anne Arundell:
    i. GEORGIANA CALVERT, born Aug. 1629, died in infancy.
    ii. MARY CALVERT, born 18 July 1633, died aged two weeks.
    iii. GEORGE CALVERT, born 15 Sep. 1634, died 6 June 1636.
    iv. FRANCES CALVERT, born November 1635, died 27 Dec. 1635.
    v. ANN CALVERT, born 9 Oct. 1636, died 6 May 1661.
    vi. **CHARLES CALVERT**, born 27 Aug. 1637, 3rd Lord Baltimore, Lord Proprietor of Maryland, Governor of Maryland for his father 1661-75, and for himself 1676, and again 1679-84; deprived of the Province at the Revolution of 1689; named in the fabricated plot of Titus Oates, but not arrested; Brig. Gen. 1696, Major Gen. 1704; died testate aged seventy-seven on 21 Feb. 1714/5, buried St. Pancras, Middlesex; married, first, about 1660 MARY DARNALL, died in childbed in Maryland; second, about 1666 **JANE (LOWE) SEWALL**, died 19 Jan. 1700/1; third, MARY (BANKES) THORPE, died 13 Mar. 1710/11; fourth, MARGARET CHARLETON, died testate 20 July 1731. One son by first marriage. Three children by second marriage.
        a. CECIL CALVERT, born 1661, buried St. Giles-in-the-Fields, Middlesex, 1 July 1681.
        b. CLARE CALVERT, born 1670, died before 1694; married EDWARD MARIA

---

[1] Ancestors of **Maria Johanna Somerset**.

CALVERT (cont.)

SOMERSET.

c. ANNE CALVERT, born 1673, died 10 Feb. 1731/2; married, first, EDWARD MARIA SOMERSET (her sister's widower), second WILLIAM PASTON, of Horton, co. Gloucester.

d. BENEDICT LEONARD CALVERT, 4th Lord Baltimore, second but first surviving son and heir, by second marriage, born 21 Mar. 1678/9; conformed to the established church in 1713, and thereupon had the province of Maryland restored to him; M.P. (Tory) for Harwich 1714-15; died testate at Epsom, Surrey, 16 Apr. 1715; married 2 Jan. 1698/9 CHARLOTTE LEE, born at St. James's Park, 13 Mar. 1678, died 22 Jan. 1720/1 (M.I.), daughter of Edward Henry Lee, 1st Earl of Lichfield, by Lady Charlotte Fitzroy, base-daughter of Charles II of England, **King of England**. Issue.

vii. MARY CALVERT, born 30 Nov. 1638, died 24 Sep. 1671 *s.p.*; married WILLIAM BLAKISTON, Knt., Baronet, of Gibside, Durham.

viii. CECILIUS CALVERT, born 23 Feb. 1639/40, died 4 Feb. 1640/1.

ix. ELIZABETH CALVERT, buried 16 Jan. 1711/2.

* * *

CAREW

EDWARD I OF ENGLAND, King of England, married, second, MARGUERITE DE FRANCE.
THOMAS OF NORFOLK [of *Brotherton*], married ALICE DE HALES.
MARGARET OF NORFOLK, married JOHN DE SEGRAVE, 4th Lord Segrave.
ELIZABETH DE SEGRAVE, married JOHN DE MOWBRAY, 4th Lord Mowbray.
ALIANOR DE MOWBRAY, married JOHN DE WELLES, 5th Lord Welles.
EUDO DE WELLES, married MAUD DE GREYSTOKE.
LIONEL DE WELLES, 6th Lord Welles, married JOAN DE WATERTON.
ALIANOR DE WELLES, married THOMAS HOO, Lord Hoo [see WELLES 6].

6. ALIANOR HOO, was born about 1449 (aged six at her father's death). She was married, it is said, for the first time to THOMAS ECHINGHAM. She was married about 1468 to **JAMES CAREW**, of Beddington, Surrey, son of Nicholas Carew, of Beddington (**descendant of Charlemagne**), by Margaret, daughter of Roger Fiennes, Knt., of Herstmonceux, Sussex. JAMES CAREW died in 1493.

H.S.P. 43:17,214 (1899) (1623 Vis. Surrey). *C.P.* 6:564-565 (1926). *Beville* (1976), pp. 330-332. *Paget* (1977), pp. 262,433.

5. RICHARD CAREW, Knt., of Beddington, Surrey, Sheriff of Surrey, Lieutenant of the Castle of Calais, son and heir, was born in 1469. He was made a Knight Banneret by King Henry VII after the battle of Blackheath in 1497 defeating the Cornishmen. He was married to **MALYN OXENBRIDGE**, widow, with a son Arthur, of Arthur Darcy, of co. Huntingdon, and daughter of Robert Oxenbridge, Knt., of Brede Place, Sussex. They had one son and four daughters. SIR RICHARD CAREW died testate on 23 May 1520 (P.C.C., 3 Bodfelde). They were buried at St. Mary's, Beddington, Surrey, Lady Malyn on 3 Oct. 1544 (M.I. and brasses).

Manning-Bray 2:chart facing p. 523 (1807). *H.S.P.* 43:17,214 (1899). *Beville* (1976), pp. 332-340, 399. *Paget* (1977), p. 178.

Child of Richard Carew, by Malyn Oxenbridge:

CAREW (cont.)

i. NICHOLAS CAREW, Knt., of Beddington, married ELIZABETH BRYAN [see LAUNCE 4].[1]

* * *

CARLETON

EDWARD I OF ENGLAND, King of England, married ALIANORE DE CASTILLE.
JOAN OF ENGLAND [of Acre], married GILBERT DE CLARE, Earl of Gloucester.
MARGARET DE CLARE, married HUGH DE AUDLEY, Earl of Gloucester.
MARGARET DE AUDLEY, married RALPH DE STAFFORD, Earl of Stafford.
HUGH DE STAFFORD, 2nd Earl of Stafford, married PHILIPPE DE BEAUCHAMP.
MARGARET DE STAFFORD, married RALPH NEVILLE, Earl of Westmorland.
RALPH NEVILLE, Knt., married MARY DE FERRERS.
JOHN NEVILLE, Esq., married ELIZABETH NEWMARCH
JOAN NEVILLE, married WILLIAM GASCOIGNE, Knt. [see NEVILLE 7].

6. MARGARET GASCOIGNE, was married to CHRISTOPHER WARDE, Knt., of Givendale, co. York, Standard Bearer to King Henry VIII, Master of the Hart Hounds, son of Roger Warde, Knt., of Givendale, by Joan (of **Magna Charta Surety descent** and **descendant of Charlemagne**), daughter of Thomas Tunstall, Knt., of Thurland, co. Lancaster. They had three daughters. He was knighted in Scotland by the Duke of Gloucester on 24 July 1482. SIR CHRISTOPHER WARDE died on 31 Dec. 1521.

Foster (1874) Gascoigne chart. H.S.P. 16:135,335 (1881) (1563 Vis. Yorks). Sur.Soc. 144:143 (1930) (1480 Vis. North). TAG 17:105-107 (Oct. 1940) (descent of Edward Carleton from King Edward III). H.S.P. 96:433-434 (1944) (Yorkshire Pedigrees). Carleton (1978), chart 6.

5. ANNE WARDE, was married for the first time to JOHN WANDSFORD, of Kirklington, North Riding, co. York. She was married for the second time in 1500/1 to RALPH NEVILLE, Esq., of Thornton Bridge, son and heir of William Neville (of **Magna Charta Surety descent** and **descendant of Charlemagne**), by his first wife Joan, daughter of Christopher Boynton, Knt., of Sedbury & Castle Lemington. He was born about 1465. They had three daughters. She was dead by 26 Oct. 1521. RALPH NEVILLE, ESQ., died on 24 July 1522.

H.S.P. 16:135,335 (1881). TAG 17:108 (Oct. 1940). H.S.P. 96:434 (1944). NEHGR 106:186-190; 118:177-181. Carleton (1978), chart 6.

4. KATHERINE NEVILLE, elder daughter and co-heiress, was born about 1501. She was married for the first time to WALTER STRICKLAND, Knt., of Sizergh, co. Westmorland, son of Walter Strickland, K.B., (of **Magna Charta Surety descent** and **descendant of Charlemagne**) by Elizabeth, daughter of John Pennington, Knt. SIR WALTER STRICKLAND died on 9 Jan 1527/8. She was married for the second time in 1529 to HENRY BOROUGH, Esq., son of Edward, Lord Borough [and stepson of Queen Katherine Parr], for the third time to _____ DARCY, and for the fourth time before 3 Mar. 1535 to WILLIAM KNYVETT, of Collywerton, co. Northampton.

TAG 17:108 (Oct. 1940). H.S.P. 96:434 (1944). Carleton (1978), charts 5,6.

---

[1] Ancestors of **Essex Beville, Mary Launce**.

3. **WALTER STRICKLAND**, Esq., of Sizergh, co. Westmorland, was born on 5 Apr. 1516, and inherited Thornton Bridge, the unentailed manor of his maternal grandfather, Ralph Neville. On 8 Mar. 1535 he was contracted to be married to Margaret, under-age daughter of Stephen Hammerton. Knt. In 1537, on the occasion of his livery, he was said to be married to **AGNES** _____. She was evidently another daughter of Stephen Hammerton, Knt. (of **Magna Charta Surety descent**), by Elizabeth, daughter of John Bigod, of Settrington, co. York (**descendant of King Edward I**) [see BIGOD 4 for her ancestry], and sister of Margaret. Both Strickland and Hammerton, who had been in correspondence, were implicated in the uprising called the *Pilgrimage of Grace*. Though both were pardoned, Stephen Hamerton was attainted and executed by hanging on 25 May 1537. The will of Stephen's widow, Elizabeth, dated 3 May 1538, named only Mary and Anne [i.e. Agnes] as children, and named supervisor "Mr. Walter Strickland", then aged about twenty-two, though not identified as son-in-law. Following his pardon Walter appears to have conformed, and served on juries trying the northern rebels, his late companions. He was, however, never knighted. The marriage to Agnes may have continued during the reign of Queen Mary (whoŝe mother Katherine of Aragon's situation was imperiled as an in-law by her royal husband's self interest). Agnes was "set aside", probably after the accession of Queen Elizabeth in November 1558, presumably with the justification that she had been Walter's sister-in-law. Walter Strickland was married, aged about forty-four years, for the second time, with marriage contract dated 20 Jan. 1560/1, in the lifetime of his first wife, to ALICE TEMPEST, widow of Christopher Place, Esq., of Halnaby, co. York, and daughter of Nicholas Tempest, Esq., of Stella, Durham. They had a son and heir. WALTER STRICKLAND, ESQ., died testate on 8 Apr. 1569. His will, dated 23 Jan. 1568, bequeathed two hundred pounds to "my daughter Elyn" provided she would not marry "contrary to the wise" of Alice, his wife. In the schedule of lands drawn up by his son Thomas for purposes of livery in 1585 there are items for two surviving wives of Walter Strickland (*Agnes, nup uxor dic. Walteri Strickland et resid. rem. in possessione ... Quedam Alicia, nup uxor predic. Walteri Strickland, habet etat inde pro termi vite sue*). His widow Alice was married for the third time, between 14 June 1573 and 31 Mar. 1574 to Thomas Boynton, Knt., of Barmston, co. York. She died in 1588. The will of "Dame Alice, Lady Boynton of Rippon in the county of York, widdow", dated 18 Jan. 1586, and proved 24 Mar. 1595, made her son Thomas Strickland, Esq., her executor, and left £10 to "Ellenor Carleton base daughter of my husband Mr. Strickland".

    NEHGR 93:35 (1939) (suggestion that first wife was Agnes, daughter of Sir Stephen Hamerton). *TAG* 17:108-109 (Oct. 1940). *NEHGR* 114:51-58 (Jan. 1960) ("in 1770 a room at the top of the pele tower at Sizergh was still known as Madam Hamerton's room") (rationale for identification of first wife as Agnes Hamerton). *NEHGR* 115:316 (Oct. 1961). *Carleton* (1978), chart 5.

2. **ELLEN STRICKLAND**, was married for the first time to THOMAS NORTON, son of Richard Norton by his wife Susan Neville, and had children, Thomas and Margaret Norton (called "brother" and "sister" in the will of her son John Carlton dated 1643). She was married for the second time by 1582 to **JOHN CARLETON**, Gent., of Beeford, East Riding, co. York, son of Thomas Carleton, of Beeford, by Jennet, daughter, probably, of William Wilson, of Denton, co. Lincoln. He was born, say, 1550/5. He was steward of Manor Court of Beeford in the East Riding 1586-1614. Ellen was undoubtedly born legitimately, but was bastardized by the repudiation of the marriage to her mother. They had five sons and one daughter. JOHN CARLETON, GENT., was buried on 27 Jan. 1622/3, survived by his widow. The will of "John Carleton of Beford in Hould[e]rnes" was dated 9 Dec. 1620 and

CARLETON (cont.)

proved 22 Nov. 1626.
NEHGR 93:35-38 (Jan. 1939). *TAG* 17:108-109 (Oct. 1940).

1. **WALTER CARLTON**, Gent., of Hornsea Burton, co. York, was baptised at Beeford, co. York, on 29 Dec. 1582. He was married, with licence dated 1607, to **JANE GIBBON**, daughter of Peter Gibbon, of Great Hatfield and Hornsea, co. York, by his wife Margery. She was born about 1595 (aged twelve years and seven months on 23 Nov. 1607). WALTER CARLTON, GENT., died at Hornsea on 4 Oct. 1623. The will of "Walter Carleton of Hornsey Burton in the Countie of Yorke gent.", was dated 15 Mar. 1622 and proved 22 Nov. 1626. His widow was married for the second time in 1626 to William Birkell, Jr. She was living in 1639.
NEHGR 93:2-46 (Jan. 1939 (parentage of Walter Carleton). *TAG* 17:105-106 (Oct. 1940).

Children and grandchildren of Walter Carlton, by Jane Gibbon:

i. **EDWARD CARLETON**, born Hornsea, baptised Beeford, co. York, 20 Oct. 1610, arrived in Massachusetts in the summer of 1638 with his wife Ellen, in the group of Yorkshire settlers who followed the Rev. Ezekiel Rogers, the rector of Rowley in the East Riding, of Yorkshire, to found the town of Rowley, Massachusetts, in 1639, where for ten years Edward Carleton was one of the leading citizens, married at St. Martin Michelgate, York, 3 Nov. 1636 **ELLEN NEWTON**, baptised at Hedon 24 Feb. 1614, daughter of Launcelot Newton (**descendant of Charlemagne**), by his wife Mary Lee.

    a. **JOHN CARLETON**, born 1637-8, resided Haverhill, Massachusetts, married **HANNAH JEWETT**. Four sons.

    b. **EDWARD CARLETON**, born Rowley 28 Oct. 1639.

    c. **MARY CARLETON**, born Rowley 4 June 1642.

    d. **ELIZABETH CARLETON**, born Rowley 20 1st mo. 1644.

ii. **THOMAS CARLTON**, bapt. 1612/13, living 1643, probably buried 1657, Barmston.

iii. **WILLIAM CARLTON**, born about 1617 (aged six at father's death), called son and next heir in *Inq.p.m.* of father for the purposes of the land bequeathed to him held of the king in chief by knight's service, died 1639.

iv. **ANN CARLTON**, living 1622.

* * *

CARY

EDWARD I OF ENGLAND, King of England, married **MARGUERITE DE FRANCE**.
EDMUND OF KENT [*of Woodstock*], Earl of Kent, married **MARGARET WAKE**.
JOAN OF KENT [*the Fair Maid of Kent*], Countess of Kent, married **THOMAS DE HOLAND**.
THOMAS DE HOLAND, 2nd Earl of Kent, married **ALICE FITZ ALAN**.
MARGARET DE HOLAND, married **JOHN BEAUFORT**, Earl of Somerset.
EDMUND BEAUFORT, married **ALIANOR BEAUCHAMP** [see BEAUFORT 9].

5. **ALIANOR BEAUFORT**, Countess of Wiltshire, daughter and, in her issue, co-heiress, was married for the first time to **JAMES BUTLER** (or **ORMOND**), 5th Earl of Ormond and 1st Earl of Wiltshire. He was beheaded on 1 May 1461 *s.p.* She was married for the second time about 1465 to **ROBERT SPENCER**, Knt., of Spencercombe, co. Devon. He was born about 1435. She died on 16 Aug 1501. SIR ROBERT SPENCER was living in 1502, and died testate (will proved 1510, P.C.C., 27 Bennett).
C.P. 9:720 (1936). *TAG* 19:199 (Apr. 1943). *C.P.* 10:129 (1945). *Paget* (1977), p. 410.

CARY (cont.)

Children of Robert Spencer, by Alianor Beaufort:
 i. **MARGARET SPENCER** [see next].
 ii. **KATHERINE SPENCER**, married **HENRY ALGERNON PERCY** [see KEMPE 6].[1]

4. MARGARET SPENCER, elder daughter and co-heiress, was born about 1472 (aged thirty and more at mother's *Inq.p.m.*). She was married about 1490 to **THOMAS CARY**, of Chilton Foliot, co. Wilts, and Moulsford, co. Berks, M.P., son of William Cary, Knt., of Cockington, co. Devon, by Alice, daughter of Baldwin Fulford, Knt., of Fulford, co. Devon. He was born, say, 1460. THOMAS CARY died before 21 June 1536.

TAG 19:199-200 (Apr. 1943). *Paget* (1977), p. 251.

3. WILLIAM CARY, Esq., was born about 1495, and was Gentleman of the Privy Chamber and Esquire of the Body to King Henry VIII. He was married on 31 Jan. 1520/1 to **MARY BOLEYN**, daughter of Thomas Boleyn, K.G., Earl of Wiltshire and Earl of Ormond (**descendant of King Edward I**), by Elizabeth, daughter of Thomas Howard, Knt. (**descendant of King Edward I**) [see BUTLER 4 for her ancestry]. She was sister of Queen ANNE BOLEYN, second wife of King Henry VIII (parents of Queen Elizabeth). WILLIAM CARY, ESQ., died on 22 June 1528. His widow died on 19 July 1543.

Swyncombe and Ewelme (1858), p. 369. *C.P.* 4:160 (1916). *TAG* 19:200 (Apr. 1943). *Paget* (1977), p. 187.

2. KATHERINE CARY, was born about 1521. She was married about 1539 to **FRANCIS KNOLLYS**, Knt., K.G., of Caversham and Rotherfield Greys, co. Oxford, son of Robert Knollys, of Rotherfield Greys, by Lettice, daughter of Thomas Peynston, Knt., of Hawridge, co. Buckingham. He was born about 1514. They had five sons and four daughters. He was Vice Chamberlain of the Household and Treasurer to the Household of Queen Elizabeth, Custos Rotulorum of the County of Oxford and M.P. for co. Oxford. She was Chief Lady of the Bedchamber to Queen Elizabeth. She died at Hampton Court, while in attendance on the Queen, on 15 Jan. 1568/9, and was buried at St. Edmund's Chapel, Westminster Abbey. "Frauncys Knollys, K.G., of Caversham, Oxford" died testate (P.C.C., 67 Drake) on 19 July 1596.

Swyncombe and Ewelme (1858), pp. 360-373. *C.P.* 4:160 (1916). *TAG* 18:212-218 (1942). *TAG* 19:200 (Apr. 1943). *Paget* (1977), p. 128.

Child of Francis Knollys, by Katherine Cary:
 i. **ANNE KNOLLYS**, married **THOMAS WEST**, Knt., Lord Delaware [see HUMPHREY 3].[2]

* * *

CERGEAUX

EDWARD I OF ENGLAND, King of England, married **ALIANORE DE CASTILLE**.
JOAN OF ENGLAND [*of Acre*], married **GILBERT DE CLARE**, Earl of Gloucester.

---

[1] Ancestors of **Edmund Kemp**.
[2] Ancestors of **Anne Humphrey, Herbert Pelham, John West**.

CERGEAUX (cont.)

ALIANOR DE CLARE, married HUGH LE DESPENSER [see CLARE 11].

10. ISABEL LE DESPENSER, was born about 1312. She was married in the King's Chapel at Havering-atte-Bower on 9 Feb. 1320/1, she being about eight years of age, to RICHARD FITZ ALAN [Copped Hat], 3rd Earl of Arundel and 4th Earl of Surrey, son and heir of Edmund Fitz Alan, 8th Earl of Arundel, Baron of Oswestry, co. Salop, Baron of Clun, co. Salop (descendant of Charlemagne), by Alice, daughter of William de Warenne (descendant of Charlemagne). He was born about 1313, and was about seven years of age at time of marriage. In 1330-1 he was fully restored in blood and honours and obtained restitution of the Castle and Honour of Arundel, becoming Earl of Arundel. Their marriage was annulled by Papal mandate on 4 Dec. 1344 on the ground of his minority and of his never having willingly consented to the match. He took a distinguished part in the wars with France, was Admiral of the West 1340-41 and 1345-47, commanded the second division at the Battle of Crécy, and was at the fall of Calais in 1347. He was married for the second time at Ditton, in the presence of King Edward, on 5 Feb. 1344/5 to ALIANOR DE LANCASTER, widow of John Beaumont, 2nd Lord Beaumont, and daughter of Henry of Lancaster, Earl of Lancaster (grandson of King Henry III), by Maud, daughter and heiress of Patrick de Chaworth, Knt. She was first cousin to his first wife and a Papal dispensation was granted on 4 Mar. 1344/5 [see FITZ ALAN 13 for descendants of this marriage]. She died at Arundel on 11 Jan. 1372, and was buried at Lewes. On 30 June 1347 he succeeded to the vast estates of the family of Warenne, by the death of his mother's brother, John, Earl of Surrey and Sussex *s.p.legit.* RICHARD FITZ ALAN, Earl of Arundel, died testate in his seventieth year at Arundel on 24 Jan. 1375/6, and was buried at Lewes.

    C.P. 1:242-244, 243 footnote *d* (1910) ("The powerful Earl desired to get rid of the woman to whom he had been married as a child, and who, since her father's attainder and execution, had ceased to be of any importance, that he might marry the woman with whom he was then living in adultery; and the Pope very obligingly annulled the marriage and bastardised the issue: a very unfair proceeding as far as Edmund d'Arundel was concerned"), 244 footnote *b.* C.P. 7:156 (1929).

Children of Richard fitz Alan, by Isabel le Despenser:

    i. EDMUND FITZ ALAN, Knt, born about 1327 [see next].

    ii. MARY FITZ ALAN, died 29 Aug. 1363; married JOHN LE STRANGE, 4th Lord Strange, born at Whitchurch about Easter 1332, summoned to Parliament 3 Apr. 1360 by writ directed *Johanni Lestraunge*, died 12 May 1361. C.P. 12(1):344-345. *Paget* (1957) 509:3.

        a. ANKARET LE STRANGE, married RICHARD TALBOT [see TALBOT 8].[1]

9. EDMUND FITZ ALAN, Knt., second son, by first marriage, was born about 1327. He was bastardized by the annulment of his parents' marriage. He was married before July 1349 to SIBYL DE MONTAGU, daughter of William de Montagu, 1st Earl of Salisbury, Earl Marshal of England (of baronial descent), by Katharine (descendant of Charlemagne), daughter of William de Grandison, 1st Lord Grandison. She died on 30 Jan. 1343/4. SIR EDMUND FITZ ALAN was living in 1377.

    C.P. 1:244b (1910).

8. PHILIPPE FITZ ALAN, daughter and co-heiress, was married by 1378 to RICHARD CERGEAUX (or SERGEAUX), Knt., of Colquite, Cornwall, M.P., Cornwall, Sheriff of Cornwall, son and heir of Richard Cergeaux, of Colquite, by

---

[1] Ancestors of **Robert Abell, Grace Chetwode, Anne & Catherine Marbury.**

CERGEAUX (cont.)

Margaret, daughter and heiress of John Seneschal, Knt., of Predarwolas, Cornwall. He had been married previously before 1362 to Elizabeth Bodrugan, daughter and heiress of William Bodrugan, Knt., of Bodrugan, Cornwall, with one daughter. Richard & Philippe had one son and four daughters. SIR RICHARD CERGEAUX died on 30 Sep. 1393. His widow was married for the second time to JOHN CORNWALL, Knt. (afterwards Lord Fanhope), and died on 13 Sep. 1399.

> C.P. (1910) 1:244 footnote b (1910) (incorrect identification of parentage of Philippe). C.P. 10:236 footnote a (correction of parentage of Philippe). Roskell (1992) 2:506-507.

Children of Richard Cergeaux, by Philippe fitz Alan:

  i. ELIZABETH CERGEAUX, married WILLIAM MARNEY, Knt. [see JENNINGS 10].[1]
  ii. PHILIPPE CERGEAUX, married ROBERT PASHLEY, Knt. [see FLEETE 8].[2]
  iii. ALICE CERGEAUX [see next].

7. ALICE CERGEAUX, third daughter and co-heiress, was born about 1384 (aged fifteen in 1399). She was married for the first time to GUY SAINT AUBYN. She was married for the second time about 1405 to RICHARD DE VERE, K.G., 11th Earl of Oxford, son and heir of Aubrey de Vere, 10th Earl of Oxford (of **Magna Charta Surety descent** and **descendant of Charlemagne**), by Alice, daughter of John Fitz Walter, 2nd Lord Fitz Walter, **Baron** of Little Dunmow, Essex (of **Magna Charta Surety descent** and **descendant of Charlemagne**). He was born, probably, in 1385, and had been married previously to _____ de Holand (died *s.p.*), daughter of John de Holand, 1st Duke of Exeter, by Elizabeth, daughter of John of Lancaster [*of Gaunt*], 1st Duke of Lancaster. RICHARD DE VERE, Earl of Oxford, died testate on 15 Feb. 1416/17, and was buried at Earls Colne. His widow was married for the third time before 13 Oct. 1421 to NICHOLAS THORLEY (died 5 May 1442). She died on 18 May 1452 and was buried at Earls Colne with the Earl.

> C.P. 10:234-236, 236 footnote a (1945).

6. JOHN DE VERE, Knt., 12th Earl of Oxford, son and heir, was born at Hedingham Castle on 23 Apr. 1408. He was married between 22 May and 31 Aug. 1425 to ELIZABETH HOWARD, daughter and heiress of John Howard, Knt., of Wiggenhall (of **Magna Charta Surety descent** and **descendant of Charlemagne**), by Joan, daughter of John Walton, of Wivenhoe. She was born about 1410 (aged fourteen and more in 1424). They had five sons and three daughters. He was arrested with his eldest son for plotting against the King, tried for high treason, and condemned to death. JOHN DE VERE, Earl of Oxford, was beheaded on Tower Hill on 26 Feb. 1462/2. His widow died soon after Christmas 1475 or later, apparently at Stratford Nunnery. They were buried in Austin Friars', London.

> C.P. 10:237-239 (1945).

5. GEORGE DE VERE, Knt., third son, Chief Steward of St. Osyth's Priory, Essex, was married to MARGARET STAFFORD, daughter and heiress of William Stafford, Knt., of Bishop's Frome, co. Hereford. His will, dated 21 Aug. 1500, names older daughters, but not the youngest.

> C.P. 10:244 (1945). C.P. 12(2):795 footnote a (1959). H.S.P. 111:219 (1984) (1561 Vis. Suffolk).

Child of George de Vere, by Margaret Stafford:

---

[1] Ancestors of **Edmund Jennings**.

[2] Ancestors of **St. Leger Codd, Henry Fleete, Warham Horsmanden, Anne Lovelace, Katherine Saint Leger, John Throckmorton**.

CERGEAUX (cont.)

i. **ELIZABETH DE VERE**, married **ANTHONY WINGFIELD**, Knt. [see HANKFORD 4].[1]

* * *

CHERLETON

EDWARD I OF ENGLAND, King of England, married **ALIANORE DE CASTILLE**.
JOAN OF ENGLAND [*of Acre*], married **GILBERT DE CLARE**, Earl of Gloucester.
MARGARET DE CLARE, married **HUGH DE AUDLEY**, 8th Earl of Gloucester.
MARGARET DE AUDLEY, married **RALPH DE STAFFORD** [see AUDLEY 12].

12. **JOAN DE STAFFORD**, was married to **JOHN CHERLETON**, 3rd Lord Cherleton, feudal Lord of Powis, co. Montgomery, son and heir of John Cherleton, 2nd Lord Cherleton, feudal Lord of Powis, by Maud, daughter of Roger de Mortimer, 1st Earl of March, **Baron** of Wigmore, co. Hereford (of **Magna Charta Surety descent** and **descendant of Charlemagne**). He was born about 1334 (aged twenty-six at Easter 1360). He was summoned to Parliament from 14 Aug. 1362 by writs directed *Johanni de Cherleton de Powys*. JOHN CHERLETON, Lord Cherleton, died on 13 July 1374. His widow was married, as his second wife, before 16 Nov 1379 (when they had pardon for marrying without licence) to GILBERT TALBOT [Lord Talbot] (died 24 Apr. 1387). She died before 1397.
    C.P. (1913) 3:161.

11. **EDWARD CHERLETON**, 5th Lord Cherleton, feudal lord of Powis, K.G., younger son, was born about 1371 (aged thirty in 1401), and was brother and heir of John, 4th Lord Cherleton. He was summoned to Parliament from 2 Dec. 1401 by writs directed *Edwardo de Cherleton de Powys*. In 1410 he sustained great loss by the rebellion of Owen Glendower. He was married for the first time in June 1399 to **ALIANOR DE HOLAND**, widow of Roger de Mortimer, Earl of March and Ulster, Lord Mortimer (died 1398) [see PLANTAGENET 9 for descendants of this marriage], and fourth daughter of Thomas de Holand, Knt. (**descendant of King Edward I**), 2nd Earl of Kent, by Alice (**descendant of King Henry III**), daughter of Richard Fitz Alan, Earl of Arundel. She was sister and co-heiress of Edmund, Earl of Kent, and died in childbed on 23 Oct. 1405 [see HOLAND 8 for her ancestry]. He was married for the second time before 1408 to ELIZABETH BERKELEY, daughter of John Berkeley, Knt., of Beverstone, co. Gloucester, by Elizabeth, daughter of John Betteshorne, Knt. They had no issue. EDWARD CHERLETON, Lord Cherleton, died on 14 Mar. 1420/1 *s.p.m.* His widow was married for the second time to JOHN SUTTON, Lord Dudley (died 30 Sep. 1487), and had issue. She died shortly before 8 Dec. 1478.
    C.P. 3:161-162 footnote *b* (1913). C.P. 4:480 (1916). C.P. 6:137 (1926). C.P. 8:450 (1932). C.P. 12(1):748 (1932).

Children of Edward Cherleton, by Alianor de Holand:

i. **JOAN CHERLETON**, born about 1400, married **JOHN GREY** [see LLOYD 8].[2]

---

[1] Ancestors of **Francis Dade**.
[2] Ancestors of **Nathaniel Littleton, Thomas Lloyd**.

CHERLETON (cont.)

ii. **JOYCE CHERLETON**, born about 1403 [see next].

10. JOYCE CHERLETON, younger daughter and co-heiress, was born about 1403 (aged eighteen in 1421). She was married, with licence dated 28 Feb. 1421/2, to **JOHN TIPTOFT**, Knt., M.P. of Huntingdonshire and Somerset, Speaker of the House of Commons, son and heir of Payn Tiptoft, Knt., of Burwell, co. Cambridge (of **Magna Charta Surety descent**), by Agnes, daughter of John Wroth, Knt., of Enfield, Middlesex. He had been married previously, before 24 Feb. 1407/8, to Philippe Talbot, widow, first, of Robert de Assheton, Knt. (died 9 Jan. 1383/4), and second, of Matthew de Gournay (died 26 Sep. 1406, aged ninety-six), and daughter of John Talbot, Knt., of Richard's Castle, co. Hereford, by his wife Katherine. She was born about 1367 (aged twenty-one in July 1388), and was sister and co-heiress of John Talbot, of Richard's Castle. She died on 2 or 3 May 1417 *s.p.* Shortly after his second marriage he was summoned to Parliament from 7 Jan. 1425/6 by writs directed *Johanni Tiptoft chivaler*, whereby he is held to have become **Lord Tiptoft**. John & Joyce had one son and three daughters. JOHN TIPTOFT, Lord Tiptoft, died on 27 Jan. 1442/3. His widow died on 22 Sep. 1446, and was buried at Enfield (M.I.).

C.P. 3:162 footnote *b* (1913). *C.P.* 4:480 footnote *c* (1916). *C.P.* 12(1):746-749 (1953). *Roskell* (1992) 4:620-628.

Children of John Tiptoft, by Joyce Cherleton:
  i. **PHILIPPE TIPTOFT**, married **THOMAS DE ROS**, 10th Lord Ros [see ROS 8].[1]
  ii. **JOAN TIPTOFT** [see next].
  iii. **JOYCE TIPTOFT**, married **EDMUND SUTTON**, Knt. [see DUDLEY 5].[2]

9. JOAN TIPTOFT, second daughter, was born before 1425 (aged sixty and more in 1485). She was married to **EDMUND INGOLDISTHORPE**, Knt., of Borough Green, co. Cambridge, son of Thomas Ingoldisthorpe, by Margaret, daughter and heiress of Walter de la Pole, Knt., of Cambridgeshire. SIR EDMUND INGOLDISTHORPE died 1456-57.

Blomefield 9:79 (1808). *C.P.* 9:92 (1936). *TG* 9:180 (1988). *Paget* (1977), p. 439. *Roskell* (1992) 3:476.

Child of Edmund Ingoldisthorpe, by Joan Tiptoft:
  i. **ISABEL INGOLDISTHORPE**, married **JOHN NEVILLE** [see MONTHERMER 7].[3]

* * *

CHETWODE

EDWARD I OF ENGLAND, King of England, married **ALIANORE DE CASTILLE**.
ELIZABETH OF ENGLAND, married **HUMPHREY DE BOHUN**, Earl of Hereford and Essex.
ALIANORE DE BOHUN, married **JAMES BUTLER**, Earl of Ormond.
PERNEL BUTLER, married **GILBERT TALBOT**, 3rd Lord Talbot.
RICHARD TALBOT, 4th Lord Talbot, married **ANKARET LE STRANGE**.

---

[1] Ancestors of **Philip & Thomas Nelson**.

[2] Ancestors of **Agnes Mackworth, John Washington**, and, probably, **Thomas Dudley**.

[3] Ancestors of **John Nelson**.

CHETWODE (cont.)

MARY TALBOT, married THOMAS GREENE, Knt.
THOMAS GREENE, Knt., married PHILIPPE DE FERRERS.
ELIZABETH GREENE, married WILLIAM RALEIGH, Esq.
EDWARD RALEIGH, Esq., married MARGARET VERNEY.
EDWARD RALEIGH, Knt., married ANNE CHAMBERLAIN [see MARBURY 4].

4. MARY RALEIGH, was married about 1508 to NICHOLAS WODHULL, Esq., of Warkworth, Sheriff of Northamptonshire, son and heir of Fulk Wodhull, of Warkworth and Thenford (of **baronial** descent), by Anne, daughter of William Newenham, of Thenford, co. Northampton. He was born in 1482. They had one son and one daughter. She died before 1522/3. He was married for the second time about 1523 to ELIZABETH PARR, daughter and co-heiress of William Parr (descendant of King Edward I), of Horton, co. Northampton, by Mary, daughter and co-heiress of William Salisbury, Knt., of Horton [see BULL 5 for descendants of this marriage]. They had one son and two daughters. She predeceased her husband. NICHOLAS WODHULL, ESQ., died testate on 6 May 1531. His will, dated 29 Mar. 1531, included the bequest of the reversion of the manor of Thenford to son Fulk, bequests to his daughters Joyce, Mary and Anne, and to his brothers Thomas and Laurence, and a request for burial in the chapel of Warkworth church.
Metcalfe (1887), p. 56 (1564 Vis. Northants) ("Nicholas, Lord Woodhull") (Woodhull arms: Or, three crescents *gules*). *TG* 7:41-42 (1987). *Bulkeley* (1933), pp. 61-62. *NEHGR* 145:20 (Jan. 1991).

3. ANTHONY WODHULL, of Warkworth, son and heir by first marriage, was born about 1517. He was married to ANNE SMITH, daughter of John Smith, Esq., of Cressing, Essex, Baron of the Exchequer, by Agnes, daughter of John Harewell, Esq., of Wootton Wawen, co. Warwick. ANTHONY WODHULL died testate aged about twenty-five, on 4 Feb. 1541/2. His will, dated 1 Feb. 1541/2 and proved 11 Oct. 1542, made bequests to his sisters Joyce, Mary, and Anne, his brother Fulk, and his uncles Lawrence and Thomas. His widow was married for the second time to John Leveson, Esq., of Halling, Kent, and Wolverhampton, co. Stafford (died 1549), and for the third time to Edward Griffin, Knt., of Dingley, Attorney General under King Edward VI (died 16 Dec. 1569). She predeceased her third husband.
Metcalfe (1887), p. 56 ("Anthony, Lord Woodhull of Woodhull, co. Bedford"). *Bulkeley* (1933), p. 62. *TG* 7:43 (1987). *NEHGR* 145:20 (Jan. 1991).

2. AGNES WODHULL, daughter and heiress, was born in 1542. She was married for the first time between 1 Dec. 1558 and 19 Apr. 1559 to RICHARD CHETWODE, Esq., son of Roger Chetwode, of Worleston, co. Chester, by Ellen, daughter of Thomas Masterson, of Nantwich, co. Chester. He was born, say, 1526-7. RICHARD CHETWODE, ESQ., died at White Friars', and was buried at St. Dunstan's-in-the-West, London, on 12 Jan. 1559/60. His will was dated 6 Jan. 1559/60. She was married for the second time, without issue, to GEORGE CALVELEY, Knt., of Lea, co. Chester. She died in 1575/6.
Metcalfe (1887), pp. 56,159 (1618/9 Vis. Northants). *Bulkeley* (1933), p. 62. *Chetwode* (1945), pp. 37-41 ("probably the heir to very little property [married to] one of the greatest heiresses of her time"). *NEHGR* 145:20 (Jan. 1991).

1. RICHARD CHETWODE, Knt., of Warkworth, co. Northampton, Sheriff of Northampton, son and heir, was born about 1560 (aged sixteen or more at mother's *Inq.p.m.*). He was married for the first time to JANE DRURY, daughter and co-heiress of William Drury, sometime Deputy Lieutenant of Ireland. They had two sons and three daughters. He was married for the second time to DOROTHY NEEDHAM, daughter of Robert Needham, of Shavington, co. Salop (**descendant of King Edward I**), by Frances, daughter of Edward Aston, Knt., of Tixall, co. Stafford.

CHETWODE (cont.)

She was born in 1570, and was named, with her husband and children, in the will of her sister Elizabeth Needham. They had four sons and seven daughters. She died in 1629 [see TALBOT 2 for her ancestry]. He attempted to establish his right to the Barony of Woodhull but his claim was not accepted by King James who offered only (doubtless on payment) a new patent which Sir Richard refused as a "derogation of his claim". He had the advowson of Odell, co. Bedford, and presented Edward Bulkeley, D.D., in 1605, and later his son Peter [see below]. SIR RICHARD CHETWODE died after 1631.

Metcalfe (1887), p. 159. *DAB* 3:249-250 (1929). *Bulkeley* (1933), pp. 57-58. *Chetwode* (1945), pp. 42-46. *NEHGR* 107:44 (Jan. 1953) (Chetwood arms: Quarterly silver and gules four crosses patty counter-changed).

Child and grandchildren of Richard Chetwode, by Dorothy Needham:

i. **GRACE CHETWODE**, born 1602, died New London, Connecticut, 21 Apr. 1669; married **REV. PETER BULKELEY**, born 31 Jan. 1582/3, M.A. St. John's College, Cambridge, Rector, Odell, co. Bedford, minister, Concord, Massachusetts, died there 9 Mar. 1658/9.

    a. **GERSHOM BULKELEY**, born Cambridge, Massachusetts, January 1635/6, "Practioner in Physick", died Glastonbury, Connecticut, 2 Dec. 1713; married **SARAH CHAUNCY**. Seven children.

    b. **ELEAZER BULKELEY**, born 1638, attended Harvard College, died unmarried.

    c. **DOROTHY BULKELEY**, born Concord 2 Aug. 1640.

    d. **PETER BULKELEY**, born Concord 12 Aug. 1643, attended Harvard College, physician, died Fairfield, Connecticut, 1691; married **MARGARET** _____. Five children.

* * *

CLARE

EDWARD I OF ENGLAND, married **ALIANORE DE CASTILLE** [see PLANTAGENET 14].

12. JOAN OF ENGLAND [*of Acre*], second daughter, was born at Acre in the Holy Land probably early in 1272. She was married for the first time at Westminster Abbey about 30 Apr. 1290 to **GILBERT DE CLARE** *the Red*, Knt., **Baron** of Clare, Suffolk, 9th Earl of Clare, 3rd Earl of Gloucester, 6th Earl of Hertford, son and heir of Richard de Clare (of **Magna Charta Surety descent** and **descendant of Charlemagne**), by Maud, daughter of John de Lacy, Earl of Lincoln, **Magna Charta Surety** (and **descendant of Charlemagne**). He was born at Christ Church, co. Hants, on 2 Sep. 1243. He had been married for the first time in the spring of 1253 to **ALICE DE LUSIGNAN**, daughter of Hughes XI de Lusignan *le Brun*, Comte de la Marche et de Angoulême (uterine brother of King Henry III), by Yolande, daughter of Pierre *Mauclerk*, Duc de Bretagne. They had two daughters, and were divorced, his wife Alice said to have become hypochondriacal in 1271. At the death of King Henry III on 16 Nov. 1272, the Earl took the lead in swearing fealty to Edward I, who was then in Sicily returning from the Crusade. He was Joint Guardian of England during the King's absence. Proposals for his marriage to the King's daughter were made as early as May 1283. Their daughter Margaret is probably the daughter born at Caerphilly Castle in October 1292, her mother having been purified there on 23 November following the birth of a daughter. **GILBERT DE CLARE**, Earl of Hertford and Gloucester, died at Monmouth Castle on 7 Dec. 1295, and was

CLARE (cont.)

buried at Tewkesbury. JOAN OF ENGLAND was married for the second time, clandestinely (to her father, the King's, great displeasure), presumably early in 1297, to RALPH DE MONTHERMER who had been a member of the late Earl's household [see MONTHERMER 13 for descendants of this marriage]. JOAN OF ENGLAND died, aged thirty-five, on 23 Apr. 1307, and was buried in the Austin Friars' at Clare, Suffolk. Ralph de Monthermer died on 10 May 1325.
 C.P. 1:346 (1910). *C.P.* 3:244 (1913). *C.P.* 4:269 (1916). *C.P.* 5:346, 373, 702-712 (1926). *C.P.* 6:503 (1926). *C.P.* 9:140-142 (1936). *Sanders* (1960), pp. 6, 34-35. *TAG* 69:138 (July 1994) (birthdates of daughters Alianor and Margaret).

Children of Gilbert de Clare, by Joan of England:
    i.   ALIANOR DE CLARE [see next].
    ii. MARGARET DE CLARE, married HUGH DE AUDLEY [see AUDLEY 13].[1]
    iii. ELIZABETH DE CLARE, three marriages [see BURGH 13].[2][3][4]

11. ALIANOR DE CLARE, was sister and co-heiress of Gilbert de Clare. She was married at Westminster in 1306, after 14 June, to HUGH LE DESPENSER, Knt., 2nd Lord Despenser, son and heir of Hugh le Despenser, Knt., of Loughborough, co. Leicester, etc. (**descendant of Charlemagne**), by Isabel (of **Magna Charta Surety descent**), daughter of William de Beauchamp, of Elmley, co. Worcester, 9th Earl of Warwick (**descendant of Charlemagne**). He was summoned to Parliament from 29 July 1314 by writs directed *Hugoni le Despenser juniori*. He was disinherited and exiled on 19 Aug. 1321. He took refuge in the Cinque Ports, and, engaging in piracy, with the King's connivance, did considerable damage. After the battle of Boroughbridge, he received large grants of the lands forfeited by the rebels. He accompanied the King in his flight to Wales in October 1326, and with the King, was captured near Llantrisant, co. Glamorgan, on 16 Nov. 1326. HUGH LE DESPENSER, Lord Le Despenser, was taken to Hereford, tried, without being allowed to speak in his own defence, condemned to death as a traitor, and hanged on 24 Nov. 1326, buried some years afterwards at Tewkesbury Abbey. His widow was married for the second time, as his second wife, about January 1328/9 to WILLIAM LA ZOUCHE DE MORTIMER, Knt., who had abducted her from Hanley Castle. He died 28 Feb. 1336/7. ALIANOR DE CLARE died on 30 June 1337.
 C.P. 1:243 (1910). *C.P.* 4:267-271 (1916). *TAG* 69:138 (July 1994).

---

[1]Ancestors of **Robert Abell, Dannett Abney, Richard & William Bernard, Elizabeth Bosvile, Charles Calvert, Edward Carleton, Grace Chetwode, St. Leger Codd, Francis Dade, Humphrey Davie, Edward Digges, William Farrar, John Fenwick, Henry Fleete, Muriel Gurdon, John Harleston, Warham Horsmanden, Nathaniel Littleton, Thomas Lloyd, Thomas Lunsford, Agnes Mackworth, Anne & Catherine Marbury, Elizabeth Marshall, Anne Mauleverer, John Nelson, Philip & Thomas Nelson, George Reade, William Randolph, William Rodney, Katherine Saint Leger, Richard Saltonstall, William Skepper, Maria Johanna Somerset, John Washington, Olive Welby, Thomas Wingfield, Mary Wolseley, Hawte Wyatt,** and, probably, **Thomas Dudley, Jane Haviland.**

[2]Ancestor, with first husband John de Burgh, of **St. Leger Codd, Edward Digges, Humphrey Davie, Warham Horsmanden, Agnes Mackwroth, John Nelson, Philip & Thomas Nelson, Katherine Saint Leger,** and, probably, **Jane Haviland.**

[3]Ancestor, with second husband Theobald de Verdun, of **Alice Baynton, Elizabeth Bosvile, George, Giles & Robert Brent, Charles Calvert, Jeremy Clarke, St. Leger Codd, Edward Digges, Warham Horsmanden, Anne Humphrey, Anne Mauleverer, Philip & Thomas Nelson, Herbert Pelham, Katherine Saint Leger, John Stockman, John West, Thomas Wingfield.**

[4]Ancestor, with third husband Roger de Damory, of **George & Robert Brent, Nathaniel Burrough, William Clopton, Muriel Gurdon, John Harleston, Elizabeth Haynes, Edmund Kempe, Robert Peyton.**

CLARE (cont.)

Children of Hugh le Despenser, by Alianor de Clare:
  i. EDWARD LE DESPENSER, Knt. [see next].
  ii. ISABEL LE DESPENSER, married RICHARD FITZ ALAN [see CERGEAUX 10].[1]
  iii. ELIZABETH LE DESPENSER, married MAURICE DE BERKELEY [see DEIGHTON 9].[2]

10. EDWARD LE DESPENSER, Knt., of Buckland, co. Buckingham, Eyworth, co. Bedford, West Winterslow, co. Wilts, Essendine, Rutland, etc., second son, was married by Groby, co. Leicester, on 20 Apr. 1335 to ANNE DE FERRERS, daughter of William Ferrers, Knt., of Groby, co. Leicester (of **Magna Charta Surety descent** and **descendant of Charlemagne**), by Ellen (possibly daughter of John de Segrave, Knt., of Chacombe, co. Northampton). She died on 8 Aug. 1367. SIR EDWARD LE DESPENSER was slain at Morlaix on 30 Sep. 1342 *v.f.* (P.C.C., 97 Beck).
   C.P. 4:272 footnote *j*, 274 (1916). *TAG* 69:138 (July 1994).

9. EDWARD LE DESPENSER, Knt., K.G., 4th Lord Despenser, of Glamorgan and Morgannwg, Wales, son and heir, was born at Essendine, Rutland, about 24 Mar. 1335/6, and was nephew and heir of Hugh Le Despenser. He was married before 2 Aug. 1354 to **ELIZABETH DE BURGHERSH**, daughter and heiress of Bartholomew de Burghersh of Ewyas Lacy, co. Hereford, Stert and Colerne, co. Wilts, 4th Lord Burghersh (of **Magna Charta Surety descent** and **descendant of Charlemagne**), by his first wife Cecily, daughter of Richard de Weyland, Knt. She was born in 1342 (aged twenty-seven at her father's death). He accompanied the Prince of Wales to Gascony in September 1355. He was summoned to Parliament from 15 Dec. 1357 by writs directed *Edwardo le Despenser*, whereby he is held to have become **Lord Le Despenser**. He was with the King in the invasion of France, October 1359 to 1360. "Edward le Despenser, lord of Glowmorg" died testate (P.C.C., 163 Bokingham) aged thirty-nine at Llanbethian, co. Glamorgan, on 11 Nov. 1375. "Elizabeth de Burghersh, Dame le Despencer" died testate about 26 July 1409. They were buried at Tewkesbury Abbey.
   C.P. 1:247, 260 (1910). *C.P.* 2:426-427 (1912). *C.P.* 4:274-278 (1916). *C.P.* 5:316 (1926). *C.P.* 6:356 (1926). *TAG* 69:138 (July 1994).

Children of Edward le Despenser, by Elizabeth de Burghersh:
  i. THOMAS LE DESPENSER, married CONSTANCE OF YORK [see OXENBRIDGE 8].[3]
  ii. ANNE LE DESPENSER, married, first, HUGH HASTINGS, Knt. [see ELSING 8].[4]
  iii. ELIZABETH LE DESPENSER, married JOHN DE ARUNDEL, Knt. [see BROWNE 10].[5]
  iv. MARGARET LE DESPENSER, married ROBERT DE FERRERS [see FERRERS 10].[6]

---

[1] Ancestors of **Robert Abell, Grace Chetwode, St. Leger Codd, Francis Dade, Henry Fleete, Warham Horsmanden, Edmund Jennings, Anne Lovelace, Anne & Catherine Marbury, Katherine Saint Leger, John Throckmorton**.

[2] Ancestors of **Elizabeth Bosvile, George, Giles & Robert Brent, St. Leger Codd, Frances, Jane & Katherine Deighton, Edward Digges, Warham Horsmanden, Anne Humphrey, Thomas Ligon, Anne Mauleverer, Philip & Thomas Nelson, Herbert Pelham, Katherine Saint Leger, John West**.

[3] Ancestors of **St.Leger Codd, Edward Digges, John Fisher, Warham Horsmanden, Katherine Saint Leger, Maria Johanna Somerset**.

[4] Ancestors of **James Claypoole, Francis Dade, William Farrar, Richard Palgrave, William Skepper, Thomas Wingfield**.

[5] Ancestors of **Alice Baynton, Mary Gye, Gabriel, Roger & Sarah Ludlow, Thomas Lunsford, John Oxenbridge**.

[6] Ancestors of **Robert Abell, Grace Chetwode, Anne & Catherine Marbury**.

EDWARD I OF ENGLAND, King of England, married **ALIANORE DE CASTILLE**.
JOAN OF ENGLAND [*of Acre*], married **GILBERT DE CLARE**, Earl of Gloucester.
ELIZABETH DE CLARE, married **THEOBALD DE VERDUN** [see BURGH 13].

10. ISABEL DE VERDUN, fourth daughter and co-heiress, was born at Amesbury, co. Wilts, on 21 Mar. 1316/7. She was married before 20 Feb. 1330/1 to **HENRY DE FERRERS**, 2nd Lord Ferrers of Groby, son and heir of William de Ferrers, Knt., of Groby, co. Leicester (of **Magna Charta Surety** descent and **descendant of Charlemagne**), by Ellen, said to be daughter of John de Segrave, Knt., of Chacombe, co. Northampton, Lord Segrave. He was born about 1294 (aged twenty-two and more at his father's death). He was summoned to Parliament from 25 Jan. 1329/30 by writs directed *Henrico de Ferariis*. He was Chamberlain to the King from March 1336/7 till November 1340, being with the King at the battle of Sluys on 24 June 1340. HENRY DE FERRERS, Lord Ferrers, died at Groby, co. Leicester, on 15 Sep. 1343. His widow died aged thirty-two on 25 July 1349.

Baddesley Clinton (1907), pp. 113-114. *C.P.* 5:344-348, 351 footnote *b* (1926). *C.P.* 12(2):252 (1959).

9. WILLIAM DE FERRERS, Knt., 3rd Lord Ferrers of Groby, son and heir, was born at Newbold Verdon, co. Leicester, on 28 Feb. 1332/3. He was married for the first time before 25 Apr. 1344 to **MARGARET DE UFFORD**, third daughter of Robert de Ufford, 1st Earl of Suffolk (of **baronial** descent), by Margaret, daughter of Walter de Norwich, Knt., of Sculthorpe, Norfolk. She was sister, and in her issue, co-heiress of William, Earl of Suffolk. He accompanied the Prince of Wales to Gascony in September 1355, and was at the Battle of Poitiers. He was with the King in the invasion of France in October 1359 to 1360. He was summoned to Parliament from 15 Mar. 1353/4 by writs directed *Willelmo de Ferariis*. He was married for the second time before 25 May 1368 to MARGARET DE PERCY, widow of Robert de Umfreville, Knt., of Pallethorp and Hessle, co. York (died *s.p.*), and daughter of Henry de Percy, Knt., of Alnwick, Northumberland, 2nd Lord Percy, by Idoine, daughter of Robert de Clifford, 1st Lord Clifford of Appleby, Westmorland. WILLIAM DE FERRERS, Lord Ferrers, died testate aged thirty-seven at Stebbing on 8 Jan. 1370/1 (will requesting burial at Ulverscroft, co. Leicester). His widow died testate at Gyng (now Buttsbury), Essex, on 2 Sep. 1375.

Baddesley Clinton (1907), p. 114. *C.P.* 5:348-351 (1926).

Children of William de Ferrers, by Margaret de Ufford:
  i. **HENRY DE FERRERS**, born 16 Feb. 1355/6 [see next].
  ii. **MARGARET DE FERRERS**, married **THOMAS BEAUCHAMP** [see BEAUCHAMP 10].[1]

8. HENRY DE FERRERS, 4th Lord Ferrers of Groby, son and heir, was born at the Abbey of Tilty on 16 Feb. 1355/6. He was married before 27 Apr. 1371 to **JOAN** _____, daughter, probably, of Thomas de Hoo, Knt., of Luton Hoo, co. Bedford (**descendant of Charlemagne**), by Isabel, daughter and heiress of John de Seint Leger, Knt. In August 1385 he accompanied King Richard II in his invasion of Scotland. He was summoned to Parliament from 4 Aug. 1377 by writs directed *Henrico de Ferrariis de Groby*. HENRY DE FERRERS, Lord Ferrers, died on 3 Feb. 1387/8. His widow died on 30 May 1394.

Baddesley Clinton (1907), pp. 114-115. *C.P.* 5:351-353 (1926).

---

[1]Ancestors of **Elizabeth Bosvile, George, Giles & Robert Brent, St. Leger Codd, Edward Digges, Warham Horsmanden, Anne Humphrey, Anne Mauleverer, Herbert Pelham, Katherine Saint Leger, Philip & Thomas Nelson, John West.**

CLARKE (cont.)

7. WILLIAM DE FERRERS, 5th Lord Ferrers of Groby, was born at the manor house of Hoo, and was baptised at Luton, co. Bedford, on 25 Apr. 1372. He was summoned to Parliament from 30 Nov. 1396 by writs directed *Willelmo de Ferrariis de Groby*. He was married for the first time after 10 Oct. 1388 to **PHILIPPE DE CLIFFORD**, daughter of Roger de Clifford, Knt., Lord Clifford (of **Magna Charta Surety descent** and **descendant of Charlemagne**), by Maud, daughter of Thomas de Beauchamp, Earl of Warwick (**descendant of Charlemagne**). They had three sons and three daughters. She was living on 4 July 1405. He was married for the second time before 9 Aug. 1416 to MARGARET DE MONTAGU, daughter of John de Montagu, 3rd Earl of Salisbury, by Maud, daughter of Adam Fraunceys, Knt., of London. He was married for the third time before 26 Oct. 1416 to ELIZABETH STANDISH, widow, first, of John de Wrottesley, of Wrottesley, co. Stafford (died 7 Sep. 1402), second, of William Botiller, Knt., of Warrington, co. Lancaster (died at the siege of Harfleur 26 Sep. 1415), and daughter of Robert Standish, of Ulnes-Walton, co. Lancaster, by his wife Iseude. She died in January or February 1441/2. WILLIAM DE FERRERS, Lord Ferrers, died testate aged seventy-three on 18 May 1445 (his will, made the previous day at Woodham Ferrers, Essex, and desiring burial at Ulverscroft Priory, was witnessed by William Culpeper).

Baddesley Clinton (1907), p. 115. *C.P.* 5:354-358 (1926). *C.P.* 6:178 (1926). *Paget* (1957) 207:507, 372:11. *Abel Lunt* (1963), pp. 238-241 (identification of daughter Elizabeth).

Children of William de Ferrers, by Philippe de Clifford:
    i. **HENRY FERRERS**, son and heir apparent, married, **ISABEL MOWBRAY** [see GREY 8].[1]
    ii. **THOMAS FERRERS**, second son, born about 1405 [see next].
    iii. **ELIZABETH FERRERS**, married **WILLIAM CULPEPER**, Knt. [see STOCKMAN 7].[2]

6. THOMAS FERRERS, Esq., second son by first marriage, and heir male, was born about 1405 (aged forty at father's death). His father settled the manors of Hethe, Flecknoe, Champeyns in Woodham Ferre on him on 20 Jan. 1442. He was married to **ELIZABETH FREVILLE**, daughter of Baldwin Freville, Knt., of Tamworth Castle, co. Warwick (**descendant of Charlemagne**), by his wife Maud. She was eldest sister and co-heiress of Baldwin de Freville, of Tamworth, inheriting that Castle and lordship. THOMAS FERRERS, ESQ., died on 6 Jan. 1458/9.

Baddesley Clinton (1907), pp. 115-116. *C.P.* 5:357 footnote *a* (1926). *Paget* (1957) 207:6-7.

5. HENRY FERRERS, Knt., Peckham, Kent, and Hambleton, co. Rutland, second son, Sheriff of Kent, M.P. for Kent, was married to **MARGARET HECKSTALL**, daughter and co-heiress of William Heckstall, Knt., of Heckstall, co. Stafford, and Peckham, Kent. They had four sons and five daughters. SIR HENRY FERRERS died testate on 28 Dec. 1500 (will, P.C.C., 4 Moore desiring burial at Peckham). His widow was married for the second time to WILLIAM WHETENHALL, of East Peckham, Kent, and had issue.

Baddesley Clinton (1907), pp. 115-116. *H.S.P.* 62:166 (1889) (1682 Vis. Warwick). *C.P.* 5:332, 357 footnote *a* (1926).

4. ELIZABETH FERRERS, was married about 1508 to **JAMES CLERKE**, Esq., of Forde Hall, son and heir of John Clerke, Esq., of Forde, Kent, by Lucy, daughter of Walter Moyle, Knt. They had four sons. JAMES CLERKE, ESQ., died at

---

[1] Ancestors of **Elizabeth Bosvile, Charles Calvert, Thomas Wingfield**, and, probably, **Thomas Dudley**.

[2] Ancestors of **Alice Baynton, John Stockman**.

CLARKE (cont.)

Wrotham, Kent, on 20 Sep. 1553.
Arch.Cant. 4:247 (1861) (1619 Vis. Kent) (Elizabetha, filia Ed'ri Ferrers, de Badesley et Peckham, in co. Cantii, militis). *H.S.P.* 62:166 (1889). *NEHGR* 74:74-75 (Jan. 1920) (Forde Hall lay about a mile and a half eastward from Wrotham church, near Addington Common, said to be still standing in 1920). *H.S.P.* 74:38 (1923) (1574 Vis. Kent).

3. **GEORGE CLERKE**, Gent., son and heir, of Wrotham, Kent, was born in 1510, was married about 1533 to **ELIZABETH WILSFORD**, daughter of Thomas Wilsford, Esq., of Hartridge in Cranbrook, Kent, by his wife Elizabeth Culpeper. They had six sons and two daughters. He participated in the suppression of Wyatt's Rebellion with a defeat of rebels at Blackesol Field, Wrotham, on 10 Feb. 1553/4. GEORGE CLERKE, GENT., died at Wrotham on 6 Mar. 1558/9.
Arch.Cant. 4:247 (1861). *NEHGR* 74:75-76 (Jan. 1920). *H.S.P.* 74:38 (1923).

2. **JAMES CLERKE**, Gent., of East Farleigh, Kent, second son, was born about 1540. He was married about 1565 to **MARY SAXBY**, daughter of Edward Saxby (or Saxilby), Knt., Baron of the Exchequer, by his second wife Elizabeth, daughter of _____ Fisher, of Longworth, co. York. They had eight children. The will of JAMES CLERKE, GENT., was dated 13 July and proved 1 Nov. 1614.
Arch.Cant. 4:247 (1861). *NEHGR* 74:130-131 (Apr. 1920) (arms of James Clerke, as given in the Visitions of Sussex: *Or*, a bend engrailed *azure*, impaling *gules*, a bend vaire between six escallops *argent*). *H.S.P.* 74:38 (1923).

1. **WILLAM CLERKE**, Gent., of East Farleigh, Kent, and St. Botolph, Aldgate, London, younger son, was born, say, 1569. He was married at St. Andrew's, Holborn, London, with licence dated 10 Feb. 1598/9, to **MARY WESTON**, daughter of Jerome Weston, Knt., of Skreens in Roxwell, Essex, by his wife Mary, daughter of Anthony Cave, Esq., of Chicheley, co. Buckingham. She was baptised at Roxwell, Essex, on 26 Apr. 1579. Their children were baptised at East Farleigh. WILLIAM CLERKE, GENT., was buried at East Farleigh on 12 June 1610. His widow probably died before 13 July 1614.
Chester of Chicheley (1878), pp. 96-97. *NEHGR* 74:131-132, 137-140 (Apr. 1920). *NEHGR* 82:154 (Apr. 1928) (Arms of Jeremy Clarke: Gold on a bend engrailed azure a cinqfoil of the field). *H.S.P.* 74:38 (1923).

Children of William Clerke, by Mary Weston:

i. WESTON CLERKE, baptised 24 Feb. 1599/1600, merchant of St. Alban's, Wood Street, London, married DORCAS SMITH.

ii. WILLIAM CLERKE, baptised 5 July 1601, probably died before 1633 *s.p.*

iii. JAMES CLERKE, baptised 31 Oct. 1602, of Aldgate Ward, London, grocer; married, first, SARAH HARVEY, second HELEN _____. Issue.

iv. REV. ESSEX CLERKE, baptised 4 Dec. 1603, rector of Pulford, co. Chester, 1648.

v. GEORGE CLERKE, baptised 2 Dec. 1604.

vi. JEREMY CLARKE, baptised East Farleigh, Kent, 1 Dec. 1605, emigrated about 1637, resided Newport, Rhode Island, freeman 16 Mar. 1640/1; treasurer of Rhode Island; buried Newport 11 mo. [Jan.] 1651/2; married, in England, about 1637 to **FRANCES (LATHAM) DUNGAN**, baptised at Kempston, co. Bedford, 15 Feb. 1609/10, died September 1677, buried Newport, widow of Thomas Dungan, Gent., of Lincoln's Inn, Middlesex, and daughter of Lewis Latham, Gent., Sergeant Falconer to King Charles I, by his wife Elizabeth. She married, third, before 18 Jan. 1656 to REV. WILLIAM VAUGHAN, died on or before 2 Sep. 1677.

a. GOV. **WALTER CLARKE**, of Newport, born about 1638, died 23 May 1714; married, first, **CONTENT FREEMAN**, second **HANNAH SCOTT**, third, **FREEBORN (WILLIAMS) HART**, fourth, **SARAH (PRIOR) GOULD**. Three children by first marriage. Six children by second marriage.

b. **MARY CLARKE**, born 1641, died 7 Apr. 1711; married, first, **JOHN CRANSTON**, Governor

CLARKE (cont.)

of Rhode Island, second, **PHILIP JONES**, merchant of New York City, third, **JOHN STANTON**. Ten children by first marriage. One child by third husband.

    c. **JEREMIAH CLARKE**, born 1643, died 16 Jan. 1728/9; married **ANN AUDLEY**. Nine children.

    d. **LATHAM CLARKE**, born 1645, died 1 Aug. 1719; married, first **HANNAH WILBUR**, second, **ANNE (COLLINS) NEWBERRY**. Nine children by first marriage.

    e. **WESTON CLARKE**, born 1648, died 1728; married **MARY EASTON**, second **REBECCA (THURSTON) EASTON**. Eight children by first marriage. Four children by second marriage.

    f. **REV. JAMES CLARKE**, of Newport, born 1649, died 1 Dec. 1736; married **HOPESTILL POWER**. Four or more children.

    g. **SARAH CLARKE**, born 1651, died about 1706; married, first, **JOHN PINNER**, second, **CALEB CARR**, Governor of Rhode Island. Four children by second marriage.

  vii. RICHARD CLERKE, baptised 12 Apr. 1607, living 6 Dec. 1647; married. Issue.

  viii. JOHN CLERKE, baptised 10 Apr. 1608.

  ix. MARY CLERKE, born posthumously, baptised 16 Sep. 1610.

* * *

CLAYPOOLE

EDWARD I OF ENGLAND, King of England, married **ALIANORE DE CASTILLE**.
JOAN OF ENGLAND [*of Acre*], married **GILBERT DE CLARE**, Earl of Gloucester.
ALIANORE DE CLARE, married **HUGH LE DESPENSER**, 2nd Lord Despenser.
EDWARD LE DESPENSER, Knt., married **ANNE DE FERRERS**.
EDWARD LE DESPENSER, 4th Lord le Despenser, married **ELIZABETH DE BURGHERSH**.
ANNE LE DESPENSER, married **HUGH HASTINGS**, Knt.
MARGARET HASTINGS, married **JOHN WINGFIELD**, Knt.
ROBERT WINGFIELD, Knt., married **ELIZABETH RUSSELL**.
ROBERT WINGFIELD, Knt., married **ELIZABETH GOUSHILL**.
HENRY WINGFIELD, Knt., married **ELIZABETH ROOKES**.
ROBERT WINGFIELD, Esq. married **MARGERY QUARLES**.
ROBERT WINGFIELD, Esq., married **ELIZABETH CECIL** [see LETHERINGHAM 4].

2. **DOROTHY WINGFIELD**, younger daughter, was married at St. George's, Stamford, co. Lincoln, on 30 Sep. 1586 to **ADAM CLAYPOOLE**, Esq., of Northborough, co. Northampton, second son of James Claypoole, of Northborough. He was baptised there on 20 June 1565, and succeeded his elder brother, John Claypoole, Knt., in possession of Northborough manor about 1615. Adam & Dorothy had eight sons and two daughters. She was buried at Northborough on 7 Nov. 1619. He was married for the second time at Northborough on 25 Sep. 1620 to JANE BIRD. They had two sons and one daughter. ADAM CLAYPOLE, GENT., died on 2 Mar. 1631/2.

    H.S.P. 3:32 (1870) (1618-19 Vis. Rutland) (daughter of Robert Wingfield identified as "Dorothy ux. Adam Claypole of Latham in Com' Lincon"). *Metcalfe* (1887), p. 82 (1618/9 Vis. Northants), p. 204 (Appendix). *Claypoole* (1893), pp. 10-15. *TAG* 47:204 (1971) (father received grant of arms: *Or*, a chevron *azure* between three hurts). *TAG* 67:104-105 (Apr. 1992).

1. **JOHN CLAYPOOLE**, Gent., of Northborough, third son, was baptised at Maxey, co. Lincoln, on 13 Apr. 1595. He was married at St. Thomas the Apostle, London, on 8 July 1622 to **MARY ANGELL**, daughter of William Angell, Esq., of Peakirk, co.

CLAYPOOLE (cont.)

Northampton, Citizen and Fishmonger of London. They had eight sons and four daughters. In 1637 John Claypoole was summoned to the Star Chamber for opposing payment of ship-money. He was a member of Gray's Inn, and was M.P. for co. Northampton in 1654 and co. Carmarthen in 1656. She died on 10 Apr. 1661, and was buried at Northborough. JOHN CLAYPOOLE, GENT., was living in 1664.
Claypoole (1893), pp. 15-52. *V.C.H. Northants.* 2:508 (1906). *TAG* 18:201-206 (Apr. 1942). *Welcome Claimants* (1970), pp. 117-120. *TAG* 47:205 (1971). *TAG* 67:104-106 (Apr. 1992).

Children and grandchildren of John Claypoole, by Mary Angell:

i. MARY CLAYPOOLE, married WILLIAM SHIELD, Esq., M.P.

ii. JOHN CLAYPOOLE, eldest son, fought in the Civil War against King Charles I, M.P., 1654-, 1656, sat in Cromwell's House of Lords, 1657, died London 26 June 1688; married, first, 1646 ELIZABETH CROMWELL, daughter of Oliver Cromwell, Lord Protector, second, BLANCHE (_____) STAVELY. Three sons and one daughter (with no descendants) by first marriage. Two children by second marriage. *D.N.B.* 4:467-469 (1908).

iii. ELIZABETH CLAYPOOLE, married DR. ALEXANDER STAPLE.

iv. ROBERT CLAYPOOLE, linen draper, died unmarried.

v. WINGFIELD CLAYPOOLE, Captain of Horse.

vi. GRANELEY CLAYPOOLE, Cornet.

vii. DOROTHY CLAYPOOLE, married. Descendants in England.

viii. FRANCES CLAYPOOLE, married, died *s.p.s.*

ix. **JAMES CLAYPOOLE**, sixth son and ninth child, born 8th mo. [Oct.] 1634, apprenticed to a merchant in Bremen about 1650, merchant of Bush Lane, London, joined the Society of Friends with wife by 1661, and William Penn and George Fox were frequent visitors at their London home, emigrated on the *Concord* arriving Philadelphia 8th day 8th mo. [Oct.] 1683, treasurer of the Free Society, died testate 6 6th mo. [Aug.] 1687, buried Friends' ground, Mulberry Street, Philadelphia; married at Bremen, Germany, 12 day 12th mo. [Feb.] 1657/8 **HELENA MERCER**, died 19 Aug. 1688, buried with husband. Thirteen children, of whom six left descendants.

   a. **JOHN CLAYPOOLE**, born Nicholas Lane, London, 15th day 9th mo. [Nov.] 1658, emigrated on ship *Amity* on 23 Apr. 1682, settled in Pennsylvania, married **MARY** _____. One daughter.

   b. **MARY CLAYPOOLE**, born Minsing Lane, London, 14th day 8th mo. [Oct.] 1660, married FRANCIS COOKE. No children.

   c. **HELEN CLAYPOOLE**, born Scots yard near London stone 6th day 9th mo. [Nov.] 1662, married Philadelphia **WILLIAM BETHELL**. Two children in Barbadoes.

   d. **JAMES CLAYPOOLE**, born Scots yard 12th day 6th mo. [Aug.] 1664, resided New Castle, Delaware, married _____. Two children.

   e. **PRISCILLA CLAYPOOLE**, born Scots yard 25th day 2nd mo. [Apr.] 1666, married **DR. JOHN CRAPPE**. One daughter.

   f. **NATHANIEL CLAYPOOLE**, born "at the signe of the Still upon Horsly Downe in Southwark" 23rd day 7th mo. [Sep.] 1668, died young.

   g. **JOSIAH CLAYPOOLE**, born Scots yard 9th day 9th mo. [Nov.] 1669, died Kingston upon Thames 2nd day 3rd mo. [May] 1670, "there buried in our friends burying place".

   h. **SAMUEL CLAYPOOLE**, born Scots Yard 19th day 1st mo. [Mar.] 1670/71, died Edmonton 11th day 1st mo. [Mar.] 1680/81, buried Moorfields.

   i. **NATHANIEL CLAYPOOLE**, born Scots yard 4th day 8th mo. [Oct.] 1672, married. Three sons. One daughter.

   j. **GEORGE CLAYPOOLE**, born Scots yard 14th day 11th mo. [Jan.] 1674, merchant at Philadelphia, married, first, MARY RIGHTON, second, MARTHA HOSKINS, third, DEBORAH HARDIMAN. Children, but no grandchildren.

   k. _____ CLAYPOOLE, stillborn son end of the year 1673.

   l. **JOSEPH CLAYPOOLE**, born Lambeth 30th day 6th mo. [Aug.] 1676, buried "in friends

CLAYPOOLE (cont.)

burying place by Moorfields".

m. JOSEPH CLAYPOOLE, born Scots yard 14th day 5th mo. [July] 1677, married, first, REBECCA JENNINGS, second, EDITH WARD. Seven children by first marriage. Four children by second marriage.

n. ELIZABETH CLAYPOOLE, born Scots Yard 25th day 5th mo. [July] 1678, died 31st day 5th mo. [July] 1678, "buryed in friends burying place by Moorfields".

x. EDWARD CLAYPOOLE, Captain of Foot, married, died Barbadoes 11 Sep. 1699. Two daughters.

xi. MARTHA CLAYPOOLE, died young.

xii. MARTHA CLAYPOOLE, died unmarried.

xiii. NORTON CLAYPOOLE, married, embarked on the ship *Bachelor's Delight* 22 Feb. 1678, settled at Lewes, Sussex County, Delaware, died 1688.

    a. JAMES CLAYPOOLE, born about 1677, emigrated with mother 1681; married JEAN _____. One son.

    b. JEREMIAH CLAYPOOLE, married, first, SARAH SHEPPARD, second, MARY DAROCH.

    c. MARY CLAYPOOLE, married RICHARD COOPER.

    d. ROBERT CLAYPOOLE, died before 22 Mar. 1727.

xiv. BENJAMIN CLAYPOOLE, baptised 15 Feb. 1642/3.

* * *

CLERKE see CLARKE

CLIFFORD see MACKWORTH

* * *

CLOPTON

EDWARD I OF ENGLAND, King of England, married ALIANORE DE CASTILLE.
JOAN OF ENGLAND [*of Acre*], married GILBERT DE CLARE, Earl of Gloucester.
ELIZABETH DE CLARE, married ROGER DAMORY, Lord Damory.
ELIZABETH DAMORY, married JOHN BARDOLF, 3rd Lord Bardolf.
WILLIAM BARDOLF, 4th Lord Bardolf, married AGNES DE POYNINGS.
CECILY BARDOLF, married BRIAN STAPLETON, Knt.
MILES STAPLETON, Knt., married KATHERINE DE LA POLE.
ELIZABETH STAPLETON, married WILLIAM CALTHORPE, Knt.
ANNE CALTHORPE, married ROBERT DRURY, Knt.
ANNE DRURY, married GEORGE WALDEGRAVE, Esq. [see WALDEGRAVE 3].

4. EDWARD WALDEGRAVE, Esq., of Rivers Hall in Boxted, later of Lawford Hall, Essex, third son, was born in 1514 (aged seventy at time of death). In December 1541 Edward Waldegrave with many others, including his future wife, were indicted in connection with the trial for adultery of Katherine Howard, Queen of King Henry VIII. His offence was "with-holding from his Majesty the King, knowledge of certain letters which have been confiscated from a chest". He was confined in the Tower during the trial, received a sentence of life imprisonment, but was later pardoned.

CLOPTON (cont.)

He was married between May and June 1556 to **JOAN ACKWORTH**, childless widow of William Bulmer, Gent. (died 1556), and daughter of George Ackworth, of Toddington, co. Bedford, by Margaret, daughter of _____ Wilberforce, of Eggleston, Durham, with whom he had property at Lawford, Essex. She was born about 1519 and was heiress of her mother. They had one son and four daughters. The will of "Edwarde Waldegrave esquier of Lalford hall", dated 12 Aug. 1584 and proved on 5 Dec. 1584 (P.C.C., 42 Watson), names his daughter "Margerie Clopton". His widow was buried, with her husband, at Lawford on 10 Dec. 1590.

H.S.P. 13:120 (1878) (1558 Vis. Essex). *H.S.P.* 32:299 (1891) (Vis. Northants). *Clopton* (1939), pp. 44-45, 75-78 (Joan "was implicated with Agnes, Duchess of Norfolk and many others for failing to inform the King of the Queen's supposed intrigue with Francis Dereham. Although she was convicted with many others, she received full pardon." *H.S.P. (n.s.)* 2:94 (1981) (1561 Vis. Suffolk).

3. **MARGARET WALDEGRAVE**, was married to **WILLIAM CLOPTON**, Esq., of manor of Castelyns in Groton, Suffolk, son of Richard Clopton, of Fore Hall in Melford, Sussex, by his second wife Margaret, daughter of William Playters, of Setterley, Suffolk. They had four sons and six daughters. WILLIAM CLOPTON, ESQ., died testate (P.C.C., 83 Cope) on 9 Aug. 1616, and was buried at Groton Church.

H.S.P. 13:309 (1878) (1612 Vis. Essex). *Muskett* (1900), pp. 26,144. *Clopton* (1939), pp. 10-13, 29-30 (descent of William Clopton from King Edward I). *TAG* 46:116 (April 1970).

Children of William Clopton, by Margaret Waldegrave:

  i. **WALTER CLOPTON**, second son, baptized 30 June 1585 [see next].

  ii. **THOMASINE CLOPTON**, baptised Groton 18 Feb. 1583, buried Groton with her infant child 11 Dec. 1616; married, as his second wife, 6 Dec. 1615, GOV. JOHN WINTHROP, of Massachusetts.

2. **WALTER CLOPTON**, Gent., of Boxted, Essex, second son, was baptised at Groton, Suffolk, on 30 June 1585. He was married at Boxted on 21 Apr. 1612 to **MARGARET MAIDSTONE**, daughter of Robert Maidstone, Gent., of Great Horkesley, Essex. They had two sons and one daughter. WALTER CLOPTON, GENT., died testate at Boxted in 1622. His widow was married for the second time to Robert Crane, Gent., of Coggeshall, Essex, grocer, and died in 1666.

Muskett (1900), p. 144. *Clopton* (1939), pp. 13-14. *TAG* 46:118 ("Walter Clopton, to New England but returned to England").

1. **REV. WILLIAM CLOPTON**, was baptised at Boxted, Essex, on 19 Apr. 1613. He attended Emmanuel College, Cambridge University, receiving B.A. in 1634 and M.A. in 1637. He was Rector of Much Horkesley, Essex, then in 1654 Rector at All Saints, Rettendon, Essex. He was married before 1653 to **ELIZABETH SUTCLIFFE**, daughter of Rev. Isaiah Sutcliffe, of Rettendon, Essex, by Elizabeth, daughter of Rev. Thomas Jolye. They were devised part of the Manor of Eastwoodbury after her mother's death. He was ejected "for conscience sake" in 1662, and thereafter resided at or near Eastwood, Essex. The will of REV. WILLIAM CLOPTON, of Eastwood, was dated 24 Oct. 1670 and proved 14 June 1671. His widow died at Paglesham, Essex, in 1683.

Muskett (1900), p. 144. *Clopton* (1939), pp. 14-18. *NEHGR* 107:190 (July 1953) (Clopton arms: Sable a bend silver cotised dancetty gold).

Children & grandchildren of Rev. William Clopton, by Elizabeth Sutcliffe:

  i. **WILLIAM CLOPTON**, Gent. born 1655, of Paglesham, Essex, apprenticed in London to Joshua White, emigrated about 1675, clerk of York County, Virginia, died New Kent County, Virginia, before 1733; married **ANNE (BOOTH) DENNETT**.

  a. **ANNE CLOPTON**, born before 1682, married **NICHOLAS MILLS**, of Goochland County,

CLOPTON (cont.)

Virginia. Seven children.

b. **ELIZABETH CLOPTON**, born before 1682, married, first, **WILLIAM WALKER**, second, **ALEXANDER MOSS**. One daughter by second marriage.

c. **ROBERT CLOPTON**, born 27 Jan. 1683, died 30 Dec. 1742; married, first, **SARAH SCOTT**, second, **MARY CRUMP**. Three children by first marriage. Four children by second marriage.

d. **WILLIAM CLOPTON**, born about 1685, died before 1733, married **JOYCE WILKINSON**. Four children.

e. **WALTER CLOPTON**, born about 1687/8, married **MARY JARRATT**. Ten children.

ii. MARGARET CLOPTON, married HENRY HAMMOND, clothworker, his will dated 27 Aug. 1713 mentioned "the children of my wife's brother William Clopton, now living in Virginia".

* * *

COBHAM see WYATT

COLPEPPER see STOCKMAN

CONSTABLE see STAPLETON

* * *

CONYERS

EDWARD I OF ENGLAND, King of England, married **ALIANORE DE CASTILLE**.
ELIZABETH OF ENGLAND, married **HUMPHREY DE BOHUN**, Earl of Hereford and Essex.
ALIANOR DE BOHUN, married **JAMES BUTLER**, Earl of Ormond.
PERNEL BUTLER, married **GILBERT TALBOT**, 3rd Lord Talbot.
ELIZABETH TALBOT, married **HENRY DE GREY**, 5th Lord Grey of Wilton.
MARGARET GREY, married **JOHN DARCY**, 4th Lord Darcy of Knaith.
PHILIP DARCY, Knt., married **ALIANOR FITZ HUGH** [see DARCY 10.i].

8. **MARGERY DARCY**, younger daughter and co-heiress, was born posthumously at Ravensworth on 1 Sep. 1418. She was married before 20 Nov. 1431 to **JOHN CONYERS**, Knt., K.G., of Hornby, North Riding, co. York, Sheriff of Yorkshire, son of Christopher Conyers, by his first wife Eleanor Rolston. They had seven sons and five daughters. She died between 20 Mar. 1468/9 and 20 Apr. 1469. SIR JOHN CONYERS died on 14 Mar. 1489/90, and was buried at Hornby (M.I.).

Sur.Soc. 41:48-49 (1862) (1530 Vis. North). *H.S.P.* 16:73 (1881) (1563 Vis. Yorks). *Northumberland* 5:411 (1899). *Clay* (1913), p. 34. *C.P.* 4:67, 71 (1916). *Sur.Soc.* 144:92 (1930) (1480 Vis. North).

7. **JOHN CONYERS**, of Hornby, K.G., son and heir apparent, was married to **ALICE NEVILLE**, third daughter and co-heiress of William Neville, Lord Fauconberge and Earl of Kent, by Joan, daughter of Thomas Fauconberg, of Shelton, co. York (of **Magna Charta Surety descent** and **descendant of Charlemagne**) (see BEAUFORT 11.iv.c. for her ancestry). She was born about 1437 (aged twenty-six and more in 1463). They had two sons and two daughters. SIR JOHN CONYERS survived his mother but died *v.p.*, being slain at Edgcote Field near Banbury on 26 July 1469.

CONYERS (cont.)

Sur.Soc. 41:49 (1862) (1530 Vis. North). *H.S.P.* 16:73 (1881). *Clay* (1913), p. 34. *C.P.* 3:404 (1913). *C.P.* 4:67, 71 (1916). *C.P.* 5:286-287 (1926). *Sur.Soc.* 144:93 (1930) (1480 Vis. North).

6. WILLIAM CONYERS, Knt., second but first surviving son and heir, was born on 21 Dec. 1468. He was married for the first time, with licence dated 24 Sep. 1479, to **MARY LE SCROPE**, daughter of John le Scrope, Lord Scrope of Bolton (**descendant of King Edward I**), by his first wife Joan, daughter of William Fitzhugh, Lord Fitzhugh, being related to her in the fourth degree [see SCROPE 6.i for her ancestry]. He succeeded his grandfather on 14 Mar. 1489/90, and built Hornby Castle. He was summoned to Parliament from 17 Oct. 1509 by writs directed *Willelmo Conyers de Conyers chivaler*, whereby he became Lord Conyers. He fought at the battle of Flodden in 1513. He was married for the second time to **ANNE NEVILLE**, daughter of Ralph Neville, 3rd Earl of Westmorland, by Margaret, daughter of Roger Booth. WILLIAM CONYERS, Lord Conyers, died aged fifty-five in 1524 before 14 April. His widow was married for the second time, with licence dated 29 Apr. 1525, to Anthony Saltmarsh, Gent., of Hornby.

Sur.Soc. 41:49 (1862) (1530 Vis. North) ("Willyam, furst Lord Coniers, son of Syr John"). *H.S.P.* 16:73 (1881) (identifies son Christopher as son of second marriage). *Clay* (1913), pp. 34-35. *C.P.* 3:404 (1913) (doesn't identify mother of heir). *C.P.* 4:67, 71 (1916). *C.P.* 5:286-287 (1926).

5. CHRISTOPHER CONYERS, of Hornby, Knt., 2nd Lord Conyers, son and heir, was married at Kirkoswald on 28 Sep. 1515 to **ANNE DACRE**, daughter of Thomas Dacre, Lord Dacre of Gillesland (**descendant of King Edward I**), by Elizabeth (**descendant of King Edward III**), daughter and heiress of Robert Greystoke, Knt. [see DACRE 6 for her ancestry]. They had two sons and two daughters. He was summoned to Parliament from 9 Aug. 1529 by writs directed *Christofero domino Conyers chivaler*. CHRISTOPHER CONYERS, Lord Conyers, died on 14 June 1538. The will of his widow was dated 16 Dec. 1547, and proved 21 Apr. 1548. They were buried at Skelton.

Sur.Soc. 41:49 (1862) (1530 Vis. North). *H.S.P.* 16:73 (1881). *Clay* (1913), p. 35. *C.P.* 3:404-405 (1913). *C.P.* 4:71 (1916).

Child of Christopher Conyers, by Anne Dacre:
  i. **JANE CONYERS**, married **MARMADUKE CONSTABLE** [see STAPLETON 4].[1]

* * *

COPE see MARBURY

COPLEY see WELLES

CORBET see FERRERS

CORBETT see DRURY

CORNWALLIS see DADE

COTTON see ABELL

---

[1] Ancestors of **Philip & Thomas Nelson**.

COURTENAY

EDWARD I OF ENGLAND, King of England, married **ALIANORE DE CASTILLE**.
ELIZABETH OF ENGLAND, married **HUMPHREY DE BOHUN** [see BOHUN 12].

10. MARGARET DE BOHUN, first surviving daughter, was born on 3 Apr. 1311. She was married on 11 Aug. 1325 to **HUGH DE COURTENAY**, K.G., 10th Earl of Devon, Lord Courtenay, son and heir of Hugh de Courtenay, Knt., **Baron** of Okehampton, Devon (of **Magna Charta Surety** descent and **descendant of Charlemagne**), by Agnes (descendant of Charlemagne), daughter of John de Saint John, Knt., **Baron** of Basing, co. Hants. He was born on 12 July 1303. He served in the Scottish and French wars, and was Knight Banneret on 20 Jan. 1327. He was summoned to Parliament on 23 Apr. 1337 by writ directed *Hugoni de Courteney juniori v.p.*, and succeeded to the Earldom three years afterwards. They had eight sons (of whom only three had issue) and nine daughters. HUGH COURTENAY, Earl of Devon, died aged seventy-three on 2 May 1377. His widow died testate (P.C.C., Rouse 2) on 16 Dec. 1391. They were buried at Exeter Cathedral (M.I.).
   Vivian (1895), p. 244 (created K.G. at the institution of the Order). C.P. 3:344 (1913). C.P. 4:324-325, 466 (1916).

Children of Hugh de Courtenay, by Margaret de Bohun:
   i. **PHILIP DE COURTENAY**, Knt., fourth son [see next].
   ii. **MARGARET DE COURTENAY**, married, first, **JOHN COBHAM** [see WYATT 10].[1]
   iii. **ELIZABETH DE COURTENAY**, married **ANDREW LUTTRELL** [see LUDLOW 10].[2]

9. PHILIP DE COURTENAY, Knt., of Powderham, Devon, fifth son, M.P. for Devon, Lord Lieutenant of Ireland, Steward of Cornwall, had Powderham settled on him by his mother. He served in the Spanish War *temp.* Edward III. He was named in the inquisition taken at the death of his brother Peter Courtenay, Knt. He was married about 1378 to **ANNE WAKE**, daughter of Thomas Wake, Knt., of Blisworth, co. Northampton (**descendant of Charlemagne**), by Alice, daughter of John de Pateshull, of Pattishall, co. Northampton, Lord Pateshulle (**descendant of Charlemagne**). They had three sons and two daughters. He was an executor of his mother's will. SIR PHILIP DE COURTENAY died on 29 July 1406.
   Vivian (1895), p. 244. C.P. 4:335 (1916). Roskell (1992) 2:670-673 ("a man of energy and ability in national and local affairs whose predilection for violence and thuggery was extreme even by medieval standards").

8. JOHN DE COURTENAY, Knt., second son, was married about 1403 to **JOAN CHAMPERNOUN**, childless widow of James Chudleigh, Knt., of Ashton and Shirwell, Devon (died 1401/2), and daughter of Alexander Champernoun, Knt., of Beer Ferrers, Devon (of **Magna Charta Surety descent** and **descendant of Charlemagne**), by Joan, daughter of Martin Ferrers, of Beer Ferrers, near Plymouth. They had two sons. SIR JOHN DE COURTENAY died before 1415 during the lives of his father and his older brother Richard, Bishop of Norwich. His widow died in 1419.
   Vivian (1895), p. 246. C.P. 4:335 (1916). Roskell (1992) 2:573,673.

7. PHILIP DE COURTENAY, Knt., of Powderham, son and heir, was born in 1404 (aged eleven at the death of his uncle Richard to whom he was heir). He was also heir to his uncle William (died 1419). He was married to **ELIZABETH**

---

[1]Ancestors of **William Randolph, Hawte Wyatt.**

[2]Ancestors of **Edmund Jennings, Gabriel, Roger & Sarah Ludlow.**

COURTENAY (cont.)

HUNGERFORD, daughter of Walter Hungerford, K.G., of Farleigh Hungerford, Somerset, and Heytesbury, co. Wilts, Lord Treasurer of England (**descendant of Charlemagne**), by Katherine, daughter and co-heiress of Thomas Peverell, of Parke, Hamatethy and Penhale, Cornwall. They had seven sons and four daughters. SIR PHILIP DE COURTENAY died on 16 Dec. 1463. His widow died on 14 Dec. 1476.

Vivian (1895), p. 246. *C.P.* 4:335 (1916). *Roskell* (1992) 3:447-448.

6. **PHILIP DE COURTENAY**, Knt., of Molland, second son, was Sheriff of Devonshire in 1471. He was married to **ELIZABETH** _____, widow of William Hyndeston, of Wonwall. They had four sons and two daughters.

Vivian (1895), p. 246.

5. **PHILIP DE COURTENAY**, of Loughtor, co. Devon, second son, was married to **JANE FOWELL**, daughter of Richard Fowell, and died on 26 Mar. 1514.

Burke's Commoners (1837) 1:204 (widow married second Humphrey Prideaux, of Adeston and Thuborough, with issue). *Crisp* Notes 12:121 (1917). *Vivian* (1895), p. 251.

4. **ELIZABETH DE COURTENAY**, daughter and heiress, was born about 1513 (aged six months at father's death). She was married to **WILLIAM STRODE**, Esq., of Newnham in Plympton St. Mary, co. Devon, son and heir of Richard Strode, of Newnham, by Agnes, daughter of John Milliton, of Meavy, co. Devon. He was born at Newnham on 16 June 1504. They have seven sons and five daughters. WILLIAM STRODE, ESQ., died at Newnham on 5 May 1579. His widow was living on 4 Oct. 1581.

Crisp Notes 12:121 (1917). *Vivian* (1895), p. 718.

Child of William Strode, by Elizabeth de Courtenay:

   i. **RICHARD STRODE**, married **FRANCES CROMWELL** [see DAVIE 3].[1]

* * *

COYTEMORE

EDWARD I OF ENGLAND, King of England, married **ALIANORE DE CASTILLE**.
ELIZABETH OF ENGLAND, married **HUMPHREY DE BOHUN**, Earl of Hereford and Essex.
WILLIAM DE BOHUN, Earl of Northampton, married **ELIZABETH DE BADLESMERE**.
ELIZABETH DE BOHUN, married **RICHARD FITZ ALAN**, Earl of Arundel.
ELIZABETH FITZ ALAN, married **ROBERT GOUSHILL**, Knt.
JOAN GOUSHILL, married **THOMAS STANLEY**, Lord Stanley of Lathom and Knowsley.
MARGARET STANLEY, married **WILLIAM TROUTBECK**, Knt. [see TROUTBECK 6].

5. **JOAN TROUTBECK**, was born in 1459. She was married for the first time to **WILLIAM BOTELER**, Knt., son of John Boteler, Knt. She was married for the second time to **WILLIAM GRIFFITH**, Knt., of Penryhn, co. Caernarvon, Chamberlain of North Wales, son of William Fychan ap Gwilym, by Alice, daughter of Richard Dalton, Knt., of Althorp, co. Northampton. They had one son and three daughters. She died 1458/9. He was married for the second time to Elsbeth Grey, daughter of Robert Grey, of Rhulhun, and had issue. SIR WILLIAM GRIFFITH was living in 1482 and dead by 1509/10 when his son William was styled "son and

---

[1]Ancestors of **Humphrey Davie**.

COYTEMORE (cont.)

heir".

    Griffith (1914), p. 185 ("The Liberal") (does not name daughter Alice by first marriage). *Chester & North Wales Arch. Soc (n.s.)* 28:167 (1929). *Gen. Mag* 8:204 (Dec. 1938). *TAG* 32:12 (Jan. 1956). *NEHGR* 108:172-174 (1948) (descent of Elizabeth Coytemore from King Edward I). *Bartrum* (1983) 8:1265, 1267 (Marchudd 6 B1 & B3).

Children of William Griffith, by Joan Troutbeck:

    i. **WILLIAM GRIFFITH**, Knt. [see next].

    ii. **ALICE GRIFFITH**, married **PIERS COYTMORE** (ancestors of Sarah Kenrick (1755-1815), wife of Ralph Eddowes of Philadelphia, Pennsylvania).

4. WILLIAM GRIFFITH, Knt., of Penrhyn Castle, co. Caernarvon, Chamberlain of North Wales, Sheriff of Caernarvonshire, son and heir, was born about 1480. He was married for the first time to **JANE STRADLING**, daughter of Thomas Stradling, of St. Donat's, co. Glamorgan, by Janet, daughter of Thomas Mathew, of Radyr, co. Glamorgan. She was born, say, 1477/1480. They had five sons and eight daughters. She died before 1520. He was married for the second time in 1520 to **JANE PULESTON**, widow of Robert ap Maredudd, of Glynllifon, and daughter of John Puleston, Constable of Caernarvon and Chamberlain of North Wales, by Eleanor, daughter of Robert Whitney, Knt., of Whitney, co. Hereford. They had three sons and two daughters. SIR WILLIAM GRIFFITH died in 1531.

    Griffith (1914), p. 185. *Gen. Mag.* 8:204 (Dec. 1938). *NEHGR* 108:172-174 (July 1954). *TAG* 32:12 (Jan. 1956) (descent of Jane Stradling from Henry Beaufort, see BEAUFORT 11.ii) (citing Lewys Dwnn, Heraldic Visitations of Wales (1846) 2:167-8; Thomas A. Glenn, Griffith of Garn and Plasnewydd (London, 1934), p, 221; John E. Griffith, Pedigrees of Anglesey and Caernarvonshire Families (Horncastle, 1914), p. 185). *Bartrum* (1983) 8:1268 (Marchudd 6 B4), 9:1454 (Puleston A1).

Child of William Griffith, by Jane Stradling:

    i. **DOROTHY GRIFFITH**, fourth daughter [see next].

Child of William Griffith, by Jane Puleston:

    ii. **SIBYL GRIFFITH**, married **OWEN AP HUGH** [see OWEN 5].[1]

3. DOROTHY GRIFFITH, fourth daughter by first marriage, was married for the first time to **WILLIAM WYNN WILLIAMS**, Esq., of Cwchwillan in Llechwedd Uchav, co. Caernarvon, Sheriff of Caernarvonshire, son of William Williams, by Lowry, daughter of Henry Salusbury, Esq., of Llanrhaidadr. They had eight sons and three daughters. She was married for the second time, as his first wife, to Robert Wynne ap John Wyn ap Maredudd, of Plas Mawr in Conway, co. Caernarvon, Sheriff of Caernarvonshire (buried Conway 30 Nov. 1598). They had no issue.

    Powys Fadog 6:200,428 (1887) (arms: *Gules*, a chevron ermine, inter three English men's heads couped in profile ppr). *Griffith* (1914), pp. 185-186 (his "will proved P.C.C. March 13, 1610"). *Gen.Mag.* 8:204 (Dec. 1938). *TAG* 32:12 (Jan. 1956). *NEHGR* 108:172-174 (July 1954). *Bartrum* (1983) 8:1268,1271 (Marchudd 6 D2) (citation of pedigrees of descendants).

2. JANE WILLIAMS, second daughter, was married to **WILLIAM COYTEMORE**, of Coetmor in Llechwedd Uchav, co. Caernarvon, son of William Coetmor, of Coetmor, by Elin, daughter of John Puleston, of Tir Môn, Anglesey. They had six sons and seven daughters. He was married for the second time to Mary Lewis, daughter of William Lewis, of Presaddfed, and had four children.

    Powys Fadog 6:200-201 (1887) (shows only a son Robert) (Ancient Coetmor arms: *Gules*, a chevron inter three stag's heads caboshed *argent*, attired *or*). *Griffith* (1914), p. 277. *Gen.Mag.* 8:204 (Dec. 1938). *TAG* 32:12 (Jan. 1956).

Children of William Coytemore, by Jane Williams:

---

[1] Ancestors of **Joshua & Rebecca Owen**.

COYTEMORE (cont.)

i. **ROWLAND COYTEMORE** [see next].

ii. **ALICE COYTEMORE**, married **HUGH WYNNE** (ancestors of Sarah Kenrick, wife of Ralph Eddowes, of Pennsylvania. See *Roberts* (1993), p. 166).

1. **ROWLAND COYTEMORE**, second son, was born, say, 1565-70. He became a mariner with several voyages to India and the East Indies as captain of ships belonging to the East India Company. He was married for the first time at Stepney, Middlesex, on 13 Jan. 1590/1 to CHRISTIAN HAYNES. He was married for the second time at St. Mary's, Whitechapel, Middlesex, on 28 Mar. 1594/5 to DOROTHY (?LANE) HARRIS, widow of William Harris, mariner of Wapping, and daughter of Dorothy (?Burton) Lane, of St. Dunstan's-in-the-East, London. They had two daughters (died *s.p.*). He was married for the third time at Harwich, Essex, on 23 Dec. 1610 to **KATHERINE (MILES) GRAY**, widow of Thomas Gray, of Harwich (buried Harwich 7 May 1607), and daughter of Robert Miles (or Myles), of Sutton, Suffolk. He was a grantee of the second Charter of Virginia, 23 May 1607. After return from Java in 1619 he resided at Wapping. The will of ROWLAND COYTEMORE, of Wapping, Middlesex, dated 5 June 1626 and proved 24 Nov. 1626 (P.C.C., 125 Hele). His widow emigrated to New England about 1636, accompanied by her son Thomas, and followed by her daughter Elizabeth. She died at Charlestown, Massachusetts, on 28 Nov. 1659.

Waters 1:158-159,160-161 (1885) (his will); *Gen.Mag.* 8:204 (Dec. 1938). *TAG* 32:14-19 (Jan. 1956). *NEHGR* 40:158. *NEHGR* 106:15-16 (Jan. 1952). *NEHGR* 108:32 (Jan. 1954) (Coytemore arms: Gules a chevron between three stag's heads cabossed silver, on the chevron a crescent for difference).

Children & grandchildren of Rowland Coytemore, by Katherine (Miles) Gray:

i. THOMAS COYTEMORE, born Prittlewell, Essex, about 1611-12, educated Charlwood School, matriculated Christ's College, Cambridge 1628, sea captain, settled Charlestown, Massachusetts, 1636, lost at sea in shipwreck off the coast of Spain, 27 Dec. 1644; married Wapping, Middlesex, 14 June 1635 MARTHA RAINSBOROUGH. Three children, all died in infancy.

ii. ELIZABETH COYTEMORE, born about 1617, emigrated with husband 1638, probably in the *Nicholas*, died Boston, Massachusetts before January 1648/9; married **CAPT. WILLIAM TYNG** of Boston, Massachusetts, Treasurer of Massachusetts Bay Colony, died Braintree, Massachusetts, 18 Jan. 1652/3.

   a. **ELIZABETH TYNG**, born, probably Wapping, Middlesex, 6 Feb. 1637/8, died Boston 9 Nov. 1682; married **THOMAS BRATTLE**, of Boston. Eight children.

   b. **ANNE TYNG**, born Boston, Massachusetts, 6 Jan. 1639/40, died Milton, Massachusetts, 5 Aug. 1709; married **THOMAS SHEPARD**. Four children.

   c. **BETHIA TYNG**, born Boston 17 Mar. 1641, died by 1670; married **RICHARD WHARTON**, Esq. One known son.

   d. **MERCY TYNG**, born Boston 13 Jan. 1642/3, died 6 Sep. 1670; married **SAMUEL BRADSTREET**. Five children.

* * *

CROMWELL see WINGFIELD

CULPEPER see STOCKMAN

CUSHIN see HAYNES

DACRE

EDWARD I OF ENGLAND, King of England, married **ALIANORE DE CASTILLE**.
JOAN OF ENGLAND [*of Acre*], married **GILBERT DE CLARE**, Earl of Gloucester.
MARGARET DE CLARE, married **HUGH DE AUDLEY**, Earl of Gloucester.
MARGARET DE AUDLEY, married **RALPH DE STAFFORD**, Earl of Stafford.
HUGH DE STAFFORD, 2nd Earl of Stafford, married **PHILIPPE DE BEAUCHAMP**.
MARGARET DE STAFFORD, married **RALPH NEVILLE** [see NEVILLE 10].

8. **PHILIPPE DE NEVILLE**, third daughter, was married before 20 July 1399 to **THOMAS DE DACRE**, 6th Lord Dacre of Gillesland, son and heir of William de Dacre, 5th Lord Dacre (of **baronial** descent), by his wife Joan Douglas. He was born at Naworth Castle on 27 Oct. 1387. They had six sons and two daughters. She was living 8 July 1453, but predeceased her husband. He was summoned to Parliament from 1 Dec. 1412 by writs directed *Thome de Dacre de Gillesland*. THOMAS DE DACRE, Lord Dacre, died on 5 Jan. 1457/8, and was buried in Lanercost Priory.

H.S.P. 16:84 (1881) (1563 Vis. Yorks). *Clay* (1913), p. 37. *C.P.* 4:7-9 (1916). *Paget* (1977), p. 416.

Children & grandchild of Thomas Dacre, by Philippe de Neville:

   i. **THOMAS DACRE**, Knt., son and heir apparent, died *v.p.*; married about 1430 **ELIZABETH BOWET**, daughter and heiress of William Bowet, Knt., of Horsford, Burgh St. Margaret's and Great Hautbois, Norfolk, by Joan, second daughter and heiress of Robert de Ufford, of Horsford, Lord Clavering (of **Magna Charta Surety descent** and **descendant of Charlemagne**). *H.S.P.* 16:85 (1881). *C.P.* 4:8-9 (1916). *Paget* (1957) 164:2. Sussex Arch. Coll. 9:87.

     a. **JOAN DE DACRE**, married **RICHARD FIENNES** [see LUNSFORD 6].[1]

   ii. **HUMPHREY DACRE**, younger son [see next].

   iii. **JOAN DACRE**, married **THOMAS DE CLIFFORD** [see MACKWORTH 6].[2]

7. **HUMPHREY DACRE**, 2nd Lord Dacre of Gillesland, younger son, Lord Warden of the Marches, was brother and heir to Randolf, Lord Dacre. He was summoned to Parliament from 15 Nov. 1482 by writs directed *Humfrido Dacre de Gillesland'*. He was married to **MABEL PARR**, daughter of Thomas Parr, Knt., of Kirkby Kendal, Westmorland (of **Magna Charta Surety descent** and **descendant of Charlemagne**), by Alice, daughter of Thomas Tunstall, Knt., of Thurland Castle, co. Lancaster. They had five sons and three daughters. HUMPHREY DACRE, Lord Dacre, died on 30 May 1485. His widow died testate on 14 Nov. 1508. They were buried at Lanercost.

H.S.P. 16:84 (1881). *Clay* (1913), p. 37. *C.P.* 4:18-20 (1916). *C.P.* 5:431 (1926). *Paget* (1977), p. 449.

6. **THOMAS DACRE**, K.B., K.G., 3rd Lord Dacre of Gillesland, son and heir, was born on 25 Nov. 1467. He was summoned to Parliament from 17 Oct. 1509 and distinguished himself at the head of a troop of horse at Flodden on 9 Sep. 1513. He was married about 1488 to **ELIZABETH GREYSTOKE**, daughter and sole heiress of Robert Greystoke, Knt. (of **Magna Charta Surety descent** and **descendant of Charlemagne**), by Elizabeth, daughter of Edmund Grey, Earl of Kent (**descendant of King Edward III**) [see HAVILAND 7.ii for her ancestry]. She was born at Morpeth on 10 July 1471 or 1472. They had two sons and five daughters. She died on 14 Aug. 1516. THOMAS DACRE, Lord Dacre, died on the Borders on 24 Oct. 1525, by a fall from his horse. They were buried at Lanercost.

H.S.P. 16:84 (1881). *Clay* (1913), p. 38. *C.P.* 4:20-21 (1916). *Paget* (1977), p. 269.

Child of Thomas Dacre, by Elizabeth Greystoke:

   i. **ANNE DACRE**, married **CHRISTOPHER CONYERS**, Lord Conyers [see CONYERS 5].[3]

---

[1] Ancestors of **Thomas Lunsford**.

[2] Ancestors of **Agnes Mackworth**.

[3] Ancestors of **Philip & Thomas Nelson**.

DADE

EDWARD I OF ENGLAND, King of England, married ALIANORE DE CASTILLE.
JOAN OF ENGLAND [*of Acre*], married GILBERT DE CLARE, Earl of Gloucester.
ALIANOR DE CLARE, married HUGH LE DESPENSER, Lord Despenser.
ISABEL LE DESPENSER, married RICHARD FITZ ALAN, Earl of Arundel and of Surrey.
EDMUND LE DESPENSER, Knt., married SIBYL DE MONTAGU.
PHILIPPE FITZ ALAN, married RICHARD CERGEAUX, Knt.
PHILIPPE SERGEAUX, married ROBERT PASHLEY, Knt. [see FLEETE 8]

7. ANNE PASHLEY, was married for the first time to JOHN BASSINGBOURNE, and had son John. She was married for the second time to EDWARD TYRRELL, Esq., of Downham, Essex, Sheriff of Essex and Hertford, M.P. for Essex, son of Walter Tyrrell, of Essex, and his wife Alianor. The will of EDWARD TYRRELL, ESQ., was dated 10 Oct. 1442.

Collins-Brydges (1812) 2:538. *H.S.P.* 4:161 (1871) (1614 Vis. Notts). *Muskett* (1908), 2:268. *Copinger* 3:239 (1909). Gen. Mag. 11:541-6 (1954). NEHGR 109:31.

6. PHILIPPE TYRRELL, daughter and heiress, was married to THOMAS CORNWALLIS, Esq., of Brome, Suffolk, M.P. for Suffolk, son and heir, of John Cornwallis, of Brome and Oakley, by Philippe, daughter and co-heiress of Robert Bucton, of Brome. He was probably born about 1420 (a minor and beyond the seas at his father's death, probably 1436/7). They had four sons and two daughters. THOMAS CORNWALLIS, ESQ., died on 24 May 1484.

Collins-Brydges (1812) 2:538. *H.S.P.* 4:161 (1871). *Dade* (1888) [n.p.]. *Muskett* (1908) 2:268. *Copinger* 3:239 (1909). *VMHB* 28:381 (Oct. 1920). *H.S.P.* (*n.s.*) 2:149-151 (1561 Vis. Suffolk).

5. WILLIAM CORNWALLIS, Esq., of Brome and Oakley, Suffolk, London, co. Bedford, and Norfolk, fourth son and eventual heir, Justice of the Peace for Suffolk, was born about 1450 (aged sixty in 1510), and was heir of his brother Edward. He was married to ELIZABETH STANFORD, daughter & co-heiress of John Stanford, Esq., of Stackden, co. Bedford, by Joan, daughter and heiress of John Boteler, of Mappershall, co. Bedford. They had five sons and six daughters. "William Cornewaleys, esquier, Ocley, Suffolk" died testate (P.C.C., 24 Ayloffe) on 20 Nov. 1519, and was buried in the chancel in St. Nicholas's, Oakley, with monumental inscription. His widow died testate on 1 Apr. 1537, and was buried in the chancel at Thrandeston.

Collins-Brydges (1812) 2:540-542. *H.S.P.* 4:161 (1871). *Muskett* (1908) 2:268. *Copinger* 3:241 (1909). *VMHB* 28:381-382 (Oct. 1920).

Children of William Cornwallis, by Elizabeth Stanford:

i. JOHN CORNWALLIS, Knt. [see next].

ii. AFFRA CORNWALLIS, married ANTHONY AUCHER, Knt. [see LOVELACE 4].[1]

4. JOHN CORNWALLIS, Knt., of Brome, Suffolk, son and heir, Steward of the Household to Edward, Prince of Wales (later King Edward VI), was married to MARY SULLIARD, daughter of Edward Sulliard (or Sulyard), of Otes in High Laver, Essex, by his wife Margaret Hungate. They had four sons and three daughters. "Sir John Cornwaleys, knight, Brome, Suffolk" died testate (P.C.C., 11 Pynnyng) at Ashridge, co. Hertford on 23 Apr. 1544, and was buried at Berkhamsted, co. Hertford, with monument in the chancel at Brome with inscription.

Collins-Brydges (1812) 2:542-544. *H.S.P.* 4:161 (1871). *Dade* (1888) [n.p.] (wife of Edward Sulyard

---

[1] Ancestors of **Anne Lovelace**.

DADE (cont.)

identified as Anne, daughter of John Norris of Essex). *Muskett* (1908) 2:268. *Copinger* 3:242-243 (1909). *Throckmorton* (1930), p. 202. *NEHGR* 98:278 (July 1944). *H.S.P. (n.s.)* 2:151 (1981).

Children of John Cornwallis, by Mary Sulyard:
  i. RICHARD CORNWALLIS, third son [see next].
  ii. ELIZABETH CORNWALLIS, mar JOHN BLENNERHASSET [see THROCKMORTON 3].[1]

3. **RICHARD CORNWALLIS**, of Shotley, Suffolk, third son, was bequeathed in his father's will his "ward Margaret Lowthe, bought of my Lord of Norfolk, to marry her himself, if they both will be so contented". He was married to **MARGARET LOWTHE**, daughter and heiress of Lionel Lowthe, of Sawtrey, co. Huntingdon. They had two sons and two daughters.

Collins-Brydges (1812) 2:543. *H.S.P.* 4:161 (1871). *Dade* (1888) [n.p.].

2. **ANNE CORNWALLIS**, was married about 1575 to **THOMAS DADE**, Gent., of Tannington, Suffolk, son and heir of William Dade, Gent., of Witton, co. Norfolk, by Margery, daughter and heiress of Nicholas Godbold, Gent., of Badingham, co. Suffolk. He was born about 1556. They had four sons and five daughters. She died on 2 May 1612, and was buried at Tannington with monumental inscription. He was married for the second time to Anne Haselop, daughter of Thomas Haselop, of Trumpington, co. Cambridge. They had one son and three daughters. THOMAS DADE, GENT., died testate (P.C.C., 80 Parker) aged sixty-three at Tannington on 13 Apr. 1619, and was buried in the chancel at Tannington with monumental inscription.

H.S.P. 4:161 (1871). *Dade* (1888) [n.p.] (Dade arms: *Gules*, a chevron between three garbs *or*, in chief a crescent *sable* for difference). *H.S.P.* 61:96 (1910) (1664 Vis. Suffolk).

1. **WILLIAM DADE**, Esq., of Tannington, Suffolk, and of Ipswich, son and heir, was born about 1580. He was married for the first time in 1612 to **MARY WINGFIELD**, daughter of Henry Wingfield, of Crowfield, Suffolk (**descendant of King Edward I**), by Elizabeth, daughter of Thomas Risby [see HANKFORD 2 for her ancestry]. They had seven sons and six daughters. She died on 3 Feb. 1624/5. He was married for the second time to ELIZABETH REVETT, "relict of Robert Armiger of Freston", and daughter of John Revett, Esq., of Brandeston, Suffolk. She died on 24 Feb. 1656/7. WILLIAM DADE, ESQ., died testate (P.C.C., 35 Nabbs) aged eighty on 22 Feb. 1659/60 (will bequeathed £300 to his son Francis), and was buried at Tannington, with both wives, monumental inscriptions.

Camden Soc. 43:127-128 (1849). *Dade* (1888) [n.p.] (identification of children). *H.S.P.* 32:318 (1891). *H.S.P.* 61:96 (1910). *NEHGR* 107:269 (Oct. 1953) (Dade arms). *Adventurers* (1987), pp. 107-109.

Child & grandchildren of William Dade, by Mary Wingfield:
  i. **CAPT. FRANCIS DADE**, born about 1622, of Tannington, Suffolk, member from Warwick County and Speaker of the House of Burgesses 1658 (under alias as John Smith), died on a return voyage from England 1662/3; married **BEHEATHLAND BERNARD**.
      a. **FRANCIS DADE**, born 7 Nov. 1659, died 1698; married **FRANCES TOWNSHEND**. Four children.
      b. **MARY DADE**, born about 1661, died about 1694; married, first, **CAPT. ROBERT MASSEY** of Stafford County, second, **COL. RICE HOOE**. Issue.

* * *

---

[1]Ancestors of **John Throckmorton**.

DAGWORTH see BUTLER

DAMORY see BURGH

DANBY see BOSVILE

DARCY see LAUNCE

* * *

DARCY

EDWARD I OF ENGLAND, King of England, married ALIANORE DE CASTILLE.
ELIZABETH OF ENGLAND, married HUMPHREY DE BOHUN, Earl of Hereford and Essex.
ALIANOR DE BOHUN, married JAMES BUTLER, Earl of Ormond.
PERNEL BUTLER, married GILBERT TALBOT, 3rd Lord Talbot.
ELIZABETH TALBOT, married HENRY DE GREY, Lord Grey of Wilton [see WILTON 9].

10. **MARGARET DE GREY**, was married to **JOHN DARCY**, 4th Lord Darcy of Knaith, son and heir of Philip Darcy, 3rd Lord Darcy of Knaith (of **Magna Charta Surety descent** and **descendant of Charlemagne**), by Elizabeth, daughter of Thomas Gray, Knt., of Heton, Northumberland. He was born about 1376 (aged twenty-two and more or twenty-three and more at father's death). They had two sons and three daughters. He was summoned to Parliament from 19 Aug. 1399 by writs directed *Johanni Darcy*. JOHN DARCY, Lord Darcy, died testate on 9 Dec. 1411 (will dated at his manor of Temple Hurst on 2 Aug. 1411, proved 18 Feb. 1411/2) (M.I. at Selby). On 14 June 1412 she had a grant of £40 a year from her late husband's lands because of her poor estate and to maintain a son and four daughters yet unmarried. His widow was married for the second time before 12 July 1421 to THOMAS SWINFORD, Knt. (died 2 Apr. 1432). "Margaret, lady Darcy" died testate (P.C.C., 18 Chedworth) on 1 June 1454.

H.S.P. 16:91 (1881) (1563 Vis. Yorks). *York.Arch.Jour.* 12:288 (1893) (arms: Semée of crosses crosslet, three cinquefoils). *Clay* (1913), p. 42. *C.P.* 4:63-65 (1916) (no reservation in identification of mother of Margaret de Grey). *TAG* 21:169-177 (Jan. 1945) (descent of Mary Launce from King Edward I).

Children & grandchildren of John Darcy, by Margaret de Grey:

    i. **PHILIP DARCY**, Knt., son and heir, born about 1398 (aged fourteen and more in June 1412); not summoned to Parliament, died aged twenty on 2 Aug. 1418 *s.p.m.*; married before 28 Oct. 1412 **ALIANOR FITZ HUGH**, died 30 Sep. 1457, daughter of Henry fitz Hugh, 3rd Lord Fitz Hugh, of Ravensworth in Richmondshire, co. York, by Elizabeth, daughter and heiress of Robert de Grey Marmion, Knt. (**descendant of Charlemagne**); two daughters and co-heiresses, the younger born posthumously; she married, second, before 18 Feb. 1426/7 to THOMAS TUNSTALL, Knt., of Thurland, co. Lancaster, third, as his second wife, HENRY BROUNFLETE, Knt., of Londesborough, co. York (afterwards Lord Vesci) (died 16 Jan. 1468/9). *H.S.P.* 16:91-92 (1881). *Northumberland* 5:411 (1899). *Clay* (1913), p. 42. *C.P.* 4:65-67 (1916). *Carleton* (1978), chart 8-19.

        a. **ELIZABETH DARCY**, married **JAMES STRANGEWAYS**, Knt. [see STRANGEWAYS 8].[1]

---

[1]Ancestors of **Edward Carleton**.

DARCY (cont.)

b. MARGERY DARCY, married JOHN CONYERS, Knt. [see CONYERS 8].[1]

ii. JOHN DARCY, second son, born about 1400 [see next].

9. JOHN DARCY, second son, was born about 1400, and became heir male of the family on the death of his brother Philip in 1418. He was married to JOAN GREYSTOKE, daughter of John de Greystoke, Baron of Greystoke (of **Magna Charta Surety** descent and **descendant of Charlemagne**), by Elizabeth, Lady of Wem, elder daughter and co-heiress of Robert de Ferrers, Knt. (of **Magna Charta Surety** descent and **descendant of Charlemagne**). They had five sons and four daughters. JOHN DARCY, Lord Darcy, died in 1458. His widow was married, with marriage dispensation dated 27 Apr. 1458, to William Stoke, Esq.

H.S.P. 16:91-92 (1881). *Clay* (1913), p. 42. *C.P.* 4:71,73 (1916). *TAG* 21:173 (Jan. 1945).

8. RICHARD DARCY, son and heir apparent, was born about 1424. He was married to ELEANOR LE SCROPE, daughter of John Le Scrope, 4th Lord Scrope of Masham, North Riding, co. York (of **Magna Charta Surety descent**), by Elizabeth, daughter of Thomas Chaworth, Knt., of Wiverton, co. Nottingham. They had three sons and one daughter. RICHARD DARCY died before 1458 *v.p.* His widow was married for the second time to William Claxton, of East Bridgford, co. Nottingham.

H.S.P. 16:92 (1881). *Clay* (1913), p. 42. *C.P.* 4:71 (1916). *TAG* 21:173 (Jan. 1945).

7. WILLIAM DARCY, Knt., 8th Lord Darcy, son and heir, was born in 1443. He was married, with licence dated 23 Jan. 1460/1, in Farnley Chapel, to EUPHEME LANGTON, daughter of John Langton, of Farnley, West Riding, co. York. They had two sons and one daughter. WILLIAM DARCY, Lord Darcy, died on 30 May 1488.

H.S.P. 16:92 (1881). *Clay* (1913), p. 42. *C.P.* 4:71, 73 (1916). *TAG* 21:173 (Jan. 1945).

6. THOMAS DARCY, Knt., K.G., of Temple Hurst, co. York, son and heir, was born about 1467 (aged twenty-one and more at his father's death). He was married for the first time to DOWSABEL TEMPEST, daughter and heiress of Richard Tempest, Knt., of Giggleswick in Ribblesdale, co. York, by Mabel, daughter of Walter Strickland, of Sizergh, Westmorland (**descendant of Charlemagne**). They had three sons and one daughter. She was living in 1503. He was summoned to Parliament, certainly from 17 Oct. 1509, by writs directed *Thome Darcy de Darcy Chl'r*, whereby he became **Lord Darcy** of Temple Hurst. He was married for the second time before 1520 to EDITH SANDYS, widow of Ralph Neville, and daughter of William Sandys, Knt., of the Vine, co. Hants, by Elizabeth, daughter of John Cheney, Knt., of Shurland. They had one daughter. She died at Stepney on 22 Aug. 1529, and was buried at the Friars Observants, Greenwich. He joined in Aske's rebellion, called *the Pilgrimage of Grace*, and was convicted of high treason on the charge of delivering up Pontefract Castle to the rebels. THOMAS DARCY, Lord Darcy, was beheaded on Tower Hill on 30 June 1537, and was buried at St. Botolph's, Aldgate.

Glover-Foster (1875), p. 47 (1584 Vis. Yorks) (Darcy arms: *Azure*, three cinquefoyles between nine crosslets *or*). *H.S.P.* 16:92 (1881). *Clay* (1913), p. 43. *C.P.* 4:71, 73-74 (1916) (was a person of some distinction in the reign of Henry VII). *TAG* 21:173-174 (Jan. 1945).

Child of Thomas Darcy, by Dowsabel Tempest:

i. ARTHUR DARCY, Knt., of Brimham, co. York, married MARY CAREW [see LAUNCE 3].[2]

---

[1] Ancestors of **Philip & Thomas Nelson**.

[2] Ancestors of **Mary Launce**.

* * *

DAVIE

EDWARD III OF ENGLAND, King of England, married PHILIPPE DE HAINAUT.
LIONEL OF CLARENCE [of Antwerp], Duke of Clarence, married ELIZABETH DE BURGH.
PHILIPPE OF CLARENCE, married EDMUND DE MORTIMER, 3rd Earl of March.
ELIZABETH MORTIMER, married HENRY PERCY, Knt.
ELIZABETH PERCY, married JOHN DE CLIFFORD, Lord Clifford.
MARY DE CLIFFORD, married PHILIP WENTWORTH, Knt.
HENRY WENTWORTH, Knt., married ANNE SAY.
MARGERY WENTWORTH, married JOHN SEYMOUR, Knt.
ELIZABETH SEYMOUR, married GREGORY CROMWELL [see WINGFIELD 5].

3. FRANCES CROMWELL, was born about 1544. She was married at Compton, co. Hants, with marriage settlement dated 3 Jan. 1560/1, to **RICHARD STRODE**, Esq., of Newnham in Plympton St. Mary, co. Devon, son and heir of William Strode, of Newnham (**descendant of Charlemagne**), by Elizabeth, daughter of Philip de Courtenay, of Loughtor, co. Devon (**descendant of King Edward I**), by Jane, daughter of Richard Fowell [see COURTENAY 4 for his ancestry]. They had one son. She died aged eighteen on 7 Feb. 1561/2, and was buried at Plympton St. Mary RICHARD STRODE, ESQ., died on 5 Aug. 1581.

Crisp Notes 12:121-122 (1917) (he was mentioned in wills of his grandfather 26 August 1550, and of his grandmother 6 November 1553). *Vivian* (1895), pp. 718-719.

2. **WILLIAM STRODE**, Knt., of Newnham, Sheriff of Devonshire, M.P. for Plympton, Recorder of Plymouth, son and heir, was born on 1 Feb. 1561/2. He was admitted to the Inner Temple in 1580. He was married for the first time on 15 July 1581 at Bovey Tracey, co. Devon, to **MARY SOUTHCOTT**, second daughter of Thomas Southcott, Esq., of Bovey Tracey, by Katherine, daughter of William Pole, Knt., of Shute, co. Devon. They had three sons and seven daughters. She was buried at Plympton St. Mary on 24 Feb. 1617/18 (M.I.). He was married for the second time at Tavistock on 31 Mar. 1624 to DEWNES GLANVILLE, widow of Stephen Vosper, of Liskeard, co. Cornwall, and daughter of Nicholas Glanville, of Tavistock. She was buried at Plympton St. Mary on 16 Sep. 1635 (M.I.). SIR WILLIAM STRODE died testate (P.C.C., 18 Lee) aged seventy-five on 27 June 1637, and was buried at Plympton St. Mary (M.I.).

Wotton (1741) 2:267 (1741). *Vivian* (1895), pp. 699, 718-719. *TAG* 23:207, 210 (Apr. 1947).

1. **JULIANA STRODE**, fifth daughter, was married to **JOHN DAVIE**, Knt., of Sandford, co. Devon, M.P. for Tiverton, Sheriff of Devonshire, son & heir of John Davie, of Sanford and Kirton, co. Devon, Mayor of Exeter, by Margaret, daughter of George Southcote, Esq., of Calverleigh, co. Devon. He was matriculated aged sixteen at Exeter College, Oxford, on 22 Feb. 1604/5. He was created a **Baronet** by King Charles I on 2 Sep. 1641. She died on 14 May 1627, and was buried at Sandford. He was married for the second time to Isabel Hele, daughter of Walter Hele, of Gnaton in Newton Ferrers, co. Devon, and had one daughter, Isabel, baptised in 1631. SIR JOHN DAVIE, BART., was buried at Sandford on 13 Oct. 1654. His widow died on 14 May 1627, and was buried at Sandford (M.I.).

Wotton (1741) 2:267-268. *Crisp* Notes 12:127 (1917). *Vivian* (1895), pp. 269-270 (Davie arms: *Azure*, three cinquefoils 2 and 1 *or*, on a chief of the last a lion passant *gules*), 698,719. *NEHGR* 86:269. *TAG* 23:206 (Jan. 1947).

Children & grandchildren of John Davie, by Juliana Strode:

DAVIE (cont.)

i. MARY DAVIE, baptised 25 Mar. 1611/12, married JOHN WILLOUGHBY, Esq., of Payhembury, co. Devon.

ii. JOHN DAVIE, Knt., 2nd Baronet, son and heir, baptised Sandford 6 Dec. 1612, Sheriff of Devonshire, buried Sandford 31 July 1678; married, first, MARY _____, second, TRYPHENA REYNELL. Two children by second marriage. No descendants.

iii. WILLIAM DAVIE, of Dura, second son, baptised Sandford 13 Nov. 1614, barrister at law, buried Sandford 28 Nov. 1663; married MARGARET CLARKE. Two sons (3rd & 4th Baronets), and five daughters.

iv. ROBERT DAVIE, third son, baptised Sandford 19 Sep. 1617, buried 28 Nov. 1617.

v. ELIZABETH DAVIE, baptised Sandford 24 Sep. 1618, married ARTHUR COPLESTON, Esq., of Bowden.

vi. ROBERT DAVIE, baptised Sandford 15 Apr. 1621, died *s.p.*

vii. JULIAN DAVIE, baptised Sandford 1 Jan. 1622/3, married THOMAS BEARE.

viii. HUMPHREY DAVIE, baptised Sandford 24 Aug. 1625, wealthy merchant in London, a zealous Puritan, emigrated in 1662 to Boston, Massachusetts, where he became a prominent man, later removed to Hartford, Connecticut, where he died 18 Feb. 1688/9; married, first, **MARY WHITE**, died after 1674; second **SARAH (GIBBON) RICHARDS**, born 17 Aug. 1645, died 8 Feb. 1714. Many descendants.

    a. EDMUND DAVIE, son, probably, graduate Harvard College, died before 1700.

    b. JOHN DAVIE, Knt., graduate Harvard College 1681, patentee of New London, Connecticut, first clerk of the town of Groton, Connecticut, returned to England in 1707 with his family, succeeding his cousin to the title as fifth Baronet and to the estates at Creedy in the parish of Sandford, co. Devon, buried Sandford 29 Dec. 1727; married ELIZABETH _____. Six sons and three daughters.

    c. ELIZABETH DAVIE, married DANIEL TAYLOR, of New London, Connecticut. Three children.

    d. ANNE DAVIE, died 12 Sep. 1662 Boston.

    e. ROWLAND DAVIE, born 23 Mar. 1664 Boston, died 17 June 1664.

    f. ANNE DAVIE, baptized 30 day 2nd mo. [Apr] 1665.

    g. MARGARET DAVIE, born 19 Feb. 1666, married **HENRY FRANKLIN**. Four children.

    h. MARY DAVIE, born 4 Nov. 1671.

    i. HUMPHREY DAVIE, born 10 June 1673.

    j. HUMPHREY DAVIE, *the Brazier*, first child by second marriage, born about 1684-5, married **MARGARET GEDNEY**. One daughter.

    k. WILLIAM DAVIE, born 27 June 1686, merchant of Boston.

ix. MARGARET DAVIE, baptised 20 May 1627, married RICHARD BEAVIS, Esq.

* * *

DEIGHTON

EDWARD I OF ENGLAND, King of England, married **ALIANORE DE CASTILLE**.
JOAN OF ENGLAND [*of Acre*], married **GILBERT OF CLARE**, Earl of Gloucester.
ALIANOR DE CLARE, married HUGH LE DESPENSER, Lord le Despenser [see CLARE 11].

9. ELIZABETH LA DESPENSER, was born no later than 1327 (father hanged 24 Nov. 1326). She was married in August 1338 to **MAURICE DE BERKELEY**, 4th Lord Berkeley, son and heir of Maurice de Berkeley, Knt., **Baron** of Berkeley, co. Gloucester (of **Magna Charta Surety descent** and **descendant of Charlemagne**, by

DEIGHTON (cont.)

Eve, daughter of Eudo la Zouche, of Harringworth, co. Northampton (**descendant of Charlemagne**). He was born about 1330 (aged eight at time of marriage). He was a commander in Gascony in 1355, and distinguished himself at the battle of Poitiers on 19 Sep. 1356, where he was severely wounded and taken prisoner, ransomed for £1000. He was summoned to Parliament 1362-1368. MAURICE DE BERKELEY, Lord Berkeley, died at Berkeley Castle aged thirty-seven on 3 June 1368 from wounds received earlier at Poitiers, and was buried at St. Augustine's, Bristol. His widow died on 13 July 1389, and was buried at St. Botolph's, London.

H.S.P. 28:30 (1889) (1623 Vis. Salop). *C.P.* 2:130-131 (1912) ("may bee called *Maurice the Valiant*").

Children & grandchild of Maurice de Berkeley, by Elizabeth Despenser:

i. THOMAS DE BERKELEY, 5th Lord Berkeley, born at Berkeley Castle 5 Jan. 1352/3, died testate 13 July 1417 *s.p.m.*, buried Wotton-under-Edge, co. Gloucester; summoned to Parliament 1381-1415; served in the wars in France, Spain, Brittany and Scotland 1378-1385; in 1386 entertained King Richard II at Berkeley Castle, for the deposition of whom, however, he was, 30 Sep. 1399, one of the Commissioners; P.C. to Kings Richard II and Henry IV; Admiral of the South and West 1403; a Regent of the Kingdom April 1416; married, aged fifteen, at Wingrave, co. Buckingham, November 1367, **MARGARET DE LISLE**, born about 1362, died 20 Mar. 1391/2, buried Wotton-under-Edge, co. Gloucester; only daughter and heiress of Warin de Lisle, Lord Lisle, by Margaret, daughter of William Pipard, Knt. *C.P.* (1932) 8:53-54.

a. ELIZABETH DE BERKELEY [see BEAUCHAMP 9].[1]

ii. JAMES DE BERKELEY, younger son, born about 1353/4 [see next].

8. JAMES DE BERKELEY, Knt., younger son, was born about 1353/4. He was married to **ELIZABETH BLUET**, daughter and heiress of John Bluet, Knt., of Raglan, co. Monmouth. SIR JAMES DE BERKELEY died on 13 June 1405 *v.f.* His widow was married for the second time to WILLIAM AP THOMAS, Knt.

H.S.P. 28:30 (1889); *C.P.* 2:132 (1912).

7. JAMES DE BERKELEY, Knt., Lord Berkeley, was born at Raglan, co. Monmouth, about 1394. He was nephew and heir male of Thomas de Berkeley, Lord Berkeley. He succeeded to the Castle of Berkeley and other estates under an entail of his great-grandfather, but was much hindered in getting possession thereof by the heir general, his cousin the Countess of Warwick. He was summoned to Parliament 1421-1461. He was married (or contracted to marry) aged sixteen to _____ SAINT JOHN, daughter of John St. John. She died young *s.p.*. He was married for the second time to _____ STAFFORD, daughter of Humphrey Stafford, Knt., of Hook. She died young *s.p.* He was married for the third time in 1423/4 to **ISABEL DE MOWBRAY**, widow (with one daughter) of HENRY FERRERS, Knt. (died shortly before 5 Dec. 1463 *s.p.m., v.p.*) [see GREY 8 for descendants of this marriage], and first daughter and in her issue co-heiress of Thomas de Mowbray, Duke of Norfolk (**descendant of King Edward I**), by Elizabeth (**descendant of King Edward I**), daughter of Richard Fitz Alan, Earl of Arundel and Surrey. She was, while about to appeal to the King in Council on behalf of her husband, arrested by order of Margaret, Countess of Shrewsbury (granddaughter and co-heiress of the last Lord Berkeley, and step-mother of James de Berkeley's fourth wife), and imprisoned at Gloucester, where she died on 23 Sep. 1452, and was buried in the church of the Greyfriars there [see MOWBRAY 9 for her ancestry]. James de Berkeley was

---

[1]Ancestors of **Elizabeth Bosvile, George, Giles & Robert Brent, St. Leger Codd, Edward Digges, Warham Horsmanden, Anne Humphrey, Anne Mauleverer, Philip & Thomas Nelson, Herbert Pelham, Katherine Saint Leger, John West.**

DEIGHTON (cont.)

married for the fourth time, with settlement dated 25 July 1457, to JOAN TALBOT, daughter of John Talbot, 1st Earl of Shrewsbury, by his first wife Maud, daughter of Thomas Neville, Lord Furnival. JAMES DE BERKELEY, Lord Berkeley, died at Berkeley Castle in November 1463, and was buried at Berkeley. His widow was married for the second time before 26 May 1474 to Edmund Hungerford.

H.S.P. 28:31 (1889). *C.P.* 2:132-135, 145 (1912) ("may bee called *James the Just*"). *C.P.* 9:610 footnote *d*.

Children of James de Berkeley, by Isabel de Mowbray:
  i. MAURICE BERKELEY, second son, born about 1435 [see next].
  ii. ISABEL BERKELEY, married WILLIAM TRYE [see TRYE 6].[1]

6. MAURICE BERKELEY, Lord Berkeley *de jure*, second son, was born about 1435 (aged fifty-six in 1492). He was disinherited by his brother, and though fifty-six years of age at his brother's death, was able to recover, within seven years, upwards of fifty manors and other lands, that had been alienated illegally. He was never summoned to Parliament. He was married in his thirtieth year in 1465 to ISABEL MEAD (at that time a widow with three children who all died young), only daughter of Philip Mead, of Mead's Place in Wraxall, Somerset, Mayor of Bristol, by his wife Isabel. She was born about or after 1444, and was heiress to her brother Thomas Mead. MAURICE BERKELEY died aged seventy years in September 1506. His widow died aged seventy at Coventry after 29 May 1514. They were buried at Austin Friars', London.

C.P. 2:135, 145 (1912) ("may bee called *Maurice the Lawier*"). *H.S.P.* 28:31 (1889). *Paget* (1977), p. 403.

5. ANNE BERKELEY, was married to WILLIAM DENNIS, Knt. of Dyrham, co. Gloucester, son of Walter Dennis, Knt., by his second wife Agnes, daughter and coheiress of Robert Danvers, Knt. They had seven sons and seven daughters. He was married for the second time to Edith Twinihoe.

Smyth-Maclean (1883) 2:178-187. *H.S.P.* 21:51 (1885) (1623 Vis. Glouc.) (Dennis arms: *Gules*, a bend engrailed *azure* between two leopards' faces jessant de lis *or*). *H.S.P.* 28:31 (1889) (1623 Vis. Salop). *Virginia Gen.* 38:49.

Children of William Dennis, by Anne Berkeley:
  i. ISABEL DENNIS [see next].
  ii. ELEANOR DENNIS, married WILLIAM LYGON [see LIGON 3].[2]

4. ISABEL DENNIS, was married for the first time to JOHN BERKELEY, Knt., of Stoke Gifford, co. Gloucester, son and heir of Richard Berkeley, of Stoke Gifford (of **Magna Charta Surety descent** and **descendant of Charlemagne**), by Elizabeth, daughter of Humphrey Conningsby, Knt. SIR JOHN BERKELEY died in 1546. She was married for the second time to ARTHUR PORTER.

Smyth-Maclean (1883) 2:180. *H.S.P.* 21:51 (1885). *C.P.* 2:234 (1912).

3. ELIZABETH BERKELEY, was married to HENRY LYGON, of Upton St. Leonard's, Gloucester, co. Gloucester, third son of Richard Lygon, Knt., of Arle Court, Sheriff of Worcester (of **Magna Charta Surety descent** and **descendant of Charlemagne**), by Margaret, daughter of William Greville, Knt., of Arle Court and Cheltenham. He was born, say, 1525. The will of HENRY LYGON was dated 30 July 1577 and proved 15 Aug. 1577).

---

[1] Ancestors of **Thomas Ligon**.
[2] Ancestors of **Thomas Ligon**.

DEIGHTON (cont.)

Smyth-Maclean (1883) 2:180. *TAG* 9:213 (Apr. 1933) (asserts descent of Richard Lygon from King Edward I through Margaret, daughter of Ralph Stafford, Earl of Stafford). *Ligon* (1947), pp. 42-43.

2. **ELIZABETH LYGON**, was born, say, 1555, and was named in her father's will. She was married to **EDWARD BASSET**, Esq., of Uley, co. Gloucester, son of William Bassett, of Uley (of **baronial** descent), by Jane, daughter of John Ashe, of co. Somerset. They had four sons and four daughters. The will of EDWARD BASSET was dated 3 June 1601 and proved 5 Nov. 1602 (P.C.C., 77 Montague).

Smyth-Maclean (1883) 1:121, 2:182-183. *H.S.P.* 21:206 (1885) (1623 Vis. Glouc.). *TAG* 9:214 (Apr. 1933). *TAG* 10:20-24 (July 1933).

1. **JANE BASSET**, was born, say, 1585, and was named in her father's will. She was married at St. Nicholas', Gloucester, co. Gloucester, on 12 Apr. 1605 to **DR. JOHN DEIGHTON**, Gent., of Gloucester, Sheriff of Gloucestershire. He was born about 1570. Their children were baptised at St. Nicholas'. She died on 23 Apr. 1631. DR. JOHN DEIGHTON died testate on 16 May 1640 (will dated 30 Jan. 1639, proved 21 May 1640, named "_____ Lugge my eldest daughter ... my daughter Francis Williams ... my daughter Katherin Haburne"). Their tombstone in the south aisle of St. Nicholas Church was inscribed with his arms: Argent a lion passant between three crosses patty fitchee gules, and this inscription: "Here lies interred the bodies of John Deighton, of this city, gent. and Jane his wife, daughter to Edward Basset, of Uley, Esq., by whom he had issue three sons and four daughters. He spent all his time in the study of chiorgery, and attained to great knowledge therein."

Smyth-Maclean (1883) 2:183. *TAG* 9:214-222 (Apr. 1933). *TAG* 10:24-29 (July 1933). *Waters* 1:551-552 (1885)). *NEHGR* 45:303 (Oct. 1891). *TG* 6:195-201 (1985). *Ligon* (1947), pp. 43-44.

Children & grandchildren of John Deighton, by Jane Basset:

   i. JOHN DEIGHTON, born about 1606, died young.

   ii. JOHN DEIGHTON, baptised 9 Apr. 1609, married MARY ANSTYE. One son.

   iii. **JANE DEIGHTON**, baptised St. Nicholas, Gloucester, 5 Apr. 1609, residing in Boston, Massachusetts, 1671; married, first, St. Nicholas, 3 Jan. 1627, **JOHN LUGG**, emigrated 1638, died after 1644; married, second, Boston, Massachusetts, 27 Oct. 1647, **JONATHAN NEGUS**, born about 1601, died before 11 Apr. 1682. Four children by first marriage born at Boston, the youngest on 4 Aug. 1644.

     a. ELIZABETH LUGG, born 7 Mar. 1638.

     b. MARY LUGG, baptised 25 Sep. 1642, married **NATHANIEL BARNARD**.

     c. JOHN LUGG, born 4 Aug. 1644.

     d. ISAAC NEGUS, baptised First Church, Boston, 3 Mar. 1650/1, died Swansea, Massachusetts, 29 Nov. 1700; married **HANNAH ANDREWS**. Five sons.

     e. MARIA NEGUS, born 6 July 1653, apparently died young.

   iv. **FRANCES DEIGHTON**, baptised St. Nicholas, Gloucester, 1 Mar. 1611, died Taunton, Massachusetts, February 1705/6; married Witcombe Magna, Gloucester, 11 Feb. 1632, **RICHARD WILLIAMS**, baptised Wootton-under-Edge, 28 Jan. 1607, emigrated about 1636 or 1637, resided Taunton, died there August 1693.

     a. JOHN WILLIAMS, baptised 27 Mar. 1634, died young.

     b. ELIZABETH WILLIAMS, baptised 7 Feb. 1635/6, died young.

     c. **SAMUEL WILLIAMS**, born about 1639, married **JANE GILBERT**.

     d. **NATHANIEL WILLIAMS**, baptized 7 Feb. 1641, married **ELIZABETH ROGERS**.

     e. **JOSEPH WILLIAMS**, born about 1643, married **ELIZABETH WATSON**.

     f. **THOMAS WILLIAMS**, born about 1645, married MARY _____.

     g. **ELIZABETH WILLIAMS**, born about 1647, married **JOHN BIRD**, of Dorchester, Massachusetts.

DEIGHTON (cont.)

    h. HANNAH WILLIAMS, born about 1650, married JOHN PARMENTER.

    i. BENJAMIN WILLIAMS, born about 1652, married REBECCA MACY.

 v. KATHERINE DEIGHTON, baptised Gloucester, England, 16 Jan. 1614/5, married, first, SAMUEL HACKBURNE, married, second, as his second wife, Roxbury, Massachusetts, 14 Apr. 1644, GOV. THOMAS DUDLEY, died 31 Jul. 1653; married, third, REV. JOHN ALLIN of Dedham, and had children by all three husbands.

    a. ELIZABETH HAGBURNE, born England 7 May 1635, married JOHN CHICKERING.

    b. SAMUEL HAGBURNE, born 20 Jan. 1637, resided New London, Connecticut.

    c. JOHN HAGBURNE, born 26 Mar. 1640.

    d. HANNAH HAGBURNE, born 5 Jan. 1642, married SAMUEL HUNTING.

For descendants of second marriage, see DUDLEY 1.

    h. BENJAMIN ALLIN, born 11 Aug. 1654.

    i. DANIEL ALLIN, born 31 July 1656.

    j. ELIEZER ALLIN, born 26 May 1658.

 vi. DAMARIS DEIGHTON, baptised 22 Mar. 1616, living 1640.

vii. MARY DEIGHTON, born about 1618, probably died young.

viii. THOMAS DEIGHTON, baptised 19 Aug. 1621, living 1640.

 ix. Son, died before 1624.

* * *

DELAWARE see HUMPHREY

DENNIS see DEIGHTON

DENNIS see also TRYE

DERING see FISHER

DESPENSER see CLARE

DEVEREUX see FERRERS

* * *

DIGGES

EDWARD III OF ENGLAND, King of England, married PHILIPPE DE HAINAUT.
LIONEL OF CLARENCE [*of Antwerp*], Duke of Clarence, married ELIZABETH DE BURGH.
PHILIPPE OF CLARENCE, married EDMUND DE MORTIMER, 3rd Earl of March.
ELIZABETH MORTIMER, married HENRY PERCY, Knt.
HENRY PERCY, Earl of Northumberland, married ALIANOR NEVILLE.
HENRY PERCY, 3rd Earl of Northumberland, married ALIANOR POYNINGS.
HENRY PERCY, 4th Earl of Northumberland, married MAUD HERBERT.
ELEANOR PERCY, married EDWARD STAFFORD, 3rd Duke of Buckingham.
MARY STAFFORD, married GEORGE NEVILLE, 5th Lord Bergavenny.

DIGGES (cont.)

URSULA NEVILLE, married **WARHAM SAINT LEGER,** Knt. [see SAINT LEGER 3].

2. ANNE SAINT LEGER, was born about 1555. She was married to **THOMAS DIGGES,** Esq., of Digges Court in Barham, Kent, son of Leonard Digges, of Wotten Court, Kent, by Bridget, daughter of Thomas Wilford, of Hartridge in Cranbrook, Kent. They had six children. He was an English mathematician, A.B., Cambridge, 1551, M.P., 1572, muster-master-general of the armies in the Low Countries, 1586-1594. "Thomas Diggs, esquier, par. of St. Alphage within Creplegate, London" died testate (P.C.C., 59 Scott) in London on 24 Aug. 1595, and was buried at St Mary Aldermansbury, London. His widow died aged eighty-one in 1636, and was buried at Chilham.

<small>Berry (1830), p. 143. H.S.P. 42:65 (1898) (1619 Vis. Kent). Mortimer-Percy (1911), pp. 30,501. Adventurers (1987), p. 247.</small>

1. DUDLEY DIGGES, Knt., of Chilham Castle, Kent, was born in 1583. He was admitted as a Gentleman Commoner aged seventeen to Christ Church College, Oxford University, on 18 July 1600, and received a B.A. degree in 1601. He was knighted at Whitehall on 29 Apr. 1607, and was a member of the Virginia Company. He was admitted to Gray's Inn on 2 Feb. 1617/8, and succeeded to the office of Master of the Rolls in 1636. He and associates were assigned land in Virginia in May 1622. He served as one of the commissioners of the East India Company to draw up a treaty between the Dutch and the English over eastern trade, and was also a member of the Muscovy Company, supporting three expeditions to discover a northeast passage to the Orient. He was married to **MARY KEMPE,** youngest daughter and co-heiress of Thomas Kempe, Knt., of Ollantigh, Kent (**descendant of King Henry III**), by Dorothy, daughter of John Thompson, of London, and through this marriage and by purchase acquired the manor and castle of Chilham in Kent [see OLLANTIGH 2 for her ancestry]. SIR DUDLEY DIGGES died testate on 18 Mar. 1638/9. She rebuilt Chilham Castle. They were buried at Chilham.

<small>Stemmata Chicheleana (1765), p. 5 (names only sons Thomas, John and Dudley). Berry (1830), p. 143. H.S.P. 42:65 (1898) (Digges arms: *Gules,* on a cross *argent* five eaglets displayed *sable*). Kemp (1902), pp. 35-36. Mortimer-Percy (1911), p. 501 (sons including "Edward Digges of Virginia, in 1684"). NEHGR 107:188 (July 1953) (Digges arms). Adventurers (1987), pp. 247-253.</small>

Children & grandchildren of Dudley Digges, by Mary Kempe:

    i. THOMAS DIGGES, of Chilham, born about 1610, B.A. University College, Oxford, died 1687, married MARY ABBOTT. Twelve children.

    ii. JOHN DIGGES, of Faversham.

    iii. DUDLEY DIGGES, born Chilham about 1614, B.A., University College, Oxford, Fellow of All Souls, a Royalist political writer, died 1 Oct. 1643, unmarried.

    iv. ANNE DIGGES, married ANTHONY HAMMOND, of St. Alban's Court, Canterbury, Kent.

    v. ELIZABETH DIGGES, baptised 28 Oct. 1617, married ARNOLD BRAYNING.

    vi. MARY DIGGES, died unmarried, will dated 4 May 1643.

    vii. FRANCIS DIGGES, fourth son, baptised 18 Jan. 1620/1, buried with mother at Chilham.

    viii. **EDWARD DIGGES,** baptised Chilham 29 May 1621, entered Gray's Inn 19 May 1637, emigrated to Virginia by 11 Dec. 1650, elected Governor of Virginia 1655, attempted silk culture on his plantation "Belfield" in York County, died 15 Mar. 1675/6; married **ELIZABETH PAGE,** daughter of Francis Page, of Bedfont, Middlesex, emigrated by 1653, died by 24 Sep. 1691. Thirteen children of whom three sons and five daughters died in infancy, or by 1691 without issue.

        a. **WILLIAM DIGGES,** supporter of Governor Berkeley during Bacon's Rebellion, and fled to Maryland, merchant and planter in St. Mary's County, Maryland, returned to Virginia after 1689, will proved 24 July 1697; married **ELIZABETH (WHARTON) SEWALL,** daughter of Henry Sewall of Patuxent, St. Mary's County. Ten children.

DIGGES (cont.)

    a. **ANN DIGGES**, born about 1658, died 22 Nov. 1686, married **WILLIAM COLE**. Two sons, no descendants.

    a. **MARY DIGGES**, born about 1660, died 18 Mar. 1690, married **FRANCIS PAGE**. One daughter.

    a. **DUDLEY DIGGES**, born about 1666, member of House of Burgesses, Colonel of Warwick County militia, prominent tobacco planter, died 18 Jan. 1710/11; married **SUSANNAH COLE**. Four children.

        a. **EDWARD DIGGES**, living 1691, died unmarried.

  ix. **LEONARD DIGGES**, baptised 11 Dec. 1622, admitted Gray's Inn, 19 May 1637.

   x. **HERBERT DIGGES**, baptised 4 June 1628.

 xi. **RICHARD DIGGES**, eighth son, baptised 1 May 1631, buried with mother at Chilham.

* * *

DRURY

EDWARD III OF ENGLAND, King of England, married **PHILIPPE DE HAINAUT**.
LIONEL OF CLARENCE [*of Antwerp*], Duke of Clarence, married **ELIZABETH DE BURGH**.
PHILIPPE OF CLARENCE, married **EDMUND DE MORTIMER**.
ELIZABETH MORTIMER, married **HENRY PERCY**, Knt.
ELIZABETH PERCY, married **JOHN DE CLIFFORD**, 7th Lord Clifford.
THOMAS DE CLIFFORD, 8th Lord Clifford, married **JOAN DACRE** [see MACKWORTH 6].

8. ELIZABETH CLIFFORD, was married to **WILLIAM PLUMPTON**, Knt., of Knaresborough, West Riding, co. York, son of William Plumpton, Knt., of Plumpton, co. York (of **Magna Charta Surety descent**), by his first wife Elizabeth, daughter of Brian Stapleton, Knt., of Carleton, co. York (**descendant of Charlemagne**). He was born in 1435. They had two daughters. SIR WILLIAM PLUMPTON died 1461/2 (1 Edw. 4) *v.p.*

    Sur Soc. 36:191 (1859) (1665 Vis. Yorks). *Sur.Soc.* 144:82-84 (1930) (1480 Vis. North). *Paget* (1957) 134:10 ("Robert" Plumpton). *Carleton* (1978), chart 7.

7. ELIZABETH PLUMPTON, younger daughter and co-heiress, was married, with marriage contract dated 1463/64, to **JOHN SOTHILL**, Esq., son of Henry Sothill, by Anne, daughter and heiress of John Boyville, of Stock Faston, co. Leicester. They had six sons and two daughters. The will of "John Sotehyll esquire of Stokefaston" was dated 2 June 1493 and proved 7 Oct. 1494 (with request for burial in the chapel of St. Botolph's, Stock Faston) (P.C.C., 15 Vox). "Dame Elisabeth Sothill of Stokefaston" died testate on 21 Sep. 1506 ("to be buried at the Gray Freres at London in the same place that my sone Henry Sotehill is buryed; and my hert to be take out of my body, and buryed at Stockfaston by my housbande") (P.C.C., 19 Adeane).

    Sur Soc. 36:191 (1859). *Sur.Soc.* 53:168-171 (1868). *Glover-Foster* (1875), p. 275 (1584 Vis. Yorks). *Sur.Soc.* 116:65-66 (1908) (her will). *Sur.Soc.* 144:84 (1930) (1480 Vis. North). *H.S.P.* 95:344-345 (Yorkshire Pedigrees).

6. HENRY SOTHILL, Esq., of Stoke Faston, co. Leicester, Attorney-General to King Henry VII, was married to **JOAN EMPSON**, daughter of [the notorious] Richard Empson, Knt. They had twin daughters. The will of "Henry Sothyll of Stokefaston in the countie of Leycestre, esquyer" was dated 16 Feb. 1505/6, and proved 16 May 1506 (with request to be buried at Grey Friars', London) (P.C.C., 31 Holgrave). His

DRURY (cont.)

widow was married for the second time to **William Pierrepoint**, Knt., of Holme Pierre Pont, co. Nottingham.

Sur.Soc. 53:169 (1868). *Glover-Foster* (1875), p. 275. *Norf.Arch.Soc.* 2:219 (1895) (1563 Vis. Norf.). *Ancient Deeds* 5:449 (1906) (A.13122: settlement of manors on Henry and Joan and their heirs). *Sur.Soc.* 116:64-65 (1908) (his will). *Sur.Soc.* 144:84 (1930). *H.S.P.* 95:345.

5. ELIZABETH SOTHILL, twin daughter and co-heiress, was born about 1505 (aged one year at father's death). She was married to **WILLIAM DRURY**, Knt., of Hawstead, Suffolk, Sheriff of Suffolk and Norfolk, Privy Councillor to Queen Mary, son of Robert Drury, Knt., of Hawstead, by Anne (**descendant of King Edward I**), daughter of William Calthorpe, Knt., of Burnham Thorpe, Norfolk [see BARDOLF 6 for his ancestry]. He was born about 1500 (aged thirty-six and more in 1536). He had been married previously to Joan St. Mawr, daughter and heiress of William St. Mawr, Knt. She died in 1517. William & Elizabeth had three sons and six daughters. "Sir William Drurye, knight of Hawstede" died testate (P.C.C., 16 Noodes) at Hawstead on 11 Jan. 1557/8. His widow died testate on 19 May 1575. They were buried at Hawstead (with monumental inscription).

Sur.Soc. 53:169 (1868). *Norf.Arch.Soc.* 1:267 (1878) (1563 Vis. Norf.). *Norf.Arch.Soc.* 2:188-189,219 (1895). *Muskett* (1900), p. 354. *Campling* (1937), pp. 47-50. *H.S.P.* 95:345. *TG* 9:192 (1988) (no reference to Elizabeth's Plantagenet ancestry).

Children of William Drury, by Elizabeth Sothill:

    i. **ANNE DRURY**, born 19 Aug. 1523, married **CHRISTOPHER HEYDON**, Knt., of Baconsthorpe, Norfolk (ancestors of Nicholas Spencer of Westmoreland County, Virginia. See *Roberts* (1993), p. 120).

    ii. **BRIDGET DRURY**, born 11 Sep. 1534, married **HENRY YELVERTON** [see PEYTON 4].[1]

    iii. **MARY DRURY**, born 30 June 1526 [see next].

4. MARY DRURY, second daughter, was born on 30 June 1526. She was married for the first time to **RICHARD CORBETT**, Knt., of Assington, Suffolk, son of Richard Corbett, Knt., of Assington, by his wife Jane. He was born in May 1524. SIR RICHARD CORBETT died before 24 June 1565. She was married for the second time in 1565 to JOHN TYRRELL, of Gipping, Suffolk. She was buried at Cotton, Suffolk, on 16 June 1594 (will proved 29 June 1594).

Norf.Arch.Soc. 2:219 (1895). *Muskett* (1900), p. 354. *Campling* (1937), p. 49. *TG* 9:192 (1988).

Child of Richard Corbett, by Mary Drury:

    i. **ELIZABETH CORBETT**, married **PHILIP WENTWORTH** [see HARLESTON 3].[2]

* * *

DRYDEN see MARBURY

* * *

---

[1] Ancestors of **Robert Peyton**.

[2] Ancestors of **John Harleston**.

DUDLEY

EDWARD I OF ENGLAND, King of England, married ALIANORE DE CASTILLE.
JOAN OF ENGLAND [of Acre], married GILBERT DE CLARE, Earl of Gloucester.
MARGARET DE CLARE, married, second, HUGH DE AUDLEY, 8th Earl of Stafford.
MARGARET DE AUDLEY, married RALPH DE STAFFORD, Lord Stafford [see AUDLEY 12].

9. KATHERINE DE STAFFORD, youngest daughter, was born on or before 16 Sep. 1348. She was married, aged nine or ten, on 25 Dec. 1357 to JOHN DE SUTTON, Baron of Dudley, co. Worcester, son and heir of John de Sutton, Baron of Dudley (descendant of Charlemagne), by Isabel, daughter of John de Cherleton, Lord of Powis. He was born in or before November 1338 (of age in 1359). She died, probably aged about fourteen, before 25 Dec. 1361, probably in the childbirth of her only child on 6 December. He was married for the second time after 1361 to his cousin Joan Clinton, widow, with issue, of John Montfort, Knt. (last of record on 25 May 1361), and daughter and heiress of John Clinton, Knt., of Coleshill, co. Warwick (of baronial descent), by Joan, younger daughter of Roger Hillary, Knt., of Bescote). She was born 1341/2 (aged twelve at the death of her father), and was granddaughter of John's paternal aunt, Katherine Sutton, wife of Roger Hillary, of Bescote. They had a son John (who predeceased his mother *s.p.*) and two daughters. JOHN DE SUTTON served in the army in France, and died aged about thirty-one, probably in France, in 1369 or early 1370. She was married for the third time in 1370 to Henry ap Griffith, Knt., of Wichnor, co. Stafford. She died by 1386.
Her. & Gen. 5:114-116 (1870). *C.P.* 4:479 footnote *e* (1916). DNB 16:107-109. *Nicholas Davis* (1956), p. 182. *TG* 5:133-137 (1984) (evidence that son John was by first wife Katherine, and not by second wife Joan) (until recent boundary changes, Dudley Castle was in co. Stafford, though the town was in co. Worcester).

8. JOHN DE SUTTON, of Dudley Castle, co. Stafford, son and heir by first marriage, was born at Coleshill in Arden, co. Warwick, on 6 Dec. 1361, his mother probably dying in childbirth. His birth occurred at Coleshill probably because it was the home of his father's nearest cousin, Joan (later his father's second wife), while Dudley Castle was occupied by his father's widowed mother and (since November 1359) her second husband, Richard le Fissher, with whom John de Sutton was in frequent litigation. After the death of his father about 1369 his wardship and marriage were granted to Richard FitzAlan, Earl of Arundel. During this period he was married to JOAN _____. He served in the King's Fleet under the Earl of Arundel after he came of age. JOHN DE SUTTON died on 10 Mar. 1395/6. His widow died in April 1408.
Her. & Gen. 5:115-116 (1870). *C.P.* 4:479 footnote *e* (1916). *Nicholas Davis* (1956), pp. 180-181. *TG* 5:137-138 (1984) (when John died the barony of Dudley was still in the possession of his grandmother Isabel) (Joan possibly daughter of John, Lord Arundel).

7. JOHN SUTTON, of Dudley Castle, co. Stafford, son and heir, was born in February 1380 (aged seventeen years and three weeks on death of father), or a few days before 23 Mar. 1379/80 (inquest into his inheritance from his great-grandmother Isabel). In 1401 he did homage and had livery of the Barony of Dudley and other family lands (the first time they had been vested in a male heir since the death of his great-grandfather in 1359). He was married before 10 Dec. 1401 to CONSTANCE BLOUNT, childless widow of Hugh Hastings, of Elsing, Norfolk, 7th Lord Hastings (died 2 Nov. 1396 *s.p.*), and daughter of Walter Blount, Knt., of Barton Blount, co. Derby, by Sancha de Ayala, daughter of Diego Gomez de Toledo, *alcalde maior* de Toledo. JOHN SUTTON died on 28 Aug. 1406. His widow died on 23 Sep. 1432.
Her. & Gen. 5:115-116 (1870). *C.P.* 4:479 (1916). *Nicholas Davis* (1956), pp. 167-168. *TG* 5:138

DUDLEY (cont.)

(1984).

6. JOHN SUTTON (or **DUDLEY**), Knt., K.G., son and heir, was born at Barton on 25 Dec. 1400, and was baptised at Barton-under-Needwood, co. Derby. He was married after 14 Mar. 1420/1 to **ELIZABETH BERKELEY**, childless widow of Edward Cherleton, 5th Lord Cherleton (died 14 Mar. 1420/1), and daughter of John Berkeley, Knt., of Beverstone, co. Gloucester (**descendant of Charlemagne**), by Elizabeth, daughter of John Betteshorne, Knt., of Bisterne, co. Hants. They had one son and three daughters. As Lord Steward in 1422 he brought home the body of King Henry V to England, and was chief mourner and carried the Standard of King Henry V at his funeral. He fought throughout the wars with France and was a firm supporter of the House of Lancaster in the Wars of the Roses. He was summoned to Parliament from 15 Feb. 1439/40 by writs directed *Johanni de Sutton de Duddeley militi*, whereby he is held to have become **Lord Dudley**. He was the first of his family to adopt the surname of Dudley as an alias for Sutton. He was taken prisoner with King Henry VI on 23 May 1455 at the first Battle of St. Albans, and was wounded at Blore Heath on 23 Sep. 1459. ELIZABETH BERKELEY died shortly before 8 Dec. 1478. "John Dudley knyght, lord Dudley" died testate (P.C.C., 8 Milles) in his 87th year on 30 Sep. 1487. They were buried in St. James's Priory, Dudley.

Twamley (1867), pp. 14-19. *Her. & Gen.* 5:115-118 (1870) ("authorities differ ... this confusion has been caused in a great measure by the labours of the genealogists of former times to engraft the plebeian blood of the Duke of Northumberland upon the patrician stock of Sutton"). *C.P.* 3:161-162 (1913). *C.P.* 4:479-480 (1916). *TG* 5:138-139 (1984) (the new surname of Dudley was perpetuated among the descendants of John's younger son, Dudley, John, Knt., of Atherington in Clymping, near Arundel, co. Sussex. The latter's grandson was John Dudley, Duke of Northumberland, who came to power in the reign of King Edward VI, and had a son who was Queen Elizabeth's Earl of Leicester). *TG* 5:164 (1984).

Children of John de Sutton, by Elizabeth Berkeley:

   i. **EDMUND SUTTON** (or **DUDLEY**), Knt., son and heir apparent [see next].

   ii. **JANE SUTTON**, married **THOMAS MAINWARING** [see MAINWARING 6].[1]

   iii. **ELEANOR SUTTON**, married twice [see MARSHALL 5][2] & [see WOLSELEY 6].[3]

5. EDMUND SUTTON (or **DUDLEY**), Knt., of Dudley Castle and Gatcombe, son and heir apparent, was married for the first time to **JOYCE TIPTOFT**, third and youngest daughter of John Tiptoft, Lord Tiptoft, by his second wife, Joyce (**descendant of King Edward I**), younger daughter and co-heiress of Edward Cherleton, Lord Cherleton [see CHERLETON 10 for her ancestry]. She was sister of John, Earl of Worcester. Through this alliance the Lords Dudley became co-heirs of the Baronies of Tibetot and of Cherleton. They had two sons and a daughter. He was married for the second time to **MAUD DE CLIFFORD**, widow of John Harington, Knt., and daughter of Thomas de Clifford, 8th Lord Clifford (descendant of King Edward III), by Joan Dacre (descendant of King Edward I), daughter of Thomas Dacre, Lord Dacre of Gillesland. They had seven sons and four daughters. SIR EDMUND SUTTON died between 6 July 1483 and 30 Sep. 1487 *v.p.*

Twamley (1867), pp 18-19. *Her. & Gen.* 5:117-122 (1870). *C.P.* 4:480 (1916). *NEHGR* 108:176-177 (July 1954). *TG* 5:139 (1984).

Children & grandchild of Edmund Sutton, by Joyce Tiptoft:

---

[1]Ancestors of **Robert Abell**.

[2]Ancestor, by first husband Henry Beaumont, of **Elizabeth Marshall**.

[3]Ancestor, by second husband George Stanley, of **Dannett Abney, Mary Wolseley**.

DUDLEY (cont.)

    i. **EDWARD SUTTON** (or **DUDLEY**), 2nd Lord Dudley, son and heir, born about 1459 [see next].

    ii. **JOHN SUTTON**, Knt., younger son, married _____ **CHARROLL** [see **WASHINGTON** 5].[1]

For descendants of Edmund Sutton, by Maud Clifford, see MACKWORTH 5.

4. EDWARD DUDLEY, 2nd Lord Dudley, K.B., son and heir, was born about 1459 (aged twenty-six when found to be cousin and co-heir of Edward Tiptoft, Earl of Worcester in 1 Hen. VII). He was married to **CECILY WILLOUGHBY**, daughter and co-heiress of William Willoughby, Knt., of Boston, co. Lincoln (**descendant of King Edward I**), by Joan (of **Magna Charta Surety** descent and **descendant of Charlemagne**), daughter and co-heiress of Thomas Strangeways [see WILLOUGHBY 5 for her ancestry]. In 1522 he rented a house in Tothill Street, Westminster, and presumably resided there. EDWARD DUDLEY, Lord Dudley, died aged about seventy-two on 31 Jan. 1531/2.

    Top. & Gen. 2:317 (1853). Twamley (1867), pp. 19-25. *Her. & Gen.* 5:122-124 (1870). *H.S.P.* 16:301-302 (1881) (1563 Vis. Yorks). *C.P.* 6:141-142 (1926).

3. JOHN DUDLEY, "*Lord Quondam* [has-been]", 3rd Lord Dudley, son and heir, was born about 1495. He was married, with contract dated 1501, to **CECILY GREY**, daughter of Thomas Grey, 1st Marquess of Dorset (**descendant of King Edward I**), by Cecily, Baroness Harington and Bonville *suo jure*, daughter of William Bonville, 6th Lord Harington (**descendant of King Edward I**) [see GREY 5 for her ancestry]. She was born, say, 1497. They had five sons and three daughters, and presumably resided in Tothill Street, Westminster. He succeeded his father in 1532 and immediately began to sell his patrimony. He was never summoned to Parliament. JOHN DUDLEY, Lord Dudley, died at Westminster, and was buried at St. Margaret's, Westminster, on 18 Sep. 1553. His widow was buried with her husband on 28 Apr. 1554 (named in the parish register as "the Lady Cysslye Gray").

    Twamley (1867), pp. 25-28. *Her. & Gen.* 5:124-126 (1870). *Wm. Salt Soc.* 9:94-99 (1888) (Dugdale stated, "It is reported by credible tradition of this John Lord Dudley, that being a weak man of understanding, whereby he had exposed himself to some wants, and so became entangled in the usurer's bonds, John Dudley, then Viscount Lisle and Earl of Warwick (afterwards Duke of Northumberland), thirsting after Dudley Castle, the chief seat of the family, made those money merchants his instruments to work him out of it, which by some mortgage being at length effected, this poor lord became exposed to the charity of his friends for a subsistence, and spending the remainder of his life in visits amongst them, was commonly called the Lord *Quondam*"). *Wrottesley* (1903), p. 270.

2. CAPT. HENRY DUDLEY, Knt., second son, was born about 1517, and was named by his grandmother, Cecily, Marchioness of Dorset, in her will, dated 6 May 1527. He was a monastic auditor under Cromwell in 1535, and a soldier in Ireland in 1536 under his uncle Leonard Grey. He was a soldier in Scotland, say, 1540-3. He was married, say, 1545-50, perhaps at Boulogne, to _____ **ASHTON**, daughter of Christopher Ashton, Sr., of Fyfield, co. Berks. There is no record of any children. He fought valiantly at the siege of Boulogne in 1544, and was Captain from early 1545 when Edward Fiennes, Lord Clinton, was Chief Captain. He was Vice Admiral of the Narrow Seas 1552-3 when Edward Fiennes was Admiral. He was knighted at Hampton Court on 11 Oct. 1551. He was a close associate of his second cousin, Robert Dudley, Earl of Leicester, and was arrested on 25 July 1553 for complicity (with, among others, his father-in-law) in the rebellion of Robert's father, John Dudley, Duke of Northumberland. Henry Dudley was jailed in the Tower of London, and received a pardon from Queen Mary on 18 Oct. 1553. He was exiled in French service 1556-1563, but was in English service as "Capt. Dudley" in 1563,

---

[1] Ancestors of **John Washington**.

DUDLEY (cont.)

receiving an annuity later the same year from Queen Elizabeth "for his service". His wife died before November 1556. In 1567 he obtained from the Queen a year's protection from his creditors (renewed for two years in 1568). SIR HENRY DUDLEY died between 1568 and 1570. No will, administration of estate, or *Inq.p.m.* has been discovered.

Adlard (1862), pp. xiv-xvi. *Twamley* (1867), pp. 28-29,126-127. *Her. & Gen.* 5:125-126 (1870). *Wm. Salt Soc.* 9:98-99 (1888). *Dudley* (1886), p. 17-95. No study of the Dudley-Sutton families, including a thorough review in 1993 (as yet unpublished in detail) by Marshall K. Kirk, has uncovered any information providing direct identification of the father of Capt. Roger Dudley. The best clues remain (1) that the will of Gov. Thomas Dudley included a seal of the baronial Sutton-Dudley arms differenced with a crescent (i.e. indicating descent from a second son of a Sutton-Dudley baron), (2) that the known associations of Thomas as a young man are with individuals from families with prior connections with Capt. Henry Dudley, and (3) that American descendants of Thomas Dudley as early as 1820 believed they were descendants of John, Duke of Northumberland (also a crescent bearer, and who had two sons named Henry in the generation to be father of Roger, the American descendants being unaware that both Henrys, third cousins of this Capt. Henry, are known to have died as young men without issue). The only second son of a baron of the appropriate generation from whom a descent was possible is this Capt. Henry Dudley whose children, however, if any, are unknown. Mr. Kirk in preparing his review of the Dudleys, credits Prof. David H. Kelley for first observing "the complex circumstantial links between [Henry and Roger] in unpublished notes about 1968".

1. CAPT. ROGER DUDLEY, son, evidently, was born (perhaps in the fortress at Boulogne), say, 1550. He may be the Roger Dudley who was matriculated as pensioner at Christ College, Cambridge University, in 1566, but left without degree (when Capt. Henry Dudley was in financial difficulty). He was married, as "Mr." Roger Dudley, at Lidlington, co. Bedford, on 8 June 1575 to SUSAN (or SUSANNA) THORNE, daughter of Thomas Thorne, Gent., of Yardley-Hastings, co. Northampton, by Mary (of **Magna Charta Surety descent and descendant of Charlemagne**), daughter of Edward Purefoy, of Shalston, co. Buckingham. She was baptised at Yardley-Hastings on 5 Mar. 1559/60. The will of John Purefoy in 1579 mentions Thomas Dudley. CAPT. ROGER DUDLEY was slain in battle before October 1588, perhaps at the siege of Zutphen in 1586 (Rev. Cotton Mather of Boston wrote that Thomas Dudley's father was "Capt. Roger Dudley, who was slain in the wars, when this, his son, and one only daughter were very young"). The will of "Thomas Dorne of Yardley Hastings, Gent.", dated 29 Oct. 1588, bequeathed "to the children of Susan Dudley, my Daughter, widow, £10, to be equally divided". Cotton Mather also stated that Thomas Dudley was aided in obtaining his education by Mrs. Purefoy [sister-in-law of John Purefoy] "a gentlewoman famed in the parts about Northampton for wisdom, piety and works of charity".

Adlard (1862), pp. xiv-xvi,21-38,97. *NEHGR* 47:120-121 (Jan. 1893) (will of Edmund Yorke). *NEHGR* 56:206 (Apr. 1902) (marriage record of Thomas Dudley and Dorothy Yorke). *NEHGR* 65:189 (Apr. 1911). *NEHGR* 66:340-343 (Oct. 1912) (will of Thomas Thorne). *H.S.P.* 75:108 (1924) (1592 Vis. Kent). *NEHGR* 86:263 (July 1932) (Dudley arms: Gold a lion vert a crescent for difference). *TAG* 9:222 (Apr. 1933). *NEHGR* 139:60 (Jan. 1985) (marriage record). Marshall K. Kirk suggests that Roger made his home after his father's death with Peter Grey, "Queen's servant", whose manor of Segenhoe was two miles from Lidlington, co. Bedford, where Roger was later married. Any relationship of Peter with Roger's presumed grandmother Cecily Grey has not been established.

Children & grandchildren of Roger Dudley, by Susanna Thorne:

    i. **GOV. THOMAS DUDLEY**, baptised Yardley-Hastings, co. Northampton, 12 Oct. 1576, became a page for William, Lord Compton (afterwards Earl of Northampton), say, 1590-5, and steward for the latter's cousin, Thomas, Lord Clinton in 1616; resided Northampton as a young man, raised a company of soldiers to join the forces sent by Queen Elizabeth to aid King Henry IV of France, and to serve at the siege of Amiens; returned to take up practice of law; settled in Massachusetts in 1630; Governor and Deputy-Governor of Massachusetts, 1630-1653; buried

DUDLEY (cont.)

aged seventy-six years at Roxbury on 25 Apr. 1653; married, first, at Hardingstone, near Northampton, 25 Apr 1603 **DOROTHY YORKE**, buried at Roxbury 27 Dec. 1643, daughter of Edmund Yorke, of Cotton End, co. Northampton (will of Edmund Yorke, dated 18 Nov 1614, mentions his grandchildren Samuel and Anne Dudley, and appoints Thomas Dudley one of his overseers); married, second, at Roxbury 14 Apr. 1644 **KATHERINE (DEIGHTON) HACKBURNE**, baptised at Gloucester 16 Jan. 1614/5, died 20 Aug. 1671, widow of Samuel Hackburne, and daughter of Dr. John Deighton, Gent., of St. Nicholas, Gloucester, by Jane Basset; widow Katherine, married, third, REV. JOHN ALLIN of Dedham and had chldren [see DEIGHTON 1].

    a. **REV. SAMUEL DUDLEY**, baptised All Saints, Northampton, 30 Nov. 1608, of Exeter, New Hampshire, married, first, **MARY WINTHROP**, second, **MARY BYLEY**. Eighteen children.

    b. **ANNE DUDLEY**, born about 1612; married **GOV. SIMON BRADSTREET**. Eight children.

    c. **PATIENCE DUDLEY**, married **MAJ.-GEN. DANIEL DENNISON**. Two children.

    d. **SARAH DUDLEY**, baptised Sempringham, co. Lincoln, 23 July 1620, married, first, **MAJ. BENJAMIN KEAYNE**, second, **THOMAS PACY**.

    e. **MERCY DUDLEY**, born 27 Sep. 1621, died Newbury, Massachusetts, 1 July 1691; married 1639 **REV. JOHN WOODBRIDGE** of Andover, Massachusetts. Eight children.

    f. **DEBORAH DUDLEY**, born 27 Feb. 1644/5, married **JONATHAN WADE**.

    g. **GOV. JOSEPH DUDLEY**, born 23 Sep 1647; married **REBECCA TYNG**. Thirteen children.

    h. **PAUL DUDLEY**, born 8 Sep. 1650, married **MARY LEVERETT**. Three sons.

b. **MARY DUDLEY**, baptised Yardley Hastings 16 Oct. 1580 ("daughter of Mr Dudley").

* * *

DYMOKE

EDWARD I OF ENGLAND, King of England, married, second, **MARGUERITE DE FRANCE**.
THOMAS OF NORFOLK [of *Brotherton*], married **ALICE DE HALES**.
MARGARET OF NORFOLK, married **JOHN DE SEGRAVE**, 4th Lord Segrave.
ELIZABETH DE SEGRAVE, married **JOHN DE MOWBRAY**, 4th Lord Mowbray.
ALIANOR DE MOWBRAY, married **JOHN DE WELLES**, Knt., 5th Lord Welles.
EUDO DE WELLES, married **MAUD DE GREYSTOKE**.
LIONEL DE WELLES, Knt., Lord Welles, married **JOAN DE WATERTON** [see WELLES 7].

5. **MARGARET DE WELLES**, third daughter and co-heiress of John de Welles, 10th Lord Welles, was married for the first time to **THOMAS DYMOKE**, Knt., of Scrivelsby, co. Lincoln, son of Philip Dymoke, Knt., of Scrivelsby, by Joan, daughter of Robert Conyers, Knt., of Sockburn, Durham. He was born about 1428 (aged twenty-seven and more at his father's death). SIR THOMAS DYMOKE was beheaded by the Yorkists on 12 Mar. 1470, before the battle of Stamford. She was married for the second time before 8 May 1472 to **ROBERT RADCLIFFE**, son of John Radcliffe, Knt. She died on 13 July 1480.

    Gen. 4:19 (1880) (Dymoke arms: *Sable*, two lions passant *argent* crowned *or*). *H.S.P.* 55:1204 (1906) (Maddison Linc. Ped.) ("Champion to Edward IV"). *C.P.* 12(2):449 footnote *j* (1959). *Paget* (1977), p. 401.

Children of Thomas Dymoke, by Margaret de Welles:

    i. **ROBERT DYMOKE**, Knt. [see next].

DYMOKE (cont.)

    ii.   **LIONEL DYMOKE**, Knt., married **JOAN GRIFFITH** [see SKIPWITH 5].[1]

4. ROBERT DYMOKE, Knt., of Scrivelsby, co. Lincoln, Sheriff of Lincolnshire, Merchant of the Staple of Calais, son and heir, was born in 1461 (aged nine at his father's death). He was Champion to Kings Richard III, Henry VII and Henry VIII, and commander at the siege of Tournai. He was married for the first time to **ANNE SPARROW**, widow of Angel Donne, Alderman of London, and daughter and heiress of John Sparrow, of London. They had two sons and one daughter. He was married for the second time to **JANE CRESMORE**, daughter of Alexander Cresmore, and had three daughters. SIR ROBERT DYMOKE died testate on 13 Apr. 1544.
    Gen. 4:19 (1880). *H.S.P.* 55:1204-1205 (1906). *Paget* (1977), p. 255.

    Child of Robert Dymoke, by Anne Sparrow:
      i.   **EDWARD DYMOKE**, Knt., born 1508, married **ANNE TAILBOYS** [see READE 3].[2]

* * *

DYMOKE OF MAREHAM-ON-THE-HILL see SKIPWITH

* * *

ECHINGHAM

HENRY III OF ENGLAND, King of England, married **ALIANORE DE PROVENCE**.
EDMUND OF LANCASTER *Crouchback*, Earl of Lancaster, married, **BLANCHE D'ARTOIS**.
HENRY OF LANCASTER, Duke of Lancaster, married **MAUD DE CHAWORTH**.
ALIANOR OF LANCASTER, married **RICHARD FITZ ALAN**, Earl of Arundel.
JOHN DE ARUNDEL, Lord Arundel, married **ALIANOR MALTRAVERS** [see BROWNE 11].

9. JOAN DE ARUNDEL, elder daughter, was married for the first time to **WILLIAM DE BRIEN**, Knt., of Kemsing, Kent, second son of Guy de Brien, Knt. He died on 23 Sep. 1395 *s.p.*, and was buried at Seal, Kent. She was married for the second time about 1401 to **WILLIAM DE ECHINGHAM**, Knt., of Etchingham, Sussex, son of William de Echingham, Knt., of Etchingham, by his wife Elizabeth. She died on 1 Sep. 1404. SIR WILLIAM DE ECHINGHAM died on 20 Mar. 1412/13. They, and their son Thomas, were buried at Etchingham.
    Top. & Gen. 2:336 (citing Vincent's *Collections* in College of Arms). *Top. & Gen.* 3:254 (1858) (Agnes, widow of Sir William Arundel, K.G., brother of this Joan, in her will, dated 6 Sep. 1401, mentions her sister "Brian"). *Arch. Jour.* 7:264-273 (1850). *Echyngham* (1850), p. 13. *Gen. (n.s.)* 21:243-245 (1905) ("Joan, daughter of John Fitzalan, or Arundel, *jure uxoris* Lord Maltravers"). *TG* 5:137 (1984).

    Children of William de Echingham, by Joan de Arundel:
      i.   **THOMAS DE ECHINGHAM**, born about 1401 [see next].

---

[1]Ancestors of **William Asfordby, Joseph Bolles**.

[2]Ancestors of **George Reade**.

ECHINGHAM (cont.)

ii. JOAN DE ECHINGHAM, married JOHN BAYNTON [see BAYNTON 6].[1]

8. THOMAS DE ECHINGHAM, Knt., of Etchingham, was born about 1401 (aged thirteen and more at father's death). He was married for the first time to AGNES SHOYSWELL, daughter of John de Shoyswell, of Shoyswell, Sussex. He was married for the second time between 1415 and 1424 to **MARGARET KNYVETT**, childless widow of Robert de Tye, Knt., of Barsham (died 1415), and daughter of John Knyvett, Sr., of Norfolk, by his wife Joan. SIR THOMAS DE ECHINGHAM died on 15 Oct. 1444 (will dated 20 Aug., proved at Lambeth 28 Oct. 1444), and was buried at Etchingham. His widow was living in 1467.

Arch. Jour. 7:268 (1850). *Echyngham* (1850), pp. 13-14. *Gen. (n.s.)* 21:243-250 (1905). *C.P.* 1:342 (1910). *Paget* (1977), p. 445.

7. THOMAS DE ECHINGHAM, Knt., of Etchingham, Sheriff of Surrey and Sussex, was born about 1425 (aged twenty and more in 1445). He was married to **MARGARET WEST**, daughter of Reynold de West, Knt., 3rd Lord la Warre (**descendant of King Henry III**), by Margaret, daughter of Robert Thorley, of Tybeste, Cornwall [see HUMPHREY 8 for her ancestry]. SIR THOMAS DE ECHINGHAM died on 20 Jan. 1482/3, and was buried at Etchingham.

Arch. Jour. 7:268 (1850) ("although a person of some consideration, outlived both the political influence and the greatness of his family"). *C.P.* (1936) 9:336-337. *Paget* (1977), p. 445.

6. MARGARET DE ECHINGHAM, younger daughter and eventual co-heiress, was married for the first time to **WILLIAM BLOUNT**, Knt., M.P. for Derby, son and heir apparent of Walter de Blount, Knt., Lord Mountjoy, of Elvaston, co. Derby (**descendant of Charlemagne**), by Ellen, daughter of John Byron, Knt., of Clayton, near Manchester, co. Lancaster. They had two sons and two daughters. SIR WILLIAM BLOUNT died of wounds fighting for King Edward IV at the battle of Barnet on 14 Apr. 1471 *v.p.* His widow was married for the second time about 1478 to JOHN ELRINGTON, Knt., of Hackney, Middlesex, Treasurer of the Household of King Edward IV. They had a son Edward. She was living on 11 July 1482 when her second husband's will was proved. They were buried at Shoreditch, Middlesex.

Echyngham (1850), p. 14. *H.S.P.* 27:20 (1888) (1569 Vis. Worc.). *C.P.* 9:336-337 (1936). *C.P.* 12(2):794 (1959). *Paget* (1977), p. 267.

Child of William Blount, by Margaret de Echingham:
    i. **ELIZABETH BLOUNT**, married **ANDREWS WINDSOR**, Lord Windsor [see LUDLOW 5].[2]

* * *

ELLIS

EDWARD I OF ENGLAND, King of England, married MARGUERITE DE FRANCE.
THOMAS OF NORFOLK [*of Brotherton*], Earl of Norfolk, married ALICE DE HALES.
MARGARET OF NORFOLK, married JOHN DE SEGRAVE, 4th Lord Segrave.
ELIZABETH DE SEGRAVE, married JOHN DE MOWBRAY, 4th Lord Mowbray.
JOAN DE MOWBRAY, married THOMAS GRAY, Knt.

---

[1] Ancestors of **Alice Baynton, Mary Gye**.

[2] Ancestors of **Gabriel, Roger & Sarah Ludlow, John Oxenbridge**.

ELLIS (cont.)

JOHN GREY, Knt., married JOAN CHERLETON.
HENRY GREY, Knt., Earl of Tancarville, married ANTIGONE OF GLOUCESTER.
ELIZABETH GREY, married ROGER KYNASTON, Knt. [see LLOYD 6].

7. MARY KYNASTON, married HYWEL AP JENKIN.
H.S.P. 29:295 (1889) (1623 Vis. Salop) (Howell ap Jenkin ap Jerworth ap Eignion) (Arms: Ermine, a saltire *gules*).

6. HUMPHREY AP HYWEL AP IEVAN, of Yns-y-maen-gwyn, was married to ANNE HERBERT, daughter of Richard Herbert, Knt., of Colebrook.
Glenn (1896), pp. 215,307.

5. JANE FERCH HUMPHREY AP HYWEL, was married to GRUFFYDD AP HYWEL, of Nannau, son of Howell ap David ap Meuric Vaughan, of Nannau, by Ellin, daughter of Robert Salisbury, of Llanrwst. They had two sons and three daughters. He was living 1541/2.
Glenn (1896), p. 215,218 (Hugh Nannau, the eldest son, signed the pedigree as head of the family, 24 July 1588).

4. SION (or JOHN) AP GRUFFYDD, was married to ELSBETH FERCH DAFYDD LLWYD, of Trawvynydd. They had one son and two daughters. He held land in the township of Dyffrydan in Dôlgelly, co. Merioneth.
Glenn (1896), pp. 215,218.

3. LEWYS AP SION AP GRUFFYDD, Gent., of Dyffryden, co. Merioneth, was married to ELLIN FERCH HYWEL AP GRUFFYDD. They had two sons. In 1617 he built a stone house at Bryn Mawr near Dôlgelly, co. Merioneth (described in 1896 as still standing), and was living on 28 Aug. 1654.
Glenn (1896), pp. 215,219.

Children & grandchild of Lewys ap John Gruffudd, by Ellin verch Hywel ap Gruffudd:
   i. REES AP LEWYS [see next].
   ii. OWAIN AP LEWYS, married MARY FERCH TUDUR VAUGHN.
      a. ROBERT AB OWAIN, married MARGARET FERCH SION AP LEWYS. Parents of MARGARET ROBERTS [see below].

2. REES AP LEWYS AP JOHN GRUFFUDD, Gent., was married to CATRIN FERCH ELISSA AP DAFYDD, daughter of Elissa ap Davydd ap Owen ap Thomas ap Howell ap Mrhedydd ap Gruffydd Derwas, by Mary ferch Sion ap David ap Gruffydd. They had four sons.
Glenn (1896), pp. 215,219-220.

1. ELLIS AP REES (or ELLIS PRICE), Gent., of Bryn Mawr, near Dôlgelly, co. Merioneth, second son, was married, with marriage settlement dated 1 Jan. 1649, to ANNE FERCH HUMPHREY, daughter of Humphrey ap Hugh ap David ap Howell ap Gronw, Gent., of Llwyngwril, co. Merioneth, by Elizabeth (**descendant of King Edward I**), daughter of John Powell, of Llanwyddyn, co. Monmouth [see OWEN 1 for her ancestry]. They had one son. ELLIS AP REES, GENT., was living 11th 1st Mo. [Mar.] 1678/9, and was dead in 1696.
Glenn (1896), pp. 205-231 (includes manuscript pedigree of ancestors prepared by Rowland Ellis shortly before 1697) (cites "The Herald's visitations made out 1585-1601, and with parish registers and other documents remaining in Wales"). *NEHGR* 108:33 (Jan. 1954) (Ellis arms: Gold a lion azure).

Child of Ellis ap Rees, by Anne ferch Humphrey:
   i. ROWLAND ELLIS, born Bryn Mawr, Dyffrdan, co. Merioneth, Wales, 1650, became Friend in 1672, imprisoned 1676, emigrated with son Rowland from Milford Haven on 16th 8th mo. [Oct.] 1686, arriving Pennsylvania 2nd mo. [Apr.] 1687, settled at Bryn Mawr, returned spring 1688, returned with remaining family 1697, died Gwynedd, Pennsylvania 7th mo. [Sep.] 1731; married, first, about 1672, MARGARET ELLIS, second, his second cousin, MARGARET ROBERTS [see

ELLIS (cont.)

ELLIS 3.ii.a above]. Two daughters by first marriage. Five children by second marriage.
a. ANNE ELLIS, married REV. RICHARD JOHNSTON, Curate of Dôlgelly. Issue.
b. JANE ELLIS, died young.
c. ELIZABETH ELLIS, died unmarried.
d. ROWLAND ELLIS, JR, died s.p.
e. ROBERT ELLIS, died s.p.
f. ELEANOR ELLIS, born Bryn Mawr, Wales, 1685, married JOHN EVANS, of Gwynedd. Eight children.
g. CATHERINE ELLIS, born 1697, died unmarried.

* * *

ELSING

EDWARD I OF ENGLAND, King of England, married ALIANORE DE CASTILLE.
JOAN OF ENGLAND [of Acre], married GILBERT DE CLARE, Earl of Gloucester.
ALIANOR DE CLARE, married HUGH LE DESPENSER, 2nd Lord Despenser.
EDWARD DESPENSER, Knt., married ANNE DE FERRERS.
EDWARD DESPENSER, married ELIZABETH DE BURGHERSH [see CLARE 9].

8. ANNE DESPENSER, third daughter, was married for the first time before 1 Nov. 1376 to HUGH HASTINGS, Knt., of Elsing, Norfolk, and Norton, co. York, son and heir of Hugh Hastings, Knt. (of **Magna Charta Surety descent** and **descendant of Charlemagne**), by his wife Margaret. On 16 June 1386 he gave evidence in the Scrope and Grosvenor controversy. SIR HUGH HASTINGS died on an expedition to Spain with the Duke of Lancaster on 6 Nov. 1386. She was married for the second time to THOMAS DE MORLEY, Knt., of Morley, Norfolk, 4th Lord Morley (died 24 Sep. 1416). ANNE DESPENSER died testate on 30 or 31 Oct. 1426.
H.S.P. 16:155 (1881) (1563 Vis. Yorks) (names only two sons). C.P. 6:355-357 (1926).

Children of Hugh Hastings, by Anne Despenser:
i. EDWARD HASTINGS, Knt., born 21 May 1382 [see next].
ii. MARGARET HASTINGS, married JOHN WINGFIELD, Knt. [see LETHERINGHAM 9].[1]

7. EDWARD HASTINGS, Knt., of Elsing, Fenwick, etc., 8th Lord Hastings *de jure*, was born at Fenwick on 21 May 1382, and was brother and heir of Hugh Hastings. He was married for the first time to MURIEL DE DINHAM, daughter of John de Dinham, Knt., of Hartland, co. Devon (of **baronial** descent), by Muriel, daughter of Thomas de Courtenay, Knt., of Woodhuish, co. Devon (of **Magna Charta Surety descent** and **descendant of Charlemagne**). He was married for the second time to MARGERY CLIFTON, daughter of Robert Clifton, Knt., of Buckenham, Norfolk, by his wife Alice. He was committed to the Tower on 11 July 1403. The right to bear the undifferenced Arms of Hastinges was decided against him in the Court of Chivalry on 9 May 1410, and in favour of his opponent Reynold, Lord Grey of Ruthin, heir to the sister of the whole blood, in preference to his own claim as heir to the brother of the half-blood, of John, Lord Hastinges, ancestor of the Earls of

---

[1]Ancestors of **James Claypoole, Francis Dade, Richard Palgrave, Thomas Wingfield**.

ELSING (cont.)

Pembroke. On refusing to pay the costs of his suit of appeal (lest he should thereby acknowledge its justice), he was imprisoned (about 1417) in the Marshalsea apparently till his death. EDWARD HASTINGS, Lord Hastings, died aged fifty-five on 6 Jan. 1437/8. His widow was married for the second time to John Wymondham, of Felbridge and Runton, Norfok (died 4 June 1475). She died in 1456 and was buried at Austin Friars', Norwich.

H.S.P. 16:155 (1881). *C.P.* 6:358-360 (1926).

6. JOHN HASTINGS, of Gressenhall, Elsing, Fenwick, etc., 9th Lord Hastings *de jure*, son and heir by first marriage, was born about 1412 (aged twenty-six and more at his father's death). He was married after 21 Apr. 1434 to **ANNE MORLEY**, daughter of Thomas Morley, 5th Lord Morley, by Isabel (**descendant of King Edward I**), daughter of Michael de la Pole, Earl of Suffolk [see POLE 12.ii for her ancestry]. They were mentioned in the will of her mother dated 3 May 1464. She died in 1471. JOHN HASTINGS, Lord Hastings, died at Elsing on 9 Apr. 1477. They were buried in Gressenhall Church (M.I.).

H.S.P. 16:155 (1881). *C.P.* 6:360-363 (1926).

5. ELIZABETH HASTINGS, was born probably before 1440. She was married to **ROBERT HILDYARD**, Knt., of Winestead, East Riding, co. York, son of Robert Hildyard, by Katherine, daughter and co-heiress of Thomas de la Hay, of Spaldington. He was born, say, 1435. They had eleven sons and three daughters. He was knighted "on the field of Selford" by the Earl of Northumberland on 22 Aug. 1482. SIR ROBERT HILDYARD died testate on 21 May 1501.

Sur.Soc. 53:13 (will of his father) ("This is the well-known "Robin of Redesdale," as he was called, so famous in the War of the Roses"). *H.S.P.* 16:155-156 (1881) ("Elsabeth wyff to Sir Robert Hyllyard" identified as daughter of "John Hastynges of Fenwyke nigh Ardesley"). *Sur.Soc.* 144:136 (1930) (1480 Vis. North) ("Robertus Helyard = Elizabeth filia Iohannis Hastinges de Fenwicke"). *Paget* (1977), p. 420. *TAG* 69:137 (July 1994) (descent of William Skepper from King Edward I).

Children of Robert Hildyard, by Elizabeth Hastings:

i. **PETER HILDYARD**, son and heir, born about 1460 [see SKEPPER 4].[1]

ii. **KATHERINE HILDYARD**, married **WILLIAM GIRLINGTON** [see GIRLINGTON 6].[2]

* * *

FARRAR

EDWARD I OF ENGLAND, King of England, married **ALIANORE DE CASTILLE**.
JOAN OF ENGLAND [*of Acre*], married **GILBERT DE CLARE**, Earl of Gloucester.
ALIANOR DE CLARE, married **HUGH LE DESPENSER**, 2nd Lord Despenser.
EDWARD DESPENSER, Knt., married **ANNE DE FERRERS**.
EDWARD DESPENSER, 4th Lord le Despenser, married **ELIZABETH DE BURGHERSH**.
ANNE DESPENSER, married **HUGH HASTINGS**, Knt.
EDWARD HASTINGS, Knt., married **MURIEL DE DINHAM**.
JOHN HASTINGS, 9th Lord Hastings, married **ANNE MORLEY**.
ELIZABETH HASTINGS, married **ROBERT HILDYARD**.

---

[1] Ancestors of **William Skepper**.

[2] Ancestors of **William Asfordby, William Farrar**.

FARRAR (cont.)

KATHERINE HILDYARD, married WILLIAM GIRLINGTON.
ISABEL GIRLINGTON, married CHRISTOPHER KELKE [see GIRLINGTON 5].

2. **WILLIAM KELKE**, of Barnetby-le-Wold, co. Lincoln, Mercer of London, younger son, was born after 1519. He was married to **THOMASINE SKERNE**, daughter of Percival Skerne. "William Kelcke of London" died testate in 1552 (will dated 16 June 1552 and proved 28 June 1552, names brother Francis, wife Thomasyn, father-in-law Percival Skerne, and his [unnamed] children, P.C.C., 18 Powell). His widow evidently died before 31 Aug. 1566 when Jeffrey Ducket was appointed administrator of the estate "during the minority of children Elizabeth and Cicely Kelke".
H.S.P. 51:557 (1903) (Maddison Linc. Ped.). *Holmes* (1972), pp. 69-77. *Adventurers* (1987), p. 273.

1. **CECILY KELKE**, was born before 1552, and was married at St. Sepulchre's Without Newgate, London, on 25 Aug. 1574 to **JOHN FARRAR**, the elder, Esq., of Croxton, co. Lincoln, and St. Mary, Aldermanbury, London, younger son of William Farrar, of Ewood in Midgley in Halifax, co. York, by Margaret, daughter of Hugh Lacy, Esq., of Brearley Hall, Halifax, co. York. JOHN FARRAR, ESQ., died in 1628 (will dated 24 Apr. 1628, proved 28 May 1628, P.C.C., 50 Barrington, devised property to son William Farrar and £50 at his return to England).
Holmes (1972), pp. 25-32 (Farrar arms: *Argent*, on a bend engrailed *gules* three horse-shoes of the field). *NEHGR* 107:190 (July 1953) (Farrar arms: Silver a bend engrailed sable on the bend three horse-shoes of the field, a crescent for difference - as used by the immigrant and confirmed by the College of Arms 1651). *Adventurers* (1987), pp. 273-279.

Child and grandchildren of John Farrar, by Cecily Kelke:

i. **WILLIAM FARRAR**, baptised Croxton, co. Lincoln, 28 Apr. 1583, third son, emigrated 16 Mar. 1617/8 on the *Neptune* with Lord De La Warr, arriving Virginia August 1618, of Henrico County, Virginia, in London in 1631, returned to Virginia, died 1637; married **CECILY (_____) (BAYLY) JORDAN**.

   a. **CECILY FARRAR**, born 1625, living 1631, married, perhaps, ISAAC HUTCHINS. If so, issue.

   b. **WILLIAM FARRAR**, born 1627, of Henrico County, member House of Burgesses, married **MARY _____**. Five children.

   c. **JOHN FARRAR**, born about 1632, of Henrico County, member House of Burgesses, died unmarried.

* * *

FENWICK

EDWARD I OF ENGLAND, King of England, married MARGUERITE DE FRANCE.
THOMAS OF NORFOLK [*of Brotherton*], Earl of Norfolk, married ALICE DE HALES.
MARGARET OF NORFOLK, married JOHN DE SEGRAVE, 4th Lord Segrave.
ELIZABETH DE SEGRAVE, married JOHN DE MOWBRAY, 4th Lord Mowbray.
JOAN DE MOWBRAY, married THOMAS GRAY, Knt.
MAUD GRAY, married ROBERT OGLE, Knt.
MARGARET OGLE, married ROBERT HARBOTTLE, Knt.
BERTRAM HARBOTTLE, Esq., married JOAN LUMLEY [see HARBOTTLE 7].

6. **AGNES HARBOTTLE**, was married to **ROGER FENWICK**, Knt., Esquire of the Body to King Henry VIII, Constable of Newcastle, Sheriff of Northumberland, son of John Fenwick, Esq., of Newburn, by Elizabeth, daughter of Roger Widdrington, Esq., Sheriff of Northumberland. SIR ROGER FENWICK died 1513/4.

FENWICK (cont.)

Surtees (1820) 2:225. *Hodgson* (1832), pp. 75,113,234-235,262. *H.S.P.* 16:121 (1881) (1563 Vis. Yorks) ("Roger Fenwyke of Mydelton in com. Northumberland = ... doughter of Wedryngton of Wedryngton"). *Northumberland* 12:chart betw.352-353 (1926).

5. **RALPH FENWICK**, of Stanton *jure uxoris*, son and heir, was married to **MARGERY MITFORD**, heiress of Stanton, held *in capite* of the king by knight's service. They had three sons and three daughters. RALPH FENWICK, ESQ., died before 10 Aug. 1535 when his widow entailed Stanton on their son John and Langfhaws on their son Anthony. She died testate.
    Hodgson (1832), pp. 75,112-113 (Margery was a descendant (in an unknown way) of Gerard Mitford, husband, by marriage contract dated 20 July 1426, of Margery, daughter of Robert Corbet, descendant of Patrick fifth Earl of Dunbar). *H.S.P.* 16:121 (1881) ("Sir Raff Fenwyke son & heyre to Roger = Margery doughter & sole heyre to Walter Corbet of Stanton Knight"). *Northumberland* 12:chart betw. 352-353 (1926) (follows H.S.P.).

4. **JOHN FENWICK**, Esq., of Stanton, was married to **MARY GREY**, daughter and co-heiress of Ralph Grey, Knt., of Chillingham (**descendant of King Edward I**) [see GRAY 5 for her ancestry]. She was born about 1505 (aged twelve in 1517). They had four sons and two daughters. She died on 22 Nov. 1571.
    Hodgson (1832), pp. 75,113. *Raine* (1852), chart between 326-327. *H.S.P.* 16:121 (1881). *Northumberland* (1935) 14: chart following p. 328.

3. **RALPH FENWICK**, Esq., of Stanton, son and heir, was married to **BARBARA OGLE**, daughter of John Ogle, Esq., of Ogle Castle. They had two sons and one daughter.
    Hodgson (1832), p. 113. *H.S.P.* 16:121 (1881). *Ogle* (1902), pp. 178-179,181.

2. **RICHARD FENWICK**, Esq., son and heir, was born at Heaton. He was married for the first time to **MARGARET MILLS**, daughter of William Mills of Gray's Inn, London, and Croydon, Surrey. He was married for the second time to DOROTHY THORNTON, daughter of Roger Thornton, of Witton.
    Hodgson (1832), p. 113. *H.S.P.* 16:121 (1881).

1. **WILLIAM FENWICK**, Esq., of Stanton, was born on 22 Sep. 1581. He was admitted to Gray's Inn on 22 Mar. 1597/8. He was married on 27 July 1605 to **ELIZABETH GARGRAVE**, daughter of Cotton Gargrave, Knt., of Nostal, co. York, by Anne, daughter of Thomas Waterton. She was baptised at Wragby, co. York, on 19 Feb. 1577/8. WILLIAM FENWICK, ESQ., died on 12 June 1647.
    Hodgson (1832), p. 113. *PMHB* 49:151-162 (1925) (William held the manor of Stanton *in capite* of the king by knight's service). *PMHB* 50:267-272. Yorks P.R.S. 105:24,65. Misc. Gen. et Her., 1st ser. 1:226-227. *NEHGR* 82:154 (Apr. 1928) (arms of John Fenwick, et al.: Silver a chief gules six martlets three two and one counterchanged). *DAB* 6:330-331 (1931) (John Fenwick). *Roberts* (1993), p. 238 (Gargrave descent from Edward I).

Children of William Fenwick, by Elizabeth Gargrave:

  i. EDWARD FENWICK, Esq., of Stanton, eldest son and heir, born 29 Oct. 1606, married SARAH NEVILLE. Eleven children, including Robert Fenwick (father of John Fenwick of South Carolina). See *Roberts* (1993), p. 238.

  ii. JOHN FENWICK, younger son, born 1618, admitted to Gray's Inn, 15 Mar. 1638/9, cavalry major under Cromwell, joined Society of Friends, supporter of establishment of Quaker colony in America, emigrated on the *Griffin*, died testate Salem, New Jersey (will, proved 16 Apr. 1684, of "John Fenwick, late of Binfield in the Countie of Berks in the Kingdom of England Esq. the late absolute Lord or Chiefepropriate[r] by law & survivorship of the province of Nova Caesaria or New Jersey and now of Fenwick's Colony" names many grandchildren (Archives of the State of New Jersey, First Series, 23:162); married first, **ELIZABETH COVERT**, with three daughters, second MARY BURDETT (did not emigrate to New Jersey).

  iii. PRISCILLA FENWICK, married ROLAND NEVET (ancestors of Ralph Eddowes of Pennsylvania. See *Roberts* (1993), pp. 238-239).

FERRERS

EDWARD I OF ENGLAND, King of England, married ALIANORE DE CASTILLE.
JOAN OF ENGLAND [*of Acre*], married GILBERT DE CLARE, Earl of Gloucester.
MARGARET DE CLARE, married HUGH DE AUDLEY, 8th Earl of Gloucester.
MARGARET DE AUDLEY, married RALPH DE STAFFORD [see AUDLEY 12].

11. ELIZABETH DE STAFFORD, was born about 1337 (aged under thirteen at time of marriage). She was married for the first time, with contract dated 1 Mar. 1346/7, to **FULK LE STRANGE**. He died of the pestilence on 30 Aug. or 2 Sep. 1349 *s.p.* She was married for the second time, with royal licence dated 19 Oct. 1349, to **JOHN DE FERRERS**, Knt., of Chartley, son and heir by Robert de Ferrers, Knt., of Chartley, co. Stafford (of **Magna Charta Surety descent** and **descendant of Charlemagne**), by his first wife Margaret. He was born at Southoe, co. Huntingdon, on or about 10 Aug. 1331. SIR JOHN DE FERRERS died beyond seas, being slain at the battle of Najera on 3 Apr. 1367. She was married for the third time to REYNOLD DE COBHAM, Knt., of Sterborough, Surrey, Lord Cobham (died 3 or 6 July 1403). She died on 7 Aug. 1375.
 C.P. 3:353-354 (1913). *C.P.* 5:313-315, 320 chart (1926).

10. ROBERT DE FERRERS, Knt., of Chartley, was born in Staffordshire on 31 Oct. 1357 or 1359. He was married for the first time after 16 Sep. 1376 to ELIZABETH _____. She was living on 13 Jan. 1378/9. He was married for the second time to **MARGARET LE DESPENSER**, fourth and youngest daughter of Edward le Despenser, of Glamorgan and Morgannwg, 4th Lord Despenser (**descendant of King Edward I**), by Elizabeth, daughter of Bartholomew de Burghersh, of Ewyas Lacy, co. Hereford, etc., 4th Lord Burghersh [see CLARE 9 for her ancestry]. SIR ROBERT DE FERRERS died on 12 or 13 Mar. 1412/13. His widow died on 3 Nov. 1415. They were buried at Merevale Abbey.
 C.P. 5:315-317, 320 chart (1926). *Paget* (1977), p. 412.

Children of Robert de Ferrers, by Margaret le Despenser:
 i. **EDMUND DE FERRERS**, Knt., born about 1387 [see next].
 ii. **PHILIPPE DE FERRERS**, married THOMAS GREENE, Knt. [see MARBURY 7].[1]

9. EDMUND DE FERRERS, Knt., of Chartley, was born about 1387 (aged twenty-six or more in 1413). About 1413, assisted by his brothers, Thomas and Edward, he carried on a private war with the Erdeswikes of Sandon, near Chartley, receiving a pardon on 24 Jan. 1414/5. He was married to **ELLEN ROCHE**, Lady of Castle Bromwich, second daughter and co-heiress of Thomas Roche, of Castle Bromwich, co. Warwick, by Elizabeth, daughter and heiress of Thomas Birmingham, Knt., and niece and heiress of John Birmingham, Knt., of Birmingham, co. Warwick, Kingston Bagpuze, co. Berks, etc. He accompanied the King to France in August 1415, and was at the siege of Harfleur, and at the Battle of Agincourt on 25 Oct. 1415. SIR EDMUND DE FERRERS died on 17 Dec. 1435. His widow was married for the second time, as his first wife, to Philip Chetwynd, Knt., of Ingestre, co. Stafford, and Grendon, co. Warwick (died 10 May 1444 *s.p.*). She died on 4 Nov. 1440.
 C.P. 5:317-319 (1926) (usually called Lord Ferrers of Chartley), 320 chart.

8. WILLIAM DE FERRERS, Knt., of Chartley, was born about 1412 (aged twenty-three and more in 1435/6). He was married to **ELIZABETH BELKNAP**, daughter of Hamon Belknap, of Seintlynge in St. Mary Cray, Kent, Knell, Sussex, etc., by Joan (of **Magna Charta Surety descent** and **descendant of Charlemagne**), younger

---

[1] Ancestors of **Grace Chetwode, Anne & Catherine Marbury**.

FERRERS (cont.)

daughter and in her issue co-heiress of Thomas Boteler, Knt., of Sudeley, co. Gloucester (**descendant of Charlemagne**). SIR WILLIAM DE FERRERS died on 9 June 1450 *s.p.m.* His widow died on 28 May 1471.

C.P. 5:320-321 (1926) (frequently called Lord Ferrers).

7. ANNE DE FERRERS, daughter and heiress, was born about November 1438 (aged eleven years and eight months in July 1450). She was married for the first time before 26 Nov. 1446 to **WALTER DEVEREUX**, Knt., K.G., of Weobley and Bodenham, co. Hereford, Branston, Cottesbach and Newbold Verdon, co. Leicester, Market Rasen, co. Lincoln, etc., M.P. for Herefordshire, son and heir of Walter Devereux, Knt., of Weobley and Bodenham, etc., by Elizabeth, daughter and heiress of John Merbury, Chief Justice in South Wales. He was born about 1433 (aged twenty-six and more in 1459). She died aged thirty on 9 Jan. 1468/9. He was married for the second time to Jane _____. He was knighted after the Battle of Towton on 29 Mar. 1461. On account of his great services against King Henry VI he was raised to the rank of a Baron, thereby becoming **Lord Ferrers**. He was summoned to Parliament from 26 July 1461 by writs directed *Waltero Devereux de Ferrers militi*. WALTER DEVEREUX, Lord Ferrers, was slain at the battle of Bosworth on 22 Aug. 1485, and was attainted of high treason in Parliament. His widow was married for the second time to THOMAS VAUGHAN (living 18 Nov. 1492), for the third time to EDWARD BLOUNT, Knt., of Sodington, co. Worcester (died testate 6 July 1499 *s.p.*, P.C.C., 37 Horne), and for the fourth time to THOMAS POYNTZ. She was living on 9 Nov. 1512.

H.S.P. 12:279 (1877) (1619 Vis. Warwick). *C.P.* 5:321-25 (1926). *Paget* (1977), p. 440.

6. ELIZABETH DEVEREUX, was married before 1478 to **RICHARD CORBET**, Knt., of Moreton Corbet, co. Salop, son of Roger Corbet, Knt., of Moreton Corbet (**descendant of Charlemagne**), by Elizabeth (**descendant of Charlemagne**), daughter of Thomas Hopton, Knt., of Stanton, co. Salop. He was born in 1451. SIR RICHARD CORBET died on 6 Dec. 1493. His widow was married for the second time to THOMAS LEIGHTON, Knt., and died in 1541.

H.S.P. 12:279 (1877). *Paget* (1977), p. 267.

5. ROBERT CORBET, Knt., of Moreton Corbet, co. Salop, Sheriff of Shropshire, was born about 1477. He was married to **ELIZABETH VERNON**, daughter of Henry Vernon, Knt., of Haddon, co. Derby, by Anne, daughter of John Talbot, 2nd Earl of Shrewsbury (**descendant of King Edward I**) [see TALBOT 6.ii for her ancestry]. They had three sons and three daughters. "Sir Robert Corbett knyght of Morton Corbet" died testate on 11 Apr. 1513 (P.C.C., 27 Fetiplace). His widow died on 29 Mar. 1563. They were buried at Moreton Corbet.

Burke's Commoners (1838) 3:190 ("she survived her husband fifty years, and was called "the old Lady Corbet, of Shawbury""). *Paget* (1977), p. 181. *TG* 5:164 (1984).

Child of Robert Corbet, by Elizabeth Vernon:

i. **DOROTHY CORBET**, married **RICHARD MAINWARING**, Knt. [see MAINWARING 4].[1]

* * *

---

[1] Ancestors of **Robert Abell**.

FERRERS OF GROBY see CLARKE

FIENNES see LUNSFORD

* * *

FISHER

EDWARD III OF ENGLAND, King of England, married PHILIPPE DE HAINAUT.
EDMUND OF YORK [*of Langley*], Duke of York, married, ISABEL DE CASTILLE.
CONSTANCE OF YORK, married THOMAS LE DESPENSER, Earl of Gloucester.
ISABEL LE DESPENSER, married RICHARD DE BEAUCHAMP, Earl of Worcester.
ELIZABETH BEAUCHAMP, married EDWARD NEVILLE, Lord Bergavenny.
GEORGE NEVILLE, Lord Bergavenny, married MARGARET FENNE [see OXENBRIDGE 5].

5. ELIZABETH NEVILLE, was married to **THOMAS BERKELEY**, of "Auyne", co. Hants, son and heir apparent of Edward Berkeley, of Beverstone, co. Gloucester, by his second wife Alice. THOMAS BERKELEY died 1500 *v.p.*
> *Smyth-Maclean* (1883) 1:354. *H.S.P.* 74:3,33 (1923) (1530 & 1574 Vis. Kent).

4. ANNE BERKELEY, second daughter and co-heiress, was married to **JOHN BRENT**, Esq., of Charing, Kent, son of John Brent, senior, of Charing. They had two sons and two daughters. She was a widow in 1545-46 and died in 1571-72.
> *Wotton* (1741) 2:17. *H.S.P.* 42:140,207,212 (1898) (1619 Vis. Kent). *Smyth-Maclean* (1883) 1:354. *H.S.P.* 74:3,33 (1923) (Brent arms: *Gules*, a wyvern tail nowed *argent*). *Brent* (1946), pp. 31, 34.

3. MARGARET BRENT, was sister and heiress of Thomas Brent, Esq. She was married for the first time to **JOHN DERING**, Esq., of Surrenden Dering, son and heir of Nicholas Dering, Esq., of Surrenden, by Alice, daughter and heiress of William Bettenham, of Bettenham Wood, Cranbrook, Kent. They had five sons and four daughters. JOHN DERING, ESQ., died in 1550, and was buried at St. Nicholas', Pluckley. She was married for the second time to _____ MOORE.
> *Wotton* (1741) 2:15. *Arch.Cant.* 10:327 (1876) (1619 Vis. Kent). *Smyth-Maclean* (1883) 1:354 (of Puckley in Kent). *H.S.P.* 42:140.207,212 (1898) (Dering arms: *Or*, a saltire *sable*). *Gen.* (n.s.) 33:269 (1917). *H.S.P.* 74:3 (1923). *H.S.P.* 75:96 (1924) (1592 Vis. Kent). *Brent* (1946), p. 31.

2. RICHARD DERING, Esq., of Surrenden, younger son, was married to **MARGARET TWISDEN**, daughter of William Twisden, Esq., of Peckham, by Elizabeth, daughter and heir of Thomas Roydon, Esq., of Great Peckham. They had four sons and three daughters.
> *Wotton* (1741) 2:17. *Arch.Cant.* 10:327 (1876). *Smyth-Maclean* (1883) 1:354. *H.S.P.* 42:140,207 (1898). *Gen.(n.s.)* 33:269 (1917). *H.S.P.* 74:33 (1923). *H.S.P.* 75:41 (1924).

1. BENNETT DERING, was married to **JOHN FISHER**, of Maidstone, Kent, son of Alexander Fisher, by Katherine, daughter of Peter Maplesden.
> *Arch.Cant.* 10:327 (1876). *H.S.P.* 42:140 (1898) (Fisher arms: *Argent*, on a chief *gules* a dolphin embowed of the field). *H.S.P.* 75:96 (Bennett unmarried in 1592). *Adventurers* (1987), p. 279-283.

Children & grandchildren of John Fisher, by Bennett Dering:

i. GEORGE FISHER, born about 1601.

ii. JOHN FISHER, second son, was born about 1603, resided Virginia in February 1623/4, will proved 23 Mar. 1639/40; married **ELIZABETH** _____.
   a. JOHN FISHER, living 28 Apr. 1639, died *s.p.*
   b. STEPHEN FISHER, born about 1636, married REBECCA (BAGWELL) ANDREWS. One daughter.

FISHER (cont.)

    c. **PHILIP FISHER**, born about 1637, of Northampton County, Virginia; married **ELIZABETH MADDOX**. Nine children.
  iii. **HENRY FISHER**, born about 1605.
  iv. **ELIZABETH FISHER**.

* * *

FITZ ALAN

HENRY III OF ENGLAND, King of England, married **ÉLÉONORE DE PROVENCE**.
EDMUND OF LANCASTER *Crouchback*, Earl of Lancaster, married **BLANCHE D'ARTOIS**.
HENRY OF LANCASTER, married **MAUD DE CHAWORTH** [see LANCASTER 13].

13. **ALIANOR OF LANCASTER**, was married for the first time before June 1337 to **JOHN BEAUMONT**, Earl of Buchan, 2nd Lord Beaumont (died 10-25 May 1342) [see MARSHALL 10 for descendants of this marriage]. She was married for the second time at Ditton, in the presence of King Edward III, on 5 Feb. 1344/5 to **RICHARD FITZ ALAN** [*Copped Hat*], 3rd Earl of Arundel and 4th Earl of Surrey, son and heir of Edmund Fitz Alan, 8th Earl of Arundel, **Baron** of Oswestry, co. Salop, **Baron** of Clun, co. Salop (**descendant of Charlemagne**), by Alice, daughter of William de Warenne (**descendant of Charlemagne**). He was born about 1313, and had been married previously to ISABEL LE DESPENSER, daughter of Hugh le Despenser the younger, Lord Despenser, by Alianor (granddaughter of King Edward I), daughter and co-heiress of Gilbert de Clare, 9th Earl of Clare (the marriage was annulled 4 Dec. 1344) [see CERGEAUX 10 for descendants of that marriage]. In 1330-1 he was fully restored in blood and honours and obtained restitution of the Castle and Honour of Arundel, becoming Earl of Arundel. He took a distinguished part in the wars with France, was Admiral of the West 1340-41 and 1345-47, commanded the second division at the battle of Crécy, and was at the fall of Calais in 1347. She was first cousin to his first wife and a Papal dispensation was granted on 4 Mar. 1344/5. ALIANOR OF LANCASTER died at Arundel on 11 Jan. 1371/2. On 30 June 1347 he succeeded to the vast estates of the family of Warenne, by the death of his mother's brother, John, Earl of Surrey and Sussex *s.p.legit.* RICHARD FITZ ALAN, Earl of Arundel, died testate in his seventieth year at Arundel on 24 Jan. 1375/6. They were buried at Lewes.
    C.P. 1:242-244, 243 footnote *d*, 244 footnote *b* (1910). *C.P.* 7:156 (1929).
    Children of Richard Fitz Alan, by Alianor of Lancaster:
    i. **RICHARD FITZ ALAN**, son and heir, by second marriage, born 1346 [see next].
    ii. **JOHN DE ARUNDEL**, younger son, married **ALIANOR MALTRAVERS** [see BROWNE 11].[1]
    iii. **JOAN FITZ ALAN**, married **HUMPHREY DE BOHUN**, Earl of Hereford [see BOHUN 10].[2]

---

[1] Ancestors of **Robert Abell, Dannett Abney, Alice Baynton, Francis Dade, Henry Fleete, Muriel Gurdon, Mary Gye, Gabriel, Roger & Sarah Ludlow, Thomas Lunsford, Elizabeth Marshall, Philip & Thomas Nelson, John Oxenbridge, William Randolph, John Washington, Mary Wolseley, Hawte Wyatt,** and, probably, **Thomas Dudley.**

[2] Ancestors of **Essex Beville, Elizabeth Bosvile, George, Giles & Robert Brent, Muriel Gurdon, Mary Launce, Anne Mauleverer.**

FITZ ALAN (cont.)

iv. ALICE FITZ ALAN, married THOMAS DE HOLAND, Knt., Earl of Kent [see HOLAND 9].[1]

12. RICHARD FITZ ALAN, 4th Earl of Arundel, 10th Earl of Surrey, son and heir by second marriage, was born in 1346. He was married for the first time, with marriage contract dated 28 Sep. 1359, to **ELIZABETH DE BOHUN**, daughter of William de Bohun, Knt., Earl of Northampton (**grandson of King Edward I**), by Elizabeth, daughter of Bartholomew de Badlesmere. She died on 3 Apr. 1385 and was buried at Lewes [see BOHUN 11 for her ancestry]. He was married for the second time on 15 Aug. 1390 to PHILIPPE MORTIMER, widow of John Hastings, 3rd Earl of Pembroke, and daughter of Edmund Mortimer, Earl of March, by Philippe, daughter and heiress of Lionel, Duke of Clarence (third son of King Edward III). She was born at Ludlow on 21 Nov. 1375. Richard Fitz Alan distinguished himself in the French wars, and "won a brilliant naval victory over the French, Spanish and Flemish fleets off Margate in 1387." Later with the Duke of Gloucester he later took an active part in the opposition to King Richard, becoming one of the five Lords Appellant in the Parliament of 1388. RICHARD FITZ ALAN, Earl of Arundel, obtained a pardon in 1394, but was treacherously seized, tried at Westminster, and beheaded at Cheapside on 21 Sep. 1397, burial at Austin Friars', in Bread Street, London, and, having been attainted, all his honours were forfeited. His widow was married for the third time, after April 1398, to Thomas Poynings, Lord St. John of Basing. She died at Halnaker, Sussex, on 24 Sep. 1401, and was buried at Boxgrove,

C.P. 1:26, 244-245, 245c (1910) ("a gallant, hot tempered, popular man, the persistent political opponent and bitter personal enemy of Richard II. He was one of the best sea-captains of the time"). *C.P.* 3:161 (1913). *C.P.* 9:604 (1936). *TAG* 67:99 (Apr. 1992).

Children and grandchildren of Richard Fitz Alan, by Elizabeth de Bohun:

   i. ALICE FITZ ALAN, married JOHN CHERLETON, 4th Lord Cherelton of Powis; said to have been mother by HENRY BEAUFORT, Cardinal of England, of a base-born daughter, Joan, wife of Edward Stradling, Knt., of St. Donat's Castle, co. Glamorgan [see BEAUFORT 11.ii].

   ii. ELIZABETH FITZ ALAN, born about 1375 [see next].

   iii. JOAN FITZ ALAN, born 1375, sister and eventual (in 1415) co-heiress of Thomas Fitz Alan, Earl of Arundel, died testate 14 Nov. 1435; married WILLIAM DE BEAUCHAMP, K.G., Lord Bergavenny, born after 1344, died testate 8 May 1411, fourth son of Thomas Beauchamp, of Elmley, co. Worcester, 11th Earl of Warwick, **Baron** of Salwarpe, co. Worcester, of Hanslope, co. Buckingham, of Flamstead, co. Hertford, and of Warwick, co. Warwick, by Katherine, daughter of Roger de Mortimer, 1st Earl of March, **Baron** of Wigmore, co. Hereford (**descendant of Charlemagne**). *C.P.* 1:24-26 (1910). *C.P.* 10:125 (1945). *Paget* (1977), p. 423.

      a. RICHARD DE BEAUCHAMP, mar ISABEL LE DESPENSER [see OXENBRIDGE 7].[2]

      b. JOAN DE BEAUCHAMP, married JAMES BUTLER, Earl of Ormond [see BUTLER 7].[3]

11. ELIZABETH FITZ ALAN, was born about 1375 (aged forty and more in 1415), and was sister and co-heiress of Thomas Fitz Alan, 7th Earl of Arundel (died 1415

---

[1]Ancestors of **Elizabeth Bosvile, Stephen Bull, Charles Calvert, Grace Chetwode, St. Leger Codd, Edward Digges, Muriel Gurdon, Warham Horsmanden, Anne Humphrey, Nathaniel Littleton, Thomas Lloyd, John Nelson, Philip & Thomas Nelson, John Oxenbridge, Herbert Pelham, Katherine Saint Leger, Maria Johanna Somerset, John Washington, John West, Thomas Wingfield**, and probably, **Thomas Dudley, Jane Haviland.**

[2]Ancestors of **St.Leger Codd, Edward Digges, John Fisher, Warham Horsmanden, Katherine Saint Leger, Maria Johanna Somerset.**

[3]Ancestors of **Robert Abell, Grace Chetwode, Herbert Pelham, Anne Humphreys, Thomas Lunsford, John West.**

FITZ ALAN (cont.)

s.p.). She was married for the first time before December 1378 to WILLIAM DE MONTAGU, Knt., son and heir of the Earl of Salisbury. He died on 6 Aug. 1382 *v.p., s.p.* She was married for the second time in July 1384 to THOMAS DE MOWBRAY, later Duke of Norfolk. They had four children [see MOWBRAY 9 for descendants of this marriage]. He died of the pestilence at Venice, Italy, on 22 Sep. 1399. She was married for the third time, without the king's licence, before 19 Aug. 1401 (when her dower lands were ordered back into the king's hands) to **ROBERT GOUSHILL**, Esq., of Hoveringham, co. Nottingham. She was pardoned on 28 Sep. 1401 and her lands were restored. He was knighted and received control of her dower land. SIR ROBERT GOUSHILL was slain at the Battle of Shrewsbury on 21 July 1403 leaving two daughters and co-heiresses. She was married for the fourth time before 3 July 1414 to GERARD UFFLETE, Knt. His will was proved in February 1420/1. ELIZABETH FITZ ALAN died on 8 July 1425.

C.P. 1:253, (1936) 9:604 (1910). *TAG* 67:99-100 (Apr. 1992).

Children of Robert Goushill, by Elizabeth Fitz Alan:

i. **ELIZABETH GOUSHILL**, married **ROBERT WINGFIELD**, Knt. [see LETHERINGHAM 7].[1]

ii. **JOAN GOUSHILL**, born about 1401 [see next].

10. **JOAN GOUSHILL**, daughter and co-heiress, was born about 1401 (aged two at her father's death). She was married to **THOMAS STANLEY**, Knt., K.G., Lord Stanley of Lathom and Knowsley, co. Lancaster, Lieutenant of Ireland, Chamberlain of North Wales, etc., son of John de Stanley, Knt., of Lathom, co. Lancaster (of **Magna Charta descent** and **descendant of Charlemagne**), by Isabel, daughter of Robert Harington, Knt., of Hornby (of **Magna Charta descent** and **descendant of Charlemagne**). He was born in 1406 (or in or before 1405). They had four sons and three daughters. He was summoned to Parliament on 15 Jan. 1455/6 by writ directed *Thome Stanley militi domino de Stanley*, whereby he is held to have become Lord Stanley. SIR THOMAS STANLEY died on 11 Feb. 1458/9. His widow was living in 1460.

H.S.P. 18:203 (1882) (1580 Vis. Cheshire). *H.S.P.* 21:144 (1885) (1623 Vis. Glouc.). *D.N.B.* 18:963 (1909). *C.P.* 4:205 (1916). *C.P.* 12(1):250-251 (1953). *TAG* 67:100 (Apr. 1992). *Paget* (1977), p. 406. *Roskell* (1992) 4:455-458.

Children & grandchildren of Thomas Stanley, by Joan Goushill:

i. **THOMAS STANLEY**, son and heir, born about 1435 [see next].

ii. **JOHN STANLEY**, married **ELIZABETH WEEVER** [see MANWARING 6].[2]

iii. **MARGARET STANLEY**, married **WILLIAM TROUTBECK**, Knt. [see TROUTBECK 6].[3]

iv. **KATHERINE STANLEY**, married **JOHN SAVAGE**, Knt. [see WYLLYS 6].[4]

9. **THOMAS STANLEY**, Knt., K.G., Lord Stanley, Sovereign Lord of the Isle of Man, P.C., Constable of England, son and heir, was born about 1435 (aged twenty-four on his father's death). He was married for the first time, apparently after 10 May 1457, to **ALIANOR NEVILLE**, fourth daughter of Richard Neville, Earl of Salisbury, by Alice (**descendant of King Edward I**), daughter and heiress of Thomas Montagu, Earl of Salisbury. She was sister of Richard, Earl of Warwick (the celebrated *King Maker*) [see MONTHERMER 8 for her ancestry]. They had six sons and four daughters.

---

[1] Ancestors of **Richard Palgrave, Thomas Wingfield**.

[2] Ancestors of **Oliver Manwaring**.

[3] Ancestors of **Grace Chetwode, Elizabeth Coytemore, Joshua & Rebecca Owen**.

[4] Ancestors of **Oliver Manwaring, Amy Wyllys**.

FITZ ALAN (cont.)

He was summoned to Parliament from 30 July 1460. She was buried at St. James's Garlickhithe, London. He was married for the second time in 1482 (before November) to MARGARET BEAUFORT, widow, first, of Edmund Tudor, Earl of Richmond [see BEAUFORT 10.ii.a], second, of Henry Stafford, Knt., and daughter and heiress of John Beaufort, Duke of Somerset, by Margaret, daughter of John Beauchamp, Lord Beauchamp, of Bletsoe. She was born at Bletsoe on 31 May 1443. He betrayed the cause of King Richard III at the battle of Bosworth on 22 Aug. 1485, and is said to have set that King's crown on the head of his step-son, the victorious Henry VII. He was created **Earl of Derby** on 27 Oct. 1485. On 24 June 1495, he received a visit lasting nearly a month, from the King and Queen, at Knowsley and at Lathom. "Thomas Stanley, erle of Derby and lord Stanley" died testate (P.C.C., 19 Holgrave) aged sixty-nine at Lathom on 29 July 1504, and was buried with his ancestors at Burscough Priory, co. Lancaster. His widow, who had founded Christ's and St. John's Colleges, Cambridge, died testate (P.C.C., 31 Bennett) in her sixty-seventh year on 29 June 1509 (three months after the death of her son King Henry VII), and was buried in Westminster Abbey.
   D.N.B. 18:962-965 (1909). *C.P.* 4:205-207 (1916). *C.P.* 12(1):251 (1953). *Paget* (1977), p. 447.

8. **GEORGE STANLEY**, K.B., K.G., son and heir apparent, was born about 1460. He was married, before 26 Feb. 1481, to **JOAN LE STRANGE**, daughter and heiress of John le Strange, Lord Strange, of Knokyn (of **Magna Charta Surety descent** and **descendant of Charlemagne**), by Jacquette (sister of Elizabeth, Queen Consort of Edward IV) (**descendant of Charlemagne**), daughter of Richard Wydeville, Earl Rivers. She was born about 1463, and on her father's death on 15 Oct. 1477, became Baroness Strange of Knokyn, and Mohun of Dunster *suo jure*. In consequence of his marriage, he was summoned to Parliament from 15 Nov. 1482 by writs directed *Georgio Stanley de la Strange*, whereby he became **Lord Strange**. He was in hostage to King Richard III, and ran great risk of his life through his father's treachery to that King. GEORGE STANLEY, Lord Strange, died aged about forty-three on 4 or 5 Dec. 1503 *v.p.*, being said to have been poisoned at a banquet, at Derby House, St. Paul's Wharf, London, and was buried (with his mother) at St. James's, Garlickhithe. "Jane Stanley le Strange of Hillingdon, Middlesex" died testate (P.C.C., 32 Fetiplace) on 20 Mar. 1513/4 at Colham Green, Middlesex.
   D.N.B. 18:965 (1909). *C.P.* 4:207-208 (1916). *C.P.* 12(1):48 footnote *a* (1953).
   Child of George Stanley, by Joan le Strange:
   i. **THOMAS STANLEY**, married **ANNE HASTINGS** [see NELSON 7].[1]

* * *

FITZ HUGH see BULL

* * *

---

[1] Ancestors of **John Nelson**.

FITZ WALTER

EDWARD I OF ENGLAND, King of England, married ALIANORE DE CASTILLE.
ELIZABETH OF ENGLAND, married HUMPHREY DE BOHUN, Earl of Hereford and Essex.
ALIANOR DE BOHUN, married THOMAS DE DAGWORTH [see BUTLER 10].

11. ALIANOR DE DAGWORTH, daughter and heiress, was married, with bishop's licence dated 23 June 1362, to marry in the chapel of the manor of Vachery, in Cranley, Surrey, to WALTER FITZ WALTER, 3rd Lord Fitz Walter, son of John Fitz Walter, 2nd Lord Fitz Walter, **Baron** of Little Dunmow, Essex (of **Magna Charta Surety descent** and **descendant of Charlemagne**), by Alianore, daughter of Henry de Percy, Knt., of Alnwick, Northumberland, **Baron** of Topcliffe, co. York (**descendant of Charlemagne**). He was born at Henham on 31 May 1345. He was summoned to Parliament from 6 Apr. 1369 by writs directed *Waltero fitz Wauter*. ALIANOR DE DAGWORTH, who was living on 29 Nov. 1375, was buried in Dunmow Priory. He was married for the second time before 27 June 1385 to Philippe de Mohun, second daughter and co-heiress of John de Mohun, Knt., of Dunster, Somerset [Lord Mohun], by Joan, daughter of Bartholomew de Burghersh, Knt., of Ewyas Lacy, co. Hereford [Lord Burghersh]. WALTER FITZ WALTER, Lord Fitz Walter, joined the unsuccessful expedition of the Duke of Lancaster to Spain in June 1386, and died at or near Oronse in Galicia on 26 Sep. 1386. His widow was married for the second time before 13 Nov. 1389 to John Golafre, Knt. (died 18 Nov. 1396), and for the third time before 24 Oct. 1404 to Edward of York [*of Norwich*], Duke of York (died *s.p.*, being slain at the battle of Agincourt on 25 Oct. 1415). She died on 17 July 1431 *s.p.*

    C.P. 5:477-480 (1926). *Paget* (1957) 230:6 (He was active in suppressing the rebellion of Jack Straw and Wat Tyler).

10. WALTER FITZ WALTER, 4th Lord Fitz Walter, second but first surviving son and heir by first marriage, was born at Henham on 5 Sep. 1368. He was summoned to Parliament from 12 Sep. 1390 by writs directed *Waltero fitz Wauter*. He was married to JOAN DEVEREUX, only daughter of John Devereux, Knt., of Dinton, co. Buckingham, etc. [Lord Devereux], by Margaret, daughter of John de Vere, Earl of Oxford (of **Magna Charta Surety descent** and **descendant of Charlemagne**). She was born about 1380 (aged seventeen and more in 1397), and was sister and heiress of John Devereux, Knt., of Whitechurch Maund, co. Hereford (died 13 Nov. 1396 *s.p.*). In passing by sea from Rome to Naples, he was captured by Saracens and taken prisoner to Tunis. Having been ransomed by some Genoese merchants, WALTER FITZ WALTER, Lord Fitz Walter, died aged thirty-seven at Venice on 16 May 1406. His widow was married for the second time, as his third wife, to Hugh Burnell, Knt. [Lord Burnell] (died 27 Nov. 1420). She died on 10 or 11 May 1409, and was buried in Dunmow Priory.

    C.P. 5:480-482 (1926). *Paget* (1957) 230:6.

9. WALTER FITZ WALTER, 5th Lord Fitz Walter, younger son, was born at Woodham Walter and baptised there on 22 June 1401, and brother and heir of Humphrey Fitz Walter. He was actively employed in the French wars of King Henry V, and was taken prisoner at Baugé on 22 Mar. 1421. He was Master of the King's Dogs and Harthounds on 16 July 1425. He was summoned to Parliament from 12 July 1429 by writs directed *Waltero fitz Wauter chivaler*. He was married before 1430 to ELIZABETH CHIDIOCK, widow of William Massey, King's esquire, and daughter of John Chidiock, Knt., of Chidiock, co. Dorset, by Alianor (**descendant of Charlemagne**), daughter and heiress of Ivo Fitz Warin, Knt., of Caundle Haddon,

FITZ WALTER (cont.)

Dorset. WALTER FITZ WALTER, Lord Fitz Walter, died testate aged thirty or thirty-one *s.p.m.* on 25 Nov. 1431. His widow was married for the third time before 5 Nov. 1438 to Thomas Cobham, Knt., of Sterborough, Surrey. She died on 14 June 1464, and was buried with her second husband at Dunmow Priory.

    C.P. 5:482-484 (1926). *Paget* (1957) 230:7.

    Child of Walter Fitz Walter, by Elizabeth Chidiock:

      i. ELIZABETH FITZ WALTER, born 28 July 1430, married, JOHN RADCLIFFE [see POLE 8].[1]

* * *

FLEETE

EDWARD I OF ENGLAND, King of England, married ALIANORE DE CASTILLE.
JOAN OF ENGLAND [*of Acre*], married GILBERT DE CLARE, Earl of Gloucester.
ALIANOR DE CLARE, married HUGH LE DESPENSER, 2nd Lord de Despenser.
ISABEL LE DESPENSER, married RICHARD FITZ ALAN, Earl of Arundel.
EDMUND FITZ ALAN, Knt., married SIBYL DE MONTAGU.
PHILIPPE FITZ ALAN, married RICHARD CERGEAUX, Knt. [see CERGEAUX 8]

8. PHILIPPE CERGEAUX, daughter and co-heiress, was born about 1381 (aged eighteen in 1399). She was married for the first time to ROBERT PASHLEY, Knt., son of Robert Pashley, Knt., by Anne, daughter of John Howard, Knt., of Norfolk. He was born about 1370. They had two sons and one daughter. SIR ROBERT PASHLEY was dead by 1399. She was married for the second time to WILLIAM SWINBORNE, Esq. She died in 1420.

    Scott (1876), p. 170 (identification of parents of Robert Pashley). *Gen.Mag.* 11:542-543 (Dec. 1954).

    Children of Robert Pashley, by Philippe Cergeaux:

      i. JOHN PASHLEY, Knt., eldest son, born 1406/7 [see next].

      ii. ANNE PASHLEY, married, second, EDWARD TYRRELL, Esq. [see DADE 7].[2]

7. JOHN PASHLEY, Knt., son and heir, was born in 1406/7. He was married to ELIZABETH WYDEVILLE, daughter of Richard Wydeville, Knt., of Grafton, co. Northampton. SIR JOHN PASHLEY died on 8 June 1453. His widow died on 8 June 1453.

    Scott (1876), p. 60. *Sur.Soc.* 144:57 (1930) (1480 Vis. North). *Gen.Mag.* 11:543 (Dec. 1954).

6. JOHN PASHLEY, Esq., of Smeeth, Kent, of Pashleys in Ticehurst, Sussex, was born in 1431/2. He was married to LOWYS GOWER, daughter and heiress of Thomas Gower, Knt. She was dead in 1450. JOHN PASHLEY, ESQ., died on 20 Nov. 1468.

    Scott (1876), p. 60. *H.S.P.* 74:17 (1923) (1530 Vis. Kent). *Sur.Soc.* 144:57 (1930) (1480 Vis. North). *Gen.Mag.* 11:543 (Dec. 1954) (*Inq.p.m.* states no known heirs).

5. ELIZABETH PASHLEY, said to be daughter and heiress, was married to REYNOLD PYMPE, of Pympe's Court, Nettlested, Kent, son of William Pympe, Knt. REYNOLD PYMPE was living 1448-1530/1.

---

[1] Ancestors of **John Nelson**.

[2] Ancestors of **Anne Lovelace, John Throckmorton**.

FLEETE (cont.)

Scott (1876), p. 60 (Pympe arms: Barry of four, *gules*, and *argent*, a vair in chief), p. 171 (attainted 1483 for assisting the Duke of Buckingham against King Richard III; attainder reversed 1 Hy. VII). Hasted, Kent 2:286; 3:292. *H.S.P.* 74:17 (1923). *Sur.Soc.* 144:58 (1930) (1480 Vis. North). *Mary Isaac* (1955), p. 273).

4. ANNE (or AMY) PYMPE, daughter and heiress, was born by 1485. She was also heiress of her mother Elizabeth. She was married in 1528 to **JOHN SCOTT**, Knt., of Scott's Hall in Smeeth, Kent, Sheriff of Kent, son of William Scott, Knt., of Scott's Hall, by Sibyl, daughter of John Lewknor, Knt., of Goring and West Dean, Sussex. They had four sons and seven daughters. SIR JOHN SCOTT died before 1534. She died between 1530 and 1540.
  Berry (1830), p. 170. *Scott* (1876), pp. 158-159. *H.S.P.* 42:127-128 (1898) (1619 Vis. Kent) (Scott arms: *Argent*, three roses within a bordure engrailed *gules*).

3. REYNOLD SCOTT, Knt., of Scott's Hall, Captain of Calais, Sheriff of Kent, son and heir, was married for the first time to **EMELYN KEMPE**, daughter of William Kempe, Knt., of Ollantigh, Kent, by Eleanor, daughter of Robert Browne, Knt. (**descendant of King Edward I**) [see BROWNE 8 for her ancestry]. They had one son and two daughters. He was married for the second time to **MARY TUKE**, daughter of Bryan Tuke, Knt., of Layer Marney, Essex, Secretary to Cardinal Wolsey, by Grissell, daughter of Nicholas Boughton, of Woolwich, Kent. They had five sons and four daughters. He died testate on 16 Dec. 1554. The will of "Raynolde Scott, knyght, of Smethe in the Countie of Kente", dated 4 Sep. 1554 and proved 13 Feb. 1554/5, names his wife and children (P.C.C., 40 More). His widow was living in 1555.
  Stemmata Chicheleana (1765), p. 10. *Berry* (1830), p. 170. *Scott* (1876), pp. 177-183 ("He inherited very large possessions, especially in West Kent in the valley of the Medway, in right of his mother, as heir to the Pashleys, Pympes, and Gowers) (Kempe arms: *Gules* within a bordure engrailed, three garbs, *or*), p. 184 (Tuke arms: Per fess dancettée *azure* and *gules*, three lions passant guardant). *H.S.P.* 14:610 (1879) (Misc. Essex Ped.). *H.S.P.* 42:128 (1898). *H.S.P.* 75:30 (1924) (1574 Vis. Kent).

Children & grandchild of Reynold Scott, by Emelyn Kempe:

  i. **THOMAS SCOTT**, Knt., of Scott's Hall, Sheriff of Kent, son and heir by first marriage, Sheriff of Kent 1576, M.P., Commander-in-Chief of the Kentish forces assembled on Northbourne Downs to the threatened approach of the Spanish Armada in 1588, Comptroller of the Household of Queen Elizabeth, died testate 30 Dec. 1594 (will includes bequests to "Warham Sentleger and Anthonye Sentleger, the two sonnes of my daughter Sentleger") (P.C.C., 1 Scott); married, first, **ELIZABETH BAKER**, died 17 Nov. 1583, buried Brabourn, eldest daughter of John Baker, Knt., of Sissinghurst Castle in Cranbrook, Kent, Chancellor of the Exchequer to King Henry VIII, Speaker of the House of Commons, Attorney-General to Queen Mary, by Elizabeth (**descendant of Charlemagne**), daughter and heiress of Thomas Dinley; married, second, 1583 **ELIZABETH HEYMAN**, died 29 June 1595 *s.p.*, eldest daughter of Ralph Heyman, of Somerfield, Kent, by Anne, daughter of William Nanton, of Suffolk, married, third (without issue), **DOROTHY BERE**, widow of John Heyes, of Essex, Edward Scott, Esq., of Camberwell, George Fynche, of Norton in Sheldwich, Kent, and daughter of John Bere, of Horsman's Place, Dartford, Kent. *Stemmata Chicheleana* (1765), p. 10. *Scott* (1876), pp. 194-207 (Baker arms: *Azure* on a fess between three swans' heads, erased *or*, and ducally gorged *gules*, as many cinquefoils, *or*). *H.S.P.* 42:128 (1898). Misc. Gen. et Her. (n.s.) 4:185-6.

  a. **MARY SCOTT**, married, first, **ANTHONY SAINT LEGER** [see SAINT LEGER 2].[1]

Children & grandchild of Reynold Scott, by Mary Tuke:

  ii. **CHARLES SCOTT**, younger son [see next].

  iii. **MARY SCOTT**, married, first, with five sons and six daughters, **RICHARD ARGALL**, Esq., of East Sutton, Kent, died 1588, buried in church there, son of Thomas Argall, Esq., of London,

---

[1]Ancestors of **St. Leger Codd, Warham Horsmanden, Katherine Saint Leger.**

FLEETE (cont.)

by Margaret, daughter of John Tallakarne, of Cornwall; married, second, LAURENCE WASHINGTON, Esq., of Maidstone, Kent, died 1605. *Scott* (1876), p. 185 notes *c & d*. *H.S.P.* 13:137 (1878) (1612 Vis. Essex). Hasted, Kent 2:418. *H.S.P.* 75:101 (1924) (1592 Vis. Kent).

    a. **ELIZABETH ARGALL**, died 9 Aug. 1638; married **EDWARD FILMER**, Knt., of East Sutton, Kent, died 2 Nov. 1629, buried church there. Grandparents of Capt. Charles Barham of Surry County, Virginia. See *Roberts* (1993), p. 242. *VMHB* 24:158-162 (1916).

2. CHARLES SCOTT, of Egerton in Godmersham, Kent, younger son, by second marriage, received "all the saide marshe lande lyinge in the saide parishes of Snave and Ivechurch" in his father's will. He purchased the manor of Egerton in Godmersham. He was married in 1537 to **JANE WYATT**, daughter of Thomas Wyatt, Knt., of Allington Castle, Kent (**descendant of King Edward I**), by Jane, daughter of William Haute (or Hawte), Knt., of Bisshopsborne, Kent [see WYATT 2 for her ancestry]. They had two sons and two daughters. CHARLES SCOTT died in 1617.

    Stemmata Chicheleana (1765), p. 10 (he is shown as becoming a Fellow of All Souls College, Oxford). *Berry* (1830), p. 169. *Scott* (1876), p. 185. *H.S.P.* 42:128 (1898). *Mary Isaac* (1955), pp. 191-192. *Adventurers* (1987), p. 284.

1. DEBORAH SCOTT, was married to **WILLIAM FLEETE**, of Chatham, Kent, and Gray's Inn, London, son of William Fleete, Gent., by Katherine, daughter of Robert Honywood, Esq., of Charing, Kent. They had twelve children. He was a member of the Virginia Company. The will of "Debora Fleete, of Westminster, widow" (P.C.C., 5 Bowyer), dated 27 Mar. 1651 and proved 23 Jan. 1651/2, provided for the "payment of such sums as sd. Sir R[obert] Filmer lent me & my son Henry Fleete towards the recovering of my sd. son of a great sickness & for furnishing him with provisions & necessaries for his last voyage to Virginia".

    Berry (1830), p. 169. *Top. & Gen.* 1:399 (Their son Henry was one of the three hundred sixty-seven living descendants of his great-grandmother Mary (Atwater) Honywood at her death aged ninety-three in 1620). *Scott* (1876), p. 185 (Fleet arms: Chequée *or* and *gules*, a canton *argent*). *VMHB* 2:70-76 (1894). *VMHB* 28:342-343 (Oct. 1920) (her will). *H.S.P.* 74:74 (1935) (Add. Ped. Kent). *Adventurers* (1987), p. 284.

Child & grandchild of William Fleete, by Deborah Scott:

    i. **CAPT. HENRY FLEETE**, emigrated to Virginia about 1621 "probably with the new Governor, Sir Francis Wyatt, who was a first cousin of Henry's mother", captured by Indians in 1623, learned their language during five years in captivity, ransomed, engaged in fur trade, member of Maryland Assembly 1638, acted as interpreter and mediator between the English and the Indians, died before 8 May 1661; married **SARAH (_____) BURDEN**, will proved 29 Dec. 1679.

        a. **HENRY FLEETE**, under twenty-one in 1669, justice of Lancaster County 1695, sheriff 1702, captain of militia, will dated 31 Jan. 1728/9, proved 9 May 1733, named children and grandchildren; married before 18 July 1683 **ELIZABETH WILDEY**. Seven children.

* * *

FORTESCUE see MONTHERMER

GASCOIGNE see NEVILLE

GASCOIGNE see also READE

* * *

GERARD

EDWARD I OF ENGLAND, King of England, married ALIANORE DE CASTILLE.
ELIZABETH OF ENGLAND, married HUMPHREY DE BOHUN, Earl of Hereford and Essex.
WILLIAM DE BOHUN, Earl of Northampton, married ELIZABETH DE BADLESMERE.
ELIZABETH DE BOHUN, married RICHARD FITZ ALAN, Earl of Arundel.
ELIZABETH FITZ ALAN, married ROBERT GOUSHILL, Knt.
JOAN GOUSHILL, married THOMAS STANLEY, Lord Stanley of Lathom and Knowsley.
KATHERINE STANLEY, married JOHN SAVAGE, Knt. [see WYLLYS 6].

5. MARGARET SAVAGE, was married for the first time to JOHN HONFORD, of Honford, son of John Honford, of Honford, by Margery, daughter of Laurence Warren, Knt., of Poynton, co. Chester. He was born about 1435, and died about 1480. She was married for the second time after 1480 to EDMUND TRAFFORD, Knt., K.B., of Trafford, co. Lancaster, son of John Trafford, Knt., by Elizabeth, daughter of Thomas Ashton, Knt., of Ashton-under-Lyne, co. Lancaster. They had three sons and two daughters. SIR EDMUND TRAFFORD died on 15 Aug. 1514.

> *Baines* (1836) 3:chart facing p. 110. *H.S.P.* 18:204 (1882) (1580 Vis. Cheshire) (daughter of John Savage identified as "____ uxr Sr Edw. Trafford").

Child of John Honford, by Margaret Savage:

> i. KATHERINE HONFORD, married JOHN MAINWARING [see OVER PEOVER 5].[1]

Child of Edmund Trafford, by Margaret Savage:

> ii. MARGARET TRAFFORD [see next].

4. MARGARET (or MARGERY) TRAFFORD was married for the first time to NICHOLAS LONGFORD, of Longford, co. Derby, and for the second time to THOMAS GERARD, Knt., of Kingsley & Bryn, co. Lancaster, son of Peter Gerard, of Kingsley and Bryn, co. Lancaster (of **Magna Charta Surety descent** and **descendant of Charlemagne**), by Margaret, daughter of Thomas Stanley, Knt., of Hooton, co. Chester. He was born in 1488 (aged six 10 Hen. VII, and twenty-seven 7 Hen. VIII). SIR THOMAS GERARD was slain fighting the Scots at Berwick-upon-Tweed on 7 Nov. 1523 (will dated 13 Sep. 1522 referring to wife, four [unnamed] younger sons and four daughters). His widow was married for the third time to JOHN PORT, Knt., of Etwall, co. Derby (*Inq.p.m.* dated 1540/1). She died on 10 May 1540.

> *Wotton* (1741) 1:55 (children identified as Thomas and four daughters) (Gerard arms: *Argent*, a saltire, *gules*). *Baines* (1836) 3:chart facing p. 110, 3:641 (children named as Thomas and Katherine). *Ormerod-Helsby* (1882) 2:132 (children named as Thomas, Margaret, Catherine, Elizabeth and Anne). Ormerod 2:96,131,371,372,416. VCH Lanc. 4:143-144, notes 23-33. *AR* (1992) 233A-39 (citing Letter to Mr. France, File L. 78, Lancashire Record Office).

Children of Thomas Gerard, by Margery Trafford:

> i. THOMAS GERARD, Knt., son and heir, Sheriff of Lancashire, M.P. for Lancashire, married JANE LEGH, daughter of Peter Legh, of Lyme (**descendant of King Edward** I), by his wife Jane Gerard [see WYLLYS 6.iii.a for her ancestry]. *Baines* (1836) 3:641.
>
>> a. CATHERINE GERARD, married WILLIAM TORBOCK [see MANWARING 3].[2]
>
> ii. WILLIAM GERARD, Gent., younger son [see next].

3. WILLIAM GERARD, Gent., of the New Hall, Ashton-in-Makerfield, co.

---

[1] Ancestors of **Robert Abell**.

[2] Ancestors of **Oliver Manwaring**.

GERARD (cont.)

Lancaster, younger son, was granted a messuage called the "New Hall" from his older brother Thomas Gerard, Knt., of Bryn, in 1542. He was married to CONSTANCE ROWSON. She was born about 1537 (aged thirty in 1567). WILLIAM GERARD, GENT., died before 1567 when the conveyance was challenged in a suit.

    AR (1992) 233A:40 (citing Duchy of Lancaster records: DL 1/54/B.17, DL 1/62/B.13; DL 4/7/3, DL 4/8/10, Public Record Office, London).

2. THOMAS GERARD, Gent., of the New Hall in Ashton-in-Makerfield, base-born son, was born about 1540/1. He was married for the first time to GRACE _____, and for the second time in 1586 to JANE _____. The will of THOMAS GERARD was dated 21 Dec. 1628 and proved 12 Jan. 1628/9, named his son John, requesting burial in Winwick Church. His widow was living in 1632.

    VCH Lanc. 4:144, note 34. *AR* (1992) 233A-41 (Letter of 26 Apr. 1960, File L.78, Lanc.Rec. Off).

1. JOHN GERARD, Gent., of the New Hall, was married on 16 Feb. 1607/8 to ISABEL _____. They had five sons. They were named in the marriage settlement dated 21 Sep. 1629 of Newhall on their son Thomas and his wife Susan, and in the conveyance dated 3 Apr. 1632 of property of his father in Ashton-in-Makerfield, with his son and daughter-in-law Thomas and Susan, and the widow Jane joined. JOHN GERARD, GENT., was residing at Warrington, co. Lancaster, in 1641.

    Chronicles of St. Mary's 7:100-102 (July 1959). *AR* (1992) 233A-43 (citing *Winwick Register*, Lanc. Par. Reg. Soc., p. 77; *Stemmata Varia* I, Gerard of Bryn, etc., Pedigrees XI(a) and XI(c), Lanc. Rec. Off. *A Biographical Dictionary of the Maryland Legislature, 1635-1789*, 1:348-349; Gerard Munimenti: DDGe (M) 127, 148, 149, Lanc. Rec. Off.) (contributed by Claude W. Faulkner). Second son, Marmaduke Gerard, of Warrington, had two daughters, Winifred, born 1639, and Bridget, born 1641, who appear to have been transported to Maryland by their uncle Thomas in 1658.

Child and grandchildren of John Gerard, by Isabel:

    i. THOMAS GERARD, Gent., of New Hall, son and heir, baptised Winwick 10 Dec. 1608, son and heir, surgeon and planter, emigrated to Maryland, in 1638, brought family in 1650, lord of St. Clement's, Basford & Westwood Manors, St. Mary's County, removed to Virginia 1664, died testate Westmoreland County, Virginia, 1673, buried St. Clement's Maryland; married, first, 1629 SUSANNA SNOW, daughter of John Snow, of Brookhouse in Chedulton, co. Stafford, yeoman, and sister of Abel, Justinian and Marmaduke Snow who were associated with Lord Baltimore in the Maryland enterprise; married, second, with no issue, ROSE (_____) TUCKER. *Maryland Hist. Mag.* 68:443-450 (1973).

      a. JUSTINIAN GERARD, married SARAH (_____) MAUNDERS.
      b. THOMAS GERARD, married SUSANNAH CURTIS.
      c. JOHN GERARD, born after 1650, married ELIZABETH _____.
      d. SUSANNA GERARD, married, first, ROBERT SLYE, second, JOHN COODE.
      e. FRANCES GERARD, married, first, THOMAS SPEKE, second, VALENTINE PEYTON, third, JOHN APPLETON, fourth, JOHN WASHINGTON, fifth, WILLIAM HARDWICK.
      f. TEMPERANCE GERARD, married, first, DANIEL HUTT, second, JOHN CRABBE, third, BENJAMIN BLANCHFLOWER.
      g. ELIZABETH GERARD, married, first, NEHEMIAH BLACKISTON, second, RALPH RYMER, third, JOSHUA GUIBERT.
      h. MARY GERARD, born after 1650, married KENELM CHESELDINE.

* * *

GIRLINGTON

EDWARD I OF ENGLAND, King of England, married ALIANORE DE CASTILLE.
JOAN OF ENGLAND [*of Acre*], married GILBERT DE CLARE, Earl of Gloucester.
ALIANOR DE CLARE, married HUGH LE DESPENSER, 2nd Lord Despenser.
EDWARD LE DESPENSER, Knt., married ANNE DE FERRERS.
EDWARD LE DESPENSER, 4th Lord le Despenser, married ELIZABETH DE BURGHERSH.
ANNE LE DESPENSER, married HUGH HASTINGS, Knt.
EDWARD HASTINGS, Knt., married MURIEL DE DINHAM.
JOHN HASTINGS, 9th Lord Hastings, married ANNE MORLEY.
ELIZABETH HASTINGS, married ROBERT HILDYARD [see ELSING 5].

6. KATHERINE HILDYARD was married for the first time to **JOHN HALDENBY**, of Haldenby. She was married for the second time to **WILLIAM GIRLINGTON**, of Frodington, co. Lincoln. They had three sons and three daughters. He was dead in 1540. Her will was proved on 5 Apr. 1540.

H.S.P. 16:140 (1881) (1563 Vis. Yorks). *H.S.P.* 51:404,556 (1903) (Maddison Linc. Ped.) (Isabel's father called "Robert").

5. ISABEL GIRLINGTON, was married for the first time, with marriage settlement dated 1516, to **CHRISTOPHER KELKE**, of Barnetby le Wold, co. Lincoln, and Great Kelke, co. York, son of Roger Kelke, of Barnetby. They had four sons. CHRISTOPHER KELKE died testate on 2 Feb. 1523/4. His widow was married for the second time to WILLIAM TYRWHIT, Knt., of Scotter, co. Lincoln, and had issue. The will of "Dame Isabell Tyrwhitt" of Scotter, dated 28 Dec. 1559 and proved 1 Feb. 1559/60, named sons Christopher, Roger and Francis (P.C.C., 11 Mellershe).

Gen. 4:186 (1880) (Vis. Linc.) ("Roger Kelke of Barnetby = Elizabeth, da. and coheir to Sir Martin de Lacy"). *H.S.P.* 16:140 (1881). *H.S.P.* 51:404-405,556 (1903). *Holmes* (1972), pp. 69-77 (William and Roger Kelke both mention a brother Francis in their wills) (Kelke arms: Sable, a bend cotised flory or) (no indication of Plantagenet ancestry).

Children of Christopher Kelke, by Isabel Girlington:

 i. **CHRISTOPHER KELKE**, son and heir [see next].
 ii. **WILLIAM KELKE**, married **THOMASINE SKERNE** [see FARRAR 2].[1]

4. CHRISTOPHER KELKE, of Great Grimsby, son and heir, was born about 1517 (aged under three in 1519). He was married to **JANE SAINT PAUL**, daughter and co-heiress of John Saint Paul, of Snarford. She was born about 1518 (aged thirty-eight in 1556-7). CHRISTOPHER KELKE died on 11 Aug. 1557.

Gen. 4:186 (1880). *H.S.P.* 16:140 (1881) ("of London Merchant"). *H.S.P.* 51:556 (1903).

3. CHRISTOPHER KELKE, of Barnetby le Wold, son and heir, was born about 1536 (aged twenty-one and more in 1557). He was a legatee of his grandmother on 18 Dec. 1559, and of his uncle Sir Robert Tyrwhitt on 11 Nov. 1581. He was married to **ELIZABETH CARR**, widow of William Fairfax, and daughter of Robert Carr, of Sleaford. They had three sons and four daughters. The will of "Christopher Kelke of Barnetby" was proved in 1587. She was dead before 4 Sep. 1604.

Gen. 4:186 (1880). *H.S.P.* 51:556,595 (1903).

2. ANNE KELKE, was married to **ROGER LEMING**, of Barnetby le Wold, son and heir of Roger Lemyng, of Barnetby. The will of "Roger Leminge of Bernetbie, Lincoln" was proved in 1591 (P.C.C., 73 Sainberbe). His widow was living on 4 Sep. 1604.

H.S.P. 51:556,595 (1903). *Allaben* (1908), pp. 165-66.

---

[1] Grandparents of **William Farrar**.

GIRLINGTON (cont.)

1. **ANNE LEMING**, was married at Caistor on 5 June 1604 to **WILLIAM WOLLEY**, of Cumberworth, son of William Wolley, of Cumberworth, by his wife Isabel Hooker, of Newton, Dorset. He was baptised at Cumberworth on 8 Sep. 1568, and had been previously married to Margaret Crewe, daughter of Peter Crewe, of Crewe, co. Chester. William & Anne had five sons and one daughter. She was buried at Cumberworth on 27 July 1614. He was married for the third time to Susan Kent (buried 1 May 1616), daughter of Thomas Kent, of Scamblesby, and for the fourth time to Anne Kirkman (buried 16 Aug. 1630), daughter of John Kirkman, of East Keal. WILLIAM WOLLEY was buried at Cumberworth on 17 Aug. 1638.

H.S.P. 51:595 (1903). *Allaben* (1908), p. 161 (Wolley arms: *Argent*, on a chevron *sable*, an eagle displayed of the field).

Child of William Wolley, by Anne Leming:

    i. **ALICE WOLLEY**, married **JOHN ASFORDBY**, of Saltfleetby [see ASFORDBY 1].[1]

* * *

GLEMHAM see PALGRAVE

GLOUCESTER see LAUNCE

GOODRICK see BOLLES

* * *

GRAY

EDWARD I OF ENGLAND, King of England, married **MARGUERITE DE FRANCE**.
THOMAS OF NORFOLK [*of Brotherton*], Earl of Norfolk, married **ALICE DE HALES**.
MARGARET OF NORFOLK, married **JOHN DE SEGRAVE**, 4th Lord Segrave.
ELIZABETH DE SEGRAVE, married **JOHN DE MOWBRAY** [see MOWBRAY 10].

10. **JOAN DE MOWBRAY**, said to be daughter, was married by 1384 to **THOMAS GRAY** [*with the croked foot*], Knt., of Heaton in Wark, Northumberland, M.P. for Northumberland, son and heir of Thomas Gray, Knt., of Wark, by Margaret, daughter and heiress of William de Pressen, of Presson, Northumberland. He was born about 1359 (aged ten in 1369). They had four sons and one daughter. Their eldest son was born in the castle of Alnwick. SIR THOMAS GRAY died on 26 Nov. or 3 Dec. 1400. His widow was married for the second time to THOMAS TUNSTALL, Knt., and was living on 30 Nov. 1402.

Raine (1852), chart between 326-327. *C.P.* 6:136 (1926) (no identification of parents of Joan). *Sur.Soc.* 144:53-54 (1930) (1480 Vis. North) (identifies wife of Thomas [vel Iohannes] Gray as *Ionetta filia Iohannes Moubray*) (identifies five sons and one daughter) (Gray arms: *Gules*, a lion rampant and a border engrailed *argent*). *Northumberland* (1935) 14: chart following p. 328. *Paget*

---

[1]Parents of **William Asfordby**.

GRAY (cont.)

(1957) 264:1. *C.P.* 10:29 (1945). *Roskell* (1992) 3:222-225 (citing the 1480 Visitation and C 137/24/50).

Children of Thomas Gray, by Joan de Mowbray:
- i. THOMAS GRAY, Knt., of Wark and Heton, born 30 Nov. 1384 [see next].
- ii. JOHN GRAY (or GREY), Knt., married JOAN CHERLETON [see LLOYD 8].[1]
- iii. MAUD GRAY, married ROBERT OGLE, Knt., of Bothal, Northumberland [see OGLE 9].[2]

9. THOMAS GRAY, Knt., of Wark and Heton, Sheriff of Northumberland, Constable of Bamburgh, was born in "le Midyllgathouse" of the castle of Alnwick on 30 Nov. 1384. He was married to ALICE NEVILLE, daughter of Ralph de Neville, Knt., of Raby, Durham, 1st Earl of Westmorland (of **Magna Charta Surety descent** and **descendant of Charlemagne**), by his first wife Margaret, daughter of Hugh Stafford (**descendant of King Edward I**), 2nd Earl of Stafford [see NEVILLE 10 for her ancestry]. They had four sons and four or five daughters. SIR THOMAS GRAY took part in the conspiracy of the Earl of Cambridge against King Henry V, and was beheaded at the North Gate of Southampton as a traitor on 2 or 3 Aug. 1415, and his lands confiscated. His widow was married for the second time to Gilbert Lancaster, Knt.

Raine (1852), chart between pp. 326-327. *Arch.Aeliana (n.s.)* 22:119 ("he is immortalized by Shakespeare as ' Thomas Grey, knight of Northumberland' "). *C.P.* 6:136 footnote *e* (1926). *Northumberland* (1935) 14: chart following p. 328. *Paget* (1957) 264:1. *Roskell* (1992) 3:224.

8. RALPH GRAY, Knt., Warden of Roxburgh Castle, younger son, was born about 1406 (aged twenty-one in 1427). He was married to ELIZABETH FITZ HUGH, daughter of Henry Fitz Hugh, 3rd Lord Fitz Hugh, of Ravensworth (of **Magna Charta Surety descent**), by Elizabeth, daughter of Robert de Grey Marmion, Knt. (of **Magna Charta Surety descent** and **descendant of Charlemagne**). They had four sons. SIR RALPH GRAY died (said to have occurred in France) on 17 Mar. 1442/3. They were buried at Chillingham (altar tomb with M.I.).

Raine (1852), chart between pp. 326-327. *Clay* (1913), p. 88. *Northumberland* (1935) 14: chart following p. 328. *Paget* (1977), p. 411.

7. RALPH GRAY, Knt., of Chillingham, Sheriff of Northumberland, Governor of Bamburgh Castle, son and heir, was born about 1427 (aged sixteen or more in 1443). He was married to JACQUETTA _____. They had two sons and one daughter. SIR RALPH GRAY betrayed Alnwick Castle to the Lancastrians, and was beheaded at Doncaster on 15 July 1464. His widow died on 26 Sep. 1469.

Raine (1852), chart between pp. 326-327. *Arch.Aeliana (n.s.)* 14:300 (1891). *Clay* (1913), p. 88. *Northumberland* (1935) 14: chart following p. 328. *Paget* (1977), p. 251.

6. THOMAS GRAY, Knt., of Heton and Wark, Captain of Norham Castle, son and heir, was born about 1456 (aged eight at father's death). He was married to MARGERY GREYSTOKE, daughter of Ralph Greystoke, 5th Lord Greystoke (of **Magna Charta Surety descent** and **descendant of Charlemagne**), by Elizabeth, daughter of William Fitz Hugh, 4th Lord Fitz Hugh (of **Magna Charta Surety descent** and **descendant of Charlemagne**). They had one son and three daughters. THOMAS GRAY died on 16 Aug. 1498.

Clay (1913), p. 89. *Northumberland* (1935) 14: chart following p. 328 ("first Grey of Chillingham").

5. RALPH GRAY, Knt., of Chillingham, Sheriff of Norham and Islandshire, son and

---

[1] Ancestors of **Nathaniel Littleton, Thomas Lloyd**.

[2] Ancestors of **John Fenwick, Philip & Thomas Nelson**.

GRAY (cont.)

heir, was born about 1479 (aged nineteen and more in 1498). He was married to **ELIZABETH** _____. They had one son and five daughters. SIR RALPH GRAY died on 4 Aug. 1507. His widow is said to have been married for the second time to Christopher Clapham, Esq., Captain of Norham Castle, Sheriff of Northumberland, and for the third time to Philip Dacre, Knt., Sheriff of Northumberland.

Raine (1852), chart between pp. 326-327. Clay (1913), p. 89.

Child of Ralph Gray, by Elizabeth:

i. MARY GRAY, married JOHN FENWICK, Knt. [see FENWICK 4].[1]

* * *

GRAY see also LLOYD

GREENE see MARBURY

GREVILLE see BOSVILE

* * *

GREY

EDWARD I OF ENGLAND, King of England, married **ALIANORE DE CASTILLE**.
JOAN OF ENGLAND [*of Acre*], married **GILBERT DE CLARE**, Earl of Gloucester.
ELIZABETH DE CLARE, married **THEOBALD DE VERDUN**, Lord Verdun.
ISABEL DE VERDUN, married **HENRY DE FERRERS**, 2nd Lord Ferrers of Groby.
WILLIAM DE FERRERS, 3rd Lord Ferrers of Groby, married **MARGARET DE UFFORD**.
HENRY DE FERRERS, 4th Lord Ferrers of Groby, married **JOAN DE HOO**.
WILLIAM DE FERRERS, 5th Lord Ferrers, mar **PHILIPPE DE CLIFFORD** [see CLARKE 7].

8. **HENRY FERRERS**, Knt., son and heir apparent, was born at Raglan, co. Monmouth, about 1394. He was married shortly before 13 July 1416 to **ISABEL MOWBRAY**, first daughter and in her issue co-heiress of Thomas Mowbray, Duke of Norfolk and Earl of Nottingham (**descendant of King Edward I**), by his second wife Elizabeth, daughter of Richard Fitz Alan, Earl of Arundel (**descendant of King Edward I**) [see MOWBRAY 9 for her ancestry]. SIR HENRY FERRERS died *s.p.m., v.p.* His widow was married for the second time in 1423-4 to JAMES BERKELEY, Knt., of Berkeley, co. Gloucester, Lord Berkeley [see DEIGHTON 7 for descendants of this marriage]. She died on 23 Sep. 1452 in Gloucester Castle, being there imprisoned by Margaret, Countess of Shrewsbury, and was buried at Grey Friars', Gloucester.

Baddesley Clinton (1907), p. 115. C.P. 5:357-358 (1926).

7. **ELIZABETH FERRERS**, Lady Ferrers of Groby, only daughter and heiress, was born about 1419 (aged twenty-six and more in 1445), and was heiress of her

---

[1] Ancestors of **John Fenwick**.

GREY (cont.)

grandfather William de Ferrers, Lord Ferrers of Groby. She was married for the first time to **EDWARD GREY**, Lord Ferrers of Groby *jure uxoris*, younger son, being first son of Reynold Grey, 3rd Lord Grey of Ruthin (of **Magna Charta Surety descent and descendant of Charlemagne**), by his second wife, Joan, daughter and heiress of William de Astley, 4th Lord Astley, of Astley, co. Warwick (of **Magna Charta Surety descent** and **descendant of Charlemagne**). He was born about 1415 (aged thirty and more in 1445). They had three sons and two daughters. He was summoned to Parliament from 14 Dec. 1446 by writs directed *Edwardo de Grey*, later as *militi domino de Ferrariis de Groby*. EDWARD GREY, Lord Ferrers of Groby, died on 18 Dec. 1457. She was married for the second time before 2 May 1462 to JOHN BOURGCHIER, Knt. She died on 23 Jan. 1482/3.

C.P. 5:358-361 (1926). *C.P.* 6:199 (1926). *Paget* (1957) 262:1.

6. JOHN GREY, Knt., of Groby, was born about 1432 (aged twenty-five and more at his father's death). He was married to **ELIZABETH WYDEVILLE**, first daughter of Richard Wydeville, 1st Earl Rivers, by Jacquette, Duchess of Bedford, daughter of Pierre de Luxembourg, Comte de Saint Pol, Conversano et Brienne (**descendant of Charlemagne**). She was born about 1437, and was sister and co-heiress of Richard, 3rd Earl Rivers. They had two sons. SIR JOHN GREY was slain, on the Lancastrian side, at the second battle of St. Albans on 17 Feb. 1460/1 *v.m.* His widow was married secretly for the second time at her father's manor of Grafton Regis, co. Northampton, on 1 May 1464 to EDWARD IV OF ENGLAND, **King of England**. They had ten children [see YORK 7.ii for descendants of that marriage]. She was crowned at Westminster on 26 May 1465. She died testate at Bermondsey Abbey, Surrey, where for some time she had resided, or had been compelled by King Henry VII to reside, on 7 or 8 June 1492, and was buried in St. George's Chapel, Windsor, co. Berks, with the King, her second husband.

C.P. 5:361-362 (1926). *Paget* (1957) 262:1. *Paget* (1977), p. 435.

5. THOMAS GREY, K.B., K.G., Lord Ferrers of Groby, son and heir, was born in 1451 (aged fifty at death) or before 1455 (aged thirty-seven and more in 1492). He was married for the first time in October 1466 to ANNE HOLAND, daughter of Henry Holand, 3rd Duke of Exeter, by Anne, daughter of Richard Plantagenet, Duke of York. She was living on 4 Jan. 1472/3, and died *s.p.* He was married for the second time, with marriage contract dated 18 July 1474, to **CECILY BONVILLE**, Baroness Harington and Bonville *suo jure*, daughter and heiress of William Bonville, 6th Lord Harington (**descendant of Charlemagne**), by Katherine (**descendant of King Edward I**), daughter of Richard Neville, 1st Earl of Salisbury [see BONVILLE 7 for her ancestry]. She was born in 1461, and was aged thirteen at time of marriage. They had three sons and six daughters. He was created **Marquess of Dorset** on 18 Apr. 1475. He was summoned to Parliament from 15 Nov. 1482 by writs directed *Thome Marchioni Dors'*. In January 1482/3 on the death of his grandmother, Elizabeth, Lady Ferrers of Groby, he became Lord Ferrers of Groby. "Thomas Gray, mercus Dorsett of Asteley", died testate (P.C.C., 7 Blamyr) aged fifty on 20 Sep. 1501, and was buried at Astley, co. Warwick. His widow was married for the second time to Henry Stafford, Earl of Wiltshire (died 6 Apr. 1523). "Cecill Bonville, Marquess Harrington and Bonvill" died testate (P.C.C., 22 Jankyn) on 12 Apr. 1530, and was buried with her first husband.

C.P. 4:418-419 (1916). *C.P.* 5:215 footnote *b* (1926). *C.P.* 5:327 (1926). *Paget* (1957) 262:1. *Paget* (1977), p. 262.

Children of Thomas Grey, by Cecily Bonville:

    i. **THOMAS GREY**, born 22 June 1477 [see next].

GREY (cont.)

    ii. **DOROTHY GREY**, married **ROBERT WILLOUGHBY**, Lord Willoughby [see PAULET 6].[1]
    iii. **CECILY GREY**, married **JOHN DUDLEY**, 3rd Lord Dudley [see DUDLEY 3].[2]
    iv. **ELEANOR GREY**, married **JOHN ARUNDELL** [see CALVERT 5].[3]

4. THOMAS GREY, K.B., K.G., 2nd Marquess of Dorset, Lord Ferrers of Groby, son and heir, was born on 22 June 1477 (but aged twenty-six and more in 1504). He was married in 1509 to **MARGARET WOTTON**, widow of William Medley, Esq. (living 6 Jan. 1509), and daughter of Robert Wotton, Knt., of Bocton Malherbe, Kent, by Anne, daughter of Henry Belknap, Knt. (of **Magna Charta Surety descent** and **descendant of Charlemagne**) They had four sons and three daughters. He was summoned to Parliament from 17 Oct. 1509 by writs directed *Thome Grey, Domino Ferrers de Groby*, later as *Thome Grey, Marchioni Dorset*. On the death of his mother, Cecily, Lady Harington and Bonvile, he became Lord Harington and Bonvile. He was one of the eight Challengers at the Field of Cloth of Gold in June 1520, and promoted King Henry VIII's divorce. "Thomas Grey, marques Dorset, of Astleye" died testate (P.C.C., 10 Thower) aged fifty-three on 10 Oct. 1530. His widow died after 6 Oct. 1535.

    C.P. 4:419-420 (1916). H.S.P. 75:78 (1924) (1574 Vis. Kent). C.P. 5:363 (1926). Paget (1957) 262:2. Paget (1977), p. 178.

    Children of Thomas Grey, by Margaret Wotton:
    i. **JOHN GREY**, younger son [see next].
    ii. **ANNE GREY**, married **HENRY WILLOUGHBY**, Knt., of Wollaton, co. Nottingham, died 17 Aug. 1548, son of Edward Willoughby, of Wollaton (of **Magna Charta Surety descent** and **descendant of Charlemagne**), by Anne, daughter of William Filliol. Paget (1977), p. 188.
        a. **MARGARET WILLOUGHBY**, married **MATTHEW ARUNDELL**, Knt. [see CALVERT 3].[4]

3. JOHN GREY, of Pirgo, Essex, younger son, was married to **MARY BROWNE**, daughter of Anthony Browne, of Battle Abbey, Sussex (**descendant of King Edward I**), by Alice, daughter of John Gage, K.G. [see BROWNE 6 for her ancestry].
    Yeatman (1903), pp. 59,67. Paget (1957) 262:2.

    Child of John Grey, by Mary Browne:
    i. **JANE GREY**, married **EDWARD GREVILLE**, Knt., of Harold Park, Essex [see BOSVILE 2].[5]

* * *

GREY OF RUTHIN see BONVILLE

GREY OF WILTON see HAVILAND

GRIFFITH see COYTEMORE

---

[1]Ancestors of **Thomas Wingfield**.

[2]Ancestors, probably, of **Thomas Dudley**.

[3]Ancestors of **Charles Calvert, Maria Johanna Somerset**.

[4]Ancestors of **Charles Calvert**.

[5]Grandparents of **Elizabeth Bosvile**.

EDWARD III OF ENGLAND, King of England, married PHILIPPE DE HAINAUT.
JOHN OF LANCASTER [*of Gaunt*], mar BLANCHE OF LANCASTER [see LANCASTER 10].

8. ELIZABETH OF LANCASTER, second daughter, was born before 21 Feb. 1363. She was married for the first time to JOHN HASTINGS, 3rd Earl of Pembroke. They were divorced after 24 Sep. 1383. She was married for the second time at or near Plymouth, on 24 June 1386, on the eve of her father's expedition to Spain, to **JOHN DE HOLAND**, Knt., K.G., younger son of Thomas de Holand, Knt., Earl of Kent (of **Magna Charta Surety descent and descendant of Charlemagne**), by Joan [*the Fair Maid of Kent*], daughter of Edmund of Kent [*of Woodstock*], Earl of Kent (**son of King Edward I**). He was born after 1350, and was half-brother of King Richard II [see HOLAND 9 for his ancestry]. He was appointed Constable of the army which John, Duke of Lancaster, was taking out in an attempt to obtain the Crown of Castile. It was by his advice that the Duke abandoned this unsuccessful enterprise. He was created **Earl of Huntingdon** on 2 June 1388, and **Duke of Exeter** on 29 Sep. 1397. He joined in the plot to seize King Henry IV, but took no active part. JOHN DE HOLAND, Duke of Exeter, died on 9 or 10 Jan. 1399/1400, being beheaded at Pleshey Castle, Essex, for treason against his brother-in-law King Henry IV. He was buried in the Collegiate Church at Pleshey (M.I.). She was married for the third time before 12 Dec. 1400 to JOHN CORNWALL, Knt., K.G., later Lord Fanhope and Lord Milbrook (died testate at Ampthill 11 Dec. 1443 *s.p.s.*). She died on 24 Nov. 1425, and was buried in Burford Church, co. Salop (M.I.).

C.P. 5:195-200, 253-254 (1926). *C.P.* 7:415 footnote *g*.

7. CONSTANCE DE HOLAND, was born about 1387 (aged four in October 1391). She was married for the first time to THOMAS MOWBRAY, Knt., Earl of Norfolk. He was executed, aged less than twenty, for involvement in the Scrope conspiracy, on 8 June 1405. She was married for the second time before 24 Feb. 1412/3 to **JOHN GREY**, Knt., K.G., of Badmondisfield, co. Suffolk, son and heir apparent of Reynold Grey, 3rd Lord Grey of Ruthin (of **Magna Charta Surety descent and descendant of Charlemagne**), by Margaret, daughter of Thomas de Ros, 4th Lord Ros of Helmsley (**descendant of King Edward I**) [see BONVILLE 10 for his ancestry]. She died on 12 or 14 Nov. 1437, and was buried in St. Katherine's by the Tower. SIR JOHN GREY died on 27 Aug. 1439 *v.p.*

Norf.Arch.Soc. 2:365 (1895) (1563 Vis. Norfolk). *C.P.* 6:159 (1926). *C.P.* 9:604-605 (1936).

Children of John Grey, by Constance de Holand:
  i. **EDMUND GREY**, born 26 Oct 1416, married **KATHERINE PERCY** [see HAVILAND 7].[1]
  ii. ALICE GREY [see next].

6. ALICE GREY, was married to **WILLIAM KNYVETT**, Knt., of Buckenham, Norfolk, M.P., Sheriff of Norfolk and Suffolk, son and heir of John Knyvett, Knt., of Buckenham (of **Magna Charta Surety descent and descendant of Charlemagne**), by Alice, daughter and heiress of William Lynne, Esq., of Norfolk. He was born about 1440 (aged fifty-one in 1491). They had one son and three daughters. She died on 4 Apr. 1474 (brass at Buckenham). He was married for the second time about 1477 to Joan Stafford, divorced wife of William Beaumont, Viscount Beaumont, and daughter of Humphrey Stafford, 1st Duke of Buckingham, and had three sons and

---

[1] Ancestors, probably, of **Jane Haviland**.

GURDON (cont.)

three daughters. He was married for a third time to Joan Courtenay, widow of Robert Clifford, Knt., and daughter and co-heiress of Thomas Courtenay, 5th Earl of Devon. SIR WILLIAM KNYVETT died on 2 Dec. 1515.

> Berry (1837), p. 53. Banks (1844), p. 158. Norf.Arch.Soc. 2:365 (1895). H.S.P. 16:177 (1881) (1563 Vis. Yorks). C.P. 2:63 (1912). Sur.Soc. 144:10 (1930) (1480 Vis. North). Paget (1977), p. 435.

5. EDMUND KNYVETT, Knt., of Buckenham, Norfolk, son and heir by first marriage, was married to **ELEANOR TYRRELL**, daughter of William Tyrrell, Knt., of Gipping, Suffolk, by Margaret, daughter of Robert Darcy, Knt., of Maldon. They had five sons. SIR EDMUND KNYVETT was drowned at sea in 1504. His widow died in 1514.

> Berry (1837), p. 54. Banks (1844), p. 148. Sur.Soc. 144:10 (1930) (1480 Vis. North). Paget (1977), pp. 263,276.

4. EDMUND KNYVETT, Knt., of Ashwellthorpe, co. Norfolk *jure uxoris*, Sergeant Porter to King Henry VIII, was born in 1490. He was married to **JOAN BOURGCHIER**, Baroness Berners *suo jure de jure*, second but only surviving daughter and heiress of John Bourgchier, Knt. (**descendant of King Edward III**), by Katherine, daughter of John Howard, K.G., Duke of Norfolk [see LAUNCE 6.i for her ancestry]. SIR EDMUND KNYVETT died testate on 1 May 1539. His widow died testate on 17 Feb. 1561/2. They were buried at Ashwellthorpe (M.I.).

> Collins (1734), pp. 343-347. Berry (1837), p. 55. Vivian (1895), p. 106 (1620 Vis. Devon). Saltonstall (1897), p. 93 (descent of Muriel Gurdon from King Edward III). Copinger (1910) 5:206-207. C.P. 2:155 (1912). Paget (1977), p. 276.

3. JOHN KNYVETT, Esq., of Plumstead, Norfolk, son and heir, was born about 1517 (aged twenty-two at his father's death). He was married, with marriage settlement dated 14 Feb. 1537, to **AGNES HARCOURT**, daughter of John Harcourt, Knt., of Ellen Hall, co. Stafford, and Stanton Harcourt, co. Oxford (**descendant of King Edward I**), by Margaret (**descendant of King Edward I**), daughter of William Barentyn [see HARCOURT 5 for her ancestry]. JOHN KNYVETT, ESQ., was living in 1543 and died *v.m.* His widow was married for the second time on 1 Mar. 1564/5 to William Bowyer, Gent., of Wimbledon, Surrey, and had issue.

> Collins (1734), pp. 345-348. *Stemmata Chicheleana* (1765), p. 121 (identifies children Thomas and Elizabeth Ashfield). Collins-Brydges (1812) 4:439. Berry (1837), pp. 54,57 (Knevet arms: *Argent a bend within a bordure engrailed sable*). Wm. Salt Soc. 3:93 (1882). Saltonstall (1897), p. 93. Copinger (1910) 5:207. C.P. 2:155 (1912).

2. ABIGAIL KNYVETT, was married, as his second wife, to **MARTIN SEDLEY**, Knt., of Moreley, Norfolk, son and heir of Martin Sedley, of Moreley, by Elizabeth, daughter of John Mounteney, Gent., of Mountnessing, Essex. He was born in 1531 (aged seventy-eight at death), and purchased Barford in 1580. He had been married previously, with two sons and two daughters, to Anne (buried 28 May 1571), daughter of Ralph Shelton, Esq. Martin & Abigail had two sons and two daughters. SIR MARTIN SEDLEY was buried, testate, at St. Peter's Chapel, Moreley, Norfolk, on 10 Feb. 1609/10, with monumental inscription (naming wives and children). She died on 15 Dec. 1623, and was buried at Wacton, Norfolk.

> Collins (1734), pp. 350-1. Norf.Arch.Soc. 1:111-112 (1878); 2:361,366(M.I.),368, 400(his will) (1895) (1563 Vis. Norfolk) (brass in nave at Wacton Magna reads: *Hic jacet Abigail Sedley, vid. filia Johannes Knyvet de Ashwouldthorp, Armigeri, et nuper uxor Martini Sedley de Morley, Armigeri, quae quidem obiit 15 Dec. a.d. 1623*). Saltonstall (1897) [confuses Abigail with her niece]. Muskett (1900), pp. 286-287. Waters 2:969-970 (1901) (his will). AR (1992) 4:39 (correction to Saltonstall provided by T.F. Beard).

1. MURIEL SEDLEY, was born in 1583. She was married, as his second wife, at St. Peter's, Moreley, Norfolk, on 8 July 1606 to **BRAMPTON GURDON**, Esq., of Assington Hall, Suffolk, Sheriff of Suffolk, M.P. for Sudbury, son and heir of John

GURDON (cont.)

Gurdon, Esq., of Assington, by Amy, daughter and heiress of William Brampton, of Letton, Norfolk. He had been married previously, with four sons and two daughters, to Elizabeth Barrett, daughter and co-heiress of Edward Barrett, of Belhouse in Aveley, Essex, by Elizabeth, daughter and co-heiress of Thomas Lytton, Knt. The will of BRAMPTON GURDON, Esq., was dated 19 Oct. 1647, codicil 1 Feb. 1648, proved 15 May 1650 (P.C.C., 68 Pembroke). His widow died at Letton, Norfolk, aged seventy-eight, on 22 Aug. 1661, and was buried there (M.I.).

Waters 2:956-957 (1901) (his will). *Norf.Arch.Soc.* 2:361 (marriage record). *Saltonstall* (1897), pp. 12-13, 93-101. *Muskett* (1900), pp. 286 (he entered pedigree in 1612 Vis. Suffolk), 287-288. *NEHGR* 95:72 (Jan. 1941). *NEHGR* 106:260 (Oct. 1952) (Gurdon arms: *Sable*, three leopard's faces jessant-delys *or*).

Children of Brampton Gurdon, by Muriel Sedley:
    i. BRAMPTON GURDON, M.P. for Sudbury, married MARY POLSTED. Descendants in England.
    ii. THOMAS GURDON, died *s.p.*
    iii. EDMOND GURDON, died at the "Barmoodies" [i.e. Bermuda], on way to New England *s.p.*
    iv. ABIGAIL GURDON, married ROGER HILL, M.P. for Bridgeport, Baron of the Exchequer.
    v. AMY GURDON, died *s.p.*
    vi. **MURIEL GURDON**, born about 1613 (aged twenty-two in 1635), married June 1633 **MAJ. RICHARD SALTONSTALL**, Esq., of Ipswich, Massachusetts [for children of this marriage see SALTONSTALL 1].

* * *

GWYNN see OWEN

* * *

GYE

HENRY III OF ENGLAND, King of England, married **ALIANORE DE PROVENCE**.
EDMUND OF LANCASTER *Crouchback*, Earl of Lancaster, married, **BLANCHE D'ARTOIS**.
HENRY OF LANCASTER, Duke of Lancaster, married **MAUD DE CHAWORTH**.
ALIANOR OF LANCASTER, married **RICHARD FITZ ALAN**, Earl of Arundel.
JOHN FITZ ALAN, Knt., married **ALIANOR MALTRAVERS**.
JOAN FITZ ALAN, married **WILLIAM DE ECHYNGHAM**, Knt.
JOAN DE ECHINGHAM, married **JOHN BAYNTON**, Knt. [see BAYNTON 6].

4. **HENRY BAYNTON**, of Faulstone, co. Wilts, fifth son, was married.
    H.S.P. 105:6 (1954) (1623 Vis. Wilts) (*Henricus Bainton 5 filius* [had daughter] *Jana filia et haer uxor Tho: Prouse de Com Devon*). *Abel Lunt* (1963), p. 223.

3. **JOAN BAYNTON**, daughter and heiress, was married, evidently, to **THOMAS PROWSE**, of Prowse in Sandford, Devon.
    NEHGR 115:248-253 (Oct. 1961). *NEHGR* 122:282-83 (1968).

2. **MARY PROWSE**, was married, as a child, apparently by marriage settlement in 1509, to **JOHN GYE**, son, evidently, of John Gye, by his wife, Elizabeth, daughter of Edmund Spencer. She was of full age in 1520 and brought to her husband the

GYE (cont.)

manors of Poughill and Doddridge in Sandford, with other lands in co. Devon. In 1516 she and her husband claimed the lands of Thomas Prowse in Poughill, Dodderidge, Ilsington, and elsewhere. She was heir general of Upcot in Cheriton FitzPaine, co. Devon, which had once belonged to her great-uncle, Nicholas Radford, the noted judge who was murdered about 1455. JOHN GYE died on 14 Aug. 1536.
NEHGR 115:248-253 (Oct. 1961). *NEHGR* 122:282-283 (Oct. 1968).

1. ROBERT GYE (or **GUY**), Gent., of Prowse in Sandford, Devon, was born about 1531 (aged five at father's death). He was married for the first time (with one son) to an unidentified wife, and for the second time about 1555 to **GRACE DOWRISH**, daughter of Thomas Dowrish, of Dowrish House in Sandford, Devon, by Anne, daughter of Charles Farringdon, of Farringdon, Devon. They had eleven children. She died intestate when her daughter Mary was very young. According to allegations in a suit of Robert Gye against Radford Maverick in 1604 in the Court of Requests, her father "gave great sums to Radford Maverick to bring up his daughter Mary, and that Maverick bestowed her in marriage to John Maverick, his cousin german". ROBERT GYE, GENT., died before Michaelmas, 1608.
Vivian (1895), pp. 290,340. *NEHGR* 96:232-241 (July 1942), 358-366 (Oct. 1942) (no identification of parents of Mary Gye). *NEHGR* 115:248-253 (descent from King Henry III) (corrected by next entry) (Thomas Westcote, A View of Devon in MDCXXX (1845), p. 618 "shows that Grace Dowrish descended from Thomas Fulford, of Fulford, Knt., whose wife was a Courtenay of Powderham and descended from Edward I. Westcote's account may be correct, although it disagrees with that given in Vivian, and should therefore be carefully investigated"). *NEHGR* 115:282-283 (Oct. 1968).

Child & grandchildren of Robert Gye, by Grace Dowrish:

   i. **MARY GYE**, youngest daughter, born about 1580, living 9 Oct. 1666; married, Ilsington, co. Devon, 28 Oct. 1600, **REV. JOHN MAVERICK**, baptised Awliscombe, co. Devon, 27 Oct. 1578, matriculated Exeter College, Oxford University, 24 Oct. 1595, B.A. 8 July 1599, M.A. 7 July 1603, Curate South Huish, co. Devon, Rector of Silverton, co. Devon 1615, chosen a teacher of the Puritan church organized at Plymouth, emigrated on the *Mary and John* embarking 24 Mar. 1629/30, arriving 30 May 1630, minister Dorchester, Massachusetts, died Boston, Massachusetts, 3 Feb. 1635/6.

      a. **SAMUEL MAVERICK**, born about 1602, emigrated to New England 1624, had large land grants in Massachusetts and Maine, spent year in Virginia in 1635, one of the earliest slaveholders in Massachusetts, attached to the Church of England, often at enmity with Puritan authorities, returned to England, back to New England in 1664 as a Royal Commissioner, settled in New York after unsuccessful dealings with Massachusetts; married about 1628 **AMIAS (COLE) THOMPSON**. Three children.

      b. **ELIAS MAVERICK**, born about 1604, died 8 Sep. 1684, buried Charlestown; married **ANNA HARRIS**. Eleven children.

      c. **MARY MAVERICK**, baptised South Huish 30 Nov. 1606, buried 6 Mar. 1606/7.

      d. **AARON MAVERICK**, baptised Huish 6 Mar. 1607/8, probably died young.

      e. **MARY MAVERICK**, baptised South Huish 6 Jan. 1609/10, married **REV. JAMES PARKER**, of Weymouth, Massachusetts, Portsmouth, New Hampshire, and Barbados. Six children.

      f. **MOSES MAVERICK**, baptised Huish 3 Nov. 1611, died Marblehead, Massachusetts, 28 Jan. 1685/6; married, first, **REMEMBER ALLERTON**, second, **EUNICE (_____) ROBERTS**. Seven children by first marriage. Four children by second marriage.

      g. **ABIGAIL MAVERICK**, baptised Huish 20 Mar. 1613/14, died 25 June 1644; married **JOHN MANNING**, merchant of Boston. Two children.

      h. **ANTIPAS MAVERICK**, born about 1619, drowned 2 July 1678; married. Three children.

      i. **JOHN MAVERICK**, born about 1621, sailor of Dorchester, settler of Charleston, South Carolina about 1670, married All Hallows, London Wall 15 Apr. 1649 **JANE ANDREWS**. Two children.

GYSE see HAVILAND

HALL see BOURCHIER

HAMMERTON see BIGOD

* * *

HANKFORD

EDWARD I OF ENGLAND, King of England, married **ALIANORE DE CASTILLE**.
JOAN OF ENGLAND [*of Acre*], married **RALPH DE MONTHERMER**, Lord Monthermer.
THOMAS DE MONTHERMER, 2nd Lord Monthermer, married **MARGARET** _____.
MARGARET DE MONTHERMER, married **JOHN DE MONTAGU**, Lord Montagu.
JOHN MONTAGU, 3rd Earl of Salisbury, married **MAUD FRANCIS** [see **MONTHERMER 10**].

7. **ANNE MONTAGU**, was married for the first time to **RICHARD HANKFORD**, Knt., of Hewish & Yarnscombe, co. Devon, etc., son of Richard Hankford, by Thomasine, daughter and heiress of Richard de Stapeldon, Knt., of Norton and Nonnington, Somerset, etc.. He was born about 21 July 1397, and obtained possession of the lands in Devon, Cornwall, Wilts, and Middlesex of his grandfather, William Hankford, on 5 June 1424. He had been married previously to Elizabeth fitz Warin, born about 1403, died between 10 Feb. 1425/6 and 16 Jan. 1427/8, daughter of Fulk Fitz Warin, of Whittington, co. Salop, 6th Lord Fitz Warin, by Anne, daughter of William Botreaux, of Boscastle, Cornwall, Lord Botreaux. He served in France in the retinue of the Earl of Salisbury. SIR RICHARD HANKFORD died aged thirty-three on 8 Feb. 1430/1. ANNE DE MONTAGU was married for the second time, as his second wife, about 1433 to **JOHN [AP] LEWIS**, Knt., of West Horndon, Essex, Citizen and Vintner of London, M.P. for Essex, Sheriff of Essex and Hertfordshire, Steward of the Duchy of Cornwall within Devon. He was of Welsh origin, and had been married previously, with two sons, to Alice de Vere (died about 1431), widow of Francis Court, Knt., of Tytherley, co. Hants, and daughter of Aubrey de Vere, 10th Earl of Oxford, by Alice, daughter of John, Lord Fitzwalter. John & Anne had three sons and four daughters (the sons adopted the surname Fitz Lewis). SIR JOHN FITZ LEWIS died testate, perhaps overseas, on 27 Oct. 1442. The will of "Lowes Joh'n knyght" (P.C.C., 14 Rous), named "Dam Alyse somtyme my wyfe", Anne Mountagew my wyfe", and sons, Lowes (the eldest), Edmond, Philip, Herry and John fitz Lowes, and daughters, Margaret (the eldest), Elizabeth, Alice and Margaret (the youngest), requesting burial in the Abbey of St. Mary Graces, London. She was married for the third time, as his third wife, to **JOHN HOLAND**, Duke of Exeter (died 5 Aug. 1447). "Anne Holland, duchesse of Excester" died testate (P.C.C., 11 Stokton) on 29 Nov. 1457, and was buried with him in the Church of St. Katherine by the Tower.

Camden Soc. 43:126 (1849) (1613 Vis. Hunts). *C.P.* (1926) 5:210, 504-507. *C.P.* 10:234 footnote g (Alice m., "1stly, Guy d'Albon; 2ndly, Sir John FitzLewis"). *Paget* (1957) 372:12. *H.S.P.* 111:217 (1984) (1561 Vis. Suffolk). *Roskell* (1992) 3:494-498 ("a Welshman of dubious origin who became a financier, a landowner of substance and the son-in-law of two earls ... close association with Thomas Chaucer of Ewelme, Henry IV's chief butler and cousin of the King's half-brothers, the Beauforts ... the two men supplied wine to the households of Henry IV and Henry V").

Child of Richard Hankford, by Anne Montagu:

HANKFORD (cont.)

    i. **ANNE HANKFORD**, married **THOMAS BUTLER**, 7th Earl of Ormond [see BUTLER 6].[1]
Child of John [ap] Lewis, by Anne Montagu:

    ii. **ELIZABETH FITZ LEWIS** [see next].

6. ELIZABETH FITZ LEWIS, was married to **JOHN WINGFIELD**, Knt., K.B., of Letheringham, Sheriff of Norfolk and Surrolk, P.C., son and heir of Robert Wingfield, Knt., of Letheringham (**descendant of King Edward I**), by Elizabeth (**descendant of King Edward I**), daughter and co-heiress of Robert Goushill, Knt., of Hoveringham, co. Nottingham. They had twelve sons and four daughters [see LETHERINGHAM 7 for his ancestry]. SIR JOHN WINGFIELD died on 10 May 1481. The will of "Dame Elizabeth Wyngfeld, wyfe of Sir John Wyngfeld, Kt., of Letherynghm, wid", was proved on 22 Dec. 1500. They were buried at Letheringham.
    Camden Soc. 43:126-127 (1849); *NEHGR* 103:295 (Oct. 1949) (no indication of her Plantagenet ancestry). *H.S.P.* 111:217 (1984). *Roskell* (1992) 3:498.

Children of John Wingfield, by Elizabeth Fitz Lewis:

    i. **JOHN WINGFIELD**, Knt., son and heir [see next].

    ii. **ELIZABETH WINGFIELD**, married **FRANCIS HALL**, of Grantham [see BOURCHIER 4].[2]

5. JOHN WINGFIELD, Knt., K.B., Sheriff of Norfolk and Suffolk, son and heir, was married to **ANNE TUCHET**, daughter of John Tuchet, 6th Lord Audley (**descendant of King Edward I**), by Anne, daughter and co-heiress of Thomas Echingham, Knt. (**descendant of King Henry III**) [see TUCHET 8 for her ancestry]). They had three sons and three daughters. He fought at Bosworth on 22 Aug. 1485 against King Richard III, and was pardoned. SIR JOHN WINGFIELD died in 1509.
    Camden Soc. 43:126 (1849) ("Anna, da. of J. Touchet, Lo. Audley, Baron of Healy Castle in Staffordshire"). *Sur.Soc.* 144:122 (1930) (1480 Vis. North) (*Dominus Iohannes Wingfeld miles nupsit dominam Annam filiam domini de Audeley*). *H.S.P.* 111:219 (1984).

4. ANTHONY WINGFIELD, Knt., K.G., of Letheringham, son and heir, married **ELIZABETH DE VERE**, daughter of George de Vere (**descendant of King Edward I**), by Margaret, daughter and heiress of William Stafford, Knt., of Bishop's Frome, co. Hereford [see CERGEAUX 5 for her ancestry]. He was knighted by King Henry VIII for bravery at the battle of Spurs on 16 Aug. 1513 and was installed Knight of the Garter in 1541. He was Comptroller of the King's Household, Vice-Chamberlain of Household to King Henry VII, Privy Councillor, and executor of the King. The will of "Sir Anthony Wyngfeld, K.G." was dated 13 Aug. 1552 and proved 18 Nov. 1553 (P.C.C., 9 Tashe). The will of his widow was dated 28 July 1557 and proved 13 Nov. 1559.
    Camden Soc. 43:126 (1849). *H.S.P.* 32:317 (1891) (Vis. Norfolk) (Elizabeth was "widow of Edward Knightlye, Knt."). *Sur.Soc.* 144:122 (1930) (1480 Vis. North). *H.S.P.* 111:219-220 (1984).

3. RICHARD WINGFIELD, Esq., of Crowfield and Wantisden, Suffolk, third son, was married to **MARY HARDWICK**, daughter and heiress of John Hardwick, of Hardwick, co. Derby, by Elizabeth, daughter of Thomas Leake, of Hasland, co. Derby. They had four sons and two daughters. The will of "Richard Wingfeilde, esquire" was dated 2 May 1588 and proved 14 Aug. 1591 (P.C.C., 62 Sainberbe).
    Camden Soc. 43:127 (1849) (Mary was "sister to Eliza. the grand Countess of Shrewesburie"). *Reliquary* 22:242 (Apr. 1882). *H.S.P.* 32:318 (1891). *H.S.P.* 111:220 (1984) (Mary was sister of "Bess of Hardwick").

---

[1] Ancestors of **Anne Humphrey, Thomas Lunsford, Herbert Pelham, John West**.

[2] Ancestors of **William Asfordby, Mary Bourchier, Diana & Grey Skipwith**.

HANKFORD (cont.)

2. HENRY WINGFIELD, of Crowfield, Suffolk, married ELIZABETH RISBY, daughter of Thomas Risby, by Jane, daughter and co-heiress of John Harbottle. They had one son and two daughters.
   Camden Soc. 43:127 (1849). *H.S.P.* 32:318 (1891). *Adventurers* (1987), p. 107-108.
   Child of Henry Wingfield, by Elizabeth Risby:
   i. MARY WINGFIELD, married WILLIAM DADE, Esq. [see DADE 1].[1]

* * *

HARBOTTLE

EDWARD I OF ENGLAND, King of England, married MARGUERITE DE FRANCE.
THOMAS OF NORFOLK [*of Brotherton*], Earl of Norfolk, married ALICE DE HALES.
MARGARET OF NORFOLK, married JOHN DE SEGRAVE, 4th Lord Segrave.
ELIZABETH DE SEGRAVE, married JOHN DE MOWBRAY, 4th Lord Mowbray.
JOAN DE MOWBRAY, married THOMAS GRAY, Knt.
MAUD GRAY, married ROBERT OGLE, Knt. [see OGLE 9].

8. MARGARET OGLE, was married for the first time in June 1424 to ROBERT HARBOTTLE, Knt., of Preston, Northumberland, Sheriff of Northumberland, son and heir of Robert Harbottle, Esq., of Preston, Northumberland, by Isabel, daughter and heiress of Bertram Monboucher, Knt., of Horton, Northumberland. He was born about 1400 (aged nineteen at his father's death in 1419). SIR ROBERT HARBOTTLE died on 14 Mar. 1443. She was married for the second time to NICHOLAS BELLINGHAM.
   Surtees (1820) 2:225 (Harbottle arms: *Azure*, three icicles bendways *or*; perhaps "the charges were intended for <u>bottles</u>"). *Hodgson* (1832), p. 262. *Arch.Aeliana (n.s.)* 14:195 (1891) (marriage settlement). *Clay* (1913), p. 153. *Sur.Soc.* 144:55 (1930) (1480 Vis. North) (Margaret identified as daughter of *Dominus Robertus Ogill miles*, by *Matildis filia domini Iohannis Gray militis*). *C.P.* 10:29 (1945). *Roskell* (1992) 3:285,287,755,861.

7. BERTRAM HARBOTTLE, Esq., of Beamish and Tanfield, Durham, of Sutton in Trent, co. Nottingham, and of Dalton Travers, co. York, Sheriff of Northumberland, was born about 1426, and was eventual heir to his second cousin Bertram Monboucher (died 1425). He was married in 1439 to JOAN LUMLEY, daughter of Thomas Lumley, Lord Lumley (of **Magna Charta Surety descent** and **descendant of Charlemagne**), by Margaret, daughter of James Harington, Knt. They had one son and five daughters. He entered on the estates on the death in 1450 of Elizabeth, Baroness of Hilton, widow of Bertram Monboucher. BERTRAM HARBOTTLE, ESQ., died on 2 Aug. 1462. His widow was living on 9 Dec. 1492.
   Surtees (1820), p. 223,225. *Hodgson* (1832), p. 262.
   Children of Bertram Harbottle, by Joan Lumley:
   i. RALPH HARBOTTLE, born about 1453 [see next].
   ii. AGNES HARBOTTLE, married ROGER FENWICK, Knt., of Stanton [see FENWICK 6].[2]

6. RALPH HARBOTTLE, Knt., of Beamish, Durham, etc., was born about 1453 (aged

---

[1]Parents of **Francis Dade**.

[2]Ancestors of **John Fenwick**.

HARBOTTLE (cont.)

nine at father's death). He was married to **MARGARET PERCY**, daughter of Ralph Percy, Knt. (**descendant of King Edward III**), by Eleanor, daughter of Laurence de Acton [see KEMPE 9.ii for her ancestry]. They had two children. She was living in 1506. SIR RALPH HARBOTTLE died about 1507.
   Surtees (1820), p. 225 (no identification of wife Margaret). *Hodgson* (1832), p. 262. *Alnwick* (1866) 1:416-417. *Northumberland* 5:467 (1899).

5. **GUISCARD HARBOTTLE**, Knt., of Beamish, etc., son and heir, was married to **JANE WILLOUGHBY**, daughter of Henry Willoughby, Knt., of Wollaton, co. Nottingham (of **Magna Charta Surety descent** and **descendant of Charlemagne**), by Margaret (**descendant of Charlemagne**), daughter of Robert Markham, Knt., of East Markham, co. Nottingham. They had one son and two daughters. SIR GUISCARD HARBOTTLE died in 1516.
   Surtees (1820), p. 225. *Hodgson* (1832), p. 262.

   Child of Guiscard Harbottle, by Jane Willoughby:
   i. **ELEANOR HARBOTTLE**, married **THOMAS PERCY**, Knt. [see KEMPE 5].[1]

* * *

HARBY see OXENBRIDGE

* * *

HARCOURT

EDWARD I OF ENGLAND, King of England, married **ALIANORE DE CASTILLE**.
JOAN OF ENGLAND [*of Acre*], married **GILBERT DE CLARE**, Earl of Gloucester.
ELIZABETH DE CLARE, married **ROGER DAMORY**, Lord Damory.
ELIZABETH DAMORY, married **JOHN BARDOLF**, 3rd Lord Bardolf.
WILLIAM BARDOLF, 4th Lord Bardolf, married **AGNES DE POYNINGS**.
CECILY BARDOLF, married **BRIAN STAPLETON**, Knt.
MILES STAPLETON, Knt., married **KATHERINE DE LA POLE** [see BARDOLF 9].

7. **JOAN STAPLETON**, younger daughter and co-heiress, was born about 1444. She was married for the first time to **JOHN HUDDLESTONE**, Knt., of Millom, Cumberland, with issue. She was married for the second time to **CHRISTOPHER HARCOURT**, Knt., of Great Ashby, son and heir of Richard Harcourt, Knt., of Stanton Harcourt, co. Oxford, by Edith, daughter and heiress of Thomas St. Clere. They had three sons. SIR CHRISTOPHER HARCOURT died in 1474.
   Collins-Brydges (1812) 4:437-438. *H.S.P.* 56:9 (1907) (1532 Vis. Berks). *Paget* (1977), p. 462.

6. **SIMON HARCOURT**, Knt., of Stanton Harcourt, co. Oxford, second, but eldest surviving son and heir, was married for the first time to **AGNES DARRELL**, daughter of Thomas Darrell, of Scotney, Kent, by Thomasine, daughter of John Gresley, Knt., of Drakelowe. They had two sons and one daughter. He was married for the second

---

[1] Ancestors of **Edmund Kempe**.

HARCOURT (cont.)

time to ELIZABETH _____, widow of Richard York, Knt. SIR SIMON HARCOURT died on 16 Jan. 1547, and was buried at Stanton Harcourt.
> *Stemmata Chicheleana* (1765), pp. 64,121 (Florence Chichele, mother of Thomas Darrell, was "Founder's Kin"). *Collins-Brydges* (1812) 4:438. *Wm. Salt Soc.* 3:92-92 (1882) (1583 Vis. Staffs) (Harcourt arms: *Gules*, two bars *or*). *H.S.P.* 56:9 (1907). *Paget* (1977), p. 462.

5. JOHN HARCOURT, Knt., of Stanton Harcourt, son and heir, was married to **MARGARET BARENTYN**, daughter and co-heiress of William Barentyn, of Hasely, co. Oxford, by Jane (**descendants of King Edward I**), daughter of Roger Lewknor, Knt. [see TUCHET 6 for her ancestry]. They had six sons and eight daughters. SIR JOHN HARCOURT died on 19 Feb. 1565, and was buried at Stanton Harcourt.
> *Stemmata Chicheleana* (1765), p. 121. *Collins-Brydges* (1812) 4:438. *Wm. Salt Soc.* 3:92 (1882). *H.S.P.* 56:9 (1907). *Paget* (1977), pp. 276,462.

Child of John Harcourt, by Margaret Barentyn:

i. **AGNES HARCOURT**, married **JOHN KNYVETT**, Esq. [see GURDON 3].[1]

* * *

HARLESTON

EDWARD III OF ENGLAND, King of England, married **PHILIPPE DE HAINAUT**.
LIONEL OF CLARENCE [*of Antwerp*], Duke of Clarence, married **ELIZABETH DE BURGH**.
PHILIPPE OF CLARENCE, married **EDMUND DE MORTIMER**, 3rd Earl of March.
ELIZABETH MORTIMER, married **HENRY PERCY**, Knt.
ELIZABETH PERCY, married **JOHN DE CLIFFORD**, Lord Clifford [see MACKWORTH 7].

7. MARY DE CLIFFORD, was married to **PHILIP WENTWORTH**, Knt., of Nettlestead, Suffolk *jure uxoris*, Sheriff of Norfolk and Suffolk, M.P., son and heir apparent of Roger Wentworth, Knt., of North Elmsall, co. York, by Margery, daughter and heiress of Philip Despenser, Knt., of Nettlestead, Suffolk, 2nd Lord le Despenser (**descendant of Charlemagne**). He was born about 1424. They had one son and one daughter. SIR PHILIP WENTWORTH served in the army of King Henry VI, and died intestate on 18 May 1464 *v.m.*, being beheaded at Middleham, co. York, after the battle of Hexham, where he had been taken prisoner by the Yorkists. She was buried at Friars Minor, Ipswich.
> *Rutton* (1891), p. 138 ("? buried at Newsam Abbey, co. Lincoln"). *Clay* (1913), p. 24. *Sur.Soc.* 144:79 (1930) (1480 Vis. North) (identifies second wife of *Martinus de See* as *Elizabeth filia domini Philippi Wentworth militis*,). *C.P.* 12(2):497 footnote *c* (1953). *TAG* 69:137 (1994) (Elizabeth not named in previous accounts of daughters of Sir Philip Wentworth) (the informant for the pedigree in *Visitations of the North* was undoubtedly Sir Martin at See).

Children of Philip Wentworth, by Mary de Clifford:

i. **HENRY WENTWORTH**, Knt., about 1448 [see next].

ii. **ELIZABETH WENTWORTH**, married **MARTIN DE LA SEE**, Knt. [see SKEPPER 5].[2]

6. HENRY WENTWORTH, Knt., K.B., of Nettlestead, Sheriff of Norfolk and Suffolk, and of Yorkshire, son and heir, was born about 1448 (aged thirty and more at his grandmother's death). He was grandson and heir of Margery le Despenser, Lady

---

[1] Ancestors of **Muriel Gurdon**.

[2] Ancestors of **William Skepper**.

HARLESTON (cont.)

Roos. He was married for the first time on 20 Feb. 1484 to **ANNE SAY**, daughter of John Say, Knt., of Sawbridgeworth, Little Berkhampstead, and Broxbourne, co. Hertford, etc., by Elizabeth, daughter of Laurence Cheney, of Fen Ditton, co. Cambridge (**descendant of Charlemagne**). They had two sons and two daughters. He was married for the second time, with licence dated 22 Oct. 1494, to marry in the chapel within the manor-house at Deighton, co. York, to ELIZABETH NEVILLE, widow of Thomas Scrope, Lord Scrope of Masham and Upsall (died 23 Apr. 1493), and second daughter of John Neville, Marquess Mountagu, by Isabel, daughter and heiress of Edmund Ingoldisthorpe, Knt., of East Rainham, Norfolk, Somerton, Suffolk. The will of "syr Henry Wentworth, knyght" was dated 17 Aug. 1499 and proved 27 Feb. 1500/1 (P.C.C., 20 Moone). He was buried in Newhouse Abbey, co. Lincoln. His widow died testate (P.C.C., 21 Maynwaryng) in September 1517 *s.p.s.*, and was buried with her first husband at Black Friars', Ludgate, London.

Rutton (1891), p. 138. *C.P.* 4:292-293 (1913). *C.P.* 12(2):497 footnote *c* (1953) (*de jure* 4th Lord le Despenser).

Children of Henry Wentworth, by Anne Say:
  i. **RICHARD WENTWORTH**, Knt., born about 1485 [see next].
  ii. **MARGARET WENTWORTH**, married **JOHN SEYMOUR**, Knt. [see RODNEY 5].[1]

5. RICHARD WENTWORTH, Knt., of Nettlestead, Suffolk, Sheriff of Norfolk and Suffolk, was born about 1485 (but called aged thirty-eight and more in 1518). He was married to **ANNE TYRRELL**, daughter of James Tyrrell, Knt., of Gipping, Suffolk, by Anne, daughter of John Arundell, Knt., of Lanherne, Cornwall. They had three sons and five daughters. SIR RICHARD WENTWORTH died testate (P.C.C., 40 Porch) on 17 Oct. 1528, and was buried at Friars Minor, Ipswich. His widow was living on 11 Nov. 1529.

Rutton (1891), p. 138. *C.P.* 4:294 (1916). *C.P.* 12(2):497 (1953) (5th Lord le Despenser *de jure*).
TG 9:190 (1988) (descent of John Harleston from King Edward III) (James Tyrrell is said to have been the murderer of the young King Edward V and his brother, Richard, Duke of York, in the Tower of London in 1483).

4. THOMAS WENTWORTH, Knt., of Nettlestead, Suffolk, M.P. for Suffolk, P.C., Lord Chamberlain of the Household to King Edward VI, son and heir, was born about 1500 (aged twenty-eight and more at his father's death). He was summoned to Parliament as **Lord Wentworth of Nettlestead** on 2 Dec. 1529. He was married about 1520 to **MARGARET FORTESCUE**, daughter of Adrian Fortescue, Knt. (**descendant of Charlemagne**), by Anne (**descendant of King Edward I**), daughter of William Stonor, Knt. [see MONTHERMER 5 for her ancestry]. They had eight sons and nine daughters, sixteen of whom were living at his death. She died between 23 Apr. 1546 and 12 May 1551, presumably before her husband. "Thomas Wentworth, knight, lorde Wentworthe" died testate (P.C.C., 35 Bucke) at the King's Palace at Westminster on 3 Mar. 1550/1, and was buried in the Abbey.

Rutton (1891), pp. 139-140. *C.P.* 4:294 (1916). *C.P.* 12(2):497-499 (1953) (*de jure* 6th Lord le Despenser). *TG* 9:190 (1988).

Children of Thomas Wentworth, by Margaret Fortescue:
  i. **PHILIP WENTWORTH**, Gent., fourth son [see next].
  ii. **ANNE WENTWORTH**, married **JOHN POLEY**, of Bradley, Suffolk (ancestors of Thomas (or Sackford) Brewster, 1617-1669, of Surry County, Virginia) *VMHB* 27:295 (July 1919) ("his descendants in the male line long lived in Virginia").

---

[1] Ancestors of **Humphrey Davie, William Rodney, Thomas Wingfield**.

HARLESTON (cont.)

3. PHILIP WENTWORTH, Gent., fourth son, was married about 1572 to **ELIZABETH CORBETT**, daughter of Richard Corbett, Knt., of Assington, Suffolk, by Mary, daughter of William Drury, Knt., of Hawstead, Suffolk (**descendant of King Edward III**) [see DRURY 4 for her ancestry]. Five of their seven children were baptised at St. Margaret's, Ipswich. PHILIP WENTWORTH, GENT., died at Christ Church [mansion], St. Margaret's, Ipswich, and was buried at Nettlestead on 10 Oct. 1583. His widow was married for the second time to JOHN BARKLEY (or BERKELEY), Gent., of Stoke Hall, Headmaster of Ipswich School, and had issue. She was living on 28 Nov. 1604.

Rutton (1891), p. 139 (children: John "and several daughters"). *TG* 9:190 (1988).

2. JANE WENTWORTH, daughter and co-heiress, was married at Stepney, co. Middlesex, on 1 Sep. 1608 to **JOHN HARLESTON**, Gent., son of Thomas Harleston, Esq., of South Ockendon, Essex (of **Magna Charta Surety descent** and **descendant of Charlemagne**), by Mary, daughter of Rowland Lytton, of Knebworth, co. Hertford (of **Magna Charta Surety descent** and **descendant of Charlemagne**). He was born and baptised at Knebworth, co. Hertford, on 2 Aug. 1572. He had been married previously married at St. Paul's Walden, co. Hertford, on 26 June 1592 to Elizabeth Hoo (buried 7 July 1608), daughter of Thomas Hoo, by his wife Helen Peryent, with issue. JOHN HARLESTON, GENT., died at South Ockendon on 25 June 1624. They were buried at South Ockendon, his widow on 15 Apr. 1626.

S.C. Hist. Mag. 3:150 (1902) (Pictured arms "handed down from generation to generation in the Harleston family" in America: *Argent*, a fesse ermine cottised, *sable*, Harlstone; quartering Wentworth, *sable*, a chevron between three leopard's heads *or*) (Jane described "on back of Coat of Arms of Harleston family in So.Ca." as daughter and co-heiress of "Philip Wentworth A Younger Brother of the Lord Wentworth"). *V.C.H. Essex* 7:119 (1978). *TG* 9:179-184 (1988).

Children of John Harleston, by Jane Wentworth:

   i. **JOHN HARLESTON**, baptised 15 Nov. 1610 [see next].

   ii. **AFFRA HARLESTON**, baptised 12 Oct. 1615, emigrated on the *Carolina* in August 1669, died testate 1699 (will includes bequest to "nephew John Harleston of Dublin in the Kingdom of Ireland, Gent., the son of John Harleston late of Malling in the county of Essex in the Kingdom of England"); married **JOHN COMIN**, Gent., of Charleston, South Carolina, mate of the *Carolina* and later captain of the *Blessing*. No issue.

1. JOHN HARLESTON, Gent., of Malling, Essex, was baptised at South Ockendon on 15 Nov. 1610. He entered St. John's College, Cambridge University in 1627, and Gray's Inn on 28 Apr. 1629. He was married to **ELIZABETH** _____, living 6 Mar. 1697/8. JOHN HARLESTON, GENT., died before 28 Dec. 1698.

S.C. Hist. Mag. 3:150-154 (1902). *TG* 9:184-225 (1988).

Children & grandchildren of John Harleston, by Elizabeth:

   i. EDWARD HARLESTON, perhaps son, born 1648, buried Barbados July 1694; married three times. Issue.

   ii. CHARLES HARLESTON, perhaps son, granted land on the Wandoe River from the Lords Proprietors in 1678, supposed to have gone to Barbados.

   iii. JOHN HARLESTON, emigrated apparently shortly after the death of his aunt Affra in 1699, of Berkeley County, South Carolina, died Berkeley County, South Carolina, November 1738; married Charleston 15 Apr. 1707 **ELIZABETH WILLIS**.

      a. **JOHN HARLESTON**, born 19 Jan. 1708/9, died 26 Nov. 1767; married **HANNAH CHILD**. Ten children.

      b. **NICHOLAS HARLESTON**, born 18 Dec. 1710, died January 1768.

      c. **GEORGE HARLESTON**, born 4 June 1713, died May 1732 unmarried.

      d. **DANIEL HARLESTON**, born 29 Jan. 1715/6, died before June 1754 unmarried.

HARLESTON (cont.)

    e. ANN HARLESTON, born 12 Feb. 1719/20, died 1740; married JONATHAN SCOTT. Issue.
    f. EDWARD HARLESTON, born 13 Nov. 1722, died 24 Sep. 1775.
    g. PHILIP HARLESTON, born 13 Oct. 1724, died 5 May 1732.
  iv. ANNE HARLESTON, of Dublin and Rathdown, Co. Wicklow, will dated 17 Dec. 1753 names brother John Harleston and sister Elizabeth Ball; married REV. THOMAS BULKELEY. No issue.
   v. ELIZABETH HARLESTON, emigrated to South Carolina by 1 June 1699, died 31 Aug. 1720; married 1699 ELIAS BALL, Gent., of Berkeley County, South Carolina, by 1701.
       a. ANNE BALL, born 20 Jan. 1700/1, died 7 June 1765; married, first, CAPT. PHILIP DAWES, R.N., second, GEORGE AUSTIN, merchant. Issue by second marriage.
       b. ELIAS BALL, born 22 Dec. 1709.
       c. ELIZABETH BALL, born 31 Aug. 1711, died 4 Sep. 1746; married, first, JOHN ASHBY, second, JOHN VICARAGE, third, RICHARD SHUBRICK. Issue by third marriage.
       d. JOHN COMING BALL, born 25 Aug. 1714.

* * *

HASILDEN

EDWARD I OF ENGLAND, King of England, married ALIANORE DE CASTILLE.
JOAN OF ENGLAND [of Acre], married GILBERT DE CLARE, Earl of Gloucester.
ELIZABETH DE CLARE, married ROGER DAMORY, Lord Damory.
ELIZABETH DAMORY, married JOHN BARDOLF, Knt., 3rd Lord Bardolf.
WILLIAM BARDOLF, 4th Lord Bardolf, married AGNES DE POYNINGS.
CECILY BARDOLF, married BRIAN STAPLETON, Knt.
MILES STAPLETON, Knt., married KATHERINE DE LA POLE.
ELIZABETH STAPLETON, married WILLIAM CALTHORPE, Knt. [see BARDOLF 7].

6. ELIZABETH CALTHORPE, was married to FRANCIS HASILDEN, Esq., of Little Chesterford, Essex, Sheriff of Cambridgeshire and Huntingdonshire, son of John Hasilden, of Meldreth, co. Cambridge, by Elizabeth, daughter of John Cheney, Knt., of Fen Ditton, co. Cambridge (**descendant of Charlemagne**). "Frauncis Hasilden esquier" died testate (P.C.C., 29 Maynwaring) early in 1522, and was buried at Gilden Morden.
    H.S.P. 16:295 (1881) (1563 Vis. Yorks). *H.S.P.* 41:88,119 (1907) (1575 Vis. Camb.). *Chester of Chicheley* (1878), pp. 216-218 (Hasilden arms: *Argent* a cross patonce *sable* charged with a mullet).

5. FRANCES HASILDEN, daughter and heiress, was married in January 1515/16 to ROBERT PEYTON, Knt., of Isleham, co. Cambridge, Sheriff of Cambridgeshire, son and heir of Robert Peyton, Knt., of Wicken, Caldecote, Isleham, by Elizabeth, daughter of Robert Clere, Knt., of Ormesby, Norfolk. He was born in 1498 (aged twenty at time of father's death in 1518). They had six sons and two daughters. "Sir Robert Payton, knight, Iselham" died testate (P.C.C., 27 Coode) on 1 Aug. 1550. His widow founded Peyton's Hospital in Isleham in 1580 and died testate (P.C.C., 14 Tirwhite) on 18 Mar. 1581/2. They were buried at St. Andrew's, Isleham (with monumental inscription).
    Wotton (1741) 1:29-30 (Peyton arms: *Sable*, a cross engrailed, *or*). *H.S.P.* 12:380-318 (1877) (1619 Vis. Warwick). *Chester of Chicheley* (1878), pp. 209-210. *H.S.P.* 75:141-143 (1924) (Add. Ped. 1592 Vis. Essex). *H.S.P.* 41:4 (1907) (1619 Vis. Camb.).

4. ROBERT PEYTON, Esq., of Isleham, co. Cambridge, Sheriff of Cambridgeshire

and Huntingdonshire, M.P. for Cambridgeshire, son and heir, was born in 1523 (aged twenty-seven at father's death). He was married before 1557 to **ELIZABETH RICH**, seventh daughter of Richard Rich, of Leighs Priory, Essex, Lord Rich, Lord Chancellor of England. They had three sons and five daughters. "Robert Peyton, esquire, of Isellham" died testate (P.C.C., 74 Drury) in London on 19 Oct. 1590. His widow died testate (P.C.C., 50 Harrington) on 17 Oct. 1591. They were buried in the South Chapel at Isleham, an alabaster tomb with effigies and monumental inscription.
Wotton (1741) 1:31. *H.S.P.* 12:381 (1877). *Chester of Chicheley* (1878), pp. 218-220. *H.S.P.* 41:4 (1907). *H.S.P.* 61:97 (1910) (1664 Vis. Suffolk). *H.S.P.* 75:141-143 (1924).

3. **JOHN PEYTON**, Knt., Bart., of Isleham, Sheriff of Cambridgeshire, M.P. for Cambridgeshire, was married at St. Dionis Backchurch, London, on 29 June 1580 to **ALICE OSBORNE**, daughter of Edward Osborne, Knt., Lord Mayor of London. She was baptised on 4 Mar. 1562/3. They had seven sons and seven daughters. He was created **Baronet** by King James I on 22 May 1611. JOHN PEYTON, BART., was buried testate (P.C.C., 46 Weldon) at Isleham on 19 Dec. 1616 with portrait figures but without inscription. His widow resided at Great Bradley, Suffolk, and died in 1626.

H.S.P. 12:381 (1877). *Chester of Chicheley* (1878), pp. 220-225. *H.S.P.* 41:4 (1907). *H.S.P.* 61:97 (1910).

Children & grandchild of John Peyton, by Alice Osborne:

   i. **EDWARD PEYTON**, Knt., born about 1581 [see next].

   ii. **ALICE PEYTON**, married at Isleham 25 Nov. 1602 her father's cousin **JOHN PEYTON**, Esq., of Doddington, born 1579, died 1635, son and heir of John Peyton, Knt., by Dorothy, daughter of Edmund Beaupré, Esq. Three sons and six daughters. *Chester of Chicheley* (1878), p. 222.

      a. **ANNE PEYTON**, married **GEORGE BRENT** [see BRENT 1].[1]

2. **EDWARD PEYTON**, Knt., 2nd Baronet, of Great Bradley, Suffolk, M.P. for Cambridgeshire, son and heir was born about 1581, and educated at St. Edmundsbury school, and Cambridge. He was married for the first time at Streatham, Surrey, on 24 Apr. 1604 to **MARTHA LIVESAY**, daughter of Robert Livesay, Esq., of Tooting, Surrey. They had three sons and one daughter. He was married for the second time on 6 June 1614 to **JANE CALTHORPE**, widow of Henry Thymelthorpe, Knt., of Norfolk, and daughter of James Calthorpe, Knt., of Calthorpe, Norfolk. They had three sons and one daughter. He was married for the third time to **DOROTHY BALL**, daughter of Edward Ball, of Stockwell, Surrey. They had two sons. SIR EDWARD PEYTON died intestate at Wicken 1656/7. His widow was married for the second time to Edward Lowe, Vicar of Brighton, Sussex. She was buried at Brighton on 10 Apr. 1681.

Wotton (1741) 1:32-33 ("siding with the presbyterians in the times of the great rebellion, had his share of sufferings for that cause, while the war lasted; which so impoverish'd him that he sold Isleham and ruined the whole estate"). *Her. & Gen.* 6:63-74 (1871). *H.S.P.* 12:381 (1877). *Chester of Chicheley* (1878), pp. 238-240. *H.S.P.* 41:4 (1907).

Child of Edward Peyton, by Jane Calthorpe:

   i. **THOMAS PEYTON**, born 1617, married **ELIZABETH YELVERTON** [see PEYTON 1].[2]

---

[1]Parents of **George & Robert Brent**.
[2]Parents of **Robert Peyton**.

HASTINGS

EDWARD I OF ENGLAND, King of England, married ALIANORE DE CASTILLE.
JOAN OF ENGLAND [*of Acre*], married RALPH DE MONTHERMER, Lord Monthermer.
THOMAS DE MONTHERMER, 2nd Lord Monthermer, married MARGARET _____.
MARGARET DE MONTHERMER, married JOHN DE MONTAGU, Lord Montagu.
JOHN MONTAGU, Earl of Salisbury, married MAUD FRANCIS.
THOMAS DE MONTAGU, Earl of Salisbury, married ALIANOR DE HOLAND.
ALICE DE MONTAGU, married RICHARD NEVILLE, Earl [see MONTHERMER 8].

8. KATHERINE NEVILLE, fifth daughter, was married for the first time in or before 1458 to WILLIAM BONVILLE, 6th Lord Harington. He was slain aged twenty on 31 Dec. 1460 [see BONVILLE 7 for descendants of this marriage]. She was married for the second time before 6 Feb. 1461/2 to WILLIAM HASTINGS, Knt., K.G., of Kirby, co. Leicester, and Burton Hastings, co. Warwick, Sheriff of Warwickshire and Leicestershire, son of Leonard Hastings, Knt., of Kirby and Burton Hastings, by Alice, daughter of Thomas de Camoys, Lord Camoys (of **baronial** descent). He was born about 1431 (aged twenty-four and more at his father's death). They had three sons and one daughter. On account of his great services against King Henry VI, the Earls of Pembroke and Wiltshire, and other rebels and traitors, in 1 Edw. IV, he was raised to the rank of a Baron, thereby becoming **Lord Hastings**, and on 17 Feb. 1461/2 the King granted him the lordship, barony, and honour of Hastings. He was summoned to Parliament from 26 July 1461 by writs directed *Willelmo Hastynges militi domino Hastynges*. "William Hastyngs Knyght, lord Hastyngs" was arrested, by the order of Richard, Duke of Gloucester, at a council in the Tower of London, charged with high treason, and beheaded testate (P.C.C., 10 Logge) on 13 June 1483. He was buried at St. George's Chapel, Windsor. The will of "Kateryn lady Hastinges" was dated 22 Nov. 1503, and was proved 25 Mar. 1504/5, requesting burial at Ashby de la Zouch (P.C.C., 7 Holgrave).

Clay (1913), p. 101. *C.P.* 6:370-374, 622 footnote (1926) *f.*

7. EDWARD HASTINGS, Knt., K.B., 2nd Lord Hastings, son and heir, was born on 26 Nov. 1466. He was married before 18 Feb. 1480/1 to **MARY HUNGERFORD**, daughter and heiress of Thomas Hungerford, Knt., by Anne, daughter of Henry Percy, 3rd Earl of Northumberland **(descendant of King Edward III)**. She was born about 1467, and became Baroness Botreaux *suo jure* on the death of her great-grandmother Margaret de Botreaux on 7 Feb. 1477/8 [see BOTREAUX 9 for her ancestry]. Probably in consequence of the marriage, he was summoned to Parliament *v.p.* from 15 Nov 1482 by writs directed *Edwardo Hastyng' de Hungreford'*, whereby he is held to have become **Lord Hastings** of Hungerford. They had two children. With the reversal of the attainders of the 3rd Lord Hungerford and his son Sir Thomas Hungerford, she became in addition *suo jure* Baroness Hungerford and Baroness Moleyns in 1485. "Edward Hastynges Knight, lord Hastinges and Hungerford" died testate on 8 Nov. 1506 (P.C.C., 37 Bennett), and was buried at Grey Friars', London. His widow was married for the second time on 1 May 1509 to Richard Sacheverell, Knt., of Ratcliffe on Soar, co. Nottingham (died testate 14 Apr. 1534). She died before 10 July 1533, and was buried with her second husband in the Collegiate Church of St. Mary in the Newark at Leicester.

Clay (1913), p. 101. *C.P.* 4:209 (1916), 6:374-375, 622-623 (1926).

Children of Edward Hastings, by Mary Hungerford:1
   i. **GEORGE HASTINGS**, born 1488 [see next].

HASTINGS (cont.)

ii. ANNE HASTINGS, married THOMAS STANLEY, 2nd Earl of Derby [see NELSON 7].[1]

6. GEORGE HASTINGS, K.B., of Ashby-de-la-Zouch, co. Leicester, 3rd Lord Hastings of Hastings, and Lord Hastings of Hungerford, P.C. to King Henry VIII, son and heir, was born in or before 1488. He was summoned to Parliament from 17 Oct. 1509. He was created **Earl of Huntingdon** on 8 Dec. 1529, and about 1533 succeeded his mother as Lord Botreaux, Lord Hungerford and Lord Moleyns. In 1536 he was in command against the rebels in the rising called *the Pilgrimage of Grace*. He was married about December 1509 to **ANNE STAFFORD**, widow of Walter Herbert, Knt. (died 16 Sep. 1507), and daughter of Henry Stafford, 2nd Duke of Buckingham (**descendant of King Edward III**), by Katherine (sister of Elizabeth, the Queen Consort) (**descendant of Charlemagne**), daughter of Richard Wydeville, Earl Rivers [see AUDLEY 7 for his ancestry]. They had five sons and three daughters. GEORGE HASTINGS, Earl of Huntingdon, died testate on 24 Mar. 1543/4. They were buried at Stoke Poges, co. Buckingham.

Clay (1913), pp. 101-102. *C.P.* (1926) 6:375-376, 624, 654-655.

Child of George Hastings, by Anne Stafford:

i. **FRANCIS HASTINGS**, son and heir, married **KATHERINE POLE** [see SOMERSET 5].[2]

* * *

HAVILAND

EDWARD III OF ENGLAND, King of England, married **PHILIPPE DE HAINAUT**.
LIONEL OF CLARENCE [*of Antwerp*], Duke of Clarence, married **ELIZABETH DE BURGH**.
PHILIPPE OF CLARENCE, married **EDMUND DE MORTIMER**, 3rd Earl of March.
ELIZABETH MORTIMER, married **HENRY PERCY**, Knt.
HENRY PERCY, 5th Lord Percy, married **ALIANOR NEVILLE** [see KEMPE 9].

7. KATHERINE PERCY, was born at Leconfield on 28 May 1423. She was married before January 1458/9 to **EDMUND GREY**, Lord Grey of Ruthin, son and heir of John Grey, Knt., of Badmondisfield, Suffolk, by Constance (**descendant of King Edward III**), daughter of John de Holand, Duke of Exeter. He was born on 26 Oct. 1416 [see GURDON 7 for his ancestry]. He succeeded his grandfather to the Barony of Grey of Ruthin on 30 Sep. 1440, and was summoned to Parliament from 3 Dec. 1441 by writs directed *Edmundo de Grey de Ruthin chivaler*. At the battle of Northampton on 10 July 1460 he was in command of the Royal vanguard, but went over to the Yorkists as the battle was joined, and is considered to have been the main cause of the Lancastrian defeat. He was created **Earl of Kent** on 30 May 1465. EDMUND GREY, Earl of Kent, died aged seventy-three on 22 May 1490. The will of "Katherine Grey, countess of Kent" was proved in 1504 (P.C.C., 15 Holgrave).

C.P. 6:160 (1926). *C.P.* 7:164-165 (1929).

Children & grandchild of Edmund Grey, by Katherine Percy:

i. **ANNE GREY** [see next].

---

[1]Ancestors of **John Nelson**.

[2]Ancestors of **Maria Johanna Somerset**.

HAVILAND (cont.)

ii. **ELIZABETH GREY**, died 18 July 1472; married **ROBERT GREYSTOKE**, Knt., son and heir apparent of Ralph de Greystoke, 5th Lord Greystoke, Lord FitzWilliam, by Elizabeth, daughter of William Fitz Hugh, 4th Lord Fitz Hugh (both of **Magna Charta Surety descent** and **descendant of Charlemagne**), died 17 June 1483 *v.p. s.p.m. C.P.* 6:199 (1926).

    a. **ELIZABETH GREYSTOKE**, married **THOMAS DACRE** [see DACRE 6].[1]

6. ANNE GREY, was married to **JOHN GREY**, 8th Lord Grey, of Wilton, son and heir of Reynold Grey, 7th Lord Grey of Wilton (**descendant of King Edward I**), by Thomasine (or Tacine), base-born daughter of John Beaufort, Duke of Somerset [see WILTON 7 for his ancestry]. He was summoned to Parliament on 20 Nov. 1496 by writ directed *Johanni Grey de Wilton' chivaler*. He was married for the second time to **ELIZABETH VAUGHAN**, widow of Thomas Cokesey (otherwise Greville), Knt., of Cooksey, co. Worcester (died 6 Mar. 1497/8 *s.p.*), and daughter of Thomas Vaughan. JOHN GREY, Lord Grey, died on 3 Apr. 1499, and was buried at White Friars', London. His widow was married for the third time to Edward Stanley, Knt., afterwards Lord Mounteagle, and died on 15 Jan. 1514/5.

    C.P. 6:180-181 (1926). *C.P.* 7:165 footnote *e*, footnote *f* (1929). *NEHGR* 108:177-178 (July 1954). Paget (1957) 260:6.

5. EDMUND GREY, 9th Lord Grey, of Wilton, son and heir, by first marriage, was born about 1469 (aged thirty and more at his father's death). He was summoned to Parliament on 17 Oct. 1509. He was married before 1495 to **FLORENCE HASTINGS**, first daughter and co-heiress of Ralph Hastings, Knt., of Harrowden, co. Northampton, and Kirby, co. Leicester (of **baronial** descent), by Anne, daughter of John Tattershall. They had four sons. "Edmund lord Grey de Wilton, of Wilton on Wye, Hereford" died testate (P.C.C., 38 Bennett) on 5 May 1511 survived by his wife.

    Stemmata Chicheleana (1765), p. 31 ("Florence = Edm. Grey of Wilton [with children] William, Lord Grey ob. 1562 [&] Elizabeth ob. 1559 = John Brydges, Lord Chandos") (Agnes Chichele, mother of Anne Tattershall, was "Founder's Kin"). *C.P.* 6:181-186 (1926). *NEHGR* 108:177-178 (July 1954) (asserts Tacy was daughter of Arthur Grey, of Wilton, a grandson of Edmund Grey). *NEHGR* 110:232 (July 1956). Paget (1957) 260:6 (marriage date) (no named daughters).

4. TACY (or **THOMASINE**) **GREY**, daughter, evidently, was born about 1490-1495. She was married, as a daughter of "Lord Grey de Wilton", about 1510 to **JOHN GYSE** (or **GUISE**), Esq., of Elmore, co. Gloucester, son of John Gyse, Knt., of Apsley Gyse, co. Bedford, and Elmore, co. Gloucester, by his wife Anne Berkeley of Stoke Gifford. He was born about 1485 (aged sixteen and more at father's death). They had three sons and three daughters. JOHN GYSE, ESQ., died at Brockworth, co. Gloucester, on 20 Dec. 1556, and was buried at Elmore. His widow was buried at Elmore on 15 Nov. 1558.

    Bristol & Glouc. Soc. 3:58-61,70 (1878-9). *H.S.P.* 21:72 (1885) (1623 Vis. Glouc.) ("Tacy d. to the lord Gray de Wilton" "according to official record in the Heralds' College") (Gyse arms: *Gules*, seven lozenges vairé, three, three, and one, on a canton *or* a mullet pierced *sable*). *NEHGR* 110:232 (July 1956).

3. WILLIAM GYSE, Esq., of Elmore, second son but eventual heir to his brother Anselme, was born about 1514 (aged forty-nine or more in 1563). He was married before 1540 to **MARY ROTSY**, daughter of John Rotsy (or Ratsy), of Colmore, King's Norton, co. Worcester, by Margaret, daughter of John Walsh, of Sheldesley Walsh, co. Worcester. They had one son and three daughters. She was buried at Elmore on 24 Nov. 1558. WILLIAM GYSE, ESQ., died testate at Elmore on 7 Sep. 1574, and was buried at Elmore.

---

[1]Ancestors of **Philip & Thomas Nelson**.

HAVILAND (cont.)

Bristol & Glouc. Soc. 3:63-62,70 (1878-9). *H.S.P.* 21:72 (1885). *NEHGR* 110:232 (July 1956).

2. **JOHN GYSE**, Esq., of Elmore and Brockworth, son and heir, was born about 1540 (aged thirty-four and more at father's death). He was married at Elmore on 27 June 1564 to **JANE PAUNCEFORT**, daughter of Richard Pauncefort, of Hasefield, co. Gloucester. They had six sons and three daughters. She was buried at Elmore on 27 June 1587. "John Guise, esquier, Elmore, Gloucester" died testate (P.C.C., 6 Leicester) on 24 Jan. 1587/8, and was buried at Elmore.

Bristol & Glouc. Soc. 3:62-63,70. *H.S.P.* 21:72 (1885) (identifies six sons, but no daughters.). *Waters* 1:547 (1885). *V.C.H. Warwick* 5:148 (1949); 6:47 (1951). *NEHGR* 110:232 (July 1956). *V.C.H. Oxon.* 6:9 (1959); 8:255 (1964).

1. **ELIZABETH GYSE**, was baptised at Elmore on 1 Aug. 1576, and was named in her father's will dated 1 Dec. 1577. She was married at Kenn, Somerset, on 7 July 1604 to **ROBERT HAVILAND**, Esq., of Hawkesbury Barnes, co. Gloucester, son of Matthew Haviland, Mayor of Bristol, by Mary, daughter of Robert Kytchin, Alderman of Bristol. He was baptised at St. Werbergh's, Bristol, on 11 Feb. 1577. ROBERT HAVILAND, ESQ., was buried at St. Werburgh's on 19 July 1648.

Bristol & Glouc. Soc. 3:64,71. *H.S.P.* 21:78 (1885) (1623 Vis. Glouc.) (Haviland arms: *Argent*, three towers triple-towered *sable*). *NEHGR* 45:299 (Oct. 1891). *NEHGR* 110:232 (July 1956).

Children of Robert Haviland, by Elizabeth Gyse:

    i. MATTHEW HAVILAND, Esq., of Hawkesbury Barnes, born about 1608, Rector of Trinity Church, London, will proved 4 Feb. 1671, mentions his sister "Jane, late Wife of William Torry, Gent., of New Ingland". *Waters* 1:547 (1885) (his will).

    ii. MARY HAVILAND.

    iii. FLORENCE HAVILAND.

    iv. JANE HAVILAND, baptised St. Werbergh's Church, Briston, 2 Aug. 1612, married **CAPT. WILLIAM TORREY** of Weymouth, Massachusetts.

    v. ELIZABETH HAVILAND.

* * *

HAYNES

EDWARD I OF ENGLAND, King of England, married **ALIANORE DE CASTILLE**.
JOAN OF ENGLAND [*of Acre*], married **GILBERT DE CLARE**, Earl of Gloucester.
ELIZABETH DE CLARE, married **ROGER DAMORY**, Lord Damory.
ELIZABETH DAMORY, married **JOHN BARDOLF**, 3rd Lord Bardolf.
WILLIAM BARDOLF, 4th Lord Bardolf, married **AGNES DE POYNINGS**.
CECILY BARDOLF, married **BRIAN STAPLETON**, Knt. [see BARDOLF 9].

8. **BRIAN STAPLETON**, Esq., of Crisping's manor in Happisburgh, and of Hasilden, Norfolk, younger son, was named, with wife Isabel, in father's will dated 5 Apr. 1438. He was lieutenant of the Duke of Exeter in 1443. He was married by 1438 to **ISABEL** (or **ELIZABETH**) _____. She was living about 1456. BRIAN STAPLETON, ESQ., was living 1461/2, but dead before 1467.

Foster (1874), Stapleton chart (no identification of descendants). *NEHGR* 148:256 (July 1994) (descent of Elizabeth Haynes from King Edward I).

7. **ELIZABETH STAPLETON**, daughter and co-heiress, was born about 1440. She was married to **JOHN RICHERS**, Esq., of Swannington, Norfolk, son of John Richers

HAYNES (cont.)

(or Rychers), by his wife Margaret. He was born about 1430, and was a lawyer of Gray's Inn and commissioner of array for Norfolk in 1491. She predeceased her husband. The will of JOHN RICHERS, ESQ., was proved 1502 (P.C.C., 7 Blamyr).

H.S.P. 75:23 (1924) (1574 Vis. Kent) ("Riches" arms). *NEHGR* 148:256 (July 1994) (Richers arms: *Argent*, three annulets *azure*).

6. **JOHN RICHERS**, Esq., was born about 1478. He was married to **ELIZABETH BATCHCROFT**, daughter of Simon Batchcroft (Bachecrofte or Bagecrofte), of Bexwell, Norfolk, by Eleanor, daughter and co-heiress of Gilbert Haltoft, of Outwell, Norfolk, Baron of the Exchequer. JOHN RICHERS, ESQ., was living in 1501 (*Inq.p.m.* dated 20 Oct. 1502).

NEHGR 148:256-257 (July 1994).

5. **HENRY RICHERS**, Esq., of Swannington, Norfolk, was born about 1500. He was married to **CECILY TILLYS**, daughter and co-heiress of Robert Tillys (Tylles or Tilles), Gent., of Popes manor in Runhall, and Salthouse, Norfolk, by his wife Katherine. HENRY RICHERS, ESQ., died in 1543.

H.S.P. 75:23 (1924) (names only two sons). *NEHGR* 148:257 (July 1994).

4. **FRANCES RICHERS**, was born about 1522. She was married in 1542 to **EDMOND CUSHIN**, Gent., of Swannington and Hingham, Norfolk, son of John Cushin (or Cushyn), Gent., of Hingham, Norfolk, by his wife Alice. He was born about 1515. They had one son Henry who died young and one daughter Elizabeth. She died in 1558. The will of EDMOND CUSHIN, GENT., was proved in 1558.

NEHGR 148:257 (July 1994) (Cushin arms: *Gules*, an eagle displayed *argent*).

3. **ELIZABETH CUSHIN**, daughter and heiress, was baptised in 1543. She was married to **WILLIAM THORNTON**, of Lincoln's Inn, and Downham in Windham, Norfolk, son of Oliver Thornton, of Soham, co. Cambridge, and Exning, Suffolk, by his first wife Pernell Bugge. He was born about 1535. WILLIAM THORNTON died testate in 1570 (P.C.C., 35 Lyon). His widow was living in 1570.

NEHGR 148:257 (July 1994) (Thornton arms: *Argent*, a chevron *sable* between three hawthorn trees *vert*).

2. **ROBERT THORNTON**, Gent., of Hingham, and of Downham in Windham, Norfolk, was baptised in 1565, and succeeded to the manor of Downham when he came of age in 1586. He later purchased a house in Hingham from his uncle, Oliver Thornton. He was married to **ANNE SMITH**, daughter of Giles Smith, of Blackmore, Essex. She was born about 1565. "Robert Thorneton, gentleman" was buried at Hingham on 26 Aug. 1613. His will was dated 1 July 1612 and proved 12 July 1615 (P.C.C., 72 Rudd). The will of his widow was proved in 1624 (P.C.C., 32 Byrde).

NEHGR 148:249-251 (July 1994) (The 1619 Visitation of Cambridgeshire, prepared shortly after her marriage, identifies Mary, wife of John Heynes of Old Holt near Colchester in Essex, as daughter of Robert Thornton of Downham in com. Norff, by his wife Anne d. of ____ Smith; The 1664-1668 Visitation of Essex prepared by Mary's son, Major-General Hezekiah Haynes, then of Copford Hall, Essex, identified his mother Mary as daughter and coheir of Robert Thornton of Hingham in com. Norf.) (Smith arms: *Argent*, a cross *gules* between four peacocks *azure*).

1. **MARY THORNTON**, daughter and co-heiress, baptised at Soham, co. Cambridge, on 30 Nov. 1598, was married at Hingham, Norfolk, on 11 Apr. 1616 to **JOHN HAYNES** (or **HEYNES**), Esq., of Old Holt in Messing, Essex, son of John Haynes, Esq., of Great Haddam and Codicote, co. Hertford, and Old Holt, by his wife Mary Michel. He was born on 1 May 1594, and baptised at Messing. They had seven children. Mary "wife of John Haynes, esquire" was buried at Hingham on 18 June

1627. He was married for the second time to Mabel Harlakenden, daughter of Richard Harlakenden, of Earl's Colne, Essex, by Margaret, daughter of Edward Huberd, of Stanstead-Montifichet, Essex, with five children. He emigrated to New England in the *Griffin* in 1633, and was elected third Governor of Massachusetts in 1635. He removed to Hartford, Connecticut, and was elected the first Governor of the Connecticut Colony in April 1639. GOV. JOHN HAYNES died testate at Hartford on 1 Mar. 1654. His widow was married for the second time to Samuel Eaton.

D.N.B. 9:301-302. *NEHGR* 148:240-251 (July 1994).

Child & grandchildren of John & Mary (Thornton) Haynes:

i. **ELIZABETH HAYNES**, baptised Hingham, 19 Oct. 1624, married about 1642 **MR. JOSEPH COOKE**, of Pebmarsh, Essex, born about 1608, emigrated on the ship *Defense* in 1635, Cambridge, Massachusetts, returned to England in 1658, resided Stanway, Essex, died 1699. Two of their children remained in New England.

   a. **JOSEPH COOKE**, Jr., born 1643, died shortly after February 1690/1, of Cambridge, Massachusetts, graduated Harvard College 1661; married **MARTHA STEDMAN**. Five children.

   b. **ELIZABETH COOKE**, born 1644/5, married REV. JOSEPH CAWTHORNE, B.A., M.A., Cambridge, of London, died 1707. Two children in England.

   c. **MARY COOKE**, born 1647, married 1676 **LT.-COL. JOHN TALCOTT**, of Hartford, Connecticut. Five children.

   d. GRACE COOKE, born 1648, died young.

   e. GRACE COOKE, born 1650.

   f. RUTH COOKE.

   g. THOMAS COOKE, living 1699.

* * *

HIGHAM see BURROUGH

HILDYARD see SKEPPER

* * *

HOLAND

EDWARD I OF ENGLAND, King of England, married **MARGUERITE DE FRANCE**.
EDMUND OF KENT, married **MARGARET WAKE** [see PLANTAGENET 14.xvii].

9. **JOAN OF KENT** [*the Fair Maid of Kent*], Countess of Kent, Baroness Wake *suo jure*, eventual heiress, was born on 29 Sep. 1328, and was sister and heiress of John, Earl of Kent, Lord Wake and Lord Woodstock. She was married for the first time in or before 1339 to **THOMAS DE HOLAND**, Knt., of Broughton, co. Buckingham, Earl of Kent *jure uxoris*, younger son of Robert de Holand, Knt., 1st Lord Holand, of Upholland, co. Lancaster, by Maud, daughter and co-heiress of Alan la Zouche,

HOLAND (cont.)

Baron Zouche of Ashby (of **Magna Charta Surety descent** and **descendant of Charlemagne**). In 1340 he was in the expedition to Flanders, taking part in the Battle of Sluys on 24 June, and the siege of Tournai in July. He fought at Crécy on 26 Aug. 1346, in the Prince's division, and after the battle superintended the counting of the slain. About 1346, during his absence abroad, Joan his wife went through a form of marriage (possibly under compulsion) with William Montagu, Earl of Salisbury. He was a founder Knight of the Order of the Garter in 1348. On 17 Nov. 1349 the Pope ordered Joan to be restored to him. He was summoned to Parliament from 15 Mar. 1353/4 by writ directed *Thome de Holand'*, whereby he is held to have become **Lord Holand**. His wife may possibly be the lady in whose honour the Order of the Garter received its name. In 1360 he was summoned as Earl of Kent. THOMAS DE HOLAND, Earl of Kent, died in Normandy on 26 or 28 Dec. 1360, and was buried at Grey Friars', Stamford. His widow was married for the second time, with dispensation dated 10 Oct. 1361, at Windsor to EDWARD OF ENGLAND, Prince of Wales *[the Black Prince]*, eldest son of King Edward III [see PLANTAGENET 12.i]. He was born at Woodstock on 15 June 1330 and died at Westminster on 8 June 1376. They were the parents of Richard II, **King of England**. She died testate at Wallingford Castle, co. Berks, on 7 or 8 Aug. 1385, and was buried with her second husband.

C.P. 3:161 (1913). *C.P.* 4:325 (1916). *C.P.* 6:533 (1926). *C.P.* 7:150-154 (1929). *C.P.* 12(1):305 (1959).

Children of Thomas de Holand, by Joan of Kent:
  i. THOMAS DE HOLAND, son and heir, born about 1350 [see next].
  ii. JOHN DE HOLAND, married ELIZABETH OF LANCASTER [see GURDON 8].[1]

8. **THOMAS DE HOLAND** *[of Woodstock]*, Knt., K.G., 2nd Earl of Kent, Lord Holand, Lord Wake, Lord Woodstock, son and heir, was born about 1350 (aged nine and more or ten and more at father's death). He was summoned to Parliament from 16 July 1381 by writs directed *Thome de Holand' comiti Kanc'*. He was married shortly after 10 Apr. 1364 to **ALICE FITZ ALAN**, daughter of Richard Fitz Alan, Knt., Earl of Arundel and Warenne, by Alianor, daughter of Henry, Earl of Lancaster (**grandson of King Henry III**) [see FITZ ALAN 13 for her ancestry]. THOMAS DE HOLAND, Earl of Kent, died testate on 25 Apr. 1397, and was buried at Bourne Abbey, co. Lincoln. His widow died on 17 Mar. 1415/6.

C.P. 7:154-156 (1929). *C.P.* 11:394-5 (1949). *C.P.* 12(1):44 (1959). *C.P.* 12(2):305 (1959).

Children of Thomas de Holand, by Alice fitz Alan:
  i. EDMUND DE HOLAND, K.G., 4th Earl of Kent, Lord Wake, Lord Woodstock, Lord Holand, younger son, born apparently 6 Jan. 1382/3, brother and heir of Thomas, 3rd Earl of Kent; died 15 Sep. 1408 *s.p. legit*, being slain in the attack on the Isle of Bréhat, Brittany, buried Bourne Abbey, co. Lincoln; married 24 Jan. 1406/7 LUCY VISCONTI, died 14 Apr. 1424, buried Austin Friars', London, tenth and youngest daughter of Barnabo Visconti, by Beatrice, daughter of Mastin della Scala. By Constance of York, then the young widow of Thomas le Despenser, 5th Lord Despenser, and daughter of Edmund of York *[of Langley]*, Duke of York [see YORK 9 for her ancestry], he is said to have had a base-born daughter, Alianor, wife of James Tuchet, 5th Lord Audley [see TUCHET 9 for descendants of that marriage]. *C.P.* 4:159-163 (1916). *C.P.* 7:161 footnote *h* (1929).
  ii. MARGARET DE HOLAND, married JOHN BEAUFORT [see BEAUFORT 10].[2]

---

[1]Ancestors of **Muriel Gurdon**, and, probably, **Jane Haviland**.

[2]Ancestors of **St. Leger Codd, Edward Digges, Warham Horsmanden, Anne Humphrey, Herbert Pelham, Katherine Saint Leger, John West**.

HOLAND (cont.)

iii. **ALIANOR [I] DE HOLAND**, married [see PLANTAGENET 9],[1] [see CHERLETON 11].[2]

iv. **ALIANOR [II] DE HOLAND**, married THOMAS DE MONTAGU [see MONTHERMER 9].[3]

* * *

HONFORD see GERARD

HOO see WELLES

HOWARD see MOWBRAY

* * *

HUMPHREY

HENRY III OF ENGLAND, King of England, married ÉLÉNORE DE PROVENCE.
EDMUND OF LANCASTER, Earl of Lancaster, married BLANCHE D'ARTOIS.
HENRY OF LANCASTER, Earl of Lancaster, married MAUD DE CHAWORTH.
JOAN OF LANCASTER, married JOHN DE MOWBRAY, Lord Mowbray [see MOWBRAY 11].

10. ALIANOR MOWBRAY, was married for the first time before 23 July 1358 to ROGER LA WARRE, Knt., 3rd Lord la Warre, son and heir of John la Warre, Knt. (of **Magna Charta Surety descent** and **descendant of Charlemagne**), by Margaret (**descendant of Charlemagne**), daughter of Robert de Holand, 1st Lord of Holand, of Upholland, co. Lancaster. He was born on 30 Nov. 1326, and was grandson and heir of John la Warre, 2nd Lord la Warre. He had been married previously before 14 Oct. 1338 to Elizabeth de Welle, daughter of Adam de Welle, Knt., of Well, co. Lincoln, by his wife Margaret (and had sons, John & Thomas, 4th & 5th Lords la Warre). She was living on 24 Feb. 1344/5. He had been married previously for the second time before 3 Feb. 1353/4 to Elizabeth _____. He was at the Battle of Poitiers where he captured the King of France. He was summoned to Parliament from 14 Aug. 1362 by writs directed *Rogero de la Warre*. "Roger la Warre, Knt., of Wakerle, Northants", died testate aged forty-three in Gascony on 27 Aug. 1370. She was married for the second time to LEWIS CLIFFORD, Knt. (died testate 1404), and died testate before 10 June 1387.

C.P. 4:144-151, 147 footnote *d* (1916) (he was a Lollard). *C.P.* 7:452 chart, 453-454 (1929).
Comber (1933), pp. 302-303 (arms: *Gules*, crusilly fitchy a lion rampant *argent*).

9. JOAN LA WARRE, was sister of the half-blood and, in her issue, heiress of John

---

[1]Ancestor, by first husband Roger de Mortimer, of **Philip & Thomas Nelson**.

[2]Ancestor, by second husband Edward Cherleton, of **Nathaniel Littleton, Thomas Lloyd, Agnes Mackworth, John Nelson, Philip & Thomas Nelson, John Washington**, and, probably, **Thomas Dudley**.

[3]Ancestors of **Elizabeth Bosvile, Stephen Bull, Charles Calvert, Grace Chetwode, John Nelson, John Oxenbridge, Maria Johanna Somerset, Thomas Wingfield**, and, probably, **Thomas Dudley**.

HUMPHREY (cont).

and Thomas, 4th and 5th Lords la Warre. She was married for the first time to RALPH DE WILINGTON, of Sandhurst, co. Gloucester. He died on 16 Aug. 1382 v.p.. She was married for the second time, with pardon for marrying without licence dated 2 May 1384, to **THOMAS WEST**, Knt., of Oakhanger, co. Northampton, son and heir of Thomas West, Knt., of Hampton Cantilupe, by Alice, daughter of Reginald Fitz Herbert, of Midsomer Norton, Somerset (**descendant of Charlemagne**). He was born in 1365 (aged twenty-one on 15 Oct. 1386). They had three sons. He was summoned to Parliament from 19 June 1402 by writs directed *Thome West*, whereby he is held to have become **Lord West**. His wife died 24 Apr. 1404. THOMAS WEST, Lord West, died testate on 19 Apr. 1405 (will dated 8 Apr. 1405 requesting burial in Christchurch Priory).

    C.P. 12(2):520, 649 footnote *d* (1959). *Comber* (1933), p. 304.

8. REYNOLD WEST, Knt., 3rd Lord la Warre, younger son, was born on 7 Sep. 1395, and was brother and heir of Thomas West, Lord West. He was summoned to Parliament as Lord la Warre from 15 July 1427 by writs directed *Reginaldo la Warre*, and as Lord West from 25 Feb. 1431/2 by writs directed *Reginaldo West*. He had licence to go to Rome, and thence to the Holy Land in 1446. He was married for the first time before 17 Feb. 1428/9 to **MARGARET THORLEY**, daughter of Robert Thorley, of Thyngest, Cornwall, by his wife Anne Lisle. She died shortly before 24 Nov. 1433. He was married for the second time by 19 Nov. 1443 to **ELIZABETH GREYNDOUR**, daughter and heiress of Robert Greyndour, of Micheldean and Abenhall, co. Gloucester, Aston Ingham, co. Hereford, etc., by Joan, daughter and heiress of Thomas Rugge, of Charlecombe, Somerset. She was born about 1421 (aged twenty-three and more in January 1443/4). REYNOLD WEST, Lord de la Warre, died aged nearly fifty-five on 27 Aug. 1450, and was buried at Broadwater, Sussex. His widow was married after 10 June 1451, as his second wife, to John Tiptoft, Earl of Worcester (beheaded on Tower Hill on 18 Oct. 1470). She died on 1 Sep. 1452.

    Smyth-Maclean (1883) 1:352. *C.P.* 4:152-154 (1916). *C.P.* 12(2):521 (1959). *Comber* (1933), p. 304.

    Children of Reynold West, by Margaret Thorley:

    i. **RICHARD WEST**, Knt., born about 28 Oct 1430 [see next].

    ii. **MARGARET WEST**, married **THOMAS DE ECHYNGHAM**, Knt. [see ECHINGHAM 7].[1]

7. RICHARD WEST, 4th Lord West, 2nd Lord de la Warre, son and heir, was born about 28 Oct. 1430. He was married before 10 June 1451 to **KATHERINE HUNGERFORD**, daughter of Robert Hungerford, 2nd Lord Hungerford, of Heytesbury, co. Wilts, by Margaret (**descendant of King Henry III**), daughter of William de Botreaux, 3rd Lord Botreaux, of Boscastle, Cornwall [see BOTREAUX 11 for her ancestry]. They had four sons and two daughters. He was summoned to Parliament from 22 Jan. 1455/6 by writs directed *Ricardo West militi*. He had licence to travel abroad for three years on 1 July 1463. RICHARD WEST, Lord de la Warre, died aged forty-five on 10 Mar. 1475/6. His widow was married for the second time to NICHOLAS LEVENTHORPE, Esq., and died on 12 May 1493.

    H.S.P. 21:89 (1885) (1623 Vis. Glouc.). *C.P.* 4:154-155 (1916). *C.P.* 12(2):522 (1959). *Comber* (1933), p. 304. *NEHGR* 150:91-93 (Jan. 1996).

6. THOMAS WEST, Knt., K.G., 5th Lord West, 3rd Lord de la Warre, son and heir,

---

[1]Ancestors of **Gabriel, Roger & Sarah Ludlow, Thomas Lunsford**.

HUMPHREY (cont).

summoned to Parliament from 15 Nov. 1482. He was married for the first time to ELIZABETH MORTIMER, daughter of Hugh Mortimer, of Mortimer's Hall, co. Hants, by Eleanor, daughter of John Cornwall. They had five sons and five daughters. He was married for the second time to **ELEANOR COPLEY**, daughter of Roger Copley, Esq., of Roughey, Sussex, by Anne (**descendant of King Edward I**), second daughter and co-heiress of Thomas Hoo, Knt., Lord Hoo of Hoo in Luton, co. Bedford [see WELLES 5 for her ancestry]. They had three sons and two daughters. "Thomas West knyght Lord Laware" died testate (P.C.C., 2 Porch) aged about sixty-eight on 11 Oct. 1525. The will of "Elynour, lady Lawar" was dated 10 May 1536 and proved 14 Nov. 1536 (P.C.C., 41 Hogen). They were buried at Broadwater, Sussex.

H.S.P. 42:209-210 (1898) (1619 Vis. Kent). *H.S.P.* 64:59 (1913). *C.P.* 4:155-156 (1916), *C.P.* 12(2):522 (1959). *Comber* (1933), pp. 305-307.

5. GEORGE WEST, Knt., of Warbelton, Sussex, younger son by second marriage, was married to **ELIZABETH MORTON**, eldest daughter and co-heiress of Robert Morton, Knt., of Lechlade, co. Gloucester. They had two sons and one daughter. SIR GEORGE WEST died testate (P.C.C., 10 Crumwell) in September 1538, and was buried at Warbleton, Sussex. His widow was living in 1554.

H.S.P. 64:59,158 (1913) (1634 Vis. Hants) (identifies her father as "Sr Anthony Morton Knt"). *C.P.* 4:158. *Comber* (1933), p. 307.

Children & grandchild of George West, by Elizabeth Morton:
    i. **WILLIAM WEST**, Knt., son and heir, born about 1520 [see next].
    ii. **THOMAS WEST**, Knt., of Testwood, co. Hants, second son, married _____ **HUTTOF**.
        a. **ELIZABETH WEST**, married **JOHN LEIGH** [see STOCKMAN 3].[1]

4. WILLIAM WEST, Knt., was born about 1520. Having been adopted as heir by his uncle, the last Lord, he "being not content to stay till his uncle's natural death, prepared poison to dispatch him quickly," and was consequently, by Act of Parliament on 1 Feb. 1549/50, disabled from all honours. He was restored in blood on 10 Apr. 1563 under the style of "William West, Esquire". He was created **Baron Delaware** on 5 Feb. 1569/70. He was summoned to Parliament from 15 Sep. 1586 by writs directed *Willielmo West de la Warr Chl'r*. He was married for the first time before 1555 to **ELIZABETH STRANGE**, daughter of Thomas Strange, of Chesterton, co. Gloucester. They had one son and three daughters. He was married for the second time to **ANNE SWIFT**, widow of Thomas Oliver, and daughter of Henry Swift, of Andover, co. Hants, by his wife Elizabeth. WILLIAM WEST, Lord Delaware, died aged over seventy-five at Wherwell, co. Hants, on 30 Dec. 1595. His widow was married for the third time to Richard Kemish, of Andover (died 6 Oct. 1611), and survived him.

H.S.P. 64:59 (1913). *C.P.* 4:158-159 (1916). *Comber* (1933), p. 307.

3. THOMAS WEST, Knt., of Wherwell, co. Hants, 2nd Lord Delaware, Sheriff of Hampshire, M.P., son and heir by first marriage, was born about 1556 (aged forty in 1596). He was married on 19 Nov. 1571 to **ANNE KNOLLYS**, daughter of Francis Knollys, K.G., of Rotherfield Greys, co. Oxford, by Mary (**descendant of King Edward I**), daughter of William Cary (and first cousin of Queen Elizabeth) [see CARY 2 for her ancestry]. They had six sons and seven daughters. THOMAS WEST, Lord Delaware, died on 24 Mar. 1601/2. His widow was living at St.

---

[1]Ancestors of **John Stockman**.

HUMPHREY (cont).

WEST, Lord Delaware, died on 24 Mar. 1601/2. His widow was living at St. Catherine, Coleman, London, on 30 Aug. 1608.

H.S.P. 64:59 (1913). *C.P.* 4:159-160 (1916). *TAG* 18:211-218 (Apr. 1942). *TAG* 19:200 (Apr. 1943) (descent of Herbert Pelham from King Edward III). *NEHGR* 106:259 (Oct. 1952) (West arms: Silver a dance sable). *Adventurers* (1987), pp. 655-659. *Comber* (1933), p. 308.

Children & grandchildren of Thomas West, by Anne Knollys:

   i. **ELIZABETH WEST**, born 11 Sep. 1573 [see next].

   ii. **THOMAS WEST, Knt.**, 3rd Lord de la Warre, third child, second but first surviving son and heir, born 9 July 1577, matriculated at Queen's College, Oxford, 9 Mar. 1591/2; M.A. 30 Aug. 1605; M.P. for Lymington 1597-98; first Lord Governor and Captain General of Virginia, 28 Feb. 1610, whither he proceeded the same year with one hundred fifty artificers, returning home in 1611, after having settled that colony, saved the colony from abandonment by the disheartened settlers, died in Nova Scotia, 7 June 1618, on a return voyage to America; Delaware Bay and the State of Delaware named after him; married at St. Dunstan's in the West, Fleet Street, London, 25 Nov. 1602 CECILY SHIRLEY, buried 31 July 1662. Six children, with descendants in England, including later Lords De la Warre. *Stemmata Chicheleana* (1765), p. 89 (She was "Founder's Kin" by Kemp descent).

   iii. **PENELOPE WEST**, married HERBERT PELHAM [the younger], Esq. [see PELHAM 2].[1]

   iv. **FRANCIS WEST**, fourth son and ninth child, born 25 Oct. 1586, emigrated about 1608, elected to the Council, 1609, and was appointed Governor of Virginia, 14 Nov. 1627, died testate between 17 Dec. 1629 and 28 Apr. 1634; married, first, MARGARET _____, second, 31 Mar. 1628, TEMPERANCE (FLOWERDEW) YEARDLEY, died December 1628, third, JANE DAVYE. Two children by first marriage. No known descendants.

   v. **JOHN WEST**, fifth son and twelfth child, born co. Hants. 14 Dec. 1590, B.A. Magdalen College, Oxford, 1 Dec. 1613, emigrated to Virginia in the *Bony Bess* in 1618, associated with the military in the defence of the colony, member of the House of Burgesses, 1628, member of the Council, 1631-59, justice of York County, 1634, Governor 1635-1637, patented land on York River, plantation at the fork of York River on the site of the present town of West Point, died there 1659; married ANN _____.

      a. **COL. JOHN WEST**, born about 1632, served as captain, major and lieutenant colonel of militia, 1652-73, loyal to Governor Berkeley during Bacon's Rebellion; member House of Burgesses, died testate (will dated 15 Nov. 1689); married before 4 Nov. 1664, UNITY CROSHAW. Four children.

   vi. **LT.-COL. NATHANIEL WEST**, sixth son and thirteenth child, born 30 Nov. 1592, emigrated to Virginia, probably in 1618, died before February 1623/4; married in Virginia in 1621 FRANCES GREVILLE (married, second, Abraham Peirsey, third, Capt. Samuel Mathews).

      a. **NATHANIEL WEST**, born Virginia 1622, died 14 Jan. 1670/1, buried at Warton; co. Lancaster; married; first, JANE ADAMS, died 25 May 1657, second, at Worsall, co. York, ELIZABETH (PRESTON) SAGAR. Four children. No descendants.

2. ELIZABETH WEST, eldest child, was born 11 Sep. 1573. The sponsors at her baptism were Queen Elizabeth, the Countess of Lincoln, and the Earl of Leicester, and she was doubtless named in honor of the Queen who was a first cousin of Elizabeth's great-grandmother, Mary Cary. Her burial inscription stated that her "youth was spent in the palace of our most serene Queen Elizabeth, her godmother" [*cuj anni juveniles p'acti sunt, in aula sereniss' reginae Elizabethae, ejus e sacro fonte susceptricis*]. She was married, aged twenty years and five months, at Wherwell, co. Hants, on 12 Feb. 1593/4 to **HERBERT PELHAM** [the elder], Esq., of Fordingham, co. Dorset and Hellingly, Sussex, son and heir of Anthony Pelham, of Buxstepe in Warbleton, Sussex, by his wife Margaret Hall. He was born about 1546 (aged twenty at his father's death in 1566), and was some thirty years her senior. His father sent

---

[1]Parents of **Herbert Pelham**.

HUMPHREY (cont).

him to Cambridge where he matriculated Fellow-Commoner from Queen's, Michaelmas, 1562. He had been married previously to CATHERINE THATCHER, daughter of John Thatcher, of Priesthawes in Westham, Sussex, by Margaret, daughter of Godard Oxenbridge, Knt. (they had three children, including Herbert Pelham [the younger], husband of his Elizabeth's younger sister Penelope West [see PELHAM 2]). Herbert and Elizabeth Pelham had four sons and six daughters. He was Sheriff of Sussex, but in 1582 was described as neglecting his duties. On Oct. 31, 1587 he purchased the manor of Michelham (the site of a priory). His later years were characterized by debt and sale of property including Michelham. HERBERT PELHAM, ESQ., died on 12 Apr. 1620, and was buried at Fordington, co. Dorset. ELIZABETH WEST resided in seclusion with her eldest son Thomas at Compton Valence, co. Dorset, where she died on 15 Jan. 1632/3 (M.I. in church there).

Stemmata Chicheleana Supplement (1775), p. 106 (in error in describing Elizabeth as a daughter rather than sister of Thomas West, Lord Delaware). *NEHGR* 33:285-288 (July 1879). *H.S.P.* 20:75 (1885) (1623 Vis. Dorset). *H.S.P.* 51:767 (1903) (Maddison Linc. Ped.). *TAG* 16:128-132 (Jan. 1940). *TAG* 16:201-205 (Apr. 1940). *Saltonstall* (1897), p. 8 (Sir Richard Saltonstall [see] was married for the second time to Elizabeth, daughter of Sir Thomas West, Lord Delaware, citing Edmonson's Collections in the Heralds' College).

1. **ELIZABETH PELHAM**, seventh child and fifth daughter, was born at Hellingly on 27 Apr. 1604. She was married at Salisbury on 4 Sep. 1621 to **JOHN HUMPHREY**, of Fordingham, Dorset, son of Michael Humphrey of Chaldon, Dorset, by his wife Dorothy Bawler. He was born about 1595, and had been married previously to Isabel Williams. ELIZABETH PELHAM died on 1 Nov. 1628. He was married for the third time about 1630 to Susan Clinton (or Fiennes), daughter of Theophilus Clinton, Earl of Lincoln. They emigrated to New England in 1634 and settled at Lynn, Massahuetts. The will of "Collonel John Humfrey" of Westminster, Middlesex, was dated 16 Dec. 1651 and proved 23 Mar. 1651/2 (P.C.C., 1653, fol. 297).

Stemmata Chicheleana (1765), p. 106. *NEHGR* 33:288 (July 1879). *H.S.P.* 20:75 (1885). *TAG* 16:205 (Apr. 1940). *NEHGR* 99:227-242 (July 1945).

Child and grandchildren of John Humphrey, by Elizabeth Pelham:

i. **ANNE HUMPHREY**, baptised Fordingham, Dorset, 17 Dec. 1625; married, first, **WILLIAM PALMES**, second, **REV. JOHN MILES** of Swansea, Massachusetts.

   a. **JONATHAN PALMES**.

   b. **ANN PALMES**, married **NICHOLAS LANG**.

   c. **ELIZABETH PALMES**.

   d. **SUSANNA PALMES**, married **SAMUEL AVERY**, of New London, Connecticut. Ten children.

   e. **REV. SAMUEL MILES**, A.M. Harvard College 1684, Rector of King's Chapel, Boston.

* * *

HUMPHREY OF LLANGELYNIN see OWEN

HUNGERFORD see BOTREAUX

INGOLDISTHORPE see CHERLETON

JENNINGS

EDWARD I OF ENGLAND, King of England, married **ALIANORE DE CASTILLE**.
JOAN OF ENGLAND [*of Acre*], married **GILBERT DE CLARE**, Earl of Gloucester.
ALIANOR DE CLARE, married **HUGH LE DESPENSER**, Lord le Despenser.
ISABEL LA DESPENSER, married **RICHARD FITZ ALAN**, Earl of Arundel.
EDMUND FITZ ALAN, Knt., married **SIBYL DE MONTAGU**.
PHILIPPE FITZ ALAN, married **RICHARD CERGEAUX**, Knt. [see CERGEAUX 8].

10. **ELIZABETH CERGEAUX**, elder daughter and co-heiress, was born about 1378 (aged twenty-one in 1399), and was sister and co-heiress of Richard Cergeaux (died 1306) receiving Chipping Norton, co. Oxford, and property in Cornwall. She was married about July 1388 to **WILLIAM DE MARNEY**, Knt., of Layer Marney, Essex, and Kingsey, co. Buckingham, M.P. for Essex,, Sheriff of Cornwall, and of Essex and Hertfordshire, son and heir of Robert de Marney, Knt., of Layer Marney, by his second wife Alice, daughter of Richard Lacer, of Bromley, Kent. He was born about 1370. They had two sons and two daughters. She predeceased her husband. "Sir William de Marny, knt., Leyr Marny, Essex" died testate (P.C.C., 29 Marche, codicil 31 Marche) on 21 Aug. 1414, and was buried at Layer Marney.

Trans. Essex. Arch. Soc. 3:30 (1865) (his tomb a "very fine example of the best period of Perpendicular work in alabaster, now exists in the chancel of the Church"). *Trigg Minor* (1876), pp. 504-508. *Roskell* (1992) 2:690-695.

9. **ANNE DE MARNEY**, was married to **THOMAS TYRRELL**, Knt., of Heron, Essex, son and heir of John Tyrrell, Knt., of Heron, by Alice, daughter and heiress of William Coggeshall, Knt., of Codham Hall. They had four sons and one daughter. "Sir Thomas Tyrrell knyght of Esthornedon, Essex" died testate (P.C.C., 31 Wattys) in 1476. They were buried at East Horndon, Essex.

Wotton (1741) 3:511. *Trigg Minor* (1876), p. 507. *H.S.P.* 13:300 (1878) (1612 Vis. Essex) (citing Essex Arch. Trans. 3:78, for will). *Roskell* (1992) 3:694.

Children of Thomas Tyrrell, by Anne Marney:

i. **ROBERT TYRRELL**, married **CHRISTIAN HARTSHORN** [see TYRRELL 9].[1]
ii. **HUMPHREY TYRRELL**, Gent., third son [see next].

8. **HUMPHREY TYRRELL**, Gent., of Little Warley, Essex, third son, was married for the first time to **ISABEL HELION**, daughter and heiress of John Helion, Esq., of Belchamps Walter, Essex. They had five daughters. He was married for the second time to **ELIZABETH WALWIN**, daughter of John Walwin, Esq., and had issue.

H.S.P. 13:300 (1878). Probably the "Humfrey Tyrell esq. of Est Thorneton, Essex", with will proved 1507 (P.C.C., 26 Adeane).

7. **ANNE TYRRELL**, heiress to her mother Isabel, was married to **ROGER WENTWORTH**, Knt., of Cobham Hall, Wethersfield and Gosfield, Essex, *jure uxoris*, Sheriff of Essex and Hertfordshire, son of Henry Wentworth, of Cobham Hall (of **Magna Charta Surety descent** and **descendant of Charlemagne**), by Elizabeth, daughter of Henry Howard, of Terrington Howards, Norfolk (of **Magna Charta Surety descent** and **descendant of Charlemagne**). They had four sons and two daughters. She died in 1534. SIR ROGER WENTWORTH died on 9 Aug. 1539. They were buried at Wethersfield (altar tomb with effigies).

H.S.P. 13:301 (1878). *Rutton* (1891), p. 193 (Anne was "heiress of Helion, Rolfe, Swynburne, Botetourt, Gernon, etc.").

6. **MARGERY WENTWORTH**, was married to **JOHN BERNEY**, son of John Berney, of Reedham, Norfolk, by Elizabeth, daughter of Osbert Mundeford, Esq., of

---

[1] Ancestors of **Edmund Jennings**.

JENNINGS (cont.)

Hockford. He had been married previously to Alice, daughter of Richard Southwell, of Woodrising, Norfolk. John & Margery had two sons. Margery was living in 1532. JOHN BERNEY died on 27 Oct. 1536.

Wotton (1741) 1:379 (no identification of wife) (Berney arms: Parted per pale, *gules* and *azure*, a cross engrailed, ermine). *Blomefield* (1810) 9:125-127. *H.S.P.* 32:16 (1891) (Vis. Norfolk) ("Barney"). *Rutton* (1891), p. 193.

5. JOHN BERNEY, Esq., of Reedham, Norfolk, son and heir, was born about 1518 (aged eighteen at father's death). He was married for the first time to **MARGARET READ**, daughter of William Read, of Beecles, Sussolk. They had two sons and one daughter. He was married for the second time in 1552 to ALICE FERRER, relict of William Sydnor, Esq., and daughter of Robert Ferrer, Esq. JOHN BERNEY, ESQ., died testate in 1557.

Wotton (1741) 1:379-380. *Blomefield* (1810) 9:125-127. *H.S.P.* 32:16 (1891).

4. HENRY BERNEY, Esq., of Park Hall in Reedham, son and heir, was married to **ALICE APPLETON**, daughter of Roger Appleton, Esq., of Dartford, Kent (**descendant of King Edward I**), by his wife Agnes, daughter of Walter Clarke, Gent., of Hadleigh, Suffolk [see TYRRELL 5 for her ancestry]. "Henry Berney, esquier, Readeham, Norfolk" died testate (P.C.C., 23 Brudenell) in 1584. They were buried at Reedham (marble tomb with effigies in 1741).

Wotton (1741) 1:379-380. *Blomefield* (1810) 9:127-128. *H.S.P.* 13:135 (1878) (1612 Vis. Essex). *H.S.P.* 32:17 (1891). *H.S.P.* 85:23-24 (1933) (1664 Vis. Norfolk).

3. THOMAS BERNEY, Knt., of Park Hall in Reedham, son and heir, Sheriff of Norfolk, was married to **JULIANA GAWDY**, daughter of Thomas Gawdy, Knt., of Redenhall, Norfolk, Justice of the Common Pleas. SIR THOMAS BERNEY died intestate in 1616.

Wotton (1741) 1:380 (identifies four sons, but no daughters). *Blomefield* (1810) 9:128. *Launditch* (1878) 2:429. *H.S.P.* 32:17 (1891). *H.S.P.* 85:23-24 (1933). *Adventurers* (1987), p. 98 ("Barney").

2. FRANCES BERNEY, was married at Tottenham, Middlesex, on 31 July 1622 to **EDWARD BARKHAM**, Knt., of Tottenham, M.P. for Boston, Sheriff of Norfolk, son and heir of Edward Barkham, Knt., Draper of London, member of the Virginia Company, M.P. for Boston, by Jane, daughter of John Crouch, of Cornbury, co. Hertford. He was born about 1595. They had two sons and eight daughters. He was created a **Baronet** on 26 June 1623. She died on 1 July 1667. SIR EDWARD BARKHAM died testate four weeks later at his house at Tottenham on 2 Aug. 1667. They were buried at Southacre, Norfolk.

Sur Soc. 36:38 (1859) (1665 Vis. Yorks). *H.S.P.* 15:50 (1880) (1633 Vis. London) (daughter Margaret unmarried in 1633/4). *Cokayne Baronetage* (1909) 1:219. *V.M.H.B.* 22:158-159 (Apr. 1914). *Adventurers* (1987), pp. 97-98.

1. MARGARET BARKHAM, was married to **EDMUND JENNINGS**, Knt., of Ripon, West Riding, co. York, son of Jonathan Jennings, of Ripon, by Elizabeth, daughter and co-heiress of Giles Parker, of Newby, co. York. He was baptised at Farnham, West Riding, co. York, on 30 Nov. 1626. He represented Ripon in the Parliaments of 1660, 1661, 1678 and 1680, and was Sheriff of the City of York in 1675.

Sur Soc. 36:58 (1859) (Jennings arms: *Argent*, a chevron gules between three plummets *sable*). *VMHB* 12:309 (1905). *Adventurers* (1987), p. 98-99.

Children and grandchildren of Edmund Jennings, by Margaret Barkham:

    i. JONATHAN JENNINGS, born about 1655, M.P. for Ripon 1695-1701, died unmarried.

    ii. WILLIAM JENNINGS, born about 1658, died 1707 unmarried.

    iii. **EDMUND JENNINGS**, born about 1659 (aged six in 1665 Visitation), emigrated to Virginia in 1680, colonel of a troop of horse and commander of the York County, Virginia, militia 1698,

JENNINGS (cont.)

member of the Council 1691-1726, Attorney General 1684-91, Secretary of the Colony 1702-12, 1720-22, acting Governor of Virginia 1706-1710, resided "Ripon Hall", York County, Virginia, died 5 Dec. 1727; married **FRANCES CORBIN**, died in London 22 Nov. 1713.

    a. **ELIZABETH JENNINGS**, married **ROBERT PORTEUS**. Issue.

    b. **FRANCES JENNINGS**, married **CHARLES GRYMES**, of Richmond County, Virginia.

    c. **EDMUND JENNINGS**, Secretary of the Province of Maryland, married **ARIANA (VANDERHEYDEN) BORDLEY**. Issue.

iv. PETER JENNINGS, born about 1664, died unmarried.

v. ANNE JENNINGS, died 10 May 1691.

vi. ELIZABETH JENNINGS, married ROGER BECKWITH, Knt., of Aldsborough, co. York, created Baronet by King Charles II 15 Apr. 1681, shot himself 6 Dec. 1700.

    a. MARMADUKE BECKWITH, Knt., born 1687, died 1780, Clerk of Richmond County, Virginia.

vii. MARY JENNINGS, died in infancy.

* * *

KAYE see SALTONSTALL

KELKE see FARRAR

KELKE see also GIRLINGTON

* * *

KEMPE

EDWARD III OF ENGLAND, King of England, married **PHILIPPE DE HAINAUT**.
LIONEL OF CLARENCE [*of Antwerp*], Duke of Clarence, married **ELIZABETH DE BURGH**.
PHILIPPE OF CLARENCE, married **EDMUND DE MORTIMER** [see PLANTAGENET 10].

10. **ELIZABETH MORTIMER**, eldest daughter, was born at Usk, co. Monmouth, on 12 Feb. 1370/1. She was married for the first time before 10 Dec. 1379 to **HENRY PERCY** [*Harry Hotspur*], Knt., K.B., K.G., son and heir apparent, of Henry Percy, 4th Lord Percy (**descendant of King Edward I**), by Margaret, daughter of Ralph de Neville, 4th Lord Neville of Raby, Durham (of **Magna Charta Surety descent and descendant of Charlemagne**). He was born on 20 May 1364 [see PERCY 9 for his ancestry]. They had two children. He attended King Richard II on his expedition into Scotland in 1385, and was called by the Scots *Haatspore*. In 1399 he acted with his father in the proceedings which placed King Henry IV on the throne. With his father, he won the notable victory of Homildon Hill over the Scots. Friction with the King, however, led to open conflict. SIR HENRY PERCY was slain at Shrewsbury on 21 July 1403 *v.p.*, and was buried at York Minster. She was married for the second time to **THOMAS DE CAMOYS**, Lord Camoys (died 28 Mar. 1421). She died on 20 Apr. 1417.

KEMPE (cont.)

Mortimer-Percy (1911), p. 2. *C.P.* 2:507-508 (1912). *C.P.* 9:713-714 (1936). *Paget* (1957) 440:3.

Children of Henry Percy, by Elizabeth Mortimer:
- i. **HENRY PERCY**, born 3 Feb. 1392/3 [see next].
- ii. **ELIZABETH PERCY**, married **JOHN DE CLIFFORD**, Lord Clifford [see MACKWORTH 7].[1]

9. HENRY PERCY, Knt., K.G., 5th Lord Percy, was born on 3 Feb. 1392/3, and was heir to his grandfather, the Duke of Northumberland, who took him shortly after his father's death, to Scotland. King Henry V, probably influenced by the young exile's mother-in-law, the Countess of Westmorland, aunt to the King, interested himself in his return. He was created **Earl of Northumberland** in Parliament on 16 Mar. 1415/6, and was regranted the entailed estates. He was knighted by the King, to whom he was faithful throughout his life. He was married at Berwick shortly after October 1414 to **ALIANOR NEVILLE**, widow of Richard Despenser, Lord le Despenser, and daughter of Ralph de Neville, 1st Earl of Westmorland, by Joan Beaufort, legitimised daughter of John of Lancaster [*of Gaunt*], Duke of Lancaster (son of King Edward III) [see BEAUFORT 11.iv.f for her ancestry]. They had nine sons and three daughters. HENRY PERCY, Earl of Northumberland, a Lancastrian, was slain fighting at the first battle of St. Albans on 22 May 1455, and was buried at the Abbey there. His widow died in 1463.

Mortimer-Percy (1911), p. 2. *Clay* (1913), p. 163. *C.P.* 6:621 footnote *e* (1926). *C.P.* 9:715-716 (1936). *C.P.* 10:464 (1945). *Paget* (1957) 440:3. *Paget* (1977), p. 424.

Children and grandchild of Henry Percy, by Alianor Neville:
- i. **HENRY PERCY**, son and heir, born 25 July 1421 [see next].
- ii. **RALPH PERCY**, Knt., seventh son, steward of the Earl of Northumberland, a Lancastrian, slain at Hedgley Moor 25 Apr. 1464; married **ELEANOR DE ACTON**, daughter and heiress of Laurence de Acton, of Newcastle, with three sons and one daughters. She married second John Carlyle, with one daughter. *Hodgson* (1832), p. 262. *Alnwick* (1866) 1:416-417. *Northumberland* 5:467 (1899). *Clay* (1913), p. 163.
  - a. **MARGARET PERCY**, married **RALPH HARBOTTLE**, Knt. [see HARBOTTLE 6].[2]
- iii. **KATHERINE PERCY**, married **EDMUND GREY**, Earl of Kent [see HAVILAND 7].[3]

8. HENRY PERCY, Knt., 6th Lord Percy, 3rd Earl of Northumberland, son and heir, was born on 25 July 1421. He was married on or before 25 June 1435 to **ALIANOR POYNINGS**, Baroness Poynings *de jure suo jure*, daughter and heiress of Richard Poynings, by his second wife Alianor, daughter of John Berkeley, Knt., of Beverstone, co. Gloucester. She was born about 1422, and was granddaughter and heiress of Robert, Lord Poynings (died 2 Oct. 1446). In consequence of his marriage he was summoned *v.p.* to Parliament on 14 Dec. 1446 as Lord Poynings. HENRY PERCY, Earl of Northumberland, took part in the battle of Wakefield on 30 Dec. 1460, and was slain fighting for the king at the Battle of Towton on 29 Mar. 1461, burial, it is said, at St. Denis', co. York. His widow died in February 1483/4.

Mortimer-Percy (1911), p. 2. *Clay* (1913), p. 163. *C.P.* 6:621 (1926). *C.P.* 9:716-717 (1936). *C.P.* 10:464 (1945). *Paget* (1977), pp. 257,411. *Paget* (1977), pp. 257,411.

Children of Henry Percy, by Alianor Poynings:
- i. **HENRY PERCY**, born about 1449 [see next].

---

[1] Ancestors of **Humphrey Davie, John Harleston, Agnes Mackworth, William Rodney, William Skepper, Thomas Wingfield**.

[2] Ancestors of **Edmund Kempe**.

[3] Ancestors, probably, of **Jane Haviland**.

KEMPE (cont.)

    ii. **ANNE PERCY**, married **THOMAS HUNGERFORD**, Knt. [see BOTREAUX 9].[1]
    iii. **MARGARET PERCY**, married **WILLIAM GASCOIGNE**, Knt. [see BERNARD 5].[2]

7. **HENRY PERCY**, Knt., K.G., 7th Lord Percy, 4th Earl of Northumberland, son and heir, was born about 1449. The Earldom of Northumberland was restored to him in 1470, and he was nominated Knight of the Garter on 18 Aug 1474. He was married about 1476 to **MAUD HERBERT**, daughter of William Herbert, Earl of Pembroke, by Anne, daughter of Walter Devereux, Knt. They had four sons and three daughters. He was Lord Great Chamberlain of England for King Richard III but deserted the King on Bosworth Field. His wife died before 27 July 1485 (the date of his will), and was buried in Beverley Minster. Being employed to levy in the North an unpopular tax and to inquire into disturbances in the city of York, HENRY PERCY, Earl of Northumberland, was murdered by the rabble at his manor house, Cock Lodge, near Topcliffe, co. York, on 28 Apr 1489, aged about forty, and was buried in Beverley Minster (M.I.).

    Mortimer-Percy (1911), p. 2. *Clay* (1913), pp. 163-164. *C.P.* 2:391 (1912). *C.P.* 9:717-719 (1936). *Paget* (1977), p. 176.

Children of Henry Percy, by Maud Herbert:
    i. **HENRY PERCY** [see next].
    ii. **ELEANOR PERCY**, married **EDWARD STAFFORD** [see SAINT LEGER 5].[3]

6. **HENRY ALGERNON PERCY**, 5th Earl of Northumberland, K.G., son and heir, was born on 14 Jan. 1477/8. He was married before 1502 to **KATHERINE SPENCER**, younger daughter and co-heiress of Robert Spencer, Knt., of Spencercombe, Devon, by Alianor, daughter of Edmund Beaufort, Duke of Somerset (**descendant of King Edward I**) [see BEAUFORT 9 for her ancestry]. They had three sons and one daughter. He led five hundred Northumberland men at the battle of the Spurs near Thérouenne in August 1513, and attended the King at the Field of the Cloth of Gold in June 1520. HENRY PERCY, Earl of Northumberland, died at Wressell, East Riding, co. York, on 19 May 1527. His widow died testate on 19 Oct. 1542. They were buried at Beverley Minster.

    Mortimer-Percy (1911), p. 2. *Clay* (1913), p. 164. *C.P.* 9:719-720 (1936). *Paget* (1977), p. 272.

5. **THOMAS PERCY**, Knt., second son, was married to **ELEANOR HARBOTTLE**, elder daughter and co-heiress of Guiscard Harbottle, Knt., of Beamish, Durham (**descendant of King Edward III**), by Jane, daughter of Henry Willoughby, Knt., of Wollaton, co. Nottingham (of **Magna Charta Surety descent** and **descendant of Charlemagne**) [see HARBOTTLE 5 for her ancestry]. She received Beamish, and Tanfield on partition with her sister on 4 Dec. 1534. They had four sons and three daughters. SIR THOMAS PERCY, having participated in *the Pilgrimage of Grace*, was attainted and hanged at Tyburn on 2 June 1537, burial at Crutched Friars', London. His widow was married for the second time about 1541 to Richard Holland, Knt., of Denton, co. Lancaster (with no issue), and died testate (will dated 18 May 1566) in April 1567.

    Surtees (1820) 2:225. *Hodgson* (1832), p. 262. *H.S.P.* 16:244 (1881) (1563 Vis. Yorks). *Mortimer-Percy* (1911), p. 2. *Clay* (1913), p. 164. *C.P.* 11:720 footnote d, 728 (1936). *Paget* (1977), pp. 188,275,461.

---

[1] Ancestors of **John Nelson, Maria Johanna Somerset**.

[2] Ancestors of **Anne Mauleverer, George Reade, Richard Saltonstall**.

[3] Ancestors of **St. Leger Codd, Edward Digges, Warham Horsmanden, Katherine Saint Leger**.

KEMPE (cont.)

4. JOAN PERCY, was married to **ARTHUR HARRIS**, of Prittlewell, Essex, son of William Harris, of Prittlewell, by Anne, daughter of _____ Jernegan, of Hertfordshire.

> *Morant* (1768) 1:363 ("had a large brick House [at Cricksey], in a pleasant Park, well stored with timber"). *Hodgson* (1832), p. 262. *Trans. Essex. Arch. Soc.* 3:184 (1865). *H.S.P.* 13:59 (1878) (1558 Vis. Essex) (Harris arms: *Argent*, on a chevron engrailed *sable* between three hares' heads erased *gules*, a lozenge *or* between two roaches of the first). *Mortimer-Percy* (1911), p. 2.

3. WILLIAM HARRIS, Esq., of Southminster, Essex, Sheriff of Essex, was married for the first time to **JOAN SMITH**, daughter and co-heiress of John Smith of Norton, Essex. They had four sons and two daughters. He was married for the second time to **JOAN COOKE**, daughter of _____ Cooke, of Bocking, Essex. They had one son. He was married for the third time to ANNE RUTTER. They had three sons. "Willyam Harrys, esquier" was buried at Southminster on 16 Sep. 1556 (will dated 12 Sep. and proved 14 Nov. 1556, P.C.C., 24 Ketchyn).

> *Morant* (1768) 1:363. *H.S.P.* 13:59-60 (1878). *Trans. Essex. Arch. Soc.* 3:183-186 (1865) ("a man of great wealth and large possessions") (will names wife Alice and sons Vincent, Arthur, Christopher, and Edward).

2. ARTHUR HARRIS, Esq., of Woodham Mortimer and Creeksea, Essex, son by second marriage, was son and heir to his mother. He was married to **DOROTHY WALDEGRAVE**, daughter of William Waldegrave, Knt., of Smallbridge, Suffolk, and of Walthamstow, Essex (**descendant of King Edward I**), by Julian, daughter of John Rainesford, Knt., of Bradfield Hall, Essex [see WALDEGRAVE 2 for her ancestry]. They had one son and one daughter. The will of ARTHUR HARRIS, ESQ., was proved on 29 Nov. 1626 (P.C.C., 121 Hele).

> *Morant* (1768) 1:363 (he died 18 June 1597). *H.S.P.* 13:121,213 (1878) (1612 Vis. Essex) (Harris arms: *Or*, on a bend engrailed *azure* three cinquefoils of the first). *H.S.P.* 32:176,298 (1891) (Vis. Norfolk). *Muskett* 1:45,47,121. *Muskett* (1908) 2:237. *Kemp* (1902), pp. 33-34. *H.S.P.* 85:114 (1933) (1664 Vis. Norf.).

1. DOROTHY HARRIS, was married about 1596 to **ROBERT KEMPE**, Esq., of Gissing, Norfolk, only son of Richard Kempe, Esq., of Wasbrooke, Suffolk, and Gissing, by his wife, Alice, relict of Edmund Poley, Esq., of Badley, Suffolk, only daughter of Philip Cockram, of Hampstead, Middlesex. He was baptised at Hampstead in 1567, and entered Gray's Inn on 9 May 1582 becoming a barrister-at-law. They had eight sons and three daughters (one son and one daughter dying early). ROBERT KEMPE, ESQ., died testate (P.C.C., 46 Capell) aged about forty-seven on 23 Oct. 1612, and was buried at Gissing (with monumental inscription). The will of his widow was dated 1626 (P.C.C., 120 Hele).

> *Wotton* (1741) 2:285 (Kemp arms: Gyronny of eight, ermine and ermines, a lion rampant, *or*). *H.S.P.* 13:213 (1878). *H.S.P.* 32:176. *Kemp* (1902), pp. 32-36. *VMHB* 28:135-136 (Apr. 1920) (will of Arthur Kempe of the parish of Michael at the Thorne, Norwich, dated 15 Jan. 1644-5, proved 17 May 1645, names "four of the eldest children of my brother Edmond, neece Dorothy Jackman, neece Elizabeth Kemp, my sister the Lady Kempe of Spaines Hall in Essex, every of my elder brother's sonnes"). *H.S.P.* 85:114 (1933) (names only son Robert). *Boddie* 10:164-169 (1966); 11:156-158 (1967).

Children & grandchildren of Robert Kempe, by Dorothy Harris:

   i. ROBERT KEMPE, Knt., Bart., of Gissing, Flordon and Antingham, married JANE BROWNE.

      a. ROBERT KEMPE. 2nd Baronet, born 2 Feb. 1627, died testate 1710 (will dated 3 My 1704 names Thomas and Peter Kemp, sons of his deceased brother Matthew Kemp); married, first, MARY KERRIDGE, second, MARY SONE. Seven children by second marriage.

      b. THOMAS KEMP.

      c. **COL. MATTHEW KEMP**, son, evidently the Matthew Kemp of Lancaster, later of Gloucester County, Virginia, Speaker of House of Burgesses, died 23 May 1683. Issue.

KEMPE (cont.)

  Wotton (1741) 2:286 ("married to the daughter of _____ Heyton, of Greenwich, in Kent (and had issue")).
- d. RICHARD KEMP, died 1714 *s.p.*
- e. JANE KEMP, married THOMAS WALDEGRAVE, of Smallbridge. Issue.
- f. ELIZABETH KEMP, married MAURICE SHELTON.
- ii. JOHN KEMPE, second son, married AMPHILLIS BIGOT.
- iii. RICHARD KEMPE, third son, baptised Gissing 1600, Secretary of Virginia, 1634, will proved London 1656 (P.C.C., 455 Berkly), names Uncle Ralf Wormley, brother Edward and nephew Edmund, daughter Elizabeth (died before 6 Dec. 1656); married ELIZABETH _____. She married second THOMAS LUNSFORD, KNT. [see LUNSFORD 1], third MAJ.-GEN. ROBERT SMITH.
- iv. ARTHUR KEMPE, baptised Gissing 1601, clergyman, resided St. Michael of the Thorne-Norwich, will dated 15 Jan. 1644, proved 12 May 1644.
- v. EDMUND KEMPE, born 1606, matriculated Magdalen College, Oxford, 16 Apr. 1624, estate administered 1649; married BRIDGET _____.
  - a. EDMUND KEMP, son, presumably, named as nephew in will of Richard Kempe, attorney for Robert Kemp, Knt.; married ANN _____. She married second GREY SKIPWITH, Knt [see SKIPWITH 1]. Issue.
- vi. EDWARD KEMPE, of Virginia, named as brother in will of Richard Kemp; probably issue.
- vii. THOMAS KEMPE, of Antingham, died 1642.
- viii. MATTHEW KEMPE.
- ix. DOROTHY KEMPE, married WILLIAM JACKMAN. Issue.
- x. ELIZABETH KEMPE, married ROBERT KEMPE, Knt., of Finchingfield.

* * *

KNOLLYS see CARY

KNYVETT see GURDON

KYNASTON see LLOYD

* * *

LANCASTER

HENRY III OF ENGLAND, married ÉLÉONORE DE PROVENCE [see PLANTAGENET 15].

14. EDMUND OF LANCASTER *Crouchback* [Gibbosus], fourth and youngest but second surviving son, Earl of Leicester, Derby and Lancaster, was born at London on 16 Jan. 1244/5. He was in the Holy Land in 1272. He was married for the first time at Westminster Abbey on 8 or 9 Apr. 1269 to AVELINE DE FORT, daughter of William de Fort, titular Comte d'Aumale, Lord of Holderness, by Isabel, daughter and heiress of Baldwin de Redvers, 7th Earl of Devon. She was born 20 Jan. 1259, and died at Stockwell on 10 Nov. 1274 *s.p.*, buried at Westminster Abbey. He was

LANCASTER (cont.)

married for the second time at Paris between 27 July and 29 Oct. 1276 to **BLANCHE D'ARTOIS**, widow of Henri de France, Roi de Navarre (died 22 July 1276), and daughter of Robert, Comte d'Artois (**descendant of Charlemagne**), by Mathilde, daughter of Heinrich II, Herzog von Brabant (**descendant of Charlemagne**). In consequence of this marriage he was styled Comte de Champagne et Brie in France. He was summoned to Parliament on 24 June 1295 by writ directed *Edmundo comiti Lancastr'*. EDMUND OF LANCASTER, Earl of Lancaster, died at Bayonne on 5 June 1296, and was buried at Westminster Abbey. His widow died in Paris on 2 May 1302.

C.P. (1929) 7:378-387 (1929). *Schwennicke* (1984) 2:83.

Children of Edmund of Lancaster, by Blanche d'Artois:

    i. THOMAS OF LANCASTER, son and heir, born about 1278, 2nd Earl of Lancaster, Leicester and Derby, Steward of England, present at the siege of Carlaverock 1 July 1300, Earl of Lincoln and Salisbury *jure uxoris*; throughout nearly the whole of his career his policy was one of obstruction to his cousin the King, which he carried to the extreme of having treasonable correspondence with the Scots; died 22 Mar. 1322 *s.p.*, being beheaded outside Pontefract in the presence of his cousin, King Edward II, buried St. John's Priory, Pontefract; married 28 Oct. 1294 ALICE DE LACY, born 25 Dec. 1281, died 2 Oct. 1384, *s.p.*, buried Barlings Abbey with second husband, daughter and heiress of Henry de Lacy, 3rd Earl of Lincoln, by Margaret, daughter of William Longespée, Earl of Salisbury. She married, second, Ebles le Strange, Knt. (died 8 Sep. 1335); third, Hugh de Frene, Knt. (died December 1336 or January 1337.

    ii. **HENRY OF LANCASTER**, second son, brother and heir, born about 1281 [see next].

    iii. JOHN OF LANCASTER, born before May 1286, died unmarried in France before 1327.

    iv. MARY OF LANCASTER, died young.

13. HENRY OF LANCASTER, second son, was born at Grosmont Castle about 1281, and was brother and heir of Thomas, 2nd Earl of Lancaster. He was married for the first time before 2 Mar. 1296/7 to **MAUD DE CHAWORTH**, daughter and heiress of Patrick de Chaworth, Knt., of Kidwelly and Ogmore, co. Carmarthen (of **baronial** descent), by Isabel (of **Magna Charta Surety descent**), daughter of William de Beauchamp, 1st Earl of Warwick (**descendant of Charlemagne**). She was born in 1282. She died between 19 Feb. 1317 and 3 Dec. 1322, and was buried at Mottisfont Priory, of which she was patron, as heir of William de Briwere, one of the founders. He was married for the second time to ALICE DE JOINVILLE, widow of Jean, Seigneur d'Arcies-sur-Aube et de Chacenay, and daughter of Jean de Joinville, Sénéchal de Champagne, by Alix, daughter and heiress of Gautier, Seigneur de Risnel. She died at Leicester on 22 Sep. 1345, and was buried at Newark Abbey. He was summoned to Parliament *v.p.* on 6 Feb. 1298/9 by writ directed *Henrico de Lancastre nepoti Regis*, whereby, he may be held to have become **Lord Lancaster**. He took part in the siege of Carlaverock in July 1300. He was created **Earl of Leicester** on 29 Mar. 1324, and restored as **Earl of Lancaster** between 1324 and 1326 succeeding his older brother Thomas. On the Queen's return to England with Roger de Mortimer in September 1326, he joined her party against King Edward II, which led to a general desertion of the King's cause. He was sent in pursuit and captured the King at Neath. He was appointed to take charge of the King, and was responsible for his custody at Kenilworth. About 1330 he became blind. Upon the fall of Mortimer his close personal relations with the young King were renewed. HENRY OF LANCASTER, Duke of Lancaster, died testate (P.C.C., 104 Beck) aged sixty-four on 22 Sep. 1345, and was buried in Newark Abbey, Leicester.

C.P. 1:244 (1910). *C.P.* 2:61 (1912). *C.P.* 7:156, 377, 396-401 (1929) (Froissart calls him *Tortcol* [Wryneck]).

Children of Henry of Lancaster, by Maud de Chaworth:

LANCASTER (cont.)

    i. HENRY OF LANCASTER *of Grosmont*, born about 1300 [see next].
    ii. BLANCHE OF LANCASTER, born about 1305, married THOMAS WAKE, 2nd Lord Wake.
    iii. MAUD OF LANCASTER, married WILLIAM DE BURGH, Earl of Ulster [see BURGH 12].[1]
    iv. JOAN OF LANCASTER, married JOHN DE MOWBRAY [see MOWBRAY 11].[2]
    v. ALIANOR OF LANCASTER [see MARSHALL 10][3] & [see FITZ ALAN 13].[4]
    vi. MARY OF LANCASTER, married HENRY PERCY, Lord Percy [see PERCY 11].[5]
    vii. ISABEL OF LANCASTER, married HENRY DE LA DALE.

12. HENRY OF LANCASTER [*of Grosmont*], son and heir, by first marriage, was born at Grosmont Castle about 1300. His father having become blind about 1330, he early became prominent in public affairs. He was created **Earl of Derby** on 16 Mar. 1336/7, and was summoned as such to Parliament in April 1337. He succeeded his father as Earl of Lancaster and Leicester, and Steward of England in 1345. He was a Founder Knight of the Order of the Garter. He was created **Earl of Lincoln** on 20 Aug. 1349, and **Duke of Lancaster** on 6 Mar. 1350/1. By David II, King of Scotland, he was created **Earl of Moray**. He was married about 1334 to ISABEL BEAUMONT, daughter of Henry Beaumont, 1st Lord Beaumont, by Alice, daughter of Alexander Comyn, Knt., of Buchan. She was living on 24 Mar. 1356. His military activities (at that day including fighting at sea) filled his whole life from youth to within a few months of his death. HENRY OF LANCASTER, Duke of Lancaster, died testate (P.C.C., 155 Gynwell) of the plague at Leicester on 24 Mar. 1360/1 *s.p.m.*, and was buried in the church of the Newark.
    C.P. 4:204 (1916). *C.P.* 7:377-378, 401-410 (1929).

    Children of Henry of Lancaster, by Isabel Beaumont:
        i. MAUD OF LANCASTER, elder daughter and co-heiress, born 4 Apr. 1335, received Leicester, Kidwelly, etc., died of the pestilence 10 Apr. 1362 *s.p.*; married, first, 1 Nov. 1344 RALPH STAFFORD, dead 1347 *s.p.*, son and heir of Ralph Stafford, 1st Earl of Stafford; second, 1352, William, Duke of Bavaria, Count of Holland, Hainault, and Zeeland, *s.p.*

---

[1]Ancestors of **St. Leger Codd, Humphrey Davie, Edward Digges, John Harleston, Warham Horsemanden, Agnes Mackworth, John Nelson, Philip & Thomas Nelson, George Reade, William Rodney, Katherine Saint Leger, Richard Saltonstall, Thomas Wingfield**, and, probably, **Jane Haviland**.

[2]Ancestors of **William Asfordby, Essex Beville, Joseph Bolles, Elizabeth Bosvile, Charles Calvert, Frances, Jane & Katherine Deighton, John Fenwick, Muriel Gurdon, Anne Humphrey, Thomas Ligon, Nathaniel Littleton, Thomas Lloyd, Philip & Thomas Nelson, Gabriel, Roger & Sarah Ludlow, Thomas Lunsford, Herbert Pelham, William Randolph, George Reade, Diana & Grey Skipwith, John Stockman, John West, Thomas Wingfield, Hawte Wyatt**, and, probably, **Thomas Dudley, Jane Haviland**.

[3]Ancestors of **Anne Humphrey, Elizabeth Marshall, John Nelson, John Oxenbridge, Herbert Pelham, Maria Johanna Somerset, John West**.

[4]Ancestors of **Robert Abell, Dannett Abney, Alice Baynton, Elizabeth Bosvile, Stephen Bull, Charles Calvert, Grace Chetwode, St. Leger Codd, Elizabeth Coytemore, Francis Dade, Edward Digges, Henry Fleete, Muriel Gurdon, Mary Gye, Warham Horsemanden, Anne Humphrey, Thomas Ligon, Nathaniel Littleton, Thomas Lloyd, Gabriel, Roger & Sarah Ludlow, Thomas Lunsford, Oliver Manwaring, Elizabeth Marshall, John Nelson, Philip & Thomas Nelson, John Oxenbridge, Joshua & Rebecca Owen, Richard Palgrave, Herbert Pelham, William Randolph, Katherine Saint Leger, John Washington, John West, Thomas Wingfield, Mary Wolseley, Hawte Wyatt, Amy Wyllys**, and, probably, **Jane Haviland, Thomas Dudley**.

[5]Ancestors of **St. Leger Codd, Humphrey Davie, Edward Digges, John Harleston, Warham Horsemanden, Agnes Mackworth, Anne Mauleverer, John Nelson, George Reade, William Rodney, Richard Saltonstall, Katherine Saint Leger, William Skepper, Thomas Wingfield**, and, probably, of **Jane Haviland**.

ii. BLANCHE OF LANCASTER, younger daughter and co-heiress, born 25 Mar. 1345 [see next].

11. **BLANCHE OF LANCASTER**, younger daughter and co-heiress, was born on 25 Mar. 1345, and received Pontefract, Lancashire and Cheshire, etc. She was married at Reading on 13 May 1359 to her cousin **JOHN OF LANCASTER** [*of Gaunt*], K.G., fourth but third surviving **son of King Edward III**, K.G. He was born at St. Bavon's Abbey, Ghent in Flanders in March 1340 [see PLANTAGENET 12 for his ancestry]. He was created **Earl of Richmond** on 20 Sep. 1342. He was created **Duke of Lancaster** on 13 Nov. 1362 in consequence of the marriage, and was ancestor of the Lancastrian Kings of England. BLANCHE OF LANCASTER died at Bolingbroke Castle, co. Lincoln, on 12 Sep. 1369, and was buried in St. Paul's Cathedral. Chaucer's *Boke of the Duchesse* is the author's tribute to her memory. John was married for the second time at Roquefort near Bordeaux in September 1371 to CONSTANCE DE CASTILLE, elder surviving daughter and co-heiress of Pedro I (the Cruel), Rey de Castilla, by his first wife Maria, daughter of Juan Garcías de Padilla, Lord of Villagera. She was born at Castro Kerez in 1354. In her right John assumed in September 1371 the title of King of Castille and León. From 1376 until his death his diplomatic and military services in France and Guienne, and in Scotland, and his Spanish expedition (1386-88) formed interludes in the factious life of politics in which, as eldest uncle of King Richard II and his chief subject, he was involved. He was created **Duke of Aquitaine** on 2 Mar. 1390. CONSTANCE DE CASTILLE died at Leicester on 24 Mar. 1394, and was buried in the Newark there. John was married for the third time on 13 Jan. 1396 to KATHERINE ROET [see BEAUFORT for their descendants]. JOHN OF LANCASTER [*of Gaunt*], DUKE OF LANCASTER, died testate (P.C.C., 13 Beaufort) at Leicester Castle aged fifty-nine on 3 or 4 Feb. 1398/9, and was buried in St. Paul's with his first wife. His widow died at Lincoln 10 May 1403.

C.P. 4:204 (1916). *C.P.* 5:196 (1926). *C.P.* 7:410-416 (1929) ("it is curious that this man of many titles is so familiar in our mouths as plain John of Gaunt--a name never used in his own time after his third year, when he received his first peerage title--for he was in every way a more ordinary man than his brilliant predecessor [father-in-law], who is forgotten. Perhaps it is to Shakespeare that he owes both name and lasting fame"), 416 footnote b ("The Duke was a man of culture, reading with Chaucer (whom he met first at Christmas 1357) the Latin poets as well as the fashionable French romances. Chaucer ... tells us that in his youth the Duke himself made verses. He came into contact several times with Wyclif, and was in favour of the translation of the Bible into English, but his support of anti-papal views must have been either temporary or merely political, for indulgences were sold in aid of his Spanish expeditions, 1386 ... The Duke was not in any walk of life brilliant, but won respect, even of his enemies, by good faith, tolerance, and a mind above the pettiness of revenge".). *Schwennicke* (1984) 2:85.

Children of John of Lancaster [*of Gaunt*], by Blanche of Lancaster:

    i. JOHN OF LANCASTER, born about 1362, died young.

    ii. EDWARD OF LANCASTER, born about 1365, died young.

    iii. JOHN OF LANCASTER, born before 4 May 1366, died young.

    iv. HENRY OF LANCASTER [*of Bolingbroke*], son and heir, born April 1367 [see next].

    v. PHILIPPE OF LANCASTER, born 31 Mar. 1360, married JOHN I, King of Portugal.

    vi. ELIZABETH OF LANCASTER, married **JOHN DE HOLAND** [see GURDON 8].[1]

    vii. ISABEL OF LANCASTER, born about 1368, died young

Children of John of Lancaster [*of Gaunt*], by Constance de Castille:

---

[1] Ancestors of **Muriel Gurdon**, and, probably, **Jane Haviland**.

LANCASTER (cont.)

viii. JOHN OF LANCASTER, born at Ghent 1374, died young.

ix. KATHERINE OF LANCASTER, born 1372/3, married ENRIQUE III, Rey de Castilla y Leon.

10. HENRY IV OF ENGLAND [*of Bolingbroke*], K.G., Earl of Hereford and Northampton *jure uxoris*, only surviving son and heir, was born at Bolingbroke Castle, co. Lincoln, in April 1366. He was married for the first time at Arundel Castle between 30 July 1380 and 10 Feb. 1381 to MARY DE BOHUN, younger daughter and co-heiress of Humphrey de Bohun, 7th and last Earl of Hereford, 6th Earl of Essex and 2nd Earl of Northampton, by Joan Fitz Alan, daughter of Richard Fitz Alan, 9th Earl of Arundel. She was born about 1370 and was aged about eleven at time of marriage [see BOHUN 10]. She died at Peterborough Castle aged twenty-four after the birth of her youngest child on 4 July 1394, and was buried in Canterbury Cathedral. From 1394 he devoted himself to work in Parliament and Council. He was created **Duke of Hereford** on 29 Sep. 1397. Very soon afterwards began a quarrel with Thomas Mowbray, Duke of Norfolk, which was ended by the banishment of both Dukes in September 1398. On his father's death in February 1399, Henry succeeded him as Duke of Lancaster, Earl of Lincoln and Leicester, and the banishment was rescinded. He returned to England at the end of June and deposed his cousin King Richard II. He was declared King of England by Parliament on 30 Sep. 1399, as Henry IV, and was crowned **King of England** on 13 Oct. 1399. He was married for the second time at Winchester on 7 Feb. 1403 to JEANNE DE NAVARRE, daughter of Charles II, Roi de Navarre, by Jeanne, daughter of Jean de France, Roi de France. She was born about 1370. HENRY IV, King of England, died at Westminster on 20 Mar. 1413, and was buried in Canterbury Cathedral. His widow died at Havering-at-Bower on 9 July 1437.

C.P. 6:477 (1926). C.P. 7:417-418 (1929). *Paget* (1977), p. 27.

Children of Henry IV of England, by Mary Bohun:

i. A son, born April 1382, died in infancy.

ii. HENRY V OF ENGLAND, born 9 Aug. 1387 [see next].

iii. THOMAS OF LANCASTER, born 29 Sep. 1388, created Duke of Clarence, Earl of Albemarle 9 July 1412, slain at the Battle of Beaugé 22 Mar. 1421 *s.p.*, buried at Canterbury; married MARGARET HOLAND, widow of his uncle of the half-blood, John Beaufort, 1st Earl of Somerset, and daughter of Thomas Holand, 2nd Earl of Kent, by Alice Fitz Alan, daughter of Richard, 5th Earl of Arundel.

iv. JOHN OF LANCASTER, born 20 June 1389, created Earl of Kendal, Duke of Bedford 16 May 1414, Regent of France September 1422, died at Rouen in the night of 14-15 Sep. 1435 *s.p.*, buried there; married, first, ANNE DE BOURGOGNE, daughter of Jean, Duc de Bourgogne, second, at Therouenne 22 Apr. 1433 JACQUETTE DE LUXEMBOURG, daughter of Pierre de Luxembourg, Comte de St. Pol, by Margaret, daughter of Francis de Baux, Duc d'Andria. She married second about 1436 Richard Wydeville, Knt., afterwards Earl Rivers.

v. HUMPHREY OF GLOUCESTER [*the Good*], fourth and youngest son, was born on 3 Oct. 1390 while his father was in Prussia, knighted 12 Oct. 1399, nom. K.G. about 1400, said to have been educated at Balliol College, Oxford, to which university he was a generous benefactor, presented many books to the University from about 1411, which formed the nucleus of the Bodleian Library, created Earl of Pembroke and Duke of Gloucester 16 May 1414, summoned to Parliament from 16 Sep. 1414, received command of siege of Harfleur, wounded at Agincourt on 25 Oct. 1415, and took a very active part in the King's second expedition to France, Protector of the Realm and Church of England, 5 Dec. 1423. His first marriage had disastrous effects on the relations between England and her chief ally in the field, the Duke of Burgundy, went to Hainault with his wife Jacqueline in October 1424 in an attempt to recover her lordships, soon discouraged, leaving her at Mons, returning to England in 1425 with Eleanor Cobham; after Eleanor's conviction of witchcraft and sorcery and indictment for treason as aiming at the King's life (she confessed to having used charms to obtain her husband's love), he gradually withdrew from politics and state affairs; died intestate, probably of natural causes,

LANCASTER (cont.)

on 23 Feb. 1447, *s.p. legit.*, but under suspicious circumstances, being under arrest at the time at Bury St. Edmunds, buried St. Albans Abbey; married, first, before 7 Mar. 1422/3 JACQUELINE DE HAINAULT, died at Teilingen 8 Oct. 1426, widow, first, John, Dauphin of France, second, John, Duke of Brabant (from whom she fled because of neglect and insult in 1421 to England, and procured a divorce from the Anti-Pope Benedict XIII), daughter and heiress of William VI, Count of Holland (marriage to Humphrey declared void 9 June 1428, and she married, fourth, Floris Borselen, Count of Ostrevant); Humphrey married, second, 1428, ELEANOR COBHAM, daughter of Reginald Cobham, Knt., of Sterborough, Surrey, by his first wife, Eleanor, daughter of Thomas Culpeper, Knt. She was condemned and put to public penance in London, sentenced to perpetual imprisonment, October 1441, died a prisoner at Peel Castle, Isle of Man in 1454. *C.P.* 5:730-737 (1926). *C.P.* 6:138-139 (1926).

   a. ARTHUR OF GLOUCESTER, base.

   b. ANTIGONE OF GLOUCESTER, base, born before 1428, married HENRY GREY, Knt., Earl of Tancarville [see LLOYD 7 for descendants].

  vi. BLANCHE OF LANCASTER, born 1392, married LOUIS III, Elector Palatine.

 vii. PHILIPPE OF LANCASTER, born 4 July 1394, married ERIK IV, King of Denmark, Sweden.

9. HENRY V OF ENGLAND [*of Monmouth*], son and heir, by first marriage, was born at Monmouth on 9 Aug. 1387. He was created Prince of Wales, Duke of Cornwall and Earl of Chester on 15 Oct. 1399, Duke of Aquitaine on 23 Oct. 1399, and Duke of Lancaster on 10 Nov. 1399. He succeeded his father on 21 Mar. 1412/3, and was crowned **King of England** on 9 Apr. 1413. By his French conquests leading to the Treaty of Troyes on 21 May 1420 he assumed the title of Heir and Regent of the realm of France. He was married at Troyes on 2 June 1420 to KATHERINE DE VALOIS, daughter of Charles VI, Roi de France, by Isabel, daughter of Stephen, Duke of Bavaria-Ingolstadt. HENRY V OF ENGLAND, King of England, died at Bois de Vincennes on 31 Aug. 1422, and was buried at Westminster Abbey. His widow is said to have been married for the second time (though no evidence of the marriage has been discovered) to Owen Tudor (beheaded by the Yorkists after the Battle of Mortimer's Crown at Hereford on 4 Feb. 1461), and had issue [see BEAUFORT 10.ii.a]. She died at Bermondsey Abbey on 3 Jan. 1437.

   C.P. 7:419 (1929). *Paget* (1977), pp. 27-28.

8. HENRY VI OF ENGLAND, son and heir, was born at Windsor on 6 Dec. 1421. He succeeded his father on 1 Sep. 1422, and was crowned **King of England** on 6 Nov. 1429. He was married at Titchfield, co. Hants, on 23 Apr. 1445 to MARGARET D'ANJOU, daughter of René, Duc d'Anjou, titular King of Sicily and Naples, by Isabel, daughter and heiress of Charles Duc de Lorraine. She was born at Pont-à-Mousson on 23 Mar. 1429. He was deposed by Edward, Duke of York, on 4 Mar. 1461, but was restored by Richard Neville *the Kingmaker*, Earl of Warwick, on 3 Oct. 1470. He was again deposed by the Yorkist victory at Barnet on 14 Apr. 1471. HENRY VI OF ENGLAND, King of England, died in the Tower of London on 21 or 22 May 1471. His widow died at Château de Dampierre on 25 Aug. 1482.

   Paget (1977), p. 28.

   Child of Henry VI, by Margaret d'Anjou:

   i. EDWARD OF ENGLAND, son and heir apparent, born at Westminster on 13 Oct. 1453. Prince of Wales and Earl of Chester, 15 Mar. 1454, died 4 May 1471 *s.p.*, being slain at the Battle of Tewkesbury on 4 May 1471, and with him ended the direct Line of the House of Lancaster; married at Amboise August 1470 (or affianced to) ANNE NEVILLE, younger daughter and co-heiress of Richard Neville, 1st Earl of Warwick *the Kingmaker*, on the occasion of that nobleman's espousal of the cause of Lancaster against King Edward IV, born 11 June 1456, died at Westminster 16 Mar. 1485, buried Westminster Abbey. His widow married, second, at Westminster Abbey, 12 July 1472, RICHARD OF ENGLAND, Duke of Gloucester, afterwards Richard III of England, **King of England**.

LANE see RANDOLPH

* * *

LAUNCE

EDWARD III OF ENGLAND, married PHILIPPE DE HAINAUT [see PLANTAGENET 12].
9. **THOMAS OF GLOUCESTER** [*of Woodstock*], Knt., K.G., sixth son, was born at Woodstock, co. Oxford, on 7 Jan. 1354/5. He was married before 24 Aug. 1376 to **ALIANOR DE BOHUN**, elder daughter and co-heiress of Humphrey de Bohun, Earl of Hereford and Essex (**descendant of King Edward I**), by Joan (**descendant of King Henry III**), daughter of Richard Fitz Alan, 3rd Earl of Arundel. She was born about 1366 [see BOHUN 9 for her ancestry]. He was summoned to Parliament on 1 Dec. 1376, and created **Earl of Buckingham** on 16 July 1377 at the Coronation of King Richard II when he acted as Constable, and **Duke of Gloucester** on 6 Aug. 1385. He was Earl of Essex *jure uxoris*, but not of Hereford or Northampton, and was recognised as Constable of England *jure uxoris*. He was active in the French and Scottish wars, and was the leader of the opposition against the autocratic rule of his nephew King Richard II. After ten years of quarrelling with Richard, he was said to have conspired to imprison the King. THOMAS OF GLOUCESTER, Duke of Gloucester, was arrested at Pleshey, taken to Calais where he was murdered by suffocation, it is said in a house called the Prince's Inn, on 8 or 15 Sep. 1397 according to the confessions of his murderers, and was buried at Westminster Abbey. His widow died testate at Minoresses Convent in Aldgate 3 Oct. 1399, and was buried at Westminster Abbey.
C.P. 5:710-729 (1926). *C.P.* 6:474-475 (1926). *C.P.* 12(1):180-181 (1953). *Paget* (1957) 452:1.

8. **ANNE OF GLOUCESTER**, Countess of Buckingham, Hereford, and Northampton, elder daughter and eventual sole heiress, was born in April 1383 (aged seventeen and more in 1399-1400), and was eventual sole heiress to her brother, Humphrey, Earl of Buckingham. She was married for the first time to THOMAS DE STAFFORD, 3rd Earl of Stafford. He died on 4 July 1392 *s.p.* during her childhood. She was married for the second time to her first husband's brother EDMUND STAFFORD, 5th Earl of Stafford, and had one son and two daughters. He was slain at the battle of Shrewsbury on 21 July 1403 [see AUDLEY 10 for descendants of this marriage]. She was married for the third time, with pardon for marrying without royal licence dated 20 Nov. 1405, to **WILLIAM BOURGCHIER**, Knt., M.P. for Essex, younger son of William Bourgchier, Knt., by Alianor, younger daughter and eventual sole heiress of John de Lovaine, of Little Easton, Essex (**descendant of Charlemagne**). He was born in 1374. They had four sons and one daughter. He accompanied King Henry V to France in August 1415, and was at the battle of Agincourt on 25 Oct. 1415. On 10 June 1419 he was granted the *comté* of Eu previously held by Charles d'Artois. SIR WILLIAM BOURGCHIER, Comte d'Eu, died aged forty-six at Troyes on 28 May 1420 (evidently while in the retinue of King Henry V). His widow survived eighteen years and in 1421 made partition with King Henry V of the Bohun estates, which made her the richest widow in England. The will of "Anne Countess of Stafford' Bokingh' Herford' and Northampton' and Lady of Breknoc" was dated 16

LAUNCE (cont.)

Oct. 1438. They were buried at Llanthony Abbey near Gloucester, of which she was hereditary patron.

Memoirs of Eu (1888), pp. 47-49. *C.P.* 2:153 (1912). *C.P.* 5:176-178 (1926). *Paget* (1957) 86:1. *Roskell* (1992) 2:315-317.

7. **JOHN BOURGCHIER**, Knt., K.G., fourth son, was married to **MARGERY BERNERS**, widow of John Ferreby (died between 1 Oct. and 12 Nov. 1441 *s.p.*), and daughter of Richard Berners, Knt., of West Horsley, Surrey, by Philippe, daughter of Edward Dalyngridge, Knt. They had two sons and two daughters. He was summoned to Parliament from 26 May 1455 by writs directed *Johanni Bourghchier de Berners chivaler*, whereby he is held to have become **Lord Berners**. "Sir John Bourgchier, knt., lord Barnesse" died testate (P.C.C., 15 Wattys) on 16 or 21 May 1474, and was buried at Chertsey Abbey, Surrey. His widow died on 18 Dec. 1475.

Memoirs of Eu (1888), p. 53. *C.P.* (1912) 2:153. *C.P.* 5:178 footnote *e* (1926). *Paget* (1957) 87:1.

Children of John Bourgchier, by Margery Berners:

i. **HUMPHREY BOURGCHIER**, Knt. [see next].

ii. **JOAN BOURGCHIER**, married **HENRY NEVILLE**, Knt. [see BOSVILE 6].[1]

6. **HUMPHREY BOURGCHIER**, Knt., son and heir apparent, was married to **ELIZABETH TILNEY**, daughter and sole heiress of Frederick Tilney, Knt., of Ashwellthorpe, co. Norfolk, and Boston, co. Lincoln, by Elizabeth, daughter of Laurence Cheney, of Fen Ditton, co. Cambridge (**descendant of Charlemagne**). They had one son and two daughters. SIR HUMPHREY BOURGCHIER was slain on the Yorkist side at the battle of Barnet on 14 Apr. 1471 *v.p.* His widow was married for the second time on 30 Apr. 1472 to THOMAS HOWARD, Earl of Surrey (later Duke of Norfolk), and died testate on 4 Apr. 1497 [see MOWBRAY 6 for descendants of this marriage] (her two wills written just before and just after her second marriage name her Bourgchier son John and daughters Anne and Margaret). She is said to have died in 1506.

Glover-Foster (1875) (1584 Vis. Yorks), pp. 62-63. *H.S.P.* 13:2 (1878) (1552 Vis. Essex). *Memoirs of Eu* (1888), p. 54 (no mention of marriages of daughters). *Vivian* (1895), p. 106 (1620 Vis. Devon) (will undated, proved 18 June 1470, P.C.C., Wattys 13, names only son John). *G.E.C.* (1889) 2:45. *C.P.* 2:153 (1912). *C.P.* (1916) 4:10 footnote *c*. *Allen* (1935), p. 60. *Paget* (1957) 87:1. *Beville* (1976), p. 341-346. *Paget* (1977), p. 402.

Children & grandchild of Humphrey Bourgchier, by Elizabeth Tilney:

i. **JOHN BOURGCHIER**, 2nd Lord Berners, son and heir, born about 1467 (aged seven at his grandfather's death). He was K.B. on 17 Jan. 1477/8, and was summoned to Parliament from 14 Oct. 1495. He was married to **KATHERINE HOWARD**, daughter of John Howard, K.G., Duke of Norfolk (**descendant of King Edward I**), by his second wife Margaret (Chedworth) Wyfold, daughter of John Chedworth, Knt. [see MOWBRAY 7 for her ancestry]. They had three daughters. SIR JOHN BOURGCHIER died testate (P.C.C., Wartis 15) aged sixty-seven at Calais about 19 Mar. 1532/3 *s.p.m. legit.*, and was buried in the parish church there. His widow died on 12 Mar. 1535-6. By a concubine, Elizabeth Bacon, he had children born in his wife's lifetime: James, Humphrey, George, and Ursula. For this son James Bourgchier, Knt., see BOURCHIER 2. *Collins* (1734), pp. 331-344 (marriage settlement on elder daughter Mary of the manors and other lands of his mother Elizabeth names as heirs to any remainder: Mary's sister Joan, then to "Thomas, lord Howard, knight, sir Edward Howard, knight, Edmund Howard, esq, brothers in tail male, one after the other, after to lady Muriell, Viscountess Lyell, Anne lady Dacre, wife of Thomas, lord Dacre of the South, dame Elizabeth Boleyn, wife of sir Thomas Boleyn, knight, and dame Margaret Bryan, wife of sir Thomas Bryan, knight" [all the surviving full and half brothers and sisters of John, i.e., all the surviving children of Elizabeth

---

[1]Ancestors of **Elizabeth Bosvile, George, Giles & Robert Brent, Anne Mauleverer**.

LAUNCE (cont.)

Tilney by her two marriages]). *Memoirs of Eu* (1888), p. 55. *Vivian* (1895), p. 106. *Copinger* 5:206 (1910). *H.S.P.* 16:30 (1881) (1563 Vis. Yorks). *C.P.* 2:153-154 (1912) ("he was distinguished as a soldier, a courtier, and an author of considerable note, being translator of *Froissart*"). *Allen* (1935), p. 58-63.

    a. **JOAN BOURGCHIER**, married **EDMUND KNYVET**, Esq. [see GURDON 4].[1]

    ii. **MARGARET BOURGCHIER** [see next].

5. **MARGARET BOURGCHIER**, was married for the first time to **JOHN SANDYS**, son and heir of William Sandys, Knt., of Hampshire. She was married for the second time to **THOMAS BRYAN**, Knt., of Ashridge in Chesham, co. Buckingham, son of Thomas Bryan, Knt., of Ashridge in Chesham, Chief Justice of the Common Pleas. He was knighted by King Henry VII in 1497, and was Vice Chamberlain to Queen Katherine of Aragon. She was governess to Princess Mary Tudor, later to Princess Elizabeth Tudor. "Sir Thomas Bryan, knt., of Assheruge, Bucks" died testate (P.C.C., 4 Ayloffe) between 1 Oct. 1508 and 30 Jan. 1517, probably in 1516. She died 1551/52.

    Collins (1734), pp. 331-344 (see 6.i above for identification as daughter of Elizabeth Tilney). *Glover-Foster* (1875), pp. 62-63 (identification of Margaret's parents and husbands). *H.S.P.* 13:2 (1878) (1552 Vis. Essex) (identifies "Marget wyff to Sr Thomas Bryan" as sister rather than daughter of Humphrey). *D.N.B.* 3:150 (1908). *Copinger* 5:206 (1910).

4. **ELIZABETH BRYAN**, daughter and heiress, was married in 1514 to **NICHOLAS CAREW**, Knt., of Beddington, co. Surrey, K.G., son of Richard Carew, Knt., of Beddington, Surrey (**descendant of King Edward I**), by Malyn, daughter of Robert Oxenbridge, Knt., of Brede Place, Sussex [see CAREW 5 for his ancestry]. They had one son and four daughters. He was in attendance to the court of King Henry VIII, being first mentioned as a knight at a banquet at Greenwich on 7 July 1517. He was made Sheriff of Surrey and Sussex in 1518/19. He was present at the Field of the Cloth of Gold in 1520. He was appointed Master of the Horse to King Henry VIII on 18 July 1522, and entertained the King with hunting on the grounds at Beddington. He was engaged in diplomatic missions to the court of France, and was installed Knight of the Order of the Garter on 21 May 1536. He fell into disfavour and was accused of treason. SIR NICHOLAS CAREW was attainted and beheaded on Tower Hill on 3 Mar. 1539/40. The will of "Ladye Dame Elsabeth Carewe", dated 21 May and proved 17 July 1546 (P.C.C., 13 Alen), mentioned "my ladye Darcie the wyfe of Sir Arthure Darcye knyghte my doughter", as well as her other daughters Isabel and Anne, and brother Sir Francis Bryan. They were buried at St. Botolph's, Aldersgate, London.

    H.S.P. 43:17,214 (1899). *Beville* (1976), pp. 340-399. *Paget* (1977), p. 167.

    Children of Nicholas Carew, by Elizabeth Bryan:

    i. **MARY CAREW** [see next].

    ii. **ISABEL CAREW**, married **NICHOLAS SAUNDERS** [see BEVILLE 3].[2]

3. **MARY CAREW**, second daughter and co-heiress, was married to **ARTHUR DARCY**, Knt., of Brimham, co. York, Lieutenant of the Tower of London, second son of Thomas Darcy, Knt., Lord Darcy of Temple Hurst (**descendant of King Edward I**), by Dowsabel, daughter and heiress of Richard Tempest, Knt., of Giggleswick in Ribblesdale, co. York. He was born about 1505 [see DARCY 6 for

---

[1] Ancestors of **Muriel Gurdon**.

[2] Ancestors of **Essex Beville**.

LAUNCE (cont.)

his ancestry]. They had ten sons and five daughters. "Sir Arthur Darcie, knight, York" died testate on 3 Apr. 1561 (P.C.C., 17 Loftes), and was buried at St. Botolph's, Aldgate (M.I.).

Glover-Foster (1875), p. 47 (1564 Vis. Yorks). *H.S.P.* 16:93 (1881) (1564 Vis. Yorks). *H.S.P.* 43:17,214 (1899) (1623 Vis. Surrey). *Clay* (1913), pp. 44-45. *C.P.* 4:71 (1916). *TAG* 21:174 (Jan. 1945) (no indication of wife's descent from King Edward III). *Beville* (1976), p. 386.

2. EDWARD DARCY, Knt., of Dartford, Kent, third son, was born about 1543, and was matriculated Fellow-Commoner from Trinity College, Cambridge University, Michaelmas 1561, being then of Stamford, co. York. He was admitted at the Inner Temple in November 1561, and was a Member of Parliament for Truro in 1584. He was knighted on 23 Apr. 1603, and was granted the Dartford priory for life in 1606. He was married to **ELIZABETH ASTLEY**, daughter of Thomas Astley, of Writtle, Essex. They had five sons and nine daughters. SIR EDWARD DARCY died aged sixty-nine on 28 Oct. 1612, and was buried at St. Botolph's, Aldgate (M.I.).

H.S.P. 16:93 (1881). *Clay* (1913), p. 45. *TAG* 21:169-177 (Jan. 1945).

1. ISABEL DARCY, ninth daughter and thirteenth child, was born about 1600. She was married about 1619 to **JOHN LAUNCE**, of Penneare in St. Clement's, Cornwall, son and heir, of Robert Launce, of Penneare, by his wife Susan, daughter of George Tubb, of Tringoff, Cornwall. JOHN LAUNCE was born about 1597 (aged twenty-three in 1620 Visitation of Cornwall). JOHN LAUNCE, described as a parliamentarian, died of a wound received in an altercation. She was married for the second time, as his second wife, to REV. SYDRACH SIMPSON, Master of Pembroke Hall, University of Cambridge. He died in April 1655, and was buried at St. Bartholomew's, Exchange, London, where he had been Rector. She died testate at London in 1669 (will dated 29 May 1668, proved 4 Aug. 1669, mentions her daughter Mary Sherman).

Waters 2:1186-1187 (1901) (their wills). *TAG* 20:129-135 (Jan. 1944). *TAG* 21:169-177 (Jan. 1945).

Children & grandchildren of John Launce, by Isabel Darcy:

   i. FRANCES LAUNCE, died after 1640, probably unmarried.

   ii. JAMES LAUNCE, of Penneare, married REBECCA BLACKSTON. Six children.

   iii. MARY LAUNCE, born before 1625, died Watertown, Massachusetts, 9 Nov. 1710; married as his second wife about 1645 REV. JOHN SHERMAN, born Dedham, Essex, 26 Dec. 1613, A.B., A.M., Cambridge University, emigrated in the *Elizabeth* from Ipswich, arriving at Boston in June 1634; first minister of Branford 1644-1647, minister at Watertown, Massachusetts from 1647, died there on 8 Aug 1685.

   a. SAMUEL SHERMAN, baptized at New Haven 23 Aug. 1646.

   b. ABIGAIL SHERMAN, born Watertown 1 Feb. 1647/8; married REV. SAMUEL WILLARD. Eight children.

   c. ELIZABETH SHERMAN, born about 1651, died 11 Nov. 1736; married SAMUEL GASKELL. Three children, no descendants.

   d. REV. JAMES SHERMAN, born about 1651, died 3 Mar. 1717/18; married MARY WALKER. Two sons.

   e. JOANNA SHERMAN, born Watertown 3 Sep. 1652, died young.

   f. MARY SHERMAN, born Watertown 5 Mar. 1656/7, married ELLIS BARRON, resided Groton, Massachusetts. Seven children.

   g. GRACE SHERMAN, born Watertown 10 Mar. 1658/9, married EBENEZER PROUT, of Middletown, Connecticut. Seven children.

   h. JOHN SHERMAN, born Watertown 17 Mar. 1659/60.

   i. ABIAH SHERMAN, died before 1702.

   j. HESTER SHERMAN, died Watertown 25 Aug. 1688.

LAUNCE (cont.)

k. **MERCY SHERMAN**, married **SAMUEL BARNARD**. Four children.
iv. **JOHN LAUNCE**, died young.
v. **DARCY LAUNCE**.
vi. **ISABEL LAUNCE**, died after 1640, probably unmarried.
vii. **JOHN LAUNCE**, died after 1640, unmarried.

* * *

LA WARRE see HUMPHREY

LEE see MACKWORTH

LEGARD see SKEPPER

LEIGH see STOCKMAN

* * *

LETHERINGHAM

EDWARD I OF ENGLAND, King of England, married **ALIANORE DE CASTILLE**.
JOAN OF ENGLAND [*of Acre*], married **GILBERT DE CLARE**, Earl of Gloucester.
ALIANOR DE CLARE, married **HUGH LE DESPENSER**, 2nd Lord Despenser.
EDWARD LE DESPENSER, Knt., married **ANNE DE FERRERS**.
EDWARD LE DESPENSER, 4th Lord le Despenser, married **ELIZABETH DE BURGHERSH**.
ANNE LA DESPENSER, married **HUGH HASTINGS**, Knt. [see ELSING 8].

9. **MARGARET HASTINGS**, was married for the first time to **JOHN WINGFIELD**, Knt., of Letheringham, Suffolk, M.P. for Suffolk, son and heir of Thomas Wingfield, Knt., of Letheringham, by Margaret, daughter of John de Bovile, of Letheringham. SIR JOHN WINGFIELD died in 1389, and was buried at Letheringham. She was married, as his second wife, to JOHN RUSSELL, Knt., of Strensham, co. Worcester, M.P. for Worcestershire, son of Robert Russell, of Strensham. "Margaret Russelle, late wife of John Russelle, militis, and late wife of dni. John Wingfeld, militis" died testate about 1397 (will dated August 1387 requesting burial at Letheringham beside her first husband). Sir John Russell was married for the third time to Elizabeth de la Plaunche (died 1423), widow, successively, of John Birmingham, Knt., Robert, Lord Grey of Rotherfield, and John Lord Clinton, and daughter of William de la Plaunche, of Haversham, co. Buckingham, by Elizabeth, daughter of Roger Hillary, Knt. He died testate at Letheringham in 1405, and was buried at Strensham.

Camden Soc. 43:125 (1849) (Vis. Hunts (1613) ("Margrett, daughter of Sr Hugh Hastings, of Elsing in Norff. k. by his Margret, d. of Sr Adam Everingham, k. and lyeth buried at Letheringham, as appeareth by his monument"). *NEHGR* 103:293 (Oct. 1949) (monument, now destroyed, had Wingfield arms: *argent*, on a bend *gules* cottised *sable* three wings conjoined in a lure *argent*, impaling Hastings, *or* a maunche *gules*). *H.S.P.* 111:215 (1984) (1561 Vis. Suffolk) (no mention of John Russell's third marriage). *Roskell* (1992) 4:248.

8. **ROBERT WINGFIELD**, Knt., younger son, succeeded to Letheringham on the

LETHERINGHAM (cont.)

death of his elder brother John. He was married to **ELIZABETH RUSSELL**, daughter of his step-father John Russell, Knt., of Strensham, co. Worcester, by Sir John's first wife Agnes. They had two sons and two daughters. SIR ROBERT WINGFIELD died on 3 May 1409, and was buried at Letheringham.
Camden Soc. 43:125 (1849). ("Sr Robert Wingfeild of Letheringham, k. maried Margret da. of Sr John Russell, of Strensham in Worc. k. and is buried at Letheringham, as appeareth"). *H.S.P.* 111:215 (1984).

7. ROBERT WINGFIELD, Knt., of Letheringham, son and heir, was born in 1403, and was knighted by King Henry VI at Hereford on 19 May 1426. He was steward of the lands of the Duke of Norfolk, and attended the Duke on an embassy to France in 1447. He was M.P. for Suffolk in 1427, and for Hertfordshire in 1449. He was married to **ELIZABETH GOUSHILL**, younger daughter and co-heiress of Robert Goushill, Knt., of Hoveringham, co. Nottingham, by Elizabeth (**descendant of King Edward I**), widow of Thomas de Mowbray, Duke of Norfolk, and daughter of Richard Fitz Alan, Earl of Arundel and Surrey (**descendant of King Henry III**). She was born about 1402 (aged one at her father's death). They had seven sons and five daughters [see FITZALAN 11 for her ancestry]. "Syr Roberd Wingefelde, knyght, town of Cambridge" died testate (P.C.C., 1 Stokton) in 1451, and was buried at Letheringham. A brass effigy formerly in Letheringham church showed the arms of Wingfield impaling Goushill bearing the inscription: "Her lieth S'r Thomas Wingfeld, knyght, Richard Wyngfeld and William Wyngfeld, squyres, sonns of S'r Rob't Wyngfeld, knyght, and of lady Elizabeth, his wif, syster to the duke of Norff".
Camden Soc. 3:126 (1849). *NEHGR* 103:295 (Oct. 1949). *NEHGR* 116:79 (Jan. 1962). *TAG* 47:205 (1971). *H.S.P.* 111:215-217 (1984). *TAG* 67:100-101 (April 1992).

Children of Robert Wingfield, by Elizabeth Goushill:

i. **JOHN WINGFIELD**, Knt., married **ELIZABETH FITZ LEWIS** [see HANKFORD 6].[1]

ii. **HENRY WINGFIELD**, Knt., born 1435-1440 [see next].

iii. **ELIZABETH WINGFIELD**, married **WILLIAM BRANDON**, Knt. [see PALGRAVE 5].[2]

6. HENRY WINGFIELD, Knt., of Orford, Suffolk, fifth son, was born 1435-1440 (aged under eighteen in his father's will). He was knighted with his brother Thomas at the battle of Tewkesbury in 1471, and was for many years Governor of Orford Castle, Suffolk. He was married for the first time before 1470 to **ALICE** _____, widow of George Seckford, and daughter, evidently, of John Harte. He was married for the second time, when he was probably aged over forty, to **ELIZABETH ROKES**, daughter of Thomas (or Robert) Rookes, Knt., of Fawley, co. Buckingham. They had two sons. She was buried in the chancel at Westhorpe, Suffolk. The will of "Syr Henry Wyngfeld, knyght" was dated 21 Feb. 1493/4 and proved 6 May 1494, requesting burial at Austin Friars', Orford, beside first wife Alice (P.C.C., 10 Vox). His widow was buried in the chancel of Westhorpe church.
H.S.P. 3:32 (1870) (1618-19 Vis.Rutland) (Henry called "Knt. of the Rhodes") (Wingfield arms: *Argent, on a bend gules three vols of the field*). *Metcalfe* (1887), p. 204 (Vis. Northants Appendix). *H.S.P.* 32:314 (1891) (Vis. Norfolk). *TAG* 47:205 (1971). *H.S.P.* 111:216 (1984). *TAG* 67:101 (Apr. 1992).

5. ROBERT WINGFIELD, Esq., of Upton, co. Northampton, second son, M.P. for Peterborough, may have been born as late as 1490 (aged under twenty-one at father's death). Like his elder brother Thomas, he entered royal service. As the King's

---

[1]Ancestors of **William Asfordby, Mary Bourchier, Francis Dade, Diana & Grey Skipwith**.

[2]Ancestors of **Richard Palgrave**.

163

LETHERINGHAM (cont.)

servant, he was granted the manors of Upton and Allesworth, co. Northampton (which had belonged to the late Queen Jane Seymour) on 12 July 1543, and established the family seat at Upton. He was married, evidently about 1530 when aged about forty, to **MARGERY QUARLES**, daughter of John Quarles, of Ufford, Norfolk. They had two sons and a daughter. She predeceased her husband and was buried at Ufford. "Robert Wingfield, esquire, Upton" died testate, apparently aged over eighty-five, at his manor of Upton, on 4 Feb. 1575/6 (will dated 4 June 1575 and proved 6 July 1576 (P.C.C., 19 Carew, requesting burial with his late wife). He was buried in the Castor parish church.

H.S.P. 3:32 (1870). *Metcalfe* (1887), p. 204. *H.S.P.* 32:314 (1891) (Vis. Norfolk). *TAG* 47:205 (1971). *TAG* 67:101-103 (Apr. 1992) (named as son of Henry Wingfield in his funeral certificate, part of the official records of the College of Arms) (has been confused in a number of secondary sources with his cousin, Sir Robert Wingfield (ca. 1464-1539), who was at the Field of the Cloth of Gold in 1520).

4. ROBERT WINGFIELD [*the younger*], Esq., of Upton, co. Northampton, M.P. for Peterborough, son and heir, was born about 1532 (aged forty-four at his father's death). He was married in September 1555 to **ELIZABETH CECIL**, second daughter of Richard Cecil, Esq., of Burghley, co. Northampton, by Jane, daughter and heiress of William Heckington, of Bourne, co. Lincoln. She was sister of William Cecil, Lord Burghley, the Elizabethan statesman. They had four sons and two daughters. "Robert Wingfeilde, esq., Upton, Northants" died testate on 31 Mar. 1580 (will dated 30 Mar. 1580 and proved 27 June 1580, P.C.C., 25 Arundell, requesting burial at Castor). His widow was married for the second time to Hugh Allington, and was buried at Tinwell, co. Rutland, on 6 Dec. 1611.

H.S.P. 3:32 (1870). *Metcalfe* (1887), p. 204. *H.S.P.* 32:314 (1891). *TAG* 27:205 (1971). *TAG* 67:103-5 (Apr. 1992) (funeral certificate of his father named children of Robert the younger, including daughter Dorothy) (confused with his cousin Robert, second son of Sir Robert Wingfield, of Letheringham, and is incorrectly called a knight in a number of secondary sources).

Children of Robert Wingfield, by Elizabeth Cecil:
   i. **JOHN WINGFIELD**, second son [see next].
   ii. **DOROTHY WINGFIELD**, married **ADAM CLAYPOOLE** [see CLAYPOOLE 2].[1]

3. JOHN WINGFIELD, Esq., second son, of Tickencote, co. Rutland *jure uxoris*, barrister-at-law, officer of the Exchequer, M.P. for Grantham, was married for the first time about 1593 to **ELIZABETH GRESHAM**, daughter of Paul Gresham, Esq., of Tickencote, co. Rutland, by his wife Margaret Lynne, of Tickencote. They had three sons and one daughter. She died on 14 Feb. 1601/2. He was married for the second time to **MARGARET THOROLD**, widow of John Blyth, Esq., and daughter of Robert Thorold, Esq., of Haigh, co. Lincoln. They had two sons and three daughters. She died in 1618. JOHN WINGFIELD, ESQ., was buried at Tickencote on 29 July 1626.

Burke's Commoners (1838) 2:480. *Camden Soc.* 4:128 (1849) (1613 Vis. Hunts). *H.S.P.* 32:314 (1891).

Child of John Wingfield, by Elizabeth Gresham:
   i. **JOHN WINGFIELD**, Knt., married **FRANCES CROMWELL** [see WINGFIELD 2].[2]

* * *

---

[1] Ancestors of **James Claypoole**.

[2] Ancestors of **Thomas Wingfield**.

LEWKNOR see TUCHET

* * *

LIGON

EDWARD I OF ENGLAND, King of England, married **ALIANORE DE CASTILLE**.
JOAN OF ENGLAND [*of Acre*], married **GILBERT OF CLARE**, Earl of Gloucester.
ALIANOR DE CLARE, married **HUGH LE DESPENSER**, 2nd Lord Le Despenser.
ELIZABETH LA DESPENSER, married **MAURICE DE BERKELEY**, 4th Lord Berkeley.
JAMES DE BERKELEY, Knt., married **ELIZABETH BLUET**.
JAMES DE BERKELEY, Lord Berkeley, married **ISABEL DE MOWBRAY**.
MAURICE BERKELEY, Lord Berkeley, married **ISABEL MEAD**.
ANNE BERKELEY, married **WILLIAM DENNIS**, Knt. [see DEIGHTON 5].

3. **ELEANOR DENNIS**, was married, with contract dated 1529, to **WILLIAM LYGON**, Esq., of Redgrove and Madresfield, co. Worcester, Sheriff of Worcestershire, son and heir of Richard Lygon, Knt., Madresfield, by Margaret, daughter and heiress of William Greville, Knt., of Arle Court and Cheltenham, Judge of the Common Pleas. She brought him Arles Court, near Cheltenham, co. Gloucester. He was born about 1512 (aged forty-four in 1556). They had seven sons and four daughters. "William Ligon, esquier, Madresfelde, Worcester" died testate (P.C.C., 15 Babington) at Madresfield on 8 Sep. 1567, and was buried at Austin Friars', London. His widow was living in 1579, but died before 2 Mar. 1585/6.

Collins-Brydges (1812) 9:358 (identifies children as Richard and Elizabeth). *Smyth-Maclean* (1883) 2:183-185. *H.S.P.* 21:51 (1885) (1623 Vis. Glouc.). *DAB* 2:217-218 (1929) (Gov. Berkeley). *Throckmorton* (1930), pp. 117-118. *Wm. & Mary Quart. (2nd ser.)* 16:289-307 (Apr. 1936). *Ligon* (1947), pp. 45-46,101-104,172-181. *Virginia Gen.* 22:253-255 (Oct. 1978). *TAG* 64:100 (Apr. 1989). *Virginia Gen.* 38:48-51 (Jan. 1994).

Children, grandchildren & great-grandchildren of William Lygon, by Eleanor Dennis:

   i. **THOMAS LYGON**, second son, born, say, 1545 [see next].
   ii. **MARGARET LYGON**, married, first, **THOMAS RUSSELL**, Knt., second, **HENRY BERKELEY**, Knt., of Bruton, co. Somerset. *Smyth-Maclean* (1883) 1:266. *Wm. & Mary Quart. (2nd ser.)*. 16:302-303 (Apr. 1936).
      a. **MAURICE BERKELEY**, Knt., of Bruton, Somerset, M.P., born 1577, died 15 Jan. 1617; married **ELIZABETH KILLIGREW**.
         WILLIAM BERKELEY, Knt., baptised Hansworth, Middlesex, 16 July 1608, Governor of Virginia, encouraged Cavaliers to emigrate, gave asylum to persecuted English clergy, died 9 July 1677; married **FRANCES (CULPEPER) STEPHENS** [see SAINT LEGER 1.iv.e].
   iii. **CECILY LYGON**, of Madresfield, co. Worcester, married **EDWARD GORGES**, Esq., of Wraxall, co. Somerset.
      a. **FERDINANDO GORGES**, born about 1565, Lord Proprietor of Maine, died 1647; married, first, **ANNE BELL**, second, **MARY (FULFORD) ACHIMS**, third, **ELIZABETH GORGES**, fourth, **ELIZABETH (GORGES) SMITH**.
   iv. **KATHERINE LYGON**, married **THOMAS FOLIOT**, of Pirton, co. Worcester.
      a. **JOHN FOLIOT**, Knt., married **ELIZABETH AYLMER**.
         REV. EDWARD FOLIOT, born about 1610, resided York County, Virginia. Two daughters. *Wm. & Mary Quart.* 2nd Ser., 16:304-305 (Apr. 1936), for descendants in Virginia.
   v. **ELIZABETH LYGON**, married **WILLIAM NORWOOD**. of Leckhampton, co. Gloucester, died

LIGON (cont.)

23 Sep. 1632.

a. **HENRY NORWOOD**, Esq., of West Camell, co. Somerset, educated Oxford University, member Middle Temple 1598, died testate 1616; married **ELIZABETH RODNEY**, widow of James Kirton of Somerset, and daughter of John Rodney, Knt., by Jane, daughter of Henry Seymour, Knt. [see RODNEY 3 for her ancestry]. *VMHB* 33:1-10 (Jan. 1925).

    CHARLES NORWOOD, Clerk of the Virginia Assembly 1654-1656, returned to England.

    COL. HENRY NORWOOD, of Bishampton, co. Worcester, and Leckhampton, Treasurer of Virginia 1661-1673, author of *A Voyage to Virginia* (1649), died 14 Sep. 1689 *s.p.*, buried Leckhampton, co. Gloucester. *VMHB* 33:1-10 (Jan. 1925).

2. THOMAS LYGON, of Elkstone, co. Gloucester, second son, was born, say, 1545. He was married to his cousin **FRANCES DENNIS**, daughter of Hugh Dennis, Esq., of Pucklechurch, by Katherine, daughter of Edward Trye, of Hardwicke (**descendant of King Edward I**) [see TRYE 3 for her ancestry]. They had five sons and three daughters. She was fined as a recusant in 1592, and later resided with her son Thomas at Calouden. "Thomas Ligon, Gent." was buried at Elkstone on 14 Aug. 1603. His widow was buried at Walsgrave-on-Sowe on 30 Jan. 1624/5. The will of "Frances Lygon, now being at Merson Co. Wilts., Widow", dated 17 Oct. 1622, and proved at Coventry on 1 June 1625 (P.C.C.), names sons Thomas and Richard.

    Smyth-Maclean (1883) 2:184. *Wm. & Mary Quart.* (2nd ser.) 16:307-308 (Apr. 1936). *Ligon* (1947), pp. 103-106. *Virginia Gen.* 22:253-255 (Oct. 1978).

Children of Thomas Lygon, by Frances Dennis:

    i. **THOMAS LIGON**, eldest son [see next].

    ii. **RICHARD LIGON**, Gent., of Pill, Somerset, author of *Exact and Veritable History of Barbadoes* (London, 1650), died 1662 unmarried.

1. THOMAS LIGON, farmer, of Calouden, near Coventry, co. Warwick, was born about 1577 (aged about forty-four in 1621). He was married, perhaps for the second time, at Walsgrave-on-Sowe, on 18 Aug. 1623, to **ELIZABETH PRATT**, daughter of Dennis Pratt, of Stoke, co. Warwick, by his wife Anne. She was baptised at Stoke-Biggin on 10 Oct. 1602. Their two children were baptised at Walsgrave-on-Sowe. "Mr. Thomas Ligon from Stoke" was buried at Walsgrave-on-Sowe on 20 Dec. 1626. His widow was buried there on 19 Aug. 1631.

    Smyth-Maclean (1883) 2:178,183-184 ("Receivour to Henry Lord Berkeley, and is now farmer of Callowdon ... by his wife daughter of Denys Pratt hath issue"). *Wm. & Mary Quart.* 2nd Ser., 16:307-314 (asserts this Thomas as the emigrant to Virginia and husband of Mary Harris). *Ligon* (1947), pp. 105-106. *NEHGR* 108:32 (Jan. 1954) (Ligon arms: Silver two lions passant in pale gules (another, sable)). *Virginia Gen.* 22:253-5 (Oct. 1978); 23:80 (1979); 38:49 (Jan. 1994). *Adventurers* (1987), pp. 356-360.

Child and grandchildren of Thomas Ligon, by Elizabeth Pratt:

    i. **THOMAS LIGON**, baptised 11 Jan. 1623/4, evidently the emigrant in 1640s to Virginia, Lt. Col., surveyor and Burgess of Henrico Co., married **MARY HARRIS**.

        a. **THOMAS LIGON**, born about 1651, died before 20 Aug. 1678, unmarried.

        b. **WILLIAM LIGON**, born 1653, married **MARY TANNER**. Four sons, four daughters.

        c. **JOAN LIGON**, born 1653, married **ROBERT HANCOCK**. Two sons, five daughters.

        d. **RICHARD LIGON**, born 1657, married **MARY WORSHAM**. Three sons, two daughters.

        e. **MATHEW LIGON**, born about 1659, died before 1 May 1689, unmarried.

        f. **HUGH LIGON**, born about 1661, married, first, **ELIZABETH WALTHALL**, second, **JANE (PEW) PRICE**. No known issue.

        g. **MARY LIGON**, born 1663, married **THOMAS FARRAR**. Five sons, one daughter.

    ii. **JOAN LIGON**, baptised 3 Apr. 1625.

* * *

LIGON see also DEIGHTON

* * *

LITTLETON

EDWARD I OF ENGLAND, King of England, married MARGUERITE DE FRANCE.
THOMAS OF NORFOLK [*of Brotherton*], Earl of Norfolk, married ALICE DE HALES.
MARGARET OF NORFOLK, married JOHN DE SEGRAVE, 4th Lord Segrave.
ELIZABETH DE SEGRAVE, married JOHN DE MOWBRAY, 4th Lord Mowbray of Axholme.
JOAN DE MOWBRAY, married THOMAS GRAY, Knt.
JOHN GRAY, Knt., married JOAN CHERLETON.
HENRY GRAY, Earl of Tancarville, married ANTIGONE OF GLOUCESTER.
ELIZABETH GREY, married ROGER KYNASTON, Knt. [see LLOYD 6].

5. **JANE KYNASTON**, was born about 1470. She was married to **ROGER THORNES**, of Shelvock, co. Salop [*the wyse Thornes of Shrewsbury*], son of Thomas Thornes, of Shelvock. He was six times Bailiff of Shrewsbury. ROGER THORNES died in 1531 and was buried at St. Mary's, Shrewsbury.

> H.S.P. 29:295,458-459 (1889) (1623 Vis. Salop) (Thornes arms: *Sable*, a lion rampant-guardant *argent*) (wife of Thomas Thornes: *Maria fil. Rogeri Corbet de Morton in co. Salop mil.* [or] *Isabel fil. SrRobert Corbett of Morton* [by] *Ciclie da. to Sr Henry Vernon Kt*) [note TALBOT 6.ii]. Bartrum (1983) 1:131 (Bleddyn ap Cynfyn 38 A3).

4. **JOHN THORNES**, of Shelvock, co. Salop, son and heir, was married to **ELIZABETH ASTLEY**, of Richard Astley, of Patishull, co. Stafford. JOHN THORNES was living in 1535.

> H.S.P. 29:459 (1889).

3. **RICHARD THORNES**, of Condover, co. Salop, second son, was married to **Margaret _____**, or to Joan, daughter of Ieuan Llwyd Fychan, of Abertenent.

> H.S.P. 29:460 (1889). Trans. Shrop. Arch. Soc. (4th ser.) 3:303 (1913). H.S.P. 90:64 (1938) (1634 Vis. Worc.). Bartrum (1983) 1:23 (Bleddyn ap Cynfyn 10 F2).

2. **ALICE THORNES**, was born about 1530. She was married about 1548 to **REV. JOHN LITTLETON**, second son of Thomas Littleton, of Spetchley, near Worcester, by Anne, daughter and heiress of John Botreaux, of Abbot's Salford, co. Warwick. He was heir to his elder brother Thomas, of Elmley Castle, and was Rector of Munslow. They had five sons. REV. JOHN LITTLETON died testate (P.C.C., 15 Streat) and was buried at Munslow on 30 Nov. 1560. His widow died testate at Rushbury in Munslow, co. Salop, and was buried on 21 Mar. 1596/7.

> NEHGR 41:364-365 (Oct. 1887) (no mention of Alice's Plantagenet ancestry). H.S.P. 27:93 (1888) (1569 Vis. Worc.) ("John, a prest"). H.S.P. 29:460 (1889). Trans. Shrop. Arch. Soc. (4th ser.) 3:302-303 (1913) (biographical information, will). H.S.P. 90:64 (1938).

1. **EDWARD LITTLETON**, Knt., of Munslow and Henley in Bitterley, and Hopton Castle, co. Salop., Chief Justice of North Wales, second son, was baptised at Munslow, co. Salop, on 23 Mar. 1550. He was married at Ludlow, co. Salop, on 9 Apr. 1588 to **MARY WALTER**, daughter of Edward Walter, Knt., of Ludlow, Chief Justice of South Wales. She was born at Ludlow on 1 Nov. 1565. They had seven

LITTLETON (cont.)

sons and seven daughters. Their son Nathaniel was born at Hopton Castle, co. Salop. SIR EDWARD LITTLETON died at Llanfaire, co. Denbigh, on 25 Sep. 1622. His widow was buried at Ludlow on 23 Oct. 1633.
NEHGR 41:364-368 (Oct. 1887). *VMHB* 18:20-21 (Jan. 1910) ("Col. Nathaniel Littleton, is referred to in the family pedigree book, in the possession of Lord Hatherton, as "Nathaniel emigrated to Virginia in 1635, a gentleman of the Earl of Southampton's Company in the Low Countries, 1625."'"). *Trans. Shrop. Arch. Soc. (4th ser.)* 3:310 (1913) (Nathaniel "died without issue"). *H.S.P.* 90:64 (1938). *NEHGR* 112:246 (Oct. 1958) (Littleton arms: Silver a chevron between three scallops sable). *Adventurers* (1987), pp. 578-580.

Child & grandchildren of Edward Littleton, by Mary Walter:

i. **NATHANIEL LITTLETON**, sixth son, baptised Hopton Castle 22 Dec. 1605, emigrated to Virginia about 1635, resided on Nandua Creek, Accomack (later Northampton), member of House of Burgesses, died about 1654; married **ANN SOUTHY**, widow of Charles Harmar.

    a. **EDWARD LITTLETON**, elder son, married, first, SARAH DOUGLASS, died in childbirth, second, FRANCES ROBINS. One daughter by second marriage, died unmarried.

    b. **SOUTHEY LITTLETON**, born about 1646, of Northampton County, Virginia, and Somerset County, Maryland, died before 12 Oct. 1679; married SARAH BOWMAN. Seven children.

    c. **ESTHER LITTLETON**, born about 1648, married COL. JOHN ROBINS, of "Salt Grove", Northampton County, Virginia. Eight children.

* * *

LLOYD

EDWARD I OF ENGLAND, King of England, married **MARGUERITE DE FRANCE**.
THOMAS OF NORFOLK [*of Brotherton*], Earl of Norfolk, married **ALICE DE HALES**.
MARGARET OF NORFOLK, married **JOHN DE SEGRAVE**, 4th Lord Segrave.
ELIZABETH DE SEGRAVE, married **JOHN DE MOWBRAY**, 4th Lord Mowbray.
JOAN DE MOWBRAY, married **THOMAS GRAY**, Knt. [see GRAY 10].

8. **JOHN GREY**, Knt., K.G., younger son, was born after 1384. He fought at the battle of Agincourt on 25 Oct. 1415. On 31 Jan 1418/9 he was granted the *comté* of Tancarville in Normandy, in tail male. He was married to **JOAN CHERLETON**, elder daughter and co-heiress of Edward Cherleton, Knt., 5th Lord Cherleton, of Powis, co. Montgomery, by his first wife, Alianor, eldest daughter of Thomas de Holand, Earl of Kent (**descendant of King Edward I**). She was born about 1400 (aged twenty-one in 1421), and inherited the Lordship of Powis [see CHERLETON 11 for her ancestry]. SIR JOHN GREY was slain at the battle of Baugé in Anjou on 22 Mar 1420/1. His widow died on 17 Sep. 1425.
Northumberland (1835) 14: chart following p. 328. *H.S.P.* 29:105 (1889) (1623 Vis. Salop) (*Johannes Grey miles Dominus Powys uxoris jure*). *C.P.* 3:162 footnote *b* (1913). *C.P.* 6:136-138 (1926). Roskell (1992) 3:225.

7. **HENRY GREY**, Knt., Earl of Tancarville in Normandy, was born about 1418 (aged one and a half and more at his father's death). He was married after 3 Jan. 1434/5 to **ANTIGONE OF GLOUCESTER**, base-born daughter of Humphrey, Duke of Gloucester (son of King Henry IV). She was born before 1428 [see LANCASTER 9.v for her ancestry]. SIR HENRY GREY died on 13 Jan. 1449/50. His widow was married for the second time to JEAN D'AMANCIER, Seigneur d'Amancier.
H.S.P. 29:105 (1889) (*Henricus Grey Dom. de Powys et Tylle Comes de Tancarville et Camerarius Normanniae*). *C.P.* 5:736 footnote *g* (1926). *C.P.* 6;138-141, 699 (1926). *Evans* (1984), p. 9.

LLOYD (cont.)

6. **ELIZABETH GREY**, was born about 1440. She was married for the first time to _____ _____. She was married for the second time in 1465 to **ROGER KYNASTON**, Knt., of Middle, co. Salop, Constable of Harlech Castle, Sheriff of Shropshire, son of Gruffudd ap John Kynaston, of Stokes, co. Salop, by Margred ferch John Hord, of Walford, co. Salop. He was born about 1430, and had been married previously to Elizabeth, widow of "Richard Lord Strange of Knockin" (died 1450), and daughter of "Lord Cobham, of Sterborough", and had one son Thomas. His first wife died in 1453. Roger and Elizabeth had two sons and six daughters. SIR ROGER KYNASTON died in 1495/6. His widow died in Shropshire after 1501.

> H.S.P. 29:105,295,459 (1889) (1623 Vis. Salop) (*Rogerus ... 4 filius Griffini Kynaston de Stokkes in com. Salop senescallus de Ellesmere* [by] *Margaretta fil. et haeres Johannis Hoord de Walford in com. Salop*). *Trans. Shrop. Arch. Soc. (2nd ser.)* 6:214 (1894) ("Roger was a personage of great renown in the troublous times in which he lived. He was a zealous partisan of the House of York, and at the Battle of Bloreheath, 23rd September, 1459, he slew the Lancastrian leader, Lord Audley, and assumed his arms (ermine, a chevron, gules) which are quartered ever since by the Kynaston family"). *Bartrum* (1983) 1:129,131 (Bleddyn ap Cynfyn 38 A1 & A3). *Evans* (1984), p. 7.

Children of Roger Kynaston, by Elizabeth Grey:

  i. **HUMPHREY KYNASTON**, second son [see next].
  ii. **JANE KYNASTON**, married **ROGER THORNES**, of Shelvock, co. Salop [see LITTLETON 5].[1]
  iii. **MARY KYNASTON**, married **HYWEL AP JENKIN** [see ELLIS 7].[2]

5. **HUMPHREY KYNASTON**, of Marton in Middle, co. Salop, Constable of MIDDLE Castle, first son by second marriage, was married for the first time to **MARGRED FERCH WILLIAM**, daughter of William ap Griffith ap Robin, and had one son and one daughter. He was married for the second time to **ELSBETH FERCH MAREDUDD AP HYWEL** (or **ELIZABETH KYFFIN**), daughter of Maredudd ap Hywel ap Maurice of Glascoed, ap Ievan Gethyn of Gartheyr, by Tomasin ferch Richard. They had three sons and two daughters. The will of HUMPHREY KYNASTON was dated 1 May 1534, and proved 16 Jan. 1534/5.

> H.S.P. 29:295 (1889). *Trans. Shrop. Arch. Soc. (2nd ser.)* 6:212-214 (1894) ("The quaint historian of Middle says that he 'for his dissolute and ryotous liveing was called the wild Humphry. Hee had two wives but both of soe meane birth that they could not claim to any Coat of Armes ... being outlawed in debt, hee left Myddle Castle (which he had suffered to grow ruinous for want of repaire) and went and sheltered himself in a Cave neare to Nescliffe, which to this day is called Kinaston's Cave, and of him the people tell almost as many romantick storyes as of the great outlawe Robin Whood". He was outlawed in 1491, and pardoned two years later). *Bartrum* (1983) 1:86 (Bleddyn ap Cynfyn 11 A3), 131. *Evans* (1984), p. 6.

4. **MARGARET KYNASTON**, was married to **JOHN AP IEUAN AB OWAIN**, of Dyffryn, son of Ieuan ab Owain ap Ieuan Deg, by Gwenhwyuar ferch Maredudd Llwyd, of Meifod.

> H.S.P. 29:295 (1889). *Glenn* (1896), p. 340. *Bartrum* (1983) 1:21 (Aleth 6A), 131. *Evans* (1984), pp. 6-7.

3. **HUMPHREY WYNNE**, of Duffryn in Meifod, co. Montgomery, was married to **MAWD FERCH OLIVER AP THOMAS PRYCE**, daughter of Oliver ap Thomas Pryce, of Newtown, co. Montgomery, by Catrin ferch Morus of Llangedwyn in Mochnant Is Rhaiadr.

> *Glenn* (1896), p. 340. *Bartrum* (1983) 1:21. *Evans* (1984), p. 5 ("Surely he was named after his grandfather Humphrey Kynaston, who in turn was named after his great-grandfather Humphrey, Duke of Gloucester, who in turn was named after his grandfather Humphrey de Bohun, Earl of Hereford,

---

[1]Ancestors of **Nathaniel Littleton**.

[2]Ancestors of **Rowland Ellis**.

LLOYD (cont.)

a descendant of Humphrey de Bohun, Steward to King Henry I").

2. CATRIN (or **KATHERINE**) **WYNNE**, daughter and co-heiress, was married about 1612 to her cousin **JOHN LLOYD**, Gent., of Dolobran Hall in Meiford, co. Montgomery, Wales, son of Dafydd Llwyd, of Dolobran, by Ales, daughter of Dafydd Llwyd, of Llanarmon Mynydd Mawr, Esq. He was born in 1575, and resided at Coedcowryd. JOHN LLOYD, GENT., was buried at Meifod on 25 May 1636.

> *Glenn* (1896), p. 340. *Evans* (1984), p. 5.

1. CHARLES LLOYD, Esq., of Dolobran Hall, son and heir, was born in 1613. He was married to **ELIZABETH STANLEY**, daughter of Thomas Stanley, of Knockin, co. Salop. They had three sons. He built a Friends meeting house near Dolobran Hall about 1660. CHARLES LLOYD, ESQ., was buried in Meivod parish on 17 Aug. 1657 (will dated 17 June 1651).

> *Burke's Commoners* (1838) 4:108,114. *Glenn* (1896), pp. 337,340-354 ("Charles was esteemed one of the most eminent genealogists and antiquarians of his time). *NEHGR* 106:166 (July 152) (Lloyd arms: *Azure*, a chevron between three cocks *argent*, legs crests and wattles *or*, on the chevron a crescent *sable*).

Children & grandchildren of Charles Lloyd, by Elizabeth Stanley:

i. **CHARLES LLOYD**, of Dolobran, son and heir, born 9 Dec. 1637, joined Society of Friends 1662; married, first, **ELIZABETH LORT**, second, **ANN LAWRENCE**. Issue.

ii. **JOHN LLOYD**, born 1638, of Jesus College, Oxford, grad. M.D., clerk in chancery; married **JANE GRESHAM**. Three children.

iii. **ELIZABETH LLOYD**, born 1639, married **HENRY PARRY**, of Penamser, co. Merioneth.

iv. **GOV. THOMAS LLOYD**, of Dolobran, born 17 Feb. 1640, member Society of Friends, resided Merion Township, Deputy-Governor and President of the Provincial Council of Pennsylvania, died 10 Sep. 1694; married, first, **MARY JONES**, second **PATIENCE (GARDINER) STORY**.

   a. **HANNAH LLOYD**, born 1666; married, first, **JOHN DELAVAL**, second, **RICHARD HILL**. Issue.

   b. **RACHEL LLOYD**, born 1667-8, married **SAMUEL PRESTON**. Issue.

   c. **MORDECAI LLOYD**, born 1669, lost at sea 1694 *s.p.*

   d. **JOHN LLOYD**, born 1671, died Jamaica 1692 *s.p.*

   e. **MARY LLOYD**, born 1674, married **ISAAC NORRIS**. Issue.

   f. **THOMAS LLOYD**, born 1675, of Goodmansfields, London; married **SARAH YOUNG**. Issue.

   g. **ELIZABETH LLOYD**, born 1677, married **DANIEL ZACHARY**. Issue.

   h. **MARGARET LLOYD**, born 1685, died 1693.

   i. **DEBORAH LLOYD**, born 1682, married **DR. MORDECAI MOORE**.

   j. **SAMUEL LLOYD**, born 1684, died in infancy.

* * *

LOVELACE

EDWARD I OF ENGLAND, King of England, married **ALIANORE DE CASTILLE**.
JOAN OF ENGLAND [*of Acre*], married **GILBERT DE CLARE**, Earl of Gloucester.
ALIANOR DE CLARE, married **HUGH LE DESPENSER**, Lord le Despenser.
ISABEL LA DESPENSER, married **RICHARD FITZ ALAN**, Earl of Arundel.
EDMUND FITZ ALAN, Knt., married **SIBYL DE MONTAGU**.
PHILIPPE FITZ ALAN, married **RICHARD CERGEAUX**, Knt.
PHILIPPE CERGEAUX, married **ROBERT PASHLEY**, Knt.
ANNE PASHLEY, married **EDWARD TYRRELL**, Esq.
PHILIPPE TYRRELL, married **THOMAS CORNWALLIS**, Esq.
WILLIAM CORNWALLIS, Esq., married **ELIZABETH STANFORD** [see DADE 5].

4. AFFRA CORNWALLIS, was named in her father's will dated 8 Nov. 1519. She was married to **ANTHONY AUCHER**, Knt., of Bishopsbourne and Otterden, Kent, Marshal of Calais, Governor of Guisnes, Master of the Jewel House of the Tower of London, son of James Aucher, Gent., of Otterden, Kent (of **Magna Charta Surety descent**), by Alice, daughter of Thomas Hill, of Eggarton, Kent. He was born about 1500, and was one of the agents of King Henry VIII in the suppression of the monasteries. They had four sons and one daughter. SIR ANTHONY AUCHER, the military commander at the siege of Calais, died intestate of wounds on 9 Jan. 1558 two days after the surrender of Calais. They were buried at Bishopsbourne, Kent, with monumental inscription.

Collins-Brydges (1812) 2:542. *H.S.P.* 4:161 (1871) (1614 Vis. Notts). *H.S.P.* 42:181 (1898) (1619 Vis. Kent). *Copinger* (1909) 3:241. *VMHB* 28:291-295 (July 1920), 375-378 (Oct. 1920). *H.S.P.* 74:1 (1923) (1530 Vis. Kent) ("Auger" arms: Ermine, on a chief *azure*, three lions rampant, *or*). *H.S.P.* 74:24-25 (1923) (1574 Vis. Kent). *Gen. (n.s.)* 33:186 (1917). *H.S.P. (n.s.)* 2:150 (1981) (1561 Vis. Suffolk).

3. EDWARD AUCHER, Esq., of Bishopsbourne, Kent, second son, was born about 1539, and inherited the entailed manor of Bishopsbourne, and other property, on the failure of the male heirs of his older brother John. He was married on 10 June 1560 to **MABEL WROTH**, daughter of Thomas Wroth, Knt., M.P., by Mary, daughter of Richard, Lord Rich, Lord Chancellor of England. She was born about 1542. They had two chidlren. EDWARD AUCHER, ESQ., died testate on 14 Feb. 1567/8. His widow was married for the second time to Richard Hardres, of Hardres, Kent. She died in 1597.

Arch.Cant. 10:204 (1876). *H.S.P.* 42:181 (1898). *Gen. (n.s.)* 33:186 (1917). *VMHB* 28:378-381 (his will can not be found), 383-390 (Oct. 1920). *H.S.P.* 74:1 (1923) (1530 Vis. Kent). *H.S.P.* 74:24-25 (1574 Vis. Kent).

2. ELIZABETH AUCHER, was born between 1561 and 1565, and was sister of Anthony Aucher, Knt., member of the Virginia Company and of the Council for Virginia in London in 1619. She was married about 1580/1 to **WILLIAM LOVELACE**, Knt., of Lovelace Bethersden, Kent, son of William Lovelace, Esq., Sergeant at Law, by Anne, daughter of Robert Lewes, Alderman of Canterbury. He was baptised at St. Alphage's, Canterbury, on 30 Sep. 1561, and was admitted to Gray's Inn in 1580. He was a member of the Virginia Company and incorporator of the Third Virginia Charter in 1614. They had two sons and one daughter. She was buried at Canterbury Cathedral on 3 Dec. 1627. The will of "Sir William Lovelace in my house of the Gray Friers within the Walles of the Citty of Canterbury, Knight" was dated 6 Oct. 1629 and proved on 19 Oct. 1629 (requesting burial "in the South Chappell of the Parish Church of Bethersden in the County of Kent near unto the south wall therein").

Arch.Cant. 10:197-208 (1876). *H.S.P.* 42:181 (1898). *Gen. (n.s.)* 33:186 (1917). *H.S.P.* 74:25 (1923). *VMHB* 28:83-90 (Apr. 1920), 380-381 (Oct. 1920). *VMHB* 29:123-4 (Jan. 1921).

LOVELACE (cont.)

1. **WILLIAM LOVELACE**, Knt., of Bethersden and Woolwich, Kent, was baptised at St. Alphage's, Canterbury, Kent, on 12 Feb. 1583/4, and was a member of the Virginia Company, and a subscriber to the second Charter in 1609. He was married about 1610 to **ANNE BARNE**, daughter of William Barne, Knt., of Woolwich, Kent, member of the Virginia Company, by Anne, daughter of the Rt. Rev. Edwin Sandys, D.D., Archbishop of York. They had five sons and three daughters. SIR WILLIAM LOVELACE, a soldier by profession, died testate at the siege of Groll in Holland, on 12 Aug. 1627. His will, dated 15 July 1622 and proved 23 June 1628 (P.C.C., Barrington 60), left "all my stock and adventures in the East India Company" to his daughter Anne. His widow was married for the second time at Greenwich, Kent, on 20 Jan. 1630/1 to DR. JONATHAN BROWNE, Dean of Hereford, Canon of Westminster (died December 1643), and had one daughter. Her will was dated 15 May 1632 and proved on 22 May 1633 (P.C.C., Russell 51).

Arch.Cant. 10:208-216. *H.S.P.* 15:327 (1880) (1633 Vis. London) (names John & Anne Gorsuch and their four oldest children). *VMHB* 24:90-93,214-221,317-321,425-440 (1916). *VMHB* 27:384-388 (1919). *VMHB* 28:170-187 (Apr. 1920) (includes portrait of William on page 177). *VMHB* 29:123-124 (Jan. 1921). *Adventurers* (1987), pp. 401-408.

Children of William Lovelace, by Anne Barne:

   i. **ANNE LOVELACE**, born Woolwich, Kent, about 1611, emigrated to Virginia with children after death of husband, letter of administration of estate in England of "Anne Gorsuch, late of Weston, co. Hertford, but deceased in parts beyond the seas, widow" issued to her son Daniel on 2 June 1652; married 1628 **REV. JOHN GORSUCH**, D.D. rector of Walkern, co. Hertford, ejected 1642, "pursued by Parliamentary officers in 1647, he took refuge in a haymow and was there smothered".

     a. DANIEL GORSUCH, born about 1629, resided England, married. Issue.

     b. JOHN GORSUCH, born about 1630, may have died young.

     c. WILLIAM GORSUCH, of Weston, co. Hertford, born about 1631, married CATHERINE MORGAN. Issue in England.

     d. **KATHERINE GORSUCH**, baptised Walkern 26 Nov. 1633, married **WILLIAM WHITBY**, of Warwick County, Virginia. Two children.

     e. **ROBERT GORSUCH**, baptised Walkern 19 Nov. 1635, of Maryland. One son in Maryland.

     f. **RICHARD GORSUCH**, baptised Walkern 19 Apr. 1637, of Talbot County, Maryland, married **ELIZABETH** _____. Six children.

     g. ANNA GORSUCH, baptised 13 Mar. 1638/9, evidently died young.

     h. **ANNA GORSUCH**, baptised Walkern 15 Mar. 1639/40, married, first, **CAPT. THOMAS TODD**, of Baltimore County, Maryland, second, **CAPT. DAVID JONES**, of Baltimore County, third, **CAPT. JOHN OLDTON**. Seven children by first marriage.

     i. **ELIZABETH GORSUCH**, baptised Walkern 13 May 1641, married **HOWELL POWELL**, of Talbot County, Maryland. Four children.

     j. **CHARLES GORSUCH**, baptised Walkern 25 Aug. 1642, of Baltimore County, Maryland; married, first, **SARAH COLE**, second, **ANNE HAWKINS**. Three sons by first marrige.

     k. **LOVELACE GORSUCH**, born about 1644, of Dorchester County, Maryland, married, first, **REBECCA PRESTON**, second **HANNAH WALLEY**. One son by first marriage. Two sons by second marriage.

     a. FRANCES GORSUCH, born about 1647, living 1662, probably died young.

  ii. **RICHARD LOVELACE**, son and heir, born 9 Dec. 1617, the poet and Cavalier; as one of the justices of Kent, presented to the House of Commons "the celebrated Kentish petition for the restoration of the king to his rights, for which he was committed in April 1642, to Gatehouse Prison, London, where he wrote his most celebrated poem *To Althea from Prison*", died London April 1658 unmarried, buried St. Bride's.

  iii. **THOMAS LOVELACE**, born about 1619, Alderman New York City 1671, Sheriff of Richmond County, New York; married **MARY** _____. One known son died young.

LOVELACE (cont.)

iv. FRANCIS LOVELACE, born about 1621, Governor of New York 1668-1673, died before 22 Dec. 1675, unmarried.
v. JOAN LOVELACE, born 1622, married ROBERT CAESAR. Three daughters in England (on whom their uncle wrote *Paris's Second Judgment*).
vi. WILLIAM LOVELACE, born about 1624, slain at Caermarthen in Royalist army 1664 or 1645, unmarried.
vii. ELIZABETH LOVELACE, born about 1625, married DANIEL HAYNE, of Wallington in Kintbury, co. Berks. Eight children in England.
viii. DUDLEY LOVELACE *Posthumus*, born about 1627, army officer in New York militia, married MARY _____.

* * *

LUDLOW

EDWARD I OF ENGLAND, King of England, married ALIANORE DE CASTILLE.
ELIZABETH OF ENGLAND, married HUMPHREY DE BOHUN, Earl of Hereford and Essex.
MARGARET DE BOHUN, married HUGH DE COURTENAY [see COURTENAY 10].

10. ELIZABETH DE COURTENAY, was married for the first time to JOHN DE VERE, Knt., son of Aubrey de Vere, Earl of Oxford. She was married for the second time in summer 1359 to **ANDREW LUTTRELL**, Knt., of Chilton, Devon, son of John Luttrell, Knt., by his wife Joan. He was born about or before 1330. In 1361 Sir Andrew Luttrell and his wife went on a pilgrimage to the shrine of Santiago de Compostella in Spain with a retinue of twenty-four men and women and as many horses. She was in attendance on her cousins, Edward *the Black Prince* and his wife Princess Joan. SIR ANDREW LUTTRELL died in 1378. His widow died at Bermondsey on 7 Aug. 1395, and was buried in the Benedictine Church of St. Nicholas, Exeter.

Vivian (1895), pp. 244,537. *Dunster* (1909), pp. 75-77. *C.P.* 10:225 (1945). *TAG* 15:132-133 (Jan. 1939). *Roger Ludlow* (1964), pp. 2,345-2,346. Roskell (1992) 3:656.

9. HUGH LUTTRELL, Knt., of Dunster, co. Somerset, M.P. for Somerset and Devon, younger son and eventual heir, was born about or probably before 1364. He was married before 1384 to **KATHERINE BEAUMONT**, widow of JOHN STRECCHE, of Wambrook, Somerset (died *s.p.*), and daughter of John Beaumont, Knt., of Saunton and Sherwell, Devon, by his wife Joan Stockhay. They had two sons and four daughters. SIR HUGH LUTTRELL died aged about sixty-four on 24 Mar. 1428, apparently while on a visit to one of his daughters, a nun at Shaftesbury, Dorset. His widow died on 28 Aug. 1435. A monument in their memory was erected on the north side of the chancel of Dunster Church.

Vivian (1895), p. 537. *Dunster* (1909), pp. 78-108. *TAG* 15:133-134 (Jan. 1939). *Roger Ludlow* (1964), pp. 2,341-2345. Roskell (1992) 3:655-660 ("one of the most outstanding west country figures of the period. His career had spanned three reigns, in all of which he was prominent in different spheres").

8. ELIZABETH LUTTRELL, was married for the first time shortly after 24 Apr. 1406 to WILLIAM HARLESTON, Esq., (died between 1418 and 1423) (with a son William Harleston, died 4 Nov. 1480). She was married for the second time after 1423 to **JOHN STRATTON**, Esq., of Tys Hall in Weston, Norfolk, citizen and mercer of London. JOHN STRATTON, ESQ., was living in 1459, and died before 8 Nov.

1469.
Dunster (1909), pp. 106-107. *TAG* 15:134-136 (Jan. 1939). *Roger Ludlow* (1964), pp. 2,337-2,339.

7. ELIZABETH STRATTON, was born about 1425. She was married about 1439 to **JOHN ANDREWS**, Esq., of Baylham, Suffolk, M.P. for Ipswich, and for Bletchingly, Suffolk, son of James Andrews, by Alice, daughter of John Weyland. He was born perhaps about 1415. He was admitted to Lincoln's Inn in 1453, and was a lawyer. They had two daughters. JOHN ANDREWS, ESQ., died in 1473, and was buried at Stoke near Ipswich, Suffolk. The will of "dame Elizabeth Andrewes, widow" was dated 18 Oct. 1474 and proved 11 Dec. 1474 (P.C.C., 11 Wattys). She was buried at St. Dionis Backchurch, London.

Dunster (1909), p. 107. *TAG* 15:136-137 (Jan. 1939). *Roger Ludlow* (1964), p. 2,322-2,324,2,335-2,337. *Paget* (1977), p. 436.

Children & grandchild of John Andrews, by Elizabeth Stratton:

  i. **ELIZABETH ANDREWS**, elder daughter and co-heiress [see next].

  ii. **ANNE ANDREWS**, younger daughter and co-heiress, died testate (P.C.C., 32 Ayloffe) 25 July 1520; married, first, **JOHN SULLIARD**, Knt., of Weston, Norfolk, previously married, with issue, to AGNES HUNGATE, daughter of John Hungate, of York, died testate (P.C.C., 21 Milles) 18 Mar. 1487/8; Judge of the King's Bench 1486; Lord Chief Justice of England; Justice of Assize in Essex, co. Hertford, Surrey, Sussex, Kent, and Middlesex; founded a chantry in Wetherden Church; two sons and three daughters, married, second, THOMAS BOURCHIER, Knt. *Paget* (1977), p. 263.

    a. **ANNE SULLIARD**, married **ROGER APPLETON**, of Dartford, Kent [see TYRRELL 7].[1]

6. ELIZABETH ANDREWS, elder daughter and co-heiress, was married for the first time before 1 Feb. 1465/6 to **THOMAS WINDSOR**, Esq., of Stanwell, Middlesex, Constable of Windsor Castle, son of Miles Windsor, Esq., of Stanwell (of **baronial** descent), by Joan, daughter of Walter Greene, of Bridgnorth. He was born about 1441 (aged eleven at father's death). He came of age before 8 Nov. 1461. "Thomas Wydnesor esquyr" died testate on 29 Sep. 1485 (P.C.C., 14 Logge, requested burial at Stanwell). His widow was married for the second time to **ROBERT LYTTON**, Knt., of Lytton and Knebworth, co. Hertford.

C.P. 12(2):792 (1959). *TAG* 15:137-139 (Jan. 1939). *Roger Ludlow* (1964), pp. 2,321-2,321. *Paget* (1977), p. 267. *H.S.P.* (n.s.) 2:111-112 (1981) (1561 Vis. Suffolk).

5. ANDREWS WINDSOR, Knt., of Stanwell, K.B., M.P. for Buckinghamshire, heir, was born in February 1467 (aged eighteen and more at father's death). He was created **Lord Windsor** of Stanwell, being admitted to the House of Lords on 1 Dec. 1529. He was married to **ELIZABETH BLOUNT**, daughter of William Blount, Knt., by Margaret, daughter and eventual heiress of Thomas Echyngham, Knt., of Etchingham, Sussex (**descendant of King Henry III**) [see ECHINGHAM 6 for her ancestry]. She was born shortly before 1471 and was elder sister and co-heiress of Edward Blount, 2nd Baron Mountjoy. They had eight children. She died after 22 Feb. 1513/4 and before her husband. On 27 Apr. 1542 he was compelled to surrender to the Crown his Manor of Stanwell in exchange for the Manor of Minchhampton, co. Gloucester, which had belonged to Sion Monastery. "Andrew Wyndesore knyght" died testate aged about seventy-six on 30 Mar. 1543 (will dated 26 Mar. 1543, proved 31 July 1543, P.C.C., 23 Spert). They were buried in the choir of the Church of the Holy Trinity, Hounslow, Middlesex.

C.P. 9:337 footnote *d* (1936). *C.P.* 12(2):792-794 (1959). *TAG* 15:138-139 (Jan. 1944). *Paget*

---

[1] Ancestors of **Edmund Jennings**.

LUDLOW (cont.)

(1977), p. 181.

Children of Andrews Windsor, by Elizabeth Blount:
  i. **EDITH WINDSOR** [see next].
 ii. **ELEANOR WINDSOR**, married, second, **EDWARD NEVILLE**, Knt. [see OXENBRIDGE 4].[1]

4. EDITH WINDSOR, may have been born about 1515 (when her mother was aged about forty-five or more). She was married before 26 Mar. 1543 (when her father's will mentioned his daughter "Edith, wife of George Ludlow of Hill-Deverill in Wilts, Esq.") to **GEORGE LUDLOW**, Esq., of Hill Deverill, co. Wilts, Sheriff of Wiltshire, son of William Ludlow, of Hill Deverill, by Jane, daughter of Nicholas Moore. He was born, probably at the Manor of Hill Deverill, in or shortly before 1522 (aged "forty" at time of his mother's *Inq.p.m.*). In 1565 he declared before a Herald of the College of Arms that his wife was "Edith, daughter of Sir Andrew Windsor, Knight, Lord of Stanwell, co. Midd'x". They had two sons and six daughters. The will of "George Ludlowe, esq., West Shireborne" was dated 25 May 1580 and proved on 4 Feb. 1580/1 (P.C.C., 4 Darcy).

Waters 1:275-276 (1885). *TAG* 15:139-141 (Jan. 1944). *Roger Ludlow* (1964), pp. 2,100-2,106.

3. THOMAS LUDLOW, Gent., of Dinton, co. Wilts, second son, was born about 1550-55. He was married about 1582 to **JANE PYLE**, daughter of Thomas Pyle, by his wife Elizabeth Langrish. She was born about 1560. Their children were baptised at Dinton, co. Wilts, from 1583 to 1596 except for Thomas baptised at Baverstock co. Wilts in 1593. THOMAS LUDLOW, GENT., was buried at Dinton on 25 Nov. 1607 (will proved June 1608, P.C.C., 61 Windebanck). The will of JANE LUDLOW of Baycliffe, Wilts, widow, was dated 10 Dec. 1646, and proved 6 July 1650.

Waters 1:275-276 (1885). *NEHGR* 86:270 (July 1932) (Ludlow arms: Silver a chevron between three marten's heads erased sable). *TAG* 15:129-143 (Jan. 1939) ("There may be Virginia families descended from [Sarah's] brothers Francis, and Thomas). *Roger Ludlow* (1964), pp. 2095-2099.

Children & grandchildren of Thomas Ludlow, by Jane Pyle:
  i. GEORGE LUDLOW, baptised 7 Sep. 1583, died young.
 ii. **GABRIEL LUDLOW**, second son, baptised 10 Feb. 1587, admitted to the Inner Temple, London, in November, 1610, as from Butleigh, Somerset; married **PHYLLIS** _____; children baptised at Warminster, co. Wilts in 1622, 1624, 1626, 1628, and at Maiden Bradley, co. Wilts on 18 Oct. 1632; called to the Bar as a barrister on 15 Oct. 1620 and elected Bencher on 3 Nov. 1637; Particular Receiver of the Duchy of Lancaster for its possessions in Norfolk, Suffolk and Cambridge; Deputy Ranger of Sellwood Forest; died shortly after 1639, certainly before 1646. The will of Phyllis Ludlow was dated 12 Sep. 1657, and proved 18 Dec. 1657. *Waters* 1:276 (1885). *Roger Ludlow* (1964), pp. 2096-2097.
    a. GABRIEL LUDLOW, baptised 18 June 1622, admitted to the Inner Temple 13 June 1638, killed at the battle of Newbury 1644.
    b. **THOMAS LUDLOW**, baptised 1 Nov. 1624, of York County, Virginia, married **MARY** _____.
    c. **FRANCIS LUDLOW**, baptised 10 Sep. 1626, of Lancaster County, Virginia, married.
    d. ANNE LUDLOW, baptised 4 Dec. 1628.
    e. ELIZABETH LUDLOW, baptised 18 Oct. 1632.
    f. **JOHN LUDLOW**, born about 1634, of Virginia.
    g. **SARAH LUDLOW**, born about 1635, married **COL. JOHN CARTER**, of Lancaster County, Virginia (see).
iii. **ROGER LUDLOW**, third son, baptised at Dinton 7 Mar. 1590, Balliol College, 1610; emigrated

---

[1] Ancestors of **John Oxenbridge**.

LUDLOW (cont.)

to America in the Winthrop Fleet 1630; Deputy-Governor of Massachusetts, 1634, and of Connecticut, returned to Great Britain in 1654, Commissioner in Dublin, Ireland; died there in 1666; married **MARY COGAN**, born about 1604, buried Dublin 3 June 1664.

- a. **SARAH LUDLOW**, born 1639; married, evidently, **REV. NATHANIEL BREWSTER** of Dublin, Ireland, and Brookhaven, Long Island. Issue.
- iv. **ANNE LUDLOW**, baptised 5 July 1591, buried Dinton 8 July 1613.
- v. **THOMAS LUDLOW**, baptised 3 Mar. 1593 [see next].
- vi. **GEORGE LUDLOW**, baptised 15 Sep. 1596, emigrated to Massachusetts Bay in 1630, then about 1635 to York County, Virginia, married **ELIZABETH** _____ . *Waters* 1:172-173 (1885) (his will).

2. **THOMAS LUDLOW**, of Warminster, co. Wilts, was baptised at Baverstock, co. Wilts, on 3 Mar. 1593. He was married at Warminster in 1624 to **JANE BENNETT**, daughter of John Bennett, of Steeple Ashton, co. Oxford. She was baptised at Warminster on 15 Apr. 1604. Their four sons were baptised at Warminster from 1631 to 1640. THOMAS LUDLOW died in 1646, inventory of his estate taken 16 June 1646. His widow died on 19 Dec. 1683.

Waters 1:276-277 (1885). *Roger Ludlow* (1964), p. 2097.

1. **GABRIEL LUDLOW**, was baptised at Warminster, co. Wilts, on 27 Aug. 1634. He was married to **MARTHA** _____ . They resided at Frome, Somerset.

Waters 1:277 (1885). *Roger Ludlow* (1964), p. 2097.

Child of Gabriel Ludlow, by Martha:

- i. **GABRIEL LUDLOW**, born Castle Cary, Somerset, 2 Nov. 1663, resided New York City, New York, married **SARAH HANMER**. Issue.

* * *

LUNSFORD

EDWARD I OF ENGLAND, King of England, married **ALIANORE DE CASTILLE**.
JOAN OF ENGLAND [*of Acre*], married **GILBERT DE CLARE**, Earl of Gloucester.
MARGARET DE CLARE, married **HUGH DE AUDLEY**, Earl of Gloucester.
MARGARET DE AUDLEY, married **RALPH DE STAFFORD**, Earl of Stafford.
HUGH DE STAFFORD, 2nd Earl of Stafford, married **PHILIPPE DE BEAUCHAMP**.
MARGARET DE STAFFORD, married **RALPH DE NEVILLE**, Earl of Westmorland.
PHILIPPE NEVILLE, married **THOMAS DACRE**, Lord Dacre of Gilsland.
THOMAS DACRE, Knt., married **ELIZABETH BOWET** [see DACRE 8.i].

6. **JOAN DACRE**, Baroness Dacre of Gillesland *suo jure*, daughter and eventual sole heiress, was born about 1433. She was married in June 1446 to **RICHARD FIENNES** (or **FENYS**), Knt., 1st Lord Dacre of the South, P.C., Sheriff of Sussex and Surrey, Constable of the Tower of London, son and heir of Roger Fiennes, Knt. (of **Magna Charta Surety descent** and **descendant of Charlemagne**), by his wife Elizabeth Holand. He was accepted by the King as 7th Lord Dacre, and was summoned to Parliament in that Barony from 9 Oct. 1459 by writs directed *Ricardo Fenys domino Dacre chivaler*. RICHARD FIENNES, Lord Dacre, died testate on 25 Nov. 1483. The will of "Jane Fenys Lady Dacre" of Herstmounceux, Sussex, died testate on 8 Mar. 1485/6 (P.C.C., 24 Logge). They were buried at Herstmounceux.

Clay (1913), p. 37. *C.P.* 4:8-9 (1916). *Sussex Arch. Coll.* 58: chart facing p. 64 (1916). *Paget* (1957) 164:2; 210:3 (identifies children, John and Elizabeth, but not Thomas).

LUNSFORD (cont.)

5. THOMAS FIENNES, Knt., of Claverham Manor, Arlington, Sussex, second son, was married to **ANNE URSWICK**, daughter of Thomas Urswick or Urdiswick, Knt., Baron of the Exchequer. SIR THOMAS FIENNES died testate (P.C.C., 7 Porch) on 8 Feb. 1525/6.

Sussex Arch. Coll. 58: chart facing p. 64 (1916).

4. MARGARET FIENNES, was married to **WILLIAM LUNSFORD**, Esq., of Lunsford and Wilegh, Sussex, son of William Lunsford, of Lunsford and Wilegh, by Cecily, daughter of John Pelham, Knt., of Laughton, Sussex. They had one son and six daughters. "William Lonsforde, esquire", died testate on 3 May 1531 (P.C.C., 17 Thower), and was buried at East Hoathly, Sussex. His widow was living on 26 Sep. 1533.

Coll. Top. & Gen. 4:139-141 (1837). *H.S.P.* 12:84-85 (1877) (1619 Vis. Warwick)(Lunsford arms: *Azure*, a chevron between three boars' heads couped *gules*). *Sussex Arch. Coll.* 58: chart facing p. 64 (1916).

3. JOHN LUNSFORD, Esq., of Lunsford and Wilegh, son and heir, was born about 1510 (aged twelve in 1532). He was married to **MARY SACKVILLE**, daughter of John Sackville, of Withyham and Chiddingley, Sussex, by Margaret (**descendant of King Edward I**), daughter of William Boleyn, Knt. [see BUTLER 5.ii for her ancestry]. They had two sons and two daughters. The will of "John Lunsford, esquier", then of Clerkenwell, Middlesex, was dated 19 Oct. 1581 and proved on 29 Jan. 1581/2 (P.C.C., 5 Tirwhite). They were buried at East Hoathly, Mary on 30 June 1571, John on 28 Nov. 1581.

Collins-Brydges (1812) 2:106. *Coll. Top. & Gen.* 4:141 (1837). *H.S.P.* 12:85 (1877).

2. JOHN LUNSFORD, Knt., of Lunsford and Wilegh, Sheriff of Sussex and Surrey, son and heir, was born about 1551 (aged twenty-three in 1574). He was married for the first time to **BARBARA LEWKNOR**, daughter and heiress of John Lewknor, Gent., of Buckingham, Sussex. He was married for the second time at Horsham on 2 Sep. 1577 to **ANNE APSLEY**, daughter of John Apsley, of Thaneham. She was baptised at Horsham on 2 Mar. 1557. They had three sons and five daughters. She was buried at East Hoathly on 10 Sep. 1612. SIR JOHN LUNSFORD was buried at East Hoathly on 5 May 1618.

Coll. Top. & Gen. 4:141 (1837) (identifies first wife as mother of son Thomas). *H.S.P.* 12:85 (1877).

1. THOMAS LUNSFORD, Gent., of Lunsford and Wilegh, son by second marriage, was born about 1586. He was married to **KATHERINE FLUDD**, daughter of Thomas Fludd, Knt., of Milgate, Kent, Treasurer of War to Queen Elizabeth, and sister of Robert Fludd, M.D., Christ Church, Oxon., Fellow of the College of Physicians, the eminent Rosicrucian. THOMAS LUNSFORD, who is said to have wasted the estate inherited from his father, died at Greenwich where he was buried on 4 Nov. 1637. His widow was buried at East Hoathley on 19 May 1642.

Coll. Top. & Gen. 4:141-142 (1837). *D.N.B.* 12:281 (1909). *VMHB* 17:26-33 (1909). *Lomax* (1913), p. 22 (son Thomas Lunsford "mentioned in Clarendon's History, who after the fall of Charles I, whose cause he had espoused, came to Virginia"), 46-47,57-63 (includes miniature of Sir Thomas Lunsford).

Children and grandchildren of Thomas Lunsford, by Katherine Fludd:

   i. ANNE LUNSFORD, eldest daughter, married _____ COOPER.

   ii. SARA LUNSFORD, second daughter, married THOMAS PRICE, of Cardigan.

   iii. WILLIAM LUNSFORD, baptised Framfield, 6 Nov. 1608, buried East Hoathly 17 May 1628.

   iv. LISLE LUNSFORD (a daughter), buried Framfield, Sussex, 17 Nov. 1610.

   v. COL. HENRY LUNSFORD, baptised Framfield 29 Sep. 1611, Colonel in the army of King Charles I, slain at the capture of Bristol 25 July 1643.

   vi. COL. HERBERT LUNSFORD, Knt. [twin to Thomas], Royalist Colonel, married

LUNSFORD (cont.)

MARGARET ENGHAM. Three children.

vii. **THOMAS LUNSFORD**, Knt., of Lunsford and Wilegh, Sussex, said to have been born about 1610, but shown as fourth son in pedigree, described by Clarendon: "a man, though of ancient family in Sussex, of very small and decayed fortune, and of no good education", described in youth as "of lawless disposition and violent temper", committed to Newgate in 1633, escaped next year, fled to the Continent and entered the French service, gaining military reputation, returned to England 1639, granted royal pardon, appointed Lieutenant of the Tower of London by King Charles I, 22 Dec. 1641, knighted 28 Dec. 1641, a commander of Royalist forces against the Parliamentarians until the execution of King Charles in January 1649, license to go to Virginia granted 7 Aug. 1649, member of the Council and Lieutenant-General of Virginia troops, 1651, died 1653, buried "Richneck", tombstone, inscribed 1727, later removed to Bruton Church, Williamsburg; will, then of Tooting Graveney, Surrey, dated 4 Jan. 1688, proved 13 June 1691, by "Lady Elizabeth Lunsford, alias Thomas, relict of the deceased"; married, first, ANNE HUDSON, of Peckham, Surrey, buried at East Hoathly, 28 Nov. 1638, one son died as infant; married, second, 1640, KATHERINE NEVILLE, died Virginia 1649, daughter of Henry Neville, Knt., of Billingbear, co. Berks (three daughters returned to England as wards of their grandmother, Dame Elizabeth Neville); married, third, **ELIZABETH** (_____) **KEMP**, widow of Richard Kemp, of "Richneck", James City County, Virginia. *D.N.B.* 12:281-283 (1909).

   a. ELIZABETH LUNSFORD, baptised Framfield, Sussex, 24 Aug. 1642, married at Lawrence Waltham, co. Berks, DANIEL NORTON, Gent.
   b. PHILIPPA LUNSFORD, second daughter.
   c. MARY LUNSFORD, born in Tower of London 1647; married at Lawrence Waltham THOMAS COLLIER, Brewer, of Shoe-lane, London. Issue.
   d. KATHARINE LUNSFORD, born about 1652, married RALPH WORMELEY, of "Rose Gill", Middlesex County, Virginia. Two daughters.

* * *

LUTTRELL see LUDLOW

LYGON see LIGON

LYGON see also DEIGHTON

* * *

EDWARD III OF ENGLAND, King of England, married **PHILIPPE DE HAINAUT**.
LIONEL OF CLARENCE [*of Antwerp*], Duke of Clarence, married **ELIZABETH DE BURGH**.
PHILIPPE OF CLARENCE, married **EDMUND DE MORTIMER**.
ELIZABETH MORTIMER, married **HENRY PERCY**, Knt. [see KEMPE 10]

8. ELIZABETH PERCY, was married for the first time between August 1403 and November 1412, probably in 1404, to **JOHN DE CLIFFORD**, K.G., 7th Lord Clifford, Hereditary Sheriff of Westmorland, M.P., only son and heir of Thomas de Clifford, 6th Lord Clifford (of **Magna Charta Surety** descent and **descendant of Charlemagne**), by Elizabeth (**descendant of King Edward I**), daughter of Thomas de Ros, 5th Lord Ros of Helmesley. He was born about 1388 (aged three at his father's death) [see ROS 11.ii for his ancestry]. They had two sons and one daughter. He took part in a great tournament at Carlisle between six English and six Scottish Knights. He was summoned to Parliament from 21 Sep. 1412. JOHN DE CLIFFORD, Lord Clifford, was slain at the siege of Meaux, France, on 13 Mar. 1421/2, and was said to have been buried at Bolton Priory. His widow was married for the second time in 1426 to RALPH NEVILLE, 2nd Earl of Westmorland (died 3 Nov. 1484). She died on 26 Oct. 1437, and was buried at Staindrop.

Collins-Brydges (1812) 6:516 (names only son and heir). *Clay* (1913), pp. 23-24. *C.P.* 3:293 (1913). *C.P.* 9:741 footnote *f* (1936). *C.P.* 12(2):549-50 (1959). *Paget* (1977), p. 416.

Children of John de Clifford, by Elizabeth de Percy:

    i. **THOMAS DE CLIFFORD**, born 26 Mar. 1414 [see next].

    ii. **MARY DE CLIFFORD**, married **PHILIP WENTWORTH** [see HARLESTON 7].[1]

7. THOMAS DE CLIFFORD, 8th Lord Clifford, Hereditary Sheriff of Westmorland, M.P., only son and heir, was born on 25 Mar. 1414. He was married after March 1424 to **JOAN DACRE**, daughter of Thomas Dacre, 6th Lord Dacre of Gillesland, by Philippe (**descendant of King Edward I**), daughter of Ralph de Neville, Earl of Westmorland [see DACRE 8 for her ancestry]. They had four sons and five daughters. She predeceased her husband. He was summoned to Parliament from 19 Dec. 1436. THOMAS DE CLIFFORD, Lord Clifford, a Lancastrian, was slain at the first battle of St. Albans on 22 May 1455, and was buried in the Abbey church there (former M.I.).

Collins-Brydges (1812) 6:516-517. *Clay* (1913), p. 24. *C.P.* 3:293 (1913).

Children of Thomas de Clifford, by Joan Dacre:

    i. **MAUD CLIFFORD** [see next].

    ii. **ELIZABETH CLIFFORD**, married **WILLIAM PLUMPTON**, Knt. [see DRURY 8].[2]

6. MAUD CLIFFORD, was married for the first time to **JOHN HARINGTON**, Knt., of Hornby, son of Thomas Harington, Knt., and had two daughters. She was married for the second time to **EDMUND SUTTON** (or **DUDLEY**), Knt., of Dudley Castle and Gatcombe, son and heir apparent of John Sutton (or Dudley), Knt. (**descendant of King Edward I**), by Elizabeth, daughter of John Berkeley, Knt., of Beverstone, co. Gloucester (**descendant of Charlemagne**) [see DUDLEY 6 for his ancestry]. He had been married previously to JOYCE TIPTOFT, daughter of John Tiptoft, Lord Tiptoft, by Joyce, daughter of Edward Cherleton, Lord Cherleton [see DUDLEY 5 for descendants of this marriage]. Edmund & Maud had seven sons and five

---

[1]Ancestors of **Humphrey Davie, John Harleston, William Rodney, William Skepper, Thomas Wingfield**.

[2]Ancestors of **John Harleston, Robert Peyton**.

MACKWORTH (cont.)

daughters. SIR EDMUND SUTTON died between 6 July 1483 and 30 Sep. 1487 v.p.
Collins-Brydges (1812) 6:517. *Twamley* (1867), chart between pp.16-17. *H.S.P.* 16:104 (1881) (1563 Vis. Yorks). *Wrottesley* (1903), p. 244 (Sutton of Dudley arms: *Or*, two lions passant *azure*). *C.P.* 4:480 (1916). *NEHGR* 108:176-177 (July 1954). *TG* 5:139 (1984).

5. **DOROTHY SUTTON**, was married for the first time to **JOHN MUSGRAVE**, Knt. She was married for the second time, probably before 1473, to **RICHARD WROTTESLEY**, Esq., of Wrottesley, co. Stafford, Sheriff of Staffordshire, son and heir of Walter Wrottesley, Knt., by Jane, daughter and heiress of Hugh Barry, Esq., of Berkshire. He was born about 1457 (aged sixteen at his father's death), and seems to have been brought up until the age of twenty at the Priory of St. Mary of Mount Carmel, Coventry. They had nine sons and seven daughters (four sons died before the parents). She died in 1517. RICHARD WROTTESLEY, ESQ., died testate between 12 Mar. 1520/1 and 6 Dec. 1521. They were buried, with incised slab, at St. Michael's, Tettenhall.
Wotton (1741) 2:345-346. *Twamley* (1867), chart between pp. 16-17 (names first husband only). *Her. & Gen.* 5:121 (1870). *H.S.P.* 16:105 (1881). *Wm. Salt Soc.* 5 (pt.2):33 (1885) (1614 Vis. Stafford). *Wrottesley* (1903), p. 244-266 (Wrottesley arms: *Or*, three piles *sable*, a quarter ermine). *NEHGR* 108:176-177 (July 1954).

4. **WALTER WROTTESLEY**, Esq., of Wrottesley, co. Stafford, son and heir, was married in 1501 to **ISABEL HARCOURT**, daughter of John Harcourt, Esq., of Ranton. They had one son and five daughters. The will of "Walter Rottysley of Rottysley Ysquire" was dated 13 Dec. 1562. WALTER WROTTESLEY, Esq., died before 1 July 1563.
Wotton (1741) 2:346 (Isabel identified as daughter of "Sir Thomas" Harcourt). *Wm. Salt Soc.* 3:153 (1882) (1583 Vis. Staffs) ("Isabell, da. of John Harecourt, sonne of Thomas"). *Wrottesley* (1903), p. 250, 256-277 (signed an indictment in 1536 as "Walter Wrotyssley"). *NEHGR* 108:176-77 (July 1954) (omits this generation).

3. **ELEANOR WROTTESLEY**, was married to **RICHARD LEE**, Esq., of Langley, co. Salop.
Wrottesley (1903), p. 274. *NEHGR* 108:176-177 (July 1954).

2. **DOROTHY LEE**, was married, with marriage settlement dated 27 July 1566, to **THOMAS MACKWORTH**, of Betton Grange, son of John Mackworth, by his wife Elizabeth Hosier. THOMAS MACKWORTH was living on 10 Jan. 1585.
NEHGR 108:176-177 (July 1954).

1. **RICHARD MACKWORTH**, of Betton Grange, was married to **DOROTHY CRANAGE**, daughter of Laurence Cranage, Gent.
NEHGR 108:176-177 (July 1954) (descent of Dorothy Lee from King Edward III).

Child of Richard Mackworth, by Dorothy Cranage:
    i. **AGNES MACKWORTH**, married, first, RICHARD WATTS, second **COL. WILLIAM CROWNE**, Gent., of Boston, Massachusetts.

* * *

MAINWARING

EDWARD I OF ENGLAND, King of England, married **ALIANORE DE CASTILLE**.
JOAN OF ENGLAND [*of Acre*], married **GILBERT DE CLARE**, Earl of Gloucester.
MARGARET DE CLARE, married, second, **HUGH DE AUDLEY**, 8th Earl of Stafford.
MARGARET DE AUDLEY, married **RALPH DE STAFFORD**, 2nd Lord Stafford.
KATHERINE DE STAFFORD, married **JOHN DE SUTTON**, Baron of Dudley.
JOHN DE SUTTON, Baron of Dudley, married **JOAN** _____.
JOHN SUTTON, Baron of Dudley, married **CONSTANCE BLOUNT**.
JOHN SUTTON, Lord Dudley, married **ELIZABETH BERKELEY** [see DUDLEY 6].

6. **JANE SUTTON**, was married to **THOMAS MAINWARING**, of Ightfield, co. Salop, second son of William Mainwaring of Ightfield, by Margaret, daughter of John Warren of Ightfield. He was born about 1450. He was tenant of two copyhold estates in Edstaston and Cotton, in Wem, co. Salop. THOMAS MAINWARING died in 1508.

Twamley (1867), chart between 16 and 171 (citing Blore and Baker). *H.S.P.* 29:348 (1889) (1623 Vis. Salop) (*Thomas Manwaring 2 filius = Jana fil. Joh'is Sutton Do[minus] [de] Dudley* [as her parents were married in 1421 she would appear to be considerably older than her husband]). *Clarkson* (1971), p. 10. *TG* 5:163-164 (1984).

Children of Thomas Mainwaring, by Jane Sutton:
  i. **JOHN MAINWARING**, Knt., son and heir, born about 1475 [see next].
  ii. **CECILY MAINWARING**, married **JOHN COTTON**, of Cotton, co. Salop [see ABELL 4].[1]

5. **JOHN MAINWARING**, Knt., of Ightfield, son and heir, was born about 1475. He was knighted at Lille on 16 Jun 1513, and was captain in the army of King Henry VIII. He was married to **JOAN LACON**, daughter of Richard Lacon, Knt., of Willey, co. Salop. The will of "sir John Maynwaryng, knight" was dated 7 July 1516, codicil 28 Jan 1517/8, proved May 1518. His widow died on 13 Apr. 1524.

H.S.P. 29:348 (1889). *TG* 5:163-164 (1984).

4. **RICHARD MAINWARING**, Knt., of Ightfield, was born about 1499. He was knighted by September 1536, Commissioner of Peace May 1538, among the knights who welcomed Queen Anne of Cleves to England on 3 Jan. 1539/40, Sheriff of Shropshire in 1544 and on other occasions. He was married to **DOROTHY CORBET**, daughter of Robert Corbet, Knt., of Moreton Corbet (**descendant of King Edward I**), by Elizabeth (**descendant of King Edward I**), daughter of Henry Vernon, Knt., of Haddon, co. Derby [see FERRERS 5 for her ancestry]. They had twelve sons and four daughters. SIR RICHARD MAINWARING died at St. Albans on 30 Sep. 1558, and was buried at Ightfield on 7 Oct, 1558.

H.S.P. 29:348 (1889). *TG* 5:163-164 (1984).

3. **ARTHUR MAINWARING**, Knt., of Ightfield, was born at Ightfield about 1520. He was knighted 1547, M.P. for Shropshire, Commissioner of Peace 1561/2, Sheriff 1563 and 1577. He was married about 1540 to **MARGARET MAINWARING**, daughter of Randall Mainwaring, Knt. (**descendant of King Edward I**), of Over Peover, by Elizabeth, daughter of Randall Brereton, Knt., of Malpas, Ipstones and Shocklach, co. Chester. She was born about 1521. They had one son and three daughters. She died before her husband [see OVER PEOVER 4 for her ancestry]. "Arthur Maynwaringe, knighte" died testate (will dated 2 Sep. 1590 and proved 21 June 1591, P.C.C., 49 Sainberbe) at Ightfield on 4 Sep. 1590.

---

[1] Ancestors of **Robert Abell**.

181

MAINWARING (cont.)

H.S.P. 29:349 (1889). *TG* 5:163-165 (1984).
Child of Arthur Mainwaring, by Margaret Mainwaring:
   i. MARY MAINWARING, married RICHARD COTTON, Esq. [see ABELL 2] .[1]

* * *

MANNERS see OGLE

* * *

MANWARING

EDWARD I OF ENGLAND, King of England, married ALIANORE DE CASTILLE.
ELIZABETH OF ENGLAND, married HUMPHREY DE BOHUN, Earl of Hereford and Essex.
WILLIAM DE BOHUN, Earl of Northampton, married ELIZABETH DE BADLESMERE.
ELIZABETH DE BOHUN, married RICHARD FITZ ALAN, 4th Earl of Arundel.
ELIZABETH FITZ ALAN, married ROBERT GOUSHILL, Knt.
JOAN GOUSHILL, married THOMAS STANLEY, Knt., Lord Stanley [see FITZ ALAN 10].

6. JOHN STANLEY, of Weever, co. Chester *jure uxoris*, third son, was married ELIZABETH WEEVER, daughter and heiress of Thomas de Weever, of Weever and Over Alderley, co. Chester, by his wife Elizabeth. JOHN STANLEY died before 1485. His widow was married for the second time to JOHN DONE, Knt.
   Baines (1836) 4:chart facing p. 10 (for issue see Ormerod 3:306).

5. MARGERY STANLEY, was married to WILLIAM TORBOCK, Knt., of Torbock, co. Lancaster, son of Richard Torbock, by _____, daughter of Thomas Daniell. They had three sons and one daughter. SIR WILLIAM TORBOCK died about 1509.
   Baines (1836) 4:9. *Gregson* (1869), p. 242. *Reliquary* 11:chart facing p. 97. *Roberts* (1993), p. 256.

4. THOMAS TORBOCK, Esq., of Torbock, son and heir, married ELIZABETH MOORE, daughter of William Moore, Esq., of Bank-house. They had two sons and three daughters.
   Baines (1836) 4:9. *Gregson* (1869), p. 242. *Reliquary* 11:chart facing p. 97.

3. WILLIAM TORBOCK, Esq., of Torbock Hall, co. Lancaster, was married to KATHERINE GERARD, daughter of Thomas Gerard, Knt. (**descendant of King Edward I**), by Jane, daughter of Peter Legh (**descendant of King Edward I**) [see GERARD 4.i for her ancestry]. They had two sons and three daughters. WILLIAM TORBOCK, ESQ., died testate in 1558 *s.p.m.*
   Baines (1836) 3:641; 4:9. *Gregson* (1869), p. 242. *Ormerod-Helsby* (1882) 2:132 ("Catherine, wife of Thomas Hoghton of Hoghton Tower, esq. o.s.p.m."). *Devon N.& Q.* 9:3-4 (1913). *Reliquary* 11:chart.

2. MARGARET TORBOCK, second surviving daughter and co-heiress, was married to OLIVER MAINWARING, Gent., of Exeter, and of Windleshaw, co. Lancaster,

---

[1] Grandparents of **Robert Abell**.

MANWARING (cont.)

seventh son of George Mainwaring, of Exeter, by Juliana, daughter of Thomas Spurway, Mayor of Exeter.

Baines (1836) 4:9 (no identification of husband). *Devon N.& Q.* 5:61 (1909)). *Trans.Hist.Soc.Lancs. (n.s.)* 31:212 (1916) (note from Howard M. Buck: "deposition by Oliver Mainwaring, jun., of Dawlish, gent. (1666), aged 79 and upwards, son of Oliver Mainwaring of Windleshawe, Lancs., gent. deceased"). *Devon N.& Q.* 9:3-4 (1917) (evidence of marriage provided by Howard M. Buck) (probably was "one Olyver Manwayringe, servant to the right wo' Sr George Peckham, Knight, being authorized for that purpose came in and declared the pretence and order of a voyage pretended to the western parte of America" from "proceedings of the Society of Merchant Adventurers, Exeter, under the dates of the 11th and 30th January 1583").

Children of Oliver Mainwaring, by Margaret Torbock:

i. OLIVER MAINWARING, born about 1587 [see next].

ii. MARY MAINWARING, probably married BENJAMIN GILL of Charles County Maryland [parents of Anna Maria Gill, wife of Capt. James Neale of Charles County, Maryland. See *Roberts* (1993), p. 255].

1. OLIVER MAINWARING, Gent., of Exeter and Dawlish, was born about 1587, and was heir of his father's older brother Christopher (died intestate 1634 *s.p.*). He was married at Heavitree in 1618 to **PRUDENCE ESSE**, daughter of Henry Esse (or Aishe), Gent., of Sowton, co. Devon (**descendant of Charlemagne**), by Loveday, daughter of Richard Moyle, of St. Austle, Cornwall. She was baptised at Sowton on 23 Dec. 1599. OLIVER MAINWARING, GENT., died on 14 Mar. 1672, and was buried at Dawlish (M.I.).

Devon N.& Q. 5:50-62 (1909). *NEHGR* 51:307 (Oct. 1920). *NEHGR* 79:110-111 (Jan. 1925). *NEHGR* 82:153 (Apr. 1928) (Manwaring arms: Silver six bars gules on the second an annulet for a second difference; also entitled to Mainwaring, ancient: Silver two bars gules & Tarbock heiress, cadet of house of Lathom: Gold an eagle's leg erased at the thigh gules on a chief indented azure a mullet between two roundles silver). *TAG* 41:225 (Oct. 1965).

Children & grandchildren of Oliver Mainwaring, by Prudence Esse:

i. ANNE MAINWARING.

ii. CHRISTOPHER MAINWARING, died *s.p.*

iii. ESSE MAYNWARING, of Dawlish, co. Devon, died 13 May 1674 (had son Oliver, 1663-1740, evidently "my nephew Oliver Manwaring in England" named in the will of Oliver Manwaring of Connecticut).

iv. [perhaps] RICHARD MANNERING, of Hempstead, Long Island; married MARY _____.

v. OLIVER MANWARING, baptised Dawlish, co. Devon, 16 Mar. 1633/4, younger son, mariner, resided Salem, Massachusetts and New London, Connecticut, died New London aged eighty-nine on 3 Nov. 1723; married **HANNAH RAYMOND**, baptized Salem, Massachusetts, 1634, died at New London, Connecticut, 18 Dec. 1717.

  a. HANNAH MANWARING, baptized 10 Sep. 1671, married, perhaps, JOHN HARRIS.

  b. ELIZABETH MANWARING, baptized 10 Sep. 1671, married PETER HARRIS.

  c. PRUDENCE MANWARING, baptized 10 Sep. 1671, married JOHN BECKWITH.

  d. LOVE MANWARING, baptized 10 Sep. 1671, married JOHN RICHARDS.

  e. RICHARD MANWARING, baptized 13 July 1673, married ELINOR JENNINGS.

  f. JUDITH MANWARING, baptized 2 Apr. 1676, married SIMON RAY, of Block Island.

  g. OLIVER MANWARING, baptized 2 Feb. 1679, married HANNAH HOUGH.

  h. BATHSHEBA MANWARING, baptized 9 May 1680.

  i. ANNE MANWARING, baptized 8 June 1682, married JEREMIAH WILSON.

  j. MERCY MANWARING, married JONATHAN PALMER, of Stonington, Connecticut.

* * *

MARBURY

EDWARD I OF ENGLAND, King of England, married ALIANORE DE CASTILLE.
ELIZABETH OF ENGLAND, married HUMPHREY DE BOHUN, Earl of Hereford and Essex.
ALIANOR DE BOHUN, married JAMES BUTLER, Earl of Ormond.
PERNEL BUTLER, married GILBERT TALBOT, 3rd Lord Talbot.
RICHARD TALBOT, 4th Lord Talbot, married ANKARET LE STRANGE [see TALBOT 8].

8. MARY TALBOT, was married to THOMAS GREENE, Knt., of Greene's Norton, co. Northampton, Sheriff of Northamptonshire, son of Thomas Greene, of Boughton, by _____, daughter of John Mablethorp, Knt., of co. Lincoln. He was born in 1369. SIR THOMAS GREENE died on 14 Dec. 1417. His widow died on 13 Apr. 1433.

    Collins-Brydges (1812) 3:9. *Colket* (1936), p. 36 (citing Baker 1:32). *Paget* (1977), p. 412.

7. THOMAS GREENE, Knt., of Greene's Norton, Sheriff of Northamptonshire, was born at Norton on 10 Feb. 1399/1400. He was married for the first time to PHILIPPE DE FERRERS, daughter of Robert de Ferrers, Knt., of Chartley. co. Stafford (**descendant of King Edward I**), by Margaret, daughter of Edward Despenser, Knt., 4th Lord Despenser (**descendant of King Edward I**) [see FERRERS 10 for her ancestry]. SIR THOMAS GREENE died 18 Jan. 1461/2. They were buried at Norton.

    C.P. 5:320 chart (1926). *Colket* (1936), p. 37 (citing Baker 1:32). *NEHGR* 123: 180-181 (Jan. 1969). *Paget* (1977) p. 251.

6. ELIZABETH GREENE, daughter, evidently, was married about 1440 to WILLIAM RALEIGH, Esq., of Farnborough, co. Warwick, son of John Raleigh, of Thornborow, co. Warwick, by Idonea, daughter and heiress of Thomas Cotesford, Knt. He was born, say, 1420. They had four sons and one daughter. On 4 July 1452 William Raleigh (with other feoffees chiefly related to the Throckmorton family) released the manor of Kegworth, co. Leicester, to Thomas Greene (brother of his wife Elizabeth), and his wife Maud Throckmorton. WILLIAM RALEIGH, ESQ., died on 15 Oct. 1460.

    Dugdale, Antiquities of Warwickshire (1760), p. 382. *H.S.P.* 12:77 (1877) (1619 Vis. Warwick) (*William Raleigh Kt. = Elizb. Da. of Sr Tho. Greene Kt.*). *Colket* (1936), pp. 37, 53 (rationale for marriage). NEHGR 123:180-181 (Jan. 1969). NEHGR 145:14-16 (Jan. 1991). *Paget* (1977), p. 422 (no identification of wife).

5. EDWARD RALEIGH, Knt., of Farnborough, co. Warwick, and Ilfracombe, co. Devon, Sheriff of Warwickshire and Leicestershire, was born about 1442 (of age in 1463). He was married in 1467 to MARGARET VERNEY, daughter of Ralph Verney, Knt., Lord Mayor of London, by his wife Emme. They had two sons and five daughters. She was living in 1478. The will of "sir Edward Ralegh, knyght" was dated 20 June 1509 and proved in 1513 (P.C.C., 14 Fetiplace) (requesting burial in the Chapel of Our Lady at Farnborough).

    H.S.P. 12:77 (1877). *Colket* (1936), p. 37. *Paget* (1977), p. 257. NEHGR 145:16-18 (Jan. 1991).

4. EDWARD RALEIGH, Esq., of Farnborough, was born about 1470. He was married between 1496 and 1505 to ANNE CHAMBERLAIN, daughter of Richard Chamberlain, of Sherburne, of **Magna Charta Surety descent** and **descendant of Charlemagne**), by Sibyl, daughter of Richard Fowler, of Sherburne, Chancellor of the Exchequer to King Edward IV. They had five sons and three daughters. "Edward Rawley" died *v.p.* (will, dated 25 Aug. 1508 and proved in 1508, P.C.C., 5 Bennett). His widow was married for the second time to Ralph Foulshurst, whose will (proved 1530, P.C.C. 20 Jankyn) mentions his wife Anne and "my sonne

MARBURY (cont.)

Cope").
H.S.P. 12:77 (1877) (names daughters Bridget and Margaret, but not Mary). *Metcalfe* (1887), pp. 15,56 (1564 Vis. Northants) ("Nicholas, Lord Woodhull, co. Bedford mar, to his first wife, the da. to ... Rawley of Thornbury, co. Oxon, Esq."). *Colket* (1936), p. 37. *Paget* (1977), p. 175. *NEHGR* 145:18-20 (Jan. 1991).

Children of Edward Raleigh, by Anne Chamberlain:
  i. BRIDGET RALEIGH [see next].
  ii. MARY RALEIGH, married NICHOLAS WODHULL, Knt. [see CHETWODE 4].[1]

3. **BRIDGET RALEIGH**, was married to **JOHN COPE**, Knt., of Canons Ashby, co. Northampton, Sheriff of Northamptonshire, M.P., second son of William Cope, Esq., of Banbury, co. Oxford, Cofferer to King Henry VIII, by his wife Jane, daughter of John Spencer, Gent., of Hodnell, co. Warwick. They had three sons and two daughters. He was married for the second time, without issue, to Mary Mallory, and for the third time, also without issue, to Margaret (Tame) Stafford. "Sir John Coope, knt., Asheby, Northants" died testate on 22 Jan. 1558/9 (P.C.C., 25 Noodes).

Wotton (1741) 1:113-114 (Cope arms: *Argent*, on a chevron *azure*, between three roses *gules*, flipt proper, as many fleur de lis, *or*). *H.S.P.* 12:77 (1877). *Metcalfe* (1887), p. 15. *Colket* (1936), p. 37 (citing Baker 2:13, Bridges 1:224, Barron, p. 370). VCH Warwick (1951) 6:115f. *NEHGR* 145:20-21 (Jan. 1991).

2. **ELIZABETH COPE**, was married to **JOHN DRYDEN**, Gent., of Canons Ashby, co. Northampton, son of David Dryden, Esq., of Staffle Hill, Cumberland, by Isabel, daughter and heiress of William Nicholson, of Staffle Hill. They had five sons and four daughters. "John Drydon, gent." died testate (P.C.C., 24 Watson) on 3 Sep. 1584, and was buried at Canons Ashby.

Wotton (1741) 1:114,349-350. *Metcalfe* (1887), pp. 15,178. *H.S.P.* 87:66 (1935) (1681 Vis. Northants) (only child named: Erasmus, grandfather of John Dryden, poet laureate to King Charles II). *Colket* (1936), p. 37 (citing Baker 2:6, Bridges 1:225). *NEHGR* 98:18-19 (Jan. 1944) (Dryden arms: *Azure*, a lion rampant and in chief a sphere betw. two estoiles, *or*). *NEHGR* 145:21 (Jan. 1991).

1. **BRIDGET DRYDEN**, was born about 1563, and named in her father's will. She was married for the first time about 1587 to **REV. FRANCIS MARBURY**, son of William Marbury, Gent., of Girsby in Burgh-upon-Bain, co. Lincoln (**descendant of Charlemagne**), by his wife Agnes, daughter of John Lenton, Esq., probably of Aldwinkle, co. Northampton. He was baptised at St. Pancras, Soper Lane, London, on 27 Oct. 1555. He was matriculated pensioner from Christ College, Cambridge, in May, 1571, but did not receive a degree. He was ordained deacon in 1578. He was married for the first time about 1580 to Elizabeth Moore, with three children. His reformist preaching led to imprisonment in the Marshalsea where he wrote an allegorical play entitled *The Contract of Marriage between Wit and Wisdom* in 1579. By 1585 he was a curate and schoolmaster in Alford, co. Lincoln. Francis & Bridget had fifteen children. He was ordained priest in 1605 and became successively Rector of Martin's Vintry, London, of St. Pancras, Soper Lane, and of St. Margaret's, New Fish Street. The will of the REV. FRANCIS MARBURY was dated 25 Jan. 1610/11 and proved 14 Feb. 1610/11. She was married for the second time to REV. THOMAS NEWMAN, of Berkhamsted, co. Hertford. Her will was dated 12 Feb. 1644, and her estate administered on 2 Apr. 1645.

Wotton (1741) 1:351. *NEHGR* 86:262 (July 1932) (Marbury arms). *Colket* (1936), pp. 25-34. *NEHGR* 98:11-25 (Jan. 1944 (Marbury arms: *Argent*, on a fess engrailed *gules*, three sheaves *or*). *NEHGR* 145:21 (Jan. 1991).

---

[1]Ancestors of **Grace Chetwode**.

MARBURY (cont.)

1644, and her estate administered on 2 Apr. 1645.
Wotton (1741) 1:351. *NEHGR* 86:262 (July 1932) (Marbury arms). *Colket* (1936), pp. 25-34. *NEHGR* 98:11-25 (Jan. 1944 (Marbury arms: *Argent*, on a fess engrailed *gules*, three sheaves *or*). *NEHGR* 145:21 (Jan. 1991).

Children of Rev. Francis Marbury, by Bridget Dryden:
  i. ANNE MARBURY, baptised 20 July 1591, married WILLIAM HUTCHINSON, emigrated to New England in 1634 in the ship *Griffin*. Issue.
  ii. CATHERINE MARBURY, born about 1610, married RICHARD SCOTT of Providence, Rhode Island. Issue.

* * *

MARKENFIELD see MAULEVERER

MARNEY see JENNINGS

* * *

MARSHALL

HENRY III OF ENGLAND, King of England, married ALIANORE DE PROVENCE.
EDMUND OF LANCASTER, Earl of Lancaster, married BLANCHE D'ARTOIS.
HENRY OF LANCASTER, married MAUD DE CHAWORTH [see LANCASTER 13].

10. ALIANOR OF LANCASTER, was married for the first time before June 1337 to JOHN DE BEAUMONT, Knt., Earl of Buchan, 2nd Lord Beaumont, son and heir of Henry de Beaumont, Lord Beaumont, Earl of Buchan (**descendant of Charlemagne**), by Alice, daughter of Alexander Comyn, Sheriff of Aberdeen (of **Magna Charta Surety descent** and **descendant of Charlemagne**). He was born about 1318 (aged twenty-two at his father's death). He was summoned to Parliament on 23 Feb. 1342/3 by writ directed *Johanni de Bello Monte*, but never as Earl of Buchan. JOHN DE BEAUMONT, Lord Beaumont, died between 10 and 25 May 1342. She was married for the second time at Ditton on 5 Feb. 1344/5 to RICHARD FITZ ALAN, Earl of Arundel and Warenne (died 1376). She had intrigued with Richard in her husband's lifetime [see FITZALAN 13 for descendants of this marriage]. She died at Arundel on 11 Jan. 1371/2, and was buried at Lewes.
C.P. 1:243-244 (1910). *C.P.* 2:60-61 (1912). *TAG* 19:10-16 (July 1942) (descent of Elizabeth Marshall from King Henry III). *Nicholas Davis* (1956), p. 169.

9. HENRY DE BEAUMONT, of Folkingham, co. Lincoln, 3rd Lord Beaumont, son and heir, was born in Brabant (during his mother's attendance on the Queen Consort Philippe) in 1340, and had consequently to be naturalised by Act of Parliament in 1351. He was summoned to Parliament as a Baron from 14 Aug. 1362. He was married to MARGARET DE VERE, daughter of John de Vere, 7th Earl of Oxford (of **Magna Charta Surety descent** and **descendant of Charlemagne**), by Maud, daughter of Bartholomew de Badlesmere, 1st Lord Badlesmere (of **Magna Charta Surety descent** and **descendant of Charlemagne**). HENRY DE BEAUMONT, Lord

had issue. She died on 15 June 1398, and was buried at Grey Friars', Newgate, London, with her third husband.

    C.P. 2:61 (1912) (identifies wife as Maud de Vere). *C.P.* 4:298 (1916) (he died 25 July 1369). *TAG* 19:11 (July 1942). *Nicholas Davis* (1956), p. 169. *Gen. Mag.* 15:251-5 (Sep. 1966).

    8. JOHN DE BEAUMONT, Knt., K.G., 4th Lord Beaumont, son and heir, was born about 1361 (aged eight at his father's death). He was knighted by King Edward III on 23 Apr. 1377. He served in the French wars and against the partizans of Pope Clement VII. In 1389 he was P.C. and Warden of the West Marches towards Scotland, and Admiral of the North, and was Constable of Dover Castle and Warden of the Cinque Ports from 1392/3 till his death. He was summoned to Parliament from 20 Aug. 1383. He was created Knight of the Garter in 1393. He was married to **KATHERINE EVERINGHAM**, daughter and heiress of Thomas Everingham, of Laxton, co. Nottingham. "John de Beaumont lord of Folkingham" died testate (P.C.C., 435 Bokingham) at Stirling on 9 Sep. 1396, and was buried at Sempringham. His widow died in 1426.

    C.P. 2:61 (1912). *TAG* 19:11 (July 1942). *Nicholas Davis* (1956), pp. 168-171.

    Children of John de Beaumont, by Katherine Everingham:

      i. **HENRY DE BEAUMONT**, born about 1380 [see next].

      ii. **ELIZABETH DE BEAUMONT**, married **WILLIAM DE BOTREAUX** [see BOTREAUX 12].[1]

7. HENRY DE BEAUMONT, 5th Lord Beaumont, K.B., son and heir, was born about 1380 (aged sixteen at his father's death). He was summoned to Parliament as a Baron from 25 Aug. 1404, and was Commissioner to treat for peace with France in 1410-1411. He was married before July 1405 to **ELIZABETH WILLOUGHBY**, daughter of William Willoughby, Lord Willoughby, of Eresby, co. Lincoln (of **Magna Charta Surety descent** and **descendant of Charlemagne**) by Lucy, daughter of Roger Le Strange, Lord Strange of Knockyn, co. Salop (**descendant of Charlemagne**). "Henry de Beaumont lord of Folkyngham" died testate (P.C.C., 78 Repingdon) in June 1413, and was buried at Sempringham, co. Lincoln. His widow died shortly before 12 Nov. 1428.

    C.P. 2:61 (1912). *TAG* 19:12 (July 1942). *Nicholas Davis* (1956), p. 166.

6. HENRY BEAUMONT, Knt., younger son, was born about 1411. He was devised the manor of Thorpe in Balne, co. York, in his father's will dated 1413. He was married probably about 1439 to **JOAN HERONVILLE**, heiress of Wednesbury, co. Stafford, widow of William Leventhorpe (living in 1438), and daughter and eventual heiress of Henry Heronville, of Wednesbury. She was born about 1402 (aged four when her father died). She brought to him the manor of Wednesbury, where they made their home, and other Staffordshire lands. SIR HENRY BEAUMONT died between 3 Nov. 1445 and 29 Nov. 1446. His widow was married for the third time to Charles Noel (or Nowell). On 27 Oct. 1452, while hearing mass in the chapel at Thorpe, she was seized by Edward Lancaster, Gent., of Skipton in Craven, and his men, placed on horseback and taken to an unknown church where a priest performed a marriage ceremony enforced by Lancaster against her protests. Her son, Henry Beaumont, and her husband, Charles Nowell, petitioned Parliament for redress. She was living (apparently at the manor of Thorpe, after her son Henry came of age) in 1460.

---

[1]Ancestors of **John Nelson, Anne Humphrey, Herbert Pelham, Maria Johanna Somerset, John West**.

MARSHALL (cont.)

TAG 19:12 (July 1942). *TG* 5:140-151 (1984).

5. HENRY BEAUMONT, Knt., of Wednesbury, co. Stafford, Sheriff of Staffordshire, son and heir, was born about 1440. He was married to **ELEANOR SUTTON**, daughter of John Sutton (or Dudley), 1st Lord Dudley (**descendant of King Edward I**), by Elizabeth, daughter of John Berkeley, Knt., of Beverstone, co. Gloucester (**descendant of Charlemagne**) [see DUDLEY 6 for her ancestry]. They had two sons and one daughter. He was knighted by King Edward IV at Tewkesbury after the battle on 3 May 1471. "Henry Beaumount" died testate (P.C.C., 17 Wattys) aged about thirty-one on 16 Nov. 1471. His widow was married for the second time to George Stanley, of Hammerwich, Lichfield, co. Stafford, son of Thomas Stanley, of Elford (of Magna Charta Surety descent), by Elizabeth, daughter of Ralph Langton, Knt., of Walton. George & Eleanor had a son and daughter and resided at Wednesbury [see WOLSELEY 6 for descendants of this marriage]. She died about 1513.

> *Twamley* (1867), chart between pp. 16-17 (citing Baker and Blore). *TAG* 19:13 (July 1942). *Nicholas Davis* (1956), pp. 163-164 (Eleanor, Lady Beaumont, died before 11 Jan. 1503). *TG* 5:140-141 (1984) (Henry Beaumont, or more likely his widow Eleanor, rebuilt Wednesbury Church, and at this time four miserere seats for the choir stalls were set up. On one of these, now in St. James's Church, Wednesbury, is the famous Beaumont badge, an elephant with a castle strapped on its back).

4. CONSTANCE BEAUMONT, was born about 1467. She was married to **JOHN MITTON** (or **MYTTON**), Esq., Sheriff of Staffordshire, son and heir of John Mytton, Esq., of Weston under Lizard, co. Stafford, by Anne, daughter of Thomas de Swinnerton, of Hilton and Essington, co. Stafford. He was born about 1470 (aged thirty and more at his father's death). JOHN MITTON, ESQ., died on 16 Feb. 1532/3. His widow died about 1551. They were buried (with former monumental brass) at Weston.

> *H.S.P.* 29:360 (1889) (1623 Vis. Salop). *TAG* 19:13-16 (July 1942) (discussion of the evidence for the marriage). *TG* 5:140-141(1984). *Nicholas Davis* (1956), pp. 145-151, 161-163 (Mitton arms: Party per pale, *azure* and *gules*, an eagle displayed with two heads within a border engrailed *or*).

3. JOYCE MITTON, daughter and heiress, was born about 1487. She was married by 1505/6 to **JOHN HARPESFIELD**, Gent., citizen and draper of London, son and heir of Nicholas Harpesfield, of Harpesfield in St. Peters St. Albans, co. Hertford, by Agnes, daughter of John Norton, of Nutley and East Tisted, co. Hants. JOHN HARPESFIELD, GENT., died before 27 Oct. 1533. She died about 1558.

> *TAG* 19:13-14 (July 1942). *Nicholas Davis* (1956), pp. 151-153 (Harpesfield arms: *Argent*, three harps *sable*, stringed *or*).

2. EDWARD HARPESFIELD (or **MITTON**), Esq., of Weston-under-Lizard, succeeded his mother at Weston-under-Lizard. He was married in 1530, as a minor, to **ANNE SKRIMSHIRE**, daughter of Thomas Skrymsher, of Norbury, co. Stafford, prothonotary of the Court of Common Pleas, by, probably, Mary, daughter of William Swineshead, of Swineshead, co. Stafford. They had five sons and five daughters living in 1570.

> *TAG* 19:14 (July 1942). *Nicholas Davis* (1956), pp. 152-153.

1. KATHERINE MITTON, youngest daughter, was married about 1590 to **ROGER MARSHALL**, Gent., draper of Shrewsbury, Merchant of the Staple of England, son of Richard Marshall, shearman of Shrewsbury, co. Salop, by Joan, daughter of Adam Benyon, of Shrewsbury. He was born about 1561, and was entered in Shrewsbury School in 1571, and was apprenticed to a draper in 1575. They had five children. He was admitted to the Drapers Company on 2 Mar. 1597. Their house, still

MARSHALL (cont.)

retaining the original wood frame, stood in Milk street in Shrewsbury and in 1947 was used as an auctioneer's offices. ROGER MARSHALL, GENT., died testate in Shrewsbury on 4 Aug. 1612, and was buried at St. Chad's, Shrewsbury, with gravestone "neere the pulpit in the middle isle" inscribed: "Here lyeth the body / of Roger Marshall / gent. late merchant / of the Staple of England Bailiff and Al- / erman of this town of Salop. who / took to wife Katherine one of the daugh- / ters of Edward Mitton of Weston under / Kirwed Esq. and had yssue two sonnes Richard / and Thomas and three daughters Judith Mary and Eli-/zabeth and deceased the 4th day of August / 1612" [the church destroyed in 1788].

    Charity Haley (1916), pp. 51-63 (no evidence as to parentage of Thomas & Elizabeth Lewis). *NEHGR* 82:155 (Apr. 1928) (Lewis & Marshall arms). *GDMNH* (1928-1939), p. 430. *TAG* 19:14-15 (July 1942). *NEHGR* 101:1-23 (Jan. 1947). *NEHGR* 101:86-91 (Apr. 1947) (arms of Roger Marshal: *Gules,* a bend engrailed *or*) (will dated 3 Aug. 1612, proved 17 Oct. 1612, P.C.C., 82 Fenner) (gravestone inscription recorded by Sir William Dugdale in 1660) (summary descent from King Henry III) (detailed in 1956 publication). *Nicholas Davis* (1956), pp. 97-101, 139-141 (Lewis arms: *Ermine,* a lion rampant within a border, *azure*).

Children & grandchildren of Roger Marshall, by Katherine Mitton:

    i. RICHARD MARSHALL, born about 1597, married. Issue.

    ii. THOMAS MARSHALL, died before 1612.

    iii. JUDITH MARSHALL, married GEORGE PERCH, of Shrewsbury. Five children.

    iv. MARY MARSHALL, died before 1612.

    v. **ELIZABETH MARSHALL**, died before 8 Oct. 1640; married at St. Chad's, Shrewsbury, 29 Aug. 1618, **THOMAS LEWIS**, Gent., son of Andrew Lewis, Draper, of Shrewsbury, co. Salop, by Mary, daughter of Mr. William Herring, of Shrewsbury, vintner and draper, born Shrewsbury about 1590, vintner of Shrewsbury, emigrated by 28 June 1631, patentee of thirty-two square miles on the eastern bank of the Saco River in the Province of Maine granted to him and Capt. Richard Bonython by the Plymouth Company in 1629, joined by wife and three daughters in 1637, died before 1640. Their children were baptised at St. Chad's, Shrewsbury. Two of them, Elizabeth and Judith, inherited the Saco patent.

        a. MARY LEWIS, baptised 28 June 1619, married at Saco in 1638, REV. RICHARD GIBSON, A.B., Magdalen College, Oxford, Church of England clergyman, returned to England about 1641.

        b. SUSANNA LEWIS, baptised 2 Nov. 1620.

        c. MARGARET LEWIS, baptised 22 Apr. 1622.

        d. ELIZABETH LEWIS, baptised 7 Apr. 1623, married ROBERT HEYWOOD, planter, of the parish of St. Thomas, Barbadoes, died before 1680. Seven children with descendants in the Barbadoes.

        e. ANDREW LEWIS, baptised 22 Feb. 1624/5, buried 15 Nov. 1625.

        f. **JUDITH LEWIS**, baptised 23 Oct. 1626, married 1646 or 1647 **JAMES GIBBINS** of Saco, Maine, born about 1614. Nine children.

        g. ANDREW LEWIS, baptised 25 Mar. 1628, died young.

* * *

MAULEVERER

EDWARD III OF ENGLAND, King of England, married PHILIPPE DE HAINAUT.
LIONEL OF CLARENCE [*of Antwerp*], Duke of Clarence, married ELIZABETH DE BURGH.
PHILIPPE OF CLARENCE, married EDMUND MORTIMER, 3rd Earl of March.
ELIZABETH MORTIMER, married HENRY PERCY, Knt.
HENRY PERCY, 5th Lord Percy, married ALIANOR NEVILLE.
HENRY PERCY, 6th Lord Percy, married ALIANOR DE POYNINGS.
MARGARET PERCY, married WILLIAM GASCOIGNE, Knt. [see READE 6].

6. DOROTHY GASCOIGNE, was married to NINIAN MARKENFIELD, Knt., of Markenfield Hall, Ripon, co. York, son of Thomas Markenfield, Knt., by Alianor, daughter of John Conyers, Knt., K.G. They had one son and two daughters. He was a commander at Flodden Field and was knighted on the field on 9 Sep. 1513. He was married for the second time, with dispensation from Cardinal Wolsey dated 18 May 1526 they being related twice in third degree, to Eleanor Clifford, daughter of Henry Clifford, Lord Clifford, by his wife Anne St. John. "Ninean Markynfeld, knyght" died testate on 25 Mar. 1527/8.

Sur.Soc. 45:374 (1864). *H.S.P.* 16:186,197 (1881) (1563 Vis. Yorks). *Foster (1874),* Mauleverer chart. *Sur.Soc.* 79:232-235 (1884) (his will). *Sur.Soc.* 144:130 (1930) (Vis. North 1480).

5. ALICE MARKENFIELD, was married, with dispensation from Cardinal Wolsey dated 1 Dec. 1524, they being related in the fourth degree, to ROBERT MAULEVERER, second son of William Mauleverer, Knt., of Wothersome and Arncliffe, West Riding, co. York, by Jane, daughter of John Conyers, Knt., of Sockburn. They had four sons and two daughters. He was heir male to his brother, Sir William Mauleverer. In 1536 he was on a grand jury to try the prisoners from *the Pilgrimage of Grace*. ROBERT MAULEVERER was buried testate at Bardsay on 31 Jan. 1540/1. The will of his widow was dated 4 Mar. and proved 7 Mar. 1552/3.

Foster (1874), chart (marriage covenant dated 16 Oct. 1524). *Glover-Foster* (1875) (1584 Vis. Yorks), p. 201. *H.S.P.* 16:197,202 (1881). *York.Arch.Jour.* 16:196 (1902).

Children of Robert Mauleverer, by Alice Markenfield:
  i. EDMUND MAULEVERER [see next].
  ii. DOROTHY MAULEVERER, married JOHN KAYE, Esq. [see SALTONSTALL 3].[1]

4. EDMUND MAULEVERER, Knt., of Wothersome and Arncliffe, co. York, son and heir, was married, with marriage contract dated 30 Sep. 1541, to MARY DANBY, daughter of Christopher Danby, Knt., of Thorpe Perrow near Bedale, North Riding, co. York, by Elizabeth, daughter of Richard Neville, 2nd Lord Latimer (**descendant of King Edward III**) [see BOSVILE 5.ii for her ancestry]. They had two sons and two daughters. He was knighted in 1553 and served as a captain in campaigns against Scotland, raising troops at his own expense. SIR EDMUND MAULEVERER died on 27 Apr. 1571, and was buried at Bardsey, co. York.

Sur.Soc. 41:88 (1862) (1530 Vis. North). *Glover-Foster* (1875), p. 201. *H.S.P.* 16:202 (1881). *York.Arch.Jour.* 16:197-198 (1902). *TAG* 69:163 (July 1994) (does not identify parents of Edmund).

3. WILLIAM MAULEVERER, Esq., of Wothersome, son and heir, was born 30 Apr., probably 1557. He was married to ELEANOR ALDBURGH, eldest daughter of Richard Aldburgh, Esq., of Aldbrough, co. York, by Eleanor, daughter of Thomas Goldesborough, of Goldesborough. She was born about Michaelmas 1553. They had four sons and one daughter. WILLIAM MAULEVERER. ESQ., died testate before

---

[1] Ancestors of **Richard Saltonstall**.

MAULEVERER (cont.)

27 Apr. 1618, and was buried in the choir at Arncliffe. His will dated 14 Apr. 1618 bequeathed to "my sonne James my tent, drummes, and armour". His widow survived until 1642.

> *Sur.Soc.* 36:97 (1859) (1665 Vis. Yorks) (Arms of "Maleverer of Arncliffe": *Sable*, three greyhounds courant in pale *argent*). *Glover-Foster* (1875), pp. 201,279. *H.S.P.* 16:202 (1881). *York.Arch.Jour.* 16:198 (1902). *TAG* 69:163 (July 1994) (in 1602, aged forty-five, he signed a pedigree of his family, which listed among other family members his son James, his wife and her father, and his parents, Sir "Edmond" Maulverer and his wife, Mary, dau. of "Sr Chr' Danby".).

2. JAMES MAULEVERER, Esq., of Arncliffe, co. York, was born on 1 Feb. 1590/1. He was married at Richmond on 27 Nov. 1613 to **BEATRICE HUTTON**, daughter of Timothy Hutton, Knt., of Marske, co. York. She was baptised at St. Olave's, York, co. York, on 24 June 1596, and probably died about 1640-2. Early in the reign of King Charles I, James Maulverer failed to pay composition in lieu of accepting a knighthood and was fined £2000. Payment of this enormous fine and debts incurred before and during the civil wars led to his bankruptcy in 1651. JAMES MAULEVERER, ESQ., was supported by his son Timothy in his last years but died a prisoner for debt in York Castle on 24 Apr. 1664, burial the following day at St. Mary's, Castlegate, co. York, outside the castle.

> *Sur.Soc.* 36:97 (1859). *York.Arch.Jour.* 16:201-203 (1902) (lists six sons and one daughter but not Edmund). *TAG* 69:164 (July 1994).

1. EDMUND MAULEVERER, was born about 1631. He married in a Friends ceremony at Kirby Grindalythe on 3 May 1666 **ANNE PEARSON**, of Mowthorpe. Their daughter Anne was born at Scarborough, co. York, in 1678. EDMUND MAULEVERER died on 27 Nov. 1679, and was buried the following day as a Friend. His widow married for the second time in a Friends ceremony on 7 Sep 1681 with Mathew Watson. Mathew & Anne Watson, and her daughter Anne, emigrated to America, where in 1683 he was a landowner in Burlington Township, New Jersey, and was described as Mathew Watson, late of Scarbrough, co. York, chemist.

> *Sur.Soc.* 36:97 (1859). *TAG* 69:164 (July 1994).

Child & grandchildren of Edmund Maulverer, by Anne Pearson:

  i. **ANNE MAULEVERER**, born 26 Apr. 1678, married in a Friends ceremony at the house of Mathew Watson in Chesterfield, Burlington Co., New Jersey, on 26th day 3rd mo. 1696 **JOHN ABBOTT**.

   a. TIMOTHY ABBOTT.

   b. **JANE ABBOTT**, born Nottingham, Burlington County, New Jersey, 9 Mar. 1701, married **JOSEPH BURR**. Issue.

* * *

MITTON see MARSHALL

MONTAGU see MONTHERMER

* * *

MONTHERMER

EDWARD I OF ENGLAND, married **ALIANORE DE CASTILLE** [see PLANTAGENET 14].

13. **JOAN OF ENGLAND** [*of Acre*], second daughter, was born at Acre in the Holy Land probably early in 1272. She was married for the first time about 30 Apr. 1290 to GILBERT DE CLARE, **Baron** of Clare, Earl of Gloucester and Hertford (died 7 Dec. 1295) [see CLARE 12 for descendants of this marriage]. She was married, clandestinely, for the second time in 1296 or 1297 to **RALPH DE MONTHERMER**, born in 1262 of unknown parentage, and a servant to her first husband. The marriage enraged her father, the King, and he committed Ralph to prison in Bristol Castle, and all Joan's lands were seised into the King's hand. By the mediation of Anthony Bec, Bishop of Durham, however, peace was made between the King and his daughter, and her lands were restored to her on 31 July 1297, Ralph having done homage. The King afterwards became much attached to his new son-in-law, who was summoned to Parliament as Earl of Gloucester and Hertford, during the minority of his step-son, Gilbert de Clare. He was at the siege of Carlaverock in the summer of 1300. JOAN OF ENGLAND died on 23 Apr. 1307, and was buried at Clare. He was summoned to Parliament from 4 Mar. 1308/9 by writs directed *Raulpho de Monte Hermerii*, whereby he is held to have become **Lord Monthermer**. He fought at Bannockburn in 1314. In December 1315 he had permission to go to Santiago on pilgrimage. He was married for the second time before 20 Nov. 1318 to Isabel le Despenser, widow of John de Hastings, of Ashill, Norfolk (died 1313), and daughter of Hugh le Despenser, Earl of Winchester, by Isabel, daughter of William de Beauchamp, Earl of Warwick. RALPH DE MONTHERMER, Lord Monthermer, died testate aged sixty-three on 5 Apr. 1325, and was buried in the Grey Friars' church, Salisbury.

    C.P. 5:710-712 (1926). C.P. 9:140-142, 140 footnote *c* (1936) (Ralph probably pronounced his name Mehermer; it is so spelt in a deed of his, and in his petitions. His arms: *Or*, an eagle displayed *vert*--the arms of Lyndsey of Northumberland). *Paget* (1957) 130:13. *Sanders* (1960), p. 42.

12. **THOMAS DE MONTHERMER**, Knt., of Stokenham, co. Devon, 2nd Lord Monthermer, was born on 4 Oct. 1301. He was not summoned to Parliament. He was married to **MARGARET** _____, probably widow of Henry de Teyes, Lord Teyes (executed 1321). THOMAS DE MONTHERMER, Lord Monthermer, died on 24 June 1340 *s.p.m.*, being slain at the Battle of Sluys. His widow died on 15, 22 or 26 May 1349.

    C.P. 9:88, 143-144 (1936).

11. **MARGARET DE MONTHERMER**, daughter and heiress, was born at Stokenham on 14 Oct. 1329. She was married before the end of 1343 to **JOHN DE MONTAGU**, Knt., of Wark-upon-Tweed, younger son of William de Montagu, Knt., 3rd Lord Montagu (of **baronial** descent), by Katherine (**descendant of Charlemagne**), daughter of William de Grandison, 1st Lord Grandison, of Lambourn, co. Berks. He was at the battle of Crécy on 26 Aug. 1346, and fought at Poitiers on 19 Sep. 1356. He was summoned to Parliament from 15 Feb. 1357 by writs directed *Johanni de Monte Acuto*, whereby he is held to have become **Lord Montagu**. He was Steward of the Household to King Richard II, 1381-1386/7. JOHN DE MONTAGU, Lord Montagu, died testate on 25 Feb. or 4 Mar. 1389/90, and was buried at Salisbury Cathedral. His widow died intestate on 24 Mar. 1394/5.

    C.P. 9:82, 86-89, 143-144 (1936) (tomb bore his arms: *Azure* 3 fusils in fesse, within a bordure; impaling a spread-eagle). C.P. 11:388 footnote b. *Paget* (1957) 372:8-9.

MONTHERMER (cont.)

10. JOHN DE MONTAGU, Knt., K.G., Earl of Salisbury, Lord Montagu, Lord Monthermer, son and heir, was born about 1350/1 (aged thirty-nine at death of his father), and was nephew and heir of William de Montagu, Earl of Salisbury. He was summoned to Parliament from 23 Nov. 1392. He was married before 4 May 1383 to **MAUD FRANCIS**, relict of John Aubrey, of Mimms and Watford, co. Hertford (died 1380-81), and widow (with son and heir Alan Buxhall, Knt.) of Alan Buxhall, Knt., K.G., of Sussex (died 2 Nov. 1381), and daughter of Adam Francis, Knt., Lord Mayor of London. JOHN DE MONTAGU, Earl of Salisbury, having conspired against King Henry IV, was beheaded at Cirencester on 7 Jan. 1399/1400, and was buried there. "Maude Mountegu countess of Salisbury" died testate (P.C.C., 2 Luffenham) in 1424 before 5 August.

C.P. 5:210 (1926). *C.P.* 9:82, 144 (1936). *C.P.* 11:391-393 (1949) (all accounts of his death record that he was a staunch Wycliffe). *Paget* (1957) 372:10-12.

Children of John de Montagu, by Maud Francis:
 i. **THOMAS DE MONTAGU**, born about 1388 [see next].
 ii. **ANNE DE MONTAGU**, married twice [see HANKFORD 7][1],[2]

9. THOMAS MONTAGU, Knt., K.G., Earl of Salisbury, Lord Montagu, son and heir, was born about 1388 (aged twelve at his father's death). He was married for the first time on or before 23 May 1399 to **ALIANOR DE HOLAND**, third daughter of Thomas de Holand, Knt., Earl of Kent (**descendant of King Edward I**), by Alice (**descendant of King Henry III**), daughter of Richard Fitz Alan, Knt., Earl of Arundel. She was born in 1387, the fifth child and second daughter of that name, and was co-heiress of her brother Edmund Holand, Earl of Kent. She was living in 1413, and, according to her husband's will, was buried at Bisham [see HOLAND 8 for her ancestry]. He was summoned to Parliament as Earl of Salisbury on 26 Oct. 1409. In consideration of his great services in the French War, he was restored in blood to the dignities held by his father on 2 May 1421, becoming thus Lord Montagu, etc. He received a grant of the Comté de Perche, and was appointed Lieut. General of Normandy. He was married for the second time before November 1424 to **ALICE CHAUCER**, widow of John Phelip, Knt. (died at Harfleur on 2 Oct. 1415), and daughter and heiress of Thomas Chaucer, Speaker of the House of Commons, Chief Butler to Kings Richard II and Henry IV, Speaker of the House of Commons, of Ewelme, co. Oxford, by Maud, daughter and co-heiress of John Burghersh, Knt. She was born about 1404 (aged eleven at the death of her first husband). THOMAS MONTAGU, Earl of Salisbury, died at Meung-sur-Loire about 3 Nov. 1428 *s.p.m.* of wounds received a few days previously at the siege of Orléans, and was buried at Bisham. His widow was married for the third time to William de la Pole, Earl (afterwards Duke) of Suffolk (murdered 2 May 1450). She died on 20 May 1475, and was buried in Ewelme Church (M.I.).

C.P. 7:156 footnote *e* (1929). *C.P.* 9:83 (1936). *C.P.* 11:393-395 (1949). *C.P.* 12(2):305 footnote *a*. *Paget* (1957) 372:12-13.

8. ALICE MONTAGU, Countess of Salisbury *suo jure*, daughter and heiress, was born about 1408 (aged twenty-two at her father's death). She was married in or before

---

[1]Ancestor, by first husband Richard Hankford, of **Anne Humphrey, Thomas Lunsford, Herbert Pelham, John West**.

[2]Ancestor, by second husband John [ap] Lewis, of **William Asfordby, Mary Bourchier, Francis Dade, Diana & Grey Skipwith**.

February 1420/1 to **RICHARD NEVILLE,** Earl of Salisbury, younger son of Ralph Neville, 1st Earl of Westmorland (of **Magna Charta Surety descent** and **descendant of Charlemagne**), being first son by his second wife, Joan Beaufort, legitimised daughter of John of Lancaster [*of Gaunt*], Duke of Lancaster [see BEAUFORT 11.iv for his ancestry]. He was said to have been born in 1400. He was Warden of the West March of Scotland, and Constable of Pontefract Castle. "Richard Nevil, earl of Salisbury" was killed testate (P.C.C., 22 Stokton) at the battle of Wakefield on 30 Dec 1460 (or was captured after the battle and beheaded after at Pontefract), and was buried at Bisham. His widow died between 3 Apr. and 9 Dec. 1462.
C.P. 5:429 (1926). *C.P.* 9:89 (1936). *TG* 9:189 (1988).

Children & grandchildren of Richard Neville, by Alice Montagu:

i. **RICHARD NEVILLE** [*the Kingmaker*], Knt., Earl of Warwick *jure uxoris*, Earl of Salisbury (succeeding his mother), son and heir, born 22 Nov. 1428; after the recovery of King Henry VI from madness he became a staunch Yorkist and at the first battle of St. Albans on 22 May 1455 "had the good fortune to decide the day and win somewhat easily a military reputation"; defeated the Lancastrians at Northampton on 10 July 1460, and captured King Henry VI whom he brought to London; still in charge of the King in London when the Yorkists were defeated at the battle of Wakefield on 30 December (in which his father was taken prisoner, being beheaded the next day, when he succeeded to the great Neville estate of Middleham, co. York); on 17 Feb. 1460/1 put to flight by the Lancastrians at the 2nd battle of St. Albans, and allowed King Henry VI to be recaptured, but having joined the young Duke of York, they entered London; one of the peers who declared the Duke to be King, as Edward IV; commanded the centre in the decisive Yorkist victory at Towton on 29 Mar. 1461. The King's marriage, however, in May 1464, to Elizabeth Wydeville and the favour shown to the Queen's relatives alienated him; secretly planned his restoration to authority throughout 1468; allowed to cross to Calais early in 1469; joined by his brother George, Archbishop of York, and by the King's brother, the Duke of Clarence, to whom he there married Isabel, his eldest daughter and co-heiress presumptive; these three joined the Yorkshire insurgents; then suppressed the Lancastrian rising in the North; slain at Barnet on Easter Sunday 14 Apr. 1471 *s.p.m.*, buried Bisham Abbey, co. Berks; married **ANNE BEAUCHAMP,** Countess of Warwick *suo jure*, born Caversham about September 1426, died shortly before 20 Sep. 1492, fourth daughter of Richard Beauchamp, 13th Earl of Warwick (**descendant of King Edward** I), by his second wife Isabel (**descendant of King Edward III**), daughter of Thomas le Despenser, Earl of Gloucester [see BEAUCHAMP 9 for her ancestry].

    a. **ISABEL NEVILLE,** born 5 Sep. 1451, married **GEORGE PLANTAGENET** [see YORK 6].[1]
    b. **ANNE NEVILLE,** born 11 June 1456, betrothed to Edward, Prince of Wales, married **RICHARD III OF ENGLAND, King of England** [see YORK 7.viii].

ii. **JOHN NEVILLE,** Knt., third son, born about 1431 [see next].
iii. **ALICE NEVILLE,** married **HENRY FITZHUGH,** Lord Fitz Hugh [see BULL 8].[2]
iv. **ALIANOR NEVILLE,** married **THOMAS STANLEY,** Earl of Derby [see FITZ ALAN 9].[3]
v. **KATHERINE NEVILLE** [see BONVILLE 7][4] & [see HASTINGS 8].[5]

7. **JOHN NEVILLE,** Knt., K.G., third son, was born about 1431, and was knighted by King Henry VI at Greenwich on Christmas Day 1449. A quarrel with Sir Thomas Percy developed into a clan war throughout the Northern counties, and was a prelude

---

[1] Ancestors of **Maria Johanna Somerset.**

[2] Ancestors of **Stephen Bull, John Oxenbridge.**

[3] Ancestors of **John Nelson.**

[4] Ancestor, by first husband, William Bonville, of **Elizabeth Bosvile, Charles Calvert, Thomas Wingfield,** and, probably, **Thomas Dudley.**

[5] Ancestor, by second husband, William Hasting, of **Maria Johanna Somerset.**

MONTHERMER (cont.)

to the Wars of the Roses. He was married on 25 Apr. 1457 to **ISABEL INGOLDISTHORPE**, daughter and co-heiress of Edmund Ingoldisthorpe, Knt., of Borough Green, co. Cambridge, by Joan, daughter of John Tiptoft, Lord Tiptoft (**descendant of King Edward I**) [see CHERLETON 9 for her ancestry]. They had one son and five daughters. When his brother Richard [*the King Maker*] came into control of the country, he received advancement and many grants. He was summoned to Parliament on 23 May 1461 by writ directed *Johanni Neville domino de Mountague chivaler*, whereby he is held to have become **Lord Montagu**. He was created **Marquess of Montagu** on 25 Mar. 1470. JOHN NEVILLE, Marquess of Montagu, was slain with his brother Richard at Barnet 14 Apr. 1471, buried, with his brother, at Bisham Abbey, co. Berks. His widow was married the second time (with issue) on 25 Apr. 1472, William Norreys, Knt. She died on 20 May 1476, and was buried at Bisham.

    C.P. 9:89-93 (1936). *TG* 9:189 (1988). *Paget* (1977), p. 439.

    Children of John Neville, by Isabel Ingoldisthorpe:

      i. **ANNE NEVILLE** [see next].

      ii. **LUCY NEVILLE**, married, second, **ANTHONY BROWNE**, Knt. [see BROWNE 7].[1]

6. ANNE NEVILLE, daughter and co-heiress, was married in Autumn 1481 to **WILLIAM STONOR**, Knt., son of Thomas Stonor, of Stonor, co. Oxford, by Joan, base daughter of William de la Pole, Duke of Suffolk. SIR WILLIAM STONOR died on 21 May 1474. His widow died shortly before 5 Nov. 1486.

    TG 9:189 (1988).

5. ANNE STONOR, was born about 1484. She was married by 17 Oct. 1499 to **ADRIAN FORTESCUE**, Knt., son of John Fortescue, Knt. (**descendant of Charlemagne**), of Punsbourne, Cornwall, by Alice, daughter of Geoffrey Boleyn, Knt. He was born in 1476. She died at Stonor on 14 June 1518. He was married for the second time. SIR ADRIAN FORTESCUE was beheaded on Tower Hill on 10 July 1539.

    TG 9:189 (1988) (the reason for his detention, attainder and execution remains to be understood).

    Child of Adrian Fortescue, by Anne Stonor:

      i. **MARGARET FORTESCUE**, married **THOMAS WENTWORTH**, Knt. [see HARLESTON 4].[2]

* * *

MORLEY see POLE

MORTIMER see PLANTAGENET

* * *

---

[1] Ancestors of **John Nelson**.

[2] Ancestors of **John Harleston**.

MOWBRAY

HENRY III OF ENGLAND, King of England, married **ÉLÉONORE DE PROVENCE**.
EDMUND OF LANCASTER, Earl of Lancaster, married **BLANCHE D'ARTOIS**.
HENRY OF LANCASTER, married **MAUD DE CHAWORTH** [see LANCASTER 13].

11. JOAN OF LANCASTER, sixth and youngest daughter, was married about 28 Feb. 1326/7 to **JOHN DE MOWBRAY**, 3rd Lord Mowbray, son and heir of John de Mowbray, Knt., **Baron** of Axholme, co. Lincoln, **Baron** of Thirsk, co. York, 2nd Lord Mowbray (of **Magna Charta Surety descent and descendant of Charlemagne**), by Alice, daughter and co-heiress of William de Brewes, Knt., **Baron** of Bramber, Sussex, lord of Gower in Wales (of **Magna Charta Surety descent and descendant of Charlemagne**). He was born at Hovingham, co. York, on 29 Nov. 1310. He was imprisoned in the Tower with his mother on 26 Feb. 1321/2. On the accession of King Edward III, his father's attainder was reversed, and he had livery of all his lands except the Isle of Axholme. He was summoned to Parliament from 10 Dec. 1327. He was Governor of Berwick-on-Tweed 15 Apr. 1340, and served in the Scots and French wars. He was one of the Commanders of the English Army at the Battle of Neville's Cross on 17 Oct. 1346. He was continually employed in Scotland and on the Border till his death. JOAN OF LANCASTER died on 7 July 1349, and is said to have been buried before the high altar at Byland. He was married for the second time before 12 Oct. 1353 to Elizabeth de Vere, widow of Hugh de Courtenay (dead 1349) (son and heir of Hugh, 2nd Earl of Devon), and daughter of John de Vere, 7th Earl of Oxford, by Maud, daughter of Bartholomew, Lord Badlesmere. JOHN DE MOWBRAY, Lord Mowbray, died of pestilence at York on 4 Oct. 1361. His widow was married for the third time before 18 Jan. 1368/9 to William de Cosynton, Knt., son and heir of Stephen de Cosynton, of Cosynton in Aylesford, and Acrise, Kent. She died on 24 Aug. 1375.

C.P. 7:401 footnote *b* (1929). *C.P.* 9:380-383, 383 footnote *c* (1936). *Paget* (1957) 391:6-7. *Sanders* (1960), p. 147.

Children of John de Mowbray, by Joan of Lancaster:

i. **JOHN DE MOWBRAY**, son and heir, born 25 June 1340 [see next].

ii. **ALIANOR DE MOWBRAY**, married **ROGER LA WARRE** [see HUMPHREY 10].[1]

10. JOHN DE MOWBRAY, Knt., 4th Lord Mowbray of Axholme, co. Lincoln, son and heir, was born at Epworth on 25 June 1340. He was knighted in July 1335 when the King was with his fleet in the Downs on his way to an invasion of France. Next year he served in the Brittany campaign. He was summoned to Parliament from 14 Aug. 1362. He was married about 1349, and before 24 Sep. 1353, to **ELIZABETH DE SEGRAVE**, daughter and eventual heiress of John de Segrave, Lord Segrave, by Margaret, Duchess of Norfolk, daughter and heiress of Thomas of Norfolk [*of Brotherton*], Earl of Norfolk (**son of King Edward I**) [see NORFOLK 11 for her ancestry]. She was born at Croxton Abbey on 25 Oct. 1338, and is said to have become Baroness Segrave *suo jure* on the death of her father on 1 Apr. 1353. She predeceased her husband. "John de Mowbray, knt., lord of Axiholm," died testate, being slain by the Turks in Thrace near Constantinople on 9 Oct. 1368. His widow died shortly before 9 May 1376.

C.P. 9:383-384 (1936). *C.P.* 11:610 (1949). *Paget* (1957) 391:7 (identifies children as John,

---

[1]Ancestors of **Anne Humphrey, Herbert Pelham, Gabriel, Roger & Sarah Ludlow, Thomas Lunsford, John Stockman, John West**.

MOWBRAY (cont.)

Thomas, and Eleanor, does not include Joan).

Children of John de Mowbray, by Elizabeth de Segrave:
   i. **THOMAS DE MOWBRAY**, Knt., 6th Lord Mowbray, born 22 Mar. 1365/6 [see next].
   ii. **ALIANOR DE MOWBRAY**, married **JOHN DE WELLES**, Lord Welles [see WELLES 9].[1]
   iii. **JOAN DE MOWBRAY**, married **THOMAS GRAY**, Knt., of Wark [see GRAY 10].[2]

9. THOMAS DE MOWBRAY, Knt., K.G., 6th Lord Mowbray, younger son, was born on 22 Mar. 1365/6, and was brother and heir of John de Mowbray. He was created **Earl of Nottingham** on 12 Feb. 1382/3, **Earl Marshal** on 30 June 1385, and **Duke of Norfolk** on 29 Sep. 1397. He was married for the first time to ELIZABETH STRANGE, Baroness Strange of Blackmere *suo jure*, daughter and heiress of John Strange, Lord Strange of Blackmere. She died in her tenth year on 23 Aug. 1383 *s.p.* He was married for the second time at Arundel Castle in the presence of the King and Queen in July 1384 to **ELIZABETH FITZ ALAN**, widow of William Montagu, styled Lord Montagu (died 6 Aug. 1382 *v.p., s.p.*), and daughter of Richard Fitz Alan, Earl of Arundel and Surrey, by Elizabeth, daughter of William de Bohun, Earl of Northampton (**grandson of King Edward I**) [see FITZ ALAN 11 for her ancestry]. She was born in 1375. He served under his father-in-law in the naval victory over the French, Spanish and Flemish fleets off Margate on 24 Mar. 1386/7. On his return from the Holy Land THOMAS DE MOWBRAY, Duke of Norfolk, died of the pestilence at Venice, Italy, on 22 Sep. 1399, and was buried in the abbey of St. George there. His widow was married for the third time to Robert Goushill, of Hoveringham, co. Nottingham, and had two daughters [see FITZ ALAN 11 for descendants of this marriage]. She was married for the fourth time to Gerard Ufflete, Knt. She died on 8 July 1425, and is said to have been buried with her third husband at Hoveringham.

C.P. 1:253 (1910). *C.P.* 5:357-8 (1926). *C.P.* 9:385, 601-604 (1936). *Paget* (1957) 391:7-9.

Children & grandchild of Thomas de Mowbray, by Elizabeth Fitz Alan:
   i. **ISABEL DE MOWBRAY**, married twice [see GREY 8][3] & [see DEIGHTON 7].[4]
   ii. **MARGARET DE MOWBRAY** [see next].

8. MARGARET DE MOWBRAY, daughter, and in her issue co-heiress, was married about 1420 to **ROBERT HOWARD**, of Stoke-by-Nayland, Suffolk, son of John Howard, Knt., of Wiggenhall, Norfolk (of **Magna Charta Surety descent** and **descendant of Charlemagne**), by his second wife Alice, daughter and heiress of William Tendring, Knt., of Tendring, Essex. He was born about 1383. SIR ROBERT HOWARD died in 1436 *v.p.* His widow died about 1440.

C.P. 1:30 (1910). *C.P.* 9:610 footnote *d* (1936). *Paget* (1957) 294:2. *Paget* (1977), p. 472. *Roskell* (1992) 3:431-433.

Children & grandchildren of Robert Howard, by Margaret de Mowbray:
   i. **JOHN HOWARD**, son and heir [see next].
   ii. **KATHERINE HOWARD**, married (with special dispensation dated 15 Oct. 1448) to **EDWARD**

---

[1] Ancestors of **William Asfordby, Essex Beville, Joseph Bolles, Anne Humphrey, Herbert Pelham, George Reade, Diana & Grey Skipwith, John Stockman, John West.**

[2] Ancestors of **John Fenwick, Nathaniel Littleton, Thomas Lloyd, Philip & Thomas Nelson.**

[3] Ancestor, by first husband Henry Ferrers, of **Elizabeth Bosvile, Charles Calvert, Thomas Wingfield**, and, probably, **Thomas Dudley.**

[4] Ancestor, by second husband James de Berkeley, of **Frances, Jane & Katherine Deighton, Thomas Ligon.**

MOWBRAY (cont.)

NEVILLE, Knt., Lord Bergavenny, died 18 Oct. 1476, widower of Elizabeth Beauchamp (died 18 June 1448) [see OXENBRIDGE 6 for descendants of that marriage], and eleventh and youngest son of Ralph Neville, 1st Earl of Westmorland (of **Magna Charta Surety descent** and **descendant of Charlemagne**), being ninth son by his second wife, Joan Beaufort, Dowager Lady Ferrers de Wemme, legitimised daughter of John of Lancaster [*of Gaunt*], Duke of Lancaster, by Katherine (Roet) Swynford [see BEAUFORT 11.iv.d for her ancestry]. He was summoned to Parliament as a Baron [Lord Bergavenny] from 5 Sep. 1450, by writs directed *Edwardo Nevill domino de Bergevenny militi*. Edward and Katherine had cohabited in the lifetime of his first wife, she being related to him in the third degree. His widow was living 29 June 1478. *C.P.* 1:27-30 (1910). *C.P.* 3:347 (1913). *Paget* (1957) 410:1.

   a. MARGARET NEVILLE, married JOHN BROOKE, 7th Lord Cobham [see WYATT 5].[1]

   b. KATHERINE NEVILLE, married ROBERT TANFIELD, Esq. [see RANDOLPH 7].[2]

7. **JOHN HOWARD**, Knt., K.G., Sheriff of Norfolk and Suffolk, and of Oxfordshire, M.P. for Norfolk, son and heir, succeeded his father in 1436. He was married for the first time in 1440 to **KATHERINE MOLEYNS**, daughter of William Moleyns, Knt., of Stoke Poges, co. Buckingham. He served in the war in France in 1452-53. He was a zealous Yorkist, and was knighted by King Edward IV at the Battle of Towton on 29 Mar. 1461. Under King Edward IV he held many important appointments. His first wife died at Stoke-by-Nayland on 3 Nov. 1465. He was married for the second time by 22 Jan. 1467 to **MARGARET CHEDWORTH**, widow, first (with a daughter Isabel), of Nicholas Wyfold, Lord Mayor of London (died 1456), second, of John Norreys, Esq., of Bray, co. Berks (died 1 Sep. 1466), and daughter of John Chedworth, Knt. He was summoned to Parliament from 15 Oct. 1470 by writs directed *Johanni Howard de Howard, militi*, whereby he is held to have become **Lord Howard**. By the death in 1481 of his cousin Anne, daughter and sole heiress of John de Mowbray, Duke of Norfolk, he became in right of his mother a co-heir and succeeded to a portion of the extensive Mowbray estates. He was created **Duke of Norfolk** and Marshal and Earl Marshal of England on 28 June 1483. SIR JOHN HOWARD led the van (of archers) at the battle of Bosworth Field, where he was slain on 22 Aug. 1485, burial, eventually, at Thetford. His widow died testate in 1494, and was buried at Stoke Nayland.

H.S.P. 74:81 (1923) (Add. Peds. Kent). *C.P.* 9:610-612 (1936). *Paget* (1957) 294:2. *Paget* (1977), p. 404. *Roskell* (1992) 3:433.

Child of John Howard, by Katherine Moleyns:

   i. THOMAS HOWARD, son and heir, born 1443 [see next].

Child of John Howard, by Margaret Chedford:

   ii. KATHERINE HOWARD, married JOHN BOURGCHIER, Lord Berners [see LAUNCE 6.i].[3]

6. **THOMAS HOWARD**, Knt., K.B., K.G., Sheriff of Norfolk and Suffolk, M.P. for Norfolk, P.C., son & heir by first marriage, was born at Stoke Nayland in 1443, and was educated at Thetford Grammar School. He was yeoman in the household of King Edward I. He fought at the Battle of Barnet on 14 Apr. 1471, and was severely wounded. He was married for the first time on 30 Apr. 1472 to **ELIZABETH TILNEY**, widow of Humphrey Bourgchier, Knt., and daughter and heiress of Frederick Tilney, Knt., of Ashwellthorpe, co. Norfolk, by Elizabeth, daughter of Laurence Cheney, of Fen Ditton, co. Cambridge (**descendant of Charlemagne**) [see

---

[1]Ancestors of **Henry Fleete, Hawte Wyatt.**

[2]Ancestors of **William Randolph.**

[3]Ancestors of **Muriel Gurdon.**

MOWBRAY (cont.)

LAUNCE 6 for descendants of this marriage]. After service with the Duke of Burgundy, he became Esquire of the Body to King Edward IV, whom he attended both in England and France. He was created **Earl of Surrey** on 28 June 1483 (the same day his father was created Duke of Norfolk). He was wounded and taken prisoner at the battle of Bosworth on 22 Aug. 1485. Finding favour with King Henry VII, he entered upon a career of employment for many years. He did notable service in the North, especially stamping out insurrections in 1489 and 1492. His first wife died, as Countess of Surrey, on 4 Apr. 1497. He was married for the second time (with dispensation dated 17 Aug. 1497 as related in the second degree, to marry in the chapel of the castle of Sheriff Hutton) to AGNES TILNEY, daughter of Hugh Tilney, of Skirbeck and Boston, co. Lincoln, by _____, daughter of Walter Tailboys. He was made Lieutenant General in the North in July 1513, and gained victory over the Scots at Flodden Field on 9 September. He was rewarded therefor by being created (with a grant of lands) **Duke of Norfolk** on 1 Feb. 1513/4. THOMAS HOWARD, Duke of Norfolk, died aged about eighty at Framlingham Castle on 21 May 1524, and was buried at Thetford Abbey. His widow was imprisoned in the Tower in 1541 (with her son Lord William Howard and Margaret his wife, and her daughter the Countess of Bridgwater), and attainted for misprision of treason in concealing the "evil life" of her step-granddaughter, Katherine Howard, before her marriage to the King Henry VIII. "Agnes Howard, duches of Norff" of Lambeth" was buried testate (P.C.C., 40 Pynnyng) at Thetford Abbey on 31 May 1545.

C.P. 4:210 (1913). H.S.P. 74:81 (1923). C.P. 9:612-615 (1936). C.P. 10:139 (1945). *Paget* (1957) 294:2. *Paget* (1977), p. 248.

Children of Thomas Howard, by Elizabeth Tilney:
    i. **EDMUND HOWARD**, younger son, born about 1478 [see next].
    ii. **ELIZABETH HOWARD**, married **THOMAS BOLEYN**, Earl of Wiltshire [see BUTLER 4].[1]

5. EDMUND HOWARD, younger son, was born about 1478. He was married for the first time after 1509 to **JOYCE CULPEPER**, widow (with five children) of RALPH LEIGH, of Stockwell in Lambeth, Surrey (died before 1 Feb. 1509/10), and daughter of Richard Culpeper, Knt., of West Peckham, Kent (**descendant of King Edward I**), by his second wife Isabel, daughter of Otewell Worsley, of Southwark, Surrey [see STOCKMAN 6 for her ancestry and for descendants of this marriage]. She was born about 1480 (aged twelve and more in 1492). He was Marshal of the Horse at the Battle of Flodden Field on 9 Sep. 1513 under his older brother, the Earl of Surrey. He attended King Henry VIII at the Field of the Cloth of Gold in 1520 when he was listed as one of the "challenging English knights" in the succession of tournaments which entertained the French and English courts. He was with his brother, Lord Edward Howard, in the expedition against Scotland in 1523, the year of Sir John Leigh's death. She died after 1527. He was married for the second time to DOROTHY TROYE. He became Controller of Calais. EDMUND HOWARD died aged sixty-one on 19 Mar. 1537 or 1543.

H.S.P. 74:81 (1923). *Mary Isaac* (1955), pp. 348-353. *Paget* (1957) 294:2. *Abel Lunt* (1963), p. 237.

Children of Edmund Howard, by Joyce Culpeper:
    i. **MARGARET HOWARD**, married THOMAS ARUNDELL, Knt. [see CALVERT 4].[2]
    ii. **KATHERINE HOWARD**, born about 1525, beheaded, for adultery, on Tower Green on 13

---

[1] Ancestors of **John West, Herbert Pelham, Anne Humphrey**.
[2] Ancestors of **Charles Calvert, Maria Johanna Somerset**.

MOWBRAY (cont.)

Feb. 1541/2; married at Hampton Court Palace, 28 July 1540, as his fifth wife, HENRY VIII OF ENGLAND, **King of England**.

* * *

NEEDHAM see TALBOT

* * *

NELSON

EDWARD III OF ENGLAND, King of England, married PHILIPPE DE HAINAUT.
LIONEL OF CLARENCE [*of Antwerp*], Duke of Clarence, married ELIZABETH DE BURGH.
PHILIPPE OF CLARENCE, married EDMUND DE MORTIMER, 3rd Earl of March.
ELIZABETH MORTIMER, married HENRY PERCY, Knt.
HENRY PERCY, Earl of Northumberland, married ALIANOR NEVILLE.
HENRY PERCY, 3rd Earl of Northumberland, married ALIANOR DE POYNINGS.
ANNE PERCY, married THOMAS HUNGERFORD, Knt.
MARY HUNGERFORD, married EDWARD HASTINGS [see HASTINGS 7].

7. ANNE HASTINGS, was married before 1503 to **THOMAS STANLEY**, K.B., Earl of Derby, son and heir of George Stanley, Lord Strange (**descendant of King Edward I**), by Joan, daughter and heiress of John le Strange, Lord Strange, of Knokyn (of **Magna Charta Surety descent** and **descendant of Charlemagne**). He was born before 1485, and was grandson and heir of Thomas Stanley, 1st Earl of Derby. He succeeded to the Earldom of Derby, and later succeeded his mother as Lord Strange (of Knokin), and Mohun (of Dunster) [see FITZ ALAN 8 for his ancestry]. He attended King Henry VIII in the French expedition in 1513, was at the battle of Spurs on 18 Aug. 1513, and attended the Emperor Charles V at Dover in 1520. "Thomas Stanley erle of Derby and lord Stanley" died testate (P.C.C., 21 Bodfelde) at Colham Green, Middlesex, on 23 May 1521, and was buried at Syon Monastery, Middlesex. "Anne Stanley, countess of Darbye" died testate (P.C.C., 7 Bucke) at Colham Green, and was buried on 17 Nov. 1550.
C.P. 4:208-209 (1916). *C.P.* 12(1):251 (1953). *Paget* (1977), p. 264.

6. MARGARET STANLEY, only daughter, was married, between 11 May and 1 Sep. 1532, to **ROBERT RADCLIFFE**, K.B., K.G., Lord Fitz Walter, first surviving son and heir of John Radcliffe, Lord Fitz Walter, of Guildford, Surrey (**descendant of King Edward I**), by Margaret, daughter of Richard Whetehill, Esq., Mayor of Calais. He was born about 1483 [see POLE 7 for his ancestry]. He was attached to the court of Prince Arthur as a boy. He had been married previously, shortly after 23 July 1505, to Elizabeth Stafford, daughter of Henry Stafford, 2nd Duke of Buckingham, by Katherine, sister to Elizabeth, Queen Consort of Edward IV, daughter of Richard Wydeville, 1st Earl Rivers (she died before 11 May 1532). He was summoned to Parliament from 28 Nov. 1511 by writs directed *Roberto Radclyff de FitzWater, Chivaler*. He accompanied King Henry VIII on the expedition to Tournai and Thérouanne in 1513, and was at the Field of the Cloth of Gold in 1520. He was created **Earl of Sussex** on 8 Dec. 1529. He was Great Chamberlain of England for life from 3 Aug. 1540. His wife was living in January 1533/4, and died *s.p.m.*, burial at St. Laurence Pountney, London. He was married for the third time on 14 Jan. 1536/7 to Mary Arundell, daughter of John Arundell, of Lanherne, Cornwall, by Katherine, daughter of Thomas Grenville, Knt., of Stowe, Cornwall. "Robert Ratcliffe, erle of Sussex, of St. Lauraunce pounteney, London" died testate (P.C.C., 1 Alen) at Chelsea on 27 Nov. 1542, and was buried at St. Laurence's, but subsequently removed to Boreham, Essex (M.I.). His widow was married for the second time on 19 Dec. 1545, as his second wife, to Henry Fitz Alan, Earl of Arundel (died 24 Feb. 1579/80 *s.p.m.s.*) and by whom she had no issue. She died at Arundel House, Strand, on 20 Oct. 1557, and was buried at St. Clement Danes, but afterwards removed to Arundel.

C.P. 5:487 (1926). *C.P.* 9:99 (1936). *C.P.* 12(1):517-520 (1953). *Mary Isaac* (1955), p. 271-272. *Paget* (1977), p. 179.

5. JANE RADCLIFFE, was born about 1532. She was married to **ANTHONY BROWNE**, Knt., K.B., K.G., of Battle Abbey and Cowdray Park, Sussex, Sheriff of Surrey and Sussex, son and heir of Anthony Browne, K.G. (**descendant of King Edward I**), by Alice, daughter of John Gage, K.G. He was born about 1528 [see BROWNE 6 for his ancestry]. She died aged twenty in childbed, at Cowdray, on 22 July 1552, and was buried at Midhurst. He was created **Viscount Montagu** on 2 Sep. 1554. He was married for the second time before 10 Dec. 1558 to Magdalen Dacre, daughter of William Dacre, 3rd Lord Dacre of Gilsland, by Elizabeth, daughter of George Talbot, 4th Earl of Shrewsbury. She was born at Naworth Castle, Cumberland in 1538. He was a zealous Roman Catholic, and was one of the fifteen executors of Queen Mary. He took an active part in repelling the Spanish Armada, and entertained Queen Elizabeth sumptuously at Cowdray for six days in August 1591. "Viscount Anthonye Monntague, K.G." died testate (P.C.C., 22 Nevell) at his manor house of West Horsley, Surrey, on 19 Oct 1592. His widow died testate at Battle on 8 Apr. 1608. They were buried at Midhurst.

Yeatman (1903), p. 59-61. *C.P.* 9:97-99 (1936). *TG* 2:125 (1981). *Paget* (1977), p. 123.

4. ANTHONY BROWNE, son and heir apparent, was born on 22 July 1552. He was married to **MARY DORMER**, daughter of William Dormer, K.B., of Eythorpe, co. Buckingham, by Dorothy, daughter of Anthony Catesby, of Whiston, co. Northampton. They had three sons and three daughters. ANTHONY BROWNE died aged thirty-nine (five months before his father), at Riverbank House, Cowdray Park, on 29 June 1592. His widow was married for the second time to Edmund Uvedale, Knt., of Holt Park, Dorset (will proved 12 Apr. 1606, P.C.C., 23 Stafford), and for the third time to Thomas Gerard, Knt., of Bryn, co. Lancaster, 1st Baronet. "Dame Marie Gerard of River Park in the Parish of Tilleton in the County of Sussex, widow" died testate (will dated 20 July 1637 and proved 23 Nov. 1637, requesting burial in the parish church of Midhurst near Anthony Browne, her deceased husband, P.C.C., 150 Goare).

C.P. 9:100 (1936). *TG* 2:123-128 (1981).

3. DOROTHY BROWNE, was married for the first time to **EDMUND LEE**, of Stanton Bury, co. Buckingham, son of Edmund Lee, of Pightlesthorne, by his wife Amicia, for the second time to _____ WOLVERSTONE, and for the third time to WILLIAM ASCUE, Gentleman of the Privy Chamber to King Charles I. As "daughter Dorathie Ascue" she received a bequest from her mother. The will of "Dorathie Ascue al[ia]s Lea" was dated 14 Jan. 1652/3 and proved on 11 May 1653 (P.C.C., 327 Brent), requesting burial in the church of St. Dunstan's in the West near

NELSON (cont.)

her late husband William Ascue.

TG 2:123-128 (1981) ("daughter" Dorathie Alston of her will must be her granddaughter Dorothy (Temple) Alston; both Dorathie Alston and Thomas Temple are known to have been children of Dorothy (Lee) Temple).

2. DOROTHY LEE, was married before 1613 to **JOHN TEMPLE**, Knt., of Stowe and Stanton Bury, co. Buckingham, son of Thomas Temple, Knt., 1st Baronet, of Stowe, co. Buckingham and of Burton Dasset, co. Warwick, by Hester, daughter of Miles Sandys, of Latimers, and of Eton, co. Buckingham. He was born in 1593. Their children were baptized at Stowe. She died in 1625. He was married for the second time to Frances Bloomfield, widow of Thomas Alston. SIR JOHN TEMPLE died at Biddlesden, co. Buckingham, on 23 Sep. 1632.

TG 2:125 (1981).

Children of John Temple, by Dorothy Lee:

i. PETER TEMPLE, Knt., of Stanton Barry; Sheriff of Buckinghamshire; author of *Man's Master-Piece* (1658), born 1613, buried at St. Peter's Mancroft, Norwich 14 Jan. 1659/60; married ELEANOR TYRRELL, daughter of Timothy Tyrrell, of Oakley. Issue.

ii. THOMAS TEMPLE, Knt., Baronet of Nova Scotia, baptised 10 Jan. 1614, Governor of Acadia under Cromwell and remained there after the Restoration until 1677; subsequently resided in Boston, Massachusetts, until 1672 or 1673 when he returned to London; died unmarried at London 27 Mar. 1674. DNB 56:520. *DAB* 13:417 (1934).

iii. DOROTHY TEMPLE, baptised Stowe 17 Oct. 1616, buried Pavenham, co. Bedford 5 Dec. 1668; married at Odell, co. Bedford 4 Jan. 1634 her stepbrother JOHN ALSTON of the Inner Temple and Pavenham, buried Pavenham 15 Aug. 1687. Grandchild: JOHN ALSTON, baptised Pavenham 25 Feb. 1668, probably emigrant to St. John's Parish, Berkeley County, South Carolina, with descendants. Another grandchild: JOHN ALSTON, baptised Felmersham, co. Bedford, 31 Dec. 1673, who may have been the settler of that name in Chowan Co., North Carolina.

iv. MARY TEMPLE, baptised 5 Aug. 1623 [see next].

1. MARY TEMPLE, was baptised at Stowe, co. Buckingham, on 5 Aug. 1623. She was married to **ROBERT NELSON**, member of Gray's Inn, London. They had three children all referred to in the wills of the Nelson and Temple families.

DAB 13:417-418 (1934). *NEHGR* 107:111 (Apr. 1953) (Nelson arms: Party silver and sable a chevron between three fleurs-de-lys all counterchanged). *TG* 2:126 (1981).

Children & grandchild of Robert Nelson, by Mary Temple:

i. TEMPLE NELSON.

ii. MARGARET NELSON, married, it is said, REV. THOMAS TEACKLE of Accomack Co., Virginia.

iii. JOHN NELSON, born 1654, emigrated to Boston, Massachusetts, about 1670, fur trader, statesman, died Boston 15 Nov. 1734; married ELIZABETH TAYLOR. Six children.

* * *

NELSON see also STAPLETON

* * *

NEVILLE

EDWARD I OF ENGLAND, King of England, married ALIANORE DE CASTILLE.
JOAN OF ENGLAND [*of Acre*], married GILBERT DE CLARE, Earl of Gloucester.
MARGARET DE CLARE, married HUGH DE AUDLEY, Earl of Gloucester.
MARGARET DE AUDLEY, married RALPH DE STAFFORD, Earl of Stafford.
HUGH DE STAFFORD, married PHILIPPE DE BEAUCHAMP [see AUDLEY 11].

10. **MARGARET STAFFORD**, was married to **RALPH NEVILLE**, K.G., 4th Lord Neville of Raby, P.C., son and heir of John de Neville, 3rd Lord Neville of Raby (of **Magna Charta Surety descent** and **descendant of Charlemagne**), by Maud (of **Magna Charta Surety descent** and **descendant of Charlemagne**), daughter of Henry de Percy, of Alnwick, Northumberland, **Baron** of Topcliffe, co. York, 2nd Lord Percy. She was born before 1364 (aged twenty-four at his father's death). They had nine children. She died on 9 June 1396, and was buried at Brancepeth, Durham. He took part in the Earl of Buckingham's expedition to Brittany, where he was knighted at St. Omer in July 1380. He succeeded his father on 17 Oct. 1388, and was summoned to Parliament from 6 Dec. 1389, by writs directed *Radulpho de Nevyll de Raby*. From 1389 till 1424 he was continually employed on the Border in negotiating truces and peace with Scotland. He was married for the second time before 20 Feb. 1397 to Joan Beaufort, widow of Robert Ferrers, 2nd Baron Ferrers of Wemme (died before 29 Nov. 1396), and legitimised daughter of John of Lancaster [*of Gaunt*], Duke of Lancaster (fourth son of King Edward III), by his third wife Katherine, daughter of Payn Roet, Knt. She was born about 1379 [see BEAUFORT 11.iv for descendants of this marriage]. He was created **Earl of Westmorland** on 29 Sep. 1397. His near alliance to the House of Lancaster (being son-in-law of John *of Gaunt*), led him to forsake the King, and take a prominent part in the elevation of Henry *of Bolingbroke*, the exiled Duke of Lancaster, to the throne as King Henry IV. RALPH NEVILLE, Earl of Westmorland, died testate at Raby Castle on 21 Oct. 1425, and was buried at Staindrop, Durham (M.I. to him and his two wives). His second wife, on whom the lordships of Middleham and Sheriff-Hutton, with other extensive lands, were settled, left them to her eldest son, Richard, Earl of Salisbury. This caused a feud between her and her sons on the one side, and the grandsons of her husband by his first wife on the other, which resulted in the elder branch espousing the cause of Lancaster, and Salisbury and his brothers, that of York. Joan Beaufort, Countess of Westmorland, died testate at Howden on 13 Nov. 1440, and was buried (with her mother) in Lincoln Cathedral (M.I).

Sur.Soc. 41:28 (1862) (1530 Vis. North) (called *Dawraby*, Daw as the diminutive of Randolf). *Gen.(n.s.)* 3:34 (Neville arms: *Gules*, a saltire *argent*). *C.P.* 2:389 (1912). *C.P.* 4:7 (1916). *C.P.* 9:716 (1936). *TAG* 17:106 (Oct. 1940). *C.P.* 11:542 (1949). *C.P.* 12(2):544-547 (1959). *Paget* (1957) 404:10-15. *Paget* (1957) 6-15. Notes & Queries, 3rd Series, 9: 376; 152: 219.

Children of Ralph Nevile, by Margaret Stafford:
  i. **RALPH NEVILLE**, Knt., second son [see next].
  ii. **ALICE NEVILLE**, married, first, **THOMAS GRAY**, Knt. [see GRAY 9].[1]
  iii. **PHILIPPE NEVILLE**, married **THOMAS DE DACRE**, 6th Lord Dacre [see DACRE 8].[2]
  iv. **MARGARET NEVILLE**, married **RICHARD LE SCROPE** [see SCROPE 7].[3]

---

[1] Ancestors of **John Fenwick**.

[2] Ancestors of **Thomas Lunsford, Agnes Mackworth, Philip & Thomas Nelson**.

[3] Ancestors of **Richard & William Bernard, Edward Carleton, Philip & Thomas Nelson**.

NEVILLE (cont.)

9. RALPH NEVILLE, Knt., of Oversley, co. Warwick, *jure uxoris*, second son, was married to **MARY DE FERRERS**, Lady of Oversley, daughter and co-heiress of Robert de Ferrers, Knt., of Wem, co. Salop (**descendant of Charlemagne**), by Joan Beaufort [his step-mother], legitimised daughter of John of Lancaster [*of Gaunt*], Duke of Lancaster, by Katherine, daughter of Payn Roët, Knt. [see BEAUFORT 11.iv.a for her ancestry]. She was born before 1394 (aged seventeen at the death of her paternal grandmother), and died on 25 Jan. 1457/8. SIR RALPH NEVILLE died on 26 Feb. 1457/8.
   TAG 17:106 (Oct. 1940). *Paget* (1957) 404:13. *Paget* (1957) 6:15.

8. JOHN NEVILLE, Esq., of Oversley, co. Warwick, and of Althorpe, co. Lincoln, and Wormesley, co. York, *jure uxoris*, son and heir, was Member of Parliament for Lincolnshire in 1449, and Sheriff of Lincolnshire 1439-1440, 1452-1453. He was married for the first time to **ELIZABETH NEWMARCH**, daughter and co-heiress of Robert Newmarch, of Wormsley, co. York. He was married for the second time about 1467 to MARGARET PLUMPTON, widow of George Darrell, Knt. (died 1466), and daughter of William Plumpton, Knt. JOHN NEVILLE, ESQ., died on 17 Mar. 1481/2. His widow died on 14 May 1487.
   TAG 17:106 (Oct. 1940). *Paget* (1957) 404:13. *Paget* (1957) 6:15. *NEHGR* 104:270.

7. JOAN NEVILLE, Lady of Oversley, co. Warwick, and Wormsley, co. York, daughter and heiress, was married for the first time about 1459/60 to **WILLIAM GASCOIGNE**, Knt., of Gawthorpe, co. York, son and heir of William Gascoigne, Knt., of Gawthorpe, by Margaret, daughter of Thomas Clarell, Knt., of Aldwark, co. York. They had three sons and two daughters. SIR WILLIAM GASCOIGNE died about 1463 *v.p.* She was married for the second time, with licence dated 13 Jan. 1463/4, to JAMES HARRINGTON, Knt., of Hornby, and had three sons.
   Sur.Soc. 41:14-15 (1862) (1530 Vis. North). *Foster* (1874). *H.S.P.* 16:135 (1881) (1563 Vis. Yorks).
   Sur.Soc. 144:151 (1930) (1480 Vis. North). *TAG* 17:107 (Oct. 1940). *Paget* (1977), p. 411.

   Children of William Gascoigne, by Jane Neville:

   i. **WILLIAM GASCOIGNE**, Knt., married **MARGARET PERCY** [see BERNARD 6].[1]
   ii. **MARGARET GASCOIGNE**, married **CHRISTOPHER WARDE**, Knt. [see CARLETON 6].[2]

* * *

NEVILLE (LORDS LATIMER) see BOSVILE

NEVILLE OF BERGAVENNY see OXENBRIDGE

NEVILLE OF SALISBURY see MAULEVERER

NEVILLE OF THORNTON BRIDGE see CARLETON

NEWCOMEN see ASFORDBY

---

[1]Ancestors of **Richard & William Beranrd**.
[2]Ancestors of **Edward Carleton**.

NORFOLK

EDWARD I OF ENGLAND, married **MARGUERITE DE FRANCE** [see PLANTAGENET 14].

12. THOMAS OF NORFOLK [*of Brotherton*], Knt., fifth son, was born at Brotherton, co. York, on 1 June 1300. He was assigned the estates of Roger Bigod, late Earl of Norfolk (with his brother Edmund jointly) by their brother King Edward II, and was created **Earl of Norfolk** on 16 Dec. 1312. He was summoned to Parliament on 3 Jan. 1312/3, and was created **Marshal of England** on 10 Feb. 1315/6. He was married for the first time about 1316, or about 1320, to **ALICE DE HALES**, daughter of Roger de Hales, Knt., of Harwich, Essex. Earl Thomas gave unhesitating support to the opposition by Queen Isabel, and met her in 1326 at her landing on his own property at Orwell, but in 1329 joined the alienated magnates against her and Roger de Mortimer, Earl of March, and had charge of Mortimer's execution (though his son was married to Mortimer's daughter). ALICE DE HALES died after 8 May 1326. He was married for the second time about 1328 to MARY DE BREWES, widow of Ralph de Cobham, Lord Cobham (died February 1326), and daughter of Peter de Brewes, Knt., of Tetbury, co. Gloucester, by his wife Agnes. They had no surviving issue. THOMAS OF NORFOLK, Earl of Norfolk, died testate about August 1338 *s.p.m.*, and was buried in the Abbey of Bury St. Edmunds. His widow was admitted to the sisterhood of Langley Priory on 4 Mar. 1345, and died between 17 Apr. 1361 and 15 June 1362.

C.P. 9:596-601 (1936). C.P. 9:609-610 (1949). *Paget* (1957) 455:1 (son Edward by a first wife Anne).

Children of Thomas of Norfolk, by Alice de Hales:

    i. EDWARD OF NORFOLK [*of Brotherton*], son and heir-apparent, born about 1319, died before 2 Dec. 1334 *v.p. s.p.*; married May or June 1328 BEATRICE DE MORTIMER, died 16 Oct. 1383, daughter of Roger de Mortimer, 1st Earl of March, by Joan, daughter and heiress of Peter de Geneville, Lord of Trim. She married, second, THOMAS DE BREWSE, of Tetbury.

    ii. **MARGARET OF NORFOLK**, elder daughter and co-heiress, born about 1320 [see next].

    iii. ALICE OF NORFOLK, younger daughter and co-heiress, died between 14 Nov. 1351 and 30 Jan. 1352; married EDWARD DE MONTAGU, 1st Lord Montagu. Three daughters, all died *s.p.*

11. MARGARET OF NORFOLK, Countess of Norfolk *suo jure*, elder daughter and co-heiress, eventual sole heiress, was born about 1320. She was married for the first time in 1337 or 1338 to **JOHN DE SEGRAVE**, 4th Lord Segrave, son and heir of Stephen de Segrave, 3rd Lord Segrave, by his wife Alice. He was born about 1315 (aged ten at his father's death). JOHN DE SEGRAVE, Lord Segrave, died testate on 1 Apr. 1353 *s.p.m.* She was married for the second time shortly before 30 May 1354 to WALTER DE MAUNY, Lord Mauny (died January 1371/2). MARGARET OF NORFOLK was created **Duchess of Norfolk** for life on 29 Sep. 1397, and died on 24 Mar 1398/9 *s.p.m.*, was buried in the choir of the Grey Friars', London.

C.P. 9:599-601 (1936). C.P. (1949) 11:610-611.

Child of John de Segrave, by Margaret of Norfolk:

    i. **ELIZABETH DE SEGRAVE**, married **JOHN DE MOWBRAY** [see MOWBRAY 10].[1]

---

[1] Ancestors of **William Asfordby, Essex Bevile, Joseph Bolles, Elizabeth Bosvile, Charles Calvert, Frances, Jane & Katherine Deighton, John Fenwick, Muriel Gurdon, Anne Humphrey, Thomas Ligon, Nathaniel Littleton, Thomas Lloyd, Philip & Thomas Nelson, Herbert Pelham, William Randolph, George Reade, Diana & Grey Skipwith, John Stockman, John West, Thomas Wingfield, Hawte Wyatt,** and, probably, **Thomas Dudley**.

OGLE

EDWARD I OF ENGLAND, King of England, married MARGUERITE DE FRANCE.
THOMAS OF NORFOLK [of Brotherton], Earl of Norfolk, married ALICE DE HALES.
MARGARET OF NORFOLK, married JOHN DE SEGRAVE, 4th Lord Segrave.
ELIZABETH DE SEGRAVE, married JOHN DE MOWBRAY, 4th Lord Mowbray of Axholme.
JOAN DE MOWBRAY, married THOMAS GRAY, Knt. [see GRAY 10].

9. **MAUD GRAY**, was married about 21 May 1399 to **ROBERT OGLE**, Knt., of Ogle, Northumberland, M.P. for Northumberland, Sheriff of Northumberland, son and heir of Robert Ogle, Knt., of Ogle and Bothal, Northumberland, by Joan, daughter and co-heiress of Alan Heton, Knt., of Ingram, Norfolk. He was born 1379/83 (variously aged twenty-six and thirty in 1409). They had three sons and four daughters. SIR ROBERT OGLE died on 12 Aug. 1436. His widow died after 1454.

Clay (1913), p. 153. *C.P.* 6:488 (1926). *Sur.Soc.* 144:53-55 (1930) (1480 Vis. North) (one son and seven daughters) (Maud identified as *Matildis filia domini Iohannis vel Thomas Gray militis*) (Ogle arms: *Argent*, a fess between three crescents *gules*). *Northumberland* (1935) 14: chart following p. 328. *C.P.* 10:28-29 (1945). *Roskell* (1992) 3:224,677,859-862.

Children of Robert Ogle, by Maud Gray:
  i. JOAN OGLE [see next].
  ii. MARGARET OGLE, married ROBERT HARBOTTLE, Knt. [see HARBOTTLE 8].

8. **JOAN OGLE**, was married to **ROBERT MANNERS**, Knt., of Etal, Northumberland, Sheriff of Northumberland, M.P., son and heir of John Manners, Knt., by Anne, daughter of John Middleton, Knt., of East Swinburn. He was born about 1430 (aged thirty and more at his father's death). They had two sons and one daughter. SIR ROBERT MANNERS died in 1461.

Collins-Brydges (1812) 1:460-461. *Northumberland* 11:444 (1922) ("Jenetta"). *Sur.Soc.* 144:55 (1930) (1480 Vis. North). *Roskell* (1992) 3:676,861-862.

7. **ROBERT MANNERS**, Knt., of Etal, was married, with licence dated 13 June 1469 to be married in the chapel of the manor-house at Wressell, to **ALIANOR DE ROS**, eldest daughter of Thomas de Ros, 9th Lord Ros (**descendant of King Edward I**), by Philippe, daughter of John Tiptoft, Lord Tiptoft [see ROS 8 for her ancestry]. She was born in 1449, and became sole heiress after the death of her brother and sister. Her inheritance included Belvoir and Helmesley Castles. They had two sons and three daughters. She died in 1487. SIR ROBERT MANNERS died in 1495.

Collins-Brydges (1812) 1:461-462. *Sur.Soc.* 45:340 (1865). *Northumberland* 11:444 (1922). *Clay* (1913), p. 184. *Sur.Soc.* 144:55,163 (1930) (1480 Vis. North). *Paget* (1977), p. 402.

Child of Robert Manners, by Alianor de Ros:
  i. GEORGE MANNERS, Knt., married ANNE SAINT LEGER [see STAPLETON 6].[1]

* * *

OLLANTIGH

HENRY III OF ENGLAND, King of England, married ÉLÉONORE DE PROVENCE.
EDMUND OF LANCASTER *Crouchback*, Earl of Lancaster, BLANCHE D'ARTOIS.
HENRY OF LANCASTER, Duke of Lancaster, married MAUD DE CHAWORTH.
ALIANOR OF LANCASTER, married RICHARD FITZ ALAN, 3rd Earl of Arundel.

---

[1] Ancestors of **Philip & Thomas Nelson**.

OLLANTIGH (cont.)

JOHN DE ARUNDEL, Lord Arundel, married **ALIANOR MALTRAVERS**.
JOHN DE ARUNDEL, 2nd Lord Arundel, married **ELIZABETH DESPENSER**.
THOMAS DE ARUNDEL, Knt., married **JOANE MOYNE**.
ALIANOR DE ARUNDEL, married **THOMAS BROWNE**, Knt. [see BROWNE 8].

5. ROBERT BROWNE, Esq., fifth son, was married, it is said, to **MARY MALLET**, daughter of William Mallet.

Wotton (1741) 3:5. *Top. & Gen.* 2:267 (1853) (pedigree prepared 1585 by Walter Browne, grandson of George Browne, Knt., elder brother of Robert Browne). *Kemp* (1902), pp. 20-26,184. *H.S.P.* 74:13 (1923) (1530 Vis. Kent). *Paget* (1977), p. 439.

4. ELEANOR BROWNE, daughter and heiress, was married for the first time to **THOMAS FOGGE**, Esq., of Ashford, Kent, Sergeant Porter of Calais to Kings Henry VII and Henry VIII. They had two daughters. "Thomas Fogges, esquyer, of Esshetisford" died testate (P.C.C., 9 Fetiplace) on 16 Aug. 1512, and was buried at Ashford. She was married for the second time to **WILLIAM KEMPE**, Knt., of Ollantigh in Wye, Kent, Sheriff of Kent, second son of Thomas Kempe, Knt., of Wye, by Emelyn, daughter and co-heiress of Valentine Chichele. He was born in 1487. They had six sons and five daughters. "William Kemp, knyght" died testate (P.C.C., 29 Dyngeley) on 28 Jan. 1535. The will of his widow was dated at the Savoy on 21 Aug. 1560. They were buried at Wye.

Stemmata Chicheleana (1765), p. 5 (Valentine Chichele was "Founder's Kin"). *Top. & Gen.* 2:267 (1853). *Arch.Cant.* 5:117 (1863) (monument of her first husband with arms of Browne of Betchworth quartering Fitzalan) (all Kempe memorials destroyed "by the fall of Wye steeple, in 1685"). *Scott* (1876), p. 175. *Kemp* (1902), pp. 20-26. *H.S.P.* 74:13 (1923) (1530 Vis. Kent) (Kemp arms: *Gules*, three garbs *or* within a bordure engrailed of the second). *Paget* (1977), p. 439.

Children of William Kempe, by Eleanor Browne:

i. **THOMAS KEMPE**, Knt. [see next].

ii. **EMELYN KEMPE**, married **REYNOLD SCOTT**, Knt. [see FLEETE 3].[1]

3. THOMAS KEMPE, Knt., of Ollantigh, Gentleman of the Court, Sheriff of Kent, was married for the first time to **KATHERINE CHENEY**, daughter and co-heiress of Thomas Cheney, Knt., Lord Warden of the Cinque Ports. They had five daughters. She died before 1550. He was married for the second time at Eastwell, Kent, on 19 Jan. 1550 to **AMY MOYLE**, daughter and co-heiress of Thomas Moyle, Knt., of Eastwell Place, by his wife Katherine Jordan. They had seven sons. She was buried at Wye on 17 Aug. 1557. He was married for the third time, with settlement dated 20 Dec. 1571, to **JOAN FERMOR**, sometime maid of honour to Princess Mary, widow successively of Robert Wilford, merchant tailor of London (died 1545), and of John Mordaunt, 2nd Lord Mordaunt (died 1571), and daughter of Richard Fermor, Knt., of Easton Neston, co. Northampton, by Anne, daughter of William Browne, Knt. SIR THOMAS KEMPE died on 7 Mar. 1591. His widow, a recusant, was residing with her step-son Moyle Kempe in Cornwall in 1592. The will of "dame Johann Mordaunte, widowe" was proved in 1592 (P.C.C., 25 Harrington).

Stemmata Chicheleana (1765), p. 5. *Top. & Gen.* 2:267 (1853). *Kemp* (1902), pp. 28-31. *H.S.P.* 74:13 (1923). *H.S.P.* 75:3,13 (1924) (1574 Vis. Kent). *C.P.* 9:195-196 (1936).

2. THOMAS KEMPE, Knt., of Ollantigh, son and heir, was baptised at Wye on 7 Nov. 1551. He was married for the first time to **ANNE** _____. They had three children. He was married for the second time to **DOROTHY THOMPSON**, daughter of John Thompson, Esq., of London. They had two daughters. SIR THOMAS

---

[1] Ancestors of **St.Leger Codd, Henry Fleete, Warham Horsmanden, Katherine Saint Leger**.

OLLANTIGH (cont.)

KEMPE died in 1607, and was buried at Wye. The will of "Dorothie Kempe, widow", dated 14 Nov. 1626 and proved May 1629 (P.C.C., 49 Ridley) names daughters, Lady Ann Cutts, Lady Dorothy Chichely, Lady Mary Diggs and Lady Ann Skipwith, and grandchildren Dorothie Chichely, Thomas Diggs, William Skipwith, and sons [in-law] John Cutts, Dudley Digges and Henry Skipwith.

Stemmata Chicheleana (1765), p. 5. *Kemp* (1902), pp. 34-38,60-63. *VMHB* 28:136-137 (Apr. 1920) (will of Dorothy Kempe) (daughter Dorothy married Sir John Chichley, of Wimpole, Cambridgeshire, and was mother of Sir Henry Chichley, Kt., Governor of Virginia). *H.S.P.* 75:3 (1924).

Child of Thomas Kempe, by Anne:

   i. **MARY KEMPE**, married **DUDLEY DIGGES**, Knt. [see DIGGES 1].[1]

Child of Thomas Kempe, by Dorothy Thompson:

   ii. **AMY KEMPE**, married **HENRY SKIPWITH**, Knt., Baronet [see SKIPWITH 1].[2]

* * *

OVER PEOVER

EDWARD I OF ENGLAND, King of England, married **ALIANORE DE CASTILLE**.
ELIZABETH OF ENGLAND, married **HUMPHREY DE BOHUN**, Earl of Hereford and Essex.
WILLIAM DE BOHUN, Earl of Northampton, married **ELIZABETH DE BADLESMERE**.
ELIZABETH DE BOHUN, married **RICHARD FITZ ALAN**, Earl of Arundel.
ELIZABETH FITZ ALAN, married **ROBERT GOUSHILL**, Knt.
JOAN GOUSHILL, married **THOMAS STANLEY**, Lord Stanley of Lathom and Knowsley.
KATHERINE STANLEY, married **JOHN SAVAGE**, Knt.
MARGARET SAVAGE, married **JOHN HONFORD** [see GERARD 5].

5. **KATHERINE HONFORD**, was married to **JOHN MAINWARING**, Knt., of Over Peover, Sheriff of Flintshire, son and heir of John Mainwaring, Esq., of Over Peover, by Maud, daughter of Robert Legh, Esq., of Adlington. He was born about 1471 (aged forty-five at death). They had seven sons. The will of "sir John Maynwaryng, knight" was dated 4 Mar. 1515/6, and proved 18 Nov. 1516 (P.C.C., 1 Maynwaryng). He was buried at Over Peover. His widow died in 1529.

Wotton (1741) 3:180 (Mainwaring arms: *Argent*, two bars, *gules*). *Wm. Salt Soc.* 3:113 (1882) (1583 Vis. Staffs) ("Catherin, da. of Will'm Honforde of Honforde") (Mainwaring arms: *Argent*, two bars *gules*). *TG* 5:164-165 (1984).

4. **RANDALL MAINWARING**, Knt., of Over Peover, son and heir, was born about 1495. He was married for the first time in or after 1518 to **ELIZABETH BRERETON**, widow of Richard Cholmondeley, of Cholmondeley in Malpas, co. Chester (died 1518), and daughter of Randall Brereton, Knt., of Malpas, Ipstones and Shocklach, co. Chester, by Eleanor, daughter of Peter Dutton, of Hatton, co. Chester. He was married for the second time in 1551, without issue, to **ELIZABETH LEYCESTER**, daughter of Ralph Leycester, of Toft. SIR RANDALL MAINWARING died testate on 6 Sep 1557. His will, dated 30 Nov 1545, names his three daughters and their husbands. His widow was married for the second time to Edmund Trafford, of Trafford, co. Lancaster, and had issue.

---

[1] Ancestors of **Edward Digges**.

[2] Ancestors of **Diana & Grey Skipwith**.

OVER PEOVER (cont.)

Wotton (1741) 3:180-181. *Wm. Salt Soc.* 3:113 (1882) (three [unnamed] daughters). *TG* 5:164-165 (1984).

Child of Randall Mainwaring, by Elizabeth Brereton:
   i. MARGARET MAINWARING, married ARTHUR MAINWARING [see MAINWARING 3].[1]

* * *

OWEN

EDWARD I OF ENGLAND, King of England, married ALIANORE DE CASTILLE.
ELIZABETH OF ENGLAND, married HUMPHREY DE BOHUN, Earl of Hereford and Essex.
WILLIAM DE BOHUN, Earl of Northampton, married ELIZABETH DE BADLESMERE.
ELIZABETH DE BOHUN, married RICHARD FITZ ALAN, Earl of Arundel.
ELIZABETH FITZ ALAN, married ROBERT GOUSHILL, Knt.
JOAN GOUSHILL, married THOMAS STANLEY, Lord Stanley of Lathom and Knowsley.
MARGARET STANLEY, married WILLIAM TROUTBECK, Knt.
JOAN TROUTBECK, married WILLIAM GRIFFITH, Knt.
WILLIAM GRIFFITH, married JANE PULESTON [see COYTEMORE 4].

5. **SIBYL GRIFFITH**, was married in 1563 to OWAIN AP HUW AB OWAIN, of Bodowen, Sheriff of Anglesey, son of Huw ab Owain, by Gwenllian ferch Morus. He was married for the second time to ELSBETH FERCH ROBERT AP ROLAND. OWAIN AP HUW AB OWAIN died in 1613.
   Bartrum (1983) 8:1268 (Marchudd 6 B4) (citation of pedigrees of descendants).

4. **JANE FERCH OWAIN AP HUW**, was married to HUGH GWYNN, of Penarth, Sheriff of Carnarvonshire.
   Glenn (1896), pp. 210,247. *Glenn* (1911), p. 43.

3. **SIBYL FERCH HUGH GWYNN**, was married to SION (or JOHN) AP HOWELL, of Gadfa in Llanwddyn, co. Montgomery, son of Howell Gôch, of Gadfa. They had two sons and two daughters. JOHN AP HOWELL was buried at Llanwyddyn, on 24 July 1636.
   Glenn (1896), pp. 210,247.

2. **ELIZABETH FERCH SION AP HOWELL**, was married in 1625 to HUMPHREY AP HUGH, Gent., of Llwyndu at Llwyngwrill in Llangelynin, co. Merioneth, son of Hugh ap David ap Howell ap Gronw ap Einion, by Catherine ferch Sion ap Rhydderch Abergynolwyn. They had four sons and three daughters. HUMPHREY AP HUGH, GENT., died about 1664.
   Glenn (1896), pp. 210,241-247. *Glenn* (1911), p. 44.

Children & grandchildren of Humphrey ap Hugh, by Elizabeth Powell:
   i. OWEN HUMPHREY, baptised 13 Apr. 1629, son and heir [see next].
   ii. JOHN HUMPHREY, baptised Llangelynin 16 Nov. 1632, emigrated to Pennsylvania 1683, settled at Merion; married JANE, sister of Richard Humphrey, of Llangelynin. No issue.
   iii. SAMUEL HUMPHREY, baptised Llangelynin 22 Jan. 1635, died Llangelynin 17 Sep. 1677; married ELIZABETH REES, daughter of Hugh Rees. His eight children emigrated to Pennsylvania.

---

[1] Ancestors of **Robert Abell**.

OWEN (cont.)

    a. **DANIEL HUMPHREY**, of Pennsylvania, married **HANNAH WYNNE**. Thirteen children.
    b. **LYDIA HUMPHREY**, married **ELLIS ELLIS**.
    c. **JOSEPH HUMPHREY**, married **ELIZABETH MEDFORD**.
    d. **BENJAMIN HUMPHREY**, married **MARY LLEWELYN**. Six children.
    e. **REBECCA HUMPHREY**, married **EDWARD REES**.
    f. **ANNE HUMPHREY**, married **EDWARD ROBERTS**.
    g. **GODITHA HUMPHREY**, died 1687.
    h. **ELIZABETH HUMPHREY**, married **THOMAS ABEL**.
  iv. **ANNE HUMPHREY**, married 1649 **ELLIS AP REES** (or **ELIAS PRICE**), of Bryn Mawr, co. Merioneth [see ELLIS 1].

1. OWEN HUMPHREY, of Llwyndu, Esq., son and heir, was baptised at Llangelynin, co. Merioneth, on 13 Apr. 1629. He was married for the first time to **MARGARET VAUGHAN**, and for the second time to **ELIZABETH THOMAS**. He was an officer under Oliver Cromwell, and served as a Justice of the Peace for Merionethshire under the Protectorate. He was among the first in Wales to become a member of the Society of Friends, and was prosecuted for failure to pay tithes in 1662. OWEN HUMPHREY was dead by 1699.

    Glenn (1896), pp. 210,219,241,246,247-50. *Glenn* (1911), pp. 44-46.

    Children & grandchild of Owen Humphrey, by Margaret Vaughan:

    i. **HUMPHREY OWEN**, baptised and died February 1653.
    ii. **JOHN OWEN**, baptised and died February 1653.
    iii. **HUMPHREY OWEN**, inherited paternal estate in Wales, married, with daughter.
    iv. **JOHN OWEN**, emigrated to Pennsylvania 1687, settled Merion, apparently died unmarried.
    v. **ROWLAND OWEN**, resided Wales.
    vi. **JOSHUA OWEN**, born Wales, emigrated to Pennsylvania 1683, settled Merion, a member of the Burlington monthly meeting of Friends, died Burlington County, New Jersey, 4 Mar. 1727; married 19 1st mo. [Mar.] 1697 **MARTHA SHINN**.

        a. **MARGARET OWEN**, born 1701, of Radnor monthly meeting, died May 1753; married Burlington, New Jersey, monthly meeting 21 Aug. 1722 **BENJAMIN CRISPIN**, born September 1699, died December 1753.

    vii. **OWEN OWEN**, resided Wales.
    viii. **REBECCA OWEN**, emigrated to Pennsylvania 1690, died Merion 23 8th mo. [Oct.] 1697; married, 11 1st mo. [Mar.] 1678/9 **ROBERT OWEN**, Gent.

    Child of Owen Humphrey, probably by Elizabeth Thomas:

    ix. **ELIZABETH OWEN**, born about 1676, emigrated to Pennsylvania; married 1692 **JOHN ROBERTS**. No known issue.

* * *

OXENBRIDGE

EDWARD III OF ENGLAND, King of England, married **PHILIPPE DE HAINAUT**.
EDMUND OF YORK [*of Langley*], married **ISABELLA DE CASTILLE** [see YORK 9].

8. CONSTANCE OF YORK, was born about 1374. She was married between 16 Apr.

1378 and 14 Jan. 1383/4 to **THOMAS LE DESPENSER, K.G.**, 5th Lord Despenser, third but first surviving son and heir of Edward Despenser, 4th Lord Le Despenser (**descendant of King Edward I**), by Elizabeth, daughter and heiress of Bartholomew de Burghersh, 4th Lord Burghersh (of **Magna Charta Surety** descent and **descendant of Charlemagne**) [see CLARE 9 for his ancestry]. He was born on 22 Sep. 1373. He was summoned to Parliament from 30 Nov. 1396 by writs directed *Thome le Despenser*, and was created **Earl of Gloucester**. Subsequently, on petition in the same Parliament, he obtained the reversal of the sentence of disheritance and exile on his ancestors, Hugh the elder and Hugh the younger. Having joined in the plot to seize King Henry IV, THOMAS LE DESPENSER was seized, and beheaded aged twenty-six on 13 Jan. 1399/1400 *v.m.*, and was buried in Tewkesbury Abbey. His widow appeared before the Council on a charge of being concerned in the abduction of the young Mortimers from Windsor Castle, when she incriminated her brother, the Duke of York. She was sent to Kenilworth Castle, and her property was seized, later restored. About this time she is said to have had a liaison with Edmund de Holand, Earl of Kent, and had a daughter, Alianor, wife of James Tuchet, Lord Audley [see TUCHET 9 for descendants]. She died on 29 Nov. 1416 and was buried in the Abbey of Reading.

C.P. 1:27 (1910). *C.P.* 2:427 (1912). *C.P.* 4:278-282 (1916). *C.P.* 9:217 (1936). *Paget* (1977), p. 424.

7. **ISABEL LE DESPENSER**, was born, posthumously, at Cardiff on 26 July 1400, and was sister and eventual (in 1414) sole heiress of Richard Le Despenser. She was married for the first time at Tewkesbury on 27 July 1411 to **RICHARD BEAUCHAMP**, K.B., 2nd Lord Bergavenny, son and heir of William de Beauchamp, Lord Bergavenny (**descendant of Charlemagne**), by Joan, daughter of Richard Fitz Alan, Earl of Arundel. He was born in or before 1397 (aged fourteen and more in June 1411) [see FITZALAN 12.iii for his ancestry]. He was created **Earl of Worcester** in February 1420/1. RICHARD BEAUCHAMP, Lord Bergavenny, died *s.p.m*, being mortally wounded at the siege of Meaux in France on 18 Mar. 1421/2, and was buried at Tewkesbury Abbey. His widow was married for the second time at Hanley Castle, co. Worcester, on 26 Nov. 1423, as his second wife, to her husband's cousin, RICHARD BEAUCHAMP, 5th Earl of Warwick (died 30 Apr. 1439) [see BEAUCHAMP 9 for descendants of this marriage]. "Dame Isabel Beauchamp, Countess of Warrwyk" died testate (P.C.C., 27 Luffenam) at the Friars Minoresses, London, on 27 Dec. 1439, and was buried at Tewkesbury Abbey (M.I.).

C.P. 1:26-27 (1910). *Paget* (1977), p. 257.

6. **ELIZABETH BEAUCHAMP**, daughter and heiress, was born at Hanley Castle, co. Worcester, on 16 Sep. 1415. She was married before 18 Oct. 1424 to **EDWARD NEVILLE**, Knt., eleventh and youngest son of Ralph Neville, 1st Earl of Westmorland (of **Magna Charta Surety** descent and **descendant of Charlemagne**), being ninth son by his second wife, Joan Beaufort, Dowager Lady Ferrers de Wemme, the legitimised daughter of John of Lancaster [*of Gaunt*], Duke of Lancaster [see BEAUFORT 11.iv.d for his ancestry]. They had two sons. ELIZABETH BEAUCHAMP died aged thirty-two on 18 June 1448, and was buried at the Carmelites, Coventry. He was summoned to Parliament as a Baron [Lord Bergavenny] from 5 Sep. 1450, by writs directed *Edwardo Nevill domino de Bergevenny militi*. He was married for the second time, with dispensation dated 15 Oct. 1448, to Katherine Howard, daughter of Robert Howard, Knt., by Margaret, daughter of Thomas Mowbray, Duke of Norfolk (descendant of King Edward I). They had

OXENBRIDGE (cont.)

cohabited in the lifetime of his first wife, were excommunicated but later absolved [see MOWBRAY 8.ii for descendants of this marriage]. SIR EDWARD NEVILLE died on 18 Oct. 1476. His widow was living on 29 June 1478.

C.P. 1:27-30 (1910). *C.P.* 3:347 (1913). *Paget* (1957) 410:1-2. *Paget* (1977) 176.

5. **GEORGE NEVILLE**, Knt., 4th Lord Bergavenny, second but first surviving son and heir by first marriage, was born at Raby Castle, Durham, and baptised at Staindrop, Durham, in 1435. He was summoned to Parliament from 15 Nov. 1482 by writs directed *Georgio Nevyle de Bergevenny chr*. He was married for the first time to **MARGARET FENNE**, daughter and heiress of Hugh Fenne, Esq., of Sculton Burdeleys, Norfolk, and of Braintree, Essex, Treasurer of the Household to King Henry VI. They had five sons and two daughters. She died on 28 Sep. 1485. He was married for the second time, as her fourth husband, to **ELIZABETH** _____, widow, successively of Robert Bassett, Knt., Lord Mayor of London, Richard Naylor, citizen of London and John Stokker, of St. George's, Eastcheap. "Sir George Nevill, knt., lord Bergavenny" died testate (P.C.C., 8 Horne) on 20 Sep. 1492, and was buried in Lewes Priory, Sussex. "Dame Elizabeth Nevile, lady of Bergevenne, of Chartham, Kent" died testate in 1500 (P.C.C., 8 Moore), and was buried in St. Martin's Outwich.

C.P. 1:30-31 (1910). *Paget* (1957) 410:2-4. *Paget* (1977), pp. 121,400.

Children of George Neville, by Margaret Fenne:

   i. **GEORGE NEVILLE**, Lord Bergavenny, married **MARY STAFFORD** [see SAINT LEGER 4].[1]
   ii. **EDWARD NEVILLE**, Knt., third son [see next].
   iii. **JANE NEVILLE**, married **HENRY POLE**, Lord Montagu [see SOMERSET 6].[2]
   iv. **ELIZABETH NEVILLE**, married **THOMAS BERKELEY** [see FISHER 5].[3]

4. **EDWARD NEVILLE**, Knt., of Aldington Park, Kent, third son, was Esquire of the King's Body, and was present at the Field of the Cloth of Gold in 1520. He was married to **ELEANOR WINDSOR**, widow of Ralph Scrope, Lord Scrope of Upsall, and daughter of Andrews Windsor, Lord Windsor (**descendant of King Edward I**), by Elizabeth (**descendant of King Henry III**), daughter of William Blount [see LUDLOW 5 for her ancestry]. They had two sons and five daughters. SIR EDWARD NEVILLE was implicated in the plot of his brother-in-law Henry Pole, Lord Montagu, tried at Westminster, and beheaded on 8 Dec. 1538.

H.S.P. 74:14 (1923) (1530 Vis. Kent). *Paget* (1957) 410:2-4.

3. **KATHERINE NEVILLE**, was married to **CLEMENT THROCKMORTON**, Esq., of Haseley, co. Warwick, M.P. for Warwickshire, third son of George Throckmorton, Knt., of Coughton, co. Warwick, by Katherine (**descendant of King Edward I**), daughter of Nicholas Vaux, Knt., of Harrowden, co. Northampton [see BULL 7.ii for his ancestry]. CLEMENT THROCKMORTON, ESQ., died on 14 Dec. 1573, buried at St. Mary's, Haseley, with inscription: "Here lieth the bodye of Cleme(nt) Throckmorton Esquire the thirde son of Sr. George Throkmorton Knyght and Katherine Nevell his wyffe the first and eldest daughter of Sr. Edward Nevell Knyght of whom he begat syxe Sonnes & seven Daughters".

H.S.P. 5:120 (1871) (1566 Vis. Oxon). *H.S.P.* 12:87-89,207 (1877) (1619 Vis. Warwick)

---

[1] Ancestors of **St.Leger Codd, Edward Digges, Warham Horsmanden, Katherine Saint Leger**.

[2] Ancestors of **Maria Johanna Somerset**.

[3] Ancestors of **John Fisher**.

OXENBRIDGE (cont.)

(Throckmorton arms: *Gules*, on a chevron *argent* three bars gemelles *sable*). *H.S.P.* 43:214 (1899). *H.S.P.* 74:14 (1923) (1530 Vis. Kent). *Throckmorton* (1930), pp. 164-169 (younger son Kellemn Throckmorton "accompanied the first expedition to Virginia in 1607. He was one of the original company. Died at Jamestown, 26th of August, 1607"). *H.S.P.* 87:84-85 (1935) (1681 Vis. Northants). *NEHGR* 108:178 (July 1954). *Paget* (1957) 410:3.

2. KATHERINE THROCKMORTON, was married, as his third wife, to **THOMAS HARBY**, Esq., of Adston, co. Northampton, son of William Harby, of Ashby, by Emma, daughter of William Wilmore, of Ashby. He had been married previously for the first time to Alice Fox, daughter of John Fox, of Bearfords, co. Oxford (with one daughter), and for the second time to Margaret Malyn, widow of John Marsh, and daughter of _____ Malyn, of London. Thomas & Katherine had three sons and five daughters. The will of THOMAS HARBY, ESQ., was dated 1572. She was married for the second time to **GEORGE DRYDEN** (brother to Erasmus Dryden, Knt., Bart.), and for the third time to **JOHN WILMER**, of Shrowley.

H.S.P. 12:207 (1877). *Throckmorton* (1930), p. 166 (Harby arms: *Gules*, a fess dancettee ermine, between ten billets) (citing Brydges, History of Northamptonshire). *H.S.P.* 87:84 (1935) (1681 Vis. Northants). *NEHGR* 108:178 (July 1954).

1. KATHERINE HARBY, was married for the first time to **DANIEL OXENBRIDGE**, "Dr. of Phisick," of Daventry, co. Northampton, son of Rev. John Oxenbridge, scholar and divine. DR. DANIEL OXENBRIDGE died testate on 24 Aug. 1642.

Throckmorton (1930), p. 166. *H.S.P.* 87:85 (1935). *NEHGR* 108:176-178. *NEHGR* 112:169 (July 1958) (Oxenbridge arms: Gules a lion silver in a border vert charged with scallops (gold or silver)). *TAG* 31:60-61 (1960).

Child & grandchildren of Daniel Oxenbridge, by Katherine Harby:

i. **REV. JOHN OXENBRIDGE**, born Davenport, co. Northampton, 30 Jan. 1608/9, B.A., M.A. Oxford University, resided Bermuda 1635-41, Fellow of Eton College 1652, Vice-Provost of Eton 1659, ejected for Puritanism 1660, settled in Surinam 1662, removed to Barbados and then to Boston, Massachusetts, becoming pastor of the First Church, Boston, died at Boston 28 Dec. 1674; married, first, JANE BUTLER, died 22 Apr. 1655, second, 1656, **FRANCES WOODWARD**, died July 1659, third, **MARY HACKSHAW**, fourth, **SUSANNA** _____.

   a. BATHSHUA OXENBRIDGE, daughter by first marriage, married RICHARD SCOTT, of Jamaica, West Indies. Descendants in England.

   b. THEODORA OXENBRIDGE, daughter by second marriage, married 21 Nov. 1677 REV. PETER THACHER, of Milton, Massachusetts.

* * *

PALGRAVE

EDWARD I OF ENGLAND, King of England, married ALIANORE DE CASTILLE.
JOAN OF ENGLAND [*of Acre*], married GILBERT DE CLARE, Earl of Gloucester.
ALIANOR DE CLARE, married HUGH LE DESPENSER, 2nd Lord Despenser.
EDWARD LE DESPENSER, Knt., married ANNE DE FERRERS.
EDWARD LE DESPENSER, 4th Lord le Despenser, married ELIZABETH DE BURGHERSH.
ANNE LE DESPENSER, married HUGH HASTINGS, Knt.
MARGARET HASTINGS, married JOHN WINGFIELD, Knt.
ROBERT WINGFIELD, Knt.,married ELIZABETH RUSSELL.
ROBERT WINGFIELD, Knt., married ELIZABETH GOUSHILL [see LETHERINGHAM 7].

5. ELIZABETH WINGFIELD, was married before 1462 to **WILLIAM BRANDON**, Knt., of Soham, Suffolk, son, perhaps, of Robert Brandon, Collector of Customs at

King's Lynn and Great Yarmouth, Norfolk. He was born about 1425, and rose in the service of John de Mowbray, Duke of Norfolk. They had four sons and five daughters. He was Escheator for Norfolk and Suffolk in 1454/5, Marshall of the Marchelsea, Marshall of the King's Bench, M.P. for Shoreham, Sussex, in 1467/8, and for Suffolk 1478. When Richard III usurped the throne he joined the uprising in the west, losing his eldest son (father of Charles, the future Duke of Suffolk) at Bosworth. William sought sanctuary at Westminster and was pardoned. The second will of "sir Willyam Brandon, knt." was dated 9 Apr. 1491, and proved 17 Nov. 1491 (P.C.C., 46 Milles, 7 Dogett). She died testate on 28 Apr. 1497 (will, P.C.C., 9 Horne, named, among others, her daughter Eleanor Glemham).

Sur.Soc. 144:120-122 (1930) (1480 Vis. North) (pedigree from Robert Wingfield senior to Anne wife of Henry Palgrave). *TAG* 25:26 (Jan. 1948). *NEHGR* 102:95 (Apr. 1948) (descent of Richard Palgrave from King Henry III). *NEHGR* 103:102-107 (Apr. 1949). *H.S.P.* 111:217 (1984) (1561 Vis. Suffolk). Paget (1977), p. 401.

4. **ELEANOR BRANDON**, was married, as his second wife, to **JOHN GLEMHAM**, Esq., of Glemham, Suffolk, son of John Glemham, of Glemham, by Katherine, daughter of Henry Rochford, Knt., of Kent. He had been previously married, with issue, to ANNE ____ (died 5 Mar. 1466). John and Eleanor had three sons and two daughters. She died on 30 June 1480 according to the Little Glemham Church brass, but the wording of her mother's will suggests that she was alive in the 1490s. The will of JOHN GLEMHAM, ESQ., was proved in 1499 (brass of John Glemham and his two wives in Little Glemham Church) (Eleanor was aunt of Charles Brandon, Duke of Suffolk).

TAG 25:26 (Jan. 1948). *NEHGR* 103:102-107 (Apr. 1949). *H.S.P.* 111:243 (1984) (1561 Vis. Suffolk).

3. **ANNE GLEMHAM**, was married to **HENRY PALGRAVE**, Esq., of Little Palgrave, Northwood Barningham and Thruxton, Norfolk, son of John Palgrave, Esq., of Little Palgrave, by his wife Margaret, daughter of William Yelverton, Knt., of Rougham, co. Norfolk, Judge of King's Bench. He was born about 1470. They had five sons and seven daughters. HENRY PALGRAVE, ESQ., died testate on 20 Oct. 1516. They were buried at Northwood Barningham Church (M.I.).

H.S.P. 32:212 (1891) (Vis. Norfolk). *Norf.Arch.Soc.* 2:24 (1895) (1563 Vis. Norf.). *Palgrave* (1878), pp. 16-17,27-29. *TAG* 25:26 (Jan. 1948). *NEHGR* 102:95 (Apr. 1948). *NEHGR* 103:102-107 (Apr. 1949). *H.S.P.* 111:244 (1984).

2. **THOMAS PALGRAVE**, Gent., of Thruxton, Norfolk, was born about 1505/10, and received the manor of Thruxton from his father or brother. He was married to **ALICE GUNTON**, daughter of Robert Gunton, Gent., of Thruxton. They had four sons and three daughters.

Palgrave (1878), p. 30. *H.S.P.* 32:212-213 (1891). *Norf.Arch.Soc.* 2:25,28 (1895). *TAG* 25:26 (Jan. 1948). *NEHGR* 102:95 (Apr. 1948).

1. **REV. EDWARD PALGRAVE**, was baptised at Thruxton, Norfolk, on 21 Jan. 1540/1. He was Rector of Barnham Broom, Norfolk, from 1567. He was married about 1571 to an unidentified wife. REV. EDWARD PALGRAVE died testate in December 1623.

Palgrave (1878), pp. 30,32,140 (his will, to be buried in chancel at Barnham Broom). *Norf.Arch.Soc.* 2:28,30 (1895) (son "Richard Palgrave, living 3 Dec., 1623"). *TAG* 18:206-209 (Dr. Richard of Wymondham perhaps same as Dr. Richard of Charlestown). *NEHGR* 102:96-97 (ancestry of Richard Palgrave and statement that he was a descendant of King Edward I). *TAG* 25:24-26 (Jan. 1948) (descent of Richard Palgrave from King Edward I). *NEHGR* 102:96-98 (Palgrave arms: *Azure*, a lion rampant, *argent*). *NEHGR* 107:269 (Oct. 1953) (Palgrave arms).

Children & grandchildren of Edward Palgrave:

PALGRAVE (cont.)

i. REV. EDWARD PALGRAVE, son and heir, born 1572, Rector of Litham, co. Norfolk, buried 9 Dec. 1641; married, first, ELIZABETH _____, buried 6 July 1631, second, MARTHA LYNFORD. Four children by second marriage.

ii. _____ PALGRAVE, born about 1574, married JOHN ABELL.

iii. GREGORY PALGRAVE, born 1576, matriculated Caius College, Cambridge University, drowned in the Cam, buried St. Michael's church, Cambridge, 19 Aug. 1590.

iv. _____ PALGRAVE, born about 1580, married RICHARD RUSSELL.

v. DR. RICHARD PALGRAVE, born about 1585, physician at Wymondham, Norfolk, emigrated with wife and three older daughters in the Winthrop Fleet in April or May 1630, a proprietor at Charlestown in 1630, freeman 18 May 1631, died testate October 1651; married ANNA _____, returned to England, probably to be near her two married daughters, residing at Stepney on 17 Mar. 1655/6, subsequently returned to reside at Roxbury, Massachusetts, died there testate 17 Feb. 1668/9.

　a. MARY PALGRAVE, born about 1619, married ROGER WELLINGTON of Watertown. Six children.

　b. SARAH PALGRAVE, born about 1620/1; married DR. JOHN ALCOCK, of Roxbury, Massachusetts. Nine children.

　c. BENJAMIN PALGRAVE, baptised Wymondham 19 Dec. 1622, buried 22 Feb. 1622/3.

　d. ELIZABETH PALGRAVE, baptised Wymondham 10 Apr. 1626, married JOHN EDWARDS. Two children.

　e. HANNAH PALGRAVE, baptised Barnham Broom 28 Sep. 1628, probably died young.

　f. REBECCA PALGRAVE, born Boston 25 (5) 1631, unmarried in 1651.

　g. JOHN PALGRAVE, born 6 1st mo. 1633/4, married MARY MAVERICK. One daughter died *s.p.*

　h. LYDIA PALGRAVE, born 15 (11) 1635/6, married EDMUND HEYLETT, merchant of Deptford, co. Kent, merchant. At least one son.

　i. BETHIA PALGRAVE, baptized Boston 8 July 1638, died 21 Aug. 1638.

* * *

PARR see BULL

PASHLEY see FLEETE

* * *

PAULET

EDWARD I OF ENGLAND, King of England, married ALIANORE DE CASTILLE.
JOAN OF ENGLAND [*of Acre*], married GILBERT DE CLARE, Earl of Gloucester.
ELIZABETH DE CLARE, married THEOBALD DE VERDUN, Lord Verdun.
ISABEL DE VERDUN, married HENRY DE FERRERS, 2nd Lord Ferrers of Groby.
WILLIAM DE FERRERS, 3rd Lord Ferrers of Groby, married MARGARET DE UFFORD.
HENRY DE FERRERS, 4th Lord Ferrers of Groby, married JOAN DE HOO.
WILLIAM DE FERRERS, 5th Lord Ferrers of Groby, married PHILIPPE DE CLIFFORD.
HENRY FERRERS, Knt., married ISABEL MOWBRAY.
ELIZABETH FERRERS, married EDWARD GREY, Lord Ferrers of Groby.

PAULET (cont.)

JOHN GREY, Knt., married ELIZABETH WYDEVILLE.
THOMAS GREY, Marquess of Dorset, married CECILY BONVILLE [see GREY 5].

6. DOROTHY GREY, was married for the first time to **ROBERT WILLOUGHBY**, Knt., K.B., 2nd Lord Willoughby de Broke, Lord Latimer *de jure*, son and heir of Robert Willoughby, 9th Lord Latimer *de jure* (of **Magna Charta Surety descent** and **descendant of Charlemagne**), by Blanche, daughter and co-heiress of John Champernoun, of Beer Ferrers, co. Devon (**descendant of Charlemagne**). He was born in 1472 (aged thirty and more at his father's *Inq.p.m.*). He was summoned to Parliament from 28 Nov. 1511 by writs directed *Roberto Willoughby de Brooke*, but sat in Parliament as Lord Broke, presumably so as to avoid confusion with his cousin, Lord Willoughby. He had been married previously, before 28 Feb. 1494/5, to Elizabeth Beauchamp, first daughter and co-heiress of Richard Beauchamp, 2nd Lord Beauchamp of Powick, by Elizabeth, daughter of Humphrey Stafford, Knt. She died on 10 Aug. 1503 [see BOSVILE 4 for descendants of their son Edward]. After the death of his son Edward in 1517 he settled the bulk of his family estates (including the manor of Brook) in Wiltshire, Dorset, Devon, etc., on his daughters of his second marriage). ROBERT WILLOUGHBY, Lord Willoughby, died testate aged about forty-nine "of a pestilential air", probably *s.p.m.s.*, on 10 Nov. 1521 at Bere Ferrers, and was buried in the church there. She was married for the second time before 29 July 1523, as his fourth wife, to WILLIAM BLOUNT, 4th Lord Mountjoy (died 8 Nov. 1534). "Lady Dorothy Mountjoy, formerly lady Willoughby de Broke" died testate (P.C.C., 20 Tashe) between 30 Aug. and 17 Nov. 1553.
    C.P. 12(2) 686-688, chart betw. 671-672 (1959).

5. ELIZABETH WILLOUGHBY, daughter and co-heiress, was married before 20 Oct. 1528 to **JOHN PAULET**, Knt., 2nd Marquess of Winchester, etc., son and heir of William Paulet, of Basing, co. Hants, by Elizabeth (of **Magna Charta Surety descent and descendant of Charlemagne**), daughter of William Capel, Knt. He was born about 1510. She presumably died before 4 Apr. 1552. He was married for the second time, between 10 Mar. and 24 Apr. 1554, to Elizabeth Seymour, widow, successively, of Sir Anthony Ughtred, and Gregory Cromwell, 1st Baron of Cromwell (died 4 July 1551), and sister of Jane, Queen Consort to Henry VIII, and of the Protector Edward Seymour, 1st Duke of Somerset, and daughter of Sir John Seymour, of Wolf Hall, co. Wilts, by Margery, daughter of Henry Wentworth, Knt., K.B., 4th Lord le Despenser, of Nettlestead, Suffolk (descendant of King Edward III). She probably died before 9 June 1563, and was buried at Basing [see WINGFIELD 5]. He was married for the third time, before 30 Sep. 1568, to Winifred Bruges, widow of Richard Sackville, Knt. (died 21 Apr. 1566), and daughter of John Bruges, or Brydges, Knt., sometime Lord Mayor of London, by Agnes, daughter of Thomas Ayloffe, of Bretons, Essex. "Sir John Powlett, Knt., Earl of Wilts, and Marquess of Winchester" died testate (P.C.C., 48 Daughtry) at Chelsea on 4 Nov. 1576, and was buried at Basing (will dated 6 to 8 June 1576, proved 3 Dec. 1577). His widow, by whom he had no issue, died testate on or shortly after 16 June 1586 at Chelsea and was buried in Westminster Abbey (M.I.).
    Gen. (n.s.) 3:168 (1886) (1565 Vis. Dorset). *C.P.* 12(2):796 (1959).

    Child of John Paulet, by Elizabeth Willoughby:

    i. **MARY PAULET**, married **HENRY CROMWELL**, 3rd Lord Cromwell [see WINGFIELD 4].[1]

---

[1]Ancestors of **Thomas Wingfield**.

PELHAM

HENRY III OF ENGLAND, King of England, married ÉLÉONORE DE PROVENCE.
EDMUND OF LANCASTER, Earl of Lancaster, married BLANCHE D'ARTOIS.
HENRY OF LANCASTER, Earl of Lancaster, married MAUD DE CHAWORTH.
JOAN OF LANCASTER, married JOHN DE MOWBRAY, 3rd Lord Mowbray.
ALIANOR MOWBRAY, married ROGER LA WARRE, 3rd Lord La Warre.
JOAN LA WARRE, married THOMAS WEST, 1st Lord West.
REYNOLD WEST, 3rd Lord West, married MARGARET THORLEY.
RICHARD WEST, 4th Lord West, married KATHERINE HUNGERFORD.
THOMAS WEST, 5th Lord West, married ELEANOR COPLEY.
GEORGE WEST, Knt., married ELIZABETH MORTON.
WILLIAM WEST, 1st Lord de la Warre, married ELIZABETH STRANGE.
THOMAS WEST, 2nd Lord de la Warre, married ANNE KNOLLYS [see HUMPHREY 3].

2. PENELOPE WEST, fourth daughter, was born on 9 Sep. 1582. She was married about 1599 to **HERBERT PELHAM** [the younger], Esq., of Hastings, Sussex, and Boston, co. Lincoln, son and heir of Herbert Pelham, the elder, of Fordingham, Dorset, and Hellingly, Sussex, by his first wife Catherine, daughter of John Thatcher. He was born about 1580, and was step-son of Penelope's older sister Elizabeth [see HUMPHREY 2]. On 6 Nov. 1598, described as "Herbert Pelham, son and heir apparent of Herbert Pelham of Mychelham, Sussex", he was registered as a student at Gray's Inn, London. PENELOPE WEST died about 1619 probably at or shortly after the birth of her last child who was named for her. He was married for the second time to Anne _____, and had four children. HERBERT PELHAM, ESQ., died intestate at Boston, co. Lincoln, seised of lands in Swineshead and Wigtoft, co. Lincoln, on 13 July 1624, and was buried in Rev. John Cotton's church. His widow was buried on 20 May 1637/8.

NEHGR 33:285-295 (July 1879). *H.S.P.* 51:767 (1903) (Maddison Linc. Ped.). *TAG* 16:128-132 (Jan. 1940). *TAG* 18:137-138 (Jan. 1942). *Adventurers* (1987), p. 655.

Children & grandchildren of Herbert Pelham [the younger], by Penelope West:

    i. **HERBERT PELHAM**, Esq., son and heir, born about 1600 [see next].

    ii. **WILLIAM PELHAM**, second son, sailed with the Winthrop Fleet in 1630, resided Sudbury, Massachusetts, until 1647, died in England after 8 Aug. 1667 *s.p.*

    iii. **MARGARET PELHAM**, eldest daughter, unmarried in 1647, believed to have been buried at the residence of her brother, Herbert at Bures, Suffolk, in 1661.

    iv. **JOHN PELHAM**, third son, born 1615, emigrated to New England in 1635, aged twenty.

    v. **ANTHONY PELHAM**, fourth son, baptised Boston, co. Lincoln, 24 May 1621.

    vi. **EDWARD PELHAM**, fifth son, apparently died in London, unmarried.

    vii. **THOMAS PELHAM**, apparently died young.

    viii. **KATHERINE PELHAM**, second daughter, born Dokenfield, Sussex, 22 Aug. 1606, died 19 Apr. 1659; married Compton, Dorset, 1631 REV. JAMES ASHTON, of Kilmersdon, Somerset. Five children, only survivor Catherine, wife of Thomas Shute, mother of Catherine, wife of Samuel Bennet, compiler in 1693 of the roll recording family information on their ancestry.

    ix. **HELENOR PELHAM**, third daughter, had "a black Pudding arm", died aged about nineteen.

    x. **PENELOPE PELHAM**, fourth daughter, born about 1619, emigrated aged sixteen in 1635, died 28 May 1702; married 9 Nov. 1641 **RICHARD BELLINGHAM**, Gent., born 1592, died 7 Dec. 1672, Governor of Massachusetts Bay Colony. No surviving issue.

1. HERBERT PELHAM, Esq., was born about 1600 (aged twenty-six at marriage). He was married for the first time, with licence dated 13 Oct. 1626, to **JEMIMA WALDEGRAVE**, second daughter and co-heiress of Thomas Waldegrave, Esq., of Ferriers Court in Bures-ad-montem, Essex, later of Bevers Hamlet, Essex, by Margaret, daughter and heiress of John Holmstead, Esq., of Halstead, Essex. She was born about 1606 (aged twenty at marriage). The first five children were baptised

PELHAM (cont).

at Bures in 1627, 1629, 1630 and 1633, and at St. Margaret's Westminster in 1629. As early as 1629 Herbert Pelham agreed to invest in the Winthrop project of colonization with his father-in-law, and invested some £3,000 in the venture. The two families embarked from Gravesend, but Thomas Waldegrave and his wife went ashore at Deal in Kent before leaving English waters because of her illness. Herbert Pelham appears to have sailed from Gravesend with his family sometime between September 1639 and December 1640, and his wife died during the crossing. Shortly after arrival in New England he was married for the second time to **ELIZABETH (BOSVILE) HARLAKENDEN**, widow, with two daughters, of Roger Harlakenden (died November 1638), and daughter of Geoffrey Bosvile, Esq., of Gunthwaite, co. York, by Margaret, daughter of Edward Greville, Knt., of Harold Park, Essex **(descendant of King Edward I)** [see BOSVILE 1 for her ancestry]. After marriage they lived in the Harlakenden household at Cambridge. He cleared large farms south of the river on Harlakenden property in Lexington and Bedford, and in Cambridge. At the request of Thomas Waldegrave, he returned to England in the winter of 1641 and, having come to an agreement concerning his first wife's property, returned to New England and took a prominent part in the affairs of the community. He was first Treasurer of Harvard College in 1643, and Commissioner of the United Colonies in 1645. He was active with the Society for Promoting and Propagating the Gospel in New England. He returned to England in the *Supply* on 9 Nov. 1646, and resided at Bures, Essex, on property inherited through his first wife. On 25 Aug. 1659 letters to administer the estate of ELIZABETH PELHAM, late of Ferriers, in Bures, Essex, were granted to her husband Herbert. HERBERT PELHAM, ESQ., was buried at Bures, Essex, on 1 July 1674. The will of "Herbert Pelham, of Ferrers, in Bewers Hamlet, in the County of Essex, Esquire", dated 1 Jan. 1672/3 and proved 30 Mar. 1676, distributed his estate to his children.

NEHGR 33:290-295 (July 1879) (he was not educated at Oxford, nor a lawyer). *H.S.P.* 51:768 (1903) (Maddison Linc. Ped.). *NEHGR* 82:154 (Apr. 1928) (Pelham arms: quartered. 1 & 4 Azure three pelicans silver vulning themselves proper. 2 & 3 Gules two pieces of belt issuing from the base palewise buckles upward silver). *TAG* 18:139-145 (Jan. 1942). Morant 1:182,417,436; 2:232,318,592.

Children of Herbert & Jemima (Waldegrave) Pelham:

  i. WALDEGRAVE PELHAM, baptised 26 Sep. 1627, resided in England; married ABIGAIL GLASCOCK. Nine children.

  ii. HERBERT PELHAM, baptised 5 Aug. 1629, buried St. Margaret's, Westminster 17 Aug. 1629.

  iii. JEMIMA PELHAM, baptised 14 June 1630, died 20 Aug. 1657, buried Bures; married 10 Feb. 1653/4 REV. SAMUEL KEM, Rector of Albury. Probably no issue.

  iv. NATHANIEL PELHAM, baptised 5 Feb. 1631/2, graduate Harvard College, lost at sea 1657 *s.p.*

  v. PENELOPE PELHAM, baptised 25 Apr. 1633, died 7 Dec. 1703, buried Marshfield, Massachusetts; married **JOSIAH WINSLOW**, Governor of Plymouth Colony. Issue.

  vi. KATHERINE PELHAM, youngest daughter, married _____ CLARKE.

Children of Herbert & Elizabeth (Bosvile) (Harlakenden) Pelham:

  vii. MARY PELHAM, born 12 Nov. 1640, died Essex *s.p.*

  viii. FRANCES PELHAM, born 9 Nov. 1643, married JEREMIAH STONNARD, resided Essex.

  ix. HERBERT PELHAM, born 3 Oct. 1645, buried 2 Jan. 1645/46.

  x. ANNE PELHAM, living 1673/4, living 1673, died Essex *s.p.*

  xi. **EDWARD PELHAM**, Gent., born about 1652, graduate Harvard College 1673, freeman Newport, Rhode Island, Captain of the Militia, died 20 Sep. 1730; married 18 Apr. 1682 **FREELOVE ARNOLD**, born 20 July 1661, died 8 Sep. 1711, daughter of Gov. Benedict Arnold of Rhode Island. Four children.

PELHAM (cont).

xii. WILLIAM PELHAM, died *s.p.*
xiii. HENRY PELHAM, buried Bures, Essex, married ELIZABETH _____. Descendants in England.

* * *

PELHAM see also HUMPHREY

* * *

PERCY

HENRY III OF ENGLAND, King of England, married ÉLÉONORE DE PROVENCE.
EDMUND OF LANCASTER, Earl of Lancaster, married BLANCHE D'ARTOIS.
HENRY OF LANCASTER, married MAUD DE CHAWORTH [see LANCASTER 13].

11. MARY OF LANCASTER, was born in 1320 (aged fourteen at marriage). She was married at Tutbury Castle in or before September 1334 to HENRY DE PERCY, 3rd Lord Percy, son and heir of Henry de Percy, 2nd Lord Percy, **Baron** of Topcliffe, co. York, **Baron** of Alnwick, Northumberland (**descendant of Charlemagne**), by Idoine (of **Magna Charta Surety descent** and **descendant of Charlemagne**), daughter of Robert de Clifford, 1st Lord Clifford, of Appleby, Westmorland. He was born at Seamer, North Riding, co. York, in 1320 (aged thirty and more at his father's death). They had two sons and one daughter. In March 1343/4, as Henry de Percy *le fitz*, he was going abroad with the Earl of Arundel in the King's service. He fought at Crécy on 26 Aug. 1346. MARY OF LANCASTER died 1 Sep. 1362, and was buried at Alnwick, Northumberland. He was married for the second time in or before May 1365 to Joan Orreby, daughter and heiress of John, Lord Orreby, by his wife Margaret. HENRY DE PERCY, Lord Percy, died about 18 May 1368, and was buried at Alnwick. His widow was married for the second time to Constantine Clifton, Knt. She died at the end of July 1369.

Clay (1913), pp. 161-2. *C.P.* 10:462-463 (1945).

9. HENRY DE PERCY, Knt., K.G., 4th Lord Percy, son and heir by first marriage, was born on 10 Nov. 1341. He was brought up in the King's court by his uncle, the 1st Duke of Lancaster. He was summoned to Parliament on 1 Dec. 1376, and was created **Earl of Northumberland** on 16 July 1377. He was married for the first time at Brancepeth on 12 July 1358 to MARGARET DE NEVILLE, widow of William de Ros, 3rd Lord Ros of Helmsley, co. York (died before 3 Dec. 1352 *s.p.*), and daughter of Ralph de Neville, 4th Lord Neville of Raby, Durham (of **Magna Charta Surety descent** and **descendant of Charlemagne**), by Alice (**descendant of Charlemagne**), daughter of Hugh de Audley, of Stratton Audley, co. Oxford, Lord Audley. They had four sons and one daughter. She died in May 1372. He was married for the second time on or before 15 Dec. 1381 to MAUD DE LUCY, widow of Gilbert de Umfreville, Earl of Angus (died 1381), and daughter of Thomas de Lucy, of Egremont, by Margaret, daughter of Thomas de Multon. She died on 18 Dec. 1398 *s.p.s.* For nearly twenty years various causes of discontent had been

PERCY (cont.)

gradually estranging Henry from King Richard II, and he played a prominent part in procuring Richard's abdication (and probably his subsequent death) and the elevation of King Henry IV. The Earl and his son together defeated the Scots at Homildon Hill, near Wooler, on 14 Sep. 1402. Because of their grievances, they joined the rising in favour of the Earl of March. In 1405 he was involved in treasonable plots, and was attainted in Parliament in 1406. SIR HENRY DE PERCY was slain on 19 Feb. 1407/8 when his force was defeated at Bramham Moor, near Tadcaster, co. York.

    Clay (1913), p. 162. *C.P.* 9:708-712 (1936).

    Child of Henry de Percy, by Margaret de Neville:

      i. **HENRY PERCY** [*Harry Hotspur*], married **ELIZABETH MORTIMER** [see KEMPE 10].[1]

* * *

PEYTON

    EDWARD III OF ENGLAND, King of England, married **PHILIPPE DE HAINAUT**.
    LIONEL OF CLARENCE [*of Antwerp*], Duke of Clarence, married **ELIZABETH DE BURGH**.
    PHILIPPE OF CLARENCE, married **EDMUND DE MORTIMER**, 3rd Earl of March.
    ELIZABETH MORTIMER, married **HENRY PERCY**, Knt.
    ELIZABETH PERCY, married **JOHN DE CLIFFORD**, 7th Lord Clifford.
    THOMAS DE CLIFFORD, 8th Lord Clifford, married **JOAN DACRE**.
    ELIZABETH CLIFFORD, married **WILLIAM PLUMPTON**, Knt.
    ELIZABETH PLUMPTON, married **JOHN SOTEHILL**, Esq.
    HENRY SOTEHILL, Esq., married **JOAN EMPSON**.
    ELIZABETH SOTEHILL, married **WILLIAM DRURY**, Knt. [see DRURY 5].

4. **BRIDGET DRURY**, was born on 11 Sep. 1534. She was married to **HENRY YELVERTON**, Esq., of Rougham, Norfolk, son of William Yelverton, of Rougham, by his wife Margaret Garnon. He was born about 1527 (aged fifty-nine 28 Eliz.). They had four sons and two daughters. "Henry Yelverton, esquier, Roughame, Norfolk" died testate (P.C.C., 48 Woodhall) on 26 Apr. 1601.

    Norf.Arch.Soc. 1:267 (1878) (1563 Vis. Norf.). *H.S.P.* 32:328-329 (1891) (Vis. Norfolk) (mother of Henry Yelverton identified as "Ann da. to Sir Henry Fermoure of Est Basame in co. Norf, knt."). *Norf.Arch.Soc.* 2:219 (1895).

3. **WILLIAM YELVERTON**, Knt., of Bayfield, Norfolk, son and heir, was born about 1558 (aged forty-three 12 Eliz.). He was married, with marriage settlement dated 12 Mar. 1587, to **DIONYSIA STUBBS**, eldest daughter of Richard Stubbs of Sedgeford, Norfolk. They had two sons and three daughters. He was created a **Baronet** in 1620. WILLIAM YELVERTON, BART., died on 30 Oct. 1631.

    Norf.Arch.Soc. 1:267 (1878).

2. **WILLIAM YELVERTON**, Knt., Second Baronet, was born about 1606 (aged thirty

---

    [1]Ancestors of **St. Leger Codd, Humphrey Davie, Edward Digges, William Farrar, John Harleston, Warham Horsmanden, Edmund Kempe, Agnes Mackworth, Anne Mauleverer, John Nelson, George Reade, William Rodney, Katherine Saint Leger, Richard Saltonstall, William Skepper, Thomas Wingfield**, and, probably, **Jane Haviland**.

PEYTON (cont.)

in 12 Car. 1). He was married, with marriage settlement dated 12 June 1614, to **URSULA RICHARDSON**, eldest daughter of Thomas Richardson, Knt., K.B., Lord Chief Justice. They had one son and two daughters. SIR WILLIAM YELVERTON, Bart., died on 19 July 1648. His widow died on 20 Mar. 1657.

Norf.Arch.Soc. 1:267-268 (1878).

1. **ELIZABETH YELVERTON**, was married to **THOMAS PEYTON**, Esq., of Rougham, Norfolk, younger son, of Edward Peyton, Knt., Bart. **(descendant of King Edward I)**, by Jane, daughter of James Calthorpe, Knt., of Calthorpe, Norfolk [see HASILDEN 2 for his ancestry]. He was baptised on 29 Mar. 1617. They had four sons. She died testate (P.C.C., 26 Penn) on 15 June 1668, and was buried at Rougham. THOMAS PEYTON, ESQ., died on 12 Oct. 1683.

Wotton (1741) 1:32 ("2. [son] Robert, of Virginia, who left no male issue"). *Her. & Gen.* 6:63-74 (1871). *Chester of Chicheley* (1878), pp. 239-240. *Peytons of Virginia* (1976), p. 63 (he married second "the widow Hacon").

Children and grandchildren of Thomas Peyton, by Elizabeth Yelverton:

    i. WILLIAM PEYTON, resided Dublin, died 1686 *s.p.*; married about 1656 FRANCES LUNSFORD.

    ii. BENJAMIN PEYTON, died 1637, aged thirteen weeks.

    iii. **MAJ. ROBERT PEYTON**, born about 1640, emigrated to Virginia before 1679, probably 1663, attorney, resided "Iselham", Gloucester County, Virginia, died 15 Mar. 1686; married **MARY ( ) KEEBLE**, widow of George Keeble, born 3 June 1637, died 28 June 1679.

        a. ELIZABETH PEYTON, born about 1670, married **COL. PETER BEVERLEY**. Three daughters.

        b. THOMAS PEYTON, born about 1675, died October 1738; married **FRANCES TABB**. Four children.

        c. ROBERT PEYTON, born about 1677/80, died North Carolina before 1746; married **MARY _____**. Seven children.

    iv. CHARLES PEYTON, of Grimston, Norfolk, baptised Martins-in-the-Fields, London, 16 Feb. 1648/9, died before 1721, buried Swannington, Norfolk, married ELIZABETH BLADWELL. Six sons in England including Captain Yelverton Peyton, R.N., who assumed the Baronetcy in 1721 "to the exclusion of his uncle Robert's five sons, and this usurpation was continued until the male line of Yelverton's descendants died out in 1815.

    v. YELVERTON PEYTON, "baptised at Mr. Peyton's house in Cambridge" 24 Dec. 1650, matriculated Gray's Inn, 1672, married _____ ROBERTS.

    vi. HANNAH PEYTON.

    vii. ANN PEYTON, married THOMAS WOOD.

    viii. THOMAS PEYTON, married _____ ROBERTS.

    ix. BENJAMIN PEYTON.

* * *

PEYTON see also HASILDEN

* * *

18. GEOFFROI (or **GEOFFREY**) **PLANTAGENET D'ANJOU** *le Bel* [the Fair], Comte d'Anjou (1129), Duc de Normandie (1144), son of Foulques V d'Anjou, Comte d'Anjou (**descendant of Charlemagne**), by Eremburge, Comtesse Héritière du Maine, daughter and heiress of Hélie de Baugency, Comte du Maine (**descendant of Charlemagne**), was born on 24 Nov. 1113. He was married on 22 May 1127 to **MAUD OF ENGLAND** [*the Empress Maud*], childless widow of Heinrich V Deutscher König, Römischer Kaiser (died 23 May 1125), and daughter of Henry I King of England (**descendant of Charlemagne**), by Maud (**descendant of Charlemagne**), daughter of Malcolm III, King of Scots. She was born on 7 Feb. 1102. They had three children. On Henry's death in 1135, he claimed the duchy of Normandie, conquering it in 1144. He held the duchy, with that of Anjou, until granting them to his son Henry. GEOFFROI D'ANJOU died at Le Mans, Maine, on 7 Sep. 1151. His widow died on 10 Sep. 1167.

Paget (1977), p. 14. *Schwennicke* (1984) 2:81.

17. HENRY II OF ENGLAND *Curtmantle* [or HENRY FITZ EMPRESS], King of England, was born at Le Mans on 5 Mar. 1132/3. He became Duc de Normandie et du Maine, and Comte d'Anjou by inheritance from his mother and father. He was married at Bordeaux on 18 May 1152 to **ÉLÉONORE D'AQUITAINE**, the divorced wife, with two daughters, of Louis VII, Roi de France (**descendant of Charlemagne**), and daughter and heiress of Guillaume X, Duc d'Aquitaine et Comte de Poitou, by Éléonore, daughter of Aumary I, Vicomte de Châtellerault. She was born about 1122. Their children were born in Normandy in 1153, at Bermondsey in 1155, in London in 1156, at Oxford in 1157, at Damfront in 1162, at Angers in 1165, and at Oxford in 1167. By his marriage Henry acquired the duchy of Aquitaine together with Gascony, Poitou and Auvergne. By the Treaty of Winchester in 1153 Henry was recognised as King Stephen's heir. He reached England on 8 Dec. 1154, and crowned **King of England** on 19 Dec. 1154, with direct rule over England and southern Wales, and a claim to the overlordship of northern Wales. His domain of England, Wales, and the French lands acquired from inheritance and marriage (ruled as separate components), was termed the "Angevin empire" (as his father was Comte d'Anjou). The overlord of his French lands, the king of France, had direct control of a much smaller domain than Henry himself. In 1171 Henry annexed Ireland though controlling the eastern part only. He had little difficulty in curbing the disorder of Stephen's reign and restoring the royal authority. He encouraged the development of juries of presentment of local men in the investigation of crimes, and trial of those accused by royal justices. His writs to sheriffs improved the disposition of claims over possession of property and benefices thereby discouraging local self-help of violent ejection and usurpation. By relying on financial and legal experts and a permanent court at Westminster he fostered the establishment of those two professions and the replacement of Roman law by English common law. Henry's reassertion of the king's rights over the church, in particular that clerics were subject to his courts and not solely to ecclesiastical courts, led to the quarrel with his former chancellor Thomas Becket, who, as Archbishop of Canterbury, was murdered in his cathedral at Henry's instigation in 1170. Henry spent much of his reign in France, upholding his authority in his numerous lordships and attempting to extend his rule. There he encountered the hostility of the French kings, who encouraged the grievances of his quarrelsome sons. HENRY II OF ENGLAND, King of England,

PLANTAGENET (cont.)

died at Chinon in Normandy on 8 July 1189 in the midst of a rebellion by his sons. His widow died at Fontévrault on 31 Mar. 1204. They were buried at Fontévrault Abbey in Anjou, where their tomb effigies may be seen.

Powicke (1961), pp. 32-33 (he died 6 July 1189, she died 1 Apr. 1204). DNB 26:1; 17:175. *Paget* (1977), pp. 14-15.

Children & grandchildren of Henry II of England, by Éléonore d'Aquitaine:

 i. WILLIAM OF ENGLAND, born 17 Aug. 1153, died at Wallingford Castle 1156.

 ii. HENRY OF ENGLAND, born 28 Feb. 1155, Duc de Normandie, Comte d'Anjou et du Maine, crowned joint King of England 14 June 1170, died at Martel 11 June 1183 *s.p., v.p.*; married 2 Nov. 1160 MARGUERITE DE FRANCE, daughter of Louis VII, Roi de France, by Constance, daughter of Alfonso VIII, Rey de Castilla. No children.

 iii. MAUD OF ENGLAND, born 1156, died 28 June 1189, buried Cathedral of St. Blasius, Brunswick; married 1168 HEINRICH VON SACHSEN, Herzog von Bayern und Sachsen *der Löwe* [the Lion].

 iv. RICHARD OF ENGLAND *Coeur de Lion*, third but eldest surviving son, born 8 Sep. 1157, Duc d'Aquitaine, Comte de Poitou; succeeded father as **King of England** (and the French lands) and was crowned 3 Sep. 1189; immediately set about organising an army to join the French and Germans on the Third Crusade, whose aim was to recover Jerusalem, captured from the westerners by the Muslims in 1187, to the shame of western Christendom. Richard left England on 12 Dec. 1189; secured Acre and Jaffa and defeated the Muslims in the battle of Arsuf, but his forces were not sufficiently strong to gain Jerusalem. He had to be content with making a truce with the Islamic leader Saladin, who much admired him. On Richard's journey home he was imprisoned in Germany; he was released in 1194 on payment of a huge ransom; returned to England on 13 Mar. 1194. His brother John had stirred up tensions in England by challenging the rule of his deputy (justiciar) there. His overlord in France, Philippe Augustus, encouraged dissidents there. But after his return Richard turned his formidable military talent to wage war against the French king. In 1199, during a minor siege at Chalus in Aquitaine, Richard was fatally injured by a crossbow bolt; died 6 Apr. 1199 *s.p.*, buried with his parents at Fontévrault Abbey; married at Lemesos, Cyprus, 12 May 1191 BERENGARIA DE NAVARRE, born about 1163, died at Espans Abbey, near Le Mans, about 1230, buried there, daughter of Sancho VI, Roi de Navarre, by Sanchia, daughter of Alfonso VII, Rey de Castilla. *Powicke* (1961), p. 33. *Paget* (1977), p. 15.

 v. GEOFFREY OF ENGLAND, fourth son, born 23 Sep. 1158, Duc de Bretagne and Earl of Richmond *jure uxoris*; killed in a tournament at Paris on 19 Aug. 1186, buried in the quire of Notre Dame Cathedral there; married July 1181 CONSTANCE DE BRETAGNE, daughter and heiress of Conan IV *le Petit*, Duc de Bretagne, Earl of Richmond, by Margaret, daughter of Henry of Scotland, Earl of Northumberland.

  a. ARTHUR OF ENGLAND, Duc de Bretagne, only son and heir, born 29 Mar. 1187 at Nantes, captured by King John in 1202, murdered, about 3 Apr. 1203, probably at Rouen, said to have been buried at Notre Dame des Prés.

  b. ALIANOR OF ENGLAND *la Brette* [the Damsel of Brittany], only sister of the whole blood and heiress, born 1184, imprisoned by King John, remained in prison under King Henry III, died 10 Aug. 1241, unmarried, probably in Corfe Castle, buried, eventually at the convent of Amesbury, co. Wiltshire.

 vi. ALIANOR OF ENGLAND, born 13 Oct. 1162, died at Burgos 31 Oct. 1214; married ALFONSO VIII, Rey de Castilla.

 vii. JOAN OF ENGLAND, born October 1165, died 4 Sep. 1199; married, first, 13 Feb. 1177, WILLIAM II, King of Sicily, second, October 1196, RAYMOND VI, Comte de Toulouse.

 viii. **JOHN OF ENGLAND**, born 24 Dec. 1167 [see next].

16. JOHN OF ENGLAND [*Lackland*], brother and heir, youngest son, was born at Oxford on 24 Dec. 1167. His father's attempt to provide territory in France for him provoked rebellion by his older brothers. His father granted him the lordship of Ireland in 1177, and arranged his succession to the earldom of Gloucester. His father's continued favour to him contributed to the rebellion of John's older brother

PLANTAGENET (cont.)

Richard I, though at the end of Henry's reign John deserted his father to support Richard who, on accession as king in 1189, made John Comte de Mortagne in Normandy. John was married for the first time at Marlebridge on 29 Aug. 1189 to ISABEL OF GLOUCESTER, Countess of Gloucester, youngest daughter and co-heiress of William FitzRobert, Earl of Gloucester, by Hawise, daughter of Robert de Beaumont, 2nd Earl of Leicester. Henry had arranged the marriage before his death, but it was delayed because Baldwin, Archbishop of Canterbury, had forbidden it on account of consanguinity (they were both great-grandchildren of King Henry I). On appeal to Rome the papal legate in England annulled the Archbishop's interdict. John became Earl of Gloucester *jure uxoris*. Richard, who was childless, acknowledged that his successor as King of England was his and John's nephew, Arthur, son of their deceased brother Geoffrey. While Richard was on crusade John broke his promise not to enter England during Richard's absence and, on learning of Richard's imprisonment in Germany, attempted, though unsuccessfully, to seize control of England. On Richard's return John was banished and disinherited though he was pardoned and recognized as heir when Arthur fell into the hands of the king of France, Philippe II. On the death of Richard in 1199, John took the Throne, and was crowned **King of England** on Ascension Day 27 May 1199. In 1199, through the Archbishop of Bordeaux and the Bishops of Poitier and Saintonge, and after a ten-year childless marriage, John obtained a divorce from his wife on the grounds of consanguinity. This enraged the Roman Curia as presuming to dissolve what had been joined by their authority. He intervened in the politics of his county of Poitou, and, in trying to settle the quarrel between the rival families of Lusignan and Angoulême, was married for the second time at Bordeaux on 24 Aug. 1200 to ISABELLE D'ANGOULÊME, daughter and heiress of Aymer Taillefer, Comte d'Angoulême (**descendant of Charlemagne**), by Alice, daughter of Pierre de France, Seigneur de Courtenay (**descendant of Charlemagne**). She was born in 1188, and had been betrothed to Hugues IX de Lusignan, Comte de La Marche. She was crowned on 8 Oct. 1200. War with France followed John's refusal to appear before Philippe II concerning the grievance of the Lusignans. At first John was successful in defending his French lands, capturing his nephew Arthur (who died in custody), but in 1204 lost Normandy, Anjou, Maine, and Touraine to the French king. For the next ten years John resided almost permanently in England (the first such Angevin king) and attempted to restore his finances for further warfare in France by determined taxation and exploitation of his feudal prerogatives (later the basis for the charge of tyranny). When he insisted on his, rather than the Pope's, right to nominate the Archbishop of Canterbury, Pope Innocent III in 1208 imposed an Interdict on England suspending all religious services, and excommunicating King John. After five years of amassing the revenues of vacant or appropriated sees and abbeys, John agreed to become a vassal to the Pope for an annual tribute of one thousand marks, with absolution from excommunication and the lifting of the Interdict. John continued his fight with the French, now with the Pope as his ally, but attempts finally collapsed with the defeat of his continental allies at Bouvines in 1214. An alliance of barons took advantage of this defeat to launch a rebellion which was successful in forcing John to a comprehensive and humiliating Magna Charta ensuring the feudal rights of the barons and the reinstatement of English law, signed at Runnymede on 19 June 1215. John soon repudiated the charter, and civil war resumed. JOHN OF ENGLAND, King of England, died suddenly in the midst of campaigning at Newark on 19 Oct. 1216, and was buried at Worcester Cathedral where his effigy is to be seen on his tomb. His widow was married for the second

PLANTAGENET (cont.)

time on 10 May 1220 to Hugues X de Lusignan, Comte de la Marche (died 1249), and had nine children. She died at Fontrévrault on 31 May 1246.

C.P. 5:689-692 (1926). *Paget* (1977), pp. 15-16.

Children of John of England, by Isabelle d'Angoulême:

i. HENRY III OF ENGLAND, King of England, son and heir, born 1 Oct. 1207 [see next].

ii. RICHARD OF ENGLAND, born 5 Jan. 1209; Comte de Poitou before 18 Aug. 1225, Earl of Cornwall 30 May 1227, elected King of the Romans 13 Jan. 1257, soon dispossessed, and returned to England, died 2 Apr. 1272, buried Hayles Abbey, which he had founded; married, first, 30 Mar. 1231, ISABEL MARSHAL, born 9 Oct. 1200, died in childbed 17 Jan. 1240, widow of Gilbert de Clare, Earl of Gloucester and Hertford, and daughter of William Marshal, 1st Earl of Pembroke, by Isabel, daughter of Richard de Clare, 2nd Earl of Pembroke; married, second, SANCHIA OF PROVENCE, born about 1225, died 9 Nov. 1261, third daughter and co-heiress of Raymond Berengar V, Comte de Provence, by Béatrix, daughter of Thomas I, Comte de Savoie; married, third, at Kaiserslautern 16 June 1269 BEATRICE DE FAUQUEMONT, died 17 Oct. 1277, daughter of Walram de Fauquemont, Seigneur de Montjoye, by Jutta, daughter of Otto, Graf von Ravensberg. Four children by first wife. Two sons by second wife. All died *s.p. Powicke* (1961), p. 33.

iii. JOAN OF ENGLAND, born 22 July 1210, died at London 5 Mar. 1238, buried Tarrant Crawford, Dorset; married at York 19 June 1221, ALEXANDER II, King of Scots.

iv. ISABEL OF ENGLAND, born 1214, died at Foggia 1 Dec. 1241; married at Worms 20 July 1235, Kaiser FRIEDRICH II.

v. ALIANOR OF ENGLAND, born 1215, married, first, WILLIAM MARSHAL *the younger*, 2nd Earl of Pembroke; second, SIMON DE MONTFORT, Earl of Leicester.

15. HENRY III OF ENGLAND [*of Winchester*], King of England, son and heir, was born at Winchester Castle on 1 Oct. 1207. He was crowned, aged nine, at Gloucester on 28 Oct. 1216. Henry assumed personal rule when he declared himself to be of full age in January 1227, and sought to recover the lands in France lost by his father. He was married at Canterbury on 14 Jan. 1236 to **ÉLÉONORE DE PROVENCE**, second daughter and co-heiress of Raymond Berengar V, Comte de Provence (**descendant of Charlemagne**), by Béatrix, daughter of Thomas I, Comte de Savoie (**descendant of Charlemagne**). She was born at Aix-en-Provence in 1217. Their children were born at Westminster in 1239, at Windsor Castle in 1240, at Bordeaux in 1242, in London in 1245 and at Westminster in 1253. Henry's personal rule in the direction of royal finances without the participation of the barons provoked discontent. The barons were further repelled by the influence over his government by his Queen's Savoyard kinsmen. His Lusignan half-brothers involved him in a disastrous foray in France. Henry's need for financial support compelled him in 1258 to agree to the creation of a privy council of barons to advise him and to oversee the administration of government. Henry sought help from the French king, Louis IX, and in 1259 made peace abandoning claims to the lost lands in France (the titles of Duc de Normandie and Comte d'Anjou in 1259, also renouncing claims to the counties of Maine, Touraine, and Poitou) and agreeing to hold the province still in his hands, the Duchy of Gascony, as a feudal vassal of Louis and his successors. His major baronial opponent by 1264 was his brother-in-law Simon de Montfort, Earl of Leicester. In the ensuing civil war Montfort captured Henry and his eldest son, Edward, at the battle of Lewes in Sussex on 14 May 1264. Montfort ruled England in Henry's name until he was defeated and killed at the battle of Evesham on 4 Aug. 1265 by Henry's son, the future King Edward I who assumed effective control of the government. HENRY III OF ENGLAND, King of England, died at Bury St. Edmunds, Suffolk, on 16 Nov. 1272, and was buried at Westminster Abbey. His widow died at Amesbury, co. Wilts, on 24 June 1291.

PLANTAGENET (cont.)

Paget (1977), pp. 17-18. Powicke (1961), pp. 34-35.

Children of Henry III of England, by Éléonore de Provence:

   i. EDWARD I OF ENGLAND, born 17 June 1239 [see next].

   ii. MARGARET OF ENGLAND, born 5 Oct. 1240; married ALEXANDER III, King of Scots.

   iii. EDMUND OF ENGLAND, married BLANCHE D'ARTOIS [see LANCASTER 14].[1]

   iv. RICHARD OF ENGLAND, born about 1247, died before 1256, buried Westminster Abbey.

   v. JOHN OF ENGLAND, born about 1250, died before 1256, buried Westminster Abbey.

   vi. HENRY OF ENGLAND, died young, buried Westminster Abbey.

   vii. BEATRICE OF ENGLAND, born 25 June 1242, married JEAN II DE DREUX.

   viii. KATHERINE OF ENGLAND, born 25 Nov. 1253, died at Windsor Castle 3 May 1257.

14. EDWARD I OF ENGLAND [*Longshanks*], King of England, son and heir, was born at Westminster, Middlesex, on 17 June 1239, and was named after the Anglo-Saxon King Edward the Confessor whose memory was honoured by King Henry. He was granted Gascony and was created **Earl of Chester** on 14 Feb. 1254. To prevent the rebellious Gascons from obtaining help from Castille, his marriage was arranged. He was married for the first time at the monastery of Las Huelgas in Spain on 18 Oct. 1254 (he being fifteen and she ten years of age) to **ALIANORE DE CASTILLE** [LEONOR DE CASTILLA or ELEANOR OF CASTILE], daughter of Fernando III, Rey de Castilla y León (**descendant of Charlemagne**), by his second wife Jeanne, daughter of Simon de Dammartin, Comte d'Aumale et de Ponthieu (**descendant of Charlemagne**). She was born about 1244. Their children were born at Windsor in 1264, at Windsor or Winchester in 1266, at Windsor in 1267, in the Holy Land in 1271, at Acre in 1272, at Bayonne in 1273, at Windsor in 1275, at Kennington in 1276, at Windsor in 1278, at Woodstock in 1279, at Rhuddlan in 1282, and at Caernarvon in 1284. In the conflict between his father, King Henry III, and the barons led by Simon de Montfort, Edward at first supported Montfort, but then supported his father, slaying Montfort at Evesham on 4 Aug 1265. Edward took the cross in 1268 and was on crusade at Acre in the Holy Land from May 1271 to September 1272. On his return journey to England he was in the kingdom of Sicily when he learned of his father's death, and paid homage at Paris to his cousin the French King, Philippe III, for his French lands. He landed at Dover in England on 2 Aug. 1274, and was crowned **King of England** at Westminster on 19 Aug. 1274. Having learned much from the civil war of his father's reign, he embarked on the restoration of royal authority with the institution of inquiries into the authority by which landowners held their jurisdictions and overhauled the civil and criminal law. From 1275 to 1307, he summoned, as had Montfort before him, representatives of the shires and boroughs to parliaments, that is, meetings of the king with the

---

[1] Ancestors of **Robert Abell, Dannett Abney, William Asfordby, Alice Baynton, Essex Beville, Joseph Bolles, Elizabeth Bosvile, Stephen Bull, Charles Calvert, Grace Chetwode, St. Leger Codd, Elizabeth Coytemore, Humphrey Davie, Frances, Jane & Katherine Deighton, Edward Digges, William Farrar, John Fenwick, Muriel Gurdon, Mary Gye, John Harleston, Warham Horsmanden, Anne Humphrey, Thomas Ligon, Nathaniel Littleton, Thomas Lloyd, Gabriel, Roger & Sarah Ludlow, Thomas Lunsford, Agnes Mackworth, Oliver Manwaring, Elizabeth Marshall, Anne Mauleverer, John Nelson, Philip & Thomas Nelson, John Oxenbridge, Joshua & Rebecca Owen, Richard Palgrave, Herbert Pelham, William Randolph, George Reade, William Rodney, Katherine Saint Leger, Richard Saltonstall, William Skepper, Diana & Grey Skipwith, John Stockman, John Washington, John West, Thomas Wingfield, Mary Wolseley, Hawte Wyatt, Amy Wyllys**, and, probably, **Jane Haviland, Thomas Dudley**.

PLANTAGENET (cont.)

principal men of the realm. This improved relations between the king and the borough communities and committed them to some support of his policies, although Edward had no intention of sharing royal authority. Edward was much concerned with asserting his claims to sovereignty over the whole of Britain. In 1277 he defeated Llewellyn, Prince of North Wales, and in the early 1280s conquered the latter's principality and annexed it to the English Crown. The hereditary Anglo-Norman lords continued to rule the marches of Wales with the overlordship of the English Crown. The dying out of the direct Scottish royal line in 1290 enabled Edward to press his claim to the overlordship of Scotland but he met resistance from his choice as King of the Scots, John Balliol. In 1296 Edward invaded Scotland, deposed Balliol and sought to occupy the kingdom. William Wallace, a supporter of Balliol, began a successful rebellion, but was decisively defeated by Edward at Falkirk in 1298. Robert Bruce, whose grandfather had been a claimant to the Scottish throne, and who was a rival of the Balliols, rebelled, and was crowned king in 1306. In 1294 Edward had become embroiled in war with his overlord, the French king, Philippe IV, who was asserting himself in the affairs of Edward's Duchy of Gascony. The extortionate demands for services and money to fight Philippe and to suppress Scottish resistance alienated his English subjects in his later years and provoked renewed baronial opposition. His wife and consort died at Herdeby, co. Lincoln, on 29 Nov. 1290. Edward I was married for the second time at Canterbury on 8 Sep. 1299 to **MARGUERITE DE FRANCE**, daughter of Philippe III de France *le Hardi* [the Bold], Roi de France (**descendant of Charlemagne**), by his second wife Maria von Brabant, daughter of Heinrich III Herzog von Brabant (**descendant of Charlemagne**). She was born in 1279. Their sons were born at Brotherton in 1300, and at Woodstock in 1301. EDWARD I OF ENGLAND, King of England, died at Burgh-on-Sands, near Carlisle, Cumberland, on 7 July 1307, when preparing once again to invade Scotland, and was buried at Westminster Abbey. His widow died at Marlborough Castle on 14 Feb. 1317.

East Herts.Arch.Soc. 1:333-334 (1902) (Eleanor died at the house of Richard de Weston or of Sir John Weston at Hardby in Nottinghamshire about ten miles from Clipstone) (her body was taken to Lincoln on December 4th, and the procession to Westminster Abbey stopped the next successive days at Grantham, Stamford, Geddington, Northampton, Stony Stratford, Woburn, Dunstable, St. Albans, Waltham, Westcheap and Charing. "In every town and place where the corpse rested, the King commanded a cross of admirable workmanship to be erected to the Queen's memory" of which Northampton, Geddington and Waltham remain). *D.N.B.* 6:432-456 (1908). *C.P.* 6:469 (1926). *Paget* (1977), pp. 18-20. *Powicke* (1961), pp. 34-35 (adds daughter Isabel, born 15 Mar. of unknown year to first marriage, and Alianor to second marriage).

Children of Edward I of England, by Alianore de Castille:
   i. JOHN OF ENGLAND, born 10 June 1266, died at Westminster 3 Aug. 1271.
   ii. HENRY OF ENGLAND, born 13 July 1267, died 14 Oct. 1274, buried Westminster Abbey.
   iii. ALPHONSO OF ENGLAND, born 24 Nov. 1273, Earl of Chester, died 19 Aug. 1284.
   iv. **EDWARD II OF ENGLAND**, King of England, born 25 Apr. 1284 [see next].
   v. ALIANOR OF ENGLAND, born about 17 June 1264, married HENRY III, Comte de Bar.
   vi. JOAN OF ENGLAND, died young before 7 Sep. 1265.
   vii. JULIAN (or CATHERINE) OF ENGLAND, born 1271, died there 5 Sep. (?).

PLANTAGENET (cont.)

viii. JOAN OF ENGLAND [see CLARE 12],[1] & [see MONTHERMER 13].[2]

ix. MARGARET OF ENGLAND, born 11 Sep. 1275, married JOHN II, Duke of Brabant.

x. BERENGARIA OF ENGLAND, born 1276, died 1279 (?).

xi. MARY OF ENGLAND, born 11 Mar. 1278, nun at Amesbury, died there before 8 July 1332.

xii. ALICE OF ENGLAND, born 12 Mar. 1279, died 1291.

xiii. ELIZABETH OF ENGLAND, married HUMPHREY DE BOHUN [see BOHUN 12].[3]

xiv. BEATRICE OF ENGLAND, born about 1286, died young.

xv. BLANCHE OF ENGLAND, born 1290, died young.

Children & grandchildren of Edward I of England, by Marguerite de France:

xvi. THOMAS OF NORFOLK [*of Brotherton*], married ALICE DE HALES [see NORFOLK 12].[4]

xvii. EDMUND OF KENT [*of Woodstock*], Earl of Kent, sixth son, born at Woodstock, co. Oxford, 5 Aug. 1301; created Earl of Kent 28 July 1321, beheaded on 19 Mar. 1330 for alleged treason in wishing to restore his half-brother Edward II to the throne; married about 25 Dec. 1325 MARGARET WAKE, born about 1299, died 29 Sep. 1349, widow of JOHN COMYN, of Badenoch, and daughter of John Wake, 1st Lord Wake, by Joan, daughter of William de Fiennes. *D.N.B.* 6:410-412 (1908). *Paget* (1957) 453:1. *Paget* (1977), pp. 19-20.

  a. EDMUND OF KENT, Earl of Kent, son and heir, born about 1326, died 5 Jan. 1333 *s.p.*.

  b. JOHN OF KENT, born 7 Apr. 1330, brother and heir, Earl of Kent, Lord Wake on the death of his mother, died 26 or 27 Dec. 1352 *s.p.*; married ELIZABETH OF JULICH.

---

[1]Ancestor, by first husband Gilbert de Clare, of **Robert Abell, Dannett Abney, Alice Baynton, Richard & William Bernard, Elizabeth Bosvile, George, Giles & Robert Brent, Nathaniel Burrough, Charles Calvert, Edward Carleton, Grace Chetwode, Jeremy Clarke, James Claypoole, William Clopton, St. Leger Codd, Francis Dade, Humphrey Davie, Frances, Jane & Katherine Deighton, Edward Digges, William Farrar, John Fenwick, Henry Fleete, Muriel Gurdon, Mary Gye, John Harleston, Elizabeth Haynes, Warham Horsmanden, Anne Humphrey, Edmund Jennings, Edmund Kempe, Thomas Ligon, Nathaniel Littleton, Thomas Lloyd, Anne Lovelace, Gabriel, Roger & Sarah Ludlow, Thomas Lunsford, Agnes Mackworth, Anne & Catherine Marbury, Elizabeth Marshall, Anne Mauleverer, John Nelson, Philip & Thomas Nelson, John Oxenbridge, Richard Palgrave, Herbert Pelham, William Randolph, George Reade, William Rodney, Katherine Saint Leger, Richard Saltonstall, William Skepper, John Stockman, John Throckmorton, John Washington, Olive Welby, John West, Thomas Wingfield, Mary Wolseley, Hawte Wyatt**, and, probably, **Thomas Dudley, Jane Haviland**.

[2]Ancestor, by second husband Ralph de Monthermer, of **William Asfordby, Elizabeth Bosvile, Mary Bourchier, Stephen Bull, Charles Calvert, Francis Dade, Anne Humphrey, Thomas Lunsford, John Nelson, John Oxenbridge, Herbert Pelham, Diana & Grey Skipwith, Maria Johanna Somerset, John West, Thomas Wingfield**, and, probably, **Thomas Dudley**.

[3]Ancestors of **Robert Abell, Essex Bevile, Elizabeth Bosvile, George, Giles & Robert Brent, Charles Calvert, Edward Carleton, Grace Chetwode, St. Leger Codd, Elizabeth Coytemore, Edward Digges, Thomas Gerard, Muriel Gurdon, Warham Horsmanden, Anne Humphrey, Edmund Jennings, Mary Launce, Thomas Ligon, Gabriel, Roger & Sarah Ludlow, Thomas Lunsford, Oliver Manwaring, Anne & Catherine Marbury, Anne Mauleverer, John Nelson, Philip & Thomas Nelson, Joshua & Rebecca Owen, John Oxenbridge, Richard Palgrave, Herbert Pelham, William Randolph, Katherine Saint Leger, John West, Thomas Wingfield, Hawte Wyatt, Amy Wyllys**, and, probably, **Jane Haviland**.

[4]Ancestors of **William Asfordby, Essex Bevile, Joseph Bolles, Elizabeth Bosvile, Charles Calvert, Frances, Jane & Katherine Deighton, John Fenwick, Muriel Gurdon, Anne Humphrey, Thomas Ligon, Nathaniel Littleton, Thomas Lloyd, Philip & Thomas Nelson, Herbert Pelham, William Randolph, George Reade, Diana & Grey Skipwith, John Stockman, John West, Thomas Wingfield, Hawte Wyatt**, and, probably, **Thomas Dudley**.

PLANTAGENET (cont.)

c. **JOAN OF KENT**, born 29 Sep. 1328, married **THOMAS DE HOLAND** [see HOLAND 9].[1]

xviii. ALIANOR OF ENGLAND, born 4 May 1306, died 1311.

13. **EDWARD II OF ENGLAND** [*of Caernarvon*], eldest surviving son and heir, was born at Caernarvon, co. Caernarvon, Wales, on 25 Apr. 1284. He was married at Boulogne on 25 Jan. 1308 to **ISABELLE DE FRANCE**, daughter of Philippe IV, Roi de France (**descendant of Charlemagne**), by Joan, daughter of Henri I, Roi de Navarre et Comte de Champagne (**descendant of Charlemagne**). She was born in 1292. Their children were born at Windsor in 1312, at Eltham in 1316, at Woodstock in 1318, and at the Tower of London in 1321. He was crowned on 25 Feb. 1308. He had little success in meeting the problems left by his father in Scotland and Gascony, and with the barons. He failed to appease the barons by consultation or the borough communities by curbing the activities of his officials, and angered them by the favours which he bestowed on a foreigner, Peter de Gaveston. In 1310 Edward agreed to a degree of baronial control over government. The barons seized Gaveston and executed him in June 1312. Robert I (the Bruce), King of Scotland, threatened to overthrow the English overlordship. Edward led an army into Scotland and was decisively defeated by Bruce at Bannockburn on 24 June 1314, and was unable to defend northern England against Scottish devastation. Edward found new favourites, the two Hughs le Despenser, father and son. The territorial ambitions of the Despensers in Wales antagonised the Welsh marcher lords. They made an alliance with Edward's cousin, Thomas of Lancaster, but were defeated by Edward at Boroughbridge, co. York, in March 1322. His reliance on the Despensers aroused the resentment of his queen, Isabelle. While on a diplomatic mission in 1325 to Paris involving the dispute over Edward's French lands, she became the mistress of Roger Mortimer, an exiled baronial opponent of Edward. In 1326 Isabelle and Roger invaded England, executed the Despensers, and deposed Edward on 7 Jan. 1327 in favour of his son Edward. EDWARD II OF ENGLAND, King of England, was murdered in Berkeley Castle on 21 Sep. 1327, apparently in an attempt to escape the castle, and was buried, it is said, at Gloucester. His widow died at Hertford Castle on 22 Aug. 1358.

D.N.B. 6:456-466 (1908). Paget (1977), p. 20. Powicke (1961), p. 35.

Children of Edward II of England, by Isabelle de France:

i. **EDWARD III OF ENGLAND**, born 13 Nov. 1312 [see next].

ii. JOHN OF ENGLAND, born 25 Aug. 1316, Earl of Cornwall, died unmarried 13 Sep. 1336.

iii. ALIANOR OF ENGLAND, born 8 June 1318, married REYNOLD II, Duke of Gueldres.

iv. JOAN OF ENGLAND, born 5 July 1321, married DAVID II (Bruce), King of Scots.

12. **EDWARD III OF ENGLAND**, King of England, Lord of Ireland, Duc d'Aquitaine, Earl of Chester, was born at Windsor Castle, co. Berks, on 13 Nov. 1312. He succeeded his father as from 24 Jan. 1326/7, and was crowned aged fifteen at Westminster Abbey on 29 Jan. 1326/7. He was married at York on 24 Jan. 1327/8 to **PHILIPPE DE HAINAUT**, daughter of Guillaume, Comte de Hainaut (**descendant of Charlemagne**), by Jeanne, daughter of Charles de France, Comte de Valois

---

[1]Ancestors of **Elizabeth Bosvile, Stephen Bull, Charles Calvert, Grace Chetwode, St. Leger Codd, Edward Digges, Muriel Gurdon, Warham Horsmanden, Anne Humphrey, Nathaniel Littleton, Thomas Lloyd, Agnes Mackworth, John Nelson, Philip & Thomas Nelson, John Oxenbridge, Herbert Pelham, Katherine Saint Leger, Maria Johanna Somerset, John Washington, John West, Thomas Wingfield,** and, probably, **Thomas Dudley, Jane Haviland.**

PLANTAGENET (cont.)

(descendant of Charlemagne). She was born on 24 June 1311. Their children were born at Woodstock in 1330, 1332 and 1335, at Hatfield in 1337, at Antwerp in 1338, at Ghent in Flanders in 1340, at the Tower of London in 1342, at Kings Langley, co. Hertford, in 1344, at Waltham near Winchester in 1344, at Windsor in 1346, at Windsor before 1348, and at Woodstock in 1355. During the first four years of his reign England was governed in his name by his mother and Roger Mortimer. Edward assumed personal rule on 19-20 Oct. 1330, and had Mortimer executed. In 1333 he reversed Isabelle's and Mortimer's policy of peace with Scotland by invading it, reviving the ambitions of his grandfather King Edward I. Edward III's main foreign preoccupation, however, from 1337 onwards was France, whose king, Philippe VI, then declared his Duchy of Gascony forfeited. Edward formally assumed the title of King of France in right of his mother in January 1340. Near continuous war ensued with some respite from truces. The financial burden of the war roused resentment which was assuaged somewhat when Edward negotiated the main war taxes with the representatives of the shires and the borough communities sitting in parliament. He aroused enthusiasm for the war by engaging the chivalrous interests of the nobles in it and stirring up distrust and hatred of the French. Edward won the battle of Sluys in Flanders in June 1340. Bubonic plague [the Black Death] made its first appearance in England during his reign in 1348. His son Edward *the Black Prince* captured the French king, Jean II, in his victory at Poitiers in 1356. In 1360 Edward made peace, giving up his claim to the throne of France and receiving from Jean the Duchy of Aquitaine in full sovereignty. The gains won by English armed forces however could not be sustained in the face of sustained French resources. In the war of 1369-75 Jean's son Charles V won back from Edward what had been conceded in 1360. By the time of his death he had been discredited. His wife and consort died at Windsor Castle on 15 Aug. 1369. EDWARD III OF ENGLAND, King of England, died at Sheen Palace, Richmond, Surrey, on 21 June 1377. They were buried at Westminster Abbey. The descendants of their sons, Lionel of Clarence, John of Lancaster, and Edmund of York, contested the Throne for generations ending in the Wars of the Roses from 1455 to 1485.

D.N.B. 6:466-488 (1908). *Paget* (1977), pp. 20-26. *Powicke* (1961), pp. 35-36. *TG* 1:138-139 (1980).

Children & grandchildren of Edward III of England, by Philippe de Hainault:

   i. **EDWARD OF ENGLAND** [*the Black Prince*], son and heir apparent, born at Woodstock 15 June 1330, Prince of Wales, Earl of Chester and Duke of Cornwall, died 8 June 1376 *v.p.*, buried Canterbury Cathedral; married at Windsor 10 Oct. 1361 JOAN OF KENT [*the Fair Maid of Kent*], born 29 Sep. 1328, died 8 Aug. 1385, widow of Thomas de Holand, 1st Earl of Kent (died 26 or 28 Dec. 1360), and daughter and eventual heiress of Edmund *of Woodstock*, Earl of Kent (son of King Edward I), by Margaret, daughter of John, 1st Lord Wake [see HOLAND 9]. *C.P.* (1929) 7:153.

     a. EDWARD OF ENGLAND, born at Angoulême 27 Jan. 1365, died at Bordeaux 1372 *v.p.*

     b. RICHARD II OF ENGLAND, younger son, born 6 Jan. 1367, grandson and heir of King Edward III, after his father's death created Prince of Wales, Duke of Cornwall and Earl of Chester on 20 Nov. 1376; succeeded his grandfather as **King of England** 22 June 1377, and was crowned 16 July; deposed by his cousin Henry *of Bolingbroke*, Duke of Lancaster, on 29 Sep. 1399, died in prison in Pontefract Castle 6 Jan. 1400 *s.p.*; married, first, at Westminster Palance, 14 Jan. 1382, ANNE OF BOHEMIA, daughter of Charles IV of Luxemburg, Emperor; married, second, 12 Mar. 1396 ISABELLE DE FRANCE, born at Paris 9 Nov. 1389, died at Blois 13 Sep. 1409, daughter of Charles VI, Roi de France. *Paget* (1977), p. 26. *Powicke* (1961), pp. 36-37.

  ii. WILLIAM OF ENGLAND, born before 16 Feb. 1337, died before 8 July 1337.

  iii. **LIONEL OF CLARENCE** [*of Antwerp*], Duke of Clarence, born 29 Nov. 1338 [see next].

PLANTAGENET (cont.)

- iv. JOHN OF LANCASTER [of Gaunt] [see LANCASTER 11][1] & [see BEAUFORT 11].
- v. EDMUND OF YORK [of Langley], married ISABELLA DE CASTILLE [see YORK 9].[2]
- vi. WILLIAM OF ENGLAND, born before 24 June 1348, buried 5 Sep. 1348.
- vii. THOMAS OF GLOUCESTER, married ALIANOR DE BOHUN [see BOHUN 9].[3]
- viii. ISABEL OF ENGLAND, born 16 June 1332, married ENGUERRAND VII, Sire de Couci.
- ix. JOAN OF ENGLAND, born about February 1335, died of the plague at Bordeaux en route for Spain to be married to PEDRO [the Cruel], Rey de Castilla y León 2 Sep. 1348.
- x. BLANCHE OF ENGLAND, born and died in the Tower of London Mar. 1342.
- xi. MARY OF ENGLAND, born 10 Oct. 1344, died thirty weeks after her marriage *s.p.*, buried Abingdon Abbey; married at Woodstock 1361 JOHN DE MONTFORT, Duc de Bretagne.
- xii. MARGARET OF ENGLAND, born 20 July 1346, died soon after 1 Oct. 1361, buried Abingdon Abbey; married at Reading 19 May 1359 JOHN DE HASTINGS, 2nd Earl of Pembroke.

11. LIONEL OF CLARENCE [of Antwerp], K.G., Duke of Clarence, Earl of Ulster *jure uxoris*, third but second surviving son, was born at Antwerp on 29 Nov. 1338. He was married in his fourth year at the Tower of London on 9 Sep. 1342 to **ELIZABETH DE BURGH**, daughter and heiress of William de Burgh, 4th Earl of Ulster (**descendant of King Edward I**), by Maud, daughter of Henry, Earl of Lancaster (**grandson of King Henry III**) [see BURGH 12]. She was born at Carrickfergus Castle on 6 July 1332. The marriage was consummated ten years later in 1352 and by this marriage he acquired the vast estates in Ireland of the de Burgh family, as well as a large part (including the honour of Clare) of the estates of the Earls of Gloucester and Hertford, in right of his wife's paternal grandmother. ELIZABETH DE BURGH died at Dublin on 10 Dec. 1363. LIONEL OF CLARENCE was married for the second time at Milan on 28 May 1368 to VIOLANTA DI MILANO, daughter of Galeazzo Visconti, by Blanche Maria, daughter of Aymon, Comte de Savoie. LIONEL OF CLARENCE died at Alba, Piedmont in Italy, on 17 Oct. 1368, and was buried at Clare, Suffolk. His widow was married for the second time on 2 Aug. 1377 to Otto Palaeologus, Marquis of Montferrat (murdered Dec. 1378), and for the third time on 18 Apr. 1381 to Ludovico Visconti, Signore de Lodi (died 1404). She died in November 1386.

C.P. 3:257-260 (1913). *C.P.* 8:445-448 (1932). *Paget* (1977), pp. 20-21. *TG* 2:124 (1981).

10. PHILIPPE OF CLARENCE, Countess of Ulster, daughter and heiress, was born at Eltham Palace, Kent, on 16 Aug. 1355. She was married at Reading about May 1368 to **EDMUND DE MORTIMER**, Knt., 3rd Earl of March, Lord Mortimer of Wigmore, Lord of Trim and Connaught, Ireland, son and heir of Roger de Mortimer, Knt. (of **Magna Charta Surety descent** and **descendant of Charlemagne**), by Philippe (**descendant of Charlemagne**), daughter of William de Montagu, 1st Earl of Salisbury. He was born at Llangoed in Llyswen, co. Brecon, Wales, on 1 Feb. 1351/2, and succeeded his father in his tenth year. He became a ward of King Edward III, and was closely associated with the King's sons, especially Edward *the Black Prince*. By the death of his wife's father in 1368 he became lord of Ulster and of Connaught, as

---

[1] Ancestor, by his first wife Blanche of Lancaster, of **Muriel Gurdon**, and, probably, **Jane Haviland**.

[2] Ancestors of **St.Leger Codd, Warham Horsmanden, Katherine Saint Leger, Philip & Thomas Nelson, Maria Johanna Somerset**.

[3] Ancestors of **Essex Beville, Elizabeth Bosvile, George, Giles & Robert Brent, Muriel Gurdon, Mary Launce, Anne Mauleverer, Maria Johanna Somerset**.

PLANTAGENET (cont.)

also lord of Clare in Suffolk *jure uxoris*, and was also styled Earl of Ulster. He was summoned to Parliament from 8 Jan. 1370/1 as Earl of March. In the domestic politics of the time Mortimer was on the side of the Prince of Wales and the clergy against John of Gaunt and the Barons. The death of the Black Prince weakened his position. With the accession of King Richard II, power remained with Lancaster, but the next rightful heir was Mortimer's own son. The will of PHILIPPE OF CLARENCE, Countess of March and Ulster, was dated 21 Nov. 1378 and proved 6 Dec. 1379 (P.C.C., 189 Courtenay). He was appointed lieutenant of Ireland on 22 Oct. 1379, it being convenient for the party of Lancaster to get him out of the country. Ulster, Connaught, and Meath, over which he bore nominal sway, had long been the most disorderly districts. EDMUND DE MORTIMER, Earl of March, having caught cold in crossing a river in winter time in Munster, died testate in the Dominican Friary at Cork on 27 Dec. 1381 (P.C.C., 188 Courtenay). They were buried at Wigmore Abbey.

D.N.B. 13:1016-1018 (1909). *C.P.* 1:245 (1910). *Mortimer-Percy* (1911), pp. vi, 1,2. *C.P.* 8:445-448 (1932). *C.P.* 9:714 (1936), *C.P.* 12(2):180 (1959). *Paget* (1977), p. 21.

Children of Edmund de Mortimer, by Philippe of Clarence:
   i. **ROGER DE MORTIMER**, son and heir, born 11 Apr. 1374 [see next].
   ii. **ELIZABETH DE MORTIMER**, married **HENRY PERCY**, Lord Percy [see KEMPE 10].[1]

9. ROGER DE MORTIMER, Knt., 4th Earl of March, 7th Earl of Ulster, Lord Mortimer of Wigmore, son and heir, was born at Usk on 11 Apr. 1374, and succeeded to title and estates when seven years old. He was declared heir presumptive to the Crown by King Richard II in October 1385, and was made a knight by the King on 23 Apr. 1390. He was married about 7 Oct. 1388 to **ALIANOR DE HOLAND**, daughter and in her issue co-heiress of Thomas de Holand, 2nd Earl of Kent (**descendant of King Edward I**), by Alice, daughter of Richard Fitz Alan, 5th Earl of Arundel (**descendant of King Henry III**) [see HOLAND 9.i.d for her ancestry]. He was summoned to Parliament on 15 Oct. 1397, and had a great popular welcome. He was careful to do nothing to justify the King Richard II's suspicions, but feeling his position to be somewhat insecure, he returned to Ireland, whither his enemy, the Duke of Surrey (his brother-in-law), was ordered to follow and capture him. Ireland was Mortimer's chief care, but he possessed little power there, the estates having been devastated, and engaged in petty campaigns against the native chieftains. ROGER DE MORTIMER, Earl of March and of Ulster, while engaged in a rash attack on some of the Leinster clans, was killed by O'Brien's men on 20 July 1398, and was buried at Wigmore Abbey. The Wigmore chronicler says that he was riding unattended, attired in the Irish manner, in front of his army, and was unrecognised by those who killed him. The death of the heir to the throne at the hands of the Irish induced King Richard II to undertake his last fatal expedition to Ireland. His widow was married for the second time in June 1399 to **EDWARD CHERLETON**, 5th Lord Cherleton, feudal lord of Powys (died 14 Mar. 1420/1 *s.p.m.*), and had two daughters [see CHERLETON 11 for descendants of this marriage]. She died 6 or 18 Oct 1405.

D.N.B. 13:1042-1043 (1909). *C.P.* 4:326 (1916). *C.P.* 8:448-453 (1932). *C.P.* 12(2):180 (1959).

---

[1]Ancestors of **St. Leger Codd, Humphrey Davie, Edward Digges, William Farrar, John Harleston, Warham Horsmanden, Agnes Mackworth, Anne Mauleverer, John Nelson, George Reade, William Rodney, Katherine Saint Leger, Richard Saltonstall, William Skepper, Maria Johanna Somerset, Thomas Wingfield**, and, probably, **Jane Haviland**.

PLANTAGENET (cont.)

Paget (1977), pp. 21-22.
Child of Roger de Mortimer, by Alianor de Holand:
   i. ANNE MORTIMER, married RICHARD OF YORK, Earl of Cambridge [see YORK 8].[1]

* * *

PLUMPTON see DRURY

* * *

POLE

EDWARD I OF ENGLAND, King of England, married ALIANORE DE CASTILLE.
JOAN OF ENGLAND [*of Acre*], married GILBERT DE CLARE, Earl of Gloucester.
MARGARET DE CLARE, married HUGH DE AUDLEY, Earl of Gloucester.
MARGARET DE AUDLEY, married RALPH DE STAFFORD, Earl of Stafford.
HUGH DE STAFFORD, married PHILIPPE DE BEAUCHAMP [see AUDLEY 11].

12. KATHERINE STAFFORD, was married before 23 Nov. 1383 to MICHAEL DE LA POLE, 2nd Earl of Suffolk, son and heir of Michael de la Pole, 1st Earl of Suffolk, by Katherine, daughter of John Wingfield, Knt., of Wingfield Castle, Suffolk. He was born in or before 1367. They had five sons and three daughters. He was summoned to Parliament from 19 Aug. 1399. MICHAEL DE LA POLE, Earl of Suffolk, died testate of the flux at the siege of Harfleur on 18 Sep. 1415. His widow died on 8 Apr. 1419. They were buried at Wingfield (M.I.).
   Clay (1913), pp. 51-52. *C.P.* 9:218 (1936). *C.P.* 12(1):441-442 (1953). *Paget* (1957) 176:1. *TAG* 69:139 (July 1994).

Children & grandchild of Michael de la Pole, by Katherine Stafford:
   i. PHILIPPE DE LA POLE [see next].
   ii. ISABEL DE LA POLE, died testate 8 Feb. 1466/7, will mentions grand-daughter Eleanor, and her daughter Anne, wife of John Hastings; married on or before 5 Feb. 1402/3 THOMAS MORLEY, 5th Lord Morley, of Moreley, Norfolk, born about 1393 (aged twenty-three at grandfather's death), grandson and heir of Thomas, Lord Morley; took part in the sieges of Rouen, Melun, and Meaux, and was present at the death of King Henry V; summoned to Parliament from 15 July 1427; died 6 Dec. 1435, buried Hingham, co. Norfolk, son and heir of Robert Morley, by his wife Isabel. *C.P.* 6:360 (1926). *C.P.* 9:218-219 (1936).
      a. ANNE MORLEY, married JOHN HASTINGS [see ELSING 6].[2]

11. PHILIPPE DE LA POLE, was married to HUGH BURNELL, of Holdgate, co. Salop, Weoley, co. Worcester, etc., K.G., 3rd Lord Burnell, Governor of Bridgnorth and Montgomery Castles, son and heir of Nicholas de Haudlo (later Burnell), Lord Burnell (**descendant of Charlemagne**), by his wife Mary. He was born about 1347 (aged thirty-six in 1383). He was summoned to Parliament from 20 Aug. 1383. He

---

[1]Ancestors of **Philip & Thomas Nelson, Maria Johanna Somerset**.

[2]Ancestors of **William Asfordby, William Farrar, William Skepper**.

233

POLE (cont.)

was married for the second time in 1386, before 22 May, to Joyce Botetourt, Baroness Botetourt *suo jure*. She died on 1 Jan. 1406/7 *s.p.* He was married for the third time in 1408 or 1409 to Joan Devereux, widow (with issue) of Walter Fitz Walter, Lord Fitz Walter (died at Venice 16 May 1407), and daughter of John Devereux, 1st Lord Devereux, by Maud, daughter of John de Vere, 7th Earl of Oxford (of Magna Charta Surety descent and descendant of Charlemagne). She was born about 1380 (aged seventeen and more in 1397). She died on 10 or 11 May 1409, and was buried in Dunmow Priory. HUGH BURNELL, Lord Burnell, died testate on 27 Nov. 1420 *s.p.s.m.* (will requesting burial at Hales Owen Abbey).
    C.P. 2:435 (1912). *C.P.* 5:481-2 (1926).

10. **EDWARD BURNELL,** Knt., of Billingford, Thurning, and East Ruston, Norfolk, was married to **ALIANOR** _____, said to be a daughter of a Lord le Strange. SIR EDWARD BURNELL died at battle of Agincourt on 25 Oct. 1415 *v.p.*
    C.P. 2:435 footnote *f* (1912). *Roskell* (1992) 3:155 (no identification of wife).

9. **KATHERINE BURNELL,** second daughter and co-heiress, was born about 1407, and inherited the manors of Billingford, Thurning, and East Ruston, Norfolk. She was married for the first time before June 1426 to **JOHN RADCLIFFE,** Knt., K.G., of Attleborough, Norfolk, younger son of James Radcliffe, of Radcliffe, co. Lancaster. He entered the entourage of Thomas of Lancaster, had a youthful career as a soldier, and was M.P. for Norfolk. He had been married previously, perhaps in 1405, to Cecily Mortimer, widow, with issue, of John Herling, Knt. (died before 1 July 1403), and daughter and co-heiress of Thomas Mortimer, Knt., of Newnham, co. Cambridge, and Attleborough, by Mary, daughter of Nicholas Park. She was half-sister of John Fastolf, Knt., with whom he had a life-long friendship. John and Cecily had one son. Cecily died at Bordeaux in 1423. John & Katherine Radcliffe had one son. SIR JOHN RADCLIFFE died on 26 Feb. or 4 Mar. 1440/1, and was buried in the choir of Attleborough Church. Katherine was married for the second time to JOHN FERRERS, and died on 13 Oct. 1452.
    C.P. 5:484-485, 485 footnote *a* (1926). *C.P.* 9:250 (1936). *Roskell* (1992) 3:155-159 ("one of the most important military captains of his day").

8. **JOHN RADCLIFFE,** of Attleborough, Norfolk, son and heir, was born about 1430. He was married before 27 Oct. 1444 to **ELIZABETH FITZ WALTER,** only daughter and heiress of Walter Fitz Walter, Lord Fitz Walter (**descendant of King Edward I**), by Elizabeth, daughter of John Chidiock, Knt., of Chideock, Dorset. She was born at Hexham on 28 July 1430 [see FITZ WALTER 9 for her ancestry]. JOHN RADCLIFFE was slain, on the Yorkist side, in the skirmish at Ferrybridge on the eve of the battle of Towton on 28 Mar. 1461. His widow was married about 15 Mar. 1466/7 to John Dinham, Lord Dinham (died *s.p.*). She died before 22 Aug. 1485.
    C.P. 5:484-486 (1926). *Paget* (1977), p. 439. *Roskell* (1992) 4:159.

7. **JOHN RADCLIFFE,** Lord Fitz Walter, of Guildford, Surrey, son and heir, was born on 1 Jan. 1451/2. He was appointed Steward of the King's Household before 19 Oct. 1485. On 14 Jan. 1485/6 he was appointed joint Warden and Chief Justice of the King's forests South of Trent, and 25 February following, of all the King's forests, for life. He was summoned to Parliament from 15 Sep. 1485 by writs directed *Johanni Radclyff, de FitzWauter*. He was married, evidently, about 6 July 1475, to **MARGARET WHETEHILL,** widow, with three children, of Thomas Walden, Gent., Merchant of the Staple of Calais (died 1474), and daughter of Richard Whetehill, Esq., Mayor of Calais, Merchant of the Staple, by his wife Joan. They had one son and five daughters. JOHN RADCLIFFE, Lord Fitz Walter, was attainted

POLE (cont.)

of high treason in 1495 as a confederate of Piers, or Perkin, Warbeck, and was beheaded at Calais, about 24 Nov. 1496.

    C.P. 5:486-487 (1926). *Mary Isaac* (1955), p. 268-272 (Whetehill arms: Per fesse, *azure* and *or*, a pale counterchanged, three lions rampant *or*). *Paget* (1977), p. 264.

    Child of John Radcliffe, by Margaret Whetehill:

      i. **ROBERT RADCLIFFE**, Lord Fitz Walter, married **MARGARET STANLEY** [see NELSON 6].[1]

* * *

POLE OF CHRISHALL see WYATT

POLE OF MEDMENHALL see SOMERSET

PYMPE see FLEETE

RADCLIFFE see POLE

RALEIGH see MARBURY

* * *

RANDOLPH

    EDWARD I OF ENGLAND, King of England, married **ALIANORE DE CASTILLE**.
    ELIZABETH OF ENGLAND, married **HUMPHREY DE BOHUN**, Earl of Hereford and Essex.
    MARGARET DE BOHUN, married **HUGH DE COURTENAY**, Earl of Devon.
    MARGARET DE COURTENAY, married **JOHN COBHAM**, 3rd Lord Cobham.
    JOAN COBHAM, married **JOHN DE LA POLE**, Knt.
    JOAN DE LA POLE, Baroness Cobham, married **REYNOLD BRAYBROOKE**, Knt.
    JOAN BRAYBROOKE, Baroness Cobham, married **THOMAS BROOKE**, Knt.
    EDWARD BROOKE, 5th Lord Cobham, married **ELIZABETH TUCHET** [see WYATT 6].

8. ELIZABETH BROOKE, was married to **ROBERT TANFIELD**, Esq., of Gayton, co. Northampton, son of Robert Tanfield, of Gayton and Harpole, co. Northampton, by his second wife _____ Lovell. He was born about 1441 (aged forty in 1481). ROBERT TANFIELD died on 22 Feb. 1483/4. His widow died in 1525.

    H.S.P. 13:294 (1878) (1612 Vis. Essex) (his parents: "Frauncis Tanfeild of Gayton in com. North. esquier & ____ daugh. and heire to Lovell"). *Metcalfe* (1887), p. 141 (1618/9 Vis. Northants) ("Sir Robert Tanfield, Knt").

7. ROBERT TANFIELD, Gent., of Gayton, co. Northampton, son and heir, was born about 1461 (aged twenty-two in 1483-4). He was married to **KATHERINE NEVILLE**, daughter of Edward Neville, Lord Bergavenny [see BEAUFORT 11.iv.d for his ancestry], by his second wife Katherine (**descendant of King Edward I**), daughter of Robert Howard, Knt. [see MOWBRAY 8.ii for her ancestry].

---

[1] Ancestors of **John Nelson**.

RANDOLPH (cont.)

H.S.P. 13:294 (1878) (states he was a knight). *Metcalfe* (1887), p. 49 (1564 Vis. Northants) (no identification of wife), p. 141 (citing Harl.MS.1553 for identification of wife).

6. **WILLIAM TANFIELD**, Esq., of Gayton, co. Northampton, son and heir, was born about 1489 (aged thirty-seven in 1525-6). He was married to **ISABEL STAVELY**, daughter of William Stavely, Esq., of Bignell, co. Buckingham. They had four sons and two daughters. WILLIAM TANFIELD, ESQ., died testate (P.C.C., 5 Jankyn) on 6 Apr. 1529.

H.S.P. 13:294 (1878). *Metcalfe* (1887), pp. 49,141.

5. **FRANCIS TANFIELD**, Esq., of Gayton, co. Northampton, son and heir, was born about 1508 (aged seventeen in 1525-6). He was married to **BRIDGET CAVE**, daughter of Richard Cave, Esq., of Stanford, co. Northampton, by his wife Margaret Saxby. They had four sons and three daughters. She died on 20 June 1583. "Francys Tanfelde esquire" died testate (P.C.C., 15 Welles) on 21 Nov. 1558.

H.S.P. 2:126-128 (1870) (1619 Vis. Leic.). *Chester of Chicheley* (1878) 1:79. *Metcalfe* (1887), p. 141 (Bridget "sister to Sir Ambrose Cave, Kt"). *H.S.P.* 13:295 (1878) (identifies three sons and two daughters, but not a daughter Anne). *H.S.P.* 16:51 (1881) (1563 Vis. Yorks) (identifies parents of Bridget as "Rychard Cave, by Margaret doughter of Thomas Saxby of Northampton").

4. **ANNE TANFIELD**, was married to **CLEMENT VINCENT**, Esq., of Harpole, co. Northampton, third son of George Vincent, of Peekleton, of co. Leicester.

H.S.P. 2:50-51,80 (1870). *Chester of Chicheley* (1878) 1:79. *Metcalfe* (1887), p. 107 (1618/9 Vis. Northants), p. 141.

3. **ELIZABETH VINCENT**, was married to **RICHARD LANE**, of Courteenhall, co. Northampton, son of Francis Lane, of Bromley Hall, co. Stafford. They had two sons and five daughters.

H.S.P. 2:51 (1870). *Chester of Chicheley* (1878) 1:79. *Metcalfe* (1887), p. 107. *Randolph* (1952), p. 16.

2. **DOROTHY LANE**, was baptized at Courteenhall on 4 Sep. 1589. She was married for the first time, with two children, to **THOMAS WEST**, of Cotton End, near Northampton, co. Northampton, son of John West, of Cotton End, by his wife Agnes. He was buried on 26 Jan. 1614/5. She was married for the second time at Little Houghton on 30 Mar. 1619 to **WILLIAM RANDOLPH**, of Little Houghton, co. Northampton, son of Robert Randolph, Gent., of Hams, Sussex, by Rose, daughter of Thomas Roberts, of Hawkhurst, Kent. He was born about 1570-2, and was Steward to Edward Lord Zouche for more than thirty years. He had been married previously to Elizabeth Smith, daughter of Thomas Smith, Gent., of Newnham, co. Northampton, with three sons and one daughter. WILLIAM RANDOLPH may be the William Randolph who was buried at Moreton Morrell, co. Warwick, in 1657.

Metcalfe (1887), p. 107. *Wm. & Mary Quart.* 1:158 (Jan. 1893). *Wm. & Mary Quart.* 4:125-127 (Oct. 1895). *H.S.P.* 87:176-177, 239 (1681 Vis. Northants). *NEHGR* 106:166 (July 1952) (Randolph arms: *Gules*, a cross *argent* on the cross five pierced molets *sable*). *Randolph* (1952), pp. 14-51.

Children & grandchildren of William Randolph, by Dorothy Lane:

    i. JOHN RANDOLPH, baptised Newnham 6 Feb. 1619/20, lawyer, married DOROTHY ATTERBURY. Issue in England.

    ii. RICHARD RANDOLPH, baptised Little Houghton 24 Feb. 1612/2 [see next].

    iii. HENRY RANDOLPH, baptised Little Houghton 27 Nov. 1623, emigrated to Virginia 1642, Clerk of Henrico County, Virginia, Clerk of Virginia Assembly, died 1673; married, first, 12 Oct. 1652 ELIZABETH _____, died 12 Oct. 1660; second, 12 Dec. 1661 **JUDITH SOANE**.

        a. HENRY RANDOLPH, born Appomatox 2 Sep. 1654, died 8 Oct. 1654.

        b. WILLIAM RANDOLPH, born James City 12 Sep. 1658, died before 1672 unmarried.

RANDOLPH (cont.)

 c. **CAPT. HENRY RANDOLPH**, born Appamatox 16 Jan. 1665, Clerk Henrico County, married **SARAH SWAN**. One son.
 d. **JUDITH RANDOLPH**, born Appamatox 29 July 1671, died young unmarried.
 e. **MARTHA RANDOLPH**, died young unmarried.
 iv. ANNE RANDOLPH, baptised Little Houghton 8 Feb. 1625/26, buried 28 Jan. 1626/7.
 v. GEORGE RANDOLPH, baptised Little Houghton 29 July 1627, slain in war 5 June 1645, buried Harrington, co. Northampton.
 vi. MARGARET RANDOLPH, baptised Little Houghton 30 Apr. 1629, married ROGER PHILLIPS, Apothecary, of Brentford, Middlesex.
 vii. JUDITH RANDOLPH, baptised Little Houghton 19 Aug. 1630, married HENRY WELTON, of Brentford, Middlesex.

1. RICHARD RANDOLPH, of Morton Hall in Moreton Morrell, co. Warwick, was baptised at Little Houghton, co. Northampton, on 24 Feb. 1621/2. He was married to **ELIZABETH RYLAND**, daughter of John Ryland, of co. Warwick. RICHARD RANDOLPH died at Dublin, Ireland, in May 1678.
 H.S.P. 87:176-177 (1935). *DAB* 15:371-372 (1935) (William Randolph). *Randolph* (1957), pp. 4-9. *Williams* (1970), p. 16.

Children and grandchildren of Richard Randolph, by Elizabeth Ryland:

 i. RICHARD RANDOLPH, Stationer of London, died *s.p.*
 ii. DOROTHY RANDOLPH, baptised Moreton Morrell 1 Apr. 1647.
 iii. MARY RANDOLPH, baptised Moreton Morrell 2 Nov. 1648, married in Dorset.
 iv. **COL. WILLIAM RANDOLPH**, baptised Moreton Morrell 7 Nov. 1650, emigrated to Virginia about 1673, of Turkey Island, Henrico County, Virginia, planter, merchant, clerk of Henrico County, Speaker of House of Burgesses, a founder of the College of William and Mary, died 11 Apr. 1711; married **MARY ISHAM**. Issue (ages apparently as of 1713/14).
  a. **WILLIAM RANDOLPH**, of Turkey Island, aged 31, married **ELIZABETH BEVERLEY**. Issue.
  b. **THOMAS RANDOLPH**, of Tuckahoe, aged 25; married **JUDITH FLEMING**.
  c. **ISHAM RANDOLPH**, of Dungeness, aged 27, married **JANE ROGERS**.
  d. **RICHARD RANDOLPH**, of Curles, aged 23; married **JANE BOLLING**.
  e. **JOHN RANDOLPH**, Knt., of Tazewell Hall, Williamsburg, married **SUSAN BEVERLEY**.
  f. **HENRY RANDOLPH**, of Chatworth, aged 29, died unmarried.
  g. **EDWARD RANDOLPH**, of Bremo, married _____ **GROVES**.
  h. **WILLIAM RANDOLPH**, died in infancy.
  i. **JOSEPH RANDOLPH**.
  j. **ELIZABETH RANDOLPH**, died young.
  k. **ELIZABETH RANDOLPH**, married **RICHARD BLAND**.
  l. **MARY RANDOLPH**, married **JOHN STITH**, of Swinyards, Charles City County, Virginia.
 v. THOMAS RANDOLPH, baptised Moreton Morrell 3 Feb. 1651, died *s.p.*
 vi. JOHN RANDOLPH, baptised Moreton Morrell 20 July 1653, resided in the Strand, London, 1682.
 vii. ELIZABETH RANDOLPH, baptised Moreton Morrell 1 Jan. 1655/6.
 viii. MARGARET RANDOLPH, born 25 Feb. 1656/7.

* * *

EDWARD III OF ENGLAND, King of England, married PHILIPPE DE HAINAUT.
LIONEL OF CLARENCE [*of Antwerp*], Duke of Clarence, married ELIZABETH DE BURGH.
PHILIPPE OF CLARENCE, married EDMUND DE MORTIMER, 3rd Earl of March.
ELIZABETH MORTIMER, married HENRY PERCY, Knt.
HENRY PERCY, Earl of Northumberland, married ALIANOR NEVILLE.
HENRY PERCY, Earl, married ALIANOR POYNINGS [see PERCY 8].

5. MARGARET PERCY, was married to WILLIAM GASCOIGNE, Knt., of Gawthorpe, co. York, son of William Gascoigne, Knt., of Gawthorpe, by Joan, Lady of Oversley, co. Warwick, and Wormsley, co. York, daughter and heiress of John Neville, Esq., of Oversley, co. Warwick (**descendant of King Edward I**) [see NEVILLE 7 for his ancestry]. They had six sons and seven daughters. SIR WILLIAM GASCOIGNE died on 4 Mar. 1486/7.

Sur.Soc. 41:15 (1862) (1530 Vis. North). *Foster* (1874), Gascoigne chart. *H.S.P.* 16:135 (1881) (1563 Vis. Yorks). *Sur.Soc.* 144:151 (1930) (1480 Vis. North). *C.P.* 9:717 footnote *d* (1936). *Paget* (1977), p. 251.

Children of William Gascoigne, by Margaret Percy:

  i. ELIZABETH GASCOIGNE [see next].

  ii. DOROTHY GASCOIGNE, married NINIAN MARKENFIELD, Knt. [see MAULEVERER 6].[1]

4. ELIZABETH GASCOIGNE, was married before April 1493 to GEORGE TAILBOYS, Knt., Lord Kyme *de jure*, Sheriff of Lincolnshire, son of Robert Tailboys, Knt., Lord Kyme (**descendant of King Edward I**), by Elizabeth, daughter of John Heron, Knt. He was born about 1467 (aged twenty-eight in 1495) [see TAILBOYS 5 for his ancestry]. He had been married previously to Margaret Burgh, daughter of Thomas Burgh, Knt., of Gainsborough, by Margaret, daughter of Thomas de Ros, 9th Lord Ros. On 2 Mar. 1517 he was judged a lunatic and his person and lands were taken into custody. GEORGE TAILBOYS, Lord Kyme, died on 21 Sep. 1538, and was buried at Bullington. His widow died in 1559 (M.I. Lincoln Cathedral).

H.S.P. 52:946 (1904) (Maddison Linc. Ped.). *C.P.* 7:356,361-363, 361 footnote *k* (1929) (Tailboys arms: *Argent* a saltire *gules*, on a chief 3 escallops of the field). *Paget* (1977), p. 255.

3. ANNE TAILBOYS, was sister and heir to Gilbert Tailboys, Knt., of Kyme. She was married for the first time to EDWARD DYMOKE, Knt., of Scrivelsby, co. Lincoln, Sheriff of Lincolnshire, son of Robert Dymoke, Knt., of Scrivelsby (**descendant of King Edward I**), by Anne, daughter and heiress of John Sparrow, of London. He was born in 1508 (aged thirty-six at his father's death) [see DYMOKE 4 for his ancestry]. He was Champion at the Coronation of King Edward VI in 1547, and Queens Mary in 1553 and Elizabeth in 1559. They had three sons and five daughters. SIR EDWARD DYMOKE died testate on 16 Sep. 1566. She was married for the second time to ROBERT CARRE, of Sleaford.

Gen. 4:19 (1880). *H.S.P.* 52:947 (1904). *H.S.P.* 55:1205 (1906). *Paget* (1977), p. 173.

2. FRANCES DYMOKE, fourth daughter, was married on 20 Aug. 1556 to THOMAS WINDEBANK, Knt., of Haynes Hill in Hurst, co. Berks, son of Richard Windebank, Knt., by Margaret ferch Griffith ap Henry. He was clerk of the Signet to Queen Elizabeth and King James I, and deputy clerk of the privy council. SIR THOMAS WINDEBANK died on 23 Oct. 1607. His widow died after 3 Mar. 1610/1.

Gen. 4:19 (1880). *VMHB* 4:204-205 (Oct. 1896). *H.S.P.* 55:1205 (1906). *Throckmorton* (1930), p. 321. *Paget* (1977), p. 120.

---

[1] Ancestors of **Anne Mauleverer**.

READE (cont.)

1. MILDRED WINDEBANK, was born in 1584. She was married on 31 July 1600 to **ROBERT READE**, Esq., of Linkenholt Hall, co. Hants, second son of Andrew Reade, of Linkenholt Hall, co. Hants. He was born in 1551, and had been married twice previously. The will of ROBERT READE, ESQ., was dated 10 Dec. 1626. The will of his widow was dated 15 Aug. 1630.

VMHB 4:205 (D.N.B. concerning Thomas Reade "states that he was a brother to Robert Reade, who was secretary to his uncle, Sir Francis Windebanke"). *VMHB* 27:302-306 (July 1919). *Throckmorton* (1930), pp. 321-322. *TAG* 51:167 (July 1975). *Paget* (1977), pp. 57,85. *Adventurers* (1987), pp. 419-427.

Children & grandchildren of Robert Reade, by Mildred Windebank:

   i. ANDREW READE, D.D., of Langershall, co. Wilts.

   ii. WILLIAM READE.

   iii. DR. THOMAS READE, born Linkenholt 1606, LL.D. Oxford 1638, principal of Magdalen Hall, Oxford, 1625.

   iv. COL. GEORGE READE, born 25 Oct. 1608, emigrated to Virginia 1637, member of Council, died 1671; married ELIZABETH MARTIAU.

      a. GEORGE READE, died *s.p.*

      b. ROBERT READE, married MARY LILLY. Seven children.

      c. THOMAS READE, married LUCY GWYN. Six children.

      d. FRANCIS READE, married, first, JANE CHEESMAN, second, ANNE _____. Two daughters by first marriage. Five children by second marriage.

      e. BENJAMIN READE, married LUCY _____. One son.

      f. MILDRED READE, married COL. AUGUSTINE WARNER. Six children.

      g. ELIZABETH READE, married CAPT. THOMAS CHEESMAN. Nine children.;

* * *

REED see BRENT

RICHERS see HAYNES

* * *

RODNEY

EDWARD III OF ENGLAND, King of England, married PHILIPPE DE HAINAUT.
LIONEL OF CLARENCE [*of Antwerp*], Duke of Clarence, married ELIZABETH DE BURGH.
PHILIPPE OF CLARENCE, married EDMUND DE MORTIMER, 3rd Earl of March.
ELIZABETH MORTIMER, married HENRY PERCY, Knt.
ELIZABETH PERCY, married JOHN DE CLIFFORD, Lord Clifford.
MARY DE CLIFFORD, married PHILIP WENTWORTH, Knt.
HENRY WENTWORTH, Knt., married ANNE SAY [see HARLESTON 6].

5. MARGERY WENTWORTH, was married to **JOHN SEYMOUR**, Knt., of Wolf Hall, co. Wilts, Sheriff of Wiltshire, son and heir of John Seymour, of Wolf Hall, by Elizabeth, daughter of George Darrell, Knt., of Littlecote, co. Wilts. He was born in 1476. They had six sons and four daughters. SIR JOHN SEYMOUR died in his

RODNEY (cont.)

sixtieth year on 21 Dec. 1536, and was buried at Easton Priory, later removed to the chancel at Great Bedwyn, co. Wilts (M.I.). His widow died testate in October 1550.

> *Wotton* (1741) 1:90-91 (Seymour arms: *Gules*, two wings conjoin'd in lure, tips downward, *or*). *Wilts.Arch.Mag.* 15:143 (Feb. 1875) (two other sons were "Edward Seymour, the Protector, and Thomas Seymour, Lord Sudeley, who married Queen Katherine Parr, widow of Henry VIII"). *Seymours* (1902), pp. 8-21. *C.P.* 12(1):59-60 (1953). *Paget* (1977), p. 187.

Children & grandchild of John Seymour, by Margery Wentworth:

i. **HENRY SEYMOUR**, Knt., second surviving son [see next].

ii. **JANE SEYMOUR**, born 1509, married **HENRY VIII OF ENGLAND, King of England**.

    a. **EDWARD VI OF ENGLAND, King of England**.

iii. **ELIZABETH SEYMOUR**, married, first, **GREGORY CROMWELL** [see WINGFIELD 5].[1]

4. HENRY SEYMOUR, Knt., second surviving son, of Marvel and Twyford, co. Hants, M.P. for Wiltshire, Sheriff for Hampshire, was married to **BARBARA WOLFE**, daughter of Morgan Wolfe, Esq., by Gwenllian, daughter and heiress of John de Barry. They had three sons and seven daughters. SIR HENRY SEYMOUR died in 1578.

> *Wotton* (1741) 1:92 (no identification of wife). *Burke's Commoners* (1838) 3:201-202 (identification of wife's parents; the identification of parents in her monumental inscription is in error). *Gen. (n.s.)* 17:101 (1901). *Seymours* (1902), p. 21. *TAG* 64:97-100 (Apr. 1989).

3. JANE SEYMOUR, was married to **JOHN RODNEY**, Knt., of Rodney Stoke, co. Somerset, Sheriff, M.P., son of George Rodney, of Rodney Stoke, by his wife Elizabeth Kirton, of Cheddar, Somerset. He was born at Stoke about 1551. "Hee was bred a Scoller in Corpus-Christi-Colledge in Oxford". [His wife] "was a very wise & provident woman, and brought him a thousand pound portion, with many Children ... sixteene or seventeene; but left behinde him at his death only seven". SIR JOHN RODNEY died aged sixty-one on 6 Aug. 1612. His widow died in February 1634. They were buried in the aisle at Stoke.

> *Gen. (n.s.)* 17:100-103 (1901) ("Genealogy of the Family of Rodney of Rodney Stoke as Compiled in the Seventeenth Century by Sir Edward Rodney, Knt.") ("Sir John Rodeney was Knighted in the first yeare of King James, Hee had borne all the Country Offices, which were proper to the best sort of Gentlemen, and at last being highe Shiriffe at the Assizes at Charde"). *D.N.B.* 17:1237-38 (1909). *C.P.* 11:66 footnote *e* (1949). *Welcome Claimants* (1970), pp. 447-448. *TAG* 64:97-100 (Apr. 1989) (Rodney arms: *Or*, three eagles displayed *purpure*).

Children of John Rodney, by Jane Seymour:

i. **WILLIAM RODNEY**, Gent. younger son, [see next].

ii. **ELIZABETH RODNEY**, married **HENRY NORWOOD** [see LIGON 3.v for his ancestry].

2. WILLIAM RODNEY, Gent., of Catcott in Moorlinch, Somerset, younger son, was born in 1610. He was married to **ALICE CAESAR**, youngest daughter of Thomas Caesar, Knt., cursitor [junior] baron of the Exchequer, by his third wife Susan, daughter of William Ryder, Knt., of Mucklestone, co. Stafford, Lord Mayor of London. She was born before 1611. They had eleven children. She predeceased her husband. WILLIAM RODNEY, GENT., died testate on 12 June 1669, and was buried at Huntspill, Somerset.

> *Gen. (n.s.)* 17:103 (1901). *Welcome Claimants* (1970), pp. 450-453. *TAG* 64:100-111 (Apr. 1989) (Caesar arms: 3 roses *argent*, on a chief of the second, 3 roses of the first).

Children of William Rodney, by Alice Caesar:

i. **JOHN RODNEY**, born about 1633, served in Royal Horse Guards 1659-1666, served as an

---

[1] Ancestors of **Humphrey Davie, Thomas Wingfield**.

RODNEY (cont.)

officer in the West Indies until 1672, settled Philadelphia, Pennsylvania, died there 1694; married about 1667-68 **FRANCES MALL**, second, before 1690 **ANN** _____. Two children by first marriage resided at Antigua. One son by second marriage.

   ii. **WILLIAM RODNEY**, baptised 21 June 1637 [see next].

1. **WILLIAM RODNEY**, Gent., was baptised at Catcott, co. Somerset, on 21 June 1637. He was a merchant and customs official at Bristol and New York, and was married to **RACHEL** _____. They resided at Bristol, co. Gloucester. He was made a Merchant Venturer at Bristol in 1665, and was a merchant on the ship *Robert* of Bristol bound for the Barbados in 1667. He was a resident of New York City on 28 Jan. 1674/5 and was a Royal Prosecutor there by July 1675 and Surveyor of the Customs by July 1675. While he served as a colonial official in New York, his family evidently remained in Bristol. It appears that he engaged in the trade between the West Indies and New York. WILLIAM RODNEY, GENT., died at sea while bound from the island of Nevis to New York on board the vessel *Lavrell* in the Sound off New Haven about January 1678/9. His widow was buried at Christchurch, Bristol, on 6 Aug. 1713.

   NEHGR 107:48 (Jan. 1953) (Rodney arms: Gold three eagles purpure). *Welcome Claimants* (1970), pp. 453-460. *TAG* 64:104-105 (Apr. 1989).

   Children and grandchildren of William Rodney, by Rachel:

   i. **WILLIAM RODNEY**, Esq., baptised Christchurch, Bristol, 14 Mar 1660/1, emigrated before December 1681, representative to the Pennsylvania Assembly from Kent Co. [Delaware] in May 1688, Clerk of the Kent Co. Court in 1697, Justice of the Kent Co. Court in 1703, speaker of the first General Assembly of the Lower Counties, later Delaware, died testate 8 Sep. 1708, buried on Byfield Plantation, near Dover, Kent Co.; married, first, **MARY HOLLYMAN**, died December 1692 second, 20 Feb. 1693/4 **SARAH JONES**.

     a. **WILLIAM RODNEY**, born 27 Oct. 1689, married **RUTH CURTIS**. Five children.

     b. **RACHEL RODNEY**, born 18 Nov. 1690, died 7 Sep. 1695.

     b. **THOMAS RODNEY**, born 11 Aug. 1692, buried Philadelphia 7 9th mo. [Nov.] 1709.

     c. **DANIEL RODNEY**, born 13 Feb. 1694/5, married **MARGARET** _____. Issue.

     d. **JOHN RODNEY**, born 13 Apr. 1696, died 1708 unmarried.

     e. **ANTHONY RODNEY**, born 20 Mar. 1698/9, married **SARAH** _____.

     f. **GEORGE RODNEY**, born 8 Feb. 1701/2, buried 12 Apr. 1725.

     g. **SARAH RODNEY**, born 5 Aug. 1704, died 10 Apr. 1720.

     h. **CAESAR RODNEY**, born 1707, married **ELIZABETH CRAWFORD**. Eight children.

   ii. **ROBERT RODNEY**, baptised 25 Feb. 1662/3, buried 27 Sep. 1666.

   iii. **RACHEL RODNEY**, baptised 25 Sep. 1664, married **ROBERT CURTIS**.

   iv. **GEORGE RODNEY**, baptised 1 June 1666, buried 11 Feb. 1667/8.

   v. **GEORGE RODNEY**, baptised 3 July 1668, buried 29 June 1672.

   vi. **ELIZABETH RODNEY**, unmarried 1708.

* * *

EDWARD I OF ENGLAND, King of England, married **ALIANORE DE CASTILLE.**
JOAN OF ENGLAND [*of Acre*], married **GILBERT DE CLARE,** Earl of Gloucester.
MARGARET DE CLARE, married **HUGH DE AUDLEY,** 8th Earl of Gloucester.
MARGARET DE AUDLEY, married **RALPH DE STAFFORD** [see AUDLEY 12].

11. BEATRICE DE STAFFORD, was married for the first time to **MAURICE FITZ MAURICE,** Earl of Desmond. He died in 1358. She was married for the second time, with royal license dated 1 Jan. 1358/9, to **THOMAS DE ROS,** Knt., 4th Lord Ros of Helmsley, third son of William de Ros, **Baron** of Helmsley, co. York (of **Magna Charta Surety descent**), by Margery (of **Magna Charta Surety descent** and **descendant of Charlemagne,** daughter of Bartholomew de Badlesmere, 1st Lord Badlesmere. He was born at Stoke Albany, co. Northampton, on 13 Jan. 1336/7, and was brother and heir of William de Ros. They had four sons and two daughters. He took part in the King's expedition in Normandy in 1355, and in the campaigns of 1356 and 1359-60. He was summoned to Parliament from 24 Aug. 1362. In 1368 he was ordered to reside on his lands in Ireland with his armed forces, to prevent the loss and destruction of the country. "Thomas de Roos, lord of Hamelak" died testate at Uffington, co. Lincoln (while preparing to go on pilgrimage to Jerusalem), on 8 June 1384, and was buried at Riveaulx. His widow was married for the third time, with pardon for marrying without licence dated 20 Aug. 1385, to **RICHARD BURLEY,** Knt., K.G. (died 23 May 1387 *s.p.*). She died testate on 14 Apr. 1415 (will dated 26 June 1414 requesting burial in Warter Priory).

Paget (1957) 473:7. DNB 49: 216-219. John Nichols: History of Leicestershire, II Part 1 27 ff.

Children & grandchild of Thomas de Ros, by Beatrice de Stafford:

  i. **WILLIAM DE ROS,** Knt., born about 1368 [see next].

  ii. **ELIZABETH DE ROS,** died March 1424; married **THOMAS DE CLIFFORD,** of Appleby, Westmorland, 6th Lord Clifford, Hereditary Sheriff of Westmorland, Governor of Carlisle Castle, born about 1363 (aged twenty-six at his father's death), died abroad 18 Aug. 1391, son and heir of Roger de Clifford, 5th Lord Clifford (of **Magna Charta Surety descent** and **descendant of Charlemagne**), by Maud, daughter of Thomas de Beauchamp, Earl of Warwick (of **Magna Charta Surety descent** and **descendant of Charlemagne**). They had two children. He was summoned to Parliament from 6 Dec. 1389. *C.P.* 3:292 (1913). *Clay* (1913), p. 23.

   a. **JOHN DE CLIFFORD,** married **ELIZABETH PERCY** [see MACKWORTH 7].[1]

  iii. **MARGARET DE ROS,** married **REYNOLD GREY** [see BONVILLE 10].[2]

10. WILLIAM DE ROS, of Belvoir, K.G., 6th Lord Ros of Helmesley, P.C., Lord Treasurer of England, was born about 1368 (aged twenty-four at his brother's death), and was brother and heir to John de Ros. He was summoned to Parliament from 20 Nov. 1394. He was married, with license dated 9 Oct. 1394, to **MARGARET DE ARUNDEL,** daughter of John de Arundel, Knt., of Arundel (**descendant of King Henry III**), by Alianor, younger daughter and co-heiress of John Maltravers, Lord Mautravers [see BROWNE 12 for her ancestry]. They had five sons and four daughters. "William de Roos, lord of Hamelak and Belvoir" died testate at Belvoir on 1 Sep. 1414, and was buried at Belvoir Priory. His widow died testate on 3 July 1438.

---

[1] Ancestors of **Humphrey Davie, John Harleston, Agnes Mackworth, William Rodney, William Skepper, Thomas Wingfield.**

[2] Ancestors of **Elizabeth Bosvile, Charles Calvert, Muriel Gurdon, George Reade, Richard Saltonstall, Olive Welby, Thomas Wingfield,** and, probably, **Thomas Dudley, Jane Haviland.**

ROS (cont.)

C.P. 1:341 (1910). *Clay* (1913), p. 184. *C.P.* 11:102-104 (1949). *Paget* (1957) 473:7-8). John Nichols: History of Leicestershire, II Part I 27 ff.

Children of William de Ros, by Margaret de Arundel:
  i. **THOMAS DE ROS**, Knt., younger son, born 26 Sep. 1406 [see next].
  ii. **MARGARET DE ROS**, married **JAMES TUCHET**, Lord Audley [see TUCHET 9].[1]

9. THOMAS DE ROS, Knt., 8th Lord Ros, younger son, was born in 26 Sep. 1406. He was brother and heir of John de Ros, 7th Lord Ros, and was aged fourteen at his brother's death. He was knighted by the King at Leicester on 19 May 1426, served in France under the Duke of Bedford in 1427, and was summoned to Parliament in 1429. He was married to **ALIANOR BEAUCHAMP**, second daughter of Richard Beauchamp, Earl of Warwick (**descendant of King Edward I**), by Elizabeth, daughter and heiress of Thomas Berkeley, Lord Berkeley (**descendant of King Edward I**). She was co-heiress to her mother as to the Baronies of Berkeley and Lisle [see BEAUCHAMP 9 for her ancestry]. THOMAS DE ROS, Lord Ros, died 18 Aug. 1430 "in the King's wars in France". His widow was married for the second time to Edmund Beaufort, Earl of Dorset, afterwards Duke of Somerset (slain at the first battle of St Albans on 22 May 1455) [see BEAUFORT 6 for descendants of this marriage]. She died on 4 Mar. 1467.

Clay (1913), p. 184. *C.P.* 11:104-105 (1949) (his widow, said to have been married, third, Walter Rokesley).

8. THOMAS DE ROS, 9th Lord Ros, son and heir, was born on 9 Sep. 1427. He was married to **PHILIPPE TIPTOFT**, daughter of John Tiptoft, Lord Tiptoft, by Joyce, daughter of Edward Cherleton, 5th Lord Cherleton (**descendant of King Edward I**). She was aunt and co-heiress to Edward, Earl of Worcester [see CHERLETON 10 for her ancestry]. They had two sons and four daughters. He was an ardent Lancastrian and had a grant of various manors belonging to Richard Neville, Earl of Salisbury. He was present at the Lancastrian rout at Towton on 29 Mar. 1461, and afterwards fled with the King to Berwick. He was subsequently attainted in Parliament on 4 Nov. 1461. He fled abroad, but returned secretly to England in May 1464, and made for the North. He was taken prisoner at Hexham on 15 May 1464. THOMAS DE ROS, Lord Ros, was beheaded at Newcastle on 17 May 1464. His widow was married for the second time before 23 Jan. 1469 to Thomas Wingfield. She was living on 23 Nov. 1485 when she was found to be one of the co-heirs of her nephew Edward, Earl of Worcester.

Clay (1913), pp. 184-185 (she married, third, Edward Grimston). *Paget* (1957) 473:9-10.

Child of Thomas de Ros, by Philippe Tiptoft:
  i. **ALIANOR DE ROS**, born 1449, married **ROBERT MANNERS**, Knt., of Etal [see OGLE 7].[2]

* * *

SACKVILLE see BUTLER

---

[1] Ancestors of **Francis Dade, Henry Fleete, Muriel Gurdon, William Randolph, Hawte Wyatt**.

[2] Ancestors of **Philip & Thomas Nelson**.

SAINT LEGER

EDWARD III OF ENGLAND, King of England, married **PHILIPPE DE HAINAUT.**
LIONEL OF CLARENCE [*of Antwerp*], Duke of Clarence, married **ELIZABETH DE BURGH.**
PHILIPPE OF CLARENCE, married **EDMUND DE MORTIMER,** 3rd Earl of March.
ELIZABETH DE MORTIMER, married **HENRY PERCY,** Knt.
HENRY PERCY, Earl of Northumberland, married **ALIANOR NEVILLE.**
HENRY PERCY, 3rd Earl of Northumberland, married **ALIANOR POYNINGS.**
HENRY PERCY, 4th Earl of Northumberland, married **MAUD HERBERT** [see KEMPE 7].

5. **ELEANOR PERCY,** first daughter, was married, with contract dated 14 Dec. 1490, to **EDWARD STAFFORD,** K.B., K.G., 3rd Duke of Buckingham, 8th Earl of Stafford, 9th Lord Stafford, son and heir of Henry Stafford, 2nd Duke of Buckingham (**descendant of King Edward III**), by Katherine (**descendant of Charlemagne**), daughter of Richard Wydeville, Earl Rivers. He was born at Brecknock Castle on 3 Feb. 1477/8, and was restored to all his father's honours in 1485 [see AUDLEY 7 for his ancestry]. He had licence to castellate his manor of Thornbury on 9 July 1510. EDWARD STAFFORD, Duke of Buckingham, appears to have entertained some notions of his possible right to the Crown, and having incurred the enmity of Cardinal Wolsey, was accused and found guilty, on very flimsy grounds, of high treason, and was executed aged forty-three on Tower Hill on 17 May 1521, and was buried at the Austin Friars, London. "Elianore duches of Buckingham" died testate (P.C.C., 4 Thower) on 13 Feb. 1530, and was buried at Greyfriars', London.
C.P. 2:390-391 (1912). *C.P.* 12(1):182-184 (1953). *Paget* (1977), p. 121.

4. **MARY STAFFORD,** youngest daughter, was married about 1519 to **GEORGE NEVILLE,** K.B., K.G., 5th Lord Bergavenny, son and heir of George Neville, 4th Lord Bergavenny (**descendant of King Edward III**), by Margaret, daughter and heiress of Hugh Fenne, Esq., of Sculton Burdeleys, Norfolk [see OXENBRIDGE 5 for his ancestry]. He was born about 1469 (aged sixteen or more at his mother's death). He had been married previously for the first time, with two daughters, to Joan Fitz Alan, daughter of Thomas Fitz Alan, Earl of Arundel, by Margaret, daughter of Richard Wydeville, Earl of Rivers (she died on 14 November *s.p.m.*), and for the second time to Margaret Brent, daughter of William Brent, of Charing, Kent, "gentleman" (she was living in 1515, but died *s.p.s.*). He was summoned to Parliament from 16 Jan. 1496/7. George & Mary had one son and five daughters. He was married for the fourth time to Mary Brooke, otherwise Cobham, who had been his mistress, and who survived him. The will of GEORGE NEVILLE, Lord Bergavenny, was dated 4 June 1535 and proved 24 Jan. 1535/6. He was buried at Birling, Kent.
C.P. 1:31 (1910). *Mortimer-Percy* (1911), p. 22. *H.S.P.* 74:15 (1923) (1530 Vis. Kent). *Paget* (1957) 410:4-5. *Paget* (1977), p. 86.

3. **URSULA NEVILLE,** youngest daughter, was married to **WARHAM SAINT LEGER,** Knt., of Ulcombe, co. Kent, Sheriff of Kent, second son of Anthony Saint Leger, Knt., Lord Deputy of Ireland, by Agnes, daughter of Hugh Warham, of Croydon. They had five sons and four daughters. She died in 1575. SIR WARHAM SAINT LEGER died in 1599.
Burke's Commoners (1838) 4:485 ("appointed chief governor of Munster ... in 1580 he caused James, of Desmond, who was denominated a notorious rebel, to be hanged under martial law, at Cork. He was killed eventually, in battle, (in single combat) by Hugh Maguire, Lord of Fermanagh, who fell himself, at the same time"). *Scott* (1876), p. 228. *Mortimer-Percy* (1911), p. 28,30. *H.S.P.* 75:69 (1924) (1574 Vis. Kent). *Paget* (1957) 410:5. *Paget* (1977), p. 58.

Children of Warham St. Leger, by Ursula Neville:
  i. **ANTHONY SAINT LEGER,** Knt. [see next].

SAINT LEGER (cont.)

  ii. **ANNE SAINT LEGER**, born about 1555, married **THOMAS DIGGES**, of Barham, Kent.[1]

2. **ANTHONY SAINT LEGER**, Knt., of Ulcombe, and of Leeds Castle, Kent, eldest son, was married about 1578 to **MARY SCOTT**, daughter of Thomas Scott, Knt., of Scott's Hall, Kent (**descendant of King Edward I**), by Elizabeth (**descendant of Charlemagne**), daughter of John Baker, Knt., of Sissinghurst Castle in Cranbrook, Kent [see FLEETE 3.i for her ancestry]. They had four sons and one daughter. SIR ANTHONY SAINT LEGER died in 1603. She was married for the second time to Alexander Culpeper, Knt., of Wigsell, Sussex, son of Alexander Culpeper, Knt., of Bedgebury, Sheriff of Kent (died 15 Apr. 1636).

Scott (1876), p. 228. *H.S.P.* 42:129 (1898) (1619 Vis. Kent). *Mortimer-Percy* (1911), p. 30. *H.S.P.* 75:69 (1924). *Adventurers* (1987), p. 523.

1. **WARHAM SAINT LEGER**, Knt., of Ulcombe, co. Kent, was a member of the Virginia Company and subscriber to the Third Charter, 1611/2. He accompanied Sir Walter Raleigh on his second voyage to Guiana 1617-18, being the captain of the *Thunder* with seventy-six men and twenty guns. Raleigh, in writing of the misconduct of his subordinates, stated that all wished to turn pirates except St. Leger. The losses which Sir Warham incurred on this expedition compelled him to sell Leeds Castle. He was married to **MARY HAYWARD**, daughter of Rowland Hayward, Knt., Lord Mayor of London, of Salmeston, Kent. SIR WARHAM SAINT LEGER died testate on 11 Oct. 1631. His widow, who later resided at Lenham, Kent, died in 1662.

Mortimer-Percy (1911), p. 30. *VMHB* 27:289-290 (July 1919). *NEHGR* 107:189 (July 1953) (Horsmanden arms: Gules a saltire silver and a fess azure, on the fess three leopards' faces gold). *N.& Q.* 224:411-412 (Feb. 1979). *Adventurers* (1987), 523-524 ("The name was pronounced Sillenger in England").

Children & grandchildren of Warham Saint Leger, by Mary Hayward:

  i. **ANTHONY SAINT LEGER**, Knt., Warden of the Mint, 1660, alienated Ulcombe, 1648; married, first BARBARA (SHERLEY) THORNHURST, second MARY NORWOOD, third BRIDGET _____. Daughter and heiress.

  ii. **THOMAS SAINT LEGER**, died 1608.

  iii. **URSULA SAINT LEGER**, born 1609, buried Ulcombe 18 Oct. 1672; married August 1627 at Ulcombe, Kent, to **REV. DANIEL HORSMANDEN**, baptised 16 Mar. 1583/4 at Lenham, Kent, D.D. Oxford, D.D. Cambridge, Rector of Ulcombe 1627-1639, will dated 27 Jan. 1654/5 at Maidstone, Kent, naming "brother Sir Anthony St. Leger", and his children. Their children baptised at Ulcombe.

   a. **COL. WARHAM HORSMANDEN**, baptised 5 Sep. 1628, a loyalist, emigrated to Virginia during the English Civil Wars, settled Charles City County, Virginia, by 25 Feb. 1653/4, member of the House of Burgesses, and of Council, 1658-59, returned to England, died 1691; married St. Mary, Somerset, London, 27 Feb. 1650/1 **SUSANNAH BEECHING**, died 1691 aged sixty-four. Three children.

   b. MARY HORSMANDEN, baptised 20 Sep. 1631.

   c. RICHARD HORSMANDEN, baptised 31 Oct. 1632.

   d. ANTHONY HORSMANDEN, baptised 25 Apr. 1634, resided Maidstone, Kent, and St. Dunstan's, London; married, first, ELIZABETH HORSMANDEN, second, JANE TURNER.

   e. DAVID HORSMANDEN, baptised 13 Apr. 1637, buried 7 Aug. 1637.

   f. SUSANNA HORSMANDEN, married _____ CHAPMAN.

  iv. **KATHERINE SAINT LEGER**, returned to Maidstone, Kent, after husband's death, died before 28 Aug. 1658; married at Ulcombe, Kent, 10 July 1628 to **THOMAS CULPEPER**, admitted

---

[1]Grandparents of **Edward Digges**.

SAINT LEGER (cont.)

Middle Temple 7 May 1621, member of Virginia Company 1623, an original patentee of the Northern Neck of Virginia 18 Sep. 1649, probably died in Virginia before 1652.

    a. MARY CULPEPER, baptised Ulcombe, Kent, 26 Apr. 1629, buried 3 Dec. 1630.

    b. ANNE CULPEPER, baptised Hollingbourne 16 Sep. 1630, buried York, England, 1695; married in Virginia about 1652 CHRISTOPHER DANBY, of Thorpe Perrow, co. York. Two children. No descendants in Virginia.

    c. JOHN CULPEPER, baptised Hollingbourne, Kent 4 Apr. 1633, presumably died young.

    d. FRANCES CULPEPER, baptised Hollingbourne 27 May 1634, living July 1690; married, first (with no issue), soon after 1 Jan. 1652/3 CAPT. SAMUEL STEPHENS, born about 1629, appointed Governor of Albemarle, died before 7 Mar. 1669/70; second, June 1670 WILLIAM BERKELEY, Knt., baptised Twickernham, Middlesex, 16 July 1608, Governor of Virginia, died 1677, third (with no issue), PHILIP LUDWELL, born 1638 Governor of both North and South Carolina, returned to England about 1700, buried Stratford le Bow, Middlesex, 1717.

    e. CAPT. ALEXANDER CULPEPER, ESQ., baptism not found, of full age by 1658, in Virginia some years before 1671, granted office of Surveyor General of Virginia 25 Oct. 1671 on return to England, buried at Bromfield, 26 Dec. 1694, unmarried.

    f. JOHN CULPEPER, GENT., son, presumably, born about 1644, baptism not found, Surveyor General of South Carolina, later resided Albemarle County, North Carolina; participated in Culpeper's Rebellion, tried for treason in England; married, first, JUDITH _____, second MARGARET (_____) BIRD, third, SARAH MAYO. Issue.

v. JOHN SAINT LEGER, married REBECCA HORSMANDEN.

vi. WARHAM SAINT LEGER, died 1621/2.

vii. MARY SAINT LEGER, baptised 1612, married Lenham, Kent, with licence dated 27 Nov. 1632 COL. WILLIAM CODD, Esq., born 1604, of Pelicans, Wateringbury, Kent, will proved 25 July 1653.

    a. MARY CODD, baptised Lenham 23 Sep. 1633.

    b. BARBARA CODD, married 19 May 1657 RICHARD HARWOOD, Gent., of Maidstone, Kent.

    c. DEBORAH CODD.

    d. KATHERINE CODD.

    e. ELIZABETH CODD.

    f. ANNE CODD.

    g. COL. ST. LEGER CODD, born 1635, admitted Gray's Inn 1 May 1656, emigrated to Virginia by 18 Apr. 1670, removed to Cecil County, Maryland, died 7 Nov. 1706; married, first, ANNE (MOTTROM) WRIGHT FOX, second, ANNE (BENNETT) BLAND, ANNE (HYNSON) RANDALL WICKES. Five children by first marriage.

    h. ANTHONY CODD.

    I. ROWLAND CODD.

viii. ROWLAND SAINT LEGER, Gent., baptised 1613/4, Governor of Brandon, County Cork, Ireland, 1642.

ix. DUDLEY SAINT LEGER, of St. John's, Thanet, Kent, married ANNE _____. Issue.

x. FRANCES SAINT LEGER, baptised 1617, died 1634.

xi. GEORGE SAINT LEGER, baptised 1618/9, died 1620.

xii. LT.-COL. HEYWARD SAINT LEGER, baptised 1621, of Hayward's Hall, co. Cork, married BARBARA (ST. LEGER) BARRETT. Seven children.

xiii. ALEXANDER SAINT LEGER, born 1622/3, died 1625/6.

* * *

SAINT LEGER OF ULCOMBE, KENT see YORK

* * *

SALTONSTALL

EDWARD III OF ENGLAND, King of England, married PHILIPPE DE HAINAUT.
LIONEL OF CLARENCE [*of Antwerp*], Duke of Clarence, married ELIZABETH DE BURGH.
PHILIPPE OF CLARENCE, married EDMUND DE MORTIMER, 3rd Earl of March.
ELIZABETH MORTIMER, married HENRY PERCY, Knt.
HENRY PERCY, 5th Lord Percy, married ALIANOR NEVILLE.
HENRY PERCY, 3rd Earl of Northumberland, married ALIANOR POYNINGS.
MARGARET PERCY, married WILLIAM GASCOIGNE, Knt.
DOROTHY GASCOIGNE, married NINIAN MARKENFIELD, Knt.
ALICE MARKENFIELD, married ROBERT MAULEVERER [see MAULEVERER 5].

3. DOROTHY MAULEVERER, was born about 1528 (aged fifteen at time of marriage). She was married at Bardsay on 21 Jan. 1542/3 to **JOHN KAYE**, Esq., of Woodsome, co. York, son and heir of Arthur Kaye, Esq., of Woodsome, by Beatrice, daughter of Matthew Wentworth, Esq., of Bretton, co. York. He was also born about 1528 and aged fifteen at time of marriage. They had nine sons and three daughters. JOHN KAYE, ESQ., was living in 1585.

Wotton (1741) 2:275-276. *Glover-Foster* (1875), pp. 201,320,334 (Wentworth descent from Edward I) (1584 Vis. Yorks) (Kaye arms: *Argent, 2 bendlets sable*). *H.S.P.* 16:175 (1881) (1563 Vis. Yorks). *Saltonstall* (1897), p. 84 (no indication of Plantagenet ancestry). *York.Arch.Jour.* 16:197 (1902).

2. ROBERT KAYE, Esq., of Woodsome, co. York, Justice of the Peace, and Treasurer for Lame Soldiers in the time of Queen Elizabeth, son and heir, was married to **ANNE FLOWER**, daughter of John Flower, of Whitewell, co. Rutland. They had one son and two daughters. The will of Matthew Kaye, Gent., of Eastcome in East Greenwich, Kent, dated 14 Nov. 1610 and proved 5 Oct. 1612, bequeathed "to my well beloved brother Robert Kaye of Woodsome in the County of York, Esq., a gold ring . . . to my cosen, Grace Saltonstall my saide brother's daughter, a like ring of goulde". ROBERT KAYE, ESQ., was living in 1612.

Wotton (1741) 2:276. *Glover-Foster* (1875), p. 320. *H.S.P.* 16:175 (1881). *Waters* 2:939-940 (1901) (will of Matthew Saltonstall). *Saltonstall* (1897), pp. 7-8, 84.

1. GRACE KAYE, was married, as his first wife, to **RICHARD SALTONSTALL**, Knt., of Huntwick, co. York, son of Mr. Samuel Saltonstall, of Kingston-upon-Hull, co. York, by his first wife, Anne, daughter of John Ramsden, Esq., of Longley near Hothersfield. He was baptised at Halifax on 4 Apr. 1586. After the death of his first wife he sold his lands and removed with his children to New England. Richard was First Associate, Massachusetts Bay Company, and was appointed First Assistant. He commenced the settlement of Watertown in 1630, and was an original patentee of Connecticut with Lord Saye and Sele, Lord Brooke, and others. He returned to England in 1631. He was married for the second time to Elizabeth West (died 15 Jan. 1623/3), widow of Herbert Pelham, and daughter of Thomas West, Knt., Lord Delaware [see HUMPHREY 2], and for the third time to Martha Wilfred. No children by the second and third marriages. The will of SIR RICHARD SALTONSTALL was dated 1658 (with a legacy to Harvard College).

Glover-Foster (1875), p. 320. *Glover-Foster* (1875), p. 570 (1612 Vis. Yorks) (names children born as of date: Richard *aet. 1, 1612* and Rosamond) (Saltonstall arms: *Or, a bend between two eagles*

SALTONSTALL (cont.)

displayed *sable*). *Saltonstall* (1897), pp. 7-8, 12-14, 86-97. *NEHGR* 82:152 (Apr. 1928) (Saltonstall arms). NEHGR 95:72.

Children & grandchildren of Richard Saltonstall, by Grace Kaye:

i. MAJ. RICHARD SALTONSTALL, born at Woodsome 1610, matriculated as "Mr. Fellow Commoner" in Emmanuel College, Cambridge University, 14 Dec. 1627; emigrated with father in 1630 before taking a degree, admitted freeman 18 May 1631, resided Watertown, embarked for England 23 Nov. 1631 and remained there four years, in April 1635 embarked at London in the *Susan and Ellen*, with wife Muriel, and daughter Muriel, settled Watertown, Massachusetts, 1630, returned to England 1631, returned with wife Muriel and young daughter to settle at Ipswich, Massachusetts, Deputy of Ipswich to the General Court 1635-7, Assistant from 1637 to 1649, in 1664 and from 1680 to 1683, visited England several times, visited Holland with son Henry in 1644, when Richard's portrait was painted, it is said, by Rembrandt, in 1672 in England (when his three daughters were living married there), and the last time in England in 1683, died at Hulme, co. Lancaster, the seat of his son-in-law Sir Edward Moseley, on 29 Apr. 1694; married in England in June 1633 MURIEL GURDON [see GURDON 1 for her ancestry].

   a. MURIEL SALTONSTALL, born about 1635 (aged nine months in April 1635), married EDWARD MOSELEY, Knt., of Hulme, co. Lancaster. One daughter.

   b. RICHARD SALTONSTALL, citizen of London, married ELIZABETH _____, died testate about 1666 *s.p.* (will dated 25 Aug. 1665, proved 16 Oct. 1666, names wife, parents, siblings and cousins).

   c. NATHANIEL SALTONSTALL, born Ipswich, Massachusetts, about 1639, graduate Harvard College 1659, freeman 1665, Representative 1666, Town Clerk of Haverhill 1669 to 1671, Colonel of Essex Regiment 1679 to 1686, Assistant 1679 to 1686, 1689-1692, Member of Council, Judge Oyer and Terminer Court 1692, refused to serve in witchcraft trials, died 21 May 1707; married 28 Dec. 1663 ELIZABETH WARD, born 9 Apr. 1647, died testate 29 Apr. 1741. Five children.

   d. ABIGAIL SALTONSTALL, born Woodsome 1610, married THOMAS HARLEY, of Hinsham Court, co. Hereford.

   e. ELIZABETH SALTONSTALL, married HERCULES HORSEY, Esq. One daughter.

   f. GURDON SALTONSTALL, died young.

ii. ROSAMOND SALTONSTALL, born, probably, 1612, emigrated with father in 1630, and returned with him in 1631, residing with Lord Warwick 1642-4, mentioned in brother Robert's will in 1650.

iii. GRACE SALTONSTALL, born after 1612, emigrated with father in 1630, and returned with him in 1631, residing with Lady Manchester in 1642-4, mentioned in brother Robert's will in 1650.

iv. ROBERT SALTONSTALL, emigrated with father in 1630, resided Watertown, then Boston, member of Artillery Company 1638, died testate summer 1650, unmarried.

v. SAMUEL SALTONSTALL, emigrated with father in 1630, resided Watertown, died 21 Jan. 1696, unmarried.

vi. HENRY SALTONSTALL, emigrated with father in 1630, member of Artillery Company 1639, had farm of three hundred acres and eighty-eight acres of meadow in Watertown, graduate in first class Harvard College in 1652, returned to England, visited Holland with his father 1644, at University of Padua, Italy, in 1649, at Oxford 1652, Fellow of New College, Oxford University, received M.D. degree.

* * *

SAUNDERS see BEVILLE

SAVAGE see WYLLYS

SCOTT see FLEETE

* * *

SCROPE

EDWARD I OF ENGLAND, King of England, married ALIANORE DE CASTILLE.
JOAN OF ENGLAND [*of Acre*], married GILBERT DE CLARE, Earl of Gloucester.
MARGARET DE CLARE, married HUGH DE AUDLEY, Earl of Gloucester.
MARGARET DE AUDLEY, married RALPH DE STAFFORD, Earl of Stafford.
HUGH DE STAFFORD, 2nd Earl of Stafford, married PHILIPPE DE BEAUCHAMP.
MARGARET DE STAFFORD, married RALPH NEVILLE [see NEVILLE 10].

7. MARGARET NEVILLE, sixth daughter, was married for the first time before 31 Dec. 1413 to **RICHARD LE SCROPE**, 3rd Lord Scrope of Bolton, son and heir of Roger Le Scrope, 2nd Lord Scrope of Bolton, by Margaret, daughter of Robert Tibetot, 3rd Lord Tibetot (of **Magna Charta Surety descent** and **descendant of Charlemagne**). He was born on 31 May 1394. They had two sons. He was never summoned to Parliament. He served in France, and was present at Agincourt on 25 Oct. 1415, and at the siege of Rouen 1418-19. RICHARD LE SCROPE, Lord Scrope, died testate on 29 Aug. 1420 (will dated 24 Jan. 1419/20 at Rouen, proved 8 Nov. 1420). She was married for the second time before 5 Nov. 1427 to WILLIAM CRESSENER, of Sudbury, Suffolk. She died in 1463/4, and was buried at Austin Friars', Clare, Suffolk.

C.P. 11:542-543 (1949). *Paget* (1957) 491:2. *Carleton* (1978), chart 8-6.

6. HENRY LE SCROPE, 4th Lord Scrope of Bolton, son and heir, was born at Bolton on 4 June 1418. He was married in or shortly before 1435 to **ELIZABETH LE SCROPE**, fourth daughter of John Le Scrope, 4th Lord Scrope of Masham (of **Magna Charta Surety descent**), by Elizabeth, daughter of Thomas Chaworth, of Wiverton, co. Nottingham. They had four sons and three daughters. He was summoned to Parliament from 3 Dec. 1441 by writs directed *Henrico Lescrop de Bolton, Chivaler*. HENRY LE SCROPE, Lord Scrope, died aged forty on 14 Jan. 1458/9. His widow was living on 20 Oct. 1498.

Clay (1913), p. 199. *C.P.* 11:543-544 (1949). *Carleton* (1978), chart 8.

Children & grandchildren of Henry le Scrope, by Elizabeth le Scrope:

i. **JOHN LE SCROPE**, Knt., son and heir, born 22 July 1437 or 1438 [see next].
ii. **ELIZABETH LE SCROPE**, married **JOHN BIGOD**, Knt. [see BIGOD 7].[1]
iii. **MARGARET LE SCROPE**, married **JOHN BERNARD** [see BERNARD 5].[2]

5. JOHN LE SCROPE, Knt., K.G., 5th Lord Scrope of Bolton, son and heir, was born on 22 July 1437 or 1438. He was summoned to Parliament from 30 July 1460. As a Yorkist, he was with Warwick at the Battle of Northampton on 10 July 1460, was "sore hurt" at the battle of Towton on 29 Mar. 1461. He was present at the battle of Hexham 15 May 1462. He was married for the first time, with dispensation dated 22 Nov. 1447, they being related in the fourth degree, to JOAN FITZ HUGH,

---

[1] Ancestors of **Edward Carleton**.
[2] Ancestors of **Francis & Richard Bernard**.

SCROPE (cont.)

daughter of William Fitz Hugh, 4th Lord Fitz Hugh, by Margery, daughter of William de Willoughby, Knt., Lord Willoughby. She died before 1470. He was married for the second time, before 10 Dec. 1471, to **ELIZABETH SAINT JOHN**, widow of William La Zouche, 6th Lord Zouche, of Haryngworth (died 14 Jan. 1467/8), and daughter of Oliver Saint John, Knt., by Margaret, daughter and eventual heiress of John Beauchamp, Knt., of Bletsoe, co. Bedford. She was living in 1488. He was married for the third time after 9 Feb. 1490/1 to ANNE HARLING, widow, first, of William Chamberlaine, Knt, K.G. (died March or April 1462), second, of Robert Wingfield, Knt., M.P., Controller of the Household (died shortly before 13 Nov. 1481), and daughter and heiress of Robert Harling, Knt., of East Harling, Norfolk, by Jane, daughter and heiress of Edmund Gunville. They had no issue. JOHN LE SCROPE, Lord Scrope, died testate aged sixty-three 17 Aug. 1498. His widow died testate on 18 Sep. 1498.

Clay (1913), p. 200. *C.P.* 11:544-546 (1949).

Child of John le Scrope, by Elizabeth St. John:

i. **MARY LE SCROPE**, married **WILLIAM CONYERS**, Knt. [see CONYERS 6][1].

* * *

SEDLEY see GURDON

SEGRAVE see NORFOLK

SEYMOUR see RODNEY

* * *

SKEPPER

EDWARD III OF ENGLAND, King of England, married **PHILIPPE DE HAINAUT**.
LIONEL OF CLARENCE [*of Antwerp*], Duke of Clarence, married **ELIZABETH DE BURGH**.
PHILIPPE OF CLARENCE, married **EDMUND DE MORTIMER**, 3rd Earl of March.
ELIZABETH MORTIMER, married **HENRY PERCY**, Knt.
ELIZABETH PERCY, married **JOHN DE CLIFFORD**, Lord Clifford.
MARY DE CLIFFORD, married **PHILIP WENTWORTH**, Knt. [see HARLESTON 7].

5. **ELIZABETH WENTWORTH**, daughter, evidently, was born, probably, 1440-1450. She was married, as his second wife, to **MARTIN DE LA SEE** (or **AT SEE**), Knt., of Barmston, co. York, son of Brian at See, of Hollym and Barmeston, co. York, by Maud, daughter and heiress of John Monceaux, of Barmeston. He was born about 1420. He had been married previously to Margaret Spencer with one daughter. Martin & Elizabeth had two children. He headed the local resistance to King Edward IV's landing at Ravenspur in March 1471. He was knighted in Scotland by the Earl of Northumberland on 24 July 1482, and served on eight consecutive

---

[1] Ancestors of **Philip & Thomas Nelson**.

commissions of the peace for the East Riding from 18 Sep. 1484 to 14 July 1494. "Martyn of the See, knyght" died testate between 20 Nov. and 15 Dec. 1494, and was buried in the choir in All Hallows', Barnston, with effigy (will mentioning "dame Margery my wife").

Sur.Soc. 53:100-101 (1868) (will). *Sur.Soc.* 53:100-101 (1869) (his will). *Sur.Soc.* 144:136-137 (1930) (1480 Vis. North) ("Les Armes de Martin de See Saphir a deulx undes perle).

4. **JOAN DE LA SEE**, daughter and co-heiress, was born about 1460-65. She was married in the early 1480s to **PETER HILDYARD**, Knt., of Winestead, in Holderness, East Riding, co. York, son and heir of Robert Hildyard, Knt., of Winestead, by Elizabeth, daughter of John Hastings, of Gressenhall, 9th Lord Hastings (**descendant of King Edward I**) [see ELSING 5 for his ancestry]. He was born about 1460. SIR PETER HILDYARD died testate on 20 Mar. 1501/2 (his will dated 14 Mar. 1501/2 names his wife Joan, his son Richard, and his seven [unnamed] unmarried daughters). The will of "Dame Jane Hilliarde, voisse [a widow who has taken the vow of chastity], som tyme wif of Peter Hiliarde Esquyer", dated 20 July 1527 and proved 7 Apr. 1528, bequeathed 20s. to her "doughtour Legerde".

Wotton (1741) 3:60 (Hildyard arms: *Azure,* three mullets, *or*). *Glover-Foster* (1875), p. 51 (1584 Vis. Yorks). *Sur.Soc.* 79:230-231 (1884) (her will). *Sur.Soc.* 144:136-137 (1930) (1480 Vis. North). *TAG* 69:137 (July 1994).

3. **ISABEL HILDYARD**, was born about 1498. She was married about 1520 to **RALPH LEGARD**, son and heir of Robert Legard, of Anlaby, East Riding, co. York, by his wife Joan, daughter of Robert Haldenby, of Haldenby. He was born, say, 1490. They had five sons and four daughters. RALPH LEGARD died intestate on 30 June 1540. She died after 10 July 1540.

Glover-Foster (1875), pp. 54-55. *H.S.P.* 16:186 (1881) (1563 Vis. Yorks). *TAG* 69:137 (July 1994) (she was identified in *1564 Visitation of Yorkshire*, p. 186 as "Izabell the sixe doughter to Pyers Hyllyard of wested, Esquier", this identification almost certainly made by her son Christopher).

2. **JOAN LEGARD**, was born, say, 1530. She was married for the first time, with marriage settlement dated 4 Feb. 1550/1, to **RICHARD SKEPPER**, of East Kirkby, co. Lincoln, son of Richard Skepper, of East Kirkby, by his wife Audrey, daughter of Ralph Grynne, of East Kirkby. He was born about 1495, and had been married previously to Katherine (_____) Gilden. Richard & Joan had three sons and one daughter. The will of RICHARD SKEPPER was dated 26 May 1556. She was married for the second time to **ROBERT TOWNLEY**, Alderman and Harbourmaster of Boston, co. Lincoln, and had two children. He was buried in the East Kirkby Church on 9 Mar. 1585-86. The will of ROBERT TOWNLEY was dated 7 Mar. 1585/6. His widow died after that date.

Glover-Foster (1875), p. 55. *H.S.P.* 16:186 (1881). *TAG* 20:77-85 (Oct. 1943) (identification of Joan Legard, but not her parents). *TAG* 69:137 (July 1994) (identification of parentage and ancestry of Joan Legard).

1. **EDWARD SKEPPER**, Gent., was born about 1552 (aged four at death of father). He was married for the first time to **AGNES** _____. They had two daughters. She was buried at East Kirkby on 14 Sep. 1586. He was married for the second time at Boston on 11 Apr. 1592 to **MARY ROBINSON**. They had three sons and four daughters. EDWARD SKEPPER, GENT., was buried at East Kirkby, co. Lincoln, on 10 Nov. 1629. His widow died after 1630.

TAG 20:79-85 (Oct. 1943). *TAG* 69:138 (July 1994).

Children & grandchildren of Edward Skepper, by Mary Robinson:

    i. LUCY SKEPPER, baptised Boston 18 Oct. 1589.

    ii. RICHARD SKEPPER, baptised Boston 18 Oct. 1590, resided East Kirkby, died about 1634;

SKEPPER (cont.)

married, first, ANNE KILLINGWORTH, second, ELIZABETH KELKE. Seven children by first marriage. Four children by second marriage.

iii. ELIZABETH SKEPPER, born Boston about 1593.

iv. JOHN SKEPPER, Gent., baptised Boston 3 Apr. 1595, died 1638; married, first, MARY _____, second, MARY CATER. One son by first marriage. Five children by second marriage.

v. REV. WILLIAM SKEPPER (or SKIPPER), baptised Boston, co. Lincoln, 27 Nov. 1597, B.A. 1617-8 Sidney College, Cambridge University, Rector of Thorpe-in-the-Marsh 1630, emigrated 1639, died intestate probably Boston, Massachusetts, 1640-50; married, first _____ _____, second, Boston, co. Lincoln, 17 Jan. 1638/9 SARAH FISHER, died Essex County, Massachusetts. Seven children by first marriage. One daughter by second marriage.

  a. ELIZABETH SKEPPER, born about 1626, died after 1671; married ZACHARIAH PHILIPPS. Nine children.

  b. JOHN SKEPPER, baptised Thorpe-in-the-Marsh 25 Oct. 1631, buried 18 Mar. 1631/2.

  c. MARY SKEPPER, baptised 19 July 1629, died young.

  d. THEOPHILUS SKEPPER, baptised Thorpe-in-the-Marsh 25 Oct. 1631, buried 18 Mar. 1631/2.

  e. THEOPHILUS SKIPPER, baptised Thorpe-in-the-Marsh 9 Jan. 1632/33, resided Lynn, Massachusetts 1646.

  f. JANE SKIPPER, baptised Thorpe-in-the-Marsh 9 Jan. 1634/5, died after 1682; married Boston 19 Aug. 1653 ABRAHAM BROWN, mariner of Boston, Massachusetts. Three children.

  g. KATHERINE SKIPPER, born about 1638, killed by Indians at Haverhill, Massachusetts, 29 Aug. 1708; married, first, JOHN MAVERICK, second, LIEUT. JOHN JOHNSON. Six children by first marriage. One son by second marriage.

  h. SARAH SKIPPER, born about 1640, died 18 Dec. 1711; married ENS. WALTER FAIRFIELD, of Wenham, Massachusetts. Fourteen children.

vi. MARY SKEPPER, born about 1599; married, first, REV. SAMUEL SAILBANKS, second, NICHOLAS HERRING. Issue.

vii. JANE SKEPPER, baptised East Kirkby 26 July 1601, buried there 30 Mar. 1602/3.

* * *

SKIPWITH

EDWARD I OF ENGLAND, King of England, married, second, MARGUERITE DE FRANCE.
THOMAS OF NORFOLK [of *Brotherton*], married ALICE DE HALES.
MARGARET OF NORFOLK, married JOHN DE SEGRAVE, 4th Lord Segrave.
ELIZABETH DE SEGRAVE, married JOHN DE MOWBRAY, 4th Lord Mowbray.
ALIANOR DE MOWBRAY, married JOHN DE WELLES, Knt., 5th Lord Welles.
EUDO DE WELLES, married MAUD DE GREYSTOKE.
LIONEL DE WELLES, Knt., 6th Lord Welles, married, first, JOAN DE WATERTON.
MARGARET DE WELLES, married THOMAS DYMOKE, Knt. [see DYMOKE 5].

5. LIONEL DYMOKE, Knt., of Mareham-on-the-Hill, and of Stockford, co. Lincoln *jure uxoris*, Sheriff of Lincolnshire, second son, was married for the first time to an unidentified wife, and had issue. He was married for the second time to JOAN GRIFFITH, daughter of Richard Griffith, Esq., of Stockford. They had two daughters. SIR LIONEL DYMOKE died testate on 17 Aug. 1519, and was buried at Horncastle.

SKIPWITH (cont.)

Gen. 4:19 (1880). *Goodricke* (1885), p. 4. *H.S.P.* 52:889 (1904) (Maddison Linc. Ped., citing Massingberd, History of Ormsby). *H.S.P.* 55:1204 (1906) (states children were by first marriage). *AR* (1992), p. 170 (states, in regard to daughter Anne: "Early Chancery Proceedings, Bundle 444/43, which identifies her as Anne and her mother as Johanne).

Children of Lionel Dymoke, by Joan Griffith:
 i. ALICE DYMOKE [see next].
 ii. ANNE DYMOKE, married JOHN GOODRICK, of Kirby, co. Lincoln [see BOLLES 4].[1]

4. ALICE DYMOKE, daughter and co-heiress, was married to **WILLIAM SKIPWITH**, Knt., of South Ormsby, co. Lincoln, Sheriff of Lincolnshire, son of John Skipwith, Knt., of Skipwith, by Agnes, daughter of John Constable, Knt. He was born about 1488 (aged thirty in 1518), and had been married previously to Elizabeth, daughter of William Tyrwhit, Knt., of Kettleby, with issue. William & Alice had four sons. SIR WILLIAM SKIPWITH died on 7 July 1547.

Wotton (1741) 1:536. *Glover-Foster* (1875), p. 634 (1612 Vis. Yorks). *Gen.* 4:19 (1880). *H.S.P.* 53:889 (1904). *H.S.P.* 55:1204 (1906). *Allaben* (1908), p. 191.

Children of William Skipwith, by Alice Dymoke:
 i. HENRY SKIPWITH [see next].
 ii. JOHN SKIPWITH, Esq., second son, married ELEANOR KINGSTON [see ASFORDBY 4].[2]

3. HENRY SKIPWITH, of Cotes and Prestwould, co. Leicester, M.P. for Leicestershire, son and heir, was married to **JANE HALL**, widow, and daughter of Francis Hall, of Grantham, co. Lincoln (**descendant of King Edward I**), by Ursula, daughter of Thomas Sherington [see BOURCHIER 3 for her ancestry]. They had four sons and eight daughters. HENRY SKIPWITH died in 1588.

Wotton (1741) 1:536-537. *Glover-Foster* (1875), p. 634. *Gen.* 4:24 (1880). *H.S.P.* 52:889-890 (1904).

2. WILLIAM SKIPWITH, Knt., of Prestwold in Cotes, co. Leicester, M.P. for Leicestershire, son and heir, was married for the first time to **MARGARET CAVE**, daughter of Roger Cave, of Stanford, co. Northampton. They had three sons and three daughters. She died in 1594. He was married for the second time to JANE ROBERTS, widow, first of John Walpole, Esq., of Whaplode, co. Lincoln (buried 1590), and second of John Markham, Esq., of Sedgebrook, co. Lincoln, and daughter and heiress of John Roberts, Esq., of Wollaston, co. Northampton. SIR WILLIAM SKIPWITH died testate (P.C.C., 24 Wood) on 3 May 1610, and was buried at Prestwold. His widow was buried at Prestwold on 4 Apr. 1630.

Norf.Arch.Soc. 1:453 (1563 Vis. Norfolk) (Skipwith arms: *Argent*, three bars *gules*, in chief a greyhound courant *sable*). *H.S.P.* 52:890 (1904). *VMHB* 27:50-51 (Jan. 1919) (his will). *Throckmorton* (1930), p. 294.

1. HENRY SKIPWITH, Knt., of Prestwold in Cotes, co. Leicester, son and heir, was born in 1589. He was married to **AMY KEMPE**, third daughter and co-heiress of Thomas Kempe, Knt., of Ollantigh, Kent (**descendant of King Edward I**), by Dorothy, daughter of John Thompson, of London [see OLLANTIGH 2 for her ancestry]. They had four sons and two daughters. He was created a **Baronet** by King James I in 1622. She died in 1631. He was married for the second time at St. Mary's Woolnoth, London, on 2 May 1639 to BLANDINA _____, widow of John Acton, citizen of London. SIR HENRY SKIPWITH died about 1658.

Wotton (1741) 1:537 (Skipwith arms: *Argent*, three bars *gules* in chief a greyhound currant, sable,

---

[1] Ancestors of **Joseph Bolles**.

[2] Ancestors of **William Asfordby**.

SKIPWITH (cont.)

collar'd *or*) ("Sir Grey Skipwith, Bart. who, in the time of the rebellion in England, after the death of King Charles I. went with several other gentlemen to Virginia, to avoid the usurper, Cromwell, and there married, and left only one son ... Sir William Skipwith, Bart. who also married in Virginia, and in the year 1730, was above sixty years of age, and had eight children, and dying ____, was succeeded in the title by his eldest son, Sir Grey Skipwith, the present baronet, now [1741] in Virginia, aged about thirty"). *Stemmata Chicheleana* (1765), p. 5. *VMHB* 27:51 (Jan. 1919). *Throckmorton* (1930), p. 294. *NEHGR* 106:166 (July 1952) (Skipwith arms). *Boddie* 10:166-167 (1966).

Children of Henry Skipwith, by Amy Kempe:

i. WILLIAM SKIPWITH, died unmarried *s.p. v.p.*

ii. HENRY SKIPWITH, Knt., 2nd Bart., died unmarried.

iii. THOMAS SKIPWITH, died *s.p.*

iv. GREY SKIPWITH, Knt., 3rd Baronet, settled in Lancaster County, Virginia, before 1680; married, first, ELIZABETH ____, second, ANNE ____, widow of EDMUND KEMPE, of Lancaster County, Virginia [see KEMPE 1].

    a. WILLIAM SKIPWITH, Knt., 4th Baronet, born about 1670, married SARAH PEYTON.

v. ELIZABETH SKIPWITH.

vi. DIANA SKIPWITH, of Lancaster County, Virginia, married MAJ. EDWARD DALE, clerk of Lancaster County.

    a. KATHERINE DALE, born 1652, married CAPT. THOMAS CARTER, of Barford, Lancaster County, Virginia. Issue.

vii. ANNE SKIPWITH, married ____.

* * *

SKIPWITH OF WALMSGATE see ASFORDBY

* * *

SOMERSET

EDWARD III OF ENGLAND, King of England, married PHILIPPE DE HAINAUT.
LIONEL OF CLARENCE [*of Antwerp*], Duke of Clarence, married ELIZABETH DE BURGH.
PHILIPPE OF CLARENCE, married EDMUND DE MORTIMER, 3rd Earl of March.
ROGER MORTIMER, 4th Earl of March, married ALIANOR HOLAND.
ANNE MORTIMER, married RICHARD OF YORK [*of Conisburgh*], Earl of Cambridge.
RICHARD PLANTAGENET, 3rd Duke of York, married CECILY NEVILLE.
GEORGE PLANTAGENET, Duke of Clarence, married ISABEL NEVILLE [see YORK 6].

7. **MARGARET PLANTAGENET**, Countess of Salisbury *suo jure*, was born at Farley Castle, near Bath, Somerset, on 14 Aug. 1473. She was married, probably in 1491, to **RICHARD POLE**, Knt., K.G., of Medmenham, co. Buckingham, son of Geoffrey Pole, K.G., of Medmenham and Ellesborough, co. Buckingham, by Edith (of **Magna Charta Surety descent and descendant of Charlemagne**), daughter of Oliver St. John, Knt. On the death of her brother Richard Plantagenet, Earl of Warwick, on 28 Nov. 1499, she became sole heiress, not only to her father, but to the Earls of Warwick and Earls of Salisbury. She was Lady of the Chamber to Queen Katherine of Aragon in 1509. SIR RICHARD POLE died before 18 Dec. 1505. In 1538 King Henry VIII

SOMERSET (cont.)

struck at the family of Pole, on account both of their descent from King Edward IV's brother, George, Duke of Clarence, and of the action of Cardinal Reginald Pole, who hoped that Paul III would publish a Bull of deprivation. Their youngest son, Sir Geoffrey Pole, was sent to the Tower on 29 Aug. 1538, followed on 4 November, by their first son, Henry, Lord Montagu [see next]. MARGARET PLANTAGENET, Countess of Salisbury, was sent to the Tower of London, attainted, and beheaded at the Tower on 28 May 1541. She was the last surviving member of the royal House of Anjou (usually known as the Plantagenets).

C.P. 11:399-402 (1949.

6. HENRY POLE, son and heir, was born about 1492. He was employed in the household of King Henry VIII as early as Nov. 1509, and appears to have been known as **Lord Montagu** from 1514. He was married, before May 1520, to **JANE NEVILLE**, daughter of George Neville, Lord Bergavenny (**descendant of King Edward III**), by Margaret, daughter and heiress of Hugh Fenne [see OXENBRIDGE 5 for her ancestry]. She died before 26 Oct. 1538. In 1538 he (as grandson of George, Duke of Clarence) and Henry Courtenay, Marquess of Exeter (as grandson of King Edward IV), became the victims of the King's fears that one of them might be chosen in his place if he were dethroned. HENRY POLE, Lord Montagu, was beheaded on Tower Hill on 9 Jan. 1538/9.

C.P. 9:94-96 (1936). *C.P.* (1926) 6:656 footnote *e*.

5. KATHERINE POLE, elder daughter and eventual co-heiress, was married in June 1532 to **FRANCIS HASTINGS**, K.B., K.G., 4th Lord Hastings, 2nd Earl of Huntingdon, P.C., son and heir of George Hastings, of Ashby-de-la-Zouch, co. Leicester, 3rd Lord Hastings of Hastings (**descendant of King Edward III**), by Anne, daughter of Henry Stafford, 2nd Duke of Buckingham (**descendant of King Edward III**). He was born about 1514 [see HASTINGS 6 for his ancestry]. They had six sons and four daughters. FRANCIS HASTINGS, Earl of Huntingdon, died testate aged forty-seven at Ashby on 23 June 1560 (P.C.C., Loftes 8). His widow died on 23 Sep. 1576. They were buried at Ashby-de-la-Zouch (M.I.).

Clay (1913), p. 102. DNB. *C.P.* (1926) 6:376, 655-656, 656 footnote *h* (Katherine Pole made a claim, based on the question to the legitimacy of the children of King Edward IV, to the Crown *de jure hereditario*, being great-granddaughter of Margaret Plantagenet, Countess of Salisbury). *C.P.* 7:694 (1929) 7:694.

4. ELIZABETH HASTINGS, fourth daughter, was married in December 1571 to **EDWARD SOMERSET**, K.G., Earl of Worcester, son and heir of William Somerset, Earl of Worcester (**descendant of King Edward I**), by Christian, daughter of Edward North, 1st Lord North. He was born about 1550 [see BEAUFORT 5 for his ancestry]. They had eight sons. She died at Worcester House, St. Clement Danes, Strand, on 24 Aug. 1621. EDWARD SOMERSET, Earl of Worcester, died testate at Worcester House on 3 Mar. 1627/8. They were buried at Raglan.

C.P. 12(1):854-857 (1953).

3. HENRY SOMERSET, 5th Earl of Worcester, son and heir, was born in Herefordshire in 1576-77. He was married at St. Martin's, Ludgate, on 16 June 1600 to **ANNE RUSSELL**, daughter and heiress of John Russell, Lord Russell, by Elizabeth, daughter of Anthony Cook, Knt., of Gidea Hall, Essex. They had nine sons and four daughters. She died at Worcester House on 8 Apr. 1639. He was summoned to Parliament *v.p.* as Lord Herbert by writ directed *Henr. Herbert Ch'r*. During the Civil War he advanced huge sums of money to King Charles I, for which he was created **Marquess of Worcester** on 2 Mar. 1642/3. His castle in Raglan was

SOMERSET (cont.)

one of the last places that held out against the Parliament. After surrender he was brought up to London and committed to Black Rod, in Covent Garden. HENRY SOMERSET, Marquess of Worcester, died testate in custody at Covent Garden on 18 Dec. 1646. They were buried at St. George's Chapel, Windsor (M.I.).
> *Collins-Brydges* (1812) 1:273. *C.P.* 12(1):856-858 footnote *i*, 857-859 (1953).

2. JOHN SOMERSET, Knt., second son, "commanded the horse of his brother's [Edward Lord Herbert] army". He was married to **MARY ARUNDELL**, daughter of Thomas Arundell, Baron Arundell of Wardour, co. Wilts (**descendant of King Edward I**), by Anne, daughter of Miles Philipson, of Crook, Westmorland [see CALVERT 2 for her ancestry]. They had three sons.
> *Collins-Brydges* (1812) 1:232-233.

1. CHARLES SOMERSET, Esq., of Acton Park, Middlesex, and Ross, co. Hereford, third son, was married for the first time, with no issue, to JANE THOMAS, daughter of Walter Thomas, Esq., of Swansey, co. Glamorgan. He was married for the second time to **CATHERINE BASKERVILLE**, widow of George Sawyer, Esq., and daughter of Walter Baskerville, Esq. He was married for the third time to ALICE GOODYER, daughter of John Goodyer, Esq., of Burghope, co. Hereford. The will of CHARLES SOMERSET, ESQ., was dated 1705, and proved in P.C.C. in 1712, naming, among others, "Charles Smith, son of daughter Mary Smith".
> *Collins-Brydges* (1812) 1:232-233. *Maryland Hist. Mag.* 3:66-73,384-385 (1908) (citing Maryland Chancery Lib. PC. [*recte* 3], fol. 849-850) (depositions concerning the marriage and children of Col. Richard Smith and his wife Maria Johanna commissioned by Charles, Lord Baltimore). "Smith of Calvert County: English Ancestry", a manuscript collection prepared by V. M. Dorsey and presented in 1940 to the Maryland Historical Society, including depositions supporting the inheritance of grandson Charles Somerset Smith in Maryland, including one from Nicholas Sewall as to the identity of Maria Johanna Smith as "daughter of Mr. Somerset in Herefordshire").

Children & grandchild of Charles Somerset, by Catherine Baskerville:
  i. CHARLES SOMERSET.
  ii. HENRY SOMERSET.
  iii. **MARIA JOHANNA SOMERSET**, married, first, COL. _____ LOWTHER, emigrated to Maryland as widow about 1697 with letter from Lord Baltimore to his son-in-law Nicholas Sewall, married, second, **COL. RICHARD SMITH**, of St. Leonard's Creek, Calvert County, Maryland.
      a. **CHARLES SOMERSET SMITH** of Charles County, Maryland, born February 1698, drowned about 1739; married, first, **JANE CRABB**, second **MARGARET SMITH**. Five daughters by first marriage. Two sons by second marriage. Descendants.
  iv. ELIZABETH SOMERSET.

* * *

SOTHILL see DRURY

SPENCER see CARY

STAFFORD see AUDLEY

STANLEY OF HAMMERWICH see WOLSELEY

STANLEY OF LATHOM see FITZ ALAN

STANLEY OF WEEVER see MANWARING

* * *

STAPLETON

EDWARD III OF ENGLAND, King of England, married PHILIPPE DE HAINAUT.
EDMUND OF YORK [*of Langley*], Duke of York, married ISABELLA DE CASTILLE.
RICHARD OF YORK [*of Conisburgh*], 2nd Duke of York, married ANNE MORTIMER.
RICHARD OF YORK *Plantagenet*, Duke of York, married CECILY NEVILLE [see YORK 7].

7. ANNE PLANTAGENET, was born at Fotheringay Castle on 10 Aug. 1439. She was married for the first time before 30 July 1447 to **HENRY HOLAND**, 2nd Duke of Exeter. They had one daughter Anne, and were divorced on 12 Nov. 1472. She was married for the second time about 1472/3 to **THOMAS SAINT LEGER**, Knt., son of John Saint Leger, of Ulcomb, Kent, by Margery, daughter of James Donnett, of Rainham. She died on 12 or 14 Jan. 1476, and was buried at St. George's Chapel, Windsor. SIR THOMAS SAINT LEGER was beheaded at Exeter on 8 Nov. 1483.
C.P. 5:213-216 (1926).

6. ANNE SAINT LEGER, daughter and heiress, was born in 1476. She was married about 1490 to **GEORGE MANNERS**, Knt., of East Compton, Surrey, and Etal, Northumberland, 12th Lord Ros of Hanlake, son and heir of Robert Manners, Knt., of Etal (**descendant of King Edward I**), by Alianor, daughter of Thomas de Ros, 9th Lord Ros (**descendant of King Edward I**). He was born about 1470 [see OGLE 7 for his ancestry]. They had five sons and six daughters. GEORGE MANNERS, Lord Ros, died testate of illness at the siege of Tournay on 27 Oct. 1513. His widow died on 21 Apr. 1526. They were buried at St. George's Chapel, Windsor with monumental inscription.
Collins-Brydges (1812) 1:462. *Banks* (1844), p. 379. *Northumberland* 11:445 (1922). *Exeter* (1907), p. 2. *Sur.Soc.* 144:163 (1930) (1480 Vis. North). *Paget* (1977), p. 269.

5. KATHERINE MANNERS, was married to **ROBERT CONSTABLE**, Knt., of Everingham, West Riding, co. York, son of Marmaduke Constable, Knt., of Everingham, by Barbara, daughter and heiress of John Sothill, of Everingham. They had three sons and six daughters. SIR ROBERT CONSTABLE died in 1558.
Wotton (1741) 2:328 (Constable arms: Quarterly, *gules* and *vaire*, a bend, *or*). *Collins-Brydges* (1812) 1:465. *Glover-Foster* (1875), p. 179 (1584 Vis. Yorks). *H.S.P.* 16:66 (1881) (1563 Vis. Yorks) (five sons and four daughters). *Exeter* (1907), p. 52.

4. MARMADUKE CONSTABLE, Knt., of Everingham, co. York, son and heir, was married to **JANE CONYERS**, daughter of Christopher Conyers, Lord Conyers, of Hornby, co. York (**descendant of King Edward I**), by Anne (**descendant of King Edward III**), daughter of Thomas Dacre, Lord Dacre of Gillesland (**descendant of King Edward I**) [see CONYERS 5 for her ancestry]. They had two sons and two daughters. She died on 4 Dec. 1558, and was buried at Everingham (M.I.). SIR MARMADUKE CONSTABLE died on 1 Feb. 1574.
Wotton (1741) 2:328. *Glover-Foster* (1875), p. 179. *H.S.P.* 16:66,73 (1881). *Exeter* (1907), p. 52. *Clay* (1913), p. 35.

3. KATHERINE CONSTABLE, was married to **ROBERT STAPLETON**, Knt., of Wighill, co. York, Sheriff of Yorkshire, M.P. for Yorkshire, eldest surviving son of Robert Stapleton, Knt., of Wighill, by his wife Elizabeth Mallory. He was born about

1548. They had two sons and two daughters. She died about 1580. He was married for the second time about 1584 to Olive Sherington, widow of John Talbot, of Salwarpe, co. Worcester (died 1583), and daughter and co-heiress of Henry Sherington, Knt., of Lacock, co. Wilts, by his wife Ann Paget. SIR ROBERT STAPLETON was buried at Wighill on 3 Oct. 1606. His widow was residing at Lacock Abbey in 1634.

Wotton (1741) 3:53. *Glover-Foster* (1875), p. 179. *H.S.P.* 16:66 (1881). *Exeter* (1907), p. 54. *NEHGR* 148:135-136 (Apr. 1994) (descent of Philip & Thomas Nelson from King Edward III) (He was described as "a gentleman for person, address, and skill in languages, [who] had no superior in England nor equal, except Sir Philip Sydney," and Queen Elizabeth is said to have recommended him to Olive Talbot as a suitable bridegroom. His court career was ruined through a "spectacular quarrel with Edwin Sandys, archbishop of York.").

2. **PHILIP STAPLETON**, Gent., of Milford and Bilton near Wetherby, co. York, son by first marriage, was born, say, 1578. He was married, presumably at Sherburn in Elmet, co. York, in 1607 to **DOROTHY HILL**, daughter of William Hill, of Pannall, co. York, by his wife Anne. She was baptised at Pannall, on 3 May 1587. PHILIP STAPLETON resided at Bilton, near Wetherby, in the deanery of Ainsty, co. York, and died, probably, in 1618 (administration on his estate dated 27 Jan. 1618/9), survived by his widow Dorothy and one minor daughter Dorothy. They evidently removed after his death to the parish of All Saints in the city of York. His widow was married for the second time at Everingham, co. York, in 1628 to John Twisleton, of Everingham.

Exeter (1907), p. 54. *NEHGR* 148:130-140 (Apr. 1994).

1. **DOROTHY STAPLETON**, was baptised at Pannall, co. York, on 11 Aug. 1608. She was married at All Saints, North Street, York, on 17 Jan. 1626/7 to **THOMAS NELSON**, Gent., of Cottingham, co. York. He was born, say, 1600. They resided in the parish of Cottingham where their six children were baptised. DOROTHY STAPLETON was buried at Rowley, co. York, on 27 Sep. 1637. He emigrated to New England in 1638, and settled at Rowley, Massachusetts. He was made a freeman in 1639, and was one of the chief town officers in the new community. He was married for the second time, with marriage contract dated 15 Feb. 1641/2, to Joan Dummer, daughter of Thomas Dummer of North Stoneham, co. Hants, England. Joan and her two children were mentioned in the will of her father, dated 12 Apr. 1650 and proved 9 Nov. 1650. He left a will, dated 24 Dec. 1645 in anticipation of a voyage abroad, with a codicil dated in England on 6 Aug. 1648. The will of THOMAS NELSON, who died in England, was proved on 21 Feb. 1650/1.

Exeter (1907), p. 54 (no identification of husband of Dorothy). *NEHGR* 148:130-140 (Apr. 1994).

Children of Thomas Nelson, by Dorothy Stapleton:

   i. THOMAS NELSON, baptised 26 Nov. 1628, buried Cottingham 27 Nov. 1628.

   ii. KATHERINE NELSON, baptised 18 May 1630, presumably died young.

   iii. MARY NELSON, baptised 10 Apr. 1632, buried Cottingham 6 Aug. 1636.

   iv. DOROTHY NELSON, baptised 19 Nov. 1633, buried Cottingham 13 Jan. 1633/4.

   v. **CAPT. PHILIP NELSON**, baptised 22 Jan. 1634/5, graduated Harvard College 1654, died Rowley, Massachusetts, 19 Aug. 1691; married, first, at Rowley, 24 June 1657, **SARAH JEWETT**, baptised Bradford 3 Jan. 1635/6, buried Rowley, 17 Feb. 1665/6, married, second, at Rowley, 1 Dec. 1666, **ELIZABETH LOWELL**, born at Newbury, 16 Feb. 1646, died at Rowley, 14 Dec. 1731. Issue.

   vi. **THOMAS NELSON**, baptised 14 July 1636, died at Rowley aged seventy-seven 5 Apr. 1712; married, first, at Rowley, 16 (or 10) Dec. 1659 **ANNE LAMBERT**, buried Rowley 7 Jan. 1678, married, second, at Rowley, 13 May 1680, **MARY LUNT** of Newbury, Massachusetts, died at Rowley 28 Aug. 1688; married, third, at Rowley, 9 Apr. 1690, **PHILIPPA (ANDREWS) (FELT)**

STAPLETON (cont.)

PLATTS, died at Rowley, 29 Sep. 1709, daughter of Samuel & Jane Andrews, and widow of George Felt and Samuel Platts. Issue.

* * *

STAPLETON OF BEDALE see BARDOLF

* * *

STOCKMAN

EDWARD I OF ENGLAND, King of England, married **ALIANORE DE CASTILLE**.
JOAN OF ENGLAND [*of Acre*], married **GILBERT DE CLARE**, Earl of Gloucester.
ELIZABETH DE CLARE, married **THEOBALD DE VERDUN**, Lord Verdun.
ISABEL DE VERDUN, married **HENRY FERRERS**, 2nd Lord Ferrers of Groby.
WILLIAM FERRERS, 3rd Lord Ferrers of Groby, married **MARGARET DE UFFORD**.
HENRY FERRERS, 4th Lord Ferrers of Groby, married **JOAN DE HOO**.
WILLIAM FERRERS, 5th Lord Ferrers, married **PHILIPPE DE CLIFTON** [see CLARKE 7].

8. ELIZABETH FERRERS, eldest daughter, evidently, was married to **WILLIAM CULPEPER**, Knt., of Aylesford, Kent, son, presumably, of John Culpeper, Knt., of Oxenhoath in West Peckham, Kent. They had three sons. SIR WILLIAM CULPEPER died testate on 20 July 1457. They were buried at West Peckham.
    Arch.Cant. 4:264 (1861) (1619 Vis. Kent). *H.S.P.* 42:11 (1898) (1619 Vis. Kent) (Culpeper arms: *Argent*, a bend engrailed *gules*). *Baddesley Clinton* (1907), pp. 115-116. *Mary Isaac* (1955), p. 343. *Abel Lunt* (1963), pp. 239-240.

7. RICHARD CULPEPER, of Oxenhoath in West Peckham, Kent, said to be son, was born about 1430. He was married for the first time to **SIBYL** _____, and had three daughters, the oldest born in 1450. He was married for the second time, as her first husband, about 1480 to **ISABEL WORSLEY**, daughter of Otewell Worsley, of Southwark, Surrey, by Rose Trevor, daughter of Edward ap Dafydd, of Brynkinallt. She was born about 1460. They had one son and two daughters. RICHARD CULPEPER died on 4 Oct. 1484. His widow was married for the second time to John Leigh, Knt., of Stockwell in Lambeth, Surrey (died testate 17 Aug. 1523), eldest son of Ralph Leigh, of Stockwell, by his wife Elizabeth Langley. She died testate on 18 Apr. 1527. They were buried in the chapel of St. Nicholas in Lambeth church.
    Arch.Cant. 4:264 (1861). *H.S.P.* 42:11 (1898). *Mary Isaac* (1955), pp. 343-355. *Abel Lunt* (1963), p. 238.

6. JOYCE CULPEPER, was born about 1480 (aged twelve and more in 1492). She was married for the first time before 1492 to **RALPH LEIGH**, of Stockwell in Lambeth, younger son of Ralph Leigh, of Stockwell in Lambeth, by his wife Elizabeth Langley. Ralph was younger brother of her step-father, and this child marriage secured her Culpeper inheritance to the Leigh family. The will of RALPH LEIGH was dated 9 Sep. 1509, and proved 1 Feb. 1509/10. His widow was married for the second time after 1509 to Lord **EDMUND HOWARD** (died 19 Mar. 1537), younger son of Thomas Howard, 2nd Duke of Norfolk, by his first wife Elizabeth, daughter and heiress of Frederick Tilney, Knt., of Ashwellthorpe, co. Norfolk. Edmund &

STOCKMAN (cont.)

Joyce had six children including Katherine, fifth wife of King Henry VIII [see MOWBRAY 5 for descendants of this marriage]. She died after 1527.

H.S.P. 42:11 (1898) ("Raffe Leigh, under Shreeve of London"). *H.S.P.* 64:158 (1913) (1634 Vis. Hants). *Mary Isaac* (1955), pp. 350-353 (the Howard family would have been intimately known to the Leighs for they had a house at Lambeth which they used when they came to London).

Children of Ralph Leigh, by Joyce Culpeper:

 i. RALPH LEIGH, younger son [see next].
 ii. ISABEL LEIGH, married EDWARD BAYNTON, Knt. [see BAYNTON 3].[1]

5. **RALPH LEIGH**, younger son, was provided a legal education by the will of his uncle Sir John Leigh, of Stockwell. He was married to **MARGARET IRELAND**, daughter of William Ireland. RALPH LEIGH died before 1563 leaving at least two children, John Leigh (his uncle Sir John's heir), and a daughter Frances Leigh.

H.S.P. 64:158 (1913). *Mary Isaac* (1955), p. 352.

4. **JOHN LEIGH**, Esq., of Froyle, co. Hants, was married to **MARGARET SAUNDERS**, daughter of Thomas Saunders, of Uxbridge, Middlesex. JOHN LEIGH, ESQ., was buried in the churchyard at Froyle. His widow was married for the second time to WILLIAM KILLEGRAVE, Knt., of Cornwall.

H.S.P. 64:158 (1913). *Mary Isaac* (1955), p. 352.

3. **JOHN LEIGH**, Knt., of Couldray, co. Hants, was married to **ELIZABETH WEST**, daughter and co-heiress of Thomas West, Knt., of Testwood, co. Hants (**descendant of King Edward I**), by his wife _____ Huttof [see HUMPHREY 5.ii for her ancestry].

H.S.P. 64:158 (1913).

2. **THOMAS LEIGH,**, Esq., of Couldray, was married to **MARY FLEMING**, eldest daughter of Thomas Fleming, Knt., of Stonham, co. Hants, by his wife Dorothy Cromwell. They had two daughters.

H.S.P. 64:158 (1913). *Stockman* (1992), pp. 6,80 ("of Testwood, Southampton"). *Roberts* (1993), p. 247 (Dorothy Cromwell was aunt of Oliver Cromwell, the Lord Protector).

1. **ANNE LEIGH**, eldest daughter, was married to **JOSEPH STOCKMAN**, Gent., of Bereford in Downton, co. Wilts, son of William Stockman, Esq., of Bereford, by his wife Ann (Hinton) Dove. He was baptised at Downton on 27 Oct. 1621. They had three sons and four daughters. She died on 22 Feb. 1674. JOSEPH STOCKMAN, GENT., died on 27 Oct. 1675. Their gravestones, in the choir of Saint Lawrence's, Downton, bear the arms of Stockman impaling those of Leigh of Testwood.

H.S.P. 64:158 (1913) (no identification of husband of Anne). *Stockman* (1992), pp. 1-8,42-43,114-128. *NEHGR* 125:263 (Oct. 1971).

Child of Joseph Stockman, by Anne Leigh:

 i. JOHN STOCKMAN, baptised All Saints', Whiteparish, near Salisbury, co. Wilts, 15 Dec. 1645; resided Salisbury, Massachusetts, died there 6 Dec. 1686, married SARAH (PIKE) BRADBURY. Issue.

* * *

STONOR see MONTHERMER

---

[1] Ancestors of **Alice Baynton**.

STRANGEWAYS

EDWARD I OF ENGLAND, King of England, married ALIANORE DE CASTILLE.
ELIZABETH OF ENGLAND, married HUMPHREY DE BOHUN, Earl of Hereford and Essex.
ALIANOR DE BOHUN, married JAMES BUTLER, Earl of Ormond.
PERNEL BUTLER, married GILBERT TALBOT, 3rd Lord Talbot.
ELIZABETH TALBOT, married HENRY DE GREY, 5th Lord Grey of Wilton.
MARGARET DE GREY, married JOHN DARCY, 4th Lord Darcy of Knayth.
PHILIP DARCY, Knt., married ALIANORE FITZ HUGH [see DARCY 10.i].

8. ELIZABETH DARCY, elder daughter and co-heiress, was born about May 1417 (aged two years eleven months in April 1420), and was heiress to half the Baronies of Darcy and Meinill. She was married on 20 Nov. 1431 to **JAMES STRANGEWAYS**, Knt., the younger, of West Harsley, co. York, Sheriff of Yorkshire, M.P. for Yorkshire, Speaker of the House of Commons, son of James Strangeways, Knt., of Whorlton, North Riding, co. York, by Joan, daughter of Nicholas Orrell. They had seventeen children. ELIZABETH DARCY was living 1 Sep. 1458, and died before November 1461. He was married for the second time to Elizabeth Eure, widow (with issue) of William Bulmer, Knt., of Wilton, co. York, and daughter of Henry Eure, of Bradley, co. Durham. SIR JAMES STRANGEWAYS died on 20 Aug. 1480. His widow died testate on 13 or 14 Mar. 1481/2.

Glover-Foster (1875), p. 202 (1584 Vis. Yorks). *H.S.P.* 16:299 (1881) (1563 Vis. Yorks). *Northumberland* 5:411 (1899). *C.P.* 4:66-68 (1916). *Carleton* (1978), chart 8.

7. RICHARD STRANGEWAYS, Knt., of West Harsley, co. York, Hadstone, Northumberland, Eckington, co. Derby, son and heir, was married for the first time to **ELIZABETH NEVILLE**, second daughter and co-heiress of William Neville, Earl of Kent (of **Magna Charta Surety descent** and **descendant of Charlemagne**), by Joan, daughter of Thomas Fauconberg, Knt. (of **Magna Charta Surety descent** and **descendant of Charlemagne**). She was born about 1435 (aged twenty-eight and more in 1463), and was co-heiress to half of the Barony of Fauconberge [see BEAUFORT 11.iv.c for her ancestry]. He was married for the second time to JOANNA ASHETON, widow of Roger Dutton, and daughter of John Asheton. SIR RICHARD STRANGEWAYS died on 13 Apr. 1488. The will of his widow was dated 1501/2.

Glover-Foster (1875), p. 202. *H.S.P.* 16:300 (1881). *C.P.* 4:68 (1916). *C.P.* 5:286-287 (1926). *Carleton* (1978), chart 8.

6. JAMES STRANGEWAYS, Knt., of Whorlton, son and heir, was married, with licence dated 7 Sep. 1472, to **ALICE LE SCROPE**, eldest daughter of Thomas Le Scrope, 5th Lord Scrope of Masham, North Riding, co. York (of **Magna Charta Surety descent**), by Elizabeth, daughter of Ralph de Greystoke, 5th Lord Greystoke (**descendant of Charlemagne**). She was co-heiress to half of the Barony of Scrope of Masham. SIR JAMES STRANGEWAYS died on 16 Dec. 1521.

Glover-Foster (1875), p. 203. *H.S.P.* 16:300 (1881) ("Sir James Stranguysh of Harlesey = [2nd] Margaret daughter of Sir James Danby" and had issue). *C.P.* 4:68 (1916). *C.P.* 5:286-287 (1926). *Carleton* (1978), chart 8.

Child of James Strangeways, by Alice le Scrope:

   i. **JOAN STRANGEWAYS**, married **JOHN BIGOD**, of Settrington, co. York [see BIGOD 5].[1]

* * *

---

[1] Ancestors of **Edward Carleton**.

STRATTON see LUDLOW

STRICKLAND see CARLETON

STRODE see DAVIE

SUTTON see DUDLEY

* * *

TAILBOYS

EDWARD I OF ENGLAND, King of England, married **ALIANORE DE CASTILLE**.
JOAN OF ENGLAND [*of Acre*], married **GILBERT DE CLARE**, Earl of Gloucester.
MARGARET DE CLARE, married **HUGH DE AUDLEY**, 8th Earl of Gloucester.
MARGARET DE AUDLEY, married **RALPH DE STAFFORD**, Earl of Stafford.
BEATRICE DE STAFFORD, married **THOMAS DE ROS**, 4th Lord Ros of Helmsley.
MARGARET DE ROS, married **REYNOLD GREY**, 3rd Lord Grey of Ruthin.
MARGARET GREY, married **WILLIAM BONVILLE** [see BONVILLE 9].

6. **ELIZABETH BONVILLE**, was married to **WILLIAM TAILBOYS**, Knt., of Kyme, co. Lincoln, Lord Kyme *de jure*, son and heir of Walter Tailboys, Lord Kyme (of **Magna Charta Surety descent** and **descendant of Charlemagne**). He was born about 1415 (aged about twenty-eight in 1444). He fought as a Lancastrian at the battle of St. Albans on 19 Feb. 1460/1 (where he was knighted), and at the battle of Towton on 29 Mar. 1461. As a rebel and an adherent of the enemies of the new King, Edward IV, he was attainted on 4 Nov. 1461. WILLIAM TAILBOYS, Lord Kyme, fought on the Lancastrian side at the battle of Hexham on 15 May 1464, and, escaping after the defeat, was captured in a coal pit near Newcastle-on-Tyne toward the end of the month, and beheaded about 26 May 1464, burial at Grey Friars', Newcastle. His widow died on 14 Feb. 1490/1.

H.S.P. 52:946 (1904) (Maddison Linc. Ped.). *C.P.* 7:356, 359-361 (1929).

5. **ROBERT TAILBOYS**, Knt., Lord Kyme *de jure*, Sheriff of Lincolnshire, M.P. for Lincolnshire, was born about 1451 (aged forty at mother's death). The attainder of his father was reversed in 1472. He was married before 1467 to **ELIZABETH HERON**, daughter of John Heron, Knt. ROBERT TAILBOYS, Lord Kyme, died testate on 30 Jan. 1494/5, and was buried at Kyme Priory. His will (P.C.C., Vox 24) mentions his sons George, William, Robert, John, and Richard, and a daughter Maud.

H.S.P. 16:233-234 (1881) (1563 Vis. Yorks) (.... *Heron [filia] Domini Willielmi Heron de Ford] nupta Johanni Heron de Wetynam*). *H.S.P.* 52:946 (1984). *C.P.* 7:356, 361 (1929).

Children of Robert Tailboys, by Elizabeth Heron:

i. **GEORGE TAILBOYS**, Lord Kyme, married **ELIZABETH GASCOIGNE** [see READE 4].[1]
ii. **MAUD TAILBOYS**, married **ROBERT TYRWHIT**, Knt., of Kettleby [see WELBY 4].[2]

---

[1] Ancestors of **George Reade**.
[2] Ancestors of **Richard Saltonstall, Olive Welby**.

* * *

TALBOT

EDWARD I OF ENGLAND, King of England, married ALIANORE DE CASTILLE.
ELIZABETH OF ENGLAND, married HUMPHREY DE BOHUN, Earl of Hereford.
ALIANOR DE BOHUN, married JAMES BUTLER, Earl of Ormond [see BUTLER 10].

9. PERNEL BUTLER, was married before 8 Sep. 1352 to **GILBERT TALBOT**, Knt., of Eccleswall, co. Hereford, 3rd Lord Talbot, son of Richard Talbot, 2nd Lord Talbot (**descendant of Charlemagne**), by Elizabeth, daughter and co-heiress of John Comyn, Lord of Badenoch (of **Magna Charta Surety descent** and **descendant of Charlemagne**). He was born about 1332. She was living on 28 May 1365, and is said to have died in 1368. He was summoned to Parliament from 14 Aug. 1362. He was married for the second time before 16 Nov. 1379 to Joan de Stafford, widow of John Cherleton, 3rd Lord Cherleton, lord of Powis (died 13 July 1374), and daughter of Ralph de Stafford, 1st Earl of Stafford, by Margaret (descendant of King Edward I), daughter and heiress of Hugh de Audley, Earl of Gloucester. He accompanied Edmund of York [*of Langley*], Earl of Cambridge, on his expedition to Portugal 1381-82, and was with John *of Gaunt*'s unsuccessful expedition to Spain and Portugal from July 1386. GILBERT TALBOT, Lord Talbot, died aged about fifty-five of the pestilence at Roales, Spain, on 24 Apr. 1387. His widow died before 1397.

Collins-Brydges (1812) 3:8. *C.P.* 3:161 (1913). *C.P.* 6:177 (1926). *Bulkeley* (1933), p. 72. *C.P.* 12(1):614-616 (1953).

Children of Gilbert Talbot, by Pernel Butler:
  i. **RICHARD TALBOT**, Knt., born about 1361 [see next].
  ii. **ELIZABETH TALBOT**, married HENRY GREY [see WILTON 9].[1]

8. RICHARD TALBOT, Knt., 4th Lord Talbot, son and heir by first marriage, was born about 1361 (aged twenty-six at father's death). He was married before 23 Aug. 1383 to **ANKARET LE STRANGE**, Baroness Strange of Blackmere, only daughter and eventual sole heiress of John le Strange, 1st Baron Strange of Blackmere, by Isabel (**descendant of King Edward I**), daughter of Richard Fitz Alan, Knt. She was born in 1361 (aged twenty-two in August 1383) [see CERGEAUX 10.ii for her ancestry]. They had five sons. He was summoned to Parliament *v.p.* in consequence of his marriage to the heiress of Strange of Blackmere from 3 Mar. 1383/4 by writs directed *Ricardo Talbot de Blakemere*. On succeeding his father he was summoned to Parliament on 17 Dec. 1387 by writ directed *Ricardo Talbot de Godriche Castell*. RICHARD TALBOT, Lord Talbot, died aged about thirty-five at London on 8 or 9 Sep. 1396. His widow was married for the second time between 8 Mar. and 4 July 1401 to Thomas Neville, Lord Furnival (died 14 Mar. 1406/7 *s.p.m.*). She died aged fifty-two on 1 June 1413.

Collins-Brydges (1812) 3:8-9. *Bulkeley* (1933), p. 72. *C.P.* 12(1):616-617 (1953).

Children of Richard Talbot, by Ankaret le Strange:
  i. **JOHN TALBOT**, Knt., second son, born 1384 [see next].

---

[1] Ancestors of **Edward Carleton, Mary Launce, Philip & Thomas Nelson**, and, probably, **Jane Haviland**.

TALBOT (cont.)

ii. **MARY TALBOT**, married **THOMAS GREENE**, Knt., of Greene's Norton [see MARBURY 8].[1]

7. **JOHN TALBOT**, Knt., K.G., Lord Furnival *jure uxoris*, Lord Strange of Blackmere, 7th Lord Talbot, second son, was born in 1384. He was married for the first time before 12 Mar. 1406/7 to **MAUD NEVILLE**, Baroness Furnivall *de jure*, daughter of Thomas Neville, Lord Furnivall (**descendant of Charlemagne**), by Joan, daughter of William, Lord Furnivall. She was born in 1392, and with her he acquired the great family estates of the family of Furnivall in Hallamshire, of which the castle of Sheffield was the *caput*. They had three sons. In consequence of his marriage he was summoned to Parliament from 26 Oct. 1409 by writs directed *Johanni Talbot de Furnyvall'*. She died in 1423, and was buried at Worksop Priory, co. Nottingham. On the death of his niece Ankaret in 1421, he succeeded to the Baronies of Strange (of Blackmere) and of Talbot. He was married for the second time on 6 Sep. 1425 at Warwick Castle, to MARGARET BEAUCHAMP, first daughter of Richard Beauchamp, Earl of Warwick, by his wife, Elizabeth, daughter of Thomas Berkeley, Lord Berkeley. She was born in 1404, and was co-heiress to her mother. They had four sons and two daughters. He fought in the war in France from 1424. For his services he was created **Earl of Shrewsbury** on 20 May 1442. He was appointed King's Lieutenant of Ireland (being lord of the honour of Wexford), and was created **Earl of Waterford** on 17 July 1446. JOHN TALBOT, Earl of Shrewsbury, was slain, aged seventy, together with his son John, Lord Lisle (son of that name by the second marriage), in an attack on the French at Castillon on the Dordogne on 17 July 1453, and was buried, with monumental inscription, at St. Alkmund's, Whitchurch, co. Salop. His widow died on 14 June 1467, and was buried in the Jesus Chapel of St. Paul's.

Collins-Brydges (1812) 3:11-17. *Clay* (1913), p. 217. *Bulkeley* (1933), pp. 72-73. *C.P.* 11:698-704, 704 footnote *c* (1949). *C.P.* 12(1):620 (1953). *Paget* (1977), p. 405.

6. **JOHN TALBOT**, Knt., K.G., 2nd Earl of Shrewsbury, Lord Treasurer of England, son and heir by first marriage, was born about 1413 (aged forty and more at death of father). He was betrothed (but not married) to KATHERINE BURNELL, daughter and co-heiress of Edward Burnell, Knt. He was married before March 1444 to **ELIZABETH BUTLER**, daughter of James Butler, 4th Earl of Ormond (**descendant of King Edward I**), by Joan (**descendant of King Edward I**), daughter of William Beauchamp, Lord Abergavenny. She was born in 1420 [see BUTLER 7 for her ancestry]. They had five sons and two daughters. JOHN TALBOT, Earl of Shrewsbury, was slain, with his brother Sir Christopher Talbot at the battle of Northampton on 10 July 1460, fighting on the Lancastrian side, and was buried, with monumental inscription, at Worksop Priory, co. Nottingham. His widow died on 8 Sep. 1473, and was buried at Shrewsbury Abbey (M.I.).

Collins-Brydges (1812) 3:17-19. *Clay* (1913), p. 217. *Bulkeley* (1933), p. 73. *C.P.* 11:704-705, 704 footnote *e* (1949) (corrects 2:435 footnote *f*). *Paget* (1977), p. 249.

Children of John Talbot, by Elizabeth Butler:

    i. **GILBERT TALBOT**, Knt., second son, born 1452 [see next].

    ii. **ANNE TALBOT**, died 17 May 1494; married 1467 **HENRY VERNON**, Knt., of Haddon, born 1445, Sheriff, Governor of Arthur, Prince of Wales, built Haddon Hall, died testate 13 Apr. 1515 (P.C.C. 9 Holder), son of William Vernon, Knt., of Haddon, co. Derby (of **Magna Charta Surety descent** and **descendant of Charlemagne**), by Margaret, daughter of William Swinfen. *Collins-Brydges* (1812) 3:19. *Clay* (1913), p. 217. *Paget* (1977), p. 264 (he born 1441, died 2 Apr.

---

[1] Ancestors of **Grace Chetwode, Anne & Catherine Marbury**.

TALBOT (cont.)

1515).

a. **ELIZABETH VERNON**, married **ROBERT CORBET**, Knt. [see FERRERS 5].[1]

5. GILBERT TALBOT, Knt., K.G., of Grafton, co. Worcester, P.C., Sheriff of Shropshire, Captain of Calais, second son, was born in 1452. He was married for the first time to **ELIZABETH GREYSTOKE**, widow of Thomas le Scrope, 5th Lord Scrope of Masham, and daughter of Ralph de Greystoke, 5th Lord Greystoke, by Elizabeth, daughter of William, 4th Lord Fitz Hugh, and had two sons and two daughters. He was married for the second time, as her third husband, to **AUDREY** (or **ETHELDREDA**) **COTTON**, widow, first of Thomas Barton, Esq., second, of Richard Gardiner, Knt., Lord Mayor of London, and daughter of William Cotton, Knt., of Landwade, co. Cambridge, by his wife Alice Abbot. On the landing of Henry, Earl of Richmond, he met him at Newport, co. Salop, and had the command of the right wing of the army in the battle of Bosworth. He was "then knighted for his valiant behaviour, being sore wounded". SIR GILBERT TALBOT died on 16 Aug. 1517, and was buried at Whitchurch, co. Salop.

Collins-Brydges (1812) 3:19,29-33 (he died 19 Sep. 1516). *H.S.P.* 16:310 (1881) (1563 Vis. Yorks). *Bulkeley* (1933), p. 74. *C.P.* 11:706 footnote a (1949). *Paget* (1977), p. 168.

4. JOHN TALBOT, Knt., of Albrighton, co. Salop, and Grafton, co. Worcester, Sheriff of Shropshire, was born in 1485. He was married for the first time before 1510 to **MARGARET TROUTBECK**, daughter and heiress of Adam Troutbeck, Esq., of Thornton-le-Moors, co. Chester (**descendant of King Edward I**), by his wife Joan Molyneux [see TROUTBECK 5 for her ancestry]. She was born in 1494 (aged sixteen in 1510). They had three sons and five daughters. She was living in 1521. He was married for the second time to ELIZABETH WROTTESLEY, daughter of Walter Wrottesley, of Wrottesley, co. Stafford. They had four sons and four daughters. SIR JOHN TALBOT died testate on 10 Sep. 1549, and was buried at Bromsgrove, co. Worcester (with monumental inscription). His widow was married for the second time to Edward Lyttleton. She died testate on 10 May 1559.

Collins-Brydges (1812) 3:34-35 (M.I. states his death occurred 10 Sep. 1550). *H.S.P.* 16:311 (1881). *Chester & North Wales.Arch.Soc.(n.s.).* 28:174-175 (1929). *Bulkeley* (1933), pp. 74-75. *C.P.* 11:731 chart (1949). *Paget* (1977), p. 115.

3. ANNE TALBOT, was born about 1515. She was married to **THOMAS NEEDHAM**, of Shavington, co. Salop, son of Robert Needham, Knt., of Shavington, co. Salop, by Agnes, daughter of John Mainwaring, of Over Peover, co. Chester. He was born in 1510. They had two sons and five daughters. THOMAS NEEDHAM died v.p.

Collins-Brydges (1812) 3:36 ([erroneously] describes Anne as granddaughter rather than daughter). *Bulkeley* (1933), pp. 63-64,67-71. *H.S.P.* 29:372 (1889) (1623 Vis. Salop) (he also was married, evidently, first, to Agnes Hope, with daughter Agnes).

2. ROBERT NEEDHAM, of Shavington, co. Salop, Sheriff of Shropshire, was born in 1535. He was married to **FRANCES ASTON**, daughter of Edward Aston, Knt., of Tixall, co. Stafford (**descendant of Charlemagne**), by Joan, daughter of Thomas Bowles, Knt., of Penho, co. Caernarvon. They had two sons and five daughters.

Bulkeley (1933), p. 64. *H.S.P.* 29:372 (1889) (does not name daughter Dorothy).

Child of Robert Needham, by Frances Aston:

---

[1] Ancestors of **Robert Abell**.

TALBOT (cont.)

i. DOROTHY NEEDHAM, married RICHARD CHETWODE, Knt. [see CHETWODE 1].[1]

* * *

TANFIELD see RANDOLPH

TEMPLE see NELSON

THIMBLEBY see WELBY

THORNES see LITTLETON

THORNTON see LITTLETON

* * *

THROCKMORTON

EDWARD I OF ENGLAND, King of England, married ALIANORE DE CASTILLE.
JOAN OF ENGLAND [*of Acre*], married GILBERT DE CLARE, Earl of Gloucester.
ALIANOR DE CLARE, married HUGH LE DESPENSER, Lord Despenser.
ISABEL LE DESPENSER, married RICHARD FITZ ALAN, Earl of Arundel.
EDMUND FITZ ALAN, Knt., married SIBYL DE MONTAGU.
PHILIPPE FITZ ALAN, married RICHARD CERGEAUX, Knt.
PHILIPPE CERGEAUX, married ROBERT PASHLEY, Knt.
ANNE PASHLEY, married EDWARD TYRRELL, Esq..
PHILLIPE TYRRELL, married THOMAS CORNWALLIS.
WILLIAM CORNWALLIS, Esq., married ELIZABETH STANFORD.
JOHN CORNWALLIS, Knt., married MARY SULLIARD [see DADE 4].

3. ELIZABETH CORNWALLIS, was born about 1522, and was named, with her husband, in her father's will. She was married to JOHN BLENNERHASSET, Esq., of Barsham, Suffolk, and Boyland Hall and Frenze, Norfolk, M.P. for Norwich, fourth son of Thomas Blennerhasset, Knt., of Frenze and Boyland Hall, Norfolk, by his second wife, Margaret, daughter of John Braham, Esq., of Wetheringsett, Suffolk. They had one daughter. He was married for the second time to Mary Echingham, second daughter and co-heiress of Edward Echingham, Knt., of Barsham, and had nine children. She was buried 20 Mar. 1571. JOHN BLENNERHASSET, ESQ., was buried at Barsham on 29 June 1573.

Collins-Brydges (1812) 2:544. *Copinger* 3:242 (1909). *Throckmorton* (1930), pp. 202-203. *NEHGR* 98:278 (July 1944). *H.S.P. (n.s.)* 3:360 (1984) (1561 Vis. Suffolk) (Blennerhasset arms: *Gules*, a chevron ermine between three dolphins embowed *argent*, on the chevron an annulet for a difference).

2. ELIZABETH BLENNERHASSET, was born about 1540. She was married at Barsham on 29 June 1561 to LIONEL THROCKMORTON, Gent., of South Elmham

---

[1] Ancestors of **Grace Chetwode**.

THROCKMORTON (cont.)

and Bungay, Suffolk, son of Simon Throckmorton, of Barsham, Suffolk, by Anne, daughter of Edmund Louthe, of Sawtry, co. Huntingdon. He was born in 1525, and had been married previously, without issue, to Elizabeth Kemp, daughter of Bartholomew Kemp, of Gissing, Norfolk. Lionel & Elizabeth had three sons and two daughters. He was founder of Bungay Grammar School. LIONEL THROCKMORTON, GENT., died testate on 24 Nov. 1599 and was buried at Holy Trinity church, Bungay. The will of his widow was dated 30 June and proved 7 Nov. 1608.

Throckmorton (1930), pp. 200-205. *NEHGR* 98:277-278 (July 1944). *H.S.P.* 32:283 (1891) (Vis. Norfolk). NEHGR 98:67-72,111-123. NEHGR 110:122-7. *H.S.P. (n.s.)* 3:360 (1984).

1. BASSINGBOURNE THROCKMORTON, Esq., Grocer, Citizen, and Alderman of Norwich, was born in 1564. He was married for the first time in 1591 to **MARY HILL**, daughter of William Hill, Gent., of Bury St. Edmunds, by Joan, daughter of John Annabel, of Bury St. Edmunds. She died in 1615. He was married for the second time to HESTER PYE, daughter of Henry Pye, of Norwich, by his wife Susanna Sotheron, and had issue. BASSINGBOURNE THROCKMORTON, ESQ., died testate (P.C.C., 152 Lee) on 21 Sep. 1638. In litigation involving his estate in 1640 it could not be determined if his son John was dead or alive.

H.S.P. 32:283 (1891) (identification of children, including four dying in infancy: Lionel, Elizabeth, Mary, and Ursula). *Throckmorton* (1930), pp. 205-209. *NEHGR* 86:265 (July 1932) (Throckmorton arms: Gules on a chevron silver two gemelles sable). *TAG* 12:79-85 (Oct. 1935) (Edward Covill, of Bradwell, Essex, in his will proved 1 Aug. 1679 bequeathed "six pounds to my kinsman John Throckmorton of Middle Towne in New England"). *NEHGR* 98:67-72 (Jan. 1944). *NEHGR* 98:111-123 (Apr. 1944). NEHGR 117:234 (July 1963).

Children & grandchildren of Bassingbourne Throckmorton, by Mary Hill:

  i. LIONEL THROCKMORTON, son and heir, baptised 1595, living 1677.

  ii. THOMAS THROCKMORTON.

  iii. **JOHN THROCKMORTON**, baptised Norwich 9 May 1601, apprenticed to a scrivener, his uncle Robert Debenay, at Norwich 20 Mar. 1620/1, emigrated on ship *Lyon*, embarked Bristol 1 Dec. 1630, arrived Nantasket 5 Feb. 1631, merchant and ship-owner, Salem, Massachusetts, 1634-1639, one of the original companions of Roger Williams in the settlement of Providence, Rhode Island, 1637-1642, 1647-1687, New Netherlands 1642-1643, Warwick, Rhode Island, 1651, died Middletown, New Jersey 1687; married REBECCA _____.

    a. **FREEGIFT THROCKMORTON**, born about 1635, died Jamaica, May 1669 *s.p.*

    b. **PATIENCE THROCKMORTON**, born about 1640, died 7 Sep. 1676; married December 1655 **DEP. GOV. JOHN COGGESHALL**, of Newport, Rhode Island. Nine children.

    c. **JOHN THROCKMORTON**, born about 1642, resided Middletown, New Jersey, died 17 July 1690; married 12 Dec. 1670 **ALICE STOUT**. Six children.

    d. **DELIVERANCE THROCKMORTON**, born about 1645, married 25 May 1669 **REV. JAMES ASHTON**, of Monmouth County, New Jersey. Seven children.

    e. **JOB THROCKMORTON**, born 30 Sep. 1650, resided Middletown, New Jersey, died 20 Aug. 1709; married 2 Feb. 1684/5 **SARAH LEONARD**, born 27 May 1660, died 5 Feb. 1743/4. Eight children.

    f. **JOSEPH THROCKMORTON**, born about 1652, mariner, owner of two vessels, resided Middletown, New Jersey, died shortly before 13 Oct. 1690 *s.p.*

  iv. MILES THROCKMORTON, baptised 18 June 1605.

  v. ROBERT THROCKMORTON, baptised 1610, hosier, Freeman 1632.

  vi. GEORGE THROCKMORTON, died *s.p.*

  vii. SIMON THROCKMORTON.

  viii. MARY THROCKMORTON, married WILLIAM RAWLEY, of Clay, Norfolk.

THROCKMORTON (cont.)

ix. ELIZABETH THROCKMORTON, married JOHN LAYER, of Norwich.

* * *

THROCKMORTON OF COUGHTON see BULL

THROCKMORTON OF HASELEY see OXENBRIDGE

TIPTOFT see CHERLETON

TORBOCK see MANWARING

TRAFFORD see GERARD

* * *

TROUTBECK

EDWARD I OF ENGLAND, King of England, married ALIANORE DE CASTILLE.
ELIZABETH OF ENGLAND, married HUMPHREY DE BOHUN, Earl of Hereford.
WILLIAM DE BOHUN, Earl of Northampton, married ELIZABETH DE BADLESMERE.
ELIZABETH DE BOHUN, married RICHARD FITZ ALAN, Earl of Arundel and of Surrey.
ELIZABETH FITZ ALAN, married ROBERT GOUSHILL, Knt.
JOAN GOUSHILL, married THOMAS STANLEY, Lord Stanley [see FITZ ALAN 10].

6. MARGARET STANLEY, was married for the first time, with dispensation dated 23 Jan. 1459/60, they being related in the third and third degrees, to **WILLIAM TROUTBECK**, Knt., of Dunham-on-the-Hill, co. Chester, son and heir of John Troutbeck, of Oxhay, co. Hertford, and Frodsham, co. Chester, Chamberlain of Chester, by Margery, daughter and heiress of Thomas Holes, of Brimstage, Oxton and Mobberley. He was born about 1435 (aged twenty-three at father's death in 1458). They had three sons and two daughters. SIR WILLIAM TROUTBECK was slain on the Lancastrian side at the battle of Blore Heath on 23 Sep. 1459. She was married for the second time in 1460 to JOHN BOTELER, Knt., of Bewsey in Warrington, and had a son Thomas. He died on 26 Feb. 1462/3. She was married for the third time to Henry Grey, Lord Grey of Codnor, and had a daughter Anne. She died about 1481.

Gen.Mag. 8:204 (Dec. 1938). VCH Lanc. I 345-349. *Chester & North Wales.Arch.Soc.(n.s.)* 28:159-165 (1929) (Troutbeck arms: *Azure*, three trouts fretted *argent*). *NEHGR* 108:172-174 (July 1954). *Paget* (1977), p. 249 (he was born 13.7.1436).

Children of William Troutbeck, by Margaret Stanley:
 i. **ADAM TROUTBECK**, younger son [see next].
 ii. **JOAN TROUTBECK**, born 1459, married **WILLIAM GRIFFITH**, Knt. [see COYTEMORE 5].[1]

---

[1]Ancestors of **Elizabeth Coytemore, Joshua & Rebecca Owen**.

TROUTBECK (cont.)

5. **ADAM TROUTBECK**, of Thornton-le-Moors, co. Chester, younger son, was married for the first time to **MARGARET BOTELER**, daughter of John Boteler, Knt., of Bewsey, Baron of Warrington, co. Lancaster, by Margaret, daughter of Peter Gerard, of Bryn and Kingsley, co. Lancaster. He was married for the second time before 1491 to **JOAN MOLYNEUX**, widow of Hamnet Massey of Denwall, and daughter, probably, of Robert Molyneux. ADAM TROUTBECK died between 1491 and 1510. His widow was living in 1511.

Chester & North Wales Arch.Soc.(n.s.) 28:173-176 (1929). *Paget* (1977), p. 168.

Child of Adam Troutbeck, by Joan Molyneux:

i. **MARGARET TROUTBECK**, born 1494, married **JOHN TALBOT**, Knt. [see TALBOT 4].[1]

* * *

TRYE

EDWARD I OF ENGLAND, King of England, married **ALIANORE DE CASTILLE**.
JOAN OF ENGLAND [*of Acre*], married **GILBERT OF CLARE**, Earl of Gloucester.
ALIANOR DE CLARE, married **HUGH LE DESPENSER**, 2nd Lord Le Despenser.
ELIZABETH DESPENSER, married **MAURICE DE BERKELEY**, 4th Lord Berkeley.
JAMES DE BERKELEY, Knt., married **ELIZABETH BLUET**.
JAMES DE BERKELEY, Knt., married **ISABEL DE MOWBRAY** [see DEIGHTON 7].

6. **ISABEL BERKELEY**, was married in 1477 to **WILLIAM TRYE**, Esq., of Hardwick, co. Gloucester, son of John Trye, by Elizabeth, daughter of Amery Boteler, of Hardwick Court. WILLIAM TRYE, ESQ., died in 1498.

Smyth-Maclean (1883) 2:91 (he was a descendant of Robert Berkeley). *H.S.P.* 21:170 (1885) (1623 Vis. Glouc.). *H.S.P.* 28:31 (1889 1623 Vis. Salop (Trye arms: *Argent*, a buck *gules*). *Ligon* (1947), p. 211.

5. **WILLIAM TRYE**, Esq., of Hardwick and Redwick, co. Gloucester, Seagry, co. Wilts, was married to **ANNE BAYNHAM**, daughter of Thomas Baynham. WILLIAM TRYE, ESQ., died in 1525.

H.S.P. 21:170 (1885)(omits this generation). *Paget* (1977), p. 459. *Ligon* (1947), p. 211.

4. **EDWARD TRYE**, Esq., of Hardwick, was born in 1494. He was married to **SIBYL MORNINGTON**, daughter of Thomas Mornington, Knt., of Sarnsfield, by Elizabeth, daughter and co-heiress of Simon Milborne. EDWARD TRYE, ESQ., died on 27 Sep. 1526.

Smyth-Maclean (1883) 2:92. *H.S.P.* 21:170 (1885). *Paget* (1977), p. 459. *Ligon* (1947), p. 211.

3. **KATHERINE TRYE**, was married to **HUGH DENNIS**, Esq., of Pucklechurch, co. Gloucester, son of John Dennis, of Pucklechurch, by Fortune, daughter of Thomas Norton, of Bristow. They had four sons and one daughter. HUGH DENNIS, ESQ., died in 1612.

Smyth-Maclean (1883) 2:92. *H.S.P.* 21:51 (1885) (1623 Vis. Glouc.) (does not name daughter Frances). *Ligon* (1947), p. 212.

Child of Hugh Dennis, by Katherine Trye:

---

[1] Ancestors of **Grace Chetwode**.

TRYE (cont.)

i. **FRANCES DENNIS**, married **THOMAS LYGON**, of Elkstone [see LIGON 2].[1]

* * *

TUCHET

EDWARD I OF ENGLAND, King of England, married **ALIANORE DE CASTILLE**.
JOAN OF ENGLAND [*of Acre*], married **GILBERT DE CLARE**, Earl of Gloucester.
MARGARET DE CLARE, married **HUGH DE AUDLEY**, 8th Earl of Gloucester.
MARGARET DE AUDLEY, married **RALPH DE STAFFORD**, Earl of Stafford.
BEATRICE DE STAFFORD, married **THOMAS DE ROS**, 4th Lord Ros of Helmesley.
WILLIAM DE ROS, Knt., married **MARGARET DE ARUNDEL** [see ROS 10].

9. **MARGARET DE ROS**, was married, with Papal dispensation dated 6 Kal. Mar. 1415 to remain in marriage contracted but not consummated, to **JAMES TUCHET**, 5th Lord Audley, son and heir of John Tuchet, Knt. (of **Magna Charta Surety descent** and **descendant of Charlemagne**), by his wife Isabel. He was born about 1398 (aged ten in 1408). He was summoned to Parliament on 26 Feb. 1420/1, with writs directed *Jacobo de Audley*. She was living on 15 Kal. Sep. 1423. He was married for the second time, with Papal dispensation dated 16 Kal. Mar. 1429/30, being related in the third degree, to **ALIANOR HOLAND**, base-born daughter of Edmund Holand, Earl of Kent, by Constance, daughter of Edmund of York [*of Langley*], Duke of York (fifth son of King Edward III) [see HOLAND 8.i and YORK 8 for her ancestry]. Having raised ten thousand men on behalf of King Henry VI, JAMES TUCHET, Lord Audley, aged sixty-one, was defeated and slain at the battle of Blore Heath, co. Salop, on 23 Sep. 1459.

C.P. (1910) 1:341-342, 341 footnote *c* (he was slain by Sir Roger Kynaston, of Hordley, who took his arms, Ermine a chevron *gules*, ever after borne by the branch of the Kynastons [see LLOYD 6]). *Gen.* 28:62 (pt. 1) (1912). *C.P.* 3:346 (1913). *C.P.* 6:140 (1926). *C.P.* 11:103, footnote *e* (1949). *Paget* (1977), p. 403.

Children & grandchildren of James Tuchet, by Margaret de Ros:
  i. **JOHN TUCHET**, son and heir [see next].
Children of James Tuchet, by Alianor Holand:
  ii. **ELIZABETH TUCHET**, married **EDWARD BROOKE**, 6th Lord Cobham [see WYATT 6].

8. **JOHN TUCHET**, 6th Lord Audley, P.C., Lord Treasurer, son and heir, was married before 1456 to **ANNE ECHINGHAM**, widow of John Rogers, of Bryanston, Dorset (died August 1450), and daughter of Thomas Echingham, Knt. (**descendant of King Henry III**), probably by his second wife, Margaret, daughter of John Kynvett. He was summoned to Parliament by writs directed *Johanni de Audley*. JOHN TUCHET, Lord Audley, died on 26 Sep. 1490. His widow died testate on 7 May 1498, and was buried at Bermondsey monastery.

C.P. 1:341-342 (1910). *Sur.Soc.* 144:122 (1930) (1480 Vis. North). *Paget* (1977), pp. 435,442.

Children of John Tuchet, by Anne Echingham:
  i. **ELEANOR TUCHET** [see next].

---

[1] Grandparents of **Thomas Ligon**.

TUCHET (cont.)

ii. **ANNE TUCHET**, married **JOHN WINGFIELD**, Knt. [see HANKFORD 5].[1]

7. **ELEANOR TUCHET**, was married to **ROGER LEWKNOR**, Knt., of Greatworth and Stoke Doyle, co. Northampton, Sheriff of Northampton, son of Thomas Lewknor, Knt., of Greatworth and Stoke Doyle (of **Magna Charta Surety descent and descendant of Charlemagne**), by Katherine, daughter of John Pelham, Knt., of Laughton, Sussex. He was born about 1465 (aged seventy in 1535-1536). He was married for the second time to Elizabeth Hussey (died *s.p.*), and for the third time to Ellen, daughter of Thomas Messant, Esq., and had issue. The will of SIR ROGER LEWKNOR was proved on 13 Apr. 1543. His widow was married for the second time to Richard Lewknor, Knt., of Trotton, and had ten children.

Baker (1841) 2:508. *Sussex Arch. Coll.* 3:96 (1850). *Sussex Arch. Coll.* 68:279-281 (1927). *H.S.P.* 53:26 (1905) (1633 Vis. Sussex). *Paget* (1977), p. 462.

6. **JANE LEWKNOR**, daughter and heiress, was married for the first time to **CHRISTOPHER PICKERING**, Knt. (died 7 Sep. 1516) (with one daughter, Anne, wife of Henry Knyvett, Knt., of Charlton, co. Wilts). Jane was married for the second time, with three children, to **ARTHUR POLE**, Knt. (died 1535-1536). She was married for the third time about 1539 to **WILLIAM BARENTYN**, Knt., of Hasely, co. Oxford, son of John Barentyn, by Mary, daughter of Thomas Stoner, of Oxfordshire. He was born on 31 Dec. 1481. SIR WILLIAM BARENTYN died testate (P.C.C., 5 Coode) on 12 Sep. 1550.

Collins-Brydges (1812) 4:438. *Sussex Arch. Coll.* 3:96 (1850) (names a son Drew only). *Wm. Salt Soc.* 3:92-93 (1882) ("Barantine" arms: *Sable*, three eagles displayed *argent*). *H.S.P.* 53:66-67 (1905). *Sussex Arch. Coll.* 68:279-281 (1927) (Jane was said to have been coerced by Arthur's brother, Henry Pole, Lord Montagu [see SOMERSET 6], to take a vow of perpetual chastity after Arthur's death, and the marriage to William was declared invalid by the Consistory Court of London in 1540). *Comber* (1931), p. 18 (he died 17 Nov. 1549). *Paget* (1977), p. 462.

Child of William Barentyn, by Jane Lewknor:

i. **MARGARET BARENTYN**, married **JOHN HARCOURT** [see HARCOURT 5].[2]

* * *

TYRRELL

EDWARD I OF ENGLAND, King of England, married **ALIANORE DE CASTILLE**.
JOAN OF ENGLAND [*of Acre*], married **GILBERT DE CLARE**, Earl of Gloucester.
ALIANOR DE CLARE, married **HUGH LE DESPENSER**, Lord Despenser.
ISABEL DESPENSER, married **RICHARD FITZ ALAN**, Earl of Arundel.
EDMUND FITZ ALAN, Knt., married **SIBYL DE MONTAGU**.
PHILIPPE FITZ ALAN, married **RICHARD CERGEAUX**, Knt.
ELIZABETH CERGEAUX, married **WILLIAM DE MARNEY**, Knt.
EMMA DE MARNEY, married **THOMAS TYRRELL**, Knt. [see JENNINGS 9].

9. **ROBERT TYRRELL**, Knt., of Essex, third son, was Master of the Horse to King Henry VIII. He was married to **CHRISTIAN HARTSHORN**. They had two sons and one daughter.

---

[1] Ancestors of **Francis Dade**.

[2] Ancestors of **Muriel Gurdon**.

TYRRELL (cont.)

H.S.P. 13:300-301 (1878) (1612 Vis. Essex). *Roberts* (1993), p. 287.

8. JOYCE TYRRELL, was married to **THOMAS APPLETON**, Gent., of Kent.
   H.S.P. 13:134 (1878) (1614 Vis. Essex). *Roberts* (1993), p. 287.

7. ROGER APPLETON, Esq., of Dartford, Kent, son and heir, was married to **ANNE SULLIARD**, daughter of John Sulliard (or Sulyard), Knt., of Weston, Norfolk, by Anne (**descendant of King Edward I**), daughter of John Andrews, Esq., of Baylham, Suffolk [see LUDLOW 7.ii for her ancestry].
   H.S.P. 13:134 (1878) ("John Suliard of Wetherden Hall in com. Suff"). *H.S.P. (n.s.)* 2:111 (1981) (1561 Vis. Suffolk).

6. HENRY APPLETON, Esq., of Dartford, son and heir, was married to **MARGARET ROPER**, daughter of John Roper, Esq., of Kent.
   H.S.P. 13:135 (1878). *Roberts* (1993), p. 287.

5. ROGER APPLETON, Esq., of North Benfleet, Essex, son and heir, was married to **AGNES CLARKE**, daughter of Walter Clarke, Gent., of Hadleigh, Suffolk, and sister and heiress of Edward Clarke. They had five sons and five daughters. She was married for the second time to Thomas Gibbon, Esq., of Lynne.
   H.S.P. 13:135 (1878) (but confusion on name of father and brother of wife). *Roberts* (1993), p. 287.

   Child of Roger Appleton, by Agnes Clarke:
   i. **ALICE APPLETON**, married **HENRY BERNEY**, Esq., of Reedham [see JENNINGS 4].[1]

* * *

TYRRELL OF DOWNHAM see DADE

TYRRELL OF LITTLE WARLEY see JENNINGS

TYRWHIT see WELBY

VAUX see OXENBRIDGE

VERDUN see BURGH

VERE see CERGEAUX

VINCENT see RANDOLPH

* * *

---

[1] Ancestors of **Edmund Jennings**.

EDWARD I OF ENGLAND, King of England, married **ALIANORE DE CASTILLE**.
JOAN OF ENGLAND [*of Acre*], married **GILBERT DE CLARE**, Earl of Gloucester.
ELIZABETH DE CLARE, married **ROGER DAMORY**, Lord Damory.
ELIZABETH DAMORY, married **JOHN BARDOLF**, 3rd Lord Bardolf.
WILLIAM BARDOLF, 4th Lord Bardolf, married **AGNES DE POYNINGS**.
CECILY BARDOLF, married **BRIAN STAPLETON**, Knt.
MILES STAPLETON, Knt., married **KATHERINE DE LA POLE**.
ELIZABETH STAPLETON, married **WILLIAM CALTHORPE**, Knt.
ANNE CALTHORP, married **ROBERT DRURY**, Knt. [see BARDOLF 6].

3. ANNE DRURY, was married for the first time to **GEORGE WALDEGRAVE**, Esq., of Smallbridge in Bures St. Mary, Suffolk, son and heir of William Waldegrave, Knt., of Smallbridge, by Margery, daughter of Henry Wentworth, of Cobham Hall, Wethersfield, Essex (of **Magna Charta Surety descent** and **descendant of Charlemagne**). He was born in 1483. They had five sons and two daughters. GEORGE WALDEGRAVE, ESQ., died testate (P.C.C., 36 Porch) on 8 July 1528, and was buried at All Saints, Sudbury. She was married for the second time to THOMAS JERMYN, Knt., of Rushbrook, and had two sons. She died on 7 June 1572, and was buried at Depden.

H.S.P. 13:120 (1878) (1558 Vis. Essex). *H.S.P.* 32:298 (1891) (Vis. Norfolk). *Muskett* (1900), p. 313. *Clopton* (1939), pp. 75-76. *H.S.P. (n.s.)* 2:93-95 (1561 Vis. Suffolk) (Kempe arms: Per pale *argent* and *gules*).

Children of George Waldegrave, by Anne Drury:

    i. **WILLIAM WALDEGRAVE**, Knt., son and heir [see next].
    ii. **EDWARD WALDEGRAVE**, Gent., married **JOAN ACKWORTH** [see CLOPTON 4].[1]
    iii. **PHYLLIS WALDEGRAVE**, married **THOMAS HIGHAM**, of Higham [see BURROUGH 3].[2]

2. WILLIAM WALDEGRAVE, Knt., of Smallbridge, Suffolk, and of Walthamstow, Essex, was married to **JULIAN RAINESFORD**, daughter and heiress of John Rainesford, Knt., of Bradfield Hall, Essex. She was aged under twenty and unmarried when her father made his will in 1521/2. They had one son and four daughters. SIR WILLIAM WALDEGRAVE died at Calais, France, on 2 May 1554, and was buried at Ste. Marie's there.

H.S.P. 13:121 (1878). *H.S.P.* 32:298 (1891) ("about the 36 Hen. VIII was Captain of 200 Suffolk men in France. He sold his manor of Waldegrave in co. Northampton to one Lane of that county"). *H.S.P. (n.s.)* 2:94 (1981).

Child of William Waldegrave, by Julian Rainesford:

    i. **DOROTHY WALDEGRAVE**, married **ARTHUR HARRIS**, Esq. [see KEMPE 2].[3]

* * *

WARDE see CARLETON

WARRE see HUMPHREY

---

[1] Ancestors of **William Clopton**.

[2] Ancestors of **Nathaniel Burrough**.

[3] Ancestors of **Edmund Kempe**.

* * *

WASHINGTON

EDWARD I OF ENGLAND, King of England, married ALIANORE DE CASTILLE.
JOAN OF ENGLAND [*of Acre*], married GILBERT DE CLARE, Earl of Gloucester.
MARGARET DE CLARE, married, second, HUGH DE AUDLEY, 8th Earl of Stafford.
MARGARET DE AUDLEY, married RALPH DE STAFFORD, 2nd Lord Stafford.
KATHARINE DE STAFFORD, married JOHN DE SUTTON, Baron of Dudley.
JOHN DE SUTTON, Baron of Dudley, married JOAN _____.
JOHN SUTTON, Baron of Dudley, married CONSTANCE BLOUNT.
JOHN SUTTON, Knt., married ELIZABETH BERKELEY.
EDMUND SUTTON, Knt., married, first, JOYCE TIBETOT [see DUDLEY 5].

5. JOHN SUTTON, Knt. of Dudley, of Aston le Walls, co. Northampton, was married to _____ CHARROLL.
> Roberts (1989), p. 138 citing Burke's Landed Gentry of Great Britain, 1939 ed., reprinted in 1971 as Prominent Families in America with British Ancestry, pp. 2959-63; HSF 4:149-54.

4. MARGARET SUTTON, daughter and heiress, was married to JOHN BUTLER, Gent., of Aston Le Walls, co. Northampton, second son of Ralph Butler, of Sawbridgeworth, co. Hertford. They had four sons and three daughters.
> *Metcalfe* (1887), p. 8 (1564 Vis. Northants) ("John Dudly of Aston, Esq."), p. 75 (1618/9 Vis. Northants.

3. WILLIAM BUTLER, of Tyes Hall in Cuckfield, Sussex, third son, was married to MARGARET GREEKE, daughter of Thomas Greeke, Gent., of Palsters, co. Lancaster, by Jane, daughter of George Thomson. They had four sons and two daughters.
> *Metcalfe* (1887), pp. 8,152 (1618/9 Vis. Northants). H.S.P. 109-10:99-100 (1568 Vis. London).
> Notes & Queries (n.s.) 24:499 (1977). *TAG* 53:15 (Jan. 1977).

2. MARGARET BUTLER, eldest daughter and co-heiress, brought to her husband the right to quarter the royal arms of Plantagenet. She was married at Aston-le-Walls, co. Northampton, on 3 Aug. 1588 to LAWRENCE WASHINGTON, Gent., of Sulgrave and Wicken, co. Northampton, son and heir of Robert Washington, Esq., of Sulgrave, by his first wife Elizabeth, daughter of Walter Lyte, of Radway Grange, co. Warwick. He was born about 1568. They had eight sons and nine daughters. LAWRENCE WASHINGTON, GENT., died at "Wickamon" on 13 Dec. 1616 *v.p.*, and was buried in St. Michael's, Brington, co. Northampton, with monumental inscription. His widow died on 16 Mar. 1651/2, and was buried at East Haddon, co. Northampton.
> *Metcalfe* (1887), p. 152 (Washington arms: *Argent*, two bars and in chief three mullets *gules*).
> *Washington Ancestry* (1932), pp. 94-109. *Boddie* 4:149-155,160-161 (1960). *TAG* 46:231 (Oct. 1970).
> *TAG* 51:168 (July 1975).

Children and grandchild of Lawrence Washington, by Margaret Butler:

   i. RICHARD WASHINGTON, fourth son, apprenticed to Clothworker's Company, London, 7 July 1614, probably the Richard Washington in Virginia, 1637-38; probably the Richard Washington buried St. Martin's in the Field, Middlesex, 8 Jan. 1641/2; married St. Martin's in the Field 17 Apr. 1627 FRANCES BROWNE.

   a. JOHN WASHINGTON, baptised St. Martin's in the Fields 14 Mar. 1631/2, probably the emigrant, shortly before 15 Nov. 1658, to Surry County, Virginia, died before 31 Jan. 1662/3; married MARY (_____) (BLUNT) FORD. One son.

   i. REV. LAWRENCE WASHINGTON, born about 1602 [see next].

WASHINGTON (cont.)

1. **REV. LAWRENCE WASHINGTON**, fifth son, was born at Sulgrave Manor, co. Northampton, about 1602. He was educated at Brasenose College, Oxford (B.A. 1623, Fellow 1624, M.A. 1626, Lector 1627-1631, Proctor, B.D. 1634). He was married, probably between March and December 1633, to **AMPHYLLIS TWIGDEN**, daughter and co-heiress of John Twigden of Little Creaton, co. Northampton, and his wife Anne Dickens (later wife of Andrew Knowling, of Tring, co. Hertford). She was baptised at Spratton, co. Northampton, on 2 Feb. 1601/2. They had three sons and three daughters, three of whom were baptised at Tring. He was Rector of Purleigh, Essex, until ejectment as a Royalist in 1643, later made Rector of Little Braxted, near Maldon, Essex, under the patronage of a royalist. His wife and children remained at Tring with her step-father. Andrew Knowling bequeathed his property at Tring to Amphyllis's second son and his godson, Lawrence, with Amphyllis's husband acting as surrogate for his son in January 1649/50. REV. LAWRENCE WASHINGTON was buried at Maldon on 21 Jan. 1652/3. He died intestate and without estate sufficient to warrant the grant of letters of administration. His widow was buried at Tring on 12 Jan. 1654/5.

NEHGR 82:151 (Apr. 1928) (Washington arms: Silver two bars and in chief three mullets gules). *Washington Ancestry* (1932), pp. 110-130. *Boddie*4:151-152 (1960). *TAG* 46:231 (Oct. 1970). *NEHGR* 129:106-132 (Apr. 1975). *TAG* 51:167-171 (July 1975). *TAG* 52-87 (Apr. 1976). *Roberts* (1993), p. 243.

Children and grandchildren of Lawrence Washington, by Amphyllis Twigden:

i. **COL. JOHN WASHINGTON**, born about 1634, emigrated 1656 in the *Sea Horse of London*, resided Washington Parish, Westmoreland County, Virginia, member of House of Burgesses, died 1677; married, first, 1 Dec. 1658 **ANNE POPE**, died 1668, second, ANNE (BROADHURST) BRETT, third, FRANCES (GERARD) (SPEAKE) (PEYTON) APPLETON. *Washington Ancestry* (1932), p. 139.

   a. **CAPT. LAWRENCE WASHINGTON**, Gent., eldest son, born September 1659, member House of Burgesses, Sheriff, died February 1697/8; married about 1689 **MILDRED WARNER**, buried Whitehaven, Cumberland, 26 Mar. 1701. Grandparents of President Washington.

   b. **JOHN WASHINGTON**, born 1661, resided Westmoreland and Stafford Counties, Virginia, died 22 Oct. 1748; married **ANNE WYCLIFFE**.

   c. **ANNE WASHINGTON**, born about 1662, married **MAJ. FRANCIS WRIGHT**. Issue.

ii. **LAWRENCE WASHINGTON**, baptised Tring, 18 June 1635, visited Virginia about 1658, returned to England, merchant at Luton, co. Bedford, died Rappahannock County, Virginia, 1677; married, first, Luton, 26 June 1660 MARY JONES, second, JOYCE (_____) FLEMING. *Washington Ancestry* (1932), pp. 130-139.

   a. **MARY WASHINGTON**, baptised Luton 22 Dec. 1663, married REV. EDWARD GIBSON, Vicar of Hawnes, co. Bedford. Issue.

   b. **CHARLES WASHINGTON**, baptised Luton 22 Nov. 1665, probably died young.

   c. **JOHN WASHINGTON**, born 2 Apr. 1671, Sheriff of Stafford County, Virginia, married **MARY TOWNSHEND**. Four children.

   d. **ANNE WASHINGTON**, died in infancy.

iii. **ELIZABETH WASHINGTON**, baptised Tring 17 Aug. 1636, married _____ RUMBOLD.

iv. **MARGARET WASHINGTON**, born about 1639, married GEORGE TALBOT, of St. Giles in the Fields.

v. **WILLIAM WASHINGTON**, baptised 14 Oct. 1641, apprenticed to a weaver 1653.

vii. **MARTHA WASHINGTON**, died *s.p.*, will dated 8 Dec. 1697 mentions sisters Elizabeth Rumbold and Margaret Talbot in England, and Washington nephews in Virginia; married **SAMUEL HAYWARD**, Clerk of Stafford County, Virginia.

EDWARD I OF ENGLAND, King of England, married ALIANORE DE CASTILLE.
JOAN OF ENGLAND [*of Acre*], married GILBERT DE CLARE, Earl of Gloucester.
MARGARET DE CLARE, married HUGH DE AUDLEY, 8th Earl of Gloucester.
MARGARET DE AUDLEY, married RALPH DE STAFFORD, Earl of Stafford.
BEATRICE DE STAFFORD, married THOMAS DE ROS, 4th Lord Ros of Helmsley.
MARGARET DE ROS, married REYNOLD GREY, 3rd Lord Grey of Ruthin.
MARGARET GREY, married WILLIAM BONVILLE.
ELIZABETH BONVILLE, married WILLIAM TAILBOYS, Knt.
ROBERT TAILBOYS, Lord Kyme, married ELIZABETH HERON [see TAILBOYS 5].

4. **MAUD TAILBOYS**, was married to **ROBERT TYRWHIT**, Knt., of Kettleby, son of William Tyrwhit, Knt., of Kettleby, Sheriff of Lincolnshire, by Anne, daughter of Robert Constable, Knt., of Flamborough, co. York. He was born in 1482. They had three sons and six daughters. SIR ROBERT TYRWHIT died on 4 July 1548, and was buried at Wrawby Church.

Wotton (1741) 1:179. *H.S.P.* 16:65 (1881) (1563 Vis. Yorks). *H.S.P.* 52:1019 (1904) (Maddison Linc. Ped.) (daughter Anne "mar. William Hansard of South Kelsey"). *C.P.* (1929) 7:361, footnote *h* (Maud is named in the will, dated 6 Apr. 1493, of her father).

3. **KATHERINE TYRWHIT**, was married to **RICHARD THIMBLEBY**, Knt., of Irnham, co. Lincoln, and East Bridgeford, co. Nottingham. SIR RICHARD THIMBLEBY died on 28 Sept. 1590.

Wotton (1741) 1:179 (identifies husband as "John", son and heir to Sir Richard "Thimelby", Knt.) (Thimbleby arms: *Gules*, three tyrwhitts, or lapwings, *or*). *H.S.P.* 52:1019 (1904).

2. **ELIZABETH THIMBLEBY**, was married for the first time to JOHN SAINT PAUL, of Nettleton, co. Lincoln. She was married for the second time at Irnham on 20 July 1560 to **THOMAS WELBY**, of Moulton, son of Thomas Welby, of Halsted, by Catherine, daughter of Thomas Bray, co. Middlesex. They had two sons and four daughters. THOMAS WELBY died testate at Bath in 1570, and was buried "within the Church of Stallys".

H.S.P. 55:1313-1315 (1906) (Maddison Linc. Ped.). *Jacobus* (1933), pp. 22-23.

1. **RICHARD WELBY**, of Moulton, second son, was baptised at Moulton, co. Lincoln, in 1564. He was married at Whaplode, co. Lincoln, about 1595 to **FRANCES BULKELEY**, daughter of Rev. Edward Bulkeley (**descendant of Charlemagne**), by Olive, daughter of John Irby, Gent., of Leighthorpe in Cawthorpe. She was born about 1568, and was buried at Moulton in 1610.

H.S.P. 55:1315 (1906). *Farwell* (1929), pp. 1-34. *Jacobus* (1933), pp. 22-23.

Children & grandchildren of Richard Welby, by Frances Bulkeley:

i. THOMAS WELBY, baptised Whaplode 1597, married ELIZABETH PARKE. Issue.

ii. ANN WELBY, baptised Moulton 1600.

iii. ANTHONY WELBY, baptised Whaplode 1602, buried 1603.

iv. OLIVE WELBY, baptised Moulton 1604, died Chelmsford, Massachusetts, 1 Mar. 1691/2; married St. Botolph's church, Boston, co. Lincoln, 16 Apr. 1629 DEA. HENRY FARWELL, tailor, born about 1605, emigrated about 1655, resided Chelmsford, died there 1 Aug. 1670. First three children born at Boston, co. Lincoln, last three at Concord, Massachusetts.

   a. ELIZABETH FARWELL, baptised 27 May 1630, died Taunton, Massachusetts, 9 Nov. 1670; married JOSEPH WILDBORE.

   b. SAMUEL FARWELL, baptised 9 June 1633, died 20 June 1634.

   c. JOHN FARWELL, baptised 25 Oct. 1635, died Concord, Massachusetts, 1686; married, first, SARAH WHEELER, second, SARAH FISKE.

   c. ENS. JOSEPH FARWELL, born 26 Feb. 1640/1, died Dunstable, Massachusetts, 31 Dec.

WELBY (cont.)

1722; married HANNAH LEARNED.
- d. **MARY FARWELL**, born about 1643, died Chelmsford 7 Mar. 1713/4; married **JOHN BATES**.
- e. **MARY FARWELL**, born about 1642, married **JOHN BATES**.
- f. **OLIVE FARWELL**, born about 1645; married **BENJAMIN SPALDING**, of Chelmsford, later Canterbury, Connecticut.
- v. **EDWARD WELBY**, baptised Moulton 1609.

* * *

WELLES

EDWARD I OF ENGLAND, King of England, married, second, **MARGUERITE DE FRANCE**.
THOMAS OF NORFOLK [of *Brotherton*], married **ALICE DE HALES**.
MARGARET OF NORFOLK, married **JOHN DE SEGRAVE**, 4th Lord Segrave.
ELIZABETH DE SEGRAVE, married **JOHN DE MOWBRAY** [see MOWBRAY 10].

9. ALIANOR DE MOWBRAY, first daughter, was born shortly before 25 Mar. 1364, and was sister of John de Mowbray, Earl of Nottingham, and of Thomas de Mowbray, Duke of Norfolk and Earl Marshal. She was married before May 1326 to **JOHN DE WELLES**, Knt., 5th Lord Welles, of Gainsby, son of John de Welles, 3rd Lord Welles (**descendant of Charlemagne**), by Maud, daughter, probably, of William de Ros, 2nd Lord Ros of Helmesley. He was born at Conisholme, co. Lincoln, on 20 Apr. 1352. He was summoned to Parliament from 20 Jan. 1375/6 by writs directed *Johanni de Welle*. He was frequently abroad or serving in the French wars. In May 1390 he and Sir David Lindsay, afterwards 1st Earl of Crawford, performed a notable feat of arms on London Bridge to prove "the chivalry and valiant deeds of Englishmen", in which Welles was unhorsed at the third course. Alianor may have been living in 1399. He was married for the second time before 13 Aug. 1417 to Margery _____. JOHN WELLES, Lord Welles, died aged about seventy-one on 26 Aug. 1421. His widow died on 8 Apr. 1426.
C.P. 12(2):441-443 (1959). *Paget* (1957) 571:2.

8. EUDO (or **IVES**) **DE WELLES**, son and heir apparent, took part in the rebellion of 1405, for which he was fined and pardoned on 7 Aug. 1405. He had licence to travel abroad on 20 Dec. 1407. He was married to **MAUD DE GREYSTOKE**, daughter of Ralph de Greystoke, 3rd Lord Greystoke (**descendant of Charlemagne**), by Katherine, daughter of Roger de Clifford, 5th Lord Clifford (of **Magna Charta Surety** descent and **descendant of Charlemagne**). EUDO DE WELLES died before 26 Aug. 1421 *v.p.*
C.P. 12(2):443 (1959). *Paget* (1957) 571:2. *TAG* 37:114-115 (Apr. 1961). *TAG* 38:180 (July 1962).

7. LIONEL DE WELLES, Knt., K.G., 6th Lord Welles, P.C., son and heir, was born in 1406, and was grandson and heir of John de Welles. He was married for the first time at St. Oswald's, Methley, on 15 Aug. 1417 to **JOAN DE WATERTON**, daughter, and in her issue eventual heiress, of Robert de Waterton, Knt., of Waterton and Methley, West Riding, co. York, by Joan, daughter of William de Everingham, of Laxton, co. Nottingham (of **baronial** descent). She was living on 18 Oct. 1434, and was buried in the Waterton chapel at Methley. He was married for the second time, with settlement dated 20 Apr. 1447, to **MARGARET BEAUCHAMP**, widow, first

WELLES (cont.)

(with children), of Oliver Saint John, Knt., second (with one daughter), of John Beaufort, Duke of Somerset (died 27 May 1444), and daughter of John Beauchamp, Knt., of Bletsoe, co. Bedford. He was summoned to Parliament from 25 Feb. 1431/2 by writs directed *Leoni de Welles*. A firm Lancastrian, he was taken prisoner by the Yorkists at Blore Heath on 23 Sep. 1459, and was with Queen Margaret's army which won St. Albans on 17 Feb. 1460/1. LIONEL DE WELLES, Lord Welles, was slain testate aged fifty-five at the Battle of Towton on 29 Mar. 1461, and was buried with his first wife at Methley. His widow died apparently shortly before 3 June 1482.

C.P. 6:564 (1926). *C.P.* 12(2):443-450 (1959) (wife also called Cecily). *Paget* (1977), p. 401 (states daughter Margaret was daughter of second marriage).

Children of Lionel de Welles, by Joan de Waterton:
    i. **ALIANOR DE WELLES** [see next].
    ii. **MARGARET DE WELLES**, married **THOMAS DYMOKE**, Knt. [see DYMOKE 5].[1]

6. ALIANOR DE WELLES, was sister and co-heiress of John Welles, 10th Lord Welles. She was married for the first time to **THOMAS HOO**, Knt., K.G., of Hoo in Luton, co. Bedford, Sheriff of Bedfordshire and Buckinghamshire, son and heir of Thomas de Hoo, Knt., of Hoo, by Eleanor, daughter and co-heiress of Thomas Felton, Knt., of Litcham, Norfolk. He was born before 1400, and distinguished himself in the French wars. On 2 June 1448, for his good service in England, France and Normandy, he was created **Lord Hoo** of Hoo in the county of Bedford and of Hastings in the county of Sussex. He was summoned to Parliament from 2 Jan. 1448/9 by writs directed *Thome Hoo Chivaler*. He had been married for the first time to Elizabeth Wichingham, daughter of Nicholas Wichingham, Esq., of Wichingham, Norfolk, and had one daughter, Anne, wife of Geoffrey Boleyn, by that marriage [see BUTLER 5 for descendants of Anne (Hoo) Boleyn]. THOMAS HOO, Lord Hoo, died testate on 13 Feb. 1454/5 *s.p.s.m.* His will, dated 12 Feb. 1454/5, provided bequests for the marriages of his daughters "Anne, Alyanor and Elyzabeth", and names "my lord Welles, my wyves father" and "Alyenor my wyffe". His widow was married for the second time to JAMES LAURENCE, Esq. (by whom she had two sons, Thomas and John, both of whom died *s.p.*), and for the third time, it is said, to HUGH HASTINGS.

C.P. 6:561-565 (1926). *C.P.* 12(2):449 footnote *j* (1959). *Beville* (1976), pp. 308-321 (buried in a chapel in Battle Abbey ... after the Dissolution effigy taken to All Saints', Herstmonceux, Sussex).

Children of Thomas Hoo, by Alianor de Welles:
    i. **ANNE HOO**, born about 1447 [see next].
    ii. **ALIANOR HOO**, born about 1449, **JAMES DE CAREW**, of Beddington [see CAREW 6].[2]

5. ANNE HOO, daughter and co-heiress by second marriage, was born about 1447 (aged seven at her father's death), and was the second daughter of that name. She was married for the first time before 1467 to **ROGER COPLEY**, Esq., of Roughey, near Horsham, Sussex, son of Richard Copley, Knt., of Batley, West Riding, co. York, by Elizabeth, daughter of John Harington, of Doncaster, West Riding. He was born about 1430, and was apprenticed to a London mercer, being admitted to the Mercers' Company in 1456. She brought him three manors: Roughey, near Horsham, Sussex, Gatton, Surrey, and The Maze, Southwark. They had three sons and five daughters. ROGER COPLEY, ESQ., was of record as a mercer in 1482, but died

---

[1] Ancestors of **William Asfordby, Joseph Bolles, George Reade, Diana & Grey Skipwith**.

[2] Ancestors of **Essex Beville, Mary Launce**.

WELLES (cont.)

v.p. before 21 Dec. 1490, when the will of William Copley, Gent., of Doncaster, left a bequest for masses for his brothers Oliver, Roger, and Thomas. She was married for the second time to WILLIAM GREYSTOKE.
Foster (1874) (Copley arms: *Argent,* a cross moline *sable*). *Gen. (n.s.)* 33:73-80 (1917). *C.P.* 6:564-565 (1926). *C.P.* 12(2):796 (1959).

    i. ELEANOR COPLEY, married THOMAS WEST, Lord de la Warre [see HUMPHREY 6].[1]

* * *

WENTWORTH OF GOSFIELD see JENNINGS

WENTWORTH OF NETTLESTEAD see HARLESTON

WEST see HUMPHREY

WILLIAMS see COYTEMORE

* * *

WILLOUGHBY

HENRY III OF ENGLAND, King of England, married ÉLÉONORE DE PROVENCE.
EDMUND OF LANCASTER *Crouchback,* Earl of Lancaster, married, BLANCHE D'ARTOIS.
HENRY OF LANCASTER, Duke of Lancaster, married MAUD DE CHAWORTH.
ALIANOR OF LANCASTER, married RICHARD FITZ ALAN.
JOHN DE ARUNDEL, Lord Arundel, married ALIANOR MALTRAVERS [see BROWNE 11].

7. RICHARD DE ARUNDEL, Knt., of Wychampton, Dorset, second son, was married to ALICE _____, widow of Roger Burley. They had two daughters. SIR RICHARD ARUNDEL died on 3 June 1419. His widow died on 30 Aug. 1436.
Top. & Gen. 2:317,336 (1853).

6. JOAN DE ARUNDEL, younger daughter and co-heiress, was born about 1407 (aged fourteen in 1421). She was married to THOMAS WILLOUGHBY, Knt., of Parham, second son of William Willoughby, 5th Lord of Eresby (of **Magna Charta Surety** descent and **descendant of Charlemagne**), by Lucy le Strange, daughter of Roger le Strange, 5th Lord Strange of Knockyn, co. Salop (**descendants of Charlemagne**).
Top. & Gen. 2:336 (1853).

5. WILLIAM WILLOUGHBY, Knt., of Boston, co. Lincoln, second son, was married to JOAN STRANGEWAYS, daughter of Thomas Strangeways, Knt., by Katherine, daughter of Ralph Neville, Earl of Westmorland (**descendant of Charlemagne** and of **Magna Charta Surety descent**). SIR WILLIAM WILLOUGHBY was living in 1460. His widow was married for the second time in November 1468 to WILLIAM

---

[1] Ancestors of **Anne Humphrey, Herbert Pelham, John Stockman, John West.**

WILLOUGHBY (cont.)

DE BERKELEY, Knt., Marquess of Berkeley (died February 1491 *s.p.*), son of James Berkeley, Lord Berkeley, by Isabel, eldest daughter of Thomas de Mowbray, Duke of Norfolk. They had two sons who died young. She died on 24 Feb. 1484.
Top. & Gen. 2:317 (1853). *H.S.P.* 16:301-302 (1881) (1563 Vis. Yorks).

Child of William Willoughby, by Joan Strangeways:
   i. CECILY WILLOUGHBY, married EDWARD DUDLEY, 2nd Lord Dudley [see DUDLEY 4].

* * *

WILLOUGHBY OF BROKE see PAULET

WILLOUGHBY OF BROKE see also BOSVILE

* * *

WILTON

EDWARD I OF ENGLAND, King of England, married ALIANORE DE CASTILLE.
ELIZABETH OF ENGLAND, married HUMPHREY DE BOHUN, Earl of Hereford and Essex.
ALIANOR DE BOHUN, married JAMES BUTLER, Earl of Ormond.
PERNEL BUTLER, married GILBERT TALBOT, 3rd Lord Talbot [see TALBOT 9].

9. ELIZABETH TALBOT, daughter, it is said, was married before 3 Feb. 1379/80 to HENRY GREY, Knt., 5th Lord Grey, of Wilton, son and heir of Reynold de Grey, 4th Lord of Wilton (of **Magna Charta Surety descent** and **descendant of Charlemagne**), by his wife Maud, said to have been daughter of John de Botetourt, Knt., of Weoley, co. Worcester. He was born about 1338 or 1340 (aged twenty eight or thirty and more at father's death). He fought in Gascony in 1366. He was summoned to Parliament on 1 Dec. 1376 by a writ directed *Henrico de Grey de Shirlond'*, and from 4 Aug. 1377 by writs directed *Henrico de Grey de Wilton'*. HENRY GREY, Lord Grey, died on 22 Apr. 1396. She died on 10 Jan. 1401/2.
C.P. 4:63-65 (1916) (no reservation on identification of wife), 6:177-178 (1926) (reservation on identity of wife). *Paget* (1957) 260:5 (no source cited for identification of wife).

Children of Henry Grey, by Elizabeth Talbot:
   i. RICHARD GREY, 6th Lord Grey of Wilton, son and heir, born about 1393 [see next].
   ii. MARGARET GREY, married, first, JOHN DARCY [see DARCY 10].[1]

8. RICHARD GREY, 6th Lord Grey, of Wilton, son and heir, was born about 1393 (aged three years and more at his father's death). He accompanied the King to France in August 1415, being in the retinue of the Earl of Dorset. He was married for the first time, it is said, to **BLANCHE** _____. They had two sons. He was married for the second time in 1427 to MARGARET FERRERS, daughter of William de Ferrers, Lord Ferrers, of Groby, by his wife Philippe Clifford. They had two sons. RICHARD GREY, Lord Grey, died testate on 13 or 20 Aug. 1442, and

---

[1]Ancestors of **Edward Carleton, Mary Launce, Philip & Thomas Nelson.**

WILTON (cont.)

was buried at Bletchley. His widow was married for the second time before 14 Feb. 1445/6 to Thomas Grey, Knt., of Richemount, co. Bedford, afterwards Lord Richemount Grey (a Lancastrian, captured and executed in 1461, some time after the battle of Towton). She died on 16 Jan 1451/2.

> *C.P.* 6:178-179 (1926). *Paget* (1957) 260:5 (de jure, though never summoned to Parliament) (identification of first wife).

7. REYNOLD GREY, 7th Lord Grey, of Wilton, son and heir by first marriage, was born about 1421 (aged twenty-one and more at his father's death). He was summoned to Parliament from 13 Jan. 1444/5 by writs directed *Reginaldo Grey de Wilton'*. He was with King Edward IV at the battle of Mortimer's Cross on 2 or 3 Feb. 1260/1, and accompanied the King in his expedition to the North in November 1462. He was married before 6 Oct. 1447 to THOMASINE (or TACINE) OF SOMERSET, base-born daughter of John Beaufort, Duke of Somerset [see BEAUFORT 10.ii.b for her ancestry.]. She was living in May 1469. REYNOLD GREY, Lord Grey, died on 22 Feb 1493/4, and was buried at Bletchley, co. Buckingham.

> *C.P.* 6:180, 185-186 (1926) (in the ceremonial of the funeral of his great-grandfather, William, they were named as "Reygnolde lorde Grey, and Thomasyn or Thasyna base daughter to John duke of Somersett"; "this is the only known authority for the marriage of Reynold, Lord Grey, with this Thomasyn, who, in Vincent's Baronage in the College of Arms, is called Thaceta, daughter of Owen son of Tudor"). *Paget* (1957) 260:6.

Child of Reynold Grey, by Thomasine of Somerset:

   i. **JOHN GREY**, 8th Lord Grey of Wilton, married **ANNE GREY** [see HAVILAND 6].

* * *

WINDEBANK see READE

WINDSOR see LUDLOW

* * *

WINGFIELD

EDWARD III OF ENGLAND, King of England, married **PHILIPPE DE HAINAUT**.
LIONEL OF CLARENCE [*of Antwerp*], Duke of Clarence, married **ELIZABETH DE BURGH**.
PHILIPPE OF CLARENCE, married **EDMUND DE MORTIMER**, 3rd Earl of March.
ELIZABETH MORTIMER, married **HENRY PERCY**, Knt.
ELIZABETH PERCY, married **JOHN DE CLIFFORD**, Lord Clifford.
MARY DE CLIFFORD, married **PHILIP WENTWORTH**, Knt.
HENRY WENTWORTH, Knt., married **ANNE SAY**.
MARGERY WENTWORTH, married **JOHN SEYMOUR**, Knt. [see RODNEY 5].

5. ELIZABETH SEYMOUR, was a sister of the Protector Edward Seymour, Duke of Somerset. She was married for the first time to ANTHONY OUGHTRED, Knt., Governor of Jersey, and for the second time before 1538 to **GREGORY CROMWELL**, K.B., only son and heir of Thomas Cromwell, Baron Cromwell,

WINGFIELD (cont.)

Chancellor of the Exchequer, by Elizabeth, daughter of Henry Wykes, of Putney Surrey, shearman. He was educated at Cambridge. He was, some five months after his father's death, created **Baron Cromwell** on 18 Dec. 1540. GREGORY CROMWELL, Baron Cromwell, died at Launde, co. Leicester, on 4 July 1551, and was buried in the Abbey there. His widow was married for the third time, as his second wife, to JOHN PAULET, 2nd Marquess of Winchester (died on 4 Nov. 1576) [see PAULET 5]. She was living on 25 Oct. 1551, at Launde, and probably died before 9 June 1563, burial at Basing.

Wotton (1741) 1:91. *C.P.* 3:557-558 (1913).

Children of Gregory Cromwell, by Elizabeth Seymour:
   i. **HENRY CROMWELL**, born before 1538 [see next].
   ii. **FRANCES CROMWELL**, born about 1544, married **RICHARD STRODE** [see DAVIE 3j.[1]

4. **HENRY CROMWELL**, 3rd Baron Cromwell, son and heir, was born before 1538, but a minor at his father's death. He was summoned to Parliament in 1563. He was married, before 1560, to **MARY PAULET**, daughter of John Paulet (or Powlett), 2nd Marquess of Winchester (of **Magna Charta Surety descent** and **descendant of Charlemagne**), by his first wife, Elizabeth (**descendant of King Edward I**), daughter of Robert Willoughby, 2nd Lord Willoughby of Broke (**descendant of Charlemagne**) [see PAULET 5 for her ancestry]. She died at North Elham on 10 Oct. 1592. HENRY CROMWELL, Baron Cromwell, died testate on 20 Nov. 1592. They were buried at Launde Abbey.

C.P. 3:558 (1913).

3. **EDWARD CROMWELL**, 4th Baron Cromwell, son and heir, was born about 1563 (aged thirty-three in 1593). He was married for the first time in 1581 to **ELIZABETH UPTON**, daughter of William Upton, of Puslinch, co. Devon, Serjeant at Arms, by Mary, daughter of Thomas Kirkham, of Blakedon, Devon. He was educated at Jesus College, Cambridge, M.A. 1592/3. His wife died in London *s.p.m.*, and was buried on 15 Jan. 1592/3 at Launde Abbey. He was married for the second time about 1593 to FRANCES RUGGE, first daughter of William Rugge, otherwise Repps, of Felmingham, Norfolk, by Thomasine, daughter of Robert Townshend, Knt., Justice of Chester. He served in the expedition against Spain with the Earl of Essex, by whom he was knighted, in Dublin, 12 July 1599, and joined in his rebellion, for which he was fined £3,000, and imprisoned for some months, but received a special pardon on 2 July 1601. Having alienated all his English estate, he purchased, in 1606, the Barony of Lecale, co. Down, in Ireland. EDWARD CROMWELL, Baron Cromwell, died on 27 Apr. 1607, and was buried in the Chancel of the Abbey Church at Down Patrick. His widow was married for the second time to Richard Wingfield, 1st Viscount Powerscourt (died 9 Sep. 1634 *s.p.*). She died before 30 Nov. 1631.

C.P. 3:558 (1913).

2. **FRANCES CROMWELL**, elder daughter, was married about 30 Jan. 1619 to **JOHN WINGFIELD**, Knt., of Tickencote, Rutland, Sheriff of Rutlandshire, son and heir of John Wingfield, Knt. (**descendant of King Edward I**), by Elizabeth, daughter of Paul Gresham, of Tickencote, co. Rutland [see LETHERINGHAM 3 for his ancestry]. He was born about 1594 (aged eight years at death of mother in 1602). He had been married previously to Jane Turpine, daughter of William Turpine, Knt., of Knaptoft, co. Leicester. John & Frances had four sons and two daughters. SIR

---

[1] Ancestors of **Humphrey Davie**.

WINGFIELD (cont.)

JOHN WINGFIELD died on 25 Dec. 1631. His widow died before 25 June 1662.
Burke's Commoners (1838) 2:480-481. *VMHB* 60:321 (1952) (citing VCH Rutland 2:276) (Wingfield arms: *Argent*, a bend gules cotised *sable* with three pairs of wings *argent* upon the bend).

1. **JOHN WINGFIELD**, of Tickencote, Rutland, York Herald, second son, was baptised at Tickencote, on 25 June 1623. He was married for the first time to **MARY OWEN**, daughter of George Owen, York Herald, by Rebecca, daughter of Thomas Darrell, Knt., of Lillingstone Dayrell, co. Bucks. They had three sons. JOHN WINGFIELD died "in the Kings Bench" on 30 Dec. 1678, and was buried in St. George's Church.
VMHB 60:305-322 (1952).

Child & grandchildren of John Wingfield, by Mary Owen:

   i. **THOMAS WINGFIELD**, born 1670, died St. Peter's Parish, New Kent Co., Virginia, 19 Dec. 1720; married, first, **MARY** _____, died 21 Jan. 1714, married, second, **MARY** _____.
   a. **RUTH WINGFIELD**, baptized 18 Oct. 1691.
   b. **THOMAS WINGFIELD**, born about 1693, married **SARAH GARLAND**. Eleven children.
   c. **JOHN WINGFIELD**, born about 1695, married **MARY HUDSON**. One known son.
   d. **ROBERT WINGFIELD**, born about 1697, married **ANN** _____. Eight children.
   e. **MARY WINGFIELD**, baptized 25 Feb. 1699/1700.
   f. **ELIZABETH WINGFIELD**, baptized 12 July 1702.
   e. **OWEN WINGFIELD**, baptized 23 Sep. 1719.

* * *

WINGFIELD OF CROWFIELD see HANKFORD

WINGFIELD OF LETHERINGHAM see LETHERINGHAM

WODHULL see BULL

WODHULL see also CHETWODE

* * *

WOLSELEY

EDWARD I OF ENGLAND, King of England, married **ALIANORE DE CASTILLE**.
JOAN OF ENGLAND [*of Acre*], married **GILBERT DE CLARE**, Earl of Gloucester.
MARGARET DE CLARE, married, second, **HUGH DE AUDLEY**, 8th Earl of Stafford.
MARGARET DE AUDLEY, married **RALPH DE STAFFORD**, 2nd Lord Stafford.
KATHARINE DE STAFFORD, married **JOHN DE SUTTON**. Baron of Dudley.
JOHN DE SUTTON, Baron of Dudley, married **JOAN** _____.
JOHN SUTTON, Baron of Dudley, married **CONSTANCE BLOUNT**.
JOHN SUTTON, Knt, married **ELIZABETH BERKELEY** [see DUDLEY 6].

6. **ELEANOR SUTTON**, was married for the first time to **HENRY BEAUMONT**, Knt., of Wednesbury, and of Thorpe-in-Balne, co. York, son of Henry Beaumont,

Knt., of Wednesbury *jure uxoris* (descendant of King Henry III), by his wife Joan, daughter and heiress of Henry Heronville. They had two sons and one daughter. SIR HENRY BEAUMONT died on 16 Nov. 1471 [see MARSHALL 5 for descendants of this marriage]. She was married for the second time to **GEORGE STANLEY**, of Hammerwich, Lichfield, co. Stafford, only son of Thomas Stanley, of Elford, co. Stafford (of **Magna Charta Surety descent**), by his second wife Elizabeth, daughter of Ralph Langton, Knt., of Walton le Dale, co. Lancaster. He was born about 1440. They had two children, and resided at Wednesbury, co. Stafford, the home of her first husband. He was Commissioner of Array in 1461, Escheator from 1469 to 1470, a Justice of the Peace from 1485, and a Commissioner of Gaol Delivery in 1489, all in Staffordshire. GEORGE STANLEY died 1508/9, and was buried in Lichfield Cathedral, the tomb bearing a figure apparently commemorating penitence for an unknown sin. She died about 1513 (the date of the proving of the will of her son and heir apparent, John Beaumont, who had died eleven years previously).
TG 5:141-143 (1984).

5. ANNE STANLEY, only daughter, was born after 1472, and was living in 1532. She was married to **JOHN WOLSELEY**, of Wolseley in Colwich, co. Stafford, son of Ralph Wolseley, of Wolseley, by Margaret, daughter of Robert Aston, Knt., of Heywood. He was born in 1475. They had two sons and eleven daughters. He succeeded his father at Wolseley in 1504 and inherited problems from the land enclosure and had lengthy disputes with the Bishop of Coventry and Lichfield. JOHN WOLSELEY died in 1553.
Wotton (1741) 2:136. *Wm. Salt Soc.* 5(2):323 (1885) (1614 Vis. Staffs) (Wolseley arms: *Argent*, a talbot passant *gules*). *TG* 5:143-145 (1984).

Children of John Wolseley, by Anne Stanley:
    i.   **ANTHONY WOLSELEY**, of Wolseley, son and heir, born about 1510 [see next].
    ii. **ELLEN WOLSELEY**, married **GEORGE ABNEY**, of Willesley, co. Derby [see ABNEY 4].[1]

4. ANTHONY WOLSELEY, Esq., eldest son, was born about 1510, and succeeded to Wolseley in 1553. He was married to **MARGARET BLYTHE**, daughter of William Blythe, Esq., of Norton, co. Derby. In 1532/3, in his father's lifetime, he and his wife, with their four small children, were residing at Chartley in Stowe, co. Stafford in the household of Sir Walter Devereux, Lord Ferrers. In 1563, ten years after his succession, Anthony Wolseley resettled Wolseley on his eldest son Erasmus for life, with a remainder to his issue, which failing, to Francis, his second son, and then to his right heirs. She died by 1570. ANTHONY WOLSELEY died in 1571.
Wotton (1741) 2:136. *Wm. Salt Soc.* 5(2):323 (1885). *TG* 5:145-146 (1984).

3. ERASMUS WOLSELEY, Esq., of Wolseley, eldest surviving son, was married in 1562 to **CASSANDRA GIFFARD**, daughter of Thomas Giffard, Knt., of Chillington, co. Stafford. They were Roman Catholics, and had six sons and two daughters. In 1587 (as recorded in the Wolseley archives) "Master Wolseley" was taken prisoner attending mass in a private house near Stafford, but was pardoned on the morning set for execution. In a list of recusants in Staffordshire, dated 1592, Erasmus Wolseley was one of three gentlemen recorded as having been imprisoned. He and his wife were both buried as recusants in Colwich Parish Church, he on 15 Jan. 1599 and she on 5 Jan. 1616.
Wotton (1741) 2:136. *Wm. Salt Soc.* 5(2):323 (1885). *TG* 5:146-147 (1984).

---

[1] Ancestors of **Dannett Abney**.

WOLSELEY (cont.)

2. THOMAS WOLSELEY, Knt., of Wolseley, son and heir, was born in 1564. He was married for the first time, without issue, to GRACE GRESLEY, daughter of Thomas Gresley, Knt., of Drakelow Hall, co. Derby. She was buried at Colwich on 6 Sep. 1591. He was married for the second time in 1592 to ANNE MOSELEY, daughter of Humphrey Moseley, of Dunstall Hall, near Wolverhampton, co. Stafford. They had three sons and three daughters. She died in 1606. He was married for the third time at Colwich in 1607/8 to **HELEN BROCKTON**, daughter of Edward Brockton, of Broughton Hall, in the parish of Longdon, co. Stafford. Their children were baptized at Colwich church. By 1623 he had mortaged all his estates to his cousin Robert Wolseley, grandson of Ralph Wolseley of Shugborough. Finally he conveyed to Robert (who was created a baronet in 1628) his estates and moved to Ravenstone, co. Leicester. SIR THOMAS WOLSELEY died testate, and was buried in the chancel of Colwich church on 21 Mar. 1630, near his parents. His widow was married for the second time in 1631 to John Wolley, of Sunningdale, co. Berks.

Wotton (1741) 2:136 (no mention of third marriage). *Wm. Salt Soc.* 5(2):323 (1885) (no mention of third marriage). *TG* 5:147-148 (1984).

Children of Thomas Wolseley, by Helen Brockton:

   i. **WALTER WOLSELEY**, baptised 25 Sep. 1612 [see next].
  ii. **DEVEREUX WOLSELEY**, baptised 24 Nov. 1617, Colonel in the Royalist Army; married ISABEL ZOUCHE, daughter of John Zouche, Knt., of Codnor Castle, co. Derby. Two daughters (descendants, including **Francis Scott Key**, author of The Star Spangled Banner).
 iii. **ANNE WOLSELEY**, married **PHILIP CALVERT** of St. Mary's County, Maryland, youngest son of the first Lord Baltimore, and Secretary of Maryland and a member of the Council from 1656, Governor in 1660 and Chancellor in 1682. No children.
  iv. **WINIFRED WOLSELEY**, married REV. WILLIAM MULLETT, D.D., of Maryland from 1675. No children.

1. WALTER WOLSELEY, of Wolseley Bridge, co. Stafford, later of Ravenstone, co. Leicester, elder surviving son by third marriage, was baptised at Colwich on 25 Sep. 1612. He was married to **MARY BEAUCHAMP**, widow of _____ _____, and daughter of John Beauchamp, of Reigate, co. Surrey, and of London. They had one son and six daughters. WALTER WOLSELEY died by 1661, survived by his widow. *TG* 5:148 (1984).

Child & grandchildren of Walter Wolseley, by Mary Beauchamp:

   i. **MARY WOLSELEY**, emigrated to Maryland to join her aunt Calvert in 1673/4; married, at the house of her aunt Calvert, **ROGER BROOKE** of Battle Creek, Calvert County, Maryland. Five children (including two that died in infancy).
       a. **JOHN BROOKE**.
       b. **BASIL BROOKE**.
       c. **ANNE BROOKE**, died 1733; married **JAMES DAWKINS** (died 1701), second, **JAMES MACKALL** (died 1716). Descendants by second marriage.

* * *

WROTTESLEY see MACKWORTH

WYNNE see LLOYD

EDWARD I OF ENGLAND, King of England, married ALIANORE DE CASTILLE.
ELIZABETH OF ENGLAND, married HUMPHREY DE BOHUN, Earl of Hereford and Essex.
MARGARET DE BOHUN, married HUGH DE COURTENAY [see COURTENAY 10].

10. MARGARET COURTENAY, eldest daughter, was married in 1332-33 to JOHN DE COBHAM, 3rd Lord Cobham, son and heir of John de Cobham, Knt., 2nd Lord Cobham, of Cobham, Kent, by Joan, daughter of John Beauchamp, Knt., **Baron** of Hatch Beauchamp, Somerset (**descendant of Charlemagne**), by his wife Joan (said to be Chenduit). He was married, when a minor, and apparently very young. He was summoned to Parliament from 20 Sep. 1355 by writ directed *Johanni de Cobeham*, later with the addition of *de Kent*. He founded the chantry of Cobham in 1362. He served in various French expeditions, 1359 to 1376, being made a Banneret in 1370. In 1388 he was one of the Lords Appellant who impeached de la Pole, de Veer, and others, the King's favourites. He was impeached at Shrewsbury in January 1397/8, and condemned to be hanged, but pardoned on condition of banishment to Jersey, when he returned within two years at the accession of King Henry IV. MARGARET COURTENAY died on 2 Aug 1385, and was buried at Cobham (brass and M.I.). JOHN DE COBHAM, Lord Cobham, died at an advanced age (seventy-four years after his marriage) on 10 Jan. 1407/8 *s.p.m.*, and was buried at the Grey Friars', London (brass, probably set up in his lifetime, at Cobham Church, represents him as holding the model of a church in his hands). His granddaughter and heiress was Joan de la Pole.

Arch.Cant. 11:70-87 (1870) ("His whole life was an unbroken succession of services rendered to the State, at one of the most critical periods of English domestic history, when the power of Parliament was rapidly developing and the Commons shewed themselves to be growing in strength ... [he] must be placed among the most eminent statesmen of his time") (Cobham arms: *Gules*, on a chevron *or* three lions passant *sable*). *Vivian* (1895), p. 244. *C.P.* 3:344-345 (1913).

9. JOAN COBHAM, daughter and in her issue heiress, was married, with contract dated 21 Oct. 1362 to JOHN DE LA POLE, Knt., of Chrishall, Essex, and Castle Ashby, co. Northampton, son of William de la Pole, Knt. of Castle Ashby, by his wife Margaret Peverel, daughter of Edmund Peverel, of Castle Ashby. She died about 1388 *v.p.* They were buried at Chrishall Church, Essex.

Arch.Cant. 11:87 (1870). *C.P.* 3:345 (1913). *V.C.H. Northants.* 4:233 (1937).

8. JOAN DE LA POLE, Baroness Cobham *suo jure*, daughter and heiress, was granddaughter and heiress of John, 3rd Lord Cobham. She was married for the first time at an early age before November 1380 to ROBERT HEMENALE, Knt., of Polstead Hall in Burnham Norton, Norfolk (and had a son William, idiot from birth, who died after 1391 *s.p.*). He died in September 1391 and was buried in Westminster Abbey. She was married for the second time between September 1391 and February 1392, when still underage, to **REYNOLD BRAYBROOKE**, Knt., of Cooling Castle, Kent, M.P. for Kent, son of Gerard Braybrooke, Knt., of Colmworth, co. Bedford, and Horsenden, co. Buckingham, by Margaret, daughter of John de Longueville, of Orton Longueville, co. Huntingdon. He was born about 1356. They had two sons (died *v.p.*), and one daughter. SIR REYNOLD BRAYBROOKE was wounded in the attack on the citadel of Sluys in Flanders, and died four months later at Middleburg on the Scheldt on 20 Sep. 1405 *s.p.m.s.*, and was buried in Cobham Church (brass and monumental inscription). She was married for the third time, within a year of his death, as his second wife, to NICHOLAS HAWBERK, Knt. (died 9 Oct. 1407). They had a son John who died as an infant. Within three

months of his death she succeeded her grandfather as Lady of Cobham. She was married for the fourth time, as his third wife, before 18 July 1408, to JOHN OLDCASTELL, Knt., of Almeley, near Kington, co. Hereford, M.P. for Herefordshire (hanged, as a traitor and heresy of being a Lollard, at St. Giles's Fields, on 25 Dec. 1417). She was married for the fifth time to JOHN HARPEDEN, Knt. (died 1458, buried Westminster Abbey). She died on 13 Jan. 1433/4 *s.p.m.s.*, and was buried in Cobham Church (brass and monumental inscription).

Arch.Cant. 11:87-101 (1870) (Braybrooke arms: *Argent*, seven mascles 3, 3 and 1, *gules*). *C.P.* 3:345 (1913). *V.C.H. Hunts.* 3:191-192 (1936). *Paget* (1977), p. 464. *Roskell* (1992) 2:349-350 ("his fine monumental brass may yet be seen"). *Roskell* (1992) 3:866.

7. JOAN BRAYBROOKE, Baroness Cobham *suo jure*, only surviving daughter and heiress of her mother, was born about 1404. She was married at Cooling Castle, Kent, with marriage settlement dated 20 Feb. 1409/10, to **THOMAS BROOKE**, Knt., of Brooke, Somerset, Holditch in Thorncombe, Dorset, and Weycroft, Devon, *jure uxoris* Lord Cobham, M.P. from Dorset and Somerset, Sheriff of Devonshire, son of Thomas Brooke, Knt., of Holditch, by Joan, daughter and co-heiress of Simon Hanham, of Gloucester. He was born about 1392 (aged twenty-six in January 1417/8). They had ten sons and four daughters. Although he adopted his stepfather's Lollardism he escaped execution. "Sir Thomas Brook, lord of Cobham" died testate (P.C.C., 28 Luffenam) on 12 Aug. 1439, and was buried at Thorncombe (M.I.). His widow died on 24 Nov. 1442.

Arch.Cant. 11:100-103 (1870) (Brooke arms: *Gules*, on a chevron *argent*, a lion rampant *sable*, crowned *or*) (he was never summoned to Parliament). *C.P.* 3:346 (1913). *Paget* (1977), p. 277. *Roskell* (1992) 2:350,375-377.

6. EDWARD BROOKE, 6th Lord Cobham, son and heir, M.P. for Somerset, was summoned to Parliament from 13 Jan. 1444/5 by writs directed *Edwardo Broke de Cobham Chivaler*. He was a staunch Yorkist, fought at St. Albans on 23 May 1455, and was at the battle of Northampton on 10 July 1460. He was married to **ELIZABETH TUCHET**, daughter of James Tuchet, 5th Lord Audley (of **Magna Charta Surety descent** and **descendant of Charlemagne**), by his second wife, Alianor, base-born daughter of Edmund Holand, Earl of Kent, by Constance of York [see TUCHET 9 for her ancestry]. EDWARD BROOKE, Lord Cobham, died in 1464 before 8 Nov, when his widow had pardon for having married without license Christopher Worsley, "the King's servant".

Arch.Cant. 11:101-103 (1870). *C.P.* 3:346 (1913) (for her parentage, *Gen. (n.s.)* 28, pt. 1, p. 62). *Paget* (1977), p. 282.

Children of Edward Brooke, by Elizabeth Tuchet:

i. **JOHN BROOKE**, son and heir [see next].

ii. **ELIZABETH BROOKE**, married **ROBERT TANFIELD** [see RANDOLPH 8].[1]

5. JOHN BROOKE, Knt., 7th Lord Cobham, son and heir, was under age on 10 Dec. 1467. He was summoned to Parliament from 19 Aug. 1472. He was employed by King Henry VII (1491-92) in an expedition into Flanders, and on 24 June 1497 (with Lord Abergavenny) defeated the Cornish insurrection at Blackheath, where his cousin, Lord Audley (afterwards executed), was taken prisoner. He was married for the first time to ELEANOR AUSTELL, daughter of _____ Austell, of Suffolk. She died *s.p.* He was married for the second time to **MARGARET NEVILLE**, daughter of Edward de Neville, Lord Bergavenny, by his second wife Katherine

---

[1]Ancestors of **William Randolph**.

WYATT (cont.)

(**descendant of King Edward I**), daughter of Robert Howard, Knt. [see MOWBRAY 8.ii for her ancestry]. She died on 30 Sept. 1506. JOHN BROOKE, Lord Cobham, died on 9 Mar. 1511/2. They were buried at Cobham, with monumental inscription.
> *Arch.Cant.* 11:103-106 (1870). *C.P.* 3:346-347 (1913). *Paget* (1977), p. 194.

4. **THOMAS BROOKE**, Knt., 8th Lord Cobham, son and heir by second marriage, was summoned to Parliament from 23 Nov. 1514, and took part in the wars with France. He was married for the first time to **DOROTHY HEYDON**, daughter of Henry Heydon, Knt., of Baconsthorpe, by Anne, daughter of Geoffrey Boleyn, Knt. They had seven sons and six daughters. He was married for the second time to DOROTHY SOUTHWELL, widow, who died *s.p.* He was married for the third time, without issue, to ELIZABETH HART. "Sir Thomas Broke, Knt., Lord Cobham" died testate (P.C.C., 24 Jankyn) on 19 July 1529, and was buried at Cobham (brass and monumental inscription). His widow was living on 31 Mar. 1552.
> *Arch.Cant.* 11:106-112 (1870). *H.S.P.* 14:623 (1879) (Misc. Essex Ped.). *Norf.Arch.Soc.* 2:186-187 (1895) (1563 Vis. Norf.). *C.P.* 3:347-348 (1913). *Gen. (n.s.)* 33:61 (1917) (third wife "sister of Sr Percivel Hart Kt"). *Paget* (1977), p. 133.

3. **ELIZABETH BROOKE**, was married to **THOMAS WYATT**, Knt., of Allington Castle, Kent, poet to King Henry VIII, son and heir of Henry Wyatt, Knt., of Allington, by Anne, daughter of John Skinner, of Surrey. He was was born in Kent in 1503. SIR THOMAS WYATT died at Sherborne, Dorset, on 10 Oct. 1542. She was married for the second time to EDWARD WARNER, Knt.
> *Arch.Cant.* 11:112 (1870). *VMHB* 16:204-205 (Oct. 1908) (inscription on great-grandson Edwin's tomb: "esquire of the body to King Henry the Eighth ... well known for learning and embassys in the reign of that King"). *Gen. (n.s.)* 33:62 (1917). *Mary Isaac* (1955), p. 191. *VMHB* 31:237.

2. **THOMAS WYATT**, Knt., of Allington Castle, Kent, was born about 1522. He was married in 1537 to **JANE HAUTE**, daughter of William Haute (or Hawte), Knt., of Bisshopsborne, Kent, by Mary, daughter of Richard Guildford, Knt. She was born about 1522. They are said to have had ten children, of whom only three left issue. He led an armed conspiracy against Queen Mary at the time of her marriage to King Philip of Spain. His badly organized followers fell away, and Wyatt was taken prisoner. SIR THOMAS WYATT was beheaded in the Tower of London on 11 Apr. 1554, steadfastly refusing to implicate the Princess Elizabeth in the plot. His lands were confiscated, but Queen Mary returned the manor of Boxley to his widow, and Queen Elizabeth restored to her the manor of Wavering which Sir Thomas had held in her right.
> *Scott* (1876), p. 185. *VMHB* 16:204-205 (Oct. 1908). *VMHB* 31:237-244 (July 1923). *Mary Isaac* (1955), pp. 191-192 ("The elder Thomas Wyatt was a romantic figure at the court of Henry VIII, a poet, soldier, diplomat and the traditional youthful lover of Queen Anne Boleyn. His parents having separated when he was a child, young Thomas was probably brought up by his grandparents, Sir Henry and Lady Wyatt, at Allington"). *Adventurers* (1987), pp. 718-723.

Children of Thomas Wyatt, by Jane Haute:
  i. **GEORGE WYATT**, born 1550 [see next].
  ii. **JANE WYATT**, married **CHARLES SCOTT**, of Egerton, Kent [see FLEETE 2].[1]

1. **GEORGE WYATT**, of Allington Castle and Boxley Abbey, Kent, was born in 1550. He was married on 8 Oct. 1582 to **JANE FINCH**, daughter of Thomas Finch, Knt., of Eastwell, Kent, by his wife Katherine. They had four sons and two daughters. GEORGE WYATT died in Ireland, and was buried at Boxley on 10 Nov. 1624. His

---

[1] Ancestors of **Henry Fleete**.

WYATT (cont.)

widow was living on 29 Apr. 1639.

Wm. & Mary Quart. 10:59-61 (1901). *VMHB* 16:204-205 (Oct. 1908) (restored in blood by act of Parliament). *VMHB* 31:242 (July 1923). Mary Isaac (1955), p. 192. *NEHGR* 112:249 (Oct. 1958) (Wyatt arms: Per fess azure and gules a pair of barnacles silver enclosed by a ring gold). *Adventurers* (1987), pp. 718-723. Roberts (1993), p. 123-124. VMHB 16:204-205. Wm & Mary Quart., 1st Ser., 12:34-35,111-116.

Children of George Wyatt, by Jane Finch:

- i. **FRANCIS WYATT**, Knt., of Boxley, born about 1588, died 1644, Governor of Virginia 1621-1626, and 1639-1642, married **MARGARET SANDYS**. Descendants in England.
- ii. **REV. HAWTE WYATT**, born 1596, matriculated Queen's College, Oxford, 25 Oct. 1611, aged seventeen, accompanied his brother on the *Georgia* arriving 18 Nov. 1621, served as minister of Jamestown from 1621 to 1625, returned to England, vicar of Boxley, buried there 1 Aug. 1638 *v.m.*; married, first, London 6 Feb. 1618/9 **BARBARA MITFORD**, second, **ELIZABETH** _____, third, **ANN LEE**, died Boxley 29 Feb. 1631/2. Two sons by first marriage, one son by second marriage, two children by third marriage. *Wm. & Mary Quart. (1st ser.).* 10:59-60 (July 1901); 12:35-45 (July 1903). *VMHB* 16:204-205 (Oct. 1908) (inscription on tomb of nephew Edwin: "George Wiat left also Haut Wiat, who died vicar of this parish, and hath issue living in Virginia"). *VMHB* 31:243 (July 1923).
    - a. **GEORGE WYATT**, baptised St. Helen's Worcester, 12 Dec. 1619, emigrated by 12 Apr. 1642, resided York County, died before 15 Jan. 1671/2; married **SUSANNA** _____. One son.
    - b. **EDWARD WYATT**, born about 1621, emigrated to Virginia by 29 Sep. 1643, resided at "Boxley", Gloucester County, living 8 Jan. 1667/8; married **JANE** _____. One son.
    - c. **THOMAS WYATT**, baptised Boxley 15 Oct. 1626, buried there 10 Apr. 1627.
    - d. **JOHN WYATT**, born in England 1630, living 1 Jan. 1648/9.
    - e. **ANNE WYATT**, baptised Boxley 14 Feb. 1631/2, living 1 Jan. 1648/9.
- iii. **ELEANOR WYATT**, married **JOHN FINCH**, Lord Finch, of Fordwick, Speaker of the House of Commons in 1627.

* * *

WYLLYS

EDWARD I OF ENGLAND, King of England, married **ALIANORE DE CASTILLE**.
ELIZABETH OF ENGLAND, married **HUMPHREY DE BOHUN**, Earl of Hereford and Essex.
WILLIAM DE BOHUN, Earl of Northampton, married **ELIZABETH DE BADLESMERE**.
ELIZABETH DE BOHUN, married **RICHARD FITZ ALAN**, Earl of Arundel.
ELIZABETH FITZ ALAN, married **ROBERT GOUSHILL**, Knt.
JOAN GOUSHILL, married **THOMAS STANLEY**, Lord Stanley [see FITZ ALAN 10].

6. KATHERINE STANLEY, heiress of the manor of Camden, was married to **JOHN SAVAGE**, K.G., of Clifton and Rocksavage, son of John Savage, Knt., of Clifton (**descendant of Charlemagne**), by Eleanor, daughter of William Brereton, Knt., of Brereton, Egerton, co. Chester. He was born about 1422, and fought at Bosworth in 1485. SIR JOHN SAVAGE died aged seventy-three years on 22 Nov. 1495.

H.S.P. 18:203-204 (1882) (1580 Vis. Cheshire) (they had nine sons and six daughters). Ormerod 1:712. *TAG* 39:88 (Apr. 63). *Paget* (1977), p. 255.

Children & grandchild of John Savage, by Katherine Stanley:

- i. **CHRISTOPHER SAVAGE**, Knt. [see next].

WYLLYS (cont.)

    ii. **MARGARET SAVAGE** [see GERARD 5].[1]
    iii. **ELEANOR SAVAGE**, married **PETER LEGH**, Knt., of Lyme, described in 1580 Vis. Cheshire as *Piers Leigh who after was a Preist*.
        a. **PETER LEGH**, married **JANE GERARD** [see GERARD 4.i].[2]

5. **CHRISTOPHER SAVAGE**, Knt., of Aston Subedge, Camden, Burlington, and Westington, co. Gloucester, seventh son, was married to his cousin **ANNE STANLEY**, daughter and co-heiress of John Stanley, Knt., of Elford, co. Warwick. SIR CHRISTOPHER SAVAGE died in 1513.

    H.S.P. 18:204 (1882). *H.S.P.* 21:144 (1885) (1623 Vis. Glouc.). *TAG* 39:88 (Apr. 1963).

4. **CHRISTOPHER SAVAGE**, of Aston Subedge, Camden, Burlington, and Westington, co. Gloucester, and Upton-on-Severn and Elmley Castle, co. Worcester, son and heir, was married to **ANNE LYGON**, daughter of Richard Lygon, Knt., of Arle Court, co. Worcester (of **Magna Charta Surety descent and descendant of Charlemagne**), by Margaret, daughter of William Greville, Knt., of Arle Court and Cheltenham. In 1544 he alienated the advowson of two chantries in Camden to Thomas Bonner (father of his future son-in-law Anthony Bonner). CHRISTOPHER SAVAGE died in 1546.

    H.S.P. 21:145 (1885). *Ligon* (1947), pp. 38-39. *TAG* 39:88 (Apr. 1963).

    Children of Christopher Savage, by Anne Lygon:
        i. **FRANCIS SAVAGE**, Esq., of Elmley Castle, co. Gloucester, married **ANNE SHELDON**. Ancestors, apparently, of Anthony Savage of Gloucester County, Virginia. *H.S.P.* 21:145 (1885). *Ligon* (1947), pp. 40-41. See *Roberts* (1993), p. 253.
        ii. **BRIDGET SAVAGE**, born about 1540 [see next].

3. **BRIDGET SAVAGE**, of Elmley, was born about 1540. She was married about 1557-60 to **ANTHONY BONNER**, Gent., of Camden, Burlington, and Westington, co. Gloucester, son of Thomas Bonner, of Camden, by his wife Joan Skinner. ANTHONY BONNER, GENT., died testate in 1580 (his will, P.C.C., 43 Arundell, names his brother-in-law, George Savage, Clerk). She died testate before May 1608. Her will dated January 1607 and proved June 1611 (P.C.C., 63 Wood) named her daughter Dame Elizabeth Culpepper of Coventry, Mr. John Savage, her brother, her daughters Combes and Wyat, and "my niece" [i.e. granddaughter] Bridget Yonge. The will of her brother John Savage, of Tetbury (dated May 1608, P.C.C., 92 Windebancke) named, among others, Anthony Bonner, Gent., and Elizabeth Culpepper al[ia]s Bonner, widow, and Joane Wyat al[ia]s Bonner, children of Bridget Bonner al[ia]s Savage, deceased, late sister.

    TAG 39:86-89 (Apr. 1963) (descent of Amy Wyllys from King Edward I).

2. **MARY BONNER**, was born about 1560. She was married for the first time by 1 Nov. 1579 to **WILLIAM YONGE**, Gent., son of John Yonge, of Cainton and Tibberton, co. Salop, by his wife Mathilda Bill. WILLIAM YONGE, GENT., died in December 1583. She was married for the second time on 10 Jan. 158_ to **THOMAS COMBE**, Gent., of Stratford. His will was dated 22 Dec. 1608, and proved 10 Feb. 1608/9. She died at Stratford-on-Avon, co. Warwick, on 5 Apr. 1617.

    TAG 39:89 (Apr. 1963).

1. **BRIDGET YONGE**, of Caynton and Stratford, was born in 1580. She was married

---

[1]Ancestors of **Robert Abell, Thomas Gerard, Oliver Manwaring**.

[2]Ancestors of **Oliver Manwaring**.

WYLLYS (cont.)

at Holy Trinity Church, Stratford, on 2 Nov. 1609 to **GEORGE WYLLYS**, of Fenny Compton, co. Worcester, and Hartford, Connecticut. She was buried at Fenny Compton, co. Worcester, on 11 Mar. 1629. He was married for the second time and had issue. He emigrated to Hartford, Connecticut, in 1638, and was Governor of Connecticut in 1642. GOV. GEORGE WYLLYS died 9 Mar 1645.

NEHGR 82:155 (Apr. 1928) (Wyllys arms: Silver a chevron sable between three mullets gules). *TAG* 39:86-89.

Children of George Wyllys, by Bridget Yonge:
  i. GEORGE WYLLYS, of Fenny Compton, co. Worcester.
  ii. **HESTER WYLLYS**, died *s.p.*; married CAPT. ROBERT HARDING.
  iii. **AMY WYLLYS**, born about 1625, emigrated with father, died Springfield, Massachusetts, 9 Jan. 1698/9; married Hartford, Connecticut, 6 Nov. 1645 to **MAJ. JOHN PYNCHON**, born about 1625, died 17 Jan. 1702/3.
    a. **COL. JOHN PYNCHON**, born Springfield 15 Oct. 1647, died there 25 Apr. 1721; married **MARGARET HUBBARD**. Three children left issue.
    b. **MARY PYNCHON**, born 2 Oct. 1650, died about 1674-6; married 5 Oct. 1669 **JOSEPH WHITING**. Daughter left issue.

* * *

WYNNE see LLOYD

YELVERTON see PEYTON

YONGE see WYLLYS

* * *

YORK

EDWARD I OF ENGLAND, King of England, married **ALIANORE DE CASTILLE**.
EDWARD II OF ENGLAND, King of England, married **ISABELLE DE FRANCE**.
EDWARD III OF ENGLAND, married **PHILIPPE DE HAINAUT** [see PLANTAGENET 12].

9. EDMUND OF YORK [*of Langley*], fifth son, was born at Kings Langley, co. Hertford, on 5 June 1344. He was created **Earl of Cambridge** on 13 Nov. 1362, and **Duke of York** on 6 Aug. 1385. He was married for the first time at Hertford about 1 Mar. 1372 to **ISABELLA DE CASTILLE**, base-born daughter of Pedro *the Cruel*, Rey de Castilla y León, by María, daughter of Juan Garcías de Padilla. She was born at Morales or Tordesilas in 1355. She died on 23 Nov. 1393. He was married for the second time before 4 Nov. 1393 to JOAN HOLAND, daughter of Thomas de Holand, 2nd Earl of Kent, by Alice Fitz Alan, daughter of Richard Fitz Alan, 5th Earl of Arundel. She was born about 1380. EDMUND OF YORK, Duke of York, died testate (P.C.C., 52 Beaufort) at Kings Langley on 1 Aug. 1402. His widow died on 12 Apr. 1434.

C.P. 2:494 (1912). *Paget* (1977), p. 24.

YORK (cont.)

Children of Edmund of York, by Isabella de Castille:

   i. EDWARD OF YORK [*of Norwich*], son and heir, born 1373, created Earl of Rutland 25 Feb. 1390, Duke of Aumale 29 Sep. 1397 (from this title he was degraded by Parliament in October 1399), succeeded father as 2nd Duke of York, slain at Agincourt 25 Oct. 1415 *s.p.*; married PHILIPPE MOHUN, died 17 July 1431, daughter of John, 2nd Lord Mohun of Dunster, by Joan, daughter of Bartholomew, Lord Burghersh. *C.P.* (1912) 2:494. Paget (1977), p. 24.

   ii. RICHARD OF YORK [*of Conisburgh*], born about Sep. 1376 [see next].

   iii. CONSTANCE OF YORK, married THOMAS LE DESPENSER [see OXENBRIDGE 8].[1]

8. RICHARD OF YORK [*of Conisburgh*], Knt., second son, was born at Conisburgh Castle about September 1376. He was created **Earl of Cambridge** on 1 May 1414. He was married, with papal dispensation dated 23 May 1408, to **ANNE MORTIMER**, daughter and eventual sole heiress, in her issue, of Roger Mortimer, 4th Earl of March (**descendant of King Edward III**), by Alianor, daughter of Thomas Holand, 2nd Earl of Kent (**descendant of Charlemagne**). She was born on 27 Dec. 1390, and was heir general in her issue of the Crown of England transmitting the right to the Crown to her grandson Edward IV. She died in September 1411, and was buried at Kings Langley, co. Hereford [see PLANTAGENET 9 for her ancestry]. He was married for the second time about 1414 to MAUD CLIFFORD, the divorced wife of John Neville, 6th Lord Latimer, and daughter of Thomas Clifford, Lord Clifford, by Elizabeth, daughter of Thomas de Ros, Lord Ros. Having conspired (with Scrope of Masham and Grey of Heton) to depose King Henry V and set up in his place the Earl of March (the heir general of King Edward III), RICHARD OF CAMBRIDGE, Earl of Cambridge, was attainted and beheaded at Southampton Green on 5 Aug. 1415, buried in the chapel of "God's House" at Southampton. His widow died on 26 Aug. 1446 *s.p.*, and was buried in the Abbey of Roche, co. York.
C.P. 2:494-495 (1912). *Paget* (1957) 456:1. *Paget* (1977), p. 21.

Children of Richard of York, by Anne Mortimer:

   i. RICHARD PLANTAGENET, Duke of York, born 21 Sep. 1411 [see next].

   ii. ISABEL OF YORK, born 1409, died 2 Oct. 1484; married, first, THOMAS GREY (died *s.p.*), second, HENRY BOURGCHIER, Comte d'Eu in Normandy, afterwards Viscount Bourchier and Earl of Essex.

7. RICHARD PLANTAGENET, 3rd Duke of York, son and heir, was born on 21 Sep. 1411, and was nephew and heir of Edward *of Norwich*. He was restored as 3rd Duke of York on 19 May 1426, though his father's attainder was not reversed till 1461. In right of his mother, heiress of the line of Lionel, Duke of Clarence, 3rd son of Edward III, he claimed the throne in 1460 against the Lancastrian Dynasty represented by King Henry VI. He was married before 18 Oct. 1424 to **CECILY NEVILLE**, twelfth and youngest daughter of Ralph Neville, 1st Earl of Westmorland, by his second wife Joan Beaufort, legitimised daughter of John of Lancaster [*of Gaunt*], Duke of Lancaster [see BEAUFORT 11.iv.g. for her ancestry]. She was born at Raby Castle on 3 May 1415. Their children were born at Fotheringhay Castle in 1439, Hatfield in 1441, Rouen in 1442, 1443 and 1444, Fotheringhay in 1446 and 1447, Neyte in 1448, Dublin in 1449, and Fotheringhay in 1452. Richard assumed the name "Plantagenet" apparently about 1448. RICHARD PLANTAGENET, Duke of York, was slain at Wakefield on 30 Dec. 1460, fighting against the supporters of King Henry VI. His widow died at Berkhamstead Castle on 31 May 1495.

---

[1]Ancestors of **St. Leger Codd, Edward Digges, Warham Horsmanden, Katherine Saint Leger, Maria Johanna Somerset.**

YORK (cont.)

C.P. 5:213, 361-362 (1926). *Paget* (1957) 456:1. *Paget* (1977), p. 24.

Children & grandchildren of Richard of York, by Cecily Neville:
  i. HENRY PLANTAGENET, born 10 Feb. 1441, died young.
  ii. EDWARD IV PLANTAGENET, eldest surviving son and heir, born at Rouen 28 Apr. 1442, known as Earl of March till he succeeded his father on 30 Dec. 1460 as 4th Duke of York, proclaimed **King of England** by his supporters on 4 Mar. 1461, and crowned at Westminster on 29 June 1461, deposed by Richard Neville *the Kingmaker*, 1st Earl of Warwick and 2nd Earl of Salisbury, and fled to Flanders, returned to England 14 Mar. 1471, and defeated Warwick and the Lancastrians at Barnet on 14 Apr. 1471, and at Tewkesbury, 4 May 1471, died at Westminster 9 Apr. 1483, buried St. George's Chapel, Windsor; married, privately, at the manor house of the bride's father at Grafton Regis, co. Northampton, 1 May 1464, ELIZABETH WYDEVILLE, born about 1437, crowned at Westminster 26 May 1465, died testate (P.C.C., 10 Dogett) at Bermondsey Abbey, where for some time she had resided, or had been compelled by King Henry VII to reside, on 8 June 1492, buried with the King, her second husband; she was widow of John Grey, Knt., of Groby, co Leicester (slain, on the Lancastrian side, at St. Albans 17 Feb. 1460/1), and daughter of Richard Wydeville, 1st Earl Rivers, by Jacquette, daughter of Pierre de Luxembourg, Comte de Saint Pol, Conversano and Brienne. *Powicke* (1961), p. 38.

  a. EDWARD V PLANTAGENET, son and heir, born in sanctuary at Westminster on 4 Nov. 1470 while his father was in exile, succeeded father as **King of England** 9 Apr. 1483, but was deposed by his uncle Richard, Duke of Gloucester, 25 June 1483, before he had been crowned, said to have died in the Tower, with his brother Richard, but appears to have been living at the accession of King Henry VII; if murdered, then at the direction of that King rather than by King Richard III.
  b. RICHARD PLANTAGENET, born at Shrewsbury 17 Aug. 1473, created Duke of York 28 May 1474, said to have been murdered in the Tower with his older brother; married at Westminster 15 Jan. 1478 ANNE MOWBRAY, daughter and heiress of John, 4th Duke of Norfolk, by Elizabeth, daughter of John Talbot, 1st Earl of Shrewsbury.
  c. GEORGE PLANTAGENET, born at Windsor March 1477, died in infancy at Windsor Castle March 1479, buried St. George's Chapel, Windsor.
  d. ELIZABETH PLANTAGENET, born at Westminster 11 Feb. 1465, died at the Tower of London 11 Feb. 1503; married at Westminster 18 Jan. 1486 HENRY VII OF ENGLAND, **King of England**, son of Edmund Tudor, Earl of Richmond, by Margaret, daughter and heiress of John Beaufort, 1st Duke of Somerset, regarded by the remnants of the Lancastrian party as the hope of Lancaster (though from an illegitimate line) on the extinction of the Royal line of the House of Lancaster [see BEAUFORT 10.ii.a.], having invaded England, defeated and killed Richard III at Bosworth on 22 Aug. 1485, chosen King of England on the battlefield, crowned 30 Oct. 1485. Ancestors of Tudor and later Kings of England.
  e. MARY PLANTAGENET, born at Windsor August 1467, died at Greenwich 23 May 1482, buried St. George's Chapel, Windsor.
  f. CECILY PLANTAGENET, born 20 Mar. 1469, died at Quarr Abbey, Isle of Wight, 24 Aug. 1507; married, first, JOHN, 1st Viscount Welles; married, second, THOMAS KYME.
  g. MARGARET PLANTAGENET, born at Windsor 10 Apr. 1472, died 11 Dec. 1472.
  h. ANNE PLANTAGENET, born at Westminster 2 Nov. 1475, died 23 Nov. 1511, married at Greenwich 4 Feb. 1495 THOMAS HOWARD, 3rd Duke of Norfolk.
  i. KATHERINE PLANTAGENET, born at Eltham about 14 Aug. 1479, died at Tiverton 15 Nov. 1527; married WILLIAM COURTENAY, afterwards Earl of Devon.
  j. BRIDGET PLANTAGENET, born at Eltham 10 Nov. 1480, nun, died Dartford 1517.
  iii. EDMUND PLANTAGENET, born 17 May 1443, slain with father at Wakefield, 30 Dec. 1460.
  iv. WILLIAM PLANTAGENET, born 7 July 1447, died young.
  v. JOHN PLANTAGENET, born 7 Nov. 1448, died young.
  vi. **GEORGE PLANTAGENET**, born 21 Oct. 1449 [see next].
  vii. THOMAS PLANTAGENET, born about 1451, died young.

YORK (cont.)

viii. RICHARD III PLANTAGENET, youngest son, born 2 Oct. 1452, created Duke of Gloucester by his brother King Edward IV 1 Nov. 1461, Lord Protector 1483, deposed his nephew Edward V and usurped the throne 26 June 1483, crowned **King of England** 6 July 1483, slain at the Battle of Bosworth 22 Aug. 1485 fighting against the invader Henry Tudor, Earl of Richmond; married at Westminster 12 July 1472 ANNE NEVILLE, born at Warwick Castle 11 June 1456, died at Westminster 16 Mar. 1485 [see MONTHERMER 8]. *Paget* (1977), pp. 29-30. *Powicke* (1961), p. 38.

    a. EDWARD PLANTAGENET, son and heir apparent, Prince of Wales, born at Middleham Castle 1473, died 9 Apr. 1484 unmarried, buried at Sheriff Hutton, co. York.

ix. ANNE PLANTAGENET, married THOMAS SAINT LEGER, Knt. [see STAPLETON 7].[1]

x. ELIZABETH PLANTAGENET, born 22 Apr. 1444, married JOHN DE LA POLE, 2nd Duke of Suffolk. Seven sons.

xi. MARGARET PLANTAGENET, born 3 May 1446, married CHARLES, Duc de Bourgogne.

xii. URSULA PLANTAGENET, born 22 July 1455, died young.

6. GEORGE PLANTAGENET, K.G., sixth but third surviving son, was born at Dublin Castle on 21 Oct. 1449. He was created **Duke of Clarence** by his brother King Edward IV on 28 June 1461. He was first summoned to Parliament on 28 Feb. 1466/7. He was married at Calais on 11 July 1469 to ISABEL NEVILLE, elder daughter and co-heiress of Richard Neville, 1st Earl of Warwick and 2nd Earl of Salisbury (**descendant of King Edward I**), by Anne Beauchamp, Countess of Warwick (**descendant of King Edward III**), daughter of Richard Beauchamp, 13th Earl of Warwick. She was born at Warwick Castle on 5 Sep. 1451 [see MONTHERMER 8.i for her ancestry]. Their children were born at sea off Calais in 1470, at Farley Castle near Bath in 1473, at Warwick Castle in 1475 and at Tewkesbury in 1476. He joined his father-in-law in the rebellion against the King (his brother) in favour of the deposed King, Henry VI, but, changing sides, assisted in King Edward's victory at Barnet on 14 Apr. 1471. In this battle his wife's father was slain, whereupon he, "in consideration of that his marriage", was created Earl of Warwick and Earl of Salisbury on 25 Mar. 1471/2, and on 20 May 1472 made Great Chamberlain of England. Isabel Neville died at Warwick Castle on 22 Dec. 1476, and was buried at Tewkesbury. He proposed a second marriage with Mary, daughter of the Duke of Burgundy, a match which was much opposed by the Queen Consort. He was accused of high treason against his brother King Edward IV, found guilty, and attainted on 8 Feb. 1477/8, whereby all his honours were forfeited. He was executed in the Tower aged twenty-eight on 18 Feb. 1478, said to have been drowned in a butt of malmsey wine, and was buried in Tewkesbury Abbey.

C.P. 3:260-261 (1913). *C.P.* 6:656 footnote *e* (1926). *C.P.* 11:399 (1949). *Paget* (1977), p. 25.

Children of George Plantagenet, by Isabel Neville:

i. EDWARD PLANTAGENET, son and heir, born 21 Feb. 1475, Earl of Warwick and Salisbury, beheaded on Tower Hill 28 Nov. 1499.

ii. RICHARD PLANTAGENET, born 6 Oct. 1476, died at Warwick Castle 1 Jan. 1477.

iii. ANNE PLANTAGENET, born April 1470, died young.

iv. **MARGARET PLANTAGENET**, married RICHARD POLE, Knt. [see SOMERSET 7].[2]

* * *

---

[1] Ancestors of **Philip & Thomas Nelson**.

[2] Ancestors of **Maria Johanna Somerset**.

BIBLIOGRAPHY

The following list includes the principal sources consulted for this work. A few sources cited but once are found only in the appropriate reference section in the text and are not listed here. Abbreviated sources in roman have not been examined, but have been taken from *Ancestral Roots* for this edition.

Abel Lunt (1963)	Walter Goodwin Davis, *The Ancestry of Abel Lunt, 1769-1806, of Newbury, Massachusetts* (Portland, Maine, 1963)
Adlard (1862)	George Adlard, *The Sutton-Dudleys of England and the Dudleys of Massachusetts in New England* (New York, 1862)
Adventurers (1987)	*Adventurers of Purse and Person / Virginia / 1607-1624/5*, ed. John Frederick Dorman (3rd ed., Richmond, Virginia, 1987)
Allaben (1908)	Frank Allaben, *The Ancestry of Leander Howard Crall* (New York City, 1908)
Allen (1935)	Sarah Cantey Whitaker Allen, *Our Children's Ancestry* (1935)
Alnwick (1866)	George Tate, *The History of the Borough, Castle and Barony of Alnwick* (Alnwick, 1866)
Ancient Deeds	*A Descriptive Catalogue of Ancient Deeds in the Public Record Office*
AR (1992)	Frederick Lewis Weis, *Ancestral Roots of Certain American Colonists Who Came to America Before 1700*, with Additions and Corrections by Walter Lee Sheppard, Jr. Assisted by David Faris (7th ed., Baltimore, 1992)
Arch.Cant.	*Archaeologia Cantiana: Being Transactions of the Kent Archaeological Society* (London)
Arch. Jour.	*The Archaeological Journal*
Baddesley Clinton	Rev. Henry Norris, *Baddesley Clinton* (London, 1907)
Baines (1836)	Edward Baines, *History of the County Palatine and Duchy of Lancaster* (4 vols., London, 1836)
Baker	George Baker, *The History and Antiquities of the County of Northampton* (2 vols., 1822-1841)
Banks (1844)	Sir Thomas Christopher Banks, *Baronia Anglica Concentrata, or A Concentrated Account of all the Baronies Commonly Called Baronies in Fee ...* (vol. 1, 1844)
Bartrum (1974)	Peter C. Bartrum, *Welsh Genealogies AD 300-1400* (8 vols., 1974)
Bartrum (1983)	Peter C. Bartrum, *Welsh Genealogies AD 1400-1500* (18 vols., 1983)
Bernard (1903)	Mrs. Napier Higgins, *The Bernards of Abington and Nether Winchendon / A Family History* (4 vols., London, 1903-1904)
Berry (1837)	William Berry, *County Genealogies / Pedigrees of Berkshire Families* (London, 1837)
Boddie	John Bennett Boddie, *Historical Southern Families* (23 vols., 1957-1980)
Blomefield	Francis Blomefield, completed by Rev. Charles Parkin, *An Essay Towards a Topographical History of the County of*

BIBLIOGRAPHY

Blore (1811) *Norfolk* (11 vols., 2nd ed., 1805-1810)
Thomas Blore, *The History and Antiquities of the County of Rutland* (1811)

Brent (1946) Chester Horton Brent, *The Descendants of Collo Giles Brent Capt George Brent and Robert Brent, Gent / Immigrants to Maryland and Virginia* (1946)

Bristol & Glouc. Soc. *Transactions of the Bristol and Gloucestershire Archaeological Society*

Bull (1961) Henry DeSaussure Bull, *The Family of Stephen Bull of Kinghurst Hall, County Warwick, England and Ashley Hall, South Carolina 1600-1960*

Burke's Commoners John Burke, *A Genealogical and Heraldic History of the Commoners of Great Britain and Ireland Enjoying Territorial Possessions or High Official Rank; but Uninvested with Heritable Honours* (London, 1834-1838)

Carleton (1978) Walter Lee Sheppard, Jr., *Ancestry of Edward Carleton and Ellen Newton his Wife* (microfilm, 1978)

Charity Haley (1916) Walter Goodwin Davis, *The Ancestry of Charity Haley 1755-1800 Wife of Major Nicholas Davis of Limington, Maine* (Boston, Massachusetts, 1916)

Chester of Chicheley Robert Edmond Chester Waters, *Genealogical Memoirs of the Extinct Family of Chester of Chicheley Their Ancestors and Descendants* (2 vols., London, 1878)

Chetwode (1945) Frank Bulkeley Smith, *The Chetwode Family of England* (Worcester, Massachusetts, 1945)

Clarkson (1971) J. Robert T. Craine, *The Ancestry and Posterity of Matthew Clarkson (1664-1702)*, edited by Harry W. Hazard

Claypoole (1893) Rebecca Irwin Graff, *Genealogy of the Claypoole Family of Philadelphia 1588-1893* (Philadelphia, 1893)

Clopton (1939) Lucy Lane Erwin, *The Ancestry of William Clopton of York County, Virginia* (1939)

Cokayne Baronetage George Edward Cokayne, *Complete Baronetage* (5 vols., 1900-1909)

Colket (1936) Meredith B. Colket, Jr., *The English Ancestry of Anne Marbury Hutchinson and Katherine Marbury Scott* (Philadelphia, 1936)

Coll. Top. & Gen. *Collectanea Topographica & Genealogica* (8 vols., London, 1834-1843)

Collins (1734) Arthur Collins, *Proceedings, Precedents Concerning Baronies by Writ* (London, 1754)

Collins-Brydges (1812) *Collins's Peerage of England; Genealogical, Biographical, and Historical. Greatly Augmented, and Continued to the Present Time*, by Sir Egerton Brydges (9 vols., London, 1812, reprint 1970)

Comber John Comber, *Sussex Genealogies* (vol. 1 Horsham Centre, 1931, vol. 2, Ardingly Centre, 1932, vol. 3 Lewes Centre, 1933).

Copinger W.A. Copinger, *The Manors of Suffolk* (vol. 1, 1905, 2, 1908, 3, 1909, 4, 1909)

C.P. George Edward Cokayne, et al., *The Complete Peerage of*

BIBLIOGRAPHY

	England (2nd ed., 13 vols. in 14, London, 1910-1959)
Craven (1805)	Thomas Dunham Whitaker, *The History and Antiquities of the Deanery of Craven in the County of York* (London, 1805)
Crisp	Frederick Arthur Crisp, ed., *Visitation of England and Wales*
DAB	*Dictionary of American Biography* (20 vols., 1928-1937)
Dade (1888)	*Genealogical Data Relating to the Family of Dade of Suffolk* (London, 1888)
Devon N.& Q.	*Devon Notes and Queries*
D.N.B.	*The Dictionary of National Biography* (21 vols., 2nd ed., 1908-1912)
Dudley (1886)	Dean Dudley, *History of the Dudley Family* (1886)
Dunster (1909)	Sir H.C. Maxwell Lyte, *A History of Dunster and of the Families of Mohun & Luttrell* (2 vols., London, 1909)
East Herts.Arch.Soc.	*East Herts Archaeological Society Transactions*
Echyngham (1850)	Spencer Hall, *Echyngham of Echyngham* (London, 1850)
Evans (1984)	Charles F.H. Evans and Irene Haines Leet, *Thomas Lloyd Dolobran to Pennsylvania* [1984]
Farwell (1929)	Jane Harter Abbott and Lillian M. Wilson, *The Farwell Family* (1929)
Foster (1874)	Joseph Foster, *Pedigrees of the County Families of Yorkshire* (vol. II North and East Riding, 1874)
GDMNH (1928-1939)	Sibyl Noyes, Charles Thornton Libby and Walter Goodwin Davis, *Genealogical Dictionary of Maine and New Hampshire* (Portland, Maine, 1928-1929, reprint Baltimore, 1972)
G.E.C.	George Edward Cokayne, ed., *Complete Peerage of England, Scotland, Ireland, Great Britain and the United Kingson Extant, Extinct, or Dormant* (1st ed., London, 1887-1896)
Gen.	*The Genealogist* (7 vols., London, 1877-1883)
Gen. n.s.	*The Genealogist, New Series* (London, 1884-1922)
Gen.Mag.	*Genealogists' Magazine*
Glenn (1896)	Thomas Allen Glenn, *Merion in the Welsh Tract* (1896)
Glenn (1911)	Thomas Allen Glenn, *Welsh Founders of Pennsylvania* (vol. 1, Oxford, 1911)
Glover-Foster (1875)	Joseph Foster, ed., *The Visitation of Yorkshire Made in the Years 1584/5 by Robert Glover, Somerset Herald; to Which is Added The Subsequent Visitation Made in 1612, by Richard St. George, Norroy King of Arms* (London, 1875)
Goodricke (1885)	Charles Alfred Goodricke, *History of the Goodricke Family* (London, 1885)
Gregson (1869)	Matthew Gregson, *Portfolio of Fragments Relative to the History and Antiquities Topography and Genealogies of the County Palatine and Duchy of Lancaster* (Manchester, 1869)
Griffith (1914)	John Edwards Griffith, *Pedigrees of Anglesey and Carnarvonshire Families with Their Collateral Branches in Denbighshire, Merionethshire and other Parts* (Horncastle, Lincolnshire, 1914)
Her. & Gen.	*The Herald and Genealogist* (8 vols., London, 1863-1874)

BIBLIOGRAPHY

Hodgson (1832)	John Hodgson, *A History of Northumberland, in Three Parts.* (part II, vol. II, Newcastle, 1832)
Holmes (1972)	Alvahn Holmes, *The Farrar's Island Family and its English Ancestry* (Baltimore, 1972)
H.S.P.	*Harleian Society Publications, Visitations Series*
Jacobus (1933)	Donald Lines Jacobus, *The Bulkeley Genealogy* (1933)
Kemp (1902)	Frederick Hitchin-Kemp, *A General History of the Kemp and Kempe Families of Great Britain and Her Colonies* (London, 1902)
Launditch (1878)	G.A. Carthew, *The Hundred of Launditch and Deanery of Brisley in the County of Norfolk* (part II, Norwich, 1878)
Ligon (1947)	William D. Ligon, Jr., *The Ligon Family and Connections* (3 vols., 1947)
Lomax (1913)	E.L. Lomax, *Genealogy of the Virginia Family of Lomax* (Chicago, 1913)
Manning-Bray	Rev. Owen Manning (continued by William Bray), *The History and Antiquities of the County of Surrey* (3 vols., 1804, 1807, 1814)
Mary Isaac (1955)	Walter Goodwin Davis, *The Ancestry of Mary Isaac* (1955)
MCS (1991)	Frederick Lewis Weis, *The Magna Charta Sureties, 1215,* with Additions and Corrections By Walter Lee Sheppard, Jr., with David Faris (4th ed., Baltimore, 1991)
M.G.H.	Miscellanea Genealogica et Heraldica (1st series, 2 vols., 1868-1876, 2nd series, 4 vols., 1874-1883)
Memoirs of Eu (1888)	Robert Edmond Chester Waters, *Genealogical Memoirs of the Counts of Eu in Normandy 996-1350 and of the English Earls of Eu, of the House of Bourchier, 1419-1540* (London, 1888)
Metcalfe (1887)	Walter C. Metcalfe, ed., *The Visitations of Northamptonshire Made in 1564 and 1618-19, with Northamptonshire Pedigrees from Various Harleian MSS* (1887)
Mary Isaac (1955)	Walter Goodwin Davis, *The Ancestry of Mary Isaac* (1955)
Maryland Hist. Mag.	*The Maryland Historical Magazine*
Morant (1768)	Philip Morant, *The History and Antiquities of the County of Essex* (2nd ed., 2 vols., London, 1763-1768)
Mortimer-Percy (1911)	The Marquis of Ruvigny and Raineval, *The Plantagenet Roll of the Blood Royal being a Complete Table of all the Descendants Now Living of Edward III, King of England The Mortimer-Percy Volume, Part 1* (London, 1911)
Muskett (1900)	Joseph James Muskett, *Suffolk Manorial Families being the County Visitations and other Pedigrees* (vol. 1, 1900)
NEHGR	*The New England Historical and Genealogical Register*
NGSQ	*National Genealogical Society Quarterly*
Nicholas Davis (1956)	Walter Goodwin Davis, *The Ancestry of Nicholas Davis 1753-1832 of Limington, Maine* (Portland, Maine, 1956)
Norf.Arch.Soc.	*Norfolk Archaeological Society*
Northumberland	*A History of Northumberland* (15 vols., Newcastle-upon-Tyne, 1893-1940)
N.& Q.	*Notes and Queries*

BIBLIOGRAPHY

Ogle (1902)	Sir Henry A. Ogle, *Ogle and Bothal* (Newcastle-upon-Tyne, 1902)
Ormerod-Helsby (1882)	George Ormerod and Thomas Helsby, *The History of the County Palatine and City of Chester* (2nd ed., 1882)
Palgrave (1878)	Charles John Palmer and Stephen Tucker, ed., *Palgrave Family Memorials* (Norwich, 1878)
PMHB	*The Pennsylvania Magazine of History and Biography*
Powys Fadog	J.Y.W. Lloyd, *The History of the Princes, the Lords Marcher, and the Ancient Nobility of Powys Fadog* (vol. 6, 1887)
Raine (1852)	James Raine, *The History and Antiquities of North Durham* (1852)
Randolph (1952)	Wassell Randolph, *Henry Randolph I (1623-1673) of Henrico County, Virginia and His Descendants* (1952)
Randolph (1957)	Wassell Randolph, *Pedigree of the Descendants of Henry Randolph I (1623-1673) of Henrico County, Virginia* (1957)
Reliquary	*The Reliquary, Quarterly Archaeological Journal and Review* (London)
Roberts (1993)	Gary Boyd Roberts, *The Royal Descents of 500 Immigrants to the American Colonies or the United States Who Were Themselves Notable or Left Descendants Notable in American History* (Baltimore, 1993)
Roger Ludlow (1964)	Herbert Furman Seversmith, *The Ancestry of Roger Ludlow* (vol. 5 of *Colonial Families of Long Island, New York, and Connecticut*, 1964)
Roskell (1992)	John S. Roskell, *The History of Parliament: The House of Commons 1386-1421* (1992)
Rutton (1891)	William Loftie Rutton, *Three Branches of the Family of Wentworth* (London, 1891)
Saltonstall (1897)	Leverett Saltonstall, *Ancestry and Descendants of Sir Richard Saltonstall, First Associate of the Massachusetts Bay Colony and Patentee of Connecticut* (1897)
S.C. Hist. Mag.	*The South Carolina Historical and Genealogical Magazine*
Schwennicke	Detlev Schwennicke, ed., *Europäische Stammtafeln* (16 vols., Marburg, 1980-1995)
Scott (1876)	James Renat Scott, *Memorials of the Family of Scott, of Scot's-Hall, in the County of Kent* (London, 1876)
Seymours (1902)	H. St. Maur, *Annals of the Seymours* (London, 1902)
Smith-Maclean (1883)	John Smyth, of Nibley, *The Lives of the Berkeleys Lords of the Honour, Castle and Manor of Berkeley in the County of Gloucester From 1066 to 1618*, edited by Sir John Maclean (Gloucester, 1883)
Stemmata Chicheleana	*Stemmata Chicheleana* (Oxford, 1765) [with *Supplement*, 1775]
Stockman (1992)	Katharine Dickson, *The Stockman Story / The English Ancestry of Mr. John Stockman of Salisbury, Massachusetts* (1992)
Sur.Soc.	*The Publications of the Surtees Society*
Sur. Soc. 36 (1859)	The Visitation of the County of Yorke 1665-1666 by William Dugdale, Esqr, Norroy King of Arms, *Sur.Soc.*

BIBLIOGRAPHY

	36 (1859)
Sur.Soc. 144 (1930)	A Visitation of the North of England Circa 1480-1500, *Sur.Soc.* 144 (1930)
Surtees (1820)	Robert Surtees, *The History and Antiquities of the County Palatine of Durham* (4 vols., London, 1816-1840)
Sussex Arch. Coll.	*Sussex Archaeological Collections Illustrating the History and Antiquities of the County*
Swyncombe and Ewelme	Henry Alfred Napier, *Historical Notices of the Parishes of Swyncombe and Ewelme in the County of Oxford* (Oxford, 1858)
TAG	*The American Genealogist*
TG	*The Genealogist* (New York, Salt Lake City, 1980-)
Throckmorton (1930)	C. Wickliffe Throckmorton, *Genealogical and Historical Account of the Throckmorton Family* (1930)
Top. & Gen.	*The Topographer and Genealogist* (3 vols., 1846-1858)
Trans.Essex.Arch.Soc.	*Transactions of the Essex Archaeological Society*
Trans.Hist.Soc.Lancs.	*Transactions of the Historic Society of Lancashire and Cheshire*
Trigg Minor (1876)	Sir John Maclean, *The Parochial and Family History of the Deanery of Trigg Minor in the County of Cornwall* (London, 1876)
Twamley (1867)	Charles Twamley, *History of Dudley Castle and Priory* (London, 1867)
Vaux (1953)	Godfrey Anstruther, *Vaux of Harrowden / A Recusant Family* (1953)
V.C.H.	*The Victoria History of the Counties of England*
Virginia Gen.	*The Virginia Genealogist*
Vivian (1895)	J.L. Vivian, *The Visitations of the County of Devon Comprising the Heralds' Visitations of 1531, 1564 & 1620* (Exeter, 1895)
VMHB	*The Virginia Magazine of History and Biography*
Washington Ancestry	Charles Arthur Hoppin, *The Washington Ancestry and Records of the McClain, Johnson, and Forty Other Colonial American Families* (Greenfield, Ohio, 1932)
Waters	Henry FitzGerald Waters, *Genealogical Gleanings in England* (vol. 1, 1885, vol. 2, 1901)
Welcome Claimants	George E. McCracken, *Welcome Claimants: Proved, Disproved and Doubtful, With an Account of Some of Their Descendants* (1970)
Williams (1970)	George E. Williams, *A Genealogy of the Descendants of Joseph Bolles of Wells, Maine* (1970)
Wm. & Mary Quart.	*William and Mary College Quarterly*
Wm. Salt Soc.	William Salt Archaeological Society, *Collections for a History of Staffordshire*
Wm. Salt Soc. 3	The Visitation of Staffordshire made by Robert Glover, al's Somerset Herald Anno D'ni 1583, in *Collections for a History of Staffordshire*, edited by The Wm. Salt Archaeological Society (London, 1882)
Wotton (1741)	Thomas Wotton, *The English Baronetage* (1741)
Wrottesley (1903)	George Wrottesley, *History of the Family of Wrottesley of*

BIBLIOGRAPHY

	Wrottesley, co. Stafford (Exeter, 1903)
Yeatman (1903)	John Pym Yeatman, *The Brownes of Bechworth Castle* (1903)
Yeatman (1907)	John Pym Yeatman, *The Feudal History of the County of Derby* (vol. V, section IX, Birmingham, 1907)
York.Arch.Jour.	*The Yorkshire Archaeological Journal*

ENGLISH ABBREVIATIONS

J.P.	Justice of the Peace
K.B.	Knight of the Bath
K.G.	Knight of the Garter
M.I.	monumental inscription
M.P.	Member of Parliament
P.C.	Privy Councillor
P.C.C.	Prerogative Court of Canterbury

LATIN ABBREVIATIONS

Inq.p.m.	Inquisition *post mortem*
s.p.	*sine prole* (without issue)
s.p.legit.	*sine prole legitimâ* (without legitimate issue)
s.p.m.	*sine prole masculâ* (without male issue)
s.p.m.s.	*sine prole masculâ superstite* (without surviving male issue)
v.f.	*vitâ fratris* (in lifetime of brother)
v.m.	*vitâ matris* (in the lifetime of mother)
v.p.	*vitâ patris* (in the lifetime of father)

LATIN PHRASES

de facto	in fact
de jure	of right and just title
dominus, domina	lord, lady
filius, filia	son, daughter
jure uxoris	by right of a wife
miles, militis	knight
suo jure	by his (or her) right

INDEX

The full names of individuals of Plantagenet descent appear in this index in bold face. These names are coupled with those of their spouses (in bold face only if the spouse is also of Plantagenet descent). Other related individuals, including other spouses and ancestors of spouses, are indexed only by surname. Page numbers are provided for couples only where biographical information and documentation appear. Cross-references indicate location of other pages where these individuals are named as children or parents in other families. Welsh names are indexed by "ap" (son of) and "ferch" (daughter of). The articles "de" and "le" are often omitted. Remote Continental ancestors are not indexed. Unrelated individuals are not indexed.

ab Owain 169, 269	ap John Wyn 74
Abbott 87, 265	**ap Lewys, Rees** & Catrin ferch Elissa 97
Abbott, John & **Anne Mauleverer** 191	ap Maredudd 74
Abel 210, 214	**ap Rees, Ellis** & Anne ferch Humphrey 97
Abell, George & **Frances Cotton** 1	**ap Sion, Lewys** & Ellin ferch Hywel 97
Abell, Robert & Joanna 2	ap Thomas 169
Abney, Dannett & Mary Lee 3	Appleton 114
Abney, Edmund & Katherine Ludlam 2	**Appleton, Alice** & **Henry Berney** 147
Abney, George & Bathusa 2	Appleton, Henry & Margaret Roper 272
Abney, George & **Ellen Wolseley** 2	**Appleton, Roger** & **Anne Sulliard** 272
Abney, Paul & Mary Lee 3	Appleton, Roger & Agnes Clarke 272
Abney, Paul & Mary Brokesby 2	Appleton, Thomas & **Joyce Tyrrell** 272
Ackworth, Joan & **Edward Waldegrave** 69	Apsley, Anne & **John Lunsford** 177
Acton 253	Aquitaine, Éléonore & **Henry II of England** 222
Acton, Eleanor & **Ralph Percy** 149	Argall 111
Adams 144	Arnold 218
Agard, Katherine & Josias Bull 41	Arnold, Freelove & **Edward Pelham** 218
Agard, Stephen & **Susan Burnaby** 41	Artois, Blanche & **Edmund of Lancaster** . . 53
Alcock 215	**Arundel, Alianor** & Thomas Browne 37
Aldburgh, Eleanor & **William Mauleverer** . 190	**Arundel, Joan** & William Echingham 95
Allerton 124	**Arundel, Joan** & Thomas Willoughby 279
Allibond 42	**Arundel, John** & Alianor Maltravers 36
Allin, John & **Katherine Deighton** 86	**Arundel, John** & Elizabeth Despenser 37
Allington 164	**Arundel, Margaret** & **William de Ros** 242
Alston 202	**Arundel, Richard** & Alice 279
Alwey 21	**Arundel, Thomas** & Joan Moyne 37
Amancier 169	Arundell 130, 201
Andrews 11, 85, 124, 258	**Arundell, Anne** & Cecil Calvert 49
Andrews, Anne & John Sulliard 174	Arundell, John & **Eleanor Grey** 48
Andrews, Elizabeth & Thomas Windsor . . . 174	**Arundell, Mary** & **John Somerset** 256
Andrews, John & **Elizabeth Stratton** 174	**Arundell, Matthew** & Margaret Willoughby . 48
Angell, Mary & **John Claypoole** 66	**Arundell, Thomas** & Margaret Howard 48
Angier 12	**Arundell, Thomas** & Anne Philipson 48
Angoulême, Isabelle & **John of England** . . 224	Ascue 201
Anjou 157	Asfordby 4
Anjou, Geoffrey & Maud of England 222	**Asfordby, John** & Alice Wolley 4
Anjou, Marguerite & Henry VI of England 157	Asfordby, William & **Eleanor Newcomen** . . . 4
Annabel 267	**Asfordby, William** & Martha Burton 4
Anstey 85	Ashby 132
ap Dafydd 97, 209, 259	Ashe 85
ap Gruffydd, Sion & Elsbeth ferch Dafydd . 97	Ashton 58, 113, 217, 261, 267
ap Gwilym 73	Ashton, _____ & **Henry Dudley** 92
ap Howell, Sion & **Sibyl ferch Hugh Gwynn** 209	Astley 27, 119
ap Hugh, Humphrey & **Elizabeth ferch Sion** 209	Astley, Elizabeth & **Edward Darcy** 161
ap Huw, Owain & **Sibyl Griffith** 209	Astley, Elizabeth & **John Thornes** 167
ap Hywel 169	Aston 60, 284
ap Hywel, Gruffydd & **Jane ferch Humphrey** 97	Aston, Frances & **Robert Needham** 265
ap Hywel, Humphrey & Anne Herbert 97	Atterbury 236
ap Ieuan, John & **Margaret Kynaston** 169	Aubrey 193
ap Jenkin, Hywel & **Mary Kynaston** 97	Aucher, Anthony & **Affra Cornwallis** 171
ap John Kynaston 169	**Aucher, Edward** & Mabel Wroth 171

302

INDEX

Aucher, Elizabeth & William Lovelace 171
Audley 5, 66, 219, 263
Audley, Hugh & Margaret Clare 5
Audley, Margaret & Ralph Stafford 5
Austell 287
Austin 132
Avery 145
Ayala 90
Aylmer 165
Aylmer, Elizabeth & John Foliot 165
Ayloffe 216
Ayscough 27
Bacon 159
Badlesmere 148, 186, 196
Badlesmere, Elizabeth & William Bohun ... 26
Bagwell 104
Bailey 42
Baker, Elizabeth & Thomas Scott 111
Ball 133
Ball, Elias & Elizabeth Harleston 132
Banister 33
Bankes 49
Bardolf, Cecily & Brian Stapleton 9
Bardolf, John & Elizabeth Damory 8
Bardolf, William & Agnes Poynings 8
Barentyn, Margaret & John Harcourt 129
Barentyn, William & Jane Lewknor 271
Barham 112
Barkham, Edward & Frances Berney 147
Barkham, Margaret & Edmund Jennings .. 147
Barnard 85, 188
Barne, Anne & William Lovelace 172
Barrett 123
Barron 161
Barry 180, 240
Barton 265
Baskerville, Catherine & Charles Somerset 256
Basset 6, 212
Basset, Edward & Elizabeth Lygon 85
Basset, Jane & John Deighton 85
Bassingbourne 77
Batchcroft, Elizabeth & John Richers 138
Bates 277
Batt, Christopher & Anne Baynton 12
Baugh 36
Baugh, Anne & Robert Brent 36
Bayes 13
Baynham, Anne & William Trye 269
Baynton, Anne & Christopher Batt 12
Baynton, Edward & Isabel Leigh 11
Baynton, Ferdinando & John Weare 12
Baynton, Henry 123
Baynton, Henry & Anne Cavendish 12
Baynton, Joan & Thomas Prowse 123
Baynton, John & Joan Digges 11
Baynton, John & Joan Echingham 10
Baynton, Robert & Elizabeth Haute 11
Beare 82
Beatty 4
Beauchamp 6, 7, 11, 17, 30, 31, 61, 64, 108, 153,
192, 198, 216, 242, 250, 264, 277, 286
Beauchamp, Alianor & Edmund Beaufort .. 18
Beauchamp, Alianor & Thomas de Ros ... 243
Beauchamp, Anne & Richard Neville 194
Beauchamp, Elizabeth & George Neville ... 14
Beauchamp, Elizabeth & Edward Neville .. 211
Beauchamp, Joan & James Butler 46
Beauchamp, Margaret & John Beaufort 17
Beauchamp, Mary & Walter Wolseley 285
Beauchamp, Philippe & Hugh Stafford 6
Beauchamp, Richard & Isabel Despenser .. 14
Beauchamp, Richard & Elizabeth Berkeley . 13
Beauchamp, Richard & Isabel Despenser .. 211
Beauchamp, Thomas & Margaret Ferrers .. 13
Beauchamp, William & Joan Fitzalan 106
Beaufew 20
Beaufort 7, 14, 18, 106, 108, 149, 194, 198, 203,
204, 211, 243, 278, 292, 293
Beaufort, Alianor & Robert Spencer 53
Beaufort, Edmund & Alianor Beauchamp .. 17
Beaufort, Henry & Alice Fitzalan 15
Beaufort, Henry & Jane Hill 18
Beaufort, Joan & Edward Stradling 15
Beaufort, Joan & Ralph Neville 16
Beaufort, Joan & Robert Ferrers 16
Beaufort, Joan & James I of Scotland 17
Beaufort, John & Margaret Holand 16
Beaufort, John & Margaret Beauchamp 17
Beaufort, Margaret & Humphrey Stafford ... 7
Beaufort, Margaret & Edmund Tudor 17
Beaumont 55, 121, 283
Beaumont, Constance & John Mitton 188
Beaumont, Elizabeth & William Botreaux .. 31
Beaumont, Henry & Margaret Vere 186
Beaumont, Henry & Eleanor Sutton 188
Beaumont, Henry & Joan Heronville 187
Beaumont, Henry & Elizabeth Willoughby . 187
Beaumont, Isabel & Henry of Lancaster .. 154
Beaumont, John & Alianor Lancaster 186
Beaumont, John & Katherine Everingham . 187
Beaumont, Katherine & Hugh Luttrell 173
Beaupré 133
Beavis 82
Becke 27
Beckwith 148, 183
Beeching, Susannah & Warham Horsmanden 245
Belknap 120
Belknap, Elizabeth & William Ferrers 102
Bell 165
Bellinger 41
Bellingham 217
Benjamin 12
Bennett 246
Bennett, Jane & Thomas Ludlow 176
Benyon 188
Bere 111
Berkeley 18, 46, 57, 118, 131, 136, 149, 165, 246,
264, 280
Berkeley, Anne & William Dennis 84
Berkeley, Anne & John Brent 104

303

INDEX

Berkeley, Elizabeth & Richard Beauchamp . 13
Berkeley, Elizabeth & Henry Lygon 84
Berkeley, Elizabeth & John Sutton 91
Berkeley, Isabel & William Trye 269
Berkeley, James & Isabel Mowbray 83
Berkeley, James & Elizabeth Bluet 83
Berkeley, John & Isabel Dennis 84
Berkeley, Maurice & Elizabeth Despenser .. 82
Berkeley, Maurice & Isabel Mead 84
Berkeley, Thomas & Margaret Lisle 83
Berkeley, Thomas & Elizabeth Neville 104
Bernard, Beheathland & Francis Dade 78
Bernard, Francis & Mary Woolhouse 21
Bernard, Francis & Alice Haslewood 20
Bernard, John & Margaret le Scrope 20
Bernard, John & Margaret Daundelyn 20
Bernard, John & Cecily Muscote 20
Bernard, Richard & Anne Cordray 21
Bernard, Richard & Elizabeth Woolhouse .. 20
Bernard, William & Lucy Higginson 21
Berners, Margery & John Bourgchier 159
Berney, Frances & Edward Barkham 147
Berney, Henry & Alice Appleton 147
Berney, John & Margery Wentworth 146
Berney, John & Margaret Read 147
Berney, Thomas & Juliana Gawdy 147
Berwyke 16
Bethell 67
Bettenham 104
Betteshorne 57, 91
Bevan 270
Beverley 221, 237
Beville, Essex & Amy Butler 22
Beville, John & Mary Clement 22
Beville, Robert & Mary Saunders 22
Bigod, Elizabeth & Stephen Hammerton ... 23
Bigod, John & Elizabeth le Scrope 22
Bigod, John & Joan Strangeways 23
Bigod, Ralph & Margaret Constable 23
Bigot 152
Bill 290
Birch 41
Bird 66, 85
Birkell 53
Birmingham 102, 162
Bla[c]kiston 50, 144, 161
Bladwell 221
Blanchflower 114
Bland 237
Blennerhasset Eliza' & Lionel Throckmorton 266
Blennerhasset, John & Elizabeth Cornwallis 266
Bloomfield 202
Blount 7, 46, 103, 216
Blount, Constance & John Sutton 90
Blount, Elizabeth & Andrews Windsor ... 174
Blount, William & Margaret Echingham ... 96
Bluet, Elizabeth & James Berkeley 83
Blythe, Margaret & Anthony Wolseley 284
Bodrugan 56
Bohun 7

Bohun, Alianor & James Butler 45
Bohun, Alianor & Thomas Dagworth 45
Bohun, Alianor & Thomas of Gloucester .. 158
Bohun, Elizabeth & Richard Fitzalan 106
Bohun, Humphrey & Joan Fitzalan 25
Bohun, Humphrey & Elizabeth of England . 24
Bohun, Margaret & Hugh Courtenay 72
Bohun, Mary & Henry IV of England ... 156
Bohun, William & Elizabeth Badlesmere ... 24
Boleyn 195, 278, 288
Boleyn, Anne & Henry VIII of England 47
Boleyn, Margaret & John Sackville 47
Boleyn, Mary & William Cary 54
Boleyn, Thomas & Elizabeth Howard 47
Boleyn, William & Margaret Butler 46
Bolles, Benjamin & Anne Goodrick 26
Bolles, Joseph & Mary Howell 27
Bolles, Thomas & Elizabeth Perkins 26
Bolling 237
Bonner, Anthony & Bridget Savage 290
Bonner, Mary & William Yonge 290
Bonville, Cecily & Thomas Grey 119
Bonville, Elizabeth & William Tailboys ... 262
Bonville, William & Margaret Grey 28
Bonville, William & Elizabeth Harington ... 28
Bonville, William & Katherine Neville 28
Booth 69, 71
Booth, Anne & William Clopton 69
Borough 51
Borton 26
Bostock 12, 22
Bosvile, Elizabeth & Roger Harlakenden ... 31
Bosvile, Elizabeth & Herbert Pelham 217
Bosvile, Godfrey & Margaret Greville 30
Boteler (see also Butler) . 64, 77, 103, 268, 269
Botetourt 234, 280
Botreaux 125, 167
Botreaux, Margaret & Robert Hungerford .. 31
Botreaux, William & Elizabeth Beaumont .. 31
Boughton 111
Bourchier, John & Elizabeth 33
Bourchier, Mary & Jabez Whitaker 34
Bourchier, Ralph & Elizabeth Hall 33
Bourgchier 7, 119, 174, 198, 292
Bourgchier, Humphrey & Elizabeth Tilney 159
Bourgchier, Joan & Henry Neville 29
Bourgchier, Joan & Edmund Knyvett 122
Bourgchier, John & Katherine Howard ... 159
Bourgchier, John & Margery Berners 159
Bourgchier, Margaret & Thomas Bryan ... 160
Bourgchier, William & Anne of Gloucester 158
Bourgogne 156
Bovile 162
Bowet, Elizabeth & Thomas Dacre 76
Bowles 265
Bowman 168
Bowyer 122
Boynton 51, 52
Boyville 88
Bracebridge 41

INDEX

Bradstreet 75, 94	Bull, Stephen 41
Braham 266	Bulmer 69, 261
Brampton 123	Burgh 18, 31, 45, 238
Bramswell 33	Burgh, Elizabeth & Lionel of Clarence . . . 231
Brandon, Eleanor & John Glemham 214	Burgh, John & Elizabeth Clare 42
Brandon, William & Elizabeth Wingfield . . 213	Burgh, William & Maud of Lancaster 43
Branford 41	Burghersh 109, 193, 211
Brattle 75	Burghersh, Elizabeth & Edward Despenser . 62
Bray 276	Burley 242, 279
Braybrooke, Joan & Thomas Brooke 287	Burnaby, Richard & Anne Wodhull 40
Braybrooke, Reynold & Joan de la Pole . . 286	Burnaby, Susan & Stephen Agard 41
Brayning 87	Burnaby, Thomas & Elizabeth Sapcott 41
Brent 244	Burnell 109, 264
Brent, George & Elizabeth Greene 35	Burnell, Edward & Alianor 234
Brent, George & Anne Peyton 35	Burnell, Hugh & Philippe de la Pole 233
Brent, Giles & Kittamaquund 35	Burnell, Katherine & John Radcliffe 234
Brent, John & Anne Berkeley 104	Burr 191
Brent, Margaret & John Dering 104	Burrell 44
Brent, Richard & Elizabeth Reed 34	Burrough, George & Frances Sparrow 44
Brent, Robert & Anne Baugh 36	Burrough, Nathaniel & Rebecca Style 44
Brereton 289	Burrough, Thomas & Bridget Higham 44
Brereton, Elizabeth & Randall Mainwaring 208	Burroughs, George & Mary Hathorne 44
Brewes 196, 205	Burton 41, 42
Brewster 130, 176	Burton, Martha & William Asfordby 4
Brice 41	Butler 53
Brien 95	Butler, Amy & Essex Beville 22
Brockton, Helen & Thomas Wolseley 285	Butler, James & Alianor Bohun 45
Brokesby, Mary & Paul Abney 2	Butler, James & Joan Beauchamp 46
Brooke 244	Butler, James & Elizabeth Darcy 45
Brooke, Edward & Elizabeth Tuchet 287	Butler, James & Anne Welles 46
Brooke, Elizabeth & Robert Tanfield 235	Butler, John & Margaret Sutton 274
Brooke, Elizabeth & Thomas Wyatt 288	Butler, Margaret & William Boleyn 46
Brooke, John & Margaret Neville 287	Butler, Margaret & Lawrence Washington . 274
Brooke, Roger & Mary Wolseley 285	Butler, Pernel & Gilbert Talbot 263
Brooke, Thomas & Dorothy Heydon 288	Butler, Thomas & Anne Hankford 46
Brooke, Thomas & Joan Braybrooke 287	Butler, William & Margaret Greeke 274
Brounflete 16, 79	Buxhall 193
Brown 252	Byley 94
Browne 48, 151, 172	Byron 96
Browne, Anthony & Lucy Neville 38	Caesar 173
Browne, Anthony & Alice Gage 38	Caesar, Alice & William Rodney 240
Browne, Anthony & Mary Dormer 201	Call 27
Browne, Anthony & Jane Radcliffe 200	Calthorpe 90
Browne, Dorothy & Edmund Lee 201	Calthorpe, Anne & Robert Drury 10
Browne, Eleanor & William Kempe 207	Calthorpe, Elizabeth & Francis Hasilden . . 132
Browne, Elizabeth & Henry Somerset 19	Calthorpe, Jane & Edward Peyton 133
Browne, Frances & Richard Washington . . 274	Calthorpe, William & Elizabeth Stapleton . . . 9
Browne, Mary & John Grey 120	Calveley 59
Browne, Robert & Mary Mallet 207	Calvert 36, 285
Browne, Thomas & Alianor Arundel 37	Calvert, Cecil & Anne Arundell 49
Bruges 216	Calvert, Charles & Jane Lowe 49
Bryan, Elizabeth & Nicholas Carew 160	Camoys 28, 134, 148
Bryan, Thomas & Margaret Bourgchier . . . 160	Capel 216
Bucton 77	Carent 11
Bugge 138	Carew, Isabel & Nicholas Saunders 21
Bulkeley 132	Carew, James & Alianor Hoo 50
Bulkeley, Frances & Richard Welby 276	Carew, Mary & Arthur Darcy 160
Bulkeley, Peter & Grace Chetwode 60	Carew, Nicholas & Elizabeth Bryan 160
Bull, Josias & Katherine Agard 41	Carew, Richard & Malyn Oxenbridge 50
Bull, Mary & John Limbrey 41	Carleton, John & Ellen Strickland 52

INDEX

Carlton, Edward & Ellen Newton 53
Carlton, Walter & Jane Gibbon 53
Carr, Elizabeth & Christopher Kelke 115
Carr[e] 66, 238
Carter 175, 254
Carter, John & Sarah Ludlow 175
Cary, Katherine & Francis Knollys 54
Cary, Thomas & Margaret Spencer 54
Cary, William & Mary Boleyn 54
Castille, Alianore & Edward I of England . 226
Castille, Isabella & Edmund of York 291
Cater 252
Catesby 201
Cave 65
Cave, Bridget & Francis Tanfield 236
Cave, Margaret & William Skipwith 253
Cavendish, Anne & Henry Baynton 12
Cawthorne 139
Cecil 1
Cecil, Elizabeth & Robert Wingfield 164
Cergeaux, Alice & Richard Vere 56
Cergeaux, Elizabeth & William Marney ... 146
Cergeaux, Philippe & Robert Pashley 110
Cergeaux, Richard & Philippe Fitzalan 55
Chadbourne 27
Chamberlain 250
Chamberlain, Anne & Edward Raleigh ... 184
Champernoun 216
Champernoun, Joan & John Courtenay ... 72
Chapman 245
Charroll, _____ & John Sutton 274
Chaucer 193
Chauncy 60
Chaworth 55, 80, 249
Chaworth, Maud & Henry of Lancaster ... 153
Chedworth, Margaret & John Howard 198
Cheesman 239
Cheney 9, 80, 130, 132, 159, 198, 207
Chenuit 286
Cherleton 90, 106, 179, 232, 263
Cherleton, Edward & Alianor Holand 57
Cherleton, Joan & John Grey 168
Cherleton, John & Joan Stafford 57
Cherleton, Joyce & John Tiptoft 58
Cheseldine 114
Chetwode, Grace & Peter Bulkeley 60
Chetwode, Richard & Dorothy Needham ... 59
Chetwode, Richard & Agnes Wodhull 59
Chetwynd 102
Chibnall 20
Chichele 207
Chickering 86
Chidiock, Elizabeth & Walter Fitzwalter .. 109
Child 131
Cholmondeley 208
Chudleigh 72
Clapham 118
Clare 25, 105, 225
Clare, Alianor & Hugh Despenser 61
Clare, Elizabeth & Theobald Verdun 42

Clare, Elizabeth & John Burgh 42
Clare, Elizabeth & Roger Damory 42
Clare, Gilbert & Joan of England 60
Clare, Margaret & Hugh Audley 5
Clarell 204
Clarence, Lionel & Elizabeth de Burgh ... 231
Clarence, Philippe & Edmund de Mortimer 231
Clarke (see Clerke) 82, 218
Clarke, Agnes & Roger Appleton 272
Clarke, Jeremy & Frances Latham 65
Claypoole, Adam & Dorothy Wingfield 66
Claypoole, James & Helena Mercer 67
Claypoole, John & Mary Angell 66
Clement, Mary & John Beville 22
Clere 132
Clerke, George & Elizabeth Wilsford 65
Clerke, James & Elizabeth Ferrers 64
Clerke, James & Mary Saxby 65
Clerke, William & Mary Weston 65
Clifford 63, 91, 122, 141, 190, 219, 277, 280, 292
Clifford, Elizabeth & William Plumpton ... 88
Clifford, John & Elizabeth Percy 179
Clifford, Mary & Philip Wentworth 129
Clifford, Maud & Edmund Sutton 179
Clifford, Philippe & William Ferrers 64
Clifford, Thomas & Joan Dacre 179
Clifford, Thomas & Elizabeth de Ros 242
Clifton 36, 98, 219
Clinton 38, 145, 162
Clopton, Walter & Margaret Maidstone 69
Clopton, William & Anne Booth 69
Clopton, William & Margaret Waldegrave .. 69
Clopton, William & Elizabeth Sutcliffe 69
Cobham 37, 102, 110, 157, 169, 205
Cobham, Joan & John de la Pole 286
Cobham, John & Margaret Courtenay 286
Cockram 151
Codd, St. Leger & Anne Mottrom 246
Codd, William & Mary Saint Leger 246
Cogan, Mary & Roger Ludlow 176
Coggeshall 146, 267
Cokesey 136
Cole 88, 124, 172
Colepepper (see Culpeper) ....
Collier 178
Colson 22
Colt 39
Combe 290
Comin 131
Comyn 154, 186, 228, 263
Conningsby 84
Constable 253, 276
Constable, Katherine & Robert Stapleton . 257
Constable, Margaret & Ralph Bigod 23
Constable, Marmaduke & Jane Conyers .. 257
Constable, Robert & Katherine Manners .. 257
Conyers 94, 190
Conyers, Christopher & Anne Dacre 71
Conyers, Jane & Marmaduke Constable .. 257
Conyers, John & Margery Darcy 70

INDEX

Conyers, John & Alice Neville 70
Conyers, William & Mary Scrope 71
Coode 114
Cook[e] 4, 67, 255
Cooke, Joanne & William Harris 151
Cooke, Joseph & Elizabeth Haynes 139
Cooper 5, 68, 177
Cope, Elizabeth & John Dryden 185
Cope, John & Bridget Raleigh 185
Copleston 82
Copley 30
Copley, Eleanor & Thomas West 143
Copley, Roger & Anne Hoo 278
Corbet, Dorothy & Richard Mainwaring .. 181
Corbet, Richard & Elizabeth Devereux ... 103
Corbet, Robert & Elizabeth Vernon 103
Corbett, Elizabeth & Philip Wentworth ... 131
Corbett, Richard & Mary Drury 89
Corbin, Frances & Edmund Jennings 148
Cordray, Anne & Richard Bernard 21
Cornwall 56, 121, 143
Cornwallis, Affra & Anthony Aucher 171
Cornwallis, Anne & Thomas Dade 78
Cornwallis, Elizabeth & John Blennerhasset 266
Cornwallis, John & Mary Sulliard 77
Cornwallis, Richard & Margaret Lowthe ... 78
Cornwallis, Thomas & Philippe Tyrrell 77
Cornwallis, William & Elizabeth Stanford .. 77
Cosynton 196
Cotesford 184
Cotton, Audrey & Gilbert Talbot 265
Cotton, Frances & George Abell 1
Cotton, George & Mary Onley 1
Cotton, John & Cecily Mainwaring 1
Cotton, Richard & Mary Mainwaring 1
Court 125
Courtenay 17, 19, 28, 98, 122, 196, 293
Courtenay, Elizabeth & William Strode 73
Courtenay, Elizabeth & Andrew Luttrell .. 173
Courtenay, Hugh & Margaret Bohun 72
Courtenay, John & Joan Champernoun 72
Courtenay, Margaret & John de Cobham . 286
Courtenay, Philip & Anne Wake 72
Courtenay, Philip & Elizabeth Hungerford . 72
Courtenay, Philip & Jane Fowell 73
Courtenay, Philip & Elizabeth 73
Covert, Elizabeth & John Fenwick 101
Coytemore, Elizabeth & William Tyng 75
Coytemore, Rowland & Katherine Miles ... 75
Coytemore, William & Jane Williams 74
Crabb[e] 114, 256
Cranage, Dorothy & Richard Mackworth .. 180
Crane 69
Cranston 65
Crappe 67
Crawford 241
Creffield 21
Cresmore 95
Cressener 249
Crewe 116

Crispin 210
Cromwell 67, 216, 260
Cromwell, Edward & Elizabeth Upton 282
Cromwell, Frances & Richard Strode 81
Cromwell, Frances & John Wingfield 282
Cromwell, Gregory & Elizabeth Seymour . 281
Cromwell, Henry & Mary Paulet 282
Croshaw 144
Crouch 147
Crowe 50
Crowne, William & Agnes Mackworth 180
Crump 70
Culpeper 11, 65, 165, 245
Culpeper, Joyce & Edmund Howard 199
Culpeper, Joyce & Ralph Leigh 259
Culpeper, Richard & Isabel Worsley 259
Culpeper, Thomas & Katherine Saint Leger 245
Culpeper, William & Elizabeth Ferrers ... 259
Curtis 114, 241
Cushin, Edmond & Frances Richers 138
Cushin, Elizabeth & William Thornton ... 138
Dacre 91, 201
Dacre, Anne & Christopher Conyers 71
Dacre, Humphrey & Mabel Parr 76
Dacre, Joan & Thomas Clifford 179
Dacre, Joan & Richard Fiennes 176
Dacre, Thomas & Elizabeth Greystoke 76
Dacre, Thomas & Philippe Neville 76
Dacre, Thomas & Elizabeth Bowet 76
Dade, Francis & Beheathland Bernard 78
Dade, Thomas & Anne Cornwallis 78
Dade, William & Mary Wingfield 78
Dagworth, Alianor & Walter Fitzwalter ... 109
Dagworth, Thomas & Alianor Bohun 45
Dale 41, 154
Dale, Edward & Diana Skipwith 254
Dalton 73
Dalyngridge 159
Damory, Elizabeth & John Bardolf 8
Damory, Roger & Elizabeth Clare 42
Danby 246
Danby, Christopher & Elizabeth Neville ... 29
Danby, Mary & Edmund Mauleverer 190
Daniell 182
Danvers 84
Darcy 46, 50, 51, 122
Darcy, Arthur & Mary Carew 160
Darcy, Edward & Elizabeth Astley 161
Darcy, Elizabeth & James Butler 45
Darcy, Elizabeth & James Strangeways ... 261
Darcy, Isabel & John Launce 161
Darcy, John & Joan Greystoke 80
Darcy, John & Margaret Grey 79
Darcy, Margery & John Conyers 70
Darcy, Philip & Alianor Fitzhugh 79
Darcy, Richard & Eleanor Scrope 80
Darcy, Thomas & Dowsabel Tempest 80
Darcy, William & Eupheme Langton 80
Darnall 49
Daroch 68

INDEX

Darrell 7, 204, 240, 283
Darrell, Agnes & **Simon Harcourt** 128
Daundelyn, Margaret & **John Bernard** 20
Davie, Humphrey & Mary White 82
Davie, John & **Juliana Strode** 81
Dawes 132
Dawkins 285
Deighton, Frances & Richard Williams 85
Deighton, Jane & Jonathan Negus 85
Deighton, Jane & **John Lugg** 85
Deighton, John & **Jane Basset** 85
Deighton, Katherine & Samuel Hackburne . 86
Deighton, Katherine & **Thomas Dudley** 86
Deighton, Katherine & John Allin 86
De la pole (see Pole, de la) ....
Delaval 170
De la Warre (see la Warre) ....
Dennis, Eleanor & William Lygon 165
Dennis, Frances & **Thomas Lygon** 166
Dennis, Hugh & **Katherine Trye** 269
Dennis, Isabel & John Berkeley 84
Dennis, William & **Anne Berkeley** 84
Dennison 94
Denston 10
Dering, Bennett & John Fisher 104
Dering, John & **Margaret Brent** 104
Dering, Richard & Margaret Twisden 104
Despenser 105,129, 149, 192
Despenser, Anne & Hugh Hastings 98
Despenser, Edward & Anne Ferrers 62
Despenser, Edward & Elizabeth Burghersh . 62
Despenser, Elizabeth & **John Arundel** 37
Despenser, Elizabeth & Maurice Berkeley .. 82
Despenser, Hugh & **Alianor Clare** 61
Despenser, Isabel & Richard Beauchamp .. 14
Despenser, Isabel & Richard Fitzalan 55
Despenser, Isabel & Richard Beauchamp .. 211
Despenser, Margaret & Robert Ferrers ... 102
Despenser, Thomas & **Constance York** ... 211
Devereux 150, 186, 234
Devereux, Elizabeth & Richard Corbet ... 103
Devereux, Joan & **Walter Fitzwalter** 109
Devereux, Walter & **Anne Ferrers** 103
Dickens 275
Digges 47
Digges, Dudley & Mary Kempe 87
Digges, Edward & Elizabeth Page 87
Digges, Joan & **John Baynton** 11
Digges, Thomas & **Anne Saint Leger** 87
Dinham 234
Dinham, Muriel & **Edward Hastings** 98
Dinley 111
Dixwell 41
Donnett 257
Dormer 1
Dormer, Mary & **Anthony Browne** 201
Douglas[s] 76, 168
Dowrish, Grace & **Robert Gye** 124
Doyne 36
Drury 59

Drury, Anne & George Waldegrave 273
Drury, Bridget & Henry Yelverton 220
Drury, Mary & Richard Corbett 89
Drury, Robert & **Anne Calthorpe** 10
Drury, William & **Elizabeth Sothill** 89
Dryden 213
Dryden, Bridget & Francis Marbury 185
Dryden, John & **Elizabeth Cope** 185
Dudley, Edward & Cecily Willoughby 92
Dudley, Henry & _____ Ashton 92
Dudley, John & Cecily Grey 92
Dudley, Roger & Susanna Thorne 93
Dudley, Thomas & **Katherine Deighton** 86
Dudley, Thomas & Dorothy Yorke 93
Dummer 258
Dutton 208, 261
Dyer 27
Dymoke, Alice & William Skipwith 253
Dymoke, Anne & John Goodrick 26
Dymoke, Edward & Anne Tailboys 238
Dymoke, Frances & Thomas Windebank .. 238
Dymoke, Lionel & Joan Griffith 252
Dymoke, Robert & Anne Sparrow 95
Dymoke, Thomas & **Margaret Welles** 94
Dynham 48
Easton 66
Echingham 50, 266
Echingham, Anne & John Tuchet 270
Echingham, Joan & John Baynton 10
Echingham, Margaret & William Blount ... 96
Echingham, Thomas & **Margaret West** 96
Echingham, Thomas & Margaret Knyvett .. 96
Echingham, William & **Joan Arundel** 95
Edwards 215
Ellis 210
Ellis, Margaret & **Rowland Ellis** 97
Ellis, Rowland & Margaret Ellis 97
Elrington 96
Emerson 5
Empson, Joan & **Henry Sothill** 88
Engham 178
England, Edward I & Marguerite de France 227
England, Edward I & Alianore de Castille . 226
England, Edward II & Isabelle de France . 229
England, Edward III & Philippe de Hainaut 229
England, Edward IV & Elizabeth Wydeville 293
England, Edward V 293
England, Edward VI 240
England, Elizabeth & Humphrey Bohun .. 24
England, Elizabeth Tudor 47
England, Henry II & Éléonore d'Aquitaine . 222
England, Henry III & Éléonore de Provence 225
England, Henry IV & Mary Bohun 156
England, Henry V & Katherine Valois 157
England, Henry VI & Marguerite d'Anjou . 157
England, Henry VII & Elizabeth 17. 293
England, Henry VIII & Anne Boleyn 47
England, Henry VIII & Katherine Howard . 200
England, Henry VIII & Jane Seymour 240
England, Joan & Gilbert Clare 60

308

INDEX

England, Joan & Ralph Monthermer 192
England, John & Isabelle d'Angoulême ... 223
England, Maud & Geoffrey d'Anjou ... 222
England, Richard I & Berengaria 223
England, Richard II & Anne of Bohemia .. 230
England, Richard III & Anne Neville 194
Esse, Prudence & Oliver Mainwaring 183
Eure 261
Evans 98
Everingham 277
Everingham, Katherine & John Beaumont . 187
Fairfax 115
Fairfield 252
Farrar 167
Farrar, John & Cecily Kelke 100
Farrar, William & Cecily 100
Farringdon 124
Farwell, Henry & Olive Welby 276
Fastolf 234
Fauconberg 16, 70, 261
Fauconberg, Joan & William Neville 16
Felton 278
Fenne, Margaret & George Neville 211
Fenwick, John & Elizabeth Covert 101
Fenwick, John & Mary Grey 101
Fenwick, Ralph & Margery Mitford 101
Fenwick, Ralph & Barbara Ogle 101
Fenwick, Richard & Margaret Mills 101
Fenwick, Roger & Agnes Harbottle 100
Fenwick, William & Elizabeth Gargrave .. 101
ferch Dafydd, Elsbeth & Sion ap Gruffydd . 97
ferch Elissa, Catrin & Rees ap Lewys 97
ferch Griffith 238
ferch Hugh Gwynn, Sibyl & Sion ap Howell 209
ferch Humphrey, Anne & Ellis ap Rees 97
ferch Humphrey, Jane & Gruffydd ap Hywel 97
ferch Hywel, Ellin & Lewys ap Sion 97
ferch John Hord 169
ferch Maredudd 169
ferch Morus 170, 209
ferch Oliver, Mawd & Humphrey Wynne .. 169
ferch Owain, Jane & Hugh Gwynn 209
ferch Richard 169
ferch Robert 209
ferch Sion 97, 209
ferch Sion, Elizabeth & Humphrey ap Hugh 209
ferch William 169
Fermor 207
Ferreby 159
Ferrer 147
Ferrers 16, 72, 80, 83, 203, 234, 280
Ferrers, Anne & Edward Despenser 62
Ferrers, Anne & Walter Devereux 103
Ferrers, Edmund & Ellen Roche 102
Ferrers, Elizabeth & James Clerke 64
Ferrers, Elizabeth & Edward Grey 118
Ferrers, Elizabeth & William Culpeper ... 259
Ferrers, Henry & Joan 63
Ferrers, Henry & Margaret Heckstall 64
Ferrers, Henry & Isabel Verdun 63

Ferrers, Henry & Isabel Mowbray 118
Ferrers, John & Elizabeth Stafford 102
Ferrers, Margaret & Thomas Beauchamp .. 13
Ferrers, Mary & Ralph Neville 204
Ferrers, Philippe & Thomas Greene 184
Ferrers, Robert & Joan Beaufort 16
Ferrers, Robert & Margaret Despenser ... 102
Ferrers, Thomas & Elizabeth Freville 64
Ferrers, William & Philippe Clifford 64
Ferrers, William & Margaret Ufford 63
Ferrers, William & Elizabeth Belknap 102
Fiennes 24, 42, 50, 228
Fiennes, Margaret & William Lunsford ... 177
Fiennes, Richard & Joan Dacre 176
Fiennes, Thomas & Anne Urswick 177
Filliol 120
Filmer 112
Finch 289
Finch, Jane & George Wyatt 288
Fisher 65,90
Fisher, John & Elizabeth 104
Fisher, John & Bennett Dering 104
Fisher, Sarah & William Skipper 252
Fiske 276
Fitzalan 15, 17, 156, 186, 211, 244, 291
Fitzalan, Alice & Henry Beaufort 15
Fitzalan, Alice & Thomas Holand 140
Fitzalan, Edmund & Sibyl Montagu 55
Fitzalan, Elizabeth & Robert Goushill 106
Fitzalan, Elizabeth & Thomas Mowbray .. 197
Fitzalan, Joan & Humphrey Bohun 25
Fitzalan, Joan & William Beauchamp ... 106
Fitzalan, Mary & John le Strange 55
Fitzalan, Philippe & Richard Cergeaux 55
Fitzalan, Richard & Isabel Despenser 55
Fitzalan, Richard & Alianor of Lancaster . 105
Fitzalan, Richard & Elizabeth Bohun ... 106
Fitzgerald 38, 45, 46
Fitzherbert 35, 142
Fitzhugh 117, 249, 265
Fitzhugh, Alianor & Philip Darcy 79
Fitzhugh, Elizabeth & William Parr 39
Fitzhugh, Elizabeth & Nicholas Vaux 39
Fitzhugh, Elizabeth & Ralph Gray 117
Fitzhugh, Henry & Alice Neville 39
Fitzlewis 125
Fitzlewis, Elizabeth & John Wingfield 126
Fitzmaurice 242
Fitzroger 28
Fitzroy 50
Fitzwalter 56, 125, 234
Fitzwalter, Elizabeth & John Radcliffe 234
Fitzwalter, Walter & Alianor Dagworth ... 109
Fitzwalter, Walter & Joan Devereux 109
Fitzwalter, Walter & Elizabeth Chidiock .. 109
Fitzwarin 45, 109, 125
Fitzwilliam 38
Fleete, Henry & Sarah 112
Fleete, William & Deborah Scott 112
Fleming 237

INDEX

Fleming, Mary & **Thomas Leigh** 260
Flower, Anne & Robert Kaye 247
Flowerdew 144
Fludd, Katherine & Thomas Lunsford 177
Fogge 207
Foliot, Edward 165
Foliot, John & Elizabeth Aylmer 165
Foliot, Thomas & **Katherine Lygon** 165
Forster 30
Fort 152
Fortescue 9
Fortescue, Adrian & **Anne Stonor** 195
Fortescue, Margaret & **Thomas Wentworth** 130
Foulshurst 184
Fowell, Jane & **Philip Courtenay** 73
Fowler 184
Fox 213
France, Isabelle & **Edward II of England** .. 229
France, Marguerite & **Edward I of England** 227
Francis 64
Francis, Maud & **John Montagu** 193
Franklin 82
Fray 29
Freeman 65
French 44
Freville, Elizabeth & **Thomas Ferrers** 64
Frost 27
Fry 18
Fulford 54, 165
Furnivall 264
Gage, Alice & **Anthony Browne** 38
Gardiner 265
Gargrave, Elizabeth & **William Fenwick** .. 101
Garland 283
Garnon 220
Gascoigne 4
Gascoigne, Dorothy & Ninian Markenfield . 190
Gascoigne, Elizabeth & **George Tailboys** .. 238
Gascoigne, Margaret & Christopher Warde . 51
Gascoigne, William & **Margaret Percy** 238
Gascoigne, William & **Joan Neville** 204
Gaskell 161
Gaveston 5
Gawdy, Juliana & **Thomas Berney** 147
Gedney 82
Gerard 201, 269, 275
Gerard, John & Isabel 114
Gerard, Katherine & **William Torbock** ... 182
Gerard, Thomas & Jane 114
Gerard, Thomas & **Jane Legh** 113
Gerard, Thomas & Susanna Snow 114
Gerard, Thomas & **Margaret Trafford** 113
Gerard, William 113
Gibbins 189
Gibbon 272
Gibbon, Jane & **Walter Carlton** 53
Gibson 189, 275
Giffard, Cassandra & **Erasmus Wolseley** .. 284
Gilbert 85
Gill 183

Gill, Benjamin & **Mary Mainwaring** 183
Girlington, Isabel & Christopher Kelke ... 115
Girlington, William & **Katherine Hildyard** . 115
Glanville 81
Glascock 218
Glemham, Anne & Henry Palgrave 214
Glemham, John & **Eleanor Brandon** 214
Gloucester 7, 224
Gloucester, Anne & **Edmund Stafford** 7
Gloucester, Anne & William Bourgchier .. 158
Gloucester, Antigone & **Henry Grey** .. 157, 168
Gloucester, Humphrey 156
Gloucester, Thomas & **Alianor Bohun** 158
Godbold 78
Golafre 109
Goldesborough 190
Goodrick, Anne & **Benjamin Bolles** 26
Goodrick, John & **Anne Dymoke** 26
Goodrick, Lionel & Winifred Sapcott 26
Goodyer 256
Gorges 165
Gorsuch, John & **Anne Lovelace** 172
Gournay 58
Goushill 197
Goushill, Elizabeth & **Robert Wingfield** ... 163
Goushill, Joan & Thomas Stanley 107
Goushill, Robert & **Elizabeth Fitzalan** 107
Gower, Lowys & **John Pashley** 110
Grandison 8, 55, 192
Granville 48
Gray 19, 75, 79
Gray, **Maud** & Robert Ogle 206
Gray, Ralph & Jacquetta 117
Gray, Ralph & Elizabeth Fitzhugh 117
Gray, Ralph & Elizabeth 117
Gray, Thomas & Margery Greystoke 117
Gray, Thomas & **Joan Mowbray** 116
Gray, Thomas & **Alice Neville** 117
Greeke, Margaret & **William Butler** 274
Greene 35, 39, 174
Greene, Elizabeth & **George Brent** 35
Greene, Elizabeth & William Raleigh 184
Greene, Thomas & **Mary Talbot** 184
Greene, Thomas & **Philippe Ferrers** 184
Grenville 201
Gresham, Elizabeth & **John Wingfield** 164
Gresley 128, 285
Greville 84, 144, 165, 218, 290
Greville, Edward & **Jane Grey** 30
Greville, Fulke & **Elizabeth Willoughby** ... 30
Greville, Katherine & Giles Reed 34
Greville, Margaret & Godfrey Bosvile 30
Grey .. 9, 38, 73, 76, 79, 117, 162, 268, 281, 292
Grey, Alice & William Knyvett 121
Grey, Anne & **John Grey** 136
Grey, Anne & Henry Willoughby 120
Grey, Cecily & John Dudley 92
Grey, Dorothy & Robert Willoughby 216
Grey, Edmund & Florence Hastings 136
Grey, Edmund & **Katherine Percy** 135

INDEX

Grey, Edward & **Elizabeth Ferrers** 119
Grey, **Eleanor** & John Arundell 48
Grey, **Elizabeth** & Robert Greystoke 136
Grey, **Elizabeth** & Roger Kynaston 169
Grey, **Henry** & Antigone of Gloucester 157, 168
Grey, Henry & **Elizabeth** Talbot 280
Grey, **Jane** & **Edward Greville** 30
Grey, John & Anne Grey 136
Grey, John & Elizabeth Wydeville 119
Grey, John & Constance Holand 121
Grey, John & Mary Browne 120
Grey, John & **Joan Cherleton** 168
Grey, **Margaret** & William Bonville 28
Grey, **Margaret** & John Darcy 79
Grey, **Mary** & John **Fenwick** 101
Grey, Reynold & **Margaret Ros** 27
Grey, Reynold & Tacine of Somerset 281
Grey, **Richard** & Blanche 280
Grey, **Tacy** & John Gyse 136
Grey, **Thomas** & Cecily Bonville 119
Grey, **Thomas** & Margaret Wotton 120
Greyndour 142
Greystoke 23, 261, 265, 279
Greystoke, Elizabeth & **Thomas Dacre** 76
Greystoke, Joan & **John Darcy** 80
Greystoke, Margery & **Thomas Gray** 117
Greystoke, Maud & **Eudo de Welles** 277
Greystoke, Robert & **Elizabeth Grey** 136
Griffin 59
Griffith, Dorothy & William Williams 74
Griffith, Joan & **Lionel Dymoke** 252
Griffith, Sibyl & Owain ap Huw 209
Griffith, William & Jane Puleston 74
Griffith, William & Jane Stradling 74
Griffith, William & **Joan Troutbeck** 73
Groves 237
Grymes 148
Grynne 251
Guibert 114
Guildford 38, 288
Guise (see Gyse) ....
Gunton, Alice & **Thomas Palgrave** 214
Gunville 250
Gurdon, Brampton & **Muriel Sedley** 122
Gurdon, Muriel & **Richard Saltonstall** 123, 248
Gwyn 21, 239
Gwynn, Hugh & **Jane ferch Owain** 209
Gye, John & **Mary Prowse** 123
Gye, Mary & John Maverick 124
Gye, Robert & Grace Dowrish 124
Gyse, Elizabeth & Robert Haviland 137
Gyse, John & Jane Pauncefort 136
Gyse, John & **Tacy Grey** 136
Gyse, William & Mary Rotsy 136
Hackburne, Samuel & **Katherine Deighton** . 86
Hainaut, Philippe & **Edward III of England** 229
Haldenby 115, 251
Hales, Alice & **Thomas of Norfolk** 205
Hall 144
Hall, Elizabeth & Ralph Bourchier 33

Hall, **Francis** & Ursula Sherington 33
Hall, Francis & **Elizabeth Wingfield** 33
Hall, Jane & **Henry Skipwith** 253
Haltoft 138
Hammersley 35
Hammerton, Agnes & **Walter Strickland** ... 52
Hammerton, Stephen & **Elizabeth Bigod** ... 23
Hammond 70, 87
Hancock 166
Hanham 287
Hankford, Anne & **Thomas Butler** 46
Hankford, Richard & **Anne Montagu** 125
Hanmer, Sarah & **Gabriel Ludlow** 176
Harbottle 127
Harbottle, Agnes & Roger Fenwick 100
Harbottle, Bertram & Joan Lumley 127
Harbottle, Eleanor & Thomas Percy 150
Harbottle, Guiscard & Jane Willoughby ... 128
Harbottle, Ralph & Margaret Percy 127
Harbottle, Robert & **Margaret Ogle** 127
Harby, Katherine & Daniel Oxenbridge ... 213
Harby, Thomas & **Katherine Throckmorton** 213
Harcourt, Agnes & John Knyvett 122
Harcourt, Christopher & **Joan Stapleton** .. 128
Harcourt, Isabel & **Walter Wrottesley** 180
Harcourt, John & **Margaret Barentyn** 129
Harcourt, Simon & Agnes Darrell 128
Hardiman 67
Harding 33, 291
Hardres 171
Hardwick 114
Hardwick, Mary & **Richard Wingfield** 126
Harewell 59
Harington 28, 91, 107, 128, 179, 204, 278
Harington, Elizabeth & **William Bonville** ... 28
Harlakenden 31, 218
Harlakenden, Roger & **Elizabeth Bosvile** ... 31
Harleston 173
Harleston, Elizabeth & Elias Ball 132
Harleston, John & Elizabeth Willis 131
Harleston, John & **Jane Wentworth** 131
Harleston, John & Elizabeth 131
Harley 248
Harling 250
Harpeden 287
Harpesfield, John & **Joyce Mitton** 188
Harrington (see Harington) ....
Harris 75, 124, 183
Harris, Arthur & **Joan Percy** 151
Harris, Arthur & **Dorothy Waldegrave** 151
Harris, Dorothy & Robert Kempe 151
Harris, Mary & **Thomas Ligon** 166
Harris, William & Joanne Cooke 151
Hart[e] 163, 288
Hartshorn, Christian & **Robert Tyrrell** 272
Harvey 65
Harwood 246
Haselop 78
Hasilden, Frances & Robert Peyton 132
Hasilden, Francis & **Elizabeth Calthorpe** .. 132

INDEX

Haslewood, Alice & Francis Bernard 20
Hastang 6
Hastings 28, 90, 106, 121, 192, 231, 251
Hastings, Anne & Thomas Stanley 200
Hastings, Edward & Muriel Dinham 98
Hastings, Edward & Mary Hungerford ... 134
Hastings, Elizabeth & Robert Hildyard 99
Hastings, Elizabeth & Edward Somerset .. 255
Hastings, Florence & Edmund Grey 136
Hastings, Francis & Katherine Pole 255
Hastings, George & Anne Stafford 135
Hastings, Hugh & Anne Despenser 98
Hastings, John & Anne Morley 99
Hastings, Margaret & John Wingfield 162
Hastings, William & Katherine Neville 134
Hathorne, Mary & George Burroughs 44
Haudlo 233
Haute, Elizabeth & Robert Baynton 11
Haute, Jane & Thomas Wyatt 288
Haviland, Jane & William Torrey 137
Haviland, Robert & Elizabeth Gyse 137
Hawberk 286
Hawkins 172
Hay 99
Hayne 173
Haynes 75
Haynes, Elizabeth & Joseph Cooke 139
Haynes, John & Mary Thornton 138
Hayward 275
Hayward, Mary & Warham Saint Leger ... 245
Heckington 164
Heckstall, Margaret & Henry Ferrers 64
Heigham (see Higham) ....
Hele 81
Helion, Isabel & Humphrey Tyrrell 146
Hemenale 286
Herbert 19
Herbert, Anne & Humphrey ap Hywel 97
Herbert, Elizabeth & Charles Somerset 19
Herbert, Maud & Henry Percy 150
Hereford 45
Herling 234
Heron 238
Heron, Elizabeth & Robert Tailboys 262
Heronville, Joan & Henry Beaumont 187
Herring 252
Heton 206
Heydon 90
Heydon, Dorothy & Thomas Brooke 288
Heyes 111
Heylett 215
Heyman 111
Heyton 152
Heywood 189
Higginson 21
Higginson, Lucy & William Bernard 21
Higham, Bridget & Thomas Burrough 44
Higham, Thomas & Phyllis Waldegrave ... 44
Hildyard, Isabel & Ralph Legard 251
Hildyard, Katherine & William Girlington . 115

Hildyard, Peter & Joan de la See 251
Hildyard, Robert & Elizabeth Hastings 99
Hill 18, 28, 123, 170, 171
Hill, Dorothy & Philip Stapleton 258
Hill, Jane & Henry Beaufort 18
Hill, Mary & Bassingbourne Throckmorton 267
Hillary 90, 162
Hinckley 12
Hinton 260
Holand 56, 119, 125, 141, 176, 230, 257, 270, 287, 291
Holand, Alianor & Edward Cherleton 57
Holand, Alianor & Thomas Montagu 193
Holand, Alianor & Roger de Mortimer ... 232
Holand, Constance & John Grey 121
Holand, John & Elizabeth of Lancaster ... 121
Holand, Margaret & John Beaufort 17
Holand, Thomas & Alice Fitzalan 140
Holand, Thomas & Joan of Kent 139
Holes 268
Holland 150
Hollyman, Mary & William Rodney 241
Holmstead 217
Holt 46
Honford, John & Margaret Savage 113
Honford, Katherine & John Mainwaring .. 208
Honywood 112
Hoo 47, 63, 131
Hoo, Alianor & James Carew 50
Hoo, Anne & Roger Copley 278
Hoo, Thomas & Alianor de Welles 278
Hooe 78
Hooker 116
Hopton 103
Horsey 248
Horsmanden 246
Horsmanden, Daniel & Ursula Saint Leger 245
Horsmanden, Warham & Susannah Beeching 245
Hosier 180
Hoskins 67
Hough 183
Howard 9, 110, 146, 211, 259, 293
Howard, Edmund & Joyce Culpeper 199
Howard, Elizabeth & John Vere 56
Howard, Elizabeth & Thomas Boleyn 47
Howard, John & Catherine Moleyns 198
Howard, John & Margaret Chedworth 198
Howard, Katherine & John Bourgchier ... 159
Howard, Katherine & Edward Neville ... 197
Howard, Katherine & Henry VIII of England 199
Howard, Margaret & Thomas Arundell 48
Howard, Robert & Margaret Mowbray ... 197
Howard, Thomas & Elizabeth Tilney 198
Howell, Mary & Joseph Bolles 27
Hubbard 291
Huddelstone 128
Hudson 178, 283
Huggeford 34
Humphrey, Anne & John Miles 145
Humphrey, Anne & William Palmes 145

INDEX

Humphrey, John & **Elizabeth Pelham** 145
Humphrey, Owen & Margaret Vaughan ... 209
Humphrey, Samuel & Elizabeth Rees 209
Hungate 77, 174
Hungerford 84
Hungerford, Elizabeth & **Philip Courtenay** . 73
Hungerford, Katherine & **Richard West** .. 142
Hungerford, Mary & **Edward Hastings** ... 134
Hungerford, Robert & Alianor Moleyns 32
Hungerford, Robert & **Margaret Botreaux** .. 31
Hungerford, Thomas & Anne Percy 32
Hunting 86
Hussey 271
Hutchins 100
Hutchinson, William & **Anne Marbury** 186
Hutt 114
Huttof, _____ & **Thomas West** 143
Hutton, Beatrice & **James Mauleverer** 191
Hyndeston 73
Hynson 246
Ingoldisthorpe 130
Ingoldisthorpe, Edmund & **Joan Tiptoft** 58
Ingoldisthorpe, Isabel & **John Neville** 195
Irby 276
Ireland, Margaret & **Ralph Leigh** 260
Isham, Mary & **William Randolph** 237
Jackman 152
Jarratt 70
Jennings 68, 183
Jennings, Edmund & Frances Corbin 147
Jennings, Edmund & **Margaret Barkham** .. 147
Jermyn 26, 273
Jernegan 151
Jerningham 10
Jewett 53
Jewett, Sarah & **Philip Nelson** 258
Johnson 252
Johnston 98
Joinville 153
Jolye 69
Jones 66, 172, 275
Jones, Mary & **Thomas Lloyd** 170
Jones, Sarah & **William Rodney** 241
Jordan 207
Kaye, Grace & Richard Saltonstall 247
Kaye, John & **Dorothy Mauleverer** 247
Kaye, Robert & Anne Flower 247
Keayne 94
Keeble 221
Kelke 251
Kelke, Anne & Roger Leming 115
Kelke, Cecily & John Farrar 100
Kelke, Christopher & **Isabel Girlington** ... 115
Kelke, Christopher & Jane Saint Paul 115
Kelke, Christopher & Elizabeth Carr 115
Kelke, William & Thomasine Skerne 99
Kem 218
Kemish 143
Kempe 254, 267
Kempe, Amy & **Henry Skipwith** 253

Kempe, Edmund & Bridget 152
Kempe, Emelyn & **Reynold Scott** 111
Kempe, Mary & Dudley Digges 87
Kempe, Matthew 151
Kempe, Robert & Dorothy Harris 151
Kempe, Thomas & Anne 207
Kempe, Thomas & Dorothy Thompson ... 207
Kempe, Thomas & Amy Moyle 207
Kempe, William & **Eleanor Browne** 207
Kennon 22
Kent 116, 230
Kent, Edmund & Margaret Wake 228
Kent, Joan & Thomas Holand 139
Kerridge 151
Killigrew 165
Killingworth 251
Kingston 4
Kingston, Eleanor & **John Skipwith** 4
Kirkham 116, 282
Kirton 240
Knollys, Anne & **Thomas West** 143
Knollys, Francis & **Katherine Cary** 54
Knowling 275
Knyvett 51, 271
Knyvett, Abigail & Martin Sedley 122
Knyvett, Edmund & **Joan Bourgchier** 122
Knyvett, Edmund & Eleanor Tyrrell 122
Knyvett, John & Agnes Harcourt 122
Knyvett, Margaret & **Thomas Echingham** .. 96
Knyvett, William & **Alice Grey** 121
Kyme 293
Kynaston, Humphrey & Elsbeth 169
Kynaston, Jane & Roger Thornes 167
Kynaston, Margaret & John ap Ieuan 169
Kynaston, Mary & Hywel ap Jenkin 97
Kynaston, Roger & Elizabeth Grey 169
Kytchin 137
La Warre, Joan & Thomas West 141
La Warre, Roger & **Alianor Mowbray** 141
Lacer 146
Lacon, Joan & **John Mainwaring** 181
Lacy 22, 60, 100, 153
Lambert, Anne & **Thomas Nelson** 258
Lancaster 55, 56
Lancaster, Alianor & Richard Fitzalan 105
Lancaster, Alianor & John Beaumont 186
Lancaster, Blanche & John of Lancaster .. 155
Lancaster, Edmund & Blanche d'Artois ... 152
Lancaster, Elizabeth & John Holand 121
Lancaster, Henry & Maud Chaworth 153
Lancaster, Henry & Isabel Beaumont 154
Lancaster, Joan & John Mowbray 196
Lancaster, John of & Katherine Roët 15
Lancaster, John of Blanche of Lancaster .. 155
Lancaster, Mary & Henry Percy 219
Lancaster, Maud & William Burgh 43
Lane 75
Lane, Dorothy & William Randolph 236
Lane, Richard & **Elizabeth Vincent** 236
Lang 145

313

INDEX

Langley 259
Langman 36
Langrish 175
Langton 188, 284
Langton, Eupheme & **William Darcy** 80
Latham, Frances & **Jeremy Clarke** 65
Launce, John & **Isabel Darcy** 161
Launce, Mary & John Sherman 161
Layer 268
Leake 126
Learned 277
Lee 3, 50
Lee, Dorothy & Thomas Mackworth 180
Lee, Dorothy & John Temple 202
Lee, Edmund & **Dorothy Browne** 201
Lee, Mary & **Paul Abney** & **Dannett Abney** .. 3
Lee, Richard & **Eleanor Wrottesley** 180
Legard, Joan & Richard Skepper 251
Legard, Ralph & **Isabel Hildyard** 251
Legh 208
Legh, Jane & **Thomas Gerard** 113
Legh, Peter & **Eleanor Savage** 290
Leigh 199, 259
Leigh, Anne & Joseph Stockman 260
Leigh, Isabel & **Edward Baynton** 11
Leigh, John & **Elizabeth West** 260
Leigh, John & Margaret Saunders 260
Leigh, Ralph & Margaret Ireland 260
Leigh, Ralph & **Joyce Culpeper** 259
Leigh, Thomas & Mary Fleming 260
Leighton 103
Leming, Anne & William Wolley 116
Leming, Roger & **Anne Kelke** 115
Lenton 185
Leonard 267
Lestrange (see Strange) ....
Leventhorpe 142, 187
Leverett 94
Leveson 59
Lewes 18, 171
Lewis 74
Lewis, John [ap] & **Anne Montagu** 125
Lewis, Thomas & **Elizabeth Marshall** 189
Lewknor 111
Lewknor, Jane & William Barentyn 271
Lewknor, Roger & **Eleanor Tuchet** 271
Leycester 208
Ligon (see also Lygon) ....
Ligon, Thomas & Mary Harris 166
Ligon, Thomas & Elizabeth Pratt 166
Lilly 239
Limbrey, John & **Mary Bull** 41
Lisle 13, 142
Lisle, Margaret & **Thomas Berkeley** 83
Littlebury 26
Littleton 265
Littleton, Edward & Mary Walter 167
Littleton, John & **Alice Thornes** 167
Littleton, Nathaniel & Ann Southy 168
Livesay 133

Llewelyn 210
Lloyd, Charles & **Elizabeth Stanley** 170
Lloyd, John & **Catrin Wynne** 170
Lloyd, Thomas & Mary Jones 170
Locke 27
Longford 113
Longueville 286
Lort 170
Louthe 267
Lovaine 158, 186
Lovelace, Anne & John Gorsuch 172
Lovelace, William & **Elizabeth Aucher** 171
Lovelace, William & Anne Barne 172
Lovell 235
Lowe 49, 133
Lowe, Jane & **Charles Calvert** 49
Lowell 258
Lowthe, Margaret & **Richard Cornwallis** ... 78
Lowther 256
Lucy 219
Ludlam, Katherine & **Edmund Abney** 2
Ludlow, Gabriel & Sarah Hanmer 176
Ludlow, Gabriel & Martha 176
Ludlow, Gabriel & Phyllis 175
Ludlow, George & **Edith Windsor** 175
Ludlow, Roger & Mary Cogan 175
Ludlow, Sarah & John Carter 175
Ludlow, Thomas & Jane Bennett 176
Ludlow, Thomas & Jane Pyle 175
Ludwell 246
Lugg, John & **Jane Deighton** 85
Lumley, Joan & **Bertram Harbottle** 127
Lunsford 152, 221
Lunsford, John & Anne Apsley 177
Lunsford, John & **Mary Sackville** 177
Lunsford, Thomas & Katherine Fludd 177
Lunsford, Thomas & Elizabeth 178
Lunsford, William & **Margaret Fiennes** ... 177
Lunt 258
Lusignan 60
Luttrell, Andrew & **Elizabeth Courtenay** .. 173
Luttrell, Elizabeth & John Stratton 173
Luttrell, Hugh & Katherine Beaumont 173
Luxembourg 156
Lygon (see also Ligon) ....
Lygon, Anne & **Christopher Savage** 290
Lygon, Elizabeth & Edward Basset 85
Lygon, Elizabeth & William Norwood 165
Lygon, Henry & **Elizabeth Berkeley** 84
Lygon, Katherine & Thomas Foliot 165
Lygon, Thomas & **Frances Dennis** 166
Lygon, William & **Eleanor Dennis** 165
Lynford 214
Lynne 121, 164
Lyte 274
Lytton 123, 131, 174
Mablethorp 184
Mackall 285
Mackworth, Agnes & William Crowne 180
Mackworth, Richard & Dorothy Cranage .. 180

INDEX

Mackworth, Thomas & Dorothy Lee 180
Macy 86
Maddox 105
Maidstone, Margaret & **Walter Clopton** 69
Mainwaring 1, 265
Mainwaring, Arthur & Margaret Mainwaring181
Mainwaring, Cecily & John Cotton 1
Mainwaring, John & Joan Lacon 181
Mainwaring, John & **Katherine Honford** .. 208
Mainwaring, Margaret & Arthur Mainwaring181
Mainwaring, Mary & Richard Cotton 1
Mainwaring, Mary & Benjamin Gill 183
Mainwaring, Oliver & Prudence Esse 183
Mainwaring, Oliver & **Margaret Torbock** .. 182
Mainwaring, Randall & Elizabeth Brereton 208
Mainwaring, Richard & Dorothy Corbet .. 181
Mainwaring, Thomas & **Jane Sutton** 181
Mall 241
Mallet, Mary & **Robert Browne** 207
Mallory 185, 257
Maltravers, Alianor & **John Arundel** 36
Malyn 213
Manners, George & Anne Saint Leger 257
Manners, Katherine & Robert Constable .. 257
Manners, Robert & **Joan Ogle** 206
Manners, Robert & Alianor Ros 206
Manning 124
Manningham 32
Mantell 42
Manwaring, Oliver & Hannah Raymond .. 183
Maplesden 104
Marbury, Anne & William Hutchinson ... 186
Marbury, Catherine & Richard Scott 186
Marbury, Francis & **Bridget Dryden** 185
Markenfield, Alice & Robert Mauleverer .. 190
Markenfield, Ninian & **Dorothy Gascoigne** . 190
Markham 128, 253
Marmion 20
Marney, Anne & Thomas Tyrrell 146
Marney, William & **Elizabeth Cergeaux** ... 146
Marrow 40
Marshal 225
Marshall, Elizabeth & Thomas Lewis 189
Marshall, Roger & **Katherine Mitton** 188
Martiau, Elizabeth & George Reade 239
Massey 78, 109, 269
Masterson 59
Mathew 74
Mauleverer 23
Mauleverer, Anne & John Abbott 191
Mauleverer, Dorothy & John Kaye 247
Mauleverer, Edmund & Anne Pearson 191
Mauleverer, Edmund & Mary Danby 190
Mauleverer, James & Beatrice Hutton ... 191
Mauleverer, Robert & **Alice Markenfield** .. 190
Mauleverer, William & Eleanor Aldburgh . 190
Mauntell 20
Mauny 205
Maverick 215, 252
Maverick, John & **Mary Gye** 124

Mayo 246
Mead, Isabel & **Maurice Berkeley** 84
Medford 210
Medley 120
Merbury 103
Mercer, Helena & **James Claypoole** 67
Merston 21
Messant 271
Michel 138
Middleton 23, 206
Milborne 269
Miles, John & **Anne Humphrey** 145
Miles, Katherine & **Rowland Coytemore** ... 75
Milliton 73
Mills 69
Mills, Margaret & **Richard Fenwick** 101
Mitford, Barbara & **Hawte Wyatt** 289
Mitford, Margery & **Ralph Fenwick** 101
Mitton, Edward & Anne Skrimshire 188
Mitton, John & **Constance Beaumont** 188
Mitton, Joyce & John Harpesfield 188
Mitton, Katherine & Roger Marshall 188
Mohun 109, 292
Moleyns, Alianor & **Robert Hungerford** 32
Moleyns, Catherine & **John Howard** 198
Molyneux, Joan & **Adam Troutbeck** 269
Monboucher 127
Monceaux 250
Montagu 64, 107, 140, 197, 205
Montagu, Alice & Richard Neville 193
Montagu, Anne & Richard Hankford 125
Montagu, Anne & John [ap] Lewis 125
Montagu, John & Maud Francis 193
Montagu, John & **Margaret Monthermer** .. 192
Montagu, Sibyl & **Edmund Fitzalan** 55
Montagu, Thomas & Alianor Holand 193
Montfort 90, 225
Montgomery 46
Monthermer, Margaret & John Montagu .. 192
Monthermer, Ralph & **Joan of England** ... 192
Monthermer, Thomas & Margaret 192
Moore 104, 170, 175, 182
Moore, Elizabeth & **Thomas Torbock** 182
Mordaunt 207
Morgan 172
Morley 98
Morley, Anne & John Hastings 99
Morley, Thomas & **Isabel Pole** 233
Mornington, Sibyl & **Edward Trye** 269
Mortimer 5, 6, 8, 13, 19, 25, 42, 57, 106, 143, 205, 234
Mortimer, Anne & Richard of York 292
Mortimer, Edmund & **Philippe of Clarence** 231
Mortimer, Elizabeth & Henry Percy 148
Mortimer, Roger & Alianor de Holand ... 232
Morton, Elizabeth & **George West** 143
Moseley 248, 285
Moss 70
Mottrom, Anne & **St. Leger Codd** 246
Mounteney 122

INDEX

Mowbray 121, 211, 280, 293
Mowbray, Alianor & Roger la Warre 141
Mowbray, Alianor & John de Welles 277
Mowbray, Isabel & James Berkeley 83
Mowbray, Isabel & Henry Ferrers 118
Mowbray, Joan & Thomas Gray 116
Mowbray, John & Elizabeth Segrave 196
Mowbray, John & Joan of Lancaster 196
Mowbray, Margaret & Robert Howard ... 197
Mowbray, Thomas & Elizabeth Fitzalan .. 197
Moyle 64, 183
Moyle, Amy & Thomas Kempe 207
Moyne, Joan & Thomas Arundel 37
Mudd 35
Mullett 285
Multon 219
Mundeford 146
Muscote, Cecily & John Bernard 20
Musgrave 180
Mynne 49
Nanton 111
Navarre 156
Naylor 212
Neale 36, 183
Needham, Dorothy & Richard Chetwode ... 59
Needham, Robert & Frances Aston 265
Needham, Thomas & Anne Talbot 265
Negus, Jonathan & Jane Deighton 85
Nelson, John & Elizabeth Taylor 202
Nelson, Margaret & Thomas Teackle 202
Nelson, Philip & Sarah Jewett 258
Nelson, Robert & Mary Temple 202
Nelson, Thomas & Dorothy Stapleton 258
Nelson, Thomas & Anne Lambert 258
Nevet 101
Neville 7, 16, 19, 52, 71, 80, 84, 101, 130, 148, 157, 178, 179, 238, 263, 279, 292, 294
Neville, Alianor & Thomas Stanley 107
Neville, Alianor & Henry Percy 149
Neville, Alice & John Conyers 70
Neville, Alice & Henry Fitzhugh 39
Neville, Alice & Thomas Gray 117
Neville, Anne & Humphrey Stafford 7
Neville, Anne & William Stonor 195
Neville, Anne & Richard III of England ... 194
Neville, Cecily & Richard Plantagenet 292
Neville, Edward & Elizabeth Beauchamp .. 211
Neville, Edward & Eleanor Windsor 212
Neville, Edward & Katherine Howard ... 198
Neville, Elizabeth & Christopher Danby ... 29
Neville, Elizabeth & Thomas Berkeley 104
Neville, Elizabeth & Richard Strangeways . 261
Neville, George & Elizabeth Beauchamp ... 14
Neville, George & Margaret Fenne 211
Neville, George & Mary Stafford 244
Neville, Henry & Joan Bourgchier 29
Neville, Isabel & George Plantagenet 294
Neville, Jane & Henry Pole 255
Neville, Joan & William Gascoigne 204
Neville, John & Elizabeth Newmarch 204

Neville, John & Isabel Ingoldisthorpe 194
Neville, Katherine & William Bonville 28
Neville, Katherine & Walter Strickland 51
Neville, Katherine & William Hastings 134
Neville, Katherine & Robert Tanfield 235
Neville, Katherine & Clement Throckmorton 212
Neville, Lucy & Anthony Browne 38
Neville, Margaret & Edward Willoughby ... 30
Neville, Margaret & Henry Percy 219
Neville, Margaret & Richard le Scrope ... 249
Neville, Margaret & John Brooke 287
Neville, Maud & John Talbot 264
Neville, Philippe & Thomas Dacre 76
Neville, Ralph & Joan Beaufort 16
Neville, Ralph & Anne Warde 51
Neville, Ralph & Mary Ferrers 204
Neville, Ralph & Margaret Stafford 203
Neville, Richard & Anne Stafford 29
Neville, Richard & Alice Montagu 194
Neville, Richard & Anne Beauchamp 194
Neville, Ursula & Warham Saint Leger ... 244
Neville, William & Joan Fauconberg 16
Newberry 66
Newcomen, Eleanor & William Asfordby 4
Newcomen, John & Mary Skipwith 4
Newenham 40, 59
Newman 185
Newmarch, Elizabeth & John Neville 204
Newton 19
Newton, Ellen & Edward Carlton 53
Nicholson 185
Norfolk, Margaret & John Segrave 205
Norfolk, Thomas & Alice Hales 205
Norreys 195, 198
Norris 170
North, Christian & William Somerset 19
Norton 52, 178, 188, 269
Norwich 63
Norwood 245
Norwood, Richard & Elizabeth Stuard 166
Norwood, William & Elizabeth Lygon 165
Nowell 41, 187
Ogle, Barbara & Ralph Fenwick 101
Ogle, Joan & Robert Manners 206
Ogle, Margaret & Robert Harbottle 127
Ogle, Robert & Maud Gray 206
Oldcastell 287
Oldton 172
Oliver 143
Onley, Mary & George Cotton 1
Orreby 219
Orrell 261
Osborne, Alice & John Peyton 133
Oughtred 281
Owen 210, 270
Owen, Joshua & Martha Shinn 210
Owen, Mary & John Wingfield 283
Owen, Rebecca & Robert Owen 210
Owen, Robert & Rebecca Owen 210
Oxenbridge 145

316

INDEX

Oxenbridge, Daniel & **Katherine Harby** ... 213
Oxenbridge, John & Frances Woodward .. 213
Oxenbridge, Malyn & **Richard Carew** 50
Pacy 94
Page 88
Page, Elizabeth & **Edward Digges** 87
Palgrave, Edward 214
Palgrave, Henry & **Anne Glemham** 214
Palgrave, Richard & Anna 215
Palgrave, Thomas & Alice Gunton 214
Palmer 183
Palmes, William & **Anne Humphrey** 145
Paratt 19
Park 234
Parke 276
Parker 124, 147
Parmenter 86
Parr 59
Parr, Elizabeth & Nicholas Wodhull 40
Parr, Mabel & **Humphrey Dacre** 76
Parr, William & **Elizabeth Fitzhugh** 39
Parr, William & Mary Salisbury 40
Pashley, Anne & Edward Tyrrell 77
Pashley, Elizabeth & Reynold Pympe 110
Pashley, John & Lowys Gower 110
Pashley, John & Elizabeth Wydeville 110
Pashley, Robert & **Philippe Cergeaux** 110
Paston 18, 50
Pateshull 72
Paulet 282
Paulet, John & **Elizabeth Willoughby** 216
Paulet, Mary & **Henry Cromwell** 282
Pauncefort, Jane & **John Gyse** 136
Payne 11
Pearson, Anne & **Edmund Mauleverer** 191
Pelham 31, 177, 247, 271
Pelham, Edward & Freelove Arnold 218
Pelham, Elizabeth & John Humphrey 145
Pelham, Herbert & **Elizabeth West** 144
Pelham, Herbert & Jemima Waldegrave .. 217
Pelham, Herbert & **Elizabeth Bosvile** ... 217
Pelham, Herbert & **Penelope West** 217
Pelham, Penelope & Josiah Winslow 218
Peniston 39
Pennington 51
Pennyton 20
Perch 189
Percy 63, 109, 203
Percy, Anne & **Thomas Hungerford** 32
Percy, Eleanor & **Edward Stafford** 244
Percy, Elizabeth & John Clifford 179
Percy, Henry & Alianor Neville 149
Percy, Henry & **Elizabeth Mortimer** 148
Percy, Henry & Alianor Poynings 149
Percy, Henry & Maud Herbert 150
Percy, Henry & **Mary of Lancaster** 219
Percy, Henry & Margaret Neville 219
Percy, Henry Algernon & **Katherine Spencer** 150
Percy, Joan & Arthur Harris 151
Percy, Katherine & Edmund Grey 135

Percy, Margaret & **Ralph Harbottle** 128
Percy, Margaret & **William Gascoigne** 238
Percy, Ralph & Eleanor Acton 149
Percy, Thomas & **Eleanor Harbottle** 150
Perkins, Elizabeth & **Thomas Bolles** 26
Peryent 131
Peverell 31, 73, 286
Pew 166
Peynston 54
Peyton 114, 254
Peyton, Alice & John Peyton 133
Peyton, Anne & George Brent 35
Peyton, Edward & Jane Calthorpe 133
Peyton, John & Alice Osborne 133
Peyton, John & **Alice Peyton** 133
Peyton, Robert & Elizabeth Rich 133
Peyton, Robert & **Frances Hasilden** 132
Peyton, Robert & Mary 221
Peyton, Thomas & Elizabeth Yelverton ... 221
Phelip 193
Philipps 237, 252
Philipson, Anne & **Thomas Arundell** 49
Pickering 271
Pierrepoint 89
Pike, Sarah & **John Stockman** 260
Pinner 66
Pipard 83
Pitnam 27
Place 52
Plantagenet, Anne & Thomas Saint Leger . 257
Plantagenet, George & Isabel Neville 294
Plantagenet, Margaret & Richard Pole ... 254
Plantagenet, Richard & Cecily Neville 292
Plaunche 162
Playters 69
Plumpton 204
Plumpton, Elizabeth & John Sothill 88
Plumpton, William & **Elizabeth Clifford** ... 88
Pole 81, 271, 294
Pole, de la 17, 58, 193, 195
Pole, Henry & Jane Neville 255
Pole, Isabel & Thomas Morley 233
Pole, Joan & Reynold Braybrooke 286
Pole, John & **Joan Cobham** 286
Pole, Katherine & **Miles Stapleton** 9
Pole, Katherine & Francis Hastings 255
Pole, Michael & **Katherine Stafford** 233
Pole, Philippe & Hugh Burnell 233
Pole, Richard & **Margaret Plantagenet** ... 254
Poley 130, 151
Polsted 123
Pontesbury......................... 1
Pope, Anne & **John Washington** 275
Port 113
Porteus 148
Powell 97, 172
Power 66
Poynings 106
Poynings, Agnes & **William Bardolf** 8
Poynings, Alianor & **Henry Percy** 149

INDEX

Poyntz 19, 103
Pratt, Elizabeth & **Thomas Ligon** 166
Pressen 116
Preston 144, 170, 172
Price 177
Prior 65
Prout 161
Provence, Éléonore & **Henry III of England** 225
Prowse, Mary & John Gye 123
Prowse, Thomas & **Joan Baynton** 123
Puleston, Jane & **William Griffith** 74
Purefoy 93
Pye 267
Pyle, Jane & **Thomas Ludlow** 175
Pympe, Anne & John Scott 111
Pympe, Reynold & **Elizabeth Pashley** 110
Pynchon, John & **Amy Wyllys** 291
Quarles, Margery & **Robert Wingfield** 164
Quinten 41
Radcliffe 94
Radcliffe, Jane & **Anthony Browne** 200
Radcliffe, John & Margaret Whetehill 234
Radcliffe, John & Elizabeth Fitzwalter 234
Radcliffe, John & **Katherine Burnell** 234
Radcliffe, Robert & **Margaret Stanley** 200
Rainesford, Julian & **William Waldegrave** . 273
Rainsborough 75
Raleigh 27, 40
Raleigh, Bridget & John Cope 185
Raleigh, Edward & Anne Chamberlain ... 184
Raleigh, Edward & Margaret Verney 184
Raleigh, Mary & Nicholas Wodhull 58
Raleigh, William & **Elizabeth Greene** 184
Ramsden 247
Randolph, Henry & Judith Soane 236
Randolph, Henry & Elizabeth 236
Randolph, Richard & Elizabeth Ryland ... 237
Randolph, William & Mary Isham 237
Randolph, William & **Dorothy Lane** 236
Rawley 267
Ray 183
Raymond, Hannah & **Oliver Manwaring** .. 183
Raynsford 32
Read, Margaret & **John Berney** 147
Reade, George & Elizabeth Martiau 239
Reade, Robert & **Mildred Windebank** 239
Redshaw 26
Redvers 152
Reed, Elizabeth & Richard Brent 34
Reed, Giles & **Katherine Greville** 34
Rees 209
Rees, Elizabeth & **Samuel Humphrey** 209
Revett 78
Reynell 82
Rich 171
Rich, Elizabeth & **Robert Peyton** 133
Richards 183
Richardson, Ursula & **William Yelverton** .. 221
Richers, Frances & Edmond Cushin 138
Richers, Henry & Cecily Tillys 138

Richers, John & **Elizabeth Stapleton** 137
Richers, John & Elizabeth Batchcroft 138
Righton 67
Risby, Elizabeth & **Henry Wingfield** 127
Roberts 210, 221, 236, 253
Robins 168
Robinson, Mary & **Edward Skepper** 251
Roche 10
Roche, Ellen & **Edmund Ferrers** 102
Rochford 23, 214
Rodney 166
Rodney, John & **Jane Seymour** 240
Rodney, William & Sarah Jones 241
Rodney, William & Mary Hollyman 241
Rodney, William & Rachel 241
Rodney, William & Alice Caesar 240
Roët, Katherine & John of Lancaster 15
Rogers 85, 237, 270
Rokes, Elizabeth & **Henry Wingfield** 163
Rokesley 8, 18
Rolston 70
Roper, Margaret & **Henry Appleton** 272
Ros 18, 31, 46, 121, 219, 238, 277, 292
Ros, Alianor & **Robert Manners** 206
Ros, Elizabeth & Thomas de Clifford 242
Ros, Margaret & Reynold Grey 27
Ros, Margaret & James Tuchet 270
Ros, Thomas & **Alianor Beauchamp** 243
Ros, Thomas & **Beatrice de Stafford** 242
Ros, Thomas & **Philippe Tiptoft** 243
Ros, William & **Margaret de Arundel** 242
Rotsy, Mary & **William Gyse** 136
Rowson 114
Roydon 104
Rugge 142, 282
Rumbold 275
Russell 162, 214
Russell, Anne & **Henry Somerset** 255
Russell, Elizabeth & **Robert Wingfield** 163
Rutter 151
Ryder 240
Ryland, Elizabeth & **Richard Randolph** ... 237
Rymer 114
Sacheverell 134
Sackville 216
Sackville, John & **Margaret Boleyn** 47
Sackville, Mary & John Lunsford 177
Sailbanks 252
Saint Aubyn 56
Saint Clere 128
Saint John 17, 23, 72, 83, 254, 278
Saint John, Elizabeth & **John le Scrope** ... 250
Saint Leger 63, 246
Saint Leger, Anne & Thomas Digges 87
Saint Leger, Anne & George Manners 257
Saint Leger, Anthony & **Mary Scott** 245
Saint Leger, Katherine & Thomas Culpeper 245
Saint Leger, Mary & William Codd 246
Saint Leger, Thomas & **Anne Plantagenet** . 257
Saint Leger, Ursula & Daniel Horsmanden 245

318

INDEX

Saint Leger, Warham & Ursula Neville ... 244
Saint Leger, Warham & Mary Hayward ... 245
Saint Lo 31
Saint Mawr 90
Saint Paul 276
Saint Paul, Jane & Christopher Kelke 115
Salisbury 97
Salisbury 59
Salisbury, Mary & William Parr 40
Saltmarsh 71
Saltonstall, Richard & Grace Kaye 247
Saltonstall, Richard & Muriel Gurdon 123, 248
Salusbury 74
Sandon 4
Sandys 49, 80, 160, 172, 202, 289
Sapcott, Elizabeth & Thomas Burnaby 41
Sapcott, Winifred & Lionel Goodrick 26
Saunders, Margaret & John Leigh 260
Saunders, Mary & Robert Beville 22
Saunders, Nicholas & Isabel Carew 21
Savage, Bridget & Anthony Bonner 290
Savage, Christopher & Anne Lygon 290
Savage, Christopher & Anne Stanley 290
Savage, Eleanor & Peter Legh 290
Savage, John & Katherine Stanley 289
Savage, Margaret & John Honford 113
Savage, Margaret & Edmund Trafford 113
Sawyer 256
Saxby 236
Saxby, Mary & James Clerke 65
Say, Anne & Henry Wentworth 130
Scotland 17, 225, 226, 229
Scotland, James I & Joan Beaufort 17
Scott 65, 70, 132, 213
Scott, Charles & Jane Wyatt 112
Scott, Deborah & William Fleete 112
Scott, John & Anne Pympe 111
Scott, Mary & Anthony Saint Leger 245
Scott, Reynold & Emelyn Kempe 111
Scott, Reynold & Mary Tuke 111
Scott, Richard & Catherine Marbury 186
Scott, Thomas & Elizabeth Baker 111
Scrope 23, 30, 130, 212, 265
Scrope, Alice & James Strangeways 261
Scrope, Eleanor & Richard Darcy 80
Scrope, Elizabeth & John Bigod 22
Scrope, Elizabeth & Henry le Scrope 249
Scrope, Henry & Elizabeth le Scrope 249
Scrope, John & Elizabeth Saint John 249
Scrope, Margaret & John Bernard 20
Scrope, Mary & William Conyers 71
Scrope, Richard & Margaret Neville 249
Seckford 163
Sedascue 31
Sedley, Martin & Abigail Knyvett 122
Sedley, Muriel & Brampton Gurdon 122
See, Joan & Peter Hildyard 251
See, Martin & Elizabeth Wentworth 250
Segrave 62, 63
Segrave, Elizabeth & John Mowbray 196

Segrave, John & Margaret of Norfolk 205
Seneschal 55
Sergeaux (see Cergeaux) ....
Sewall 35
Seymour 35, 216
Seymour, Elizabeth & Gregory Cromwell . 281
Seymour, Henry & Barbara Wolfe 240
Seymour, Jane & Henry VIII of England .. 240
Seymour, Jane & John Rodney 240
Seymour, John & Margery Wentworth 239
Shakerley 33
Shaver 26
Sheldon 290
Shelton 122, 152
Sheppard 68, 75
Sherington 257
Sherington, Ursula & Francis Hall 33
Sherley 245
Sherman, John & Mary Launce 161
Shield 67
Shinn, Martha & Joshua Owen 210
Shirley 144
Shoyswell 96
Shubrick 132
Simpson 161
Skepper, Edward & Mary Robinson 251
Skepper, Richard & Joan Legard 251
Skerne, Thomasine & William Kelke 100
Skinner 288, 290
Skipper, William & Sarah Fisher 252
Skipwith 152
Skipwith, Diana & Edward Dale 254
Skipwith, Grey & Elizabeth 254
Skipwith, Henry & Amy Kempe 253
Skipwith, Henry & Jane Hall 253
Skipwith, John & Eleanor Kingston 4
Skipwith, Mary & John Newcomen 4
Skipwith, William & Margaret Cave 253
Skipwith, William & Alice Dymoke 253
Skrimshire, Anne & Edward Mitton 188
Slye 114
Smith 65, 151, 152, 236
Smith, Anne & Anthony Wodhull 59
Smith, Anne & Robert Thornton 138
Smith, Richard & Maria Johanna Somerset 256
Snow 114
Snow, Susanna & Thomas Gerard 114
Soane, Judith & Henry Randolph 236
Somerset 49
Somerset, Charles & Elizabeth Herbert 19
Somerset, Charles & Catherine Baskerville 256
Somerset, Edward & Elizabeth Hastings .. 255
Somerset, Henry & Elizabeth Browne 19
Somerset, Henry & Anne Russell 255
Somerset, John & Mary Arundell 256
Somerset, Maria Johanna & Richard Smith 256
Somerset, Tacine & Reynold Grey 281
Somerset, William & Christian North 19
Sone 151
Sotheron 267

INDEX

Sothill 257
Sothill, Elizabeth & William Drury 89
Sothill, Henry & Joan Empson 88
Sothill, John & Elizabeth Plumpton 88
Southcote 81
Southwell 147, 288
Southy, Ann & Nathaniel Littleton 168
Spalding 277
Sparrow, Anne & Robert Dymoke 95
Sparrow, Frances & George Burrough 44
Speke 114
Spencer 89, 123, 185
Spencer, Katherine & Henry Algernon Percy 150
Spencer, Margaret & Thomas Cary 54
Spencer, Robert & Alianor Beaufort 53
Spurway 183
Squire 19
St. (see Saint)
Stafford 6, 12, 17, 20, 83, 108, 117, 119, 121, 154,
   158, 200, 216, 263
Stafford, Anne & Richard Neville 29
Stafford, Anne & George Hastings 135
Stafford, Beatrice & Thomas de Ros 242
Stafford, Edmund & Anne of Gloucester 7
Stafford, Edward & Eleanor Percy 244
Stafford, Elizabeth & John Ferrers 102
Stafford, Henry & Katherine Wydeville 7
Stafford, Hugh & Philippe Beauchamp 6
Stafford, Humphrey & Margaret Beaufort ... 7
Stafford, Humphrey & Anne Neville 7
Stafford, Joan & John Cherleton 57
Stafford, Katherine & John Sutton 90
Stafford, Katherine & Michael de la Pole . 233
Stafford, Margaret & George Vere 56
Stafford, Margaret & Ralph Neville 203
Stafford, Mary & George Neville 244
Stafford, Ralph & Margaret Audley 5
Standish 64
Stanford 2
Stanford, Elizabeth & William Cornwallis .. 77
Stanley 17, 113, 136, 188
Stanley, Anne & John Wolseley 284
Stanley, Anne & Christopher Savage 290
Stanley, Elizabeth & Charles Lloyd 170
Stanley, George & Joan Strange 108
Stanley, George & Eleanor Sutton 283
Stanley, John & Elizabeth Weever 182
Stanley, Katherine & John Savage 289
Stanley, Margaret & Robert Radcliffe 200
Stanley, Margaret & William Troutbeck .. 268
Stanley, Margery & William Torbock 182
Stanley, Thomas & Alianor Neville 107
Stanley, Thomas & Joan Goushill 107
Stanley, Thomas & Anne Hastings 200
Stanton 66
Staple 67
Stapledon 125
Stapleton 9, 88
Stapleton, Brian & Cecily Bardolf 9
Stapleton, Brian & Isabel 137

Stapleton, Dorothy & Thomas Nelson 258
Stapleton, Elizabeth & William Calthorpe ... 9
Stapleton, Elizabeth & John Richers 137
Stapleton, Joan & Christopher Harcourt .. 128
Stapleton, Miles & Katherine Pole 9
Stapleton, Philip & Dorothy Hill 258
Stapleton, Robert & Katherine Constable . 257
Stavely, Isabel & William Tanfield 236
Stedman 139
Stephens 246
Stewart 17
Stith 237
Stockhay 173
Stockman, John & Sarah Pike 260
Stockman, Joseph & Anne Leigh 260
Stokker 212
Stoner 271
Stonnard 218
Stonor, Anne & Adrian Fortescue 195
Stonor, William & Anne Neville 195
Stourton 17
Stout 267
Stradling 15
Stradling, Edward & Joan Beaufort 15
Stradling, Jane & William Griffith 74
Strange .. 27, 102, 153, 169, 187, 197, 234, 279
Strange, Ankaret & Richard Talbot 263
Strange, Elizabeth & William West 143
Strange, Joan & George Stanley 108
Strange, John & Mary Fitzalan 55
Strangeways, James & Alice le Scrope 261
Strangeways, James & Elizabeth Darcy ... 261
Strangeways, Joan & John Bigod 23
Strangeways, Joan & William Willoughby . 279
Strangeways, Richard & Elizabeth Neville . 261
Strangwishe 29
Stratton, Elizabeth & John Andrews 174
Stratton, John & Elizabeth Luttrell 173
Strecche 173
Strelley 21
Strickland 80
Strickland, Ellen & John Carleton 52
Strickland, Walter & Katherine Neville 51
Strickland, Walter & Agnes Hammerton ... 52
Strode, Juliana & John Davie 81
Strode, Richard & Frances Cromwell 81
Strode, William & Elizabeth Courtenay ... 73
Strode, William & Mary Southcott 81
Stuard, Elizabeth & Richard Norwood ... 166
Stubbs, Dionysia & William Yelverton ... 220
Stumpe 12
Style, Rebecca & Nathaniel Burrough 44
Sulliard 1, 11
Sulliard, Anne & Roger Appleton 272
Sulliard, John & Anne Andrews 174
Sulliard, Mary & John Cornwallis 77
Sutcliffe, Elizabeth & William Clopton 69
Sutton 19, 57
Sutton, Dorothy & Richard Wrottesley ... 180
Sutton, Edmund & Joyce Tiptoft 91

INDEX

Sutton, Eleanor & George Stanley 283
Sutton, Jane & Thomas Mainwaring 181
Sutton, John & Elizabeth Berkeley 91
Sutton, John & Joan 90
Sutton, John & Katherine Stafford 90
Sutton, John & Constance Blount 90
Sutton, John & _____ Charroll 274
Sutton, Margaret & John Butler 274
Swan 237
Swift 143
Swinborne 110
Swineshead 188
Swinfen 264
Swinford 79
Swinnerton 188
Swynford 15
Sydnor 147
Tabb 221
Tailboys 199
Tailboys, Anne & Edward Dymoke 238
Tailboys, George & Elizabeth Gascoigne .. 238
Tailboys, Maud & Robert Tyrwhit 276
Tailboys, Robert & Elizabeth Heron 262
Tailboys, William & Elizabeth Bonville ... 262
Talbot 31, 57, 58, 84, 201, 257, 275
Talbot, Anne & Thomas Needham 265
Talbot, Anne & Henry Vernon 264
Talbot, Elizabeth & Henry Grey 280
Talbot, Gilbert & Pernel Butler 263
Talbot, Gilbert & Audrey Cotton 265
Talbot, John & Elizabeth Butler 264
Talbot, John & Margaret Troutbeck 265
Talbot, John & Maud Neville 264
Talbot, Mary & Thomas Greene 184
Talbot, Richard & Ankaret le Strange 263
Talcott 139
Tallakarne 112
Tame 185
Tanfield, Anne & Clement Vincent 236
Tanfield, Francis & Bridget Cave 236
Tanfield, Robert & Katherine Neville 235
Tanfield, Robert & Elizabeth Brooke 235
Tanfield, William & Isabel Stavely 236
Tanner 166
Tattershall 136
Taylor 40, 82
Taylor, Elizabeth & John Nelson 202
Teackle, Thomas & Margaret Nelson 202
Tempest 52
Tempest, Dowsabel & Thomas Darcy 80
Temple, John & Dorothy Lee 202
Temple, Mary & Robert Nelson 202
Tendring 197
Teyes 192
Thacher 213
Thatcher 145, 217
Thimbleby, Elizabeth & Thomas Welby ... 276
Thimbleby, Richard & Katherine Tyrwhit . 276
Thomas 256
Thompson 36

Thompson, Dorothy & Thomas Kempe ... 207
Thomson 274
Thorley 56
Thorley, Margaret & Reynold West 142
Thorne, Susanna & Roger Dudley 93
Thornes, Alice & John Littleton 167
Thornes, John & Elizabeth Astley 167
Thornes, Richard 167
Thornes, Roger & Jane Kynaston 167
Thornton 101
Thornton, Mary & John Haynes 138
Thornton, Robert & Anne Smith 138
Thornton, William & Elizabeth Cushin ... 138
Throckmorton, Bassingbourne & Mary Hill 267
Throckmorton, Clement & Katherine Neville 212
Throckmorton, George & Katherine Vaux .. 40
Throckmorton, John & Rebecca 267
Throckmorton, Katherine & Thomas Harby 213
Throckmorton Lionel & Eliza' Blennerhasset 266
Thurston 66
Thymelthorpe 133
Tibetot (see also Tiptoft) 249
Tillys, Cecily & Henry Richers 138
Tilney 259
Tilney, Elizabeth & Humphrey Bourgchier 159
Tilney, Elizabeth & Thomas Howard 198
Tiptoft (see also Tibetot) 92, 142, 179
Tiptoft, Joan & Edmund Ingoldisthorpe 58
Tiptoft, John & Joyce Cherleton 58
Tiptoft, Joyce & Edmund Sutton 91
Tiptoft, Philippe & Thomas Ros 243
Todd 1, 21, 172
Tolliot 31
Toppan 12
Torbock, Margaret & Oliver Mainwaring .. 182
Torbock, Thomas & Elizabeth Moore 182
Torbock, William & Katherine Gerard ... 182
Torbock, William & Margery Stanley 182
Torrey, William & Jane Haviland 137
Townley 251
Townshend 78, 275, 282
Trafford 208
Trafford, Edmund & Margaret Savage 113
Trafford, Margaret & Thomas Gerard 113
Trevor 259
Troutbeck, Adam & Joan Molyneux 269
Troutbeck, Joan & William Griffith 73
Troutbeck, Margaret & John Talbot 265
Troutbeck, William & Margaret Stanley .. 268
Troye 199
Trusbut 39
Trye, Edward & Sibyl Mornington 269
Trye, Katherine & Hugh Dennis 269
Trye, William & Isabel Berkeley 269
Trye, William & Anne Baynham 269
Tubb 161
Tuchet 211
Tuchet, Anne & John Wingfield 126
Tuchet, Constance & Robert Whitney 270
Tuchet, Eleanor & Roger Lewknor 271

INDEX

Tuchet, Constance & Robert Whitney 270
Tuchet, Eleanor & Roger Lewknor 271
Tuchet, Elizabeth & **Edward Brooke** 287
Tuchet, James & **Margaret de Ros** 270
Tuchet, John & **Anne Echingham** 270
Tucker 114
Tudor 8, 17, 108, 293
Tudor, Edmund & Margaret Beaufort 17
Tuke, Mary & **Reynold Scott** 111
Tunstall 39, 51, 76, 79, 116,
Turner 245
Turpine 282
Twigden, Amphyllis & **Lawrence Washington** 275
Twisden, Margaret & **Richard Dering** 104
Twisleton 258
Tye 96
Tyng 94
Tyng, William & **Elizabeth Coytemore** 75
Tyrrell 89, 202
Tyrrell, Anne & **Richard Wentworth** 130
Tyrrell, Anne & Roger Wentworth 146
Tyrrell, Edward & **Anne Pashley** 77
Tyrrell, Eleanor & **Edmund Knyvett** 122
Tyrrell, Humphrey & Isabel Helion 146
Tyrrell, Joyce & Thomas Appleton 272
Tyrrell, Philippe & Thomas Cornwallis 77
Tyrrell, Robert & Christian Hartshorn 271
Tyrrell, Thomas & **Anne Marney** 146
Tyrwhit 115, 253
Tyrwhit, Katherine & Richard Thimbleby . 276
Tyrwhit, Robert & **Maud Tailboys** 276
Ufflete 107, 197
Ufford 9, 43, 76
Ufford, Margaret & **William Ferrers** 63
Ughtred 216
Umfreville 36, 63, 219
Upton, Elizabeth & **Edward Cromwell** 282
Urswick, Anne & **Thomas Fiennes** 177
Uvedale 201
Valois, Katherine & Henry V of England .. 157
Vanderheyden 148
Vaughan 37, 65, 103, 136, 270
Vaughan, Margaret & **Owen Humphrey** ... 209
Vaux, Katherine & George Throckmorton .. 40
Vaux, Nicholas & **Elizabeth Fitzhugh** 39
Verdun, Isabel & Henry Ferrers 63
Verdun, Theobald & **Elizabeth Clare** 42
Vere 109, 125, 196, 234
Vere, Elizabeth & **Anthony Wingfield** 126
Vere, George & Margaret Stafford 56
Vere, John & Elizabeth Howard 56
Vere, Margaret & **Henry Beaumont** 186
Vere, Richard & **Alice Cergeaux** 56
Verney, Margaret & **Edward Raleigh** 184
Vernon, Elizabeth & Robert Corbet 103
Vernon, Henry & **Anne Talbot** 264
Vicarage 132
Vincent, Clement & **Anne Tanfield** 236
Vincent, Elizabeth & Richard Lane 236
Visconti 140

Vosper 81
Wade 94
Wake 14, 154, 230
Wake, Anne & **Philip Courtenay** 72
Wake, Margaret & **Edmund of Kent** 228
Waldegrave 152
Waldegrave, Dorothy & **Arthur Harris** 151
Waldegrave, Edward & Joan Ackworth 68
Waldegrave, George & **Anne Drury** 273
Waldegrave, Jemima & **Herbert Pelham** .. 217
Waldegrave, Margaret & William Clopton .. 69
Waldegrave, Phyllis & Thomas Higham 44
Waldegrave, William & Julian Rainesford . 273
Walden 234
Walker 70, 161
Waller 27
Walley 172
Walpole 253
Walsh 136
Walter, Mary & **Edward Littleton** 168
Walthall 166
Walton 56
Walwin 146
Wandsford 51
Ward 68, 248
Warde, Anne & Ralph Neville 51
Warde, Christopher & **Margaret Gascoigne** . 51
Warenne 55, 105
Warham 244
Warner 239, 288
Warren 113, 181
Washington 112, 114
Washington, John & Mary 274
Washington, John & Anne Pope 275
Washington, Lawrence & Joyce 275
Washington, Lawrence & Amphyllis Twigden 275
Washington, Lawrence & **Margaret Butler** . 274
Washington, Richard & Frances Browne .. 274
Waterton 101
Waterton, Joan & **Lionel de Welles** 277
Watson 85, 191
Watts 26, 180
Weare, Joan & **Ferdinando Baynton** 12
Webb 41
Weever, Elizabeth & **John Stanley** 182
Welby, Olive & Henry Farwell 276
Welby, Richard & Frances Bulkeley 276
Welby, Thomas & **Elizabeth Thimbleby** ... 276
Welles 17, 141, 293
Welles, Alianor & Thomas Hoo 278
Welles, Anne & **James Butler** 46
Welles, Eudo & Maud de Greystoke 277
Welles, John & **Alianor de Mowbray** 277
Welles, Lionel & Joan de Waterton 277
Welles, Margaret & Thomas Dymoke 94
Wellington 214
Welton 237
Wentworth 23, 216, 247, 273
Wentworth, Elizabeth & Martin de la See . 250
Wentworth, Henry & Anne Say 129

INDEX

Wentworth, Jane & John Harleston 131
Wentworth, Margery & John Berney 146
Wentworth, Margery & John Seymour 239
Wentworth, Philip & Mary Clifford 129
Wentworth, Philip & Elizabeth Corbett ... 131
Wentworth, Richard & Anne Tyrrell 130
Wentworth, Roger & Anne Tyrrell 146
Wentworth, Thomas & Margaret Fortescue 130
West 19, 236, 247
West, Elizabeth & Herbert Pelham 144
West, Elizabeth & John Leigh 260
West, George & Elizabeth Morton 143
West, John & Ann 144
West, Margaret & Thomas Echingham 96
West, Penelope & Herbert Pelham 217
West, Reynold & Margaret Thorley 142
West, Richard & Katherine Hungerford .. 142
West, Thomas & Eleanor Copley 142
West, Thomas & Joan la Warre 142
West, Thomas & _____ Huttof 143
West, Thomas & Anne Knollys 143
West, William & Elizabeth Strange 143
Weston, Mary & William Clerke 65
Weyland 62, 174
Whalesborough 32
Wharton 75, 87
Wheeler 27, 276
Whetehill, Margaret & John Radcliffe 234
Whetenhall 64
Whitaker, Jabez & Mary Bourchier 34
Whitby 172
White, Mary & Humphrey Davie 82
Whiting 291
Whitney 74
Whitney, Robert & Constance Tuchet 270
Wichingham 278
Widdrington 100
Wilberforce 69
Wilbur 66
Wildbore 276
Wildey 112
Wilford 87, 207
Wilfred 247
Wilington 142
Wilkinson 31, 70
Willard 161
Williams 65, 145
Williams, Jane & William Coytemore 74
Williams, Richard & Frances Deighton 85
Williams, William & Dorothy Griffith 74
Williamson 26
Willis, Elizabeth & John Harleston 131
Willoughby 19, 27, 39, 82, 249
Willoughby, Cecily & Edward Duley 92
Willoughby, Edward & Margaret Neville .. 30
Willoughby, Elizabeth & Fulke Greville 30
Willoughby, Elizabeth & Henry Beaumont . 187
Willoughby, Elizabeth & John Paulet 216
Willoughby, Henry & Anne Grey 120
Willoughby, Jane & Guiscard Harbottle ... 128

Willoughby, Margaret & Matthew Arundell . 48
Willoughby, Robert & Dorothy Grey 216
Willoughby, Thomas & Joan de Arundel .. 279
Willoughby, William & Joan Strangeways . 279
Wilmer 213
Wilsford, Elizabeth & George Clerke 65
Wilson 41, 52, 138
Windebank, Mildred & Robert Reade 239
Windebank, Thomas & Frances Dymoke .. 238
Windsor, Andrews & Elizabeth Blount ... 174
Windsor, Edith & George Ludlow 175
Windsor, Eleanor & Edward Neville 212
Windsor, Thomas & Elizabeth Andrews ... 174
Wingfield 233, 243, 250
Wingfield, Anthony & Elizabeth Vere 126
Wingfield, Dorothy & Adam Claypoole 66
Wingfield, Elizabeth & Francis Hall 33
Wingfield, Elizabeth & William Brandon .. 213
Wingfield, Henry & Elizabeth Risby 127
Wingfield, Henry & Elizabeth Rokes 163
Wingfield, John & Elizabeth Fitzlewis 126
Wingfield, John & Anne Tuchet 126
Wingfield, John & Elizabeth Gresham 164
Wingfield, John & Margaret Hastings 162
Wingfield, John & Mary Owen 283
Wingfield, John & Frances Cromwell 282
Wingfield, Mary & William Dade 78
Wingfield, Richard & Mary Hardwick 126
Wingfield, Robert & Elizabeth Goushill ... 163
Wingfield, Robert & Elizabeth Cecil 164
Wingfield, Robert & Elizabeth Russell 162
Wingfield, Robert & Margery Quarles 163
Wingfield, Thomas & Mary 283
Winslow 94
Winslow, Josiah & Penelope Pelham 218
Winthrop 69
Witham 26
Withe 9
Wodhull, Agnes & Richard Chetwode 59
Wodhull, Anne & Richard Burnaby 40
Wodhull, Anthony & Anne Smith 59
Wodhull, Nicholas & Elizabeth Parr 40
Wodhull, Nicholas & Mary Raleigh 58
Wolfe, Barbara & Henry Seymour 240
Wolley 4, 285
Wolley, Alice & John Asfordby 4
Wolley, William & Anne Leming 116
Wolseley, Anthony & Margaret Blythe 284
Wolseley, Ellen & George Abney 2
Wolseley, Erasmus & Cassandra Giffard .. 284
Wolseley, John & Anne Stanley 284
Wolseley, Mary & Roger Brooke 285
Wolseley, Thomas & Helen Brockton 285
Wolseley, Walter & Mary Beauchamp 285
Wolverstone 201
Wood 221
Woodbridge 94
Woodhouse 26
Woodward, Frances & John Oxenbridge .. 213
Woolhouse, Elizabeth & Richard Bernard .. 21

INDEX

Worsham 166
Worsley, Isabel & **Richard Culpeper** 259
Wotton, Margaret & **Thomas Grey** 120
Wright 27, 275
Wriothesley 48
Wroth 58
Wroth, Mabel & **Edward Aucher** 171
Wrottesley 64, 265
Wrottesley, Eleanor & Richard Lee 180
Wrottesley, Richard & **Dorothy Sutton** ... 180
Wrottesley, Walter & Isabel Harcourt 180
Wyatt, George & Jane Finch 288
Wyatt, Hawte & Barbara Mitford 289
Wyatt, Jane & Charles Scott 112
Wyatt, Thomas & **Elizabeth Brooke** 288
Wyatt, Thomas & Jane Haute 288
Wycliffe 275
Wydeville 7, 11, 19, 108, 200, 293
Wydeville, Elizabeth & Edward IV 293
Wydeville, Elizabeth & **John Pashley** 110
Wydeville, Elizabeth & **John Grey** 119
Wydeville, Katherine & **Henry Stafford** 7
Wyfold 198
Wykes 281
Wylde 40
Wyllys, Amy & John Pynchon 291
Wyllys, George & Bridget Yonge 290
Wymondham 99
Wynne 210
Wynne, Catrin & John Lloyd 170
Wynne, Humphrey & Mawd ferch Oliver .. 169
Yelverton 214
Yelverton, Elizabeth & Thomas Peyton ... 221
Yelverton, Henry & **Bridget Drury** 220
Yelverton, William & Ursula Richardson .. 220
Yelverton, William & Dionysia Stubbs 220
Yonge 1
Yonge, Bridget & George Wyllys 290
Yonge, William & **Mary Bonner** 290
York 14, 109, 119, 129, 270, 287
York, Constance & Thomas Despenser ... 210
York, Edmund & Isabella de Castille 291
York, Richard & Anne Mortimer 292
Yorke, Dorothy & **Thomas Dudley** 93
Young 170
Zachary 170
Zouche 37, 61, 83, 139, 250, 285

CPSIA information can be obtained
at www.ICGtesting.com
Printed in the USA
LVHW020155100920
665474LV00011B/301